Integrated eBook

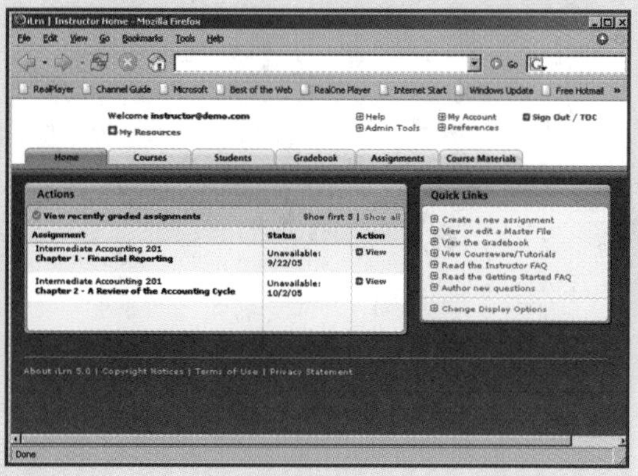

- A complete eBook is available, to be accessed and read sequentially.
- The eBook is made available to instructors as assignable content.
- The eBook is linked from specific end-of-chapter assignments to be used for remediation.

Assessment Options

- In an effort to help institutions and faculty meet AACSB/AICPA accreditation standards, Thomson South-Western has tagged all ThomsonNOW assessment activities against AACSB/AICPA standards.
- Test banks are included! Tests or quizzes created from the test bank are automatically graded and linked into the grade book.
- Select test bank questions are offered with algorithmic functionality and are easily identified.

Course Management Tools, including Grade Book

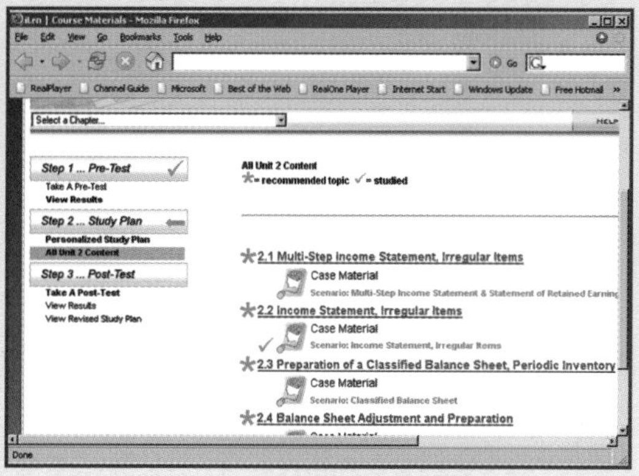

- An instructor grade book includes grades for algorithmically generated questions.
- Instructors have the ability to weight grades.
- There are options for points or percentage grading, and instructors have the ability to overwrite grades.
- WebCT® & Blackboard® Integration

Financial Accounting

Information for Decisions 6e

Robert W. Ingram
University of Alabama

Thomas L. Albright
University of Alabama

THOMSON
SOUTH-WESTERN

Australia · Brazil · Canada · Mexico · Singapore · Spain · United Kingdom · United States

THOMSON
SOUTH-WESTERN

Financial Accounting: Information for Decisions, Sixth Edition

Robert W. Ingram, Thomas L. Albright

VP/Editorial Director:
Jack W. Calhoun

Publisher:
Rob Dewey

Executive Editor:
Sharon Oblinger

Developmental Editor:
Allison Rolfes

Marketing Manager:
Chris McNamee

Production Project Manager:
Tamborah Moore

Technology Project Editor:
Robin Browning

Web Coordinator:
Scott Cook

Manufacturing Coordinator:
Doug Wilke

Production House:
LEAP Publishing Services, Inc.

Composition:
GGS Book Services, Inc.

Printer:
Transcontinental-Beauceville
Beauceville, Quebec

Art Director:
Bethany Casey

Internal Designer:
Knapke Design/Mason, Ohio

Cover Designer:
Knapke Design/Mason, Ohio

Cover Images:
© Getty Images, Inc./ The Image Bank Collection/ Photographer: Frank Pease

Photography Manager:
Deanna Ettinger

Photo Researcher:
Susan Van Etten

Printed in Canada
1 2 3 4 5 08 07 06 05

Student Edition:
ISBN 0-324-31341-1

Instructor's Edition:
ISBN 0-324-37464-X

Library of Congress Control Number: 2005936757

For more information about our products, contact us at:
Thomson Learning Academic Resource Center
1-800-423-0563

Thomson Higher Education
5191 Natorp Boulevard
Mason, OH 45040
USA

We dedicate this book to our families whose love and support have been essential to our success.

Brief Contents

FINANCIAL ACCOUNTING

Table of Contents

FINANCIAL ACCOUNTING

Instructor Preface

DRIVING EXCELLENCE THROUGH INNOVATION

Excellence . . . it is a word that is often stated, but rarely defined. Managers rely on excellence from their employees, companies expect it from their managers, and stockholders demand it from their companies.

As instructors, you see excellence through some students, a colleague's research, and in some of the resources you use. *Financial Accounting: Information for Decisions, 6e,* is proud to be one of those excellent resources.

For many of your students, this course will be the only financial accounting course they will ever take. Thus, it is essential that they take from the course the basic understanding needed to make wise financial choices. Our innovative approach to financial accounting continues to give your students this understanding and provide them with a direction for their future. For accounting majors, this innovative look at accounting and the role of accountants in the global community will serve as a firm foundation upon which they will build the more detailed skills cultivated in their higher-level courses. This sixth edition of *Financial Accounting: Information for Decisions* is the road map to assist you in teaching all of your students that accounting is the language of business. Giving them this direction will launch them toward becoming the business decision-makers of tomorrow.

Your students may or may not be aware of the concerns of large company investors or creditors. However, they probably do understand there are risks in the business world and that knowing more about the financial information of companies is helpful for controlling those risks and driving their own personal success.

DRIVE UNDERSTANDING WITH QUALITY CONTENT

NEW! Favorite Cookie Company Case

The straightforward and realistic case of a small, start-up company unfolds throughout the text and provides students with an easy-to-understand example of the purpose of accounting, its process, and its importance in decision making. As students move from chapter to chapter, they learn how the owners of the company tackle basic business decisions using accounting information and how their accounting system develops over time. At the beginning of each chapter, new information about Favorite Cookie Company sets the stage for that chapter's coverage.

Engaging Questions Give Direction for Knowledge

"What do we need to know to start a business?" "How much will it cost to borrow money?" These and other questions are asked by people in the business world everyday. Each chapter begins with its own key question to tell students upfront the overall focus of the chapter's content. The question is extended at the end of each chapter in the "Thinking Beyond the Question" feature.

WHAT DO WE NEED TO KNOW TO START A BUSINESS?

In December of 2006, Maria and Stan were very excited about starting a company to sell cookies made using old family recipes. They decided to call the business Favorite Cookie Company. Realizing they did not have much money and had little business experience, the brother and sister made plans to start with a small company. They hope the business will grow as more customers become aware of their products. Maria and Stan know that accountants provide advice to help managers of companies better understand their businesses. Because they had never started a company before, they made an appointment with Ellen Coleman, an accountant who had provided helpful business advice to several of their friends.

From page 2.

HOW MUCH WILL IT COST TO BORROW MONEY?

Maria and Stan have been successful in starting Favorite Cookie Company. The company has been profitable and is growing as more customers demand its products. Maria and Stan are now concerned about meeting the additional demand. They need to expand their operations, and they are considering producing their own products rather than purchasing them from other bakeries. Before they can expand, however, they must obtain additional financing for their company. The time value of money is an important concept that business owners need to understand before they borrow money.

From page 282.

Included with the opening questions is the "Food for Thought" feature, which asks students to think about what they would do if they were a business owner faced with the scenarios presented.

Food for Thought

If you were going to borrow money, how much would you have to pay back over the life of the loan? How much would you have to pay each period? How much interest expense would you incur? Borrowing money always involves an investment by one entity, a bank for example, in another entity, such as Favorite Cookie Company. The amount repaid by the borrower includes interest in addition to the amount borrowed. Maria and Stan are considering borrowing from a local bank but have decided to discuss the loan with their accountant, Ellen, to determine how much the loan will cost.

From page 282.

Each scenario also concludes with a discussion among the owners (Maria and Stan) and the company's accountant (Ellen) to give students a better understanding of the types of information accounting and business professionals must consider.

Stan: *Ellen, Maria and I are considering expanding our business. To finance the expansion, we will need a loan. We are concerned about how much the debt will cost us and how much cash we will need to repay the principal and interest.*

Ellen: *You should be concerned about these issues. You should never borrow money without a clear idea of how much you will have to repay.*

Maria: *We know we'll have to repay the principal of the loan plus interest. We're not sure, however, how much the bank will require us to repay each period.*

Ellen: *To understand loan payments, you need to understand time value of money concepts. Interest computations can be complex, depending on when payments are made and whether you repay the loan in a single payment or in a series of payments. Let's review these concepts.*

From page 282.

Students Choose Their Own Route—Thinking Beyond the Question

The chapter opening question is expanded in material at the end of each chapter. Students are asked to consider the question from a different perspective and use the knowledge they have gained from the chapter to provide a variety of answers.

The solution to the chapter opening question has been redesigned to clearly show the connection between the question and answer.

THINKING BEYOND THE QUESTION

HOW DO WE KNOW HOW WELL OUR BUSINESS IS DOING?

At the beginning of the chapter we asked how a business can determine how well it is performing. This chapter has described the key elements of a basic accounting system. Accounts are used to record business activities. Account balances are summarized at the end of a fiscal period, and those balances are used to prepare financial statements. Those statements help owners, creditors, and other stakeholders understand the resources available to a company, how the resources were financed, how they were used in the business, how much profit the business earned, and the events that affected the company's cash during the period.

The procedures described in this chapter may appear mechanical. Some of them are. However, sometimes judgments have to be made about when certain events should be recorded. Assuming you are making the accounting decisions for a company, what information do you think would tell you when revenues have been earned and expenses have been incurred? What events would be important for determining when to recognize revenues and expenses?

From page 63.

INNOVATIVE ORGANIZATION TO INSPIRE STUDENT COMPREHENSION

The sixth edition of the text continues to innovate on the approach to understanding financial accounting. By providing an organization around the business activities of a firm and clustering like topics to increase the clarity of information, students can easily identify why accounting information will be important to them in their career.

- **Accounting and Organizations.** Chapter 1 provides a *conceptual foundation* for understanding the purpose of accounting in business organizations. The chapter examines the need for information about business activities. Information is linked to a description of business activities and the purpose of businesses. The need for accurate and timely information leads to a brief introduction of the regulatory environment in which accounting and businesses operate. The chapter concludes with a discussion of the *importance of ethics* for accounting.
- **Business Activities—The Source of Accounting Information.** Chapter 2 *links business activities to accounting* through the *accounting equation*. The equation is used to develop a conceptual description of the accounting process for recording business activities. Simple examples are used to introduce accounting for financing, investing, and operating activities. The format used for this purpose highlights the relationships between transactions and financial statements. The chapter extends this description to a *brief introduction to financial statements* and the *analysis* of financial statement information. Thus, the chapter explains the purpose of accounting in terms of measuring and recording business activities, reporting information about those activities, and analyzing that information. The book emphasizes the importance of accounting for *decision making*. Accordingly, even procedural issues are linked to the decision focus. Accounting is not just about preparing information. It is about using that information to understand organizations and make business decisions.
- **Proven Appendix on Debits and Credits.** To provide flexibility in coverage, we have placed content explaining the basics of debits and credits, T accounts, and journal entries in an appendix to Chapter 2. The approach allows instructors the flexibility to include or exclude these topics.

Appendix ***Debits and Credits: Another Way to Record Transactions***

- **Measuring Revenues and Expenses.** Chapter 3 extends the simple description of accounting for business activities in Chapter 2 to include *timing issues associated with accrual accounting*. The chapter explains accrual accounting concepts, the importance of these concepts, and their relationship to the accounting cycle through adjusting and closing transactions. Students are provided with a solid background in *transaction analysis* developed within a conceptual model of business decision making.
- **Reporting Earnings and Financial Position.** Chapter 4 examines the *income statement, balance sheet, and statement of stockholders' equity*. Examples from both hypothetical and real companies are used to introduce basic financial reporting concepts and to provide a realistic description of variations that exist in practice.
- **Reporting Cash Flows.** Chapter 5 considers the *statement of cash flows*. Both the direct and indirect formats are included. Simple examples are used to describe the indirect format and to reemphasize the importance of accrual accounting concepts. The chapter also examines the importance of the statement of cash flows for *evaluating business performance*.
- **Full and Fair Reporting.** Chapter 6 examines the broader context of financial reporting, including information in the annual report other than financial statements. It examines the importance of disclosure, accounting regulation, auditing,

and internal control. The sixth edition pulls this material into one primary location to underscore the *importance of accounting as a validative, as well as descriptive, process.*

- **Computerized Accounting Systems.** Chapter 7 examines *accounting systems*, including the flow of data and processing in computerized systems. A goal of this chapter is to help students see *accounting as a dynamic, technological process.* Students sometimes get the impression that accounting is a clerical process without much technological sophistication. Modern accounting systems require a basic understanding of computer networks and database management systems. The world in which accountants work is not one of traditional journals and ledgers. It is one in which computer systems are essential to processing and analyzing business information. The chapter includes an *illustration of a simple accounting database system.* By working through this project, students learn how basic accounting functions are automated and how computers facilitate the accounting process. The Favorite Cookie Company database files that tie to this project are provided on the text's Web site (http://ingram.swlearning.com).

EXHIBIT 1 Components of an Accounting Information System

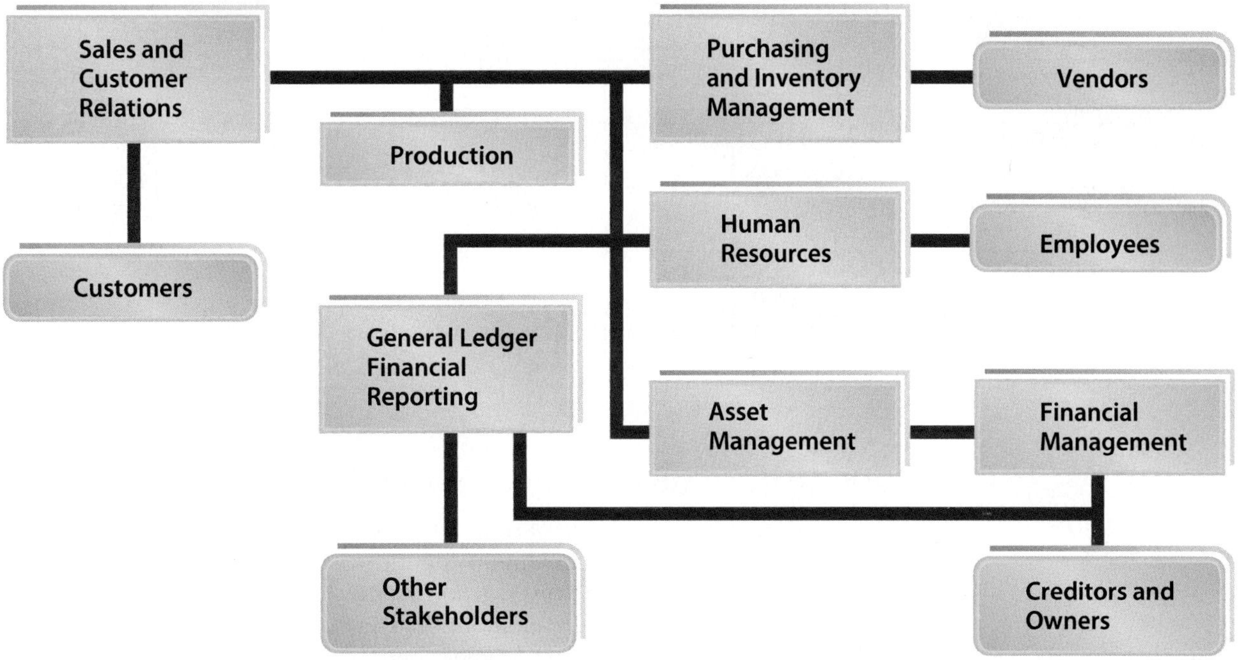

All of the components in the system are linked so they share data with each other. Some businesses use one software application that integrates all of these functions. **Systems that integrate most of the business information functions as a basis for management decisions are referred to as** *enterprise resource planning (ERP) systems*. Many large companies have implemented these systems from ERP developers such as SAP® and Oracle®.

From pages 255–256.

PEDAGOGY DRIVEN THROUGH DESIGN

The internal design of the sixth edition has been significantly revised in order to provide a more clear, concise, and directional learning path. Learning features such as the "Case in Point" boxes and the "Learning Notes" are presented within the text so they stand out visually and encourage students to read and think about the information presented in these features.

The end-of-chapter material has also been streamlined to more closely follow the direction of a student's learning path. This reorganization of the activities at the end of the chapter allows students to easily navigate their way through review materials. It also helps to enhance their learning experience by understanding the connection between questions and chapter topics.

Proven Spreadsheet Presentation

The spreadsheet presentation of transactions continues to clearly show the effect of income statement accounts on the accounting equation. Through this approach, students have seen how nominal accounts increase or decrease retained earnings. We have consistently used this format throughout this edition of the text.

EXHIBIT 10 Accounting Representation of Expenses

		Assets		=	Liabilities	+	Owners' Equity	
Date	Accounts	Cash	Other Assets				Contributed Capital	Retained Earnings
	Beginning Amounts	13,200	+32,120	=	30,000	+	10,000	+5,320
Jan. 6	Supplies Expense							−300
	Cash	−300						
Jan. 8	Rent Expense							−600
	Cash	−600						
Jan. 31	Wages Expense							−1,000
	Cash	−1,000						
Jan. 31	Utilities Expense							−200
	Cash	−200						
	Ending Amounts	11,100	+32,120	=	30,000	+	10,000	+3,220

From page 53.

Providing Direction on Business Ethics

As the headlines indicate, the coverage of ethics has never been more important—especially in accounting. That is why the sixth edition continues to introduce the importance of ethics in Chapter 1, expand on the coverage in Chapter 3, and reinforce it in the "Case in Point" boxes and assignments. In addition, Chapter 6 has been updated with information about the Sarbanes-Oxley Act of 2002. End-of-chapter activities in Chapter 6 have also been enhanced to reinforce the impact of Sarbanes-Oxley and the importance of responsible reporting in accounting.

THE IMPORTANCE OF ETHICS

Objective 8
Explain why ethics are important for business and accounting.

Ethics are important in business organizations. Ethics involve living by the norms and rules of society. In business, those norms and rules identify appropriate behavior for managers, employees, investors, and other stakeholders. Keeping their investors and other stakeholders fully informed about their business activities is an important ethical norm for managers. Managers who conceal their activities or who misrepresent those activities make it difficult for stakeholders to assess how well a business is performing. Overstating profits, for example, may result in investors allocating more resources to a company than actual results would justify. This misallocation results in a loss of value to society and often leads to financial harm for those who use this information.

From page 22.

P1-20 **ETHICS AND MORAL HAZARD**

Obj. 8

You manage an auto service store. One of your major services is brake replacement. You purchase replacement parts at an average cost of $30 per set. Each set contains parts for four wheels and will repair one car. You charge an average of $100 per car for replacing worn brakes, including an average labor cost of $40. Your current volume for brake replacements is about 700 jobs per month. A new vendor has contacted you with an offer to sell you replacement parts at an average cost of $22.50 per set. After checking on the quality of these parts, you find that their average life is about two-thirds that of the parts you are currently using.

Required

A. What are the short-run profit implications of using the $22.50 brakes instead of the $30 brakes?
B. What are the long-run profit implications?
C. What ethical issues should be considered in choosing which brakes to use?

From page 40.

P6-5 **SARBANES-OXLEY—ACHIEVING THE INTENDED EFFECT AT HEALTHSOUTH CORPORATION**[1]

Obj. 1

Publicly traded corporations traditionally have included a statement of management responsibilities as part of the annual report. This statement typically used the following language:

> The company's management is responsible for the fairness and accuracy of the consolidated financial statements. The statements have been prepared in accordance with accounting principles that are generally accepted in the United States, using management's best estimates and judgments where appropriate.

In the wake of a series of high-profile public frauds, Congress passed the Sarbanes-Oxley Act. HealthSouth Corporation was one of the first companies tried under the new SOX legislation. Management was accused of overstating earnings by $2.6 billion from 1996 to 2002. The following is an excerpt from an article appearing in the *Birmingham Post* on February 5, 2005:

> Court testimony Friday showed the fraud at HealthSouth Corp. unraveled when a newly married executive returned from his honeymoon and said he could no longer live a life of deception.
>
> Weston Smith, [HealthSouth's] chief financial officer at the time, said in August 2002 he would quit rather than certify financial statements he knew were false . . . Smith had good reason not to sign the documents. When he returned from celebrating his marriage, the financial statements requiring his signature were the first bound by the Sarbanes-Oxley Act. . . .

Required If management had been responsible for the fairness and accuracy of the financial statements prior to SOX, explain why executives would have been more hesitant to sign statements they knew were fraudulent.

From page 246.

Updated Case In Point Boxes

The content presented in these boxes provides students with a variety of enrichment information regarding ethical dilemmas. Examples from the business community in general and specific company disclosures expose students to ethical situations they may face during their business careers.

Case In Point

http://ingram.swlearning.com

Visit Procter & Gamble's home page to learn more about the company.

Disclosure of Debt Covenants

A note in Procter & Gamble's 2004 annual report describes a covenant in the company's credit facilities, which are borrowing arrangements:

> *While not considered material to the overall financial condition of the Company, there is a covenant in the credit facilities stating the ratio of net debt to earnings before interest expense, income taxes, depreciation and amortization cannot exceed four at the time of a draw on the facility. As of June 30, we are comfortably below this level, with a ratio of approximately 1.3.*

Source: Procter & Gamble's 2004 annual report.

From page 372.

Innovative and Proven Pedagogical Features

- **Learning Objectives** serve as ongoing reminders to students as to what is key in each part of the chapter and provide a basis for review. These objectives, which are written as measurable goals, are partnered with the assignments so instructors can easily select applicable coverage.
- **Learning Notes** highlight issues that frequently are troublesome for students or that enrich student understanding.
- **Self-Study Problems** provide opportunity for students to test themselves as they progress through the chapter.
- **Introducing Students to Excel as a Helpful Tool** begins with *A Short Introduction to Excel* in the Chapter 1 appendix, continues throughout the text in the *Excel in Action* problems, and is further developed in Chapters 8 and 9 through the *Using Excel* explanations. Students learn how to use this helpful tool in generating financial accounting information.

Appendix *A Short Introduction to Excel*

This introduction summarizes some of the primary operations and functions of a spreadsheet. It is intended to get you started if you have not had previous experience with Excel. There are many operations and functions in addition to those mentioned here.

Identifying and Selecting Cells

A spreadsheet consists of rows and columns. Rows are identified by numbers, and columns are identified by letters. An intersection of a row and column is a cell. A cell is identified by the column letter and row number that intersect at that cell.

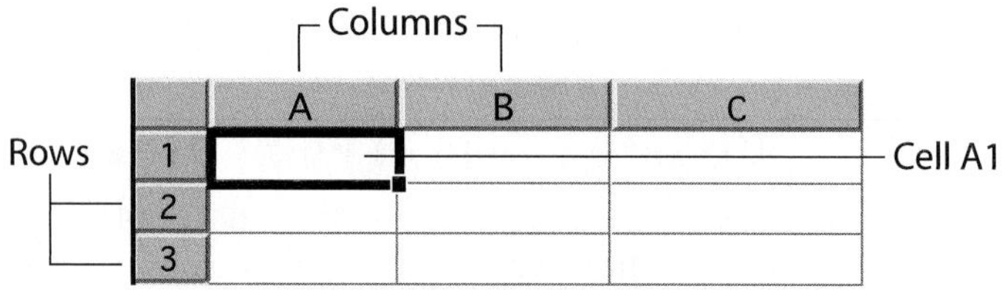

From page 23.

- **Thinking Beyond the Question** is an end-of-chapter section that revisits the chapter opening question. Students are asked a challenging question that requires them to think beyond what has been presented in the chapter.
- **Solutions to Self-Study Problems** give students the answers to the chapter Self-Study Problems as a way of reinforcing their understanding of the material.
- **Key Concepts and Terms** list, with page references, the concepts and terms that are defined in the chapter.
- **Review of Important Concepts** provides a summary in outline form of each chapter's important concepts.
- **Questions** are designed to stimulate in-class discussion of each chapter's most important concepts.
- **Exercises** are short assignments that focus on computations and are excellent for in-class demonstration and discussion.
- **Problems** provide for a more complex learning experience, taking student learning further by focusing on analysis of information. Each chapter contains a problem set of multiple-choice questions, which many instructors like to use as an in-class quiz. A spreadsheet icon identifies assignments that work well with Excel.
- **Cases** are more challenging than problems and encourage thinking and analytical skills.

EXCELLENCE CONTINUES WITH UPDATED ASSIGNMENT MATERIAL

To keep content accurate and relevant, new exercises and problems have been added to each chapter. In addition, updates to existing problems with new company data have also been included.

The HealthSouth case has been revised to address PCAOB standards and management certifications required by Sarbanes-Oxley to keep students close to the impact these rules and regulations have on the accounting industry.

REVISED! Real World Examples

Real company information usually grabs student interest and helps clarify the meaning and relevance of accounting. Throughout the text, examples involving real world information have been updated. Among the companies presented are the following featured firms:

- **General Mills, Inc.** Portions of its annual report are included at the end of the text and tied to many case assignments in the text.
- **Procter & Gamble** Key financial statements and other supporting information are included in several chapters.
- **Microsoft** General financial information is presented as a comparison company with Procter & Gamble in the analysis chapters.

Cases

C13-1 **EXAMINING OPERATING ACTIVITIES**

Objs. 2, 4, 5 Selected information from **General Mills**' 2004 annual report and 10K is provided in Appendix A at the end of the text.

Required Review the annual report and answer each of the following questions.

A. What was the primary inventory estimation method used by General Mills? What is the effect on the company's cost of goods sold and operating income of using this primary method as compared to other methods? (Hint: Look at Notes 1c and 6. The "Reserve for LIFO" is an estimate of the difference between FIFO and LIFO values.)
B. What was the amount of General Mills' allowance for doubtful accounts for 2004? Did the relationship between estimated doubtful accounts and net sales change from 2002 to 2004?
C. How much did General Mills report for depreciation and amortization and for interest expense in 2004? How much cash did General Mills pay for depreciation, amortization, and interest in 2004? (Hint: See the income statement, cash flow statement, and Note 13.)

From page 524.

INTERNATIONAL

Throughout the text, coverage relating to the international business community is identified by an icon in the margin.

BRING CONTENT ALIVE THROUGH INNOVATIVE TECHNOLOGY

Thomson™ NOW!

Your Course. Your Time. Your Way.

Introducing ThomsonNOW for Ingram/Albright *Financial Accounting: Information for Decisions, 6e!*

This powerful and fully integrated online teaching and learning system provides you with flexibility and control, saves valuable time, and improves outcomes. Your students benefit by having choices in the way they learn through our unique personalized learning path. All this is made possible by ThomsonNOW!

- Homework
- Integrated eBook
- Personalized Learning Path
- Interactive Course Assignments
- Assessment Options
- Test Delivery
- Course Management Tools, including Grade Book
- WebCT & Blackboard Integration

Thomson™ NOW!

WebTutor® Toolbox on WebCT® or Blackboard®. Available on both platforms, this rich course management product is a specially designed extension of the classroom experience that enlivens the course by leveraging the power of the Internet with comprehensive educational content. Instructors or students can use these resources along with those on the Product Web Site to supplement the classroom experience. Use this effective resource as an integrated solution for your distance learning or web-enhanced course! Contact your local sales representative for details! (http://webtutor.swlearning.com; WebTutor® Toolbox on WebCT® ISBN: 0-534-27488-9; WebTutor® Toolbox on Blackboard® ISBN: 0-534-27489-7).

Acquire, Assess, and Apply Financial Statement Analysis

Blue Company: An Interactive Approach (0-324-37764-9). Prepared by Larry Rankin and Dan Wiegand (Miami University), this powerful hands-on tool allows students to interact directly with financial statement elements. At the conslusion of the financial statement analysis exercises, students are asked to complete an Annual Report Project. Students receive a printed booklet with instructions for set-up, and exercises that demonstrate vertical, horizontal, and ratio analysis as well as financial modeling.

A grading CD-Rom for instructors (0-324-37867-X) allows for automatic batch grading of each student's Annual Report Project.

Innovate and Motivate

JoinIn on Turning Point (0-324-38072-0) is interactive PowerPoint®, simply the best classroom response system available today! JoinIn allows lectures to be transformed into powerful, two-way experiences. This lecture tool makes full use of the Instructor's PowerPoint® presentation but moves it to the next level with interactive questions that provide immediate feedback on the students' understanding of the topic at hand. Visit http://turningpoint.thomsonlearningconnections.com/index.html to find out more!

Drive Real-World Experience Into the Classroom

Business & Company Resource Center. Put a complete business library at your fingertips with The Business & Company Resource Center. The BCRC is a premiere online business research tool that allows seamless searches of thousands of periodicals, journals, references, financial information, industry reports, company histories, and much more. For more information, visit http://bcrc.swlearning.com.

Excellence Defined: Book Companion Web Site Provides Additional Resources

The book companion Web site, http://ingram.swlearning.com, for the sixth edition offers you and your student many resources for teaching and learning.

Student Resources

- **Quizzes** with feedback to enhance student comprehension.
- **Web Links** to many resources on the Web, including all of the Web sites listed in the text; this provides a quick connection to key information.
  - **Check figures** to selected assignments.
  - **Learning objectives** from the chapter are repeated as a study aid to keep clear focus on the core goals.
  - **Updates** for the latest information about changes in GAAP and other industry resources.
  - **Favorite Cookie Company Database File**
  - **Annual Report Project and Readings**
  - **"B" set problems,** which is a set of extra exercises and problems for practice.

Instructor Resources

- **Solutions Manual**
- **Cooperative Learning and Instructor's Resource Guide**
- **Solutions to Excel templates for the Excel in Action** and other assignments identified by the spreadsheet icon in the text.
- **Instructor's Manual** for the *Annual Report Project and Readings.*
- **"B" set solutions** for set of extra exercises and problems for practice.

Learn and Reinforce Concepts with These Extra Resources for Students:

- **Study Guide and Forms (0-324-40659-2).** This guide reinforces and enhances student understanding of the topics covered in the text. It is a thorough, value-adding book, prepared by Stephen Senge and George Sanders (Western Washington University). Included are working paper forms for selected text assignments.
- **Annual Report Project and Readings (0-324-40666-5).** This popular project, by Clayton Hock (Miami University), can be used by either learning teams or individual students. It is tailored to reinforce the concepts presented in the financial accounting chapters of the text. Students work with annual reports of real companies to understand, interpret, and analyze the information. The project guides them through this process. Interesting readings from publications like *The Wall Street Journal* along with supporting Questions for Consideration provide additional enrichment.

Plan and Manage Effectively with Time-Saving Resources for Instructors

- **Cooperative Learning and Instructor's Resource Guide (0-324-40664-9).** Contained in this supporting item are chapters explaining cooperative learning techniques for use in the classroom and matrices that suggest application of techniques to specific end-of-chapter items. In addition, there are outlines of each chapter, teaching notes, and descriptions of the exercises, problems, and cases to assist in class preparation. This guide's content is also available in electronic form on the Instructor's Resource CD-ROM and (restricted) on the product support Web site.
- **Solutions Manual (0-324-40661-4).** Author-prepared and carefully verified solutions to all exercises, problems, and cases are presented in this manual.
- **Test Bank (0-324-40658-4).** A complete and plentiful set of newly revised test items in print form; also available in electronic form (using ExamView® software, provided) on the Instructor's Resource CD-ROM.
- **Instructor's Resource CD-ROM with ExamView® (0-324-40662-2).** This IRCD contains the files for key instructor's ancillaries (the Cooperative Learning and Instructor's Resource Guide, the Solutions Manual, and the PowerPoint® Presentation slides). This gives instructors the ultimate tool for customizing lectures and presentations. The presentation slides reinforce chapter content and provide a rich tool for in-class lectures and out-of-class reviewing. The test bank files on the CD-ROM are provided in ExamView® format. This program is an easy-to-use test creation software compatible with Microsoft® Windows. Instructors can add or edit questions, instructions, and answers, and select questions (randomly or numerically) by previewing them on the screen. Instructors can also create and administer quizzes online, whether over the Internet, a local area network (LAN), or a wide area network (WAN).

- **Solution Transparencies (0-324-40660-6)**. Acetate transparencies of the numerical solutions to the exercises, problems, and cases are available to adopters.
- **Annual Report Project and Readings Instructor's Manual (0-324-40665-7).** Prepared by the author of the Annual Report Project and Readings, this manual provides guidance to assist instructors in maximizing the benefit of the project in their courses. In addition to the printed manual, the files are available in the Instructor Resources section of the text's Web site.

Acknowledgments

Throughout the writing and development of the six editions of our text, many colleagues have contributed creative, helpful suggestions through reviews, focus groups, surveys, etc. We have considered all of the feedback carefully as each edition has been prepared and will continue to do so in the future. Therefore, in appreciation, we thank the following reviewers who provided feedback for the sixth edition:

Roger Ames, Miami University
James Brett, Arizona State University
Nancy Csapo, Central Michigan University
Charles T. Dick, Miami University
Edmund D. Fenton, Eastern Kentucky University
Michael Flores, Wichita State University
Rochelle K. Greenberg, Florida State University
John Hathorn, Metropolitan State College of Denver
William C. Hood, Central Michigan University
Susan B. Hughes, Butler University
Sakthi Mahenthiran, Butler University
Karen B. McCarron, Gordon College
Ransom McClung, Florida State University
Debra McGilsky, Central Michigan University
Richard A. Moellenberndt, Washburn University
Ashton Oravetz, III, Tyler Junior College
Mary Ann M. Prater, Clemson University
Pamela J. Rouse, Butler University
P.N. Saksena, Indiana University South Bend
Tony Wain, Babson College

SPECIAL THANKS TO THE FOLLOWING SUPPLEMENT PREPARERS AND VERIFIERS:

Judy Beebe, Western Oregon University
Douglas Cloud, Professor Emeritus of Accounting, Pepperdine University
Christine Jonick, Gainesville State College, Gainesville, GA
Cynthia Killingsworth, Western Oregon University
Ken Martin, Martinique Development Services

Barbara Millis, University of Nevada, Reno
Ralph Millis, University of Nevada, Reno
Nancy Pernarelli, University of Nevada, Reno
George D. Sanders, Western Washington University
Stephen V. Senge
Tracy L. Smith, University of Memphis
Kathleen A. Wilcox, Kennesaw State University

About the Authors

Robert W. Ingram

Robert W. Ingram is the Ross-Culverhouse Chair and Senior Associate Dean of the College of Commerce in the Culverhouse College of Business at The University of Alabama. He teaches courses in financial accounting and has been actively involved in course curriculum development. He has served as Director of Education for the American Accounting Association, as a member of the Accounting Education Change Commission, and as editor of *Issues in Accounting Education*, a journal dedicated to accounting education research.

Professor Ingram is a Certified Public Accountant and holds a Ph.D. from Texas Tech University. Prior to joining the faculty at the University of Alabama, he held positions at the University of South Carolina and the University of Iowa, and a visiting appointment at the University of Chicago. His research, which examines financial reporting and accounting education, has been published widely in accounting and business journals. He is the recipient of the National Alumni Association Outstanding Commitment to Teaching Award and the Burlington Northern Foundation Faculty Achievement in Research Award at The University of Alabama. He has also received the Notable Contribution to Literature Award of the Government and Nonprofit Section of the American Accounting Association and the Award for Excellence and Professional Contributions of the Alabama Association for Higher Education in Business.

Professor Ingram is married and has two children. They enjoy sports, travel, reading, music, and art.

Thomas L. Albright

Thomas L. Albright is the J. Reese Phifer Faculty Fellow in the Culverhouse School of Accountancy at the University of Alabama. He teaches courses at the undergraduate and graduate levels in financial and managerial accounting. Professor Albright has received the Professor of the Year award on numerous occasions in relation to his work with MBA and Executive MBA students. In 2005, the University of Alabama National Alumni Association presented Professor Albright with the Outstanding Commitment to Teaching Award.

Professor Albright is a Certified Public Accountant (California) and holds a Ph.D. from the University of Tennessee. He has received the Certificate of Merit from the Institute of Management Accountants (IMA) for his research in the area of quality costs. Based on his work with manufacturing companies in both the United States and Mexico, he has published research in a variety of scholarly and applied journals. His work is used to help companies determine more accurate product costs and to develop better performance measures to achieve manufacturing excellence.

Professor Albright and his wife, Debby, have two children, Michael and Jenny. He enjoys sailing, scuba diving, and underwater photography.

Financial Accounting

Information for Decisions 6e

Robert W. Ingram
University of Alabama

Thomas L. Albright
University of Alabama

The Accounting Information System

SECTION 1

© PHOTODISC/GETTY IMAGES

Accounting and Organizations 1

WHAT DO WE NEED TO KNOW TO START A BUSINESS?

In December of 2006, Maria and Stan were very excited about starting a company to sell cookies made using old family recipes. They decided to call the business Favorite Cookie Company. Realizing they did not have much money and had little business experience, the brother and sister made plans to start with a small company. They hope the business will grow as more customers become aware of their products. Maria and Stan know that accountants provide advice to help managers of companies better understand their businesses. Because they had never started a company before, they made an appointment with Ellen Coleman, an accountant who had provided helpful business advice to several of their friends.

Food for Thought

Suppose you were in Maria and Stan's position. What would you want to know in order to start a business? What goals would you have for the business, and how would you plan to reach those goals? What resources would you need in your business, and how would you finance those resources? How would you organize your company? Who would your customers be? How would you know whether you are reaching your goals or not? These are issues Ellen poses to Maria and Stan.

Ellen: *Creating a successful business is not an easy task. You need a good product, and you need a plan to produce and sell that product.*

Maria: *Stan and I think we have an excellent product. We don't have a lot of money for equipment and other resources, but we have identified a bakery that could produce our products using our recipes and according to our specifications.*

Stan: *Also, we have spoken with several local grocery chains that have been impressed with samples and have agreed to sell our products.*

Ellen: *Good. A primary goal of every successful business is to create value for customers. If you focus on delivering a product that customers want at a price they are willing to pay, you are also likely to create value for yourselves as owners of the company. You have to make sure you know what it will cost to run your company and decide how you will obtain the money you need to get started.*

Stan: *We have some money in savings, and we plan to obtain a loan from a local bank. Those financial resources should permit us to rent a small office and purchase equipment we need to manage the company. Also, we will need to acquire a truck for picking up the cookies from the bakery and delivering them to the grocery stores.*

Ellen: *You will need a system for measuring your costs and the amounts you sell. That system is critical for helping you determine whether you are accomplishing your goals.*

Maria: *Stan and I don't know much about accounting. Can you help us get started?*

Ellen: *I'll be happy to help you. First, let's explore in more detail some of the issues you need to consider.*

Objectives

Once you have completed this chapter, you should be able to:

1 Identify how accounting information helps decision makers.

2 Compare major types of organizations and explain their purpose.

3 Describe how businesses create value.

4 Explain how accounting helps investors and other decision makers understand businesses.

5 Identify business ownership structures and their advantages and disadvantages.

6 Identify uses of accounting information for making decisions about corporations.

7 Explain the purpose and importance of accounting regulations.

8 Explain why ethics are important for business and accounting.

INFORMATION FOR DECISIONS

Objective 1

Identify how accounting information helps decision makers.

All of us use information to help us make decisions. *Information* **includes facts, ideas, and concepts that help us understand the world.** To use information, we must be able to interpret it and understand its limitations. Poor information or the improper use of information often leads to poor decisions.

As an example, assume you wish to drive from Sevierville to Waynesville. The drive will take several hours and require several turns on unfamiliar secondary roads. Therefore, you use a map, as illustrated in Exhibit 1, to provide information to help guide you along the way.

Why is the map useful? The map can help you plan your trip. You have selected a primary goal: arrive at Waynesville. You may have other goals as well, such as getting there as quickly as possible. Or perhaps you wish to stop at various points along the way.

EXHIBIT 1

Map from Sevierville to Waynesville

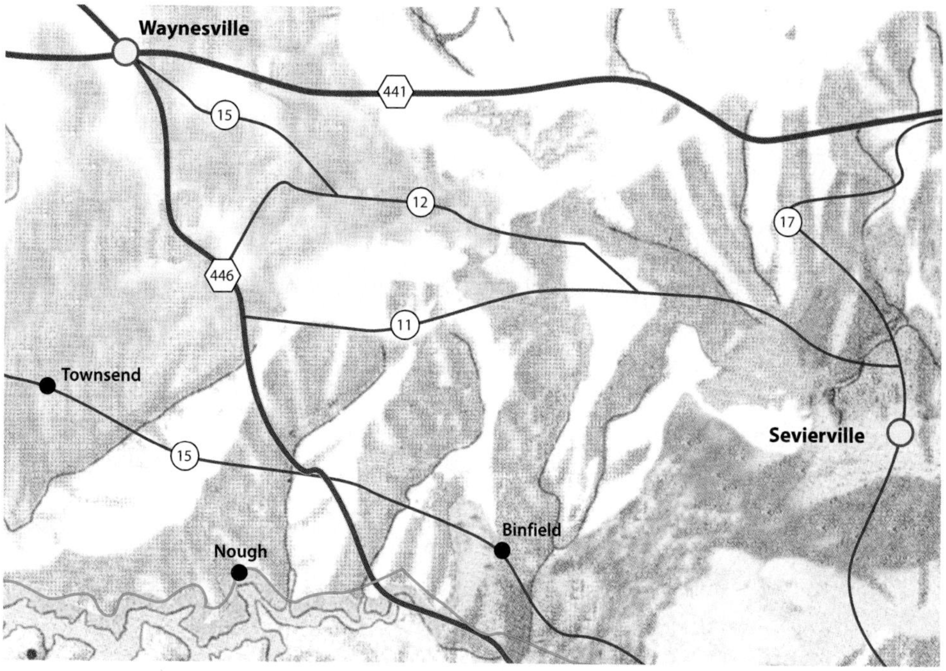

The map provides information about alternative routes so that you can select the one that is shortest, fastest, or most scenic. Using the map along the way helps you make decisions about where to turn or stop. It helps you determine how far you have traveled and how much farther you have left to go. It helps you decide whether you are on the right road or where you made a wrong turn. It helps you decide where you are, how you got there, and where you are going.

INTERNATIONAL

Accounting provides information to help in making decisions about organizations. This information is like a map of an organization. **Accounting information helps decision makers determine where they are, where they have been, and where they are going.** Rather than measuring distances in miles or kilometers, accounting measures an organization's activities by the dollar amounts associated with these activities. The primary measurement unit for accounting information is dollars in the United States or the local currency for other countries.

Maria and Stan have decided to start a business selling cookies. Their company will pay a bakery to produce the cookies and will sell the cookies to local grocery stores. An early decision they have to make is to identify the resources they will need to start and run their business. They will need merchandise (cookies) to sell and will purchase those products from a supplier (the bakery). They will need a place to operate the business and someone to pick up the products and deliver them to sellers (grocery stores). They will need money to pay for the merchandise, rent for their office, wages, equipment, and miscellaneous costs such as supplies and utilities.

As an initial step in deciding whether to start the business, Maria and Stan might consider how much they expect to sell. Suppose that after discussing this issue with grocery store owners, they determine that the company will sell about $12,000 of merchandise each month.

Next, they consider how much money they will need to operate their business. A discussion with the bakery indicates the cost of the merchandise will be $8,000 each month. After consideration of their other needs, they calculate their monthly costs will be:

Merchandise	$ 8,000
Wages	1,000
Rent	600
Supplies	300
Utilities	200
Total	$10,100

From this information, they decide they should expect to earn a profit of $1,900 ($12,000 – $10,100) each month as shown in Exhibit 2. Profit is the amount left over after the cost of doing business is subtracted from sales.

EXHIBIT 2
Expected Monthly Earnings for Favorite Cookie Company

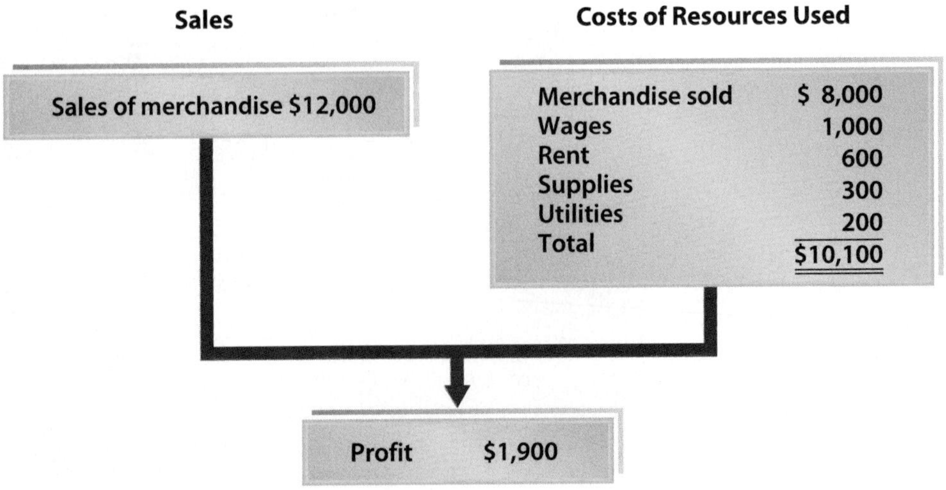

Does this appear to be a good business for Maria and Stan? Suppose they each have $5,000 to invest in the business. They will use this money to purchase merchandise and to pay for rent, wages, and the miscellaneous costs for the first month. Would investing their money in the business be a good idea?

If they don't invest in the business, they could earn interest of about $50 a month on their $10,000 of combined savings. The expected profit of $1,900 is considerably larger. However, they also should consider the wages they could earn if they worked for someone else instead of working in their own company. Additionally, they should consider how certain they are about the amount they can earn from their business and how much risk they are willing to take. Investing in a business is always risky. ***Risk*** **is uncertainty about an outcome,** such as the amount of profit a business will earn. If the company sells less than Maria and Stan expect, its earnings also will be less than expected. If the company does not do well, they could lose their investments. Are they willing to take that risk? **Accounting can help with these decisions by providing information about the results that owners and other decision makers should expect to occur.** Decision makers then have to evaluate that information and make their decisions.

Accounting is a way of looking at a business. It measures the activities of a business by the dollars it receives and spends. It helps decision makers determine where they started and where they should end up. It helps determine whether expectations are being met. In the case of Favorite Cookie Company, accounting identifies the company's starting point by the $10,000 Maria and Stan invest in their business. It identifies an expected ending point as the amount of profit of $1,900 they expect to earn each month. It provides a means of determining whether expectations are being met by measuring business activities each month to determine whether the company is actually earning $1,900 each month. Like a map, accounting can help decision makers determine that they are not where they want to be. It can help them determine what went wrong and what they might do to get back on the proper route.

Accounting provides a model of a business by measuring the business activities in dollar amounts. Underlying this model is an information system. This system provides a process for obtaining facts that can be converted into useful information. Understanding the system and its processes will help you understand the information provided by accounting.

The purpose of accounting is to help people make decisions about economic activities. Economic activities involve the allocation of scarce resources. People allocate scarce resources any time they exchange money, goods, or services. These activities are so common that almost every person in our society uses the accounting process to assist in decision making.

Accounting provides information for managers, owners, members, and other stakeholders who make decisions about organizations. ***Stakeholders*** **include those who have an economic interest in an organization and those who are affected by its activities. An *organization* is a group of people who work together to develop, produce, and/or distribute goods or services.** The next section of this chapter discusses the purpose of organizations and the role of accounting in organizations.

THE PURPOSE OF ORGANIZATIONS

Objective 2

Compare major types of organizations and explain their purpose.

Many types of organizations exist to serve society. Why do these organizations exist? Most exist because people need to work together to accomplish their goals. The goals are too large, too complex, or too expensive to be achieved without cooperation. All organizations provide goods and/or services. By working together, people can produce more and better goods and services.

Organizations differ as to the types of goods or services they offer (Exhibit 3). ***Merchandising*** **(or *retail*) *companies* sell to consumers goods that are produced by**

EXHIBIT 3
Types of Organizations

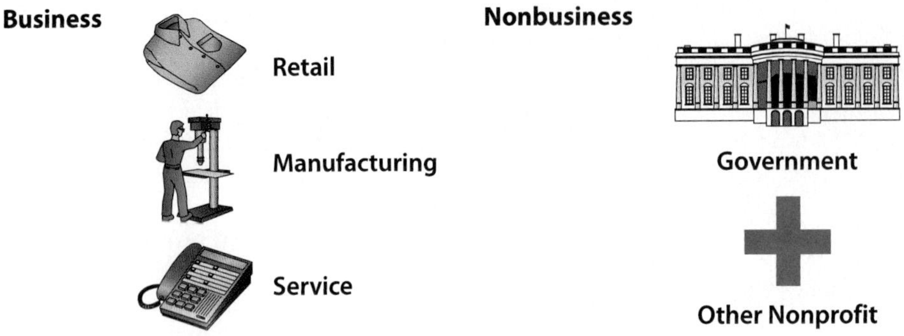

other companies. Grocery, department, and hardware stores are examples. Favorite Cookie Company is a merchandising company. It purchases merchandise from a bakery and sells the merchandise to grocery stores. *Manufacturing companies* **produce goods that they sell to consumers, to merchandising companies, or to other manufacturing companies.** Examples include automobile manufacturers, petroleum refineries, furniture manufacturers, computer companies, and paper companies. The bakery from which Favorite Cookie Company purchases its cookies is a manufacturing company. *Service companies* **sell services rather than goods.** These companies include banks, insurance companies, hospitals, universities, law firms, and accounting firms. Some companies may be a combination of types. For example, many automobile dealers are both retail and service companies. Restaurants are both manufacturing and service companies.

Organizations may be classified by whether or not they attempt to earn a profit. Profits result from selling goods and services to customers at prices greater than the cost of the items sold. **Organizations that sell their goods and services to make a profit are** *business organizations*. *Governmental and nonprofit organizations*, **sometimes referred to as nonbusiness organizations, provide goods or, more typically, services without the intent of making a profit.** Nonbusiness organizations include civic, social, and religious organizations. Some types of services, such as education and healthcare services, are provided by both business and nonbusiness organizations. Although the products are similar, the goals of the organizations providing these services are different. Nevertheless, all organizations need accounting information for decision making. This book focuses primarily on accounting for business organizations, though many of the concepts described are applicable to nonbusiness organizations as well.

Transformation of Resources

A common purpose of organizations is to transform resources from one form to a different, more valuable, form to meet the needs of people. Resources include natural resources (such as minerals and timber), physical resources (such as buildings and equipment), management skills, labor, financial resources, legal rights (such as patents and trademarks), information, and the systems that provide information. The transformation process combines these resources to create goods and services. Transformation may involve making goods or services easier or less expensive for customers to obtain, as in most merchandising and service companies. Or it may involve physically converting resources by processing or combining them, as in manufacturing companies. An easy way to understand the transformation of resources is by thinking about how a bakery takes resources like flour and sugar and transforms them through the mixing and baking process to become cookies. Exhibit 4 illustrates this transformation process.

Organizations are created because many transformations are too difficult or too expensive for individuals to accomplish without working together. By combining their managerial skills, labor, and money, individuals create organizations to provide value that otherwise would be unavailable. Value is added to society when an organization transforms resources from a less desirable form or location to a more desirable form or

EXHIBIT 4
Transformation of Resources into Goods and Services

location. **The transformation, if it meets a need of society, creates value because people are better off after the transformation than before.** For example, a company that manufactures shirts creates value because the shirts are more useful to those who purchase them than the material from which the shirts are made or the cotton or synthetic fibers used to make the material.

To improve its welfare, a society must encourage organizations to increase the value they create. Because resources are in scarce supply, a society should attempt to use its resources wisely. A major purpose of accounting information is to help decide how to get the most value from scarce resources.

Creating Value

Objective 3
Describe how businesses create value.

How can society determine how to use its resources? Decisions about using scarce resources wisely are not easy. Because society is made up of many individuals, disagreement often exists as to how resources should be used. In our society and many others, markets are the means used to promote the wise use of many resources.

Markets exist to allocate scarce resources used and produced by organizations. **A *market* is any location or process that permits resources to be bought and sold.** Competition in a market determines the amount and value of resources available for exchange. The more valuable a resource is in meeting your needs, the more you are willing to pay for it as a buyer, or the more you want for it as a seller.

The price paid for a resource in a competitive market is an indication of the value assigned to it at the particular time the buyer and seller negotiate an exchange. For example, when you buy a box of cookies, you exchange money for it. The amount of money is a measure of the value you place on the product. Thus, the price of goods and services in a market is a basis for measuring value. **Accounting measures the increase in value created by a transformation as the difference between the total price of goods and services sold and the total cost of resources consumed in developing, producing, and selling the goods and services.**

*Learning Note - Distinguish between prices charged by a business to its customers and prices paid by a business for resources it consumes. A price charged by a business is a **sales price**. A price paid by a business to purchase resources that will be consumed in providing goods and services is a **cost** to the business.*

What value results when you purchase cookies? The amount you pay for the cookies is an indication of the value you expect to receive. However, resources were consumed in producing the cookies and making them available to you as illustrated in Exhibit 5.

If you pay \$3.50 for a box of cookies and the total cost of producing the cookies and making them available to you is \$3.00, the value added by the transformation is \$0.50. The difference between the price you pay and the total cost of the cookies is profit for those who produce and sell the cookies. ***Profit* is the difference between the price a seller receives for goods or services and the total cost to the seller of all resources consumed**

EXHIBIT 5
Value Created by Transforming Resources

Sales Price of Box of Cookies		Total Cost of Resources Consumed to Produce and Make Box of Cookies Available		Value Added
$3.50	–	**$3.00**	=	**$0.50**

in developing, producing, and selling these goods or services during a particular period. Thus, profits are the net resources generated from selling goods and services (resources received from the sales minus resources used in making the sales).

Several types of markets are important in our economy. Markets exist for resources used by organizations. Organizations compete in **financial markets** for financial resources. Investors choose where to invest their money by selecting among competing organizations. Organizations compete in **supplier markets** for other resources needed to produce goods and services. Competition in these markets determines the costs of materials, labor, equipment, and other resources available to organizations. Organizations compete in **product markets** (markets for goods and services). These markets determine the prices of goods and services available to customers. From the perspective of organizations, financial and supplier markets are input markets; product markets are output markets. All of these markets allocate scarce resources.

Exhibit 6 reports the actual profit earned by Favorite Cookie Company in January 2007, its first month of operations. (Keep in mind, the information presented earlier was the estimated amount of sales, costs, and profit.) The profit of $1,700 represents the difference between the amount of resources created by selling goods to customers and the total cost of resources consumed in providing those goods. Of course, a business venture may not produce a profit. It produces a loss if it consumes more resources than it creates.

This exhibit reports results of activities that occurred during January. These results can be compared with expected results. Favorite Cookie Company had sales of $11,400 compared with expected sales of $12,000. The cost of merchandise sold during January was $7,600 rather than the expected amount of $8,000, and profit earned by the company was $1,700 rather than the expected amount of $1,900. By examining the differences between expected and actual results, Maria and Stan can determine whether they need to make changes in their business. Perhaps they need to find more stores to sell their products, or perhaps they need to advertise their products.

EXHIBIT 6
Profit Earned by Favorite Cookie Company in January

Favorite Cookie Company
Profit Earned
For January

Resources created from selling cookies		$11,400
Resources consumed:		
Cost of merchandise sold	$7,600	
Wages	1,000	
Rent	600	
Supplies	300	
Utilities	200	
Total cost of resources consumed		9,700
Profit earned		$ 1,700

THE ROLE OF ACCOUNTING IN BUSINESS ORGANIZATIONS

Objective 4

Explain how accounting helps investors and other decision makers understand businesses.

Businesses earn profits by providing goods and services demanded by society. Owners invest in a business to receive a return on their investments from profits earned by their business. By investing in a business, owners are forgoing the use of their money for other purposes. In exchange, they expect to share in a business's profits. ***Return on investment (ROI)*** **is the amount of profit earned by a business that could be paid to owners.** Return on investment often is expressed as a ratio that compares the amount of profit to the amount invested in a business by its owners:

$$\text{Return on Investment} = \frac{\text{Profit}}{\text{Amount Invested}}$$

Profits represent net resources that have been earned through sales transactions. A business may distribute profits to its owners. Alternatively, owners (or managers acting on their behalf) may decide to reinvest profits in a business to acquire additional resources. The business can use the additional resources to earn more profits by expanding its size or by expanding into new locations or product lines. Either way, the owners are usually better off. They receive cash from their investments if profits are withdrawn, or they add value to the business if profits are reinvested.

As shown in Exhibit 6, Favorite Cookie Company earned $1,700 during January. As the owners, Maria and Stan may choose to withdraw some or all of this amount for personal use. It is their return on investment. Alternatively, they might choose to reinvest all or a portion of this profit to enlarge their company by buying a larger amount of merchandise for sale in February.

Return on investment for Favorite Cookie Company for January was $1,700, or 17% ($1,700 ÷ $10,000), relative to the owners' initial investment. If Maria and Stan withdraw more than $1,700 from their business, the additional amount withdrawn is a **return *of* investment,** not a return **on** investment. That additional amount is a return of a portion of the amount they originally invested. **For a company to maintain its capital (the amount invested by its owners), it must pay a return to owners from profits the company has earned. Otherwise, the company is reducing its capital by returning a portion of owners' investments to them.**

The amount of return owners receive from a company depends on the company's success in earning a profit. If you are the primary owner of a business, you are actively involved in managing the business, and its success depends largely on your ability and effort. If you are one of many who invest in a company, you probably are not actively involved in the business, and its success depends largely on the abilities and efforts of those who are managing the business. When you invest in a business, you have no guarantee that it will be successful. You are taking a risk that you may not receive a return on your investment, that the return may be smaller than you expected, or even that you might lose your investment.

Why invest in a business if the investment is risky? If a business is successful, its owners can expect to earn a higher rate of return on their investments than they could earn on a safer alternative, such as a savings account. By investing $10,000 in Favorite Cookie Company, Maria and Stan expect to earn $1,900 each month from their investment. If they invested their money in a savings account, they would expect to earn $50 each month. In general, it is necessary to take greater risks in order to earn higher returns. Accounting information helps owners evaluate the risks and returns associated with their investments so they can make good decisions.

To earn profits and pay returns to owners, businesses must operate effectively and efficiently. **An *effective business* is one that is successful in providing goods and services demanded by customers.** Effective management involves identifying the right products and putting them in the right locations at the right times. **An *efficient business* is one that keeps the costs of resources consumed in providing goods and services low**

relative to the selling prices of these goods and services. Managers must control costs by using the proper mix, qualities, and quantities of resources to avoid waste and to reduce costs. The risk of owning a business is lower if the business is effective and efficient than if it is ineffective or inefficient. Efficient and effective businesses are competitive in financial, supplier, and product markets.

Favorite Cookie Company will be effective if it sells products desired by customers and if the products are made available in locations convenient for customers to purchase them. The company will be efficient if it can keep the costs of resources it consumes low relative to the price of the goods it sells. During January, the company was less effective than Maria and Stan had planned because it sold fewer goods than expected. The company was efficient in controlling the cost of resources consumed because its costs were less than the prices of goods sold, thus permitting the company to earn a profit.

Business owners expect to receive a return on their investments. Investors choose among alternative investments by evaluating the amount, timing, and uncertainty of the returns they expect to receive. Businesses that earn high profits and are capable of paying high returns have less difficulty in obtaining investors than other businesses. A business that cannot earn sufficient profits will be forced to become more effective and efficient or to go out of business.

The accounting information system is a major source of the information investors use in making decisions about their investments. Accounting information helps investors assess the effectiveness and efficiency of businesses. It helps them estimate the returns that can be expected from investing in a business and the amount of risk associated with their investments. Financial, supplier, and product markets create incentives for businesses to provide products that society demands. These markets help ensure that scarce resources are used to improve society's welfare. Markets help allocate scarce resources to those organizations that can best transform them to create value.

Accounting **is an information system for the measurement and reporting of the transformation of resources into goods and services and the sale or transfer of these goods and services to customers.** Accounting uses the prices and costs of resources to measure value created by the transformation process and to trace the flow of resources through the transformation process. By tracing the flow of resources, managers and other decision makers can determine how efficiently and effectively resources are being used.

Self-Study Problem #1

John Bach owns a music store in which he sells and repairs musical instruments and sells sheet music. The following transactions occurred for Bach's Music Store during December 2006:

1. Sold $8,000 of musical instruments that cost the company $4,300.
2. Sold $1,400 of sheet music that cost the company $870.
3. The price of repair services provided during the month was $2,200.
4. Rent on the store for the month was $650.
5. The cost of supplies used during the month was $250.
6. The cost of advertising for the month was $300.
7. The cost of utilities for the month was $200.
8. Other miscellaneous costs for December were $180.

Required

A. Determine the profit earned by Bach's Music Store for December.

B. Explain how profit measures the value created by Bach's Music Store.

The solution to Self-Study Problem 1 appears at the end of the chapter.

THE STRUCTURE OF BUSINESS ORGANIZATIONS

Objective 5
Identify business ownership structures and their advantages and disadvantages.

Many types of decisions are made in organizations. Accounting provides important information to make these decisions. For example, organizations require financial resources to buy other resources used to produce goods and services. Primary sources of financing for businesses are owners and creditors.

Business Ownership

Businesses may be classified into two categories: those that are distinct legal entities apart from their owners and those that are not distinct legal entities. **A *corporation* is a legal entity with the right to enter into contracts; the right to own, buy, and sell property; and the right to sell stock.** Resources are owned by the corporation rather than by individual owners.

Corporations may be very large or fairly small organizations. Small corporations often are managed by their owners. The owners of most large corporations do not manage their companies. Instead, they hire professional managers. These owners have the right to vote on certain major decisions, but they do not control the operations of their corporations on a day-to-day basis. One reason most large businesses are organized as corporations is that corporations typically have greater access to financial markets than other types of organizations.

A corporation may be owned by a large number of investors who purchase shares of stock issued by the corporation. **Each share of *stock* is a certificate of ownership that represents an equal share in the ownership of a corporation.** An investor who owns 10% of the shares of a corporation owns 10% of the company and has a right to 10% of the return available to stockholders. ***Stockholders,* or *shareholders,* are the owners of a corporation.**

Shares of stock often are traded in stock markets, such as the New York, London, and Tokyo stock exchanges, which are established specifically for this purpose. These markets facilitate the exchange of stock between buyers and sellers. Therefore, unlike other businesses, ownership in many corporations changes frequently as stockholders buy or sell shares of stock. Major corporations, such as **General Motors, Exxon,** or **Microsoft,** have received billions of dollars from stockholders.

***Proprietorships* and *partnerships* are business organizations that do not have legal identities distinct from their owners. Proprietorships have only one owner; partnerships have more than one owner.** For most proprietorships and partnerships, owners also manage the business. Owners have a major stake in the business because often much of their personal wealth is invested in it. The amount of a proprietor's personal wealth and his or her ability to borrow limit the size of a proprietorship. If a proprietorship is profitable, profits earned by the proprietor can be reinvested, and the business can become fairly large.

Partnerships can include several partners; therefore, the money available to finance a partnership depends on the money available from all the partners. New partners can be added, making new money available to the business. While most partnerships are small, large businesses (with as many as a thousand or more owners) sometimes are organized as partnerships. The profit of most proprietorships and partnerships is not taxed. Instead, the profit is income for the owners, who pay income taxes on the profit as part of their personal income taxes.

INTERNATIONAL

Percentage of Companies and Volume of Sales by Type of Organization

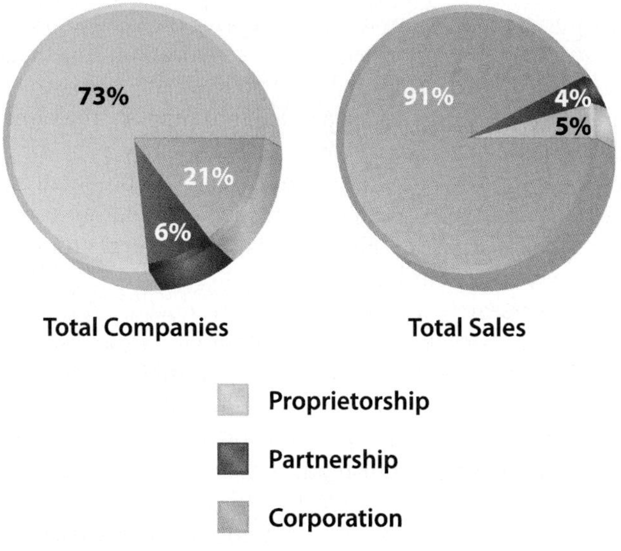

Data source: U.S. Census Bureau Web site (http://www.census.gov)

EXHIBIT 7
Corporate Management Functions

Management of Corporations

Exhibit 7 describes the organizational structure of a typical corporation. A **board of directors** oversees the decisions of management and is responsible for protecting the interests of stockholders. Normally, the board is appointed by management with the approval of stockholders. Top managers often serve on the board along with outside directors who are not part of the corporation's management. The **chairman of the board** often holds the position of **chief executive officer (CEO)** with the ultimate responsibility for the success of the business. The **president**, as **chief operating officer (COO)**, is responsible for the day-to-day management of a corporation. In some cases, the president also may be the CEO. The company may appoint any number of **vice presidents**, who are responsible for various functions in the organization. The titles and roles of these managers will vary from corporation to corporation. Along with the CEO and the president, the vice presidents constitute the top management of a corporation. Together, they make planning decisions and develop company goals and policies.

Functions performed within a corporation may be separated into support functions and primary functions. Support functions assist the primary functions by providing information and other resources necessary to produce and sell goods and services. Primary functions are those actually involved in producing and selling goods and services. These functions include distribution of goods and services to customers and servicing the goods and services to meet customer needs.

Among the support functions are research and development, product and production design, finance, legal services, accounting, purchasing, and human resources. The **chief financial officer (CFO)**, who also may be the **treasurer**, is responsible for obtaining financial resources and managing a corporation's cash. The **controller**, as the chief accounting officer, is responsible for accounting and financial reporting, developing and maintaining the accounting information system, and reporting to tax and regulatory authorities.

Primary functions involve production, distribution, sales, and service. **Plant managers** oversee production for specific product lines or geographical locations. These managers often have their own staffs at the divisional or plant level. For example, divisional or plant level controllers exist in many corporations. Research, design, and development staffs also exist at the divisional or plant level in some organizations.

Corporations may be organized by functions such as those described in Exhibit 7. Other corporations are organized primarily by region or product line. For example, multinational companies may be organized into North American, European, and Pacific divisions. Functional areas, such as development and production, report to regional or product managers. Many corporations are finding advantages in changing from a traditional organization structure to teams of managers working together on specific projects. Thus, the idea for a new product may be the responsibility of a team of employees from a company's functional areas, such as engineering, accounting, and marketing. Together, the team decides on a design for the product and on a production process to create efficiency and product quality.

Advantages of Corporations

A corporate form of organization has several advantages over proprietorships or partnerships. Corporations have **continuous lives** apart from those of their owners. If a proprietor or partner sells her or his share of a business or dies, the business ceases to exist as a legal entity. The new owner of the business must reestablish the business as a new legal entity. Most corporations, however, continue unchanged if current owners sell their stock, donate it to charity, give it to relatives, or otherwise dispose of their shares.

Shareholders normally are not liable personally for the debts of a corporation. This is a characteristic known as **limited liability**. If a corporation defaults on debt or enters bankruptcy, its owners may lose a portion or all of their investments in the company, but they are not obligated to use their personal wealth to repay creditors for losses the creditors incurred. In many cases, proprietors and partners are personally liable for the debts of their companies and can be required to use their personal wealth to repay their creditors.

*Learning Note - A partnership can be organized as a **limited liability partnership (LLP)**. The LLP restricts the personal liability of each partner for obligations created by the company. Many professional service companies, particularly accounting and legal firms, are organized as LLPs. A business also can be organized as a **limited liability company (LLC)**. An LLC combines certain advantages of a partnership and a corporation in that it combines the tax treatment of a partnership with the limited liability of corporations. While a corporation can have as few as one shareholder, an LLC usually must have at least two owners. Both LLPs and LLCs are separate legal entities from their owners.*

Shareholders of most corporations do not manage the company. They elect members of the board of directors, who then hire **professional managers** to run the corporation. Investors can own part of a corporation or parts of many corporations without having to participate in the day-to-day decisions of running those companies. Many Americans own stock in corporations through personal investments and retirement plans, but they are not required to commit large amounts of their personal time to corporate concerns.

Shareholders cannot enter into contracts or agreements that are binding on a corporation unless they are managers or directors. Therefore, investors in a corporation do not have to be concerned about the abilities of other stockholders to make good business decisions. In contrast, bad decisions by one partner can result in the personal bankruptcy of all partners in a partnership. This problem arises because partners normally are in a mutual agency relationship. *Mutual agency* **permits a partner to enter into contracts and agreements that are binding on all members of a partnership.**

By selling shares to many investors, a corporation can obtain a large amount of financial resources. The **ability to raise large amounts of capital** permits corporations to become very large organizations. Thus, corporations can invest in plant facilities and undertake production activities that would be difficult for proprietorships or partnerships.

Disadvantages of Corporations

There are several disadvantages to the corporate form of ownership. Most corporations must pay **taxes** on their incomes. Corporate taxes are separate from the taxes paid by shareholders on dividends received from the company. (Some corporations, however, especially smaller ones, are not taxed separately.) Another disadvantage is that corporations are **regulated** by various state and federal government agencies. These regulations require corporations to comply with many state and federal rules concerning business practices and reporting of financial information. Corporations must file many reports with government agencies and make public disclosure of their business activities. Compliance with these regulations is costly. Also, some of the **required disclosures** may be helpful to competitors. Partnerships and proprietorships are regulated also, but the degree of regulation normally is much less than for corporations.

Owners of corporations usually do not have access to information about the day-to-day activities of their companies. They depend on managers to make decisions that will increase the value of their investments. However, managers' personal interests sometimes conflict with the interests of stockholders. This problem produces a condition known as moral hazard. Moral hazard arises when one group, known as **agents** (such as managers), is responsible for serving the needs of another group, known as **principals** (such as investors). ***Moral hazard*** **is the condition that exists when agents have superior information to principals and are able to make decisions that favor their own interests over those of the principals.**

Without disclosure of reliable information, corporations would have difficulty in selling stock, and investors would be unable to determine whether managers were making decisions that increased stockholder value or were making decisions that took advantage of the stockholders. Accounting reports are major sources of information to help stockholders assess the performance of managers. For example, profit information helps owners evaluate how well managers have used owners' investments to earn returns for the owners. Moral hazard imposes costs on corporations because managers must report to stockholders and, generally, these reports are audited. **An audit verifies the reliability of reported information.**

The size of many corporations makes them **difficult to manage**. An individual manager cannot be involved directly with all the decisions made in operating a large organization. Top-level managers depend on other managers to make decisions and to keep them informed about a corporation's operations. This process is costly because coordination among managers may be difficult to achieve. Moral hazard also exists among managers and employees, not just between managers and investors. Corporate goals and policies provide guidance for manager decisions, but communicating goals and policies and providing incentives for managers to implement them often is difficult and expensive. Employees and low-level managers may not report reliable information about their activities to high-level managers if the information is not in their best interests. Multinational corporations, in particular, are complex and difficult to manage. Distant locations for facilities and differences in language and local custom can cause special problems.

The profits of corporations, except for those of small privately owned ones, referred to as Subchapter S corporations, are taxed separately from taxes paid by the owners of the corporation. The federal government and most state governments impose a corporate income tax on the profits of corporations. This tax is paid by the corporation. In addition, amounts distributed to shareholders are taxed as part of their personal income. Thus, the profits of corporations often are subject to **double taxation**: taxation of the corporation and taxation of the shareholders.

Creditors

In addition to money provided by owners, businesses (and other organizations) may borrow money. Money may be obtained from banks and other financial institutions, or it may be borrowed from individual lenders. **A** ***creditor*** **is someone who loans financial resources to an organization.**

Most organizations depend on banks and similar institutions to lend them money. Corporations often borrow money from individuals or other companies. Exhibit 8

EXHIBIT 8
Sources of Financing for Selected Corporations

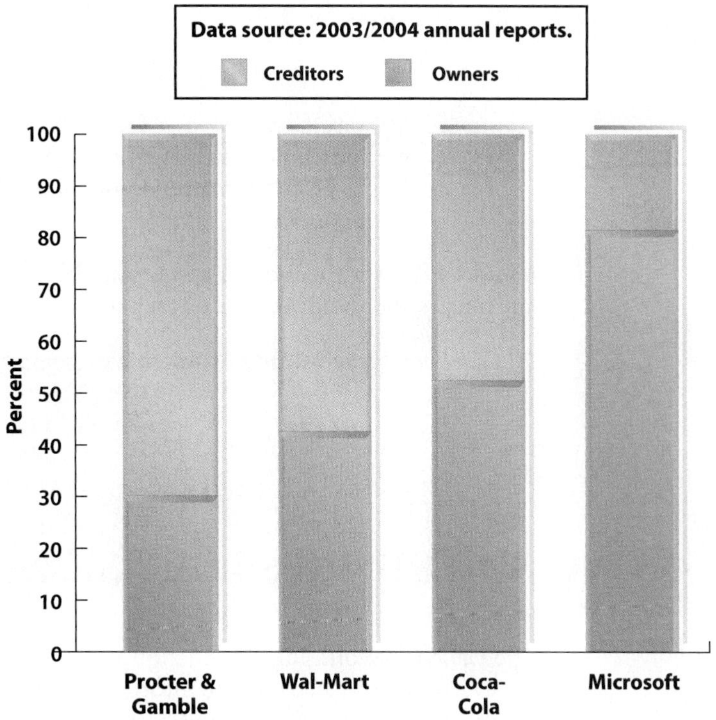

shows the amount of money several large corporations have received from owners and creditors. The amounts and proportions of financing from owners and creditors vary greatly across companies.

Creditors loan money to organizations to earn a return on their investments. They usually loan money for a specific period and are promised a specific rate of return on their investments. Usually, this is a fixed rate (say 10%). In contrast, owners invest for a nonspecific period (until they decide to sell their investments) and receive a return that depends on the profits earned by the business.

The success of a business determines whether creditors will receive the amount promised by the borrower. When a business fails to generate sufficient cash from selling goods and services to pay for resources it consumes and to pay its creditors, the creditors may not receive the amount promised. Therefore, creditors estimate the probability that an organization will be able to repay debt and interest. Risk is a concern of both creditors and owners, and accounting information is key in evaluating the risk. Exhibit 9 illustrates the role of owners and creditors in providing financial resources for businesses.

EXHIBIT 9
Obtaining Financial Resources

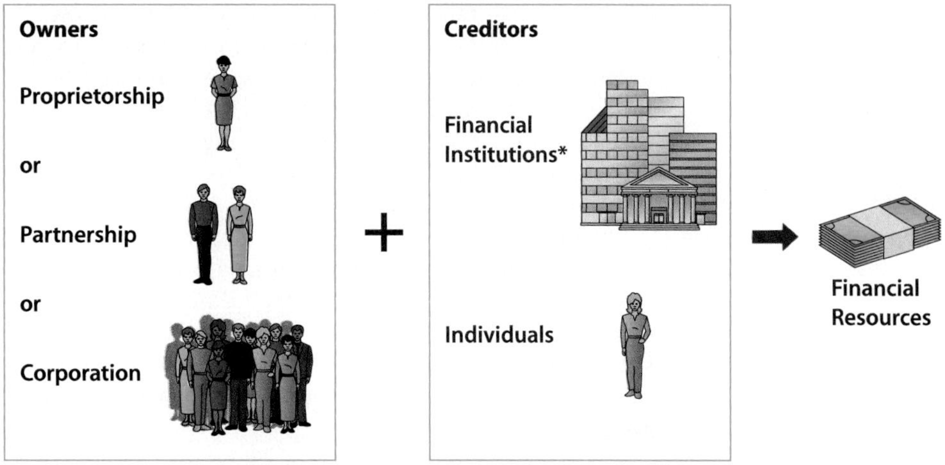

*The term "financial institutions" refers to banks, savings and loans, and similar companies.

Self-Study Problem #2

Hammer Hardware Company and **Home Depot** are both retail stores that sell tools, hardware, and household items. Hammer Hardware is owned by Harvey Hammer and is organized as a proprietorship. Home Depot is organized as a corporation and is owned by thousands of investors.

Required Why is the form of ownership different for these companies? What are the advantages and disadvantages of each form?

The solution to Self-Study Problem 2 appears at the end of the chapter.

ACCOUNTING AND BUSINESS DECISIONS

Objective 6

Identify uses of accounting information for making decisions about corporations.

The value of accounting information is determined by how well it meets the needs of those who use it. Accounting information describes economic consequences of the transformation process. Information needs of decision makers arise from the many relationships that occur within the transformation process among an organization's stakeholders: managers, investors, suppliers, employees, customers, and government authorities. These stakeholders compete in markets for resources, or they regulate these markets. They exchange resources or services with an organization as part of its transformation process.

Contracts **are legal agreements for the exchange of resources and services.** They provide legal protection for the parties to an agreement if the terms of the agreement are not honored. Contract terms establish the rights and responsibilities of the contracting parties. Contracts are "give and get" relationships. Each party to the contract expects to receive something in exchange for something given. For example, a contract by an employee to provide labor to a company involves the giving of labor services by the employee in exchange for wages and benefits. Contracts with proprietorships and partnerships are between the owners/managers and other contracting parties. In contrast, because corporations are legal entities, contracts can be formed with the corporation as one of the contracting parties. Managers make contracts on behalf of corporations and their owners.

Contracts are enforceable only to the extent that contracting parties can determine whether the terms of the contract are being met. Assume that you sign a contract with a company that calls for you to invest $1,000 in the company and for the company to pay you 10% of the amount the company earns each year. Unless you have reliable information about the company's earnings, you cannot determine whether it is paying you the agreed amount. Therefore, you probably would not agree to the contract. Contracts require information that the contracting parties accept as reliable and sufficient for determining if the terms of the contract have been met. **Accounting information is important for forming and evaluating contracts.**

Exhibit 10 identifies examples of exchanges among stakeholders for which contracts and information about organizations are important. The following sections discuss these exchanges.

Learning Note - Products can be either goods or services or both. While often we talk about companies that sell goods, you should keep in mind how accounting is important to service companies also.

EXHIBIT 10
Examples of Exchanges Requiring Information

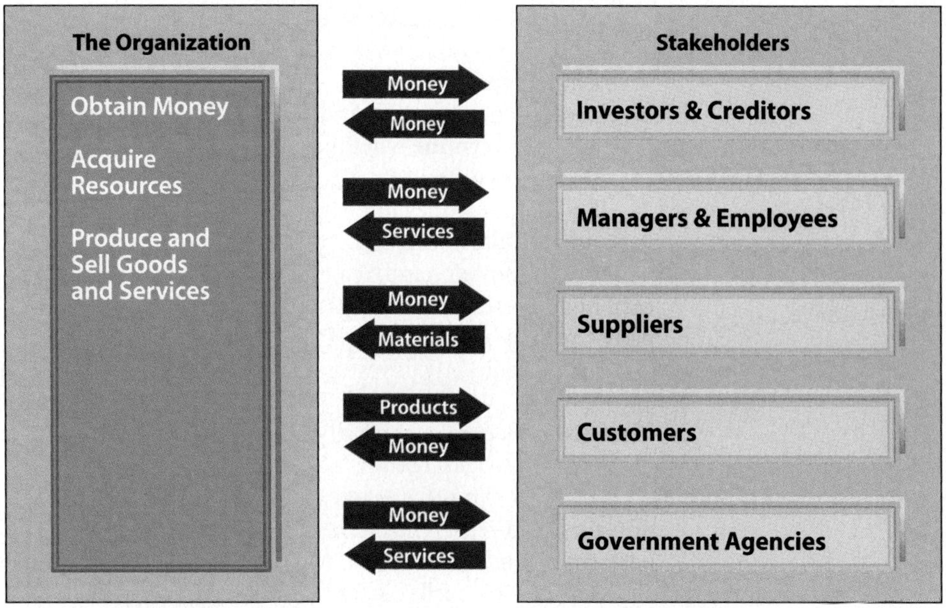

Risk and Return

Contracts are formed to identify rights and responsibilities. These rights and responsibilities establish how risk and return will be shared among contracting parties. Information about risk and return is needed to determine contract terms. Return is the amount a party to a contract expects as compensation for the exchange outlined in the contract. As noted earlier in this chapter, risk is uncertainty about an outcome; it results from uncertainty about the amount and timing of return. Exhibit 11 describes the returns of two investments (A and B) over several time periods. Which investment is riskier? Returns for Investment A are relatively stable and predictable; they are growing at a steady rate. Returns for Investment B are less predictable. Investment B is riskier than A, although it may produce higher returns over time than A.

Those who invest in a company expect to earn returns on their investments. At the same time, they must evaluate the risk inherent in investing in the company. What should they earn if the company does well? What might happen if the company does poorly? Risk and return are related in most situations; investors expect to earn higher returns on riskier investments. The higher returns compensate them for accepting higher risk. However, actual returns may differ from expected returns, and so riskier investments may actually result in higher or lower returns than less risky investments. On average, however, higher return should be associated with greater risk; otherwise, investors will not participate in risky investments. Accounting information helps investors predict risk and return associated with investments. The following sections consider the risk and return evaluations made by those who contract with an organization.

EXHIBIT 11
An Illustration of Risk and Return

	Returns	
Time Period	**Investment A**	**Investment B**
1	$6	$ 8
2	6	7
3	7	10
4	7	4
5	8	12
6	8	11

Investors and Creditors. Investors and creditors contract with companies to provide financial resources in exchange for future returns. They need information to decide whether to invest in a company and how much to invest. **Accounting information helps investors evaluate the risk and return they can expect from their investments. Also, it helps them determine whether managers of companies they invest in are meeting the terms of their contracts.**

If a company does not earn sufficient profits, it may be unable to repay its creditors, and creditors can force a company to liquidate (sell its resources) to repay its debts. On the other hand, if a company is profitable, stockholders (investors) normally earn higher returns than creditors because stockholders have a right to share in a company's profits. Creditors receive only the amount of interest agreed to when debt is issued. Consequently, investors and creditors choose between risk and return.

Managers. Owners generally do not manage large corporations. Instead, they hire managers who operate the businesses for them. Managers contract with owners to provide management services in exchange for salaries and other compensation. Owners, or directors who represent them, need information to determine how well managers are performing and to reward managers when they do well. To provide incentives for managers to perform well, owners may offer managers bonuses when a company is profitable. **Accounting information provides a means for owners and managers to determine the amount of compensation managers will receive.**

Compensation arrangements also encourage managers to present their companies' performances in the best light. Often, compensation is linked to profits and other accounting information, giving managers incentives to report numbers that will maximize their compensation. The combination of management control over information and manager incentives to make their companies look good provides an ethical dilemma for managers. Sometimes, they must choose between the company's best interests and their own best interests.

Decisions by managers have a direct effect on the risk and return of those who contract with a company. Managers decide which resources to acquire, when to acquire them, and how much to pay for them.

Each investment in a resource involves decisions about the risk and return associated with the investment. An organization is a portfolio (collection) of individual resources.

CASE IN POINT

http://ingram.swlearning.com

Visit Enron's home page to learn more about the company.

Moral Hazard—Mismanagement by Managers

In 2001, Enron Corporation, the seventh largest U.S. corporation at the time, declared bankruptcy after revealing that its profits had been overstated for several years and that it had failed to report large amounts of debt. The debt was used by the corporation to expand its business operations into new markets and products. Some of these new ventures resulted in losses that were not properly reported by the corporation's management. When revealed, these losses made it difficult for the corporation to obtain additional financing, and it was unable to meet its debt obligations. As a result of these events, the market value of the corporation decreased dramatically, creating losses for many investors. Many employees lost their jobs and retirement savings, and many creditors were unable to collect amounts owed them. In 2005, the company was in the process of selling its assets to pay its creditors.

Enron's investors and creditors sued the company's managers, claiming that they had been misled by information reported by the managers. The managers had earned high salaries and other compensation associated with the high profitability and growth they reported for the company. Investors and creditors, and many members of Congress who investigated the collapse of Enron, argued that managers had profited by operating the business for personal gain rather than for the benefit of the company's owners.

In combination, the risks and returns on the investments in these resources help determine the risk and return of the organization as a whole. One task of management is to select a portfolio of resources that will yield a desired amount of return at a level of risk that managers and owners find acceptable. Investments in proven technology and established products generally are less risky than investments in new technology or products. Investments in resources in some countries are riskier than those in other countries because of those countries' political and economic environments. **Accounting information is useful for identifying the types and locations of an organization's resources.**

A major purpose of accounting is to measure costs associated with the flow of resources through the transformation process. Accounting also measures resources obtained from selling goods and services. The profits earned by a corporation are a major determinant of risk and return. **Information about the results of the operations of a business is used to estimate, compare, and manage companies' risks and returns.**

Employees. Employees have a major effect on a company's risk and return. Wages and quality of work directly affect product quality, sales, costs, and profits. Companies evaluate the cost and productivity of their employees. They compare employee performance with management expectations, examine changes over time, and compare different divisions with each other. **Accounting information helps managers assess employee performance.**

Employees negotiate for wages, benefits, and job security. Compensation is affected by a company's performance and financial condition. Labor unions and other employee groups use accounting information to evaluate a company's ability to compensate its employees. Like other contracting parties, employees evaluate risk and return in an employment relationship. If a company does well, employees expect to be rewarded. If it does poorly, they may face layoffs, wage and benefit cuts, and loss of jobs. **Accounting information helps employees assess the risk and return of their employment contracts.**

Suppliers. An organization purchases materials, merchandise, and other resources from suppliers. These resources are a major cost for most companies. Careful negotiation of prices, credit, and delivery schedules between management and suppliers is required. If a company cannot obtain quality materials when they are needed, it may incur major losses as a result of idle production, waste, lost sales, and dissatisfied customers. If a supplier goes out of business or cannot fulfill its commitments, a company may have difficulty obtaining needed resources. **Accounting information helps companies evaluate the abilities of their suppliers to meet their resource needs.**

Suppliers often sell resources to companies on credit. These suppliers are creditors who are financing the sale of resources to a company in anticipation of future payments. Usually, these loans are for short periods (30 to 60 days), although longer financing sometimes is arranged. When a company is not profitable, its suppliers may have difficulty collecting the amounts owed them. Therefore, suppliers evaluate the risk they are taking in selling on credit to other companies. **Suppliers often use accounting information about their customers to evaluate the risk of a buyer not being able to pay for goods and services acquired.**

Customers. A company is a supplier to its customers. Thus, it evaluates customers in the same way it is evaluated by suppliers. Managers decide the terms of sales by evaluating the risk and return associated with the sales. Riskier customers normally receive less favorable terms. For example, a customer with good credit can purchase a house, car, appliances, and other goods on more favorable terms than can a customer with bad credit.

Customers' decisions to buy products often are affected by their perception of quality and dependability, as well as price. These decisions also may depend on the financial reputation of the seller. Will the company be in business in the future when maintenance, repair, or replacement is needed? Will it be able to honor warranties? Are its profits sufficient to invest in new technology and maintain quality products? **Accounting**

information is used to assess the risks of buying from specific companies and selling to specific customers.

Government Agencies. Organizations are required to provide information to government agencies. Governments require businesses to purchase licenses for selling goods and services and to pay fees and taxes for various government services. Often these amounts are determined by the amount of sales or the profitability of an organization. Governments collect information about organizations as a basis for economic forecasts and planning at the local, state, and national levels. Businesses are required to report information to state and federal authorities that regulate business activities to ensure fair trade, fair treatment of employees, and fair disclosure to investors.

Businesses report information to taxing authorities at various levels of government. Reports are required in filing sales, property, payroll, excise, and income taxes. The amount of these taxes is determined by a company's sales, the costs it incurs, and amounts paid to employees. **Government agencies use accounting information to make taxation and regulatory decisions.**

THE REGULATORY ENVIRONMENT OF ACCOUNTING

Objective 7

Explain the purpose and importance of accounting regulations.

Accounting information prepared for use by external decision makers is financial accounting information. *Financial accounting* **is the process of preparing, reporting, and interpreting accounting information that is provided to external decision makers.** It is a primary source of information for investors and creditors. Thus, it is very important to the organization when it wants to obtain resources from those external decision makers. It also may affect the decisions of suppliers, customers, and employees. Because of concerns about information reliability and moral hazard, managers of major corporations prepare financial accounting information according to specific rules called *generally accepted accounting principles* (GAAP). *GAAP* **are standards developed by professional accounting organizations to identify appropriate accounting and reporting procedures.** GAAP establish minimum disclosure requirements and increase the comparability of information from one period to the next and among different companies.

Learning Note - GAAP apply only to information prepared for use by external decision makers. Because managers control information available inside an organization, accounting standards such as GAAP are not necessary for this information.

This textbook emphasizes financial accounting for corporations. Moral hazard resulting from the separation of owners and managers has led to the creation of a strong regulatory environment for corporations. This environment oversees the development of accounting and reporting requirements for corporations. We will examine this environment and the resulting requirements.

Financial accounting usually is distinguished from managerial accounting. *Managerial* **(or** *management*) *accounting* **is the process of preparing, reporting, and interpreting accounting information that is provided to internal decision makers.** Because managers have control over the information they use internally, this information does not have to be prepared according to GAAP. Accounting information reported by managers to owners and other external decision makers is the subject of financial accounting. It is important to keep in mind, however, that this information also is used by managers. Although managers have access to information that extends beyond that reported to external decision makers, internal and external decisions are related. Therefore, this book will consider internal and external decisions that rely on financial accounting information.

Learning Note - Managers, as internal decision makers, use financial accounting information to evaluate the performance of their companies. Also, they are concerned about the effect of financial accounting information on the decisions of the other stakeholders because these decisions can affect their companies.

Accounting information reported by corporations to investors must be audited. **An *audit* is a detailed examination of an organization's financial reports.** It includes an examination of the information system used to prepare the reports and involves an examination of control procedures organizations use to help ensure the accuracy of accounting information. The purpose of an audit is to evaluate whether information reported to external decision makers is a **fair presentation** of an organization's economic activities. Standards (GAAP) for the preparation and reporting of information help ensure the reliability of accounting information. The auditors, who are independent **certified public accountants (CPAs)**, examine this information to confirm that it is prepared according to GAAP. To be a CPA, a person must pass a qualifying exam and meet education and experience requirements. CPAs are independent of the companies they audit because they are not company employees. Rather, they work for an accounting firm that is hired by the company's owners to perform the audit. In the case of a corporation, it is the board of directors, with the approval of stockholders, that hires the auditor. Also, CPAs should have no vested interests in the companies that might bias their audits.

http://ingram.swlearning.com

Learn more about the CPA exam.

Learning Note - GAAP apply to all business organizations. As long as accounting information produced by the business is used for internal purposes only, the company's managers can elect whether or not that information complies with GAAP. Conformity with GAAP is required for information produced for external users, such as creditors. Many privately-owned businesses are audited because they are required to provide accounting information to banks and other financial institutions that lend money to the businesses.

Many corporations must report audited financial accounting information to governmental agencies. Corporations whose stock is traded publicly in the United States report to the **Securities and Exchange Commission (SEC)**. This agency examines corporate financial reports to verify their conformance with GAAP and SEC requirements.

Case In Point

http://ingram.swlearning.com

Visit the Center for Public Company Audit Firms' site for general information regarding auditor responsibilities.

Auditor Responsibility

Enron Corporation's audit firm, Andersen, was investigated for its role in the misstatement of Enron's financial information. The audit firm admitted that it made mistakes in the audit but argued that Enron's managers had failed to report fully to the auditors about its questionable business activities. Andersen also was found guilty of destroying information that would have assisted the government in its investigation of Enron's activities. As a result, this industry leader could no longer perform SEC audits. Consequently, Andersen ceased to exist as an audit firm as former clients awarded their audits to other audit firms and as many Andersen employees left the firm.

Critics also questioned Andersen's independence in the audit because the firm earned large consulting fees from Enron. The critics argued that Andersen did not press Enron for proper disclosure of its business activities for fear that it would lose Enron as a client, thereby losing the consulting fees in addition to its audit fees. It is important that audit firms be *perceived* as being independent of their clients, in addition to actually *being* independent. Auditors must continuously assess their independence.

If the SEC believes a company's reports have not been prepared in conformance with GAAP, it can refer the company to the Justice Department for criminal and civil charges. In addition, the corporation's auditors can be prosecuted if they fail to meet their responsibilities for ensuring that a corporation's reports are a fair representation of its economic activities.

Financial accounting is critical for the operations of a market economy. **Full and fair disclosure** of business activities is necessary for stakeholders to evaluate the returns and risks they anticipate from investing in and contracting with business organizations. **Capital markets**, markets in which corporations obtain financing from investors, in particular, require information that permits investors to assess the risks and returns of their investments. If that information is not available or is unreliable, investors are unable to make good decisions. **Without reliable information about companies' business activities, investors cannot determine which companies are most efficient and effective and are making the best use of resources.** Consequently, resources may be allocated to less efficient and effective companies, resulting in a loss of value for society.

Without good information, contracts cannot be evaluated, and markets cannot function properly. Consequently, accounting plays a critical role in our society. For our society to continue to prosper, it is essential that those who make decisions about resource allocations understand accounting information and how to use that information to evaluate business activities. They need to understand how accounting information is created and the limitations inherent in this information. Failure to understand accounting properly is likely to lead to poor decisions and unsatisfactory economic outcomes.

This book will help you understand why accounting information is important, how this information is produced, and how you can use this information to make good business decisions. It will help you learn to evaluate business activities and to determine which companies are operating most efficiently and effectively. It will help you contribute to improving our society by becoming an informed participant in our market economy.

THE IMPORTANCE OF ETHICS

Objective 8

Explain why ethics are important for business and accounting.

Ethics are important in business organizations. Ethics involve living by the norms and rules of society. In business, those norms and rules identify appropriate behavior for managers, employees, investors, and other stakeholders. Keeping their investors and other stakeholders fully informed about their business activities is an important ethical norm for managers. Managers who conceal their activities or who misrepresent those activities make it difficult for stakeholders to assess how well a business is performing. Overstating profits, for example, may result in investors allocating more resources to a company than actual results would justify. This misallocation results in a loss of value to society and often leads to financial harm for those who use this information.

Ethical behavior is particularly important for accounting because the reliability of accounting information depends on the honesty of those who prepare, report, and audit this information. Managers may make decisions that benefit themselves at a cost to investors or other stakeholders. If they then attempt to conceal these decisions by reporting incorrect information, that information is not an accurate description of the economic activities of a business. If employees steal money or other resources from a business and the thefts are not detected, the company's accounting information also will not properly reflect the company's economic situation. If those who audit a company do not ensure that reported information is a fair representation of the company's business activities, those who rely on the information are likely to be disadvantaged.

Those who contract with businesses must consider the ethics of those who manage them. Managers who are willing to bend rules or operate outside of accepted norms are likely to be untrustworthy. An important role of accounting is to evaluate whether appropriate rules are being followed in accounting for reporting business activities. Failure to follow these rules can result in significant economic consequences, as evidenced by the collapse of Enron Corporation. Generally accepted accounting principles and other accounting and auditing rules have been created to help ensure that companies fairly report their business activities. In addition, corporations and other organizations are required to maintain elaborate systems of controls to make it difficult for managers and employees to engage in unethical behavior or misrepresent business activities. We examine ethical issues and controls throughout this book as we consider proper accounting rules and procedures.

Self-Study Problem #3

Floorshine is a manufacturer of shoes. The company operates as a corporation and has issued shares of stock to its owners and debt to creditors. It has purchased and leased buildings and equipment. It purchases materials on short-term credit and converts the materials into shoes. The shoes are sold to retail stores, also on a short-term credit arrangement.

Required Identify the primary exchanges and contracts between the company and its stakeholders. Describe the primary information needs associated with these exchanges and contracts.

The solution to Self-Study Problem 3 appears at the end of the chapter.

Appendix *A Short Introduction to Excel*

This introduction summarizes some of the primary operations and functions of a spreadsheet. It is intended to get you started if you have not had previous experience with Excel. There are many operations and functions in addition to those mentioned here.

Identifying and Selecting Cells

A spreadsheet consists of rows and columns. Rows are identified by numbers, and columns are identified by letters. An intersection of a row and column is a cell. A cell is identified by the column letter and row number that intersect at that cell.

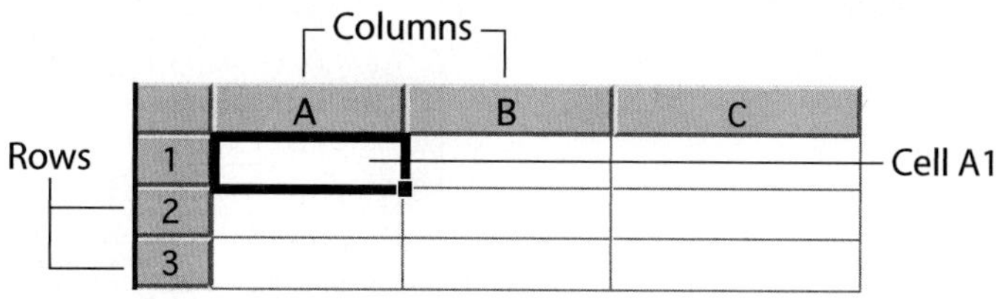

To select a cell, click on the cell using the left mouse button. A cell must be selected before you can enter data or format the cell. Enter data by typing numbers, words, or characters. Enter numbers without commas. Commas can be added using formatting procedures described later. An entire row or column can be selected by clicking on the row or column header. The row header is the leftmost cell in a row that contains the row number. A column header is the topmost cell in a column that contains the cell letter. A group of neighboring cells can be selected by clicking with the left mouse button on the cell in the upper, left corner of the group, then dragging the cursor over all the cells to be selected.

Referencing and Mathematical Operations

The contents of one or more cells can be referenced in another cell. To reference a cell, enter the equal sign followed by the cell being referenced. For example, entering =A1 in cell B1 will copy the contents of cell A1 in cell B1. If the contents of cell A1 are changed, these changes also will appear in cell B1. A common use of cell referencing is to calculate totals from data in a series of cells. For example, the following spreadsheet contains sales data for the first three months of a year. The total appears in cell B5. To calculate the total, you would enter a formula in cell B5. The formula would be =B2+B3+B4.

	A	B
1		Sales
2	January	3,457.38
3	February	3,892.90
4	March	3,204.07
5	Total	10,554.35

Normal mathematical operations can be entered in a cell:

=B2+B3 adds the contents of cells B2 and B3.
=B2−B3 subtracts the contents of cell B3 from cell B2.
=B2*B3 multiplies the contents of cell B2 by the contents of cell B3.
=B2/B3 divides the contents of cell B2 by the contents of cell B3.
=B2^B3 raises the number in cell B2 to the power of the number in cell B3.

Copying Cell Contents

The contents (including a formula) can be copied from one cell or group of cells to another cell or group of cells. To copy the contents, select the cells containing the data to be copied and click on Edit/Copy. Then select the cell you want to copy to (or the upper, left cell of a group of cells) and click Edit/Paste.

The contents of a cell also can be copied to a neighboring cell using a shortcut procedure. In the following example, we want to copy the contents of cell B4 to cell C4. Cell B4 contains the formula =B2+B3. To copy the contents, we select cell B4 and drag the cursor over the box in the lower, right corner of cell B4. The cursor changes shape and appears as crosshairs (+). If we click on the left mouse button while the cursor is in this shape, we can drag the contents of cell B4 to cell C4. The formula =B2+B3 is copied to cell C4, except that the references are automatically adjusted for the new column, and the formula appears as =C2+C3.

	A	B	C
1		Cash	Merchandise
2	Store 1	1,543.02	16,794.23
3	Store 2	4,587.45	24,586.50
4	Total	6,130.47	

Box

When you enter a formula in a cell, such as =B2+B3, the cell addresses are relative addresses. When the formula is copied to another cell, the relative addresses change. Copying the contents of cell B4 above to cell C4 results in an adjustment in the formula so that =B2+B3 is changed to =C2+C3. You can also enter absolute addresses. An absolute address results from entering a dollar sign ($) before a cell address. For example, if you enter =$B2+$B3 in cell B4 and then copy cell B4 to cell C4, the formula in

C4 remains =$B2+$B3. You can use absolute addresses for the column (=$B2), the row (=B$2), or both (=$B$2).

Changing Column Widths

You can make a column wider or narrower using the Format/Column/Width menu. A simpler approach is to move the cursor to the right-hand side of the column header of the column you wish to adjust. The cursor changes to appear as . Click and drag the cursor to the right or left to adjust the column width. The same procedure can be used for row height adjustments.

Menus

The top of an Excel spreadsheet contains menus. A brief description of the menu items you are likely to use on a regular basis follows.

File. Use the File menu to open a **New** spreadsheet, to **Open** an existing spreadsheet, to **Save** a spreadsheet, to **Print** a spreadsheet, and to **Close** the Excel program.

Edit. Use the Edit menu to **Delete** a row, column, or cell. Select the row, column, or cell and click Edit/Delete. You can delete the contents of a particular cell by selecting the cell and pressing the Backspace or Delete key.

View. Use the View menu to select which Toolbars appear on the spreadsheet. The Header and Footer command permits you to add titles and comments to spreadsheets that will appear on printed output. The Zoom command allows spreadsheets to be resized as they appear on the monitor to make them easier to see. This command does not affect printed output.

Insert. Use the Insert menu to insert **Rows, Columns,** and **Cells**. To enter a new row, select the row *below* the row you wish to add and click on Insert/Row. To enter a new column, select the column to the *left* of the column you want to add and click on Insert/Column. To enter a new cell, click on the cell where you want to add a new cell and click on Insert/Cell. A dialog box will ask whether you want the existing cell moved to the right or down. When you enter a new cell, all existing cells to the right or below the entered cell will be moved to make room for the new cell.

Format. Use the Format menu to format **Cells**. Select the cells and click on Format/Cells. A dialog box provides options. The **Number** tab provides various formatting options. The **Alignment** tab provides options for how numbers or text will be aligned. The Wrap text box can be checked (click on the box) to allow for more than one line of text to appear in a particular cell.

Tools. Use the Tools menu to check your **Spelling**.

Data. Use the Data menu to **Sort** data. To sort, select all the columns in the spreadsheet and click Data/Sort. A dialog box lets you select the column or columns you want to use to sort the data.

Help. Use the Help menu to get additional directions about using Excel. Click on Help/Contents and Index. Select a topic from the **Contents** tab or click on the **Index** tab. Type the keyword for an item to get additional information and click on the Display button.

Buttons

Several of the buttons under the menu are particularly useful. The identity of each button and its use are described below.

 **Save.** Click to save your spreadsheet. **Save your work often.**

 **Copy.** Copies the contents of a selected cell or group of cells.

 **Paste.** Pastes the contents of a copied cell or group of cells into a selected cell or group.

 **Format Painter.** Copies the format of a selected cell into another cell or group of cells. Select the cell with the format to be copied and click the button. Then click on the cell or click and drag over the cells where the format will be copied.

 **AutoSum.** Select a cell to contain the sum of a neighboring set of cells (above or to the left of the selected cell). For example, we want to sum the contents of cells E10 and E11 into cell E12. Select cell E12 and click on the AutoSum button. The =Sum formula appears in cell E12 as

shown below. You can change the cells to be included in the sum by clicking on the top cell to be included and dragging the cursor over the cells to be added as part of the sum.

412.89
84.56
=SUM(E10:E11)

Once the sum formula is correct, click on the checkmark in the selection box at the top of the spreadsheet:

X ✓ = | =SUM(E10:E11)

Click on the green checkmark to accept the cell contents. Click on the red X to remove the cell contents.

B *I* U **Format.** Select a cell or group of cells and click on B for bold, I for italics, and U for underline.

Align. Select a cell or group of cells and click on a button to align the cell contents to the left, center, or right of the cell.

Merge and Center. Select two or more neighboring cells in a row and click on the button to merge the cells into a single cell and center the cell contents. For example, the caption (The Book Wermz) in the following example was created by selecting cells B1 and C1 and clicking on the Merge and Center button.

	A	B	C
1		The Book Wermz	
2	Store 1	1,543.0	Merchandise
3	January	4,528.23	145,360.98

$ % , **Number Formatting.** Select a cell or group of cells and click on a button to include a dollar sign in the cell(s), to convert from decimals to percentages, or to add comma separators between thousands' digits in numbers.

Decimal Places. Select a cell or group of cells and click on a button to increase or decrease the number of decimal places showing in the cell(s).

Indent. Select a cell or group of cells and click on a button to indent the cell contents or to remove the indentation.

Borders. Select a cell or group of cells and click on the down arrow. Select the type of border you want for the cell(s) from the options provided. If the option you want is already showing on the button, click on the button to select that option.

THINKING BEYOND THE QUESTION

WHAT DO WE NEED TO KNOW TO START A BUSINESS?

The chapter introduction asked you to consider what you would need to know in order to start a company. This chapter identified several important considerations. How would your answer to this question differ if you were starting a service business or a nonprofit service organization as opposed to a retail business?

Self-Study Problem Solutions

SSP1-1 A.

Bach's Music Store Profit Earned For December 2006		
Resources created from selling goods and services:		
Musical instruments	$8,000	
Sheet music	1,400	
Repair of instruments	2,200	
Total resources created		$11,600
Resources consumed:		
Cost of instruments sold	$4,300	
Cost of sheet music sold	870	
Rent	650	
Supplies used	250	
Advertising	300	
Utilities	200	
Miscellaneous	180	
Total resources consumed		6,750
Profit		$ 4,850

B. The value created by a transformation of resources is the difference between the total price of the goods and services sold and the total cost of the resources consumed in producing these goods and services. This difference is profit for the seller.

SSP1-2 Hammer Hardware is owned and managed by Harvey Hammer. As a small company, Hammer Hardware does not need access to large amounts of capital. Harvey is probably more interested in maintaining control of his company rather than having others invest in it. As a proprietorship, Harvey has total control of the business. All company profits belong to him. A primary disadvantage of the proprietorship is that Harvey is personally liable for all of the company's obligations. He is responsible for paying the company's debts, even if they require use of his personal resources.

Home Depot is a large corporation. To obtain the financial resources the company needs, it sells stock to a large number of investors. These investors expect a return from their investments but have no interest in managing the company. Instead, they hire professional managers to run the company for them. Corporations permit access to large amounts of capital. Also, individual owners are not responsible for the corporation's debt, thus reducing the risk of ownership. A primary disadvantage of corporations is that owners have little access to information about the company. They depend on managers to run the business for the benefit of owners and to provide reliable information about their business activities.

SSP1-3 A. **Exchanges and contracts between managers, owners, and creditors:** Owners and creditors exchange money with Floorshine for the right to receive cash in the future from the company. Contracts exist among managers, owners, and creditors. Managers contract with owners and creditors for money to acquire resources that will generate profits for the company and to employ the resources effectively and efficiently. Managers expect to be rewarded for their effectiveness and efficiency, and owners and creditors expect a fair return on their investments. These contracting parties need information to assess how well managers have performed and to determine how much cash from the company's operations should be distributed to each party. Managers, owners, and creditors decide whether the terms of contracts are being met. Owners hire independent auditors (CPAs) to examine the financial information provided by managers to owners and creditors to ensure its reliability.

B. **Exchanges and contracts between suppliers and managers:** Suppliers exchange goods and services with the company for the right to receive cash. Contracts between suppliers and managers require information to determine that the company receives the correct types and quantities of goods and services at the appropriate times. Also, information is needed to demonstrate that the company has made timely payments for these goods and services.

C. **Exchanges and contracts between employees and managers:** Employees exchange labor services with the company for wages and benefits. Contracts between employees and managers describe the payments, benefits, and rights employees have negotiated with managers. Information is needed to demonstrate that labor services have been provided and employees have been treated fairly. The demands of employees for future wages and benefits depend, in part, on the profitability of the company. Employees and managers need information about the performance of the company to negotiate future contracts.

D. **Exchanges and contracts between customers and managers:** Customers exchange cash for goods and services provided by the company. Customers, such as retail stores, may receive the goods and pay for them later, say within 30 or 60 days. Managers expect to receive the payments when they are due. Contracts between customers and managers call for the delivery of goods to customers and payment to the company. Customers decide whether to continue to purchase the company's goods. The quality and costs of the goods and future prospects for obtaining the goods when needed are relevant pieces of information. Information about the payment history of customers helps managers decide whether to continue to extend credit to customers.

E. **Exchanges and contracts between government agencies and managers:** Government agencies monitor companies to determine if they are engaged in fair trade and labor practices. Managers provide information to demonstrate that the company is conforming to government regulations. Governments provide services to companies in the form of police and fire protection, utilities, sanitation, and streets and roads. Companies pay taxes and fees for these services. Information is required to verify that appropriate amounts of taxes and fees are being paid.

Define *Terms and Concepts Defined in This Chapter*

Review Summary of Important Concepts

1. The accounting process provides information about business activities to help decision makers allocate scarce resources.
   a. Accounting measures profits created by a business as the dollar amount of resources created from selling goods and services minus the dollar amount of resources consumed in producing and making the goods and services available to customers.
   b. Accounting helps decision makers determine the risk and return they should anticipate from a business investment or activity.
2. Organizations serve the needs of society by providing a means for people to work together to accomplish their goals.
   a. Businesses operate as merchandising, manufacturing, and service companies. Other organizations, like governments and nonprofit organizations, are nonbusiness organizations.
   b. All organizations benefit society by transforming resources from one form to another form that is more valuable in meeting the needs of people.
3. Businesses sell their products and acquire resources in competitive markets.
   a. Markets provide a way for people to express their perceptions of the value of goods and services by the products they purchase and the prices they pay. Markets allocate resources to those companies and activities that market participants believe best meet their needs.
   b. Value created by a business is measured by the difference between the dollar amount of resources created from selling goods and services and the dollar amount of resources consumed in producing and making the goods and services available to customers.
4. Owners invest in a business to receive a return on their investments from business profits. Businesses that operate effectively and efficiently normally will earn higher profits.
   a. Businesses that are not profitable will have difficulty attracting investors and will be forced to change their behavior or to go out of business.
   b. Markets make financial and other scarce resources available to organizations that can best transform them to maximize their value for society.
5. Businesses operate as corporations, proprietorships, and partnerships.
   a. Corporations can obtain large amounts of capital by selling stock to many investors.
   b. Owners of corporations usually hire professional managers to run their businesses. They depend on these managers to run the business for the benefit of owners and to report reliable information about their business activities.
6. Accounting information is used in corporations and other organizations to create and evaluate contracts and other agreements between a company and its stakeholders.
   a. Accounting information helps investors and creditors assess the return and risk associated with their investments and loans.
   b. Accounting information is useful for determining management compensation, determining an organization's resources, and evaluating results of its operating activities.
   c. Accounting information helps managers evaluate employee performance and helps employees evaluate the risk and return of their employment contracts.
   d. Accounting information helps companies evaluate their suppliers and helps customers evaluate the companies from which they make purchases.
   e. Accounting information helps government agencies make taxation and regulatory decisions.
7. Because investors and other external stakeholders have limited access to business information, information reported to external parties is regulated.
   a. Companies must prepare financial accounting information in conformity with generally accepted accounting standards.

(Continued)

b. This information is audited by an independent accountant to ensure that it fairly represents a company's business activities.
c. Reliable accounting information is essential for the proper operation of markets that depend on the information to determine how to allocate resources.

8. Ethical behavior is important to ensure that businesses are managed properly and that accounting information is reliable. Accounting rules and controls have been created to help monitor and enforce ethical behavior.

Questions

Q1-1 *Obj. 1* What is the purpose of accounting? How does accounting accomplish that purpose?

Q1-2 *Obj. 1* How can accounting information help investors understand risk?

Q1-3 *Obj. 2* How does the purpose of merchandising, manufacturing, and service companies differ? How do they each create value?

Q1-4 *Obj. 2* List an example of each of the following types of organization. Describe how each type of organization differs from each of the others.

a. Merchandising
b. Manufacturing
c. Service
d. Governmental
e. Nonprofit

Q1-5 *Obj. 3* Sandy Dune overheard some friends from your accounting class discussing the "transformation of resources." She is curious about what this term means and how it applies to organizations and accounting. Explain to Sandy your understanding of the transformation of resources and why it is an important concept in accounting.

Q1-6 *Obj. 3* Accounting is an information system that measures and reports the value created when a company transforms resources. Does an accounting system create value? If so, how? If not, why do companies have them?

Q1-7 *Obj. 4* Phillip invested $3,000 in a business at the beginning of the year. By the end of the year, the value of this investment had risen to $4,100. Near year-end, the business sent Phillip a check for $2,000. Describe the difference between a return *on* investment and a return *of* investment. What portion of the $2,000 is return on investment and what portion is return of investment?

Q1-8 *Obj. 4* How are effectiveness, efficiency, return on investment, and accounting interrelated? Be specific.

Q1-9 *Obj. 6* What is a contract, and why are contracts important for business organizations?

Q1-10 *Obj. 6* What is meant by risk, and why is it an important concept for decision makers to understand? What is the relationship between risk and accounting?

Q1-11 *Obj. 6* Your friend is puzzled that the topic of contracts has come up in your accounting class. Says he, "Contracts are the business of lawyers, not accountants. Why are we studying contracts in an accounting class?" Educate your friend.

Q1-12 *Obj. 6* Your uncle tells you that risk is to be avoided when considering potential investments. In fact, he believes the government should ban risky investments to protect the public. Do you agree with your uncle? Why or why not?

Q1-13 *Obj. 6* It is often said that there exists a risk-return tradeoff. That is, to obtain a higher return, one must be willing to accept higher risk. If one wishes to incur little risk, one must be willing to accept a smaller return. What evidence of this do you observe in the world around you, either in investments or other aspects of life?

Q1-14 *Obj. 6* Why do owners invest in businesses even though such an investment is more risky than investing in U.S. Savings Bonds? If you had $3,000 to invest, how would you decide whether to invest it in businesses or whether to invest it in U.S. Savings Bonds?

Q1-15 *Objs. 6, 7* What is the interrelationship among the concepts of risk, moral hazard (when setting executive compensation), and generally accepted accounting principles?

Q1-16 *Obj. 7* How does an audit increase the credibility of financial statements?

Q1-17 *Obj. 7* An accounting classmate notes that adherence to GAAP is not required for managerial accounting reports. She observes, "If it's so important for financial accounting, it seems reasonable that it would also be useful for managerial reporting." Explain to her why it's more important that financial accounting reports adhere to GAAP than it is for managerial accounting reports to do so. In what ways is managerial accounting different from financial accounting?

Exercises

E1-1 Write a short definition for each of the terms listed in the *Terms and Concepts Defined in This Chapter* section.

E1-2 *Obj. 1* Assume you have a friend, Edwina Polinder, who has no knowledge of accounting. Draft a short memo to Edwina that will help her understand the purpose of accounting.

DATE: (today's date)
TO: Edwina Polinder
FROM: (your name)
SUBJECT: Inquiry about accounting
(your response)

E1-3 *Objs. 1, 6* Wilma Borrelli is a stockholder of Essex International, a major supplier of building materials. Wilma received information that Essex sustained a large loss during the most recent quarter and is expecting bigger losses during the coming quarter. How might this information affect those who contract with Essex?

E1-4 *Obj. 2* Match the type of organization with the characteristics and examples provided below.

Type of organization:

1. Merchandising (or retail) companies
2. Manufacturing companies
3. Service companies
4. Governmental and nonprofit organizations

Characteristics and examples:

a. Provide goods or services without the intent of making a profit. Examples include the **IRS** and the **United Way**.
b. Produce goods that are sold to consumers or to merchandising companies. Examples include **Ford Motor Company** and **PepsiCo**.
c. Sell to consumers goods that are produced by other companies. Examples include **Wal-Mart** and **Sears.**
d. Sell services rather than goods. Examples include **H&R Block** and **Delta Air Lines**.

E1-5 *Obj. 3* Eduardo has started a small business making sundials. The following transactions occurred for the business during a recent period. How much profit did the company earn for this period?

Sales to customers	$1,050
Rent for the period	425
Supplies used during the period	250
Wages for the period	175

E1-6 *Obj. 3* Soft Light Company produces specialty lamps and sells them to retail stores. During the latest year, the company sold 40,000 lamps at an average price of $70 per lamp. The production and distribution costs per lamp were $25, on average. Other costs for the year were $1,200,000 for management salaries and facilities. Total investment in the company is $3,000,000. How much profit did Soft Light earn for the year? Describe the steps you went through to get your answer.

E1-7 *Obj. 3* Fashion Threads Company uses the following four steps to make a pair of cotton slacks:

a. Cotton is planted, grown, harvested, and shipped to a textile manufacturer. The cost to produce the cotton associated with the slacks is $5. This amount of cotton is sold to the manufacturer for $5.50.
b. Raw cotton is processed into cotton fabric. The cost of producing the fabric for the slacks, including the cost of the raw cotton, is $13.25. This fabric is sold to a garment manufacturer for $17.
c. Cotton fabric is cut and sewn to produce a pair of slacks. The cost of making the slacks, including the cost of the fabric, is $25. The slacks are sold to a retailer for $30.
d. The cost to the retailer of making the slacks available for sale, including the cost of the slacks, is $34. The retailer sells the slacks for $56.

Use Exhibits 5 and 6 to help you answer the following questions. How much profit is earned at each step in the production and selling process? How much total profit is earned by those involved in making and selling the slacks? Why are customers willing to pay the amounts involved in this process?

E1-8 *Obj. 3* Alexander makes professional baseball gloves by hand. He buys leather for $80 a yard. Padding costs $6 a pound; thread and other materials cost $16 for a month's supply. He pays $500 a month rent for a small shop, and utilities average $150 a month. Shipping costs are about $4.50 per glove. In an average month, Alexander produces and sells eight gloves. Each glove requires a half yard of leather and a half pound of padding. What is the average cost of a glove made by Alexander? How much profit does Alexander earn on each glove if he sells them for $475 each? How much profit does Alexander earn each month, on average? Exhibits 5 and 6 will help you answer these questions.

E1-9 *Obj. 3* Antonio's Restaurant specializes in Italian food. During June, Antonio's recorded the following sales to customers and costs of doing business:

Sales to customers	$20,500
Cost of food products used	6,250
Cost of rented building and equipment	4,376
Cost of employee labor services used	4,050
Maintenance and utilities used	2,000

Prepare a schedule that shows the amount of profit (or loss) earned by Antonio's Restaurant during June. (Hint: See Exhibit 6.)

E1-10 *Obj. 3* The Quick Stop is a fast-food restaurant. During March, Quick Stop recorded the following sales to customers and costs of doing business:

Sales to customers	$4,400
Cost of food products used	2,100
Cost of rented building and equipment	1,250
Cost of employee labor services used	1,000
Maintenance and utilities used	600

Prepare a schedule that shows the amount of profit (or loss) earned by Quick Stop during March. (Hint: See Exhibit 6.)

E1-11 *Obj. 3* Pam Lucas is a high school student who delivers papers to earn spending money. During May, she received $450 from customers in payment for their subscriptions for the month. She paid $300 for the papers she delivered. In addition, she paid $45 to her parents for use of their car to deliver the papers, and she paid $30 for gas. Prepare a statement to compute the amount of profit Pam earned from her paper route in May. (Hint: See Exhibit 6.)

E1-12 *Obj. 4* On January 1, 2007, Alicia invested $4,000 in a savings account. At the end of January, the account balance had increased to $4,020. The balance at the end of February was $4,040.10. The balance at the end of March was $4,060.30. The increases occurred because of interest earned on the account. What was Alicia's return on investment, in dollars and cents, for each of the three months? What was the total return for the three months taken together?

E1-13 *Obj. 4* Sam Smith invested $17,000 in Anchor Insurance Company. At the end of the year, Smith's investment was worth $19,500 because of earnings during the year. Anchor paid Smith $3,000 at the end of the year. What was Smith's return *on* investment (in dollars) for the year? What was his return *of* investment (in dollars) for the year? Did Anchor Insurance Company maintain its capital as a result of these events? Explain.

E1-14 *Obj. 4* J-mart and Buy-Lo are two companies that sell identical products. They are located in different parts of the same city. During September, J-mart sold $25,000 of goods, while Buy-Lo sold $19,000. J-mart's profit was $9,000, and Buy-Lo's profit was $3,000. Compare the efficiency and effectiveness of the two companies.

E1-15 *Obj. 4* Rogers and Hornsby are two companies that compete in the same market with the same product, a brand of steak sauce. The companies are the same size and sell to the same grocery retailers. Both products are sold by the retailers at the same price. During 2007, Rogers sold 500,000 bottles of its sauce at a profit of 10 cents per bottle. Hornsby sold 425,000 bottles at a profit of 15 cents a bottle. Which company was more effective? Which was more efficient? Which company was more profitable?

E1-16 *Obj. 4* You have a choice of investing in either of two companies, Alpha or Beta. Both companies make the same products and compete in the same markets. Over the last five years, the operating results for the two companies have been:

	Alpha	Beta
Sales to customers	$4,700,000	$6,525,000
Profit	$420,000	$913,500
Return on investment per dollar invested	4.5%	7.5%

Which company is more efficient? Which is more effective? In which company would you invest? State the reasons for your answers.

E1-17 *Obj. 5* Identify each of the following as describing corporations, proprietorships, and/or partnerships. Some items have more than one answer.

a. Distinct legal entity separate from its owners.
b. More than one owner.
c. Ownership by stockholders.
d. Controlled by a board of directors.
e. Legal identity changes when a company is sold.
f. Limited liability.
g. Mutual agency.
h. Access to large amounts of capital.
i. Direct taxation of profits.
j. Moral hazard usually not a major problem.

E1-18 *Obj. 6* Yashiko Takawsa is a loan officer at a major bank. Hendrick Swindler recently applied for a small business loan for his dry cleaning company, Take 'Em to the Cleaners. As part of the application, Swindler was asked to provide financial information about his company. The financial reports revealed that the company had been fabulously profitable. What concerns might Yashiko have about the information provided by Swindler? What actions might she take to relieve these concerns?

E1-19 *Obj. 6* Wendy Hu is considering two new products for her office products manufacturing business. One is a laser printer. Wendy has had numerous calls for the product, which will compete with existing well-known brands. The other product is a new computer projection system that permits a presenter to display color computer images without the need of a regular computer or projection system. The product would have little competition. Wendy believes the market will be receptive to this product. What are some of the risks that Wendy must consider in deciding whether to produce the two products?

E1-20
Obj. 7
To encourage its managers to earn a profit for its stockholders, Primrose Mining Company pays a bonus to top managers if the company earns at least a 15% return on investment each year. Management prepares financial reports from which the return on investment is calculated. Should the board and the stockholders be concerned about the reliability of the financial reports? Discuss. What can they do to make sure the reports faithfully represent the company's economic activities?

E1-21
Obj. 8
Andy attends college on a full-time basis and works part-time for Meredith's Garden Center. The owner, Jim Meredith, asked Andy to work late into the night to move merchandise from one warehouse to an empty warehouse located across town. Andy thought his assignment was unusual but was happy to get the extra hours of work.

The next day, Andy overheard the company's auditors discussing their visit to the warehouse where he had moved the merchandise. Apparently, Mr. Meredith was attempting to fool the auditors. They had counted the merchandise on the previous day. On the following day, they had counted the same merchandise a second time but at a different warehouse. Meredith was attempting to acquire a bank loan and wanted to impress the loan officer with a strong financial report. Andy knew Meredith would mislead the auditors and banker but did not know what to do.

What may happen to Andy if he informs the auditors of his activities from the night before? Who may be harmed by Meredith's actions?

Problems

P1-1 OBTAINING FUNDING
Obj. 1

Betsy wants to start a business making flags. She has calculated that she will need $62,500 to start the business. The money will be used to rent a building, purchase equipment, hire workers, and begin production and sales. Betsy has $12,500 in savings she can invest in the business.

Required

A. What alternatives might Betsy have for obtaining the additional $50,000 she needs for her business?
B. What information about her business will lenders or investors want to have?

P1-2 TYPES OF ORGANIZATIONS
Obj. 2

Provided below are four types of organizations and a list of organizations with which you are probably familiar. Associate each organization with a type of organization.

Types of organizations
Merchandising companies
Manufacturing companies
Service companies
Governmental or nonprofit organizations

Organizations
United Parcel Service (UPS)
Amazon.com
Dow Chemical Company
United States Postal Service (USPS)
PepsiCo
Federal Express (FedEx)
Internal Revenue Service (IRS)
March of Dimes
JCPenney
DaimlerChrysler
Sears
Verizon Communications

P1-3 DETERMINING PROFIT AND RETURN ON INVESTMENT
Obj. 3

Linda Greene owns a small car dealership. She rents the property she uses, buys cars from a manufacturer, and resells them to customers. During July, Linda sold 14 cars that cost her a total of $189,000. The total amount she received from the sale of these cars was $230,000. Other costs incurred by Linda for the month included rent, $2,550; utilities, $800; insurance, $825; maintenance of property and cars, $700; advertising, $1,250; and property taxes and business license, $200.

Required

A. Prepare a profit report that calculates the amount of profit earned during July.
B. What can Linda do with the profit she earned?
C. Assuming she invested $1,200,000 in the dealership, what was the return on her investment for July expressed as a percentage of her investment?

P1-4 DEVELOPING PROFIT AND RETURN ON INVESTMENT

Objs. 3, 4

Through hard work and careful saving, Hans and his family have $152,000 to start a small specialty foods business. The family estimates sales to customers will be about $4,500 per month during the first year. On the average, expected costs per month are budgeted as follows:

Wages for occasional labor	$ 700	Utilities	$100
Rent on land and buildings	1,200	Advertising	300
Supplies	75	Delivery costs	225

Required

A. What is the projected monthly profit?
B. What is the expected annual return on investment?

P1-5 THE RELATIONSHIP BETWEEN PROFIT AND VALUE CREATED

Obj. 3

Marty and Judi own and operate Tender Sender Company, a store providing private mail boxes, contract shipping services on commission, and a wide variety of gift and novelty items. The following transactions occurred during the month of February.

1. Sold $7,000 of gift items for which the company had paid $3,100.
2. Advertising, both newspaper and radio, was $1,500.
3. Rent for the month received from mail box customers totaled $1,640.
4. The cost of monthly rent for the store location was $2,200.
5. The cost of utilities for the month was $525.
6. Commissions earned from shipping services for the month totaled $1,588.
7. Sold $3,200 of novelty items that had cost the company $1,450.
8. The cost of supplies used during the month was $384.
9. Other miscellaneous costs for the month of February totaled $500.

Required

A. Prepare a schedule that shows the amount of profit earned by the company during the month of February.
B. Has the company created value? Explain your answer.

P1-6 HOW BUSINESSES CREATE VALUE

Objs. 1, 3

You are considering opening a shop in a nearby mall that will sell specialty T-shirts. T-shirts, containing designs and words selected by customers, will be produced for customers on order. You will need to borrow $25,000 to begin operations. A local bank has agreed to consider a loan and has asked for a summary plan to demonstrate the performance you expect from your company and your ability to repay the loan. You will pay $5.50 for T-shirts and will sell them for $8. The cost of paint and supplies will be $0.50 per shirt. An examination of similar stores at other malls indicates that you should be able to sell an average of 1,000 shirts per month. Rent for your store will be $300 per month. Utilities will be $150 per month, on average. Wages will be $800 per month.

Required

A. Calculate the expected profit of your company for the first year of operation.
B. Explain how a bank loan officer may use your profit projections to help make the lending decision.

P1-7 MEASURING VALUE CREATED

Obj. 3

T. Edison owns her own business and had the following activity during September. She earned $3,600 from royalties on inventions. She consumed resources as follows: $550 for rent, $300 for clerical salaries, $130 for legal services, $100 for office supplies, $90 for utilities, $70 for fuel, and $250 for insurance.

Required

A. Prepare a report in good form, following the example of Exhibit 6, to describe Edison's financial activities for September.
B. How might this information be useful for Edison?
C. Identify some decisions Edison might make using this information.

P1-8 THE RESULTS OF THE TRANSFORMATION PROCESS

Obj. 3

Betsy started Betsy's Flag Co. on September 1. During September, Betsy consumed the following resources:

Rent	$ 650	Utilities	$ 250
Supplies	3,000	Repairs	1,750
Fabric	8,750	Wages	2,500
Business license	500		

Betsy created resources by selling flags for $24,000 during the month of September.

Required Determine the profit earned by Betsy during September.

P1-9 USING ACCOUNTING INFORMATION FOR DECISIONS

Objs. 1, 4

The chief financial officer (CFO) of Flash Bulb and Seed Company has prepared the following projections for the month of August.

Expected sales		$480,000
Projected monthly resources consumed:		
Rent	$ 85,000	
Utilities	2,900	
Wages	274,000	
Advertising	115,000	
Repairs	12,000	
Supplies	2,500	
Total cost of resources consumed		491,400
Projected loss		$ (11,400)

Although Flash Bulb and Seed Company predicts a loss for August, the CFO is confident that sales will increase in the future.

Required

A. Why is it important that the CFO prepare a document like this?
B. If the company came to your bank requesting a loan, how would you respond? From the data given, does the firm appear that it is likely to be able to repay a loan? Why?

P1-10 RETURN ON INVESTMENT AND RETURN OF INVESTMENT

Obj. 4

John invested $250,000 into a business that earned a profit of $2,250 during the past month as shown below. John believes the business will earn an annual profit equal to twelve times the monthly profit. Assume John wants to take $20,000 from the business each year for his personal use.

Resources created from sales		$17,000
Resources consumed:		
Materials	$7,500	
Insurance	1,500	
Rent	2,000	
Utilities	950	
Wages	2,800	
Total cost of resources consumed		14,750
Profit earned		$ 2,250

Required

A. Determine the company's return on investment.
B. Determine John's return of investment.

P1-11 CHOOSING A FORM OF BUSINESS ORGANIZATION

Obj. 5

Below are three independent situations.

A. Larry, Ulysses, and Irene are three college student friends planning to set up a summer business at a nearby resort to sell T-shirts, souvenirs, and novelties to tourists. While they have no assets (to speak of) of their own, Larry's uncle has agreed to finance them with upfront capital to acquire merchandise and so on. They plan to operate for only one summer, as all expect to graduate soon and take permanent jobs in a nearby state.
B. Molly and Vicky are twin sisters who have decided to start a computer software consulting firm. Molly is the "techie," and a bit unreliable. Vicky is a highly successful manager gifted with organizational and business skills. Between the two, they believe they can attract and serve a profitable clientele. In fact, they envision rapid expansion of their practice and diversification into a variety of related business activities. Between them, they have only enough liquid capital to start a small operation.
C. Reginald and Ruth Ann are ne'er-do-well offspring of a deceased industrialist who left them each $400 million—most of which they still have. Ever the optimists, they think there is money to be made in the steel business. A friend they met at the country club has persuaded them to provide $10 million to set up a business that would manufacture and distribute a line of lightweight steel kites. Operations would be located in a nearby state.

Required For each of the three independent situations, recommend the form of business organization that you believe would be most appropriate. Explain your reasoning in each case, both in favor of your selection and any reasons against your choice.

P1-12 BUSINESS OWNERSHIP STRUCTURES

Obj. 5

Mary Jackson is graduating with a degree in business administration. She has scheduled interviews with a variety of companies. Mary found the following diagram in the packet of information provided by one of the companies:

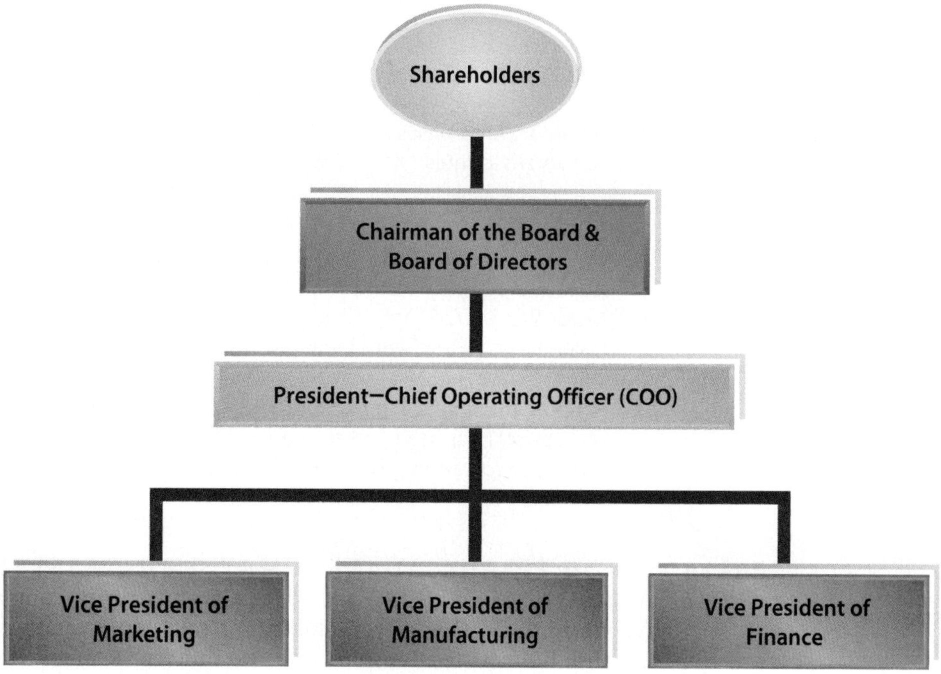

Required

A. Is Mary interviewing with a proprietorship, partnership, or corporation?
B. What are the advantages of this form of organization?
C. In this form of organization, management ultimately is responsible to whom?

P1-13 CONTRACTS, RISK, AND USES OF ACCOUNTING INFORMATION

Obj. 6

Sonny Beam established Solar Supply Corporation earlier in the current year. To obtain resources, he contributed $5,000 of his savings to the company, had the company borrow $8,000 from his mother, sold shares of company stock to friends totaling $10,000, and obtained a $25,000 bank loan. The company is obligated to buy out all investors and repay the two loans within 12 months of the business becoming profitable. Sonny located space in a nearby business park and leased it for monthly rent of $1,000 plus 1% of his company's sales. Several competing manufacturers tried to attract him as a distributor of their products. He signed an exclusive agreement with one that offered its products at 52% off their normal sales prices with 30-day free credit. Sonny hired a sales manager at a salary of $3,000 per month and promised her a profit-sharing plan payable each December 31. Sonny's credit policy is that commercial customers receive 60-day free credit and that retail customers must pay by cash or credit card. All goods carry the manufacturer's warranty and Sonny's secondary warranty of "satisfaction guaranteed or your money back." Because the company is a corporation, it will pay corporate income tax to the city, state, and federal governments. In addition, the state will levy a merchandise tax each July 1.

Required

A. Identify the primary exchanges and contracts between the company and those that interact with it.
B. Which of the parties have taken on risk? For each such party, describe that risk.
C. Which contracts will require the parties to rely on accounting information to verify performance according to the contract? Be specific.

P1-14 USING INFORMATION ABOUT RISK TO MAKE DECISIONS

Objs. 4, 6

Nancy and Mauro are reviewing the information given below for different reasons. Nancy is a bank loan officer who has received a two-year, $50,000 loan application from both firms. Mauro is an independently wealthy investor who is considering investing $50,000 in a company. The information below is just one part of a complete data set about the companies that both persons are reviewing. The data reveal the profit history of the two firms over the last seven years. The companies are very similar except for the way in which their profits vary over the years. (All dollar amounts are in thousands.)

	Profits							
	2007	**2006**	**2005**	**2004**	**2003**	**2002**	**2001**	**Total**
Hill Country Enterprises	337	315	303	268	207	225	201	1,856
Low Land Associates	730	(55)	(10)	598	(131)	619	498	2,249

Required

A. Explain the concept of risk and its usual relationship to return on investment.
B. If you were Nancy, would you be more likely to make the loan to Hill Country or to Low Land? Why?
C. If you were Mauro, would you be more likely to invest in Hill Country or Low Land? Why?
D. Suppose the financial information of Low Land Associates (but not that of Hill Country Enterprises) has been audited and verified as being in conformance with generally accepted accounting principles. Would that change your responses to parts (b) and (c) above?

P1-15 USING FINANCIAL INFORMATION TO ASSESS RISK

Obj. 6

Assume you are the credit manager for a manufacturing company that sells its products to retail businesses. One of your company's sales representatives has been working hard to establish business relationships with two different retailers. Both businesses are interested in marketing your products. Summary earnings information is presented below for each business.

	Profits (losses)			
	2004	**2005**	**2006**	**2007**
Company A	80,000	20,000	(10,000)	70,000
Company B	30,000	32,000	40,000	43,000

Required

A. Based on the summary financial information, which company is a better credit risk?
B. When a new relationship is established between two businesses, would the customer be interested in information about the supplier's financial condition? Why or why not?

P1-16 ACCOUNTING INFORMATION AND MANAGEMENT COMPENSATION

Objs. 6, 8

Taylor Grey is the sales manager of an electronics manufacturing company. His annual bonus is based on profits earned by the company. On December 30, Taylor is inquiring about the status of a very large order that he would like to include in the year-end profit figures. Unfortunately, a production machine has broken down. Taylor has been advised the order will not be completed and shipped by the end of the year. The profit figures including and excluding the order appear below.

Profit Including the Order	Profit Excluding the Order
$2,400,000	$1,600,000

Taylor's bonus is 3% of profits.

Required

A. Using the financial information provided, calculate Taylor's bonus under both scenarios.
B. Why do companies use accounting information to evaluate managerial performance?
C. Is there an economic incentive for Taylor to misrepresent the annual sales?

P1-17 THE VALUE OF AN AUDIT

Obj. 7

Assume you have inherited a sum of money from a distant relative and are looking for good investment opportunities. You are considering investing in one of two companies, Wonderworks or Hoffstetter's. Both companies are retailing organizations that have earned profits during the month of January as follows:

	Wonderworks		Hoffstetter's	
Resources created		$50,000		$60,000
Resources consumed:				
Cost of merchandise sold	$30,000		$35,000	
Wages	5,000		4,000	
Rent	2,000		2,500	
Supplies	1,500		1,700	
Utilities	700		500	
Total cost of resources consumed		39,200		43,700
Profit earned		$10,800		$16,300

You learn that a CPA examined the financial information provided by Wonderworks and confirmed the information was prepared according to GAAP.

"I don't see any reason to pay a CPA to examine my company's books," Patty Hoffstetter tells you. "They add to the cost of conducting business." Hoffstetter's brother-in-law prepared the company's financial information. He has no formal training in accounting but followed the instructions provided in the accounting software package that he purchased from an office supply company.

Required

A. Do you agree that the audit adds no value? Why or why not?
B. GAAP help ensure that users can compare the financial information of two different companies. The two sets of financial information appear identical in format. Are they comparable?

P1-18 FANNIE RESTATEMENT ORDERED

Obj. 7

http://ingram.swlearning.com

Visit Qwest's home page to learn more about the SEC.

The Securities and Exchange Commission staff has ordered Fannie Mae, the nation's largest mortgage company, to restate its last four annual reports. The SEC chief accountant announced that the company's accounting practices for 2001 through mid-2004 "did not comply in material respects" with accounting rules related to loans. The company has been accused of deliberately violating accounting rules to smooth earnings, meet financial projections, and increase bonuses for senior executives. News reports indicate the company intends to comply with the SEC ruling.

Source: TheStreet.com (15 December 2004).

Required

A. What is the SEC? What is its mission?
B. If a company's management believes they have reported earnings in a meaningful way, why can the SEC force them to restate earnings?
C. If management issued misleading financial information, do the shareholders have a reason to be upset with the company? Explain.

P1-19 ETHICS AND MORAL HAZARD

Obj. 8

You are the manager of a retail electronics store. Recently, you purchased 200 What-A-Sound portable CD players from a wholesaler in a going-out-of-business sale. These units cost you $80 each, about half of the normal cost of other brands that you sell for $260. You expected to sell these units at the regular price and earn an above-normal profit. After your purchase, you discovered that the units were poorly constructed and would probably last about a third as long as other major brands.

Customers often ask you for a recommendation when considering the purchase of a portable CD player. If you tell them the truth about the What-A-Sound model, you may have difficulty selling these units, even if you offer a steep discount.

Required

A. What will you tell a customer who asks about these units?
B. What are the short-run and long-run implications for your company's profits if (a) you conceal the quality of the units and sell them at their regular price or (b) reveal the quality problem? If you were to choose alternative b, what options might you consider in an effort to minimize the effect of these units on your profits?

P1-20 ETHICS AND MORAL HAZARD

Obj. 8

You manage an auto service store. One of your major services is brake replacement. You purchase replacement parts at an average cost of $30 per set. Each set contains parts for four wheels and will repair one car. You charge an average of $100 per car for replacing worn brakes, including an average labor cost of $40. Your current volume for brake replacements is about 700 jobs per month. A new vendor has contacted you with an offer to sell you replacement parts at an average cost of $22.50 per set. After checking on the quality of these parts, you find that their average life is about two-thirds that of the parts you are currently using.

Required

A. What are the short-run profit implications of using the $22.50 brakes instead of the $30 brakes?
B. What are the long-run profit implications?
C. What ethical issues should be considered in choosing which brakes to use?

P1-21 EXCEL IN ACTION

Millie and Milo Wermz are the owners and managers of a small bookstore, The Book Wermz, near a college campus. The store specializes in rare and out-of-print books. During September 2007, the company sold $40,000 of books. The books cost the company $28,000. The cost of other resources used during September included:

Wages	$4,200
Supplies	2,000
Rent	1,500
Utilities	300

Required Use a spreadsheet to prepare a report describing profit earned by The Book Wermz for September. The spreadsheet should contain the following heading:

The Book Wermz
Profit Earned
For September 2007

The merge and center button can be used to center the heading in the first three rows of the spreadsheet. Select the cells that will contain the heading, and then click the merge button to combine these cells.

The report should list each resource created or consumed during September and should include a formula to automatically calculate the profit earned as the difference between resources created and resources consumed. Use the appropriate format buttons to format the numbers to include commas. Show resources consumed as negative amounts. The first and last numbers in the column should include dollar signs.

The completed worksheet should look like the following example:

	A	B
1	The Book Wermz	
2	Profit Earned	
3	For September 2007	
4		
5	Sales	$ 40,000
6	Cost of goods sold	(28,000)
7	Wages	(4,200)
8	Supplies	(2,000)
9	Rent	(1,500)
10	Utilities	(300)
11	Profit	$ 4,000

Use formula to calculate total

It is important to **save your work on a regular basis.** Save your work before you make any major changes so that mistakes will not require you to redo a lot of work.

P1-22 MULTIPLE-CHOICE OVERVIEW OF THE CHAPTER

1. The basic purpose of accounting is to:
   a. minimize the amount of taxes a company has to pay.
   b. permit an organization to keep track of its economic activities.
   c. report the largest amount of earnings to stockholders.
   d. reduce the amount of risk experienced by investors.

2. A primary purpose of all organizations in our society is to:
   a. make a profit.
   b. minimize the payment of taxes.
   c. provide employment for the largest number of workers possible.
   d. create value by transforming resources from one form to another.

(Continued)

3. Value is created when organizations:
   a. raise capital by borrowing funds from banks, individuals, or other businesses.
   b. pay cash to suppliers, employees, owners, and the government.
   c. sell products or services at prices that exceed the value of resources consumed.
   d. invest in machinery.

4. Which of the following are features of the corporate form of business organization?

	Mutual Agency	Limited Liability
a.	Yes	Yes
b.	Yes	No
c.	No	Yes
d.	No	No

5. Tammy invested $2,000 in a partnership. One year later, the partnership was sold, and cash from the sale was distributed to the partners. On that date, Tammy received a check for her share of the company in the amount of $2,250. What was Tammy's return on investment?
   a. $0
   b. $250
   c. $2,000
   d. $2,250

6. Sternberg Enterprises developed a new type of roller skate that is very popular because of its high quality and reasonable price. Sternberg is losing money on the product, however, because several key production personnel recently resigned and replacements are not as skilled. Which of the following terms properly describe the firm?

	Effective	Efficient
a.	Yes	Yes
b.	Yes	No
c.	No	Yes
d.	No	No

7. The *transformation of resources* refers to:
   a. the assessment of employee performance.
   b. converting resources from one form to a more valuable form.
   c. procedures designed to reduce a company's risk.
   d. training methods by which unskilled workers become efficient and effective.

8. An investor is evaluating the potential investments described below. Past financial results of these two companies are judged to be indicative of future returns and risk.

Year	Abercrombie Profits	Fitch Profits
A	$16	$ 6
B	18	48
C	20	3

From the information provided, which investment appears to have the higher return and which the higher risk?

	Highest Return	Highest Risk
a.	Abercrombie	Abercrombie
b.	Abercrombie	Fitch
c.	Fitch	Abercrombie
d.	Fitch	Fitch

9. SEC stands for:
   a. Securities Excellence Commission
   b. Securities and Exchange Commission
   c. Standard Executive Compensation
   d. Salaried Executive's Council

10. Ethical behavior is particularly important for accounting because:
    a. companies cannot detect unethical behavior.
    b. if the reports are wrong, accountants may have to go to jail.
    c. the SEC cannot carefully audit each company's financial statements.
    d. the reliability of accounting information depends on the honesty of those who prepare, report, and audit this information.

Case

C1-1 UNDERSTANDING THE TRANSFORMATION PROCESS

Obj. 2 Environmental Housing Company designs and builds log homes. It purchases logs and other building materials from other companies. The logs are cut to the dimensions called for in a design and shipped to the customer's building site with other materials for assembly. Environmental Housing employs construction and assembly workers, maintenance personnel, and marketing and service personnel, in addition to its management and office staff. The company is in charge of the construction process until the home is completed and ready for occupancy.

Required Identify the resources, transformation activities, and goods of Environmental Housing's transformation process. Construct a diagram similar to Exhibit 4 that shows the flow of resources through the transformation process.

© PHOTODISC/GETTY IMAGES

Business Activities—The Source of Accounting Information

2

HOW DO WE KNOW HOW WELL OUR BUSINESS IS DOING?

After developing an understanding of the purpose of a business and the considerations involved in starting a business, Maria and Stan officially began Favorite Cookie Company in January of 2007. Their first task was to obtain financial resources for the business. Then, they acquired equipment and other resources for the business, and they began to produce and sell their products. In addition, they needed an accounting system to record their business activities and to report how the business was performing.

Food for Thought

If you were starting a business, what kinds of information would you want to know about your business? How would you keep track of where the company obtained financial resources, how those resources were used, and the amounts of other resources the company has available for use? How would you know how much of your product you were selling and how much it was costing you to acquire and sell the product? For answers to these questions Maria and Stan are meeting with their accountant, Ellen.

Ellen: *Once you start your business, you will need an accounting system for recording business activities and for providing reports to help you understand how your business is performing.*

Maria: *Is this something we can do ourselves?*

Ellen: *Yes, for now, since your business will not be very complicated. You can set up a basic accounting system and keep track of your activities. The system will help you understand your business and events that affect how well you are doing.*

Stan: *How do we get started?*

Ellen: *We will start with a simple set of accounts and look at how these accounts are related. As your company acquires and uses resources, we will record each event. At the end of the month, we will summarize these activities and prepare financial statements.*

Maria: *What will the statements tell us?*

Ellen: *The statements will report the resources available to your company, how you financed those resources, and how the resources were used.*

Stan: *Will we know whether our company is making money?*

Ellen: *Yes, we can prepare a statement that will tell you how much profit the company earns each month. By the time we are finished, you'll have a pretty good idea of whether the company is performing as well as you hope it will.*

Objectives

Once you have completed this chapter, you should be able to:

1. Identify financing activities and explain why they are important to a business.
2. Demonstrate how accounting measures and records business activities.
3. Identify investing activities and explain why they are important to a business.
4. Identify operating activities and explain how they create profits for a company.
5. Describe how financial reports summarize business activities and provide information for business decisions.

FINANCING ACTIVITIES

Objective 1
Identify financing activities and explain why they are important to a business.

A business is an organization that exists for the purpose of making a profit for its owners. A business creates a profit if it can sell goods and services to customers at prices that are greater than the total costs incurred to provide those goods and services. To be successful, a business must be effective in meeting the needs of customers by providing goods and services demanded by customers at prices they are willing to pay. Also, a business must be efficient in controlling costs so that the prices charged to customers exceed the costs to the company of acquiring and selling its products. If a company is successful, it creates value for its owners as well as for other stakeholders. Profit is a measure of the value created by a business for its owners.

Maria and Stan started Favorite Cookie Company in January of 2007. The goods they sell are prepared from family recipes. It is important to keep in mind that for accounting purposes a business is a separate entity from its owners. The resources and activities of the business should be kept separate from those of the owners or managers of a business. Throughout this book we will discuss accounting issues related to Favorite Cookie Company. We will be accounting for the company, not for the owners or other stakeholders.

To start their business, Maria and Stan invested $10,000 from their savings. This money enabled the company to acquire resources it would need to operate. **A contribution by owners to a business, along with any profits that are kept in the business, is known as *owners' equity*.** The contribution provides resources to the company and represents a claim by the owners. Owners have a claim to profits earned by a business and to the resources owned by the business.

Because they needed more money to get started, Maria and Stan borrowed $8,000 from a local bank to help finance the business. Borrowing is another source of money for a company and represents a claim by the lender of the money. As noted in Chapter 1, those who lend money to a business are referred to as creditors of the business. Creditors have a claim for repayment of amounts the company borrows and for interest on amounts borrowed. **The amount a company borrows is the *principal* of a loan. *Interest* is the cost of borrowing and is paid to creditors in addition to the repayment of principal.**

Learning Note - Keep in mind that the business is an accounting entity separate from its owners. From an accounting perspective, the bank lends the $8,000 to the business, Favorite Cookie Company, not to Maria and Stan.

Contributions by owners and loans from creditors are examples of business activities, as illustrated in Exhibit 1. ***Business activities* are events that occur when a business acquires, uses, or sells resources or claims to those resources.** Exhibit 1 illustrates business activities as the exchange of resources and claims between creditors and owners and the company.

EXHIBIT 1
Business Activities: Financing from Owners and Creditors

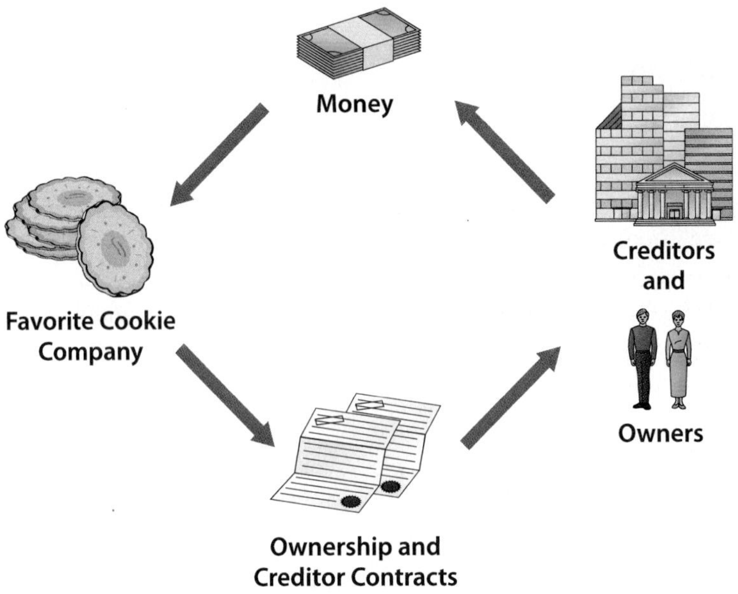

Contributions by owners and loans from creditors are examples of financing activities. *Financing activities* **occur when owners or creditors provide resources to a company or when a company transfers resources to owners or creditors,** as in the repayment of a loan principal. Financing activities provide financial resources for businesses. How businesses use those resources is a topic discussed later in this chapter when we examine investing and operating activities. First, we look at how we account for financing and other business activities.

ACCOUNTING FOR BUSINESS ACTIVITIES

Objective 2
Demonstrate how accounting measures and records business activities.

Accounting provides a basis for describing business activities. Accounting measures, records, reports, and analyzes business activities using accounts. **An *account* is a record of increases and decreases in the dollar amount associated with a specific resource or activity.** Accounting *transactions* **are descriptions of business activities (or events) that are measured in dollar values and recorded in accounts.** In general, the amount recorded for an event is the cash value of resources transferred or used in a business activity.

Financial accounting records transactions by using the accounting equation. The accounting equation shows the fundamental relationship between resources and claims to those resources:

Assets = Liabilities + Owners' Equity

Assets **are the resources controlled by a business.** *Liabilities* **are the claims of creditors to a company's resources.** Liabilities are the resources a company would have to transfer to creditors to satisfy those claims. As noted earlier, owners' equity is the claim of owners to a company's resources. Accounts are specific types of assets, liabilities, or owners' equity.

Learning Note - "Account" is the root of "accounting." The root of "account" is "count." Thus, we can observe that accounting is a process of quantifying ("counting") business activities and recording them in specific information categories as a means of understanding these activities.

EXHIBIT 2
The Effect of Financing Activities on the Accounting Equation

Assets	=	Liabilities	+	Owners' Equity
$18,000		$8,000		$10,000

EXHIBIT 3
Accounting Representation of Financing Activities

Date	Accounts	Assets	=	Liabilities	+	Owners' Equity
	Beginning Amounts	0	=	0	+	0
Jan. 2	Cash	10,000				
	Contributed Capital					10,000
Jan. 3	Cash	8,000				
	Notes Payable			8,000		
	Ending Amounts	18,000	=	8,000	+	10,000

Exhibit 2 illustrates financing activities of Favorite Cookie Company. The company received $10,000 from Maria and Stan. Then, it borrowed $8,000 from a bank. Consequently, the company has assets (cash) valued at $18,000. Creditors have a claim of $8,000, and owners have a claim of $10,000 on the company's assets.

Exhibit 3 provides an accounting representation of financing activities. On January 2, 2007, Favorite Cookie Company received $10,000 from the company's owners. On January 3, 2007, the company received $8,000 from the bank. These events are recorded as increases (or decreases, if needed) in specific accounts.

Accounts associated with these transactions include Cash, Contributed Capital, and Notes Payable. ***Cash*** **refers to financial resources in the form of coins and currency, bank deposits, and short-term investments that can be converted easily into currency and that can be used to pay for resources and obligations of a company.** *Contributed Capital* **is an owners' equity account and identifies amounts contributed to a company by its owners.** *Notes Payable* **is a liability account used to identify amounts a company owes to creditors with whom a formal agreement, or note, has been signed.**

As Exhibit 3 illustrates, accounting measures business activities in terms of dollar values, and records these activities in accounts. Thus, accounting provides a systematic way for a business to keep track of its activities. A review of a company's transactions

CASE IN POINT

http://ingram.swlearning.com
Visit the Enron site for the latest news.

Consequences of Unreported Liabilities

One of the primary criticisms of Enron Corporation's accounting was that it failed to report large amounts of debt (liabilities) that the company was responsible for repaying. The company's owners and other stakeholders were not easily able to identify or measure the amount of debt owed by the corporation. Consequently, their investments in Enron were riskier than they thought. When some of Enron's business operations proved to be less profitable than anticipated, the corporation had difficulty meeting its obligations. If owners and other stakeholders had known the true amount of the company's debt, they may have been less willing to purchase the company's stock or lend money to the company, and some owners and creditors may have avoided losses they incurred when the company's actual financial condition became known.

reveals the events that occurred, when they occurred, the amounts involved, and the resources and claims that were exchanged. Good business decisions depend on accurate and timely information about business activities. Decision makers need to know what the business did and how the business was affected by those activities. Accounting is a primary source of this information. It is important that accounting provide a complete record of a company's business activities. Only then do decision makers have a full and fair description of those activities.

INVESTING ACTIVITIES

Objective 3
Identify investing activities and explain why they are important to a business.

Before a company can sell goods and services to customers, it must acquire resources needed to operate the business. The particular resources a business needs depends on what the business is. Maria and Stan do not have sufficient resources to produce their cookies. Instead, they have contracted with a local bakery to make the cookies from their recipes. The bakery will order containers and package the cookies with the Favorite Cookie Company label. Maria and Stan have arranged to sell the cookies to local grocery stores.

The primary resources Favorite Cookie Company needs are office equipment and delivery equipment. Maria and Stan will use the office equipment to maintain information about the business and to make contacts with the bakery and grocery stores. Delivery equipment will be used to pick up cookies from the bakery and to deliver them to stores. Resources such as office equipment and delivery equipment are long-term resources because they can be used for more than one year. These resources enable a company to acquire and sell its products but are not products themselves. **Activities involving the acquisition or disposal of long-term resources used by a business are *investing activities.*** Exhibit 4 illustrates investing activities for Favorite Cookie Company. Long-term resources (such as office and delivery equipment) are acquired from suppliers. Money, or a promise of future payment, is transferred to suppliers of these resources.

Exhibit 5 provides an accounting representation of investing activities. On January 5, Favorite Cookie Company paid $6,000 for office equipment. On January 6, the company

EXHIBIT 4
Business Activities: Investing in Long-Term Resources

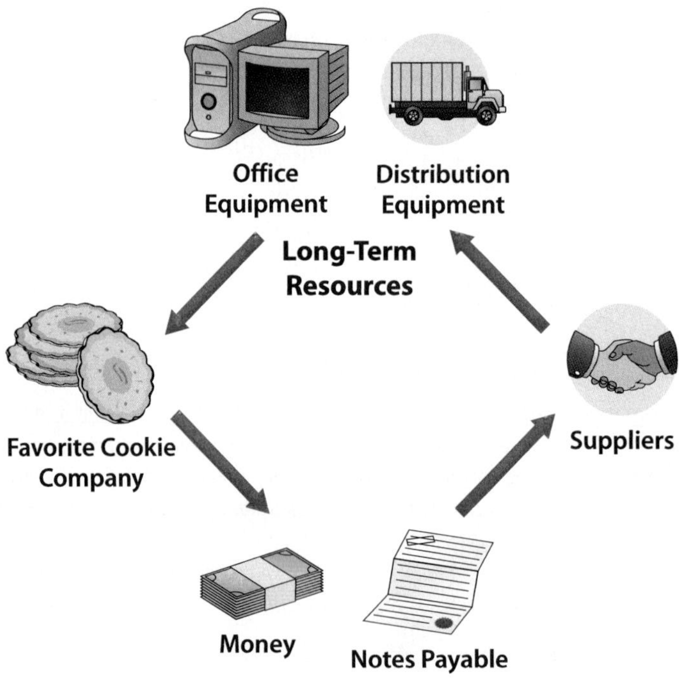

EXHIBIT 5
Accounting Representation of Investing Activities

Date	Accounts	Assets	=	Liabilities	+	Owners' Equity
	Beginning Amounts	18,000	=	8,000	+	10,000
Jan. 5	Equipment	6,000				
	Cash	−6,000				
Jan. 6	Equipment	25,000				
	Cash	−3,000				
	Notes Payable			22,000		
	Ending Amounts	40,000	=	30,000	+	10,000

bought a delivery van for $25,000. It paid $3,000 in cash and financed the remaining $22,000 of the purchase price with a note payable.

The January 6 entry shows the equipment purchase as a single transaction involving both the borrowing of $22,000 from the bank and the payment of an additional $3,000. An alternative way to record the purchase of the delivery van shows the transaction as a two-step process. First the $22,000 is borrowed from the bank and then the full $25,000 is paid to purchase the van. Recording the transaction in two steps is presented below.

Date	Accounts	Assets	=	Liabilities	+	Owners' Equity
	Beginning Amounts	18,000	=	8,000	+	10,000
Jan. 5	Equipment	6,000				
	Cash	−6,000				
Jan. 6	**Cash**	**22,000**				
	Notes Payable			**22,000**		
Jan. 6	**Equipment**	**25,000**				
	Cash	**−25,000**				
	Ending Amounts	40,000	=	30,000	+	10,000

Accounts used to record these transactions include Equipment, Cash, and Notes Payable. Observe that the second transaction involves both an investing activity (purchase of equipment) and a financing activity (borrowing to purchase van).

In each transaction, the accounting equation must balance. The January 5th transaction balances because the $6,000 increase in Equipment offsets the amount of the decrease in Cash. The January 6th transaction involves three accounts. Together the net increase in assets of $22,000 ($25,000 − $3,000) equals the increase in liabilities of $22,000.

Learning Note - Account titles vary in practice depending on the needs of a company. Accounts can be divided into as many subcategories as a business needs. For example, Favorite Cookie Company could use separate accounts for Office Equipment and Delivery Equipment if it chose to do so. Although you should not get too concerned about specific account titles, certain titles, such as Notes Payable, are used by most businesses. You should learn the titles that are listed as terms in this book. Remember, what is most important is that the account titles correctly represent the transactions.

The ending amounts in Exhibit 5 indicate that the accounting equation is in balance. Each transaction and all transactions taken together must preserve the relationship:

Assets = Liabilities + Owners' Equity

Maintaining the accounting equation is an important accounting control. If individual transactions or all transactions as a whole do not preserve the equality, an error has occurred in recording one or more of the business activities.

Self-Study Problem #1

Delphi Co. was started in 2007 when its owners contributed $100,000 to the business and borrowed $120,000 from creditors. These resources were used to purchase equipment at a cost of $160,000. In addition, the company purchased a building at a cost of $400,000, paying $40,000 in cash and signing a note for $360,000 with a local bank.

Required Using the format of Exhibit 5, record these financing and investing activities. Demonstrate that the accounting equation is in balance after the transactions have been recorded.

The solution to Self-Study Problem 1 appears at the end of the chapter.

OPERATING ACTIVITIES

Objective 4
Identify operating activities and explain how they create profits for a company.

Financing and investing activities are necessary for a company to obtain the resources it needs to operate, but these activities do not involve operating the business. A business operates by obtaining or creating products or services and selling those products or services to customers. Favorite Cookie Company acquires cookies from a bakery and sells the cookies to grocery stores. *Operating activities* **are those activities necessary to acquire and sell goods and services.** When goods or services are sold to customers, revenue is created. *Revenue* **is the amount a company expects to receive when it sells goods or services.** Revenue can be thought of as the reward earned by serving customers. In addition to goods and services for sale, operating activities use a variety of resources, including employee labor, supplies, and utilities. The consumption of these resources creates expenses. *Expense* **is the amount of resources consumed in the process of acquiring and selling goods and services.** Not all operating activities create revenues or expenses, but most do.

EXHIBIT 6
Operating Activities: Purchase of Goods for Sale

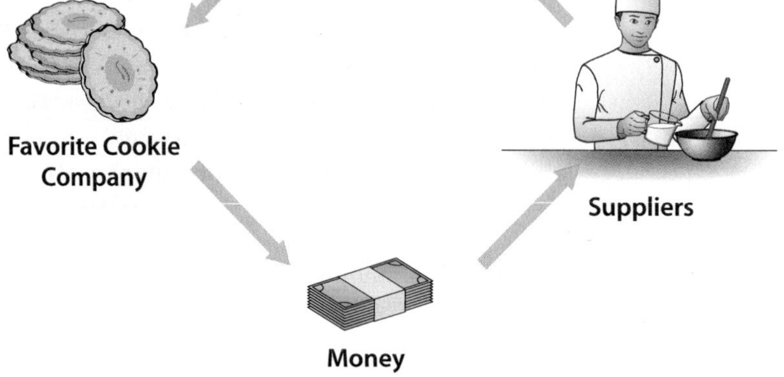

EXHIBIT 7
Accounting Representation of Purchase of Merchandise

Date	Accounts	Assets	=	Liabilities	+	Owners' Equity
	Beginning Amounts	40,000	=	30,000	+	10,000
Jan. 7	Merchandise Inventory	7,200				
	Cash	−7,200				
	Ending Amounts	40,000	=	30,000	+	10,000

Exhibit 6 illustrates the purchase of goods to sell, which is one aspect of operating activities that does not create a revenue or expense. Cookies are purchased from the bakery in exchange for cash.

Exhibit 7 describes how this type of transaction might be recorded. Favorite Cookie Company purchased cookies from the bakery at a cost of $7,200 on January 7. ***Merchandise Inventory*** **is an asset account and identifies the cost of goods a company has purchased that are available for sale to customers.** Observe that in this transaction the company's total assets have not changed. The particular assets controlled by the company have changed. The company now has $7,200 of goods for sale but $7,200 less cash than before. In fact, the company's cash balance is now $1,800 ($18,000 cash raised from financing activities minus $6,000 spent on office equipment, $3,000 for the down payment on a delivery van, and $7,200 spent on merchandise).

Exhibit 8 illustrates a company's sale of goods to a customer. When goods or services are sold to a customer, revenue is earned. The amount of revenue earned is equal to the amount of resources received from the customer in exchange for the goods. In this example, Cash is received from the customer and merchandise is delivered to the customer.

Exhibit 9 describes how this type of transaction can be recorded. Assume Favorite Cookie Company sells 380 boxes of cookies to grocery stores during January in exchange for cash. Each box, which contains several bags of cookies, costs Favorite Cookie Company $16, the amount the company pays the bakery for producing and packaging the cookies. Favorite Cookie Company sells each box to the store for $30. Therefore, 380 boxes cost the company $6,080 (380 boxes × $16) and are sold for $11,400 (380 boxes × $30).

Because revenues and expenses occurred in this transaction, we expand the accounting equation to include them. ***Retained Earnings*****, a subcategory of Owners' Equity, are the accumulated profits of a business that have been reinvested in the business.**

EXHIBIT 8
Operating Activities: Selling Goods to Customers

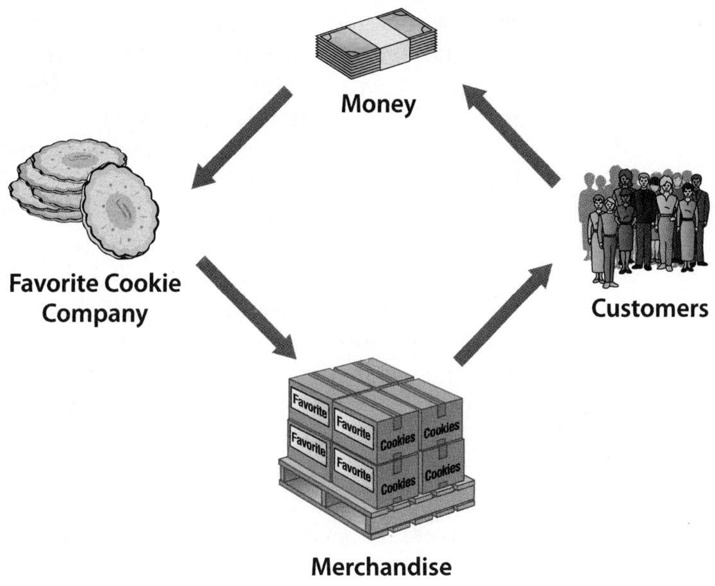

EXHIBIT 9 Accounting Representation of Operating Activities

		Assets		=	Liabilities	+	Owners' Equity	
Date	Accounts	Cash	Other Assets				Contributed Capital	Retained Earnings
	Beginning Amounts	1,800	+38,200	=	30,000	+	10,000	+0
Jan. 31	Cash	11,400						
	Sales Revenue							11,400
Jan. 31	Cost of Goods Sold							−6,080
	Merchandise Inventory		−6,080					
	Ending Amounts	13,200	+32,120	=	30,000	+	10,000	+5,320

Revenues increase Retained Earnings and expenses decrease Retained Earnings. Amounts paid to owners from a company's profits also decrease Retained Earnings. We distinguish Retained Earnings from Contributed Capital because this subcategory identifies the profits earned by a company rather than amounts contributed directly by owners.

Also, notice in Exhibit 9 that Assets have been divided into two categories: Cash (beginning amount is $1,800) and Other Assets (beginning amount is $38,200). They still total to $40,000, the ending amount in Exhibit 7. Because many transactions involve Cash, separating it from Other Assets makes it easier to keep track of the cash received and paid by a company.

In Exhibit 9, the sale of goods is recorded in two transactions. One records the revenue earned from the sale. The other records the cost of the goods sold. These transactions are central to business operations and should be examined closely.

Learning Note - The sales transaction in Exhibit 9 is a summary transaction for all sales during January. In reality, sales occur throughout the month, and each sale should be recorded as it occurs. Each transaction would follow the same pattern shown in Exhibit 9. Therefore, to avoid repeating the same transaction several times, we record one summary transaction.

Sales Revenue **identifies the amount a company earns from selling its products.** Revenue ordinarily is measured by the amount of cash received or expected from a customer in exchange for the goods or services transferred. Revenue normally is recorded at the time goods are transferred to customers. A company earns revenue for its owners. Remember that owners have a claim to profits earned by a company. Accordingly, revenue is part of owners' equity. It is an increase in the value of a company for its owners.

Cost of Goods Sold **identifies the cost to the company of the goods transferred to customers.** It is an example of an expense. Expense normally is measured by the cost of resources consumed and is recorded at the time the resources are consumed. Thus, when merchandise is sold to customers, it is consumed from the seller's viewpoint. The seller no longer has control of the resource. Consequently, merchandise has been "used up." An expense reduces owners' equity because it identifies the use of resources for which owners have a claim. It is a decrease in the value of a company for its owners. Thus, **revenues increase owners' equity and expenses decrease owners' equity.**

Revenue minus expense equals profit. Profit results from operating activities and is the difference between revenues earned from selling goods and services and expenses incurred in acquiring and selling those goods and services. Note that in Exhibit 9 the sale resulted in profit of $5,320 ($11,400 − $6,080). The company's assets and owners' equity each increased by $5,320 as a result of the sale.

Remember, Owners' Equity represents the claims of owners to a business. Those claims include contributions made by the owners (Contributed Capital) plus profits earned by the business minus amounts paid by the business to its owners (Retained Earnings).

EXHIBIT 10 Accounting Representation of Expenses

		Assets		=	Liabilities	+	Owners' Equity	
Date	Accounts	Cash	Other Assets				Contributed Capital	Retained Earnings
	Beginning Amounts	13,200	+32,120	=	30,000	+	10,000	+5,320
Jan. 6	Supplies Expense							−300
	Cash	−300						
Jan. 8	Rent Expense							−600
	Cash	−600						
Jan. 31	Wages Expense							−1,000
	Cash	−1,000						
Jan. 31	Utilities Expense							−200
	Cash	−200						
	Ending Amounts	11,100	+32,120	=	30,000	+	10,000	+3,220

Other common expenses for a company like Favorite Cookie Company include wages paid to employees, plus the cost of supplies, rent, and utilities. To illustrate, assume the following activities for Favorite Cookie Company during January:

Jan. 6 Paid $300 for supplies used during January.
8 Paid $600 for rent for January.
31 Paid $1,000 for wages for January.
31 Paid $200 for utilities for January.

Exhibit 10 illustrates how these activities are recorded. An expense is recorded for the amount of resources used in each transaction. Because these resources were paid for at the time they were consumed, Cash decreases in each transaction.

Self-Study Problem #2

The following events occurred for Mega Co. during January, its first month of business:

Jan. 3 Owners contributed $40,000 to the business.
5 The company received $25,000 from a bank in exchange for a note payable.
8 The company paid $35,000 for equipment.
10 The company paid $20,000 for merchandise.
11 The company paid $2,000 for supplies used in January.
15 The company received $12,000 from customers for the sale of merchandise. The merchandise cost Mega Co. $8,000.
22 The company received $9,000 from customers for the sale of merchandise. The merchandise cost Mega Co. $6,000.
31 The company paid $3,000 to employees for wages earned in January.
31 The company paid $800 for utilities used in January.

Required Use the format of Exhibit 10 to record the transactions of Mega Co. for January. The beginning account balances will all be zero.

The solution to Self-Study Problem 2 appears at the end of the chapter.

FINANCIAL REPORTING AND ANALYSIS

Objective 5

Describe how financial reports summarize business activities and provide information for business decisions.

The purpose of measuring and recording business activities is to provide useful information to those who need to make decisions. Accounting reports information to decision makers in the form of financial statements. *Financial statements* **are reports that summarize the results of a company's accounting transactions for a fiscal period.** Exhibit 11 lists all of Favorite Cookie Company's transactions for January using the expanded format.

To prepare financial statements, a company needs to identify the balances in its accounts at the end of the fiscal period being reported. Exhibit 12 provides a summary of account balances for Favorite Cookie Company at January 31. Balances for expenses, which reduce owners' equity, are shown in parentheses. All of the summary balances shown in this exhibit are the results of the transactions recorded for the company in Exhibit 11.

The Income Statement

The *income statement* **reports revenues and expenses for a fiscal period as a means of determining how well a company has performed in creating profit for its owners.** An income statement reports revenues, expenses, and profit for a fiscal period. **A** *fiscal period* **is any time period for which a company wants to report its financial activities.** Typical periods are months, quarters (three months), and years. Fiscal

EXHIBIT 11 Transactions for Favorite Cookie Company for January

		Assets		=	Liabilities	+	Owners' Equity	
Date	Accounts	Cash	Other Assets				Contributed Capital	Retained Earnings
	Beginning Amounts	0	+0	=	0	+	0	+0
Jan. 2	Cash	10,000						
	Contributed Capital						10,000	
Jan. 3	Cash	8,000						
	Notes Payable				8,000			
Jan. 5	Equipment		6,000					
	Cash	−6,000						
Jan. 6	Equipment		25,000					
	Cash	−3,000						
	Notes Payable				22,000			
Jan. 6	Supplies Expense							−300
	Cash	−300						
Jan. 7	Merchandise Inventory		7,200					
	Cash	−7,200						
Jan. 8	Rent Expense							−600
	Cash	−600						
Jan. 31	Cash	11,400						
	Sales Revenue							11,400
Jan. 31	Cost of Goods Sold							−6,080
	Merchandise Inventory		−6,080					
Jan. 31	Wages Expense							−1,000
	Cash	−1,000						
Jan. 31	Utilities Expense							−200
	Cash	−200						
	Ending Amounts	11,100	+32,120	=	30,000	+	10,000	+3,220

EXHIBIT 12
Summary of Account Balances for Favorite Cookie Company at January 31

Account	January 31 Balance	Explanation
Assets:		
Cash	11,100	column total
Merchandise Inventory	1,120	\$7,200 − \$6,080
Equipment	31,000	\$6,000 + \$25,000
Liabilities:		
Notes Payable	30,000	\$8,000 + \$22,000
Owners' Equity:		
Contributed Capital	10,000	
Sales Revenue	11,400	
Cost of Goods Sold	(6,080)	
Wages Expense	(1,000)	
Rent Expense	(600)	
Supplies Expense	(300)	
Utilities Expense	(200)	

months usually correspond with calendar months (January, February, etc.). Fiscal years do not have to correspond with calendar years, however. For example, a company may prepare an income statement for the year ended June 30 that would report operating activities for July 1 through June 30 of the following year. Some companies choose months that end on particular days of the week, such as Sunday. Thus, a company might prepare an income statement for the month ended January 29 if the 29th were the last Sunday in the month. For example, **General Mills'** fiscal year always ends on the last Sunday of May. Therefore, fiscal year 2004 ended on May 30, 2004 and included all operating activities since the previous year ended on May 25, 2003. General Mills' 2004 income statement is shown in Appendix B at the end of this book.

Exhibit 13 provides an example of an income statement for Favorite Cookie Company for the month ended January 31, 2007. The statement includes all the revenues and expenses recorded for January. *Net income* **is the amount of profit earned by a business during a fiscal period.** It is a measure of the value created for the owners of a business by the operating activities of the business during a fiscal period. Net income (revenue minus expense) increases owners' equity as we observed in the transactions in Exhibit 9. Information in financial statements is summarized from the transactions recorded for a fiscal period. All the sales revenue transactions are added together, for example, to calculate the total sales revenue for January.

An income statement provides information about the results of a company's operating activities for a fiscal period. Owners and other decision makers can use the statement to evaluate how well a company has performed.

EXHIBIT 13
Income Statement

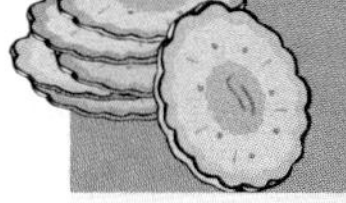

Favorite Cookie Company Income Statement For the Month Ended January 31, 2007	
Sales revenue	\$11,400
Cost of goods sold	(6,080)
Wages expense	(1,000)
Rent expense	(600)
Supplies expense	(300)
Utilities expense	(200)
Net income	\$ 3,220

EXHIBIT 14
Balance Sheet

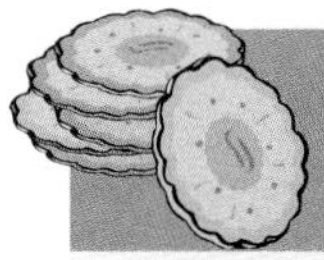

Favorite Cookie Company Balance Sheet At January 31, 2007	
Assets	
Cash	$11,100
Merchandise inventory	1,120
Equipment	31,000
Total assets	$43,220
Liabilities and Owners' Equity	
Notes payable	$30,000
Contributed capital	10,000
Retained earnings	3,220
Total liabilities and owners' equity	$43,220

The Balance Sheet

A *balance sheet* **identifies a company's assets and claims to those assets by creditors and owners at a specific date.** It is a summary of the accounting equation and, like the equation, the total of assets reported on the balance sheet must equal the combined total of liabilities and owners' equity. Exhibit 14 provides a balance sheet for Favorite Cookie Company at January 31, 2007. It reports dollar amounts associated with a company's assets and the sources of financing for those assets. It reports resources and claims at a particular point in time rather than results of activities over a period of time.

A balance sheet usually is prepared at the end of each fiscal period. It reports amounts of assets, liabilities, and owners' equity at that time. We examine the procedure for determining these amounts in more detail in Chapter 3.

Profit is earned by a business for its owners. It may be paid to the owners as a return on their investments, or it may be retained in the business as a means of acquiring additional assets. Thus, retained earnings is the total amount of net income earned over the life of a company minus the portion of net income paid out to owners. January is the first month of operations of Favorite Cookie Company, so the company has earned net income for only one month. The income statement reported net income for January of $3,220. None of the net income was paid out to owners. Consequently, retained earnings at the end of January is $3,220.

Retained earnings, January 1	$ 0
Net income for January	3,220
Less: Payment to owners in January	0
Retained earnings, January 31	$3,220

Retained earnings is separated from contributed capital in Exhibit 14 to distinguish between the amount paid into the company by Maria and Stan from the amount of profit earned and retained by the company. Amounts paid to owners normally should come from the company's profits. If a company pays its owners more than the company has earned, it is returning a portion of their investment to them. Owners need to know whether amounts paid to them are a return *on* their investments, from profits, or a return *of* their investments, from amounts invested directly by the owners. Thus, Favorite Cookie Company could pay Maria and Stan up to $3,220 from profits earned in January as a return on their investment. Any amount paid in excess of $3,220 would be a return of their investment.

The Statement of Cash Flows

A third financial statement prepared by businesses is the statement of cash flows. **The** *statement of cash flows* **reports events that affected a company's cash account during**

EXHIBIT 15
Statement of Cash Flows

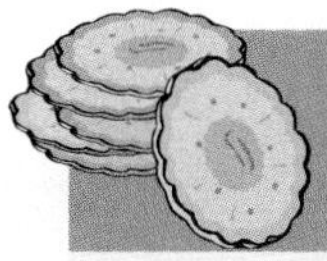

Favorite Cookie Company
Statement of Cash Flows
For the Month Ended January 31, 2007

Operating Activities		
Received from customers	$11,400	
Paid for merchandise	(7,200)	
Paid for wages	(1,000)	
Paid for rent	(600)	
Paid for supplies	(300)	
Paid for utilities	(200)	
Net cash flow from operating activities		$ 2,100
Investing Activities		
Paid for equipment*		(31,000)
Financing Activities		
Received from creditors**	$30,000	
Received from owners	10,000	
Net cash flow from financing activities		40,000
Net cash flow for January		$11,100
Cash balance, January 1		0
Cash balance, January 31		$11,100

*Office Equipment of $6,000 + Delivery Van of $25,000
**Notes Payable of $8,000 + Notes Payable of $22,000

a fiscal period. The statement contains three sections corresponding to operating, investing, and financing activities. The operating activities section reports cash from selling goods and services and cash paid for expense-related activities. The investing activities section reports cash paid for equipment and other long-term assets and cash received from selling these assets. The financing activities section reports cash received from creditors and owners, cash paid to creditors as a repayment of amounts borrowed by the company, and cash paid to owners.

Exhibit 15 provides a statement of cash flows for Favorite Cookie Company for January 2007. The source of data for the statement is the cash column for the transactions recorded in Exhibit 11. The results of these transactions are organized into the sections contained in the statement of cash flows.

Learning Note - As noted in the discussion of Exhibit 5, the purchase of the delivery van involved both investing and financing activities. On the statement of cash flows these are treated as two events. The financing transaction is treated as though the company received cash from borrowing money, and the investing transaction is treated as though the company paid cash for the delivery van.

The statement of cash flows describes the events that affected a company's cash account during a fiscal period. The amount reported as net cash flow for the period is the change in the cash balance. The final line of the statement reports the cash balance at the end of the month and corresponds with the amount reported on the company's balance sheet (see Exhibit 14). Thus, the statement of cash flows is useful for identifying how much cash a company has, where that cash came from, and how the company used its cash during a fiscal period.

The Transformation Process

Businesses transform resources into goods and services for sale to customers. Accounting measures and reports the results of that transformation process. Financing

EXHIBIT 16
Reporting the Transformation Process

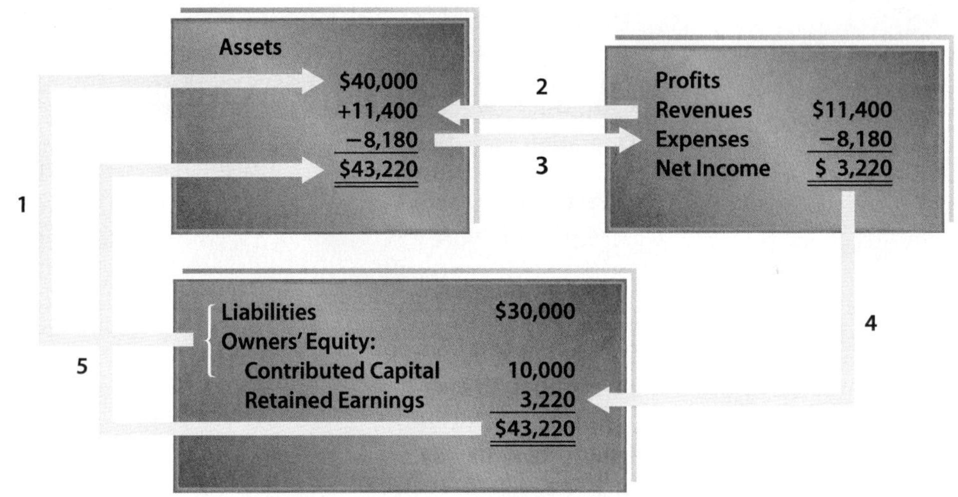

activities describe how a company obtains financial resources from owners and creditors. Investing activities describe how a company uses financial resources to acquire long-term assets to be used by the company. Operating activities describe how a company uses its financial resources and long-term assets to acquire and sell its products.

Learning Note - The statement of cash flows often is prepared using a format different than that described in Exhibit 15. We examine the alternate format in a later chapter.

Exhibit 16 illustrates the relationship among these activities as they are described in the income statement and balance sheet. The balance sheet describes a company's assets. Financial resources to acquire these assets are obtained from (1) financing activities (liabilities and owners' equity) and from (2) revenues earned by the company. When assets are consumed (3), expenses are created that reduce a company's profits. The profits earned during a period (4) increase owners' equity, as reported in retained earnings. The total amount of assets is equal to the total amount of liabilities and owners' equity (5).

Financial Analysis

Many business decisions rely on accounting information. Decision makers use accounting information to evaluate a company's performance. A variety of analysis tools are available for this purpose. We examine these in later chapters. Financial statement numbers themselves provide useful information. For example, managers need to know how much cash or merchandise inventory a company has available so they can determine whether purchases can or should be made. Creditors need to know about a company's liabilities and profits to determine whether to make additional loans. Analysis often involves a comparison of accounting numbers, such as net income, with other numbers. Sometimes comparisons are made among fiscal periods or among companies. Comparisons are also made among different divisions of a company. For example, a decision maker may be interested in how the East division of a company compares with the West division, or how the U.S. division compares with the European division.

A common analytical tool involves the calculation of ratios. Most ratios compare one financial statement number with another. One example is return on assets. *Return on assets (ROA)* **is the ratio of net income to total assets.** Because total assets are equal to the total investment in a company from creditors and owners, return on assets measures return on total investment in a company. We can calculate return on assets for Favorite Cookie Company at January 31, 2007, as:

$$\text{Return on Assets} = \frac{\text{Net Income}}{\text{Total Assets}} = \frac{\$3{,}220}{\$43{,}220} = 7.5\%$$

We can interpret the ratio as the amount a company earned for each dollar of total investment. Thus, Favorite Cookie Company earned 7.5 cents for each dollar of investment in January. It is common to report many ratios, especially those expected to be less than one, as percentages, as shown above. Whether 7.5% is a good return or not can be assessed by comparing the amount with expectations of owners, with returns for similar companies, and with returns for other periods. A good return for one company is not necessarily good for another, particularly if the companies operate in different industries, countries, or geographic regions.

Owners, creditors, and other decision makers can examine return on assets for Favorite Cookie Company to decide whether the company is earning a reasonable profit. If the return is not satisfactory, Maria and Stan can make changes in the business. We examine various means of analyzing a company's performance in this book.

Business analysis relies on accounting and other information to understand how a business is performing and to determine future business activities. Exhibit 17 describes the role of accounting in business organizations. Accounting measures and records business activities. It converts data about business activities into useful information that is reported to decision makers. The information is analyzed to evaluate the performance of a company. Then, decisions are made that affect the company's future business activities. **A primary purpose of accounting is to help people make decisions about business activities. Accounting is the link between business activities and business decisions.**

EXHIBIT 17
A Model of the Accounting Process

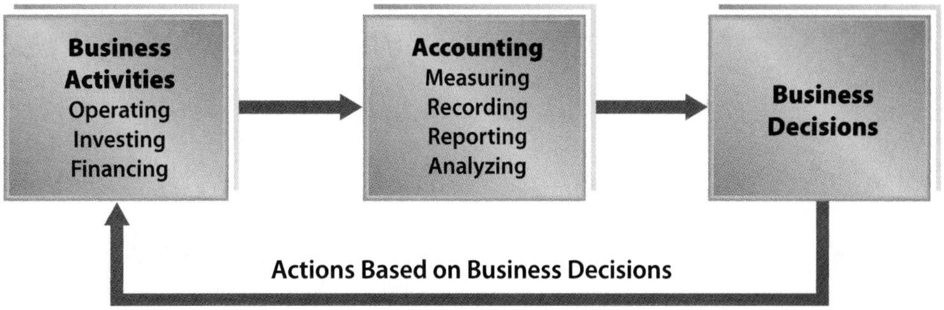

Self-Study Problem #3

Philistine Co. reported the following information for its first month of operations ended August 31, 2007:

Cash	$ 25,000
Merchandise inventory	200,000
Equipment	425,000
Notes payable	350,000
Investment by owners	250,000
Sales revenue	520,000
Cost of goods sold	300,000
Other expenses	140,000
Payments to owners	30,000

Required

A. Prepare an income statement using the format of Exhibit 13.

B. Determine how much retained earnings the company should report at the end of August.

C. Prepare a balance sheet using the format of Exhibit 14.

D. Calculate return on assets for the company for August.

The solution to Self-Study Problem 3 appears at the end of the chapter.

Appendix

Debits and Credits: Another Way to Record Transactions

For most of its history, accounting has recorded transactions using debits and credits. They were particularly useful to facilitate the calculation of account balances prior to the advent of computers. Though the accounting process is largely computerized today, debits and credits remain part of the language of accounting. To understand this method, begin with the accounting equation, including revenues and expenses as subcategories of owners' equity, as described in Exhibit 18.

Debits **are increases in elements on the left (assets) side of the accounting equation and decreases in elements on the right (liabilities and owners' equity) side.** *Credits* **are decreases in elements on the left (assets) side of the accounting equation and increases in elements on the right (liabilities and owners' equity) side.** Because expenses decrease owners' equity, they are recorded as debits (unless expense amounts are being eliminated or offset). Because revenues increase owners' equity, they are recorded as credits (unless revenue amounts are being eliminated or offset).

Each account can be divided into a debit side (on the left) and a credit side (on the right). Transactions are recorded as debits and credits to the appropriate accounts. For example, (a) an owner's contribution of $10,000 to a company could be recorded as in Exhibit 19.

Cash is increased, and because it is an asset account, the increase is represented by a debit to the cash account. Contributed Capital is increased, and because it is an owners' equity account, the increase is represented by a credit to the contributed capital account.

For the accounting equation to balance, every transaction must have an equal amount of debits and credits. Therefore, total debits must always equal total credits for a company's transactions or accounts taken as a whole. Consequently, debits and credits provide a useful control to help ensure integrity of the accounting process. If debits do not equal credits, an error has been made.

The T-account format illustrated in Exhibit 19 often is used to describe transactions. This format makes it easy to observe the debit and credit effects of a transaction. If several transactions involve the same account, this format also makes it easy to observe the cumulative effect of the transactions. For example, (b) assume that the company borrowed $8,000 from a bank. Exhibit 20 includes the effect of this transaction, in addition to the transaction shown in Exhibit 19.

EXHIBIT 18
Defining Debits and Credits

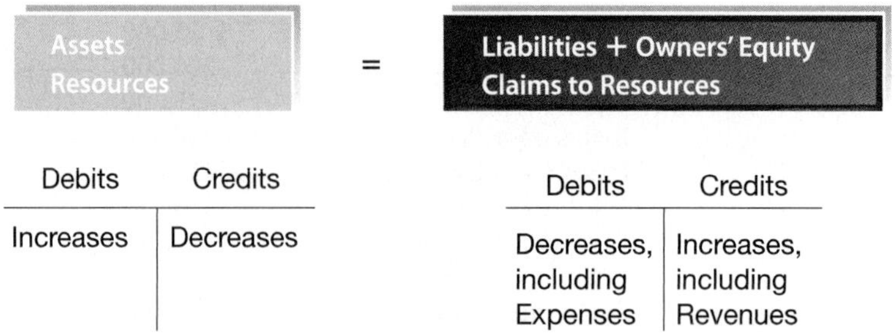

EXHIBIT 19
Recording a Transaction with Debits and Credits

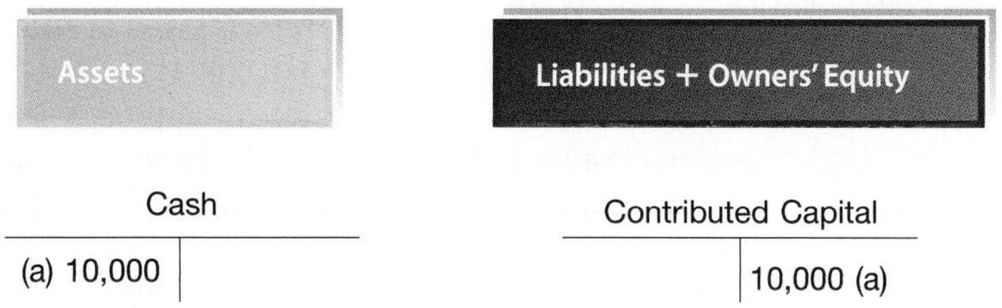

EXHIBIT 20
Recording Additional Transactions with Debits and Credits

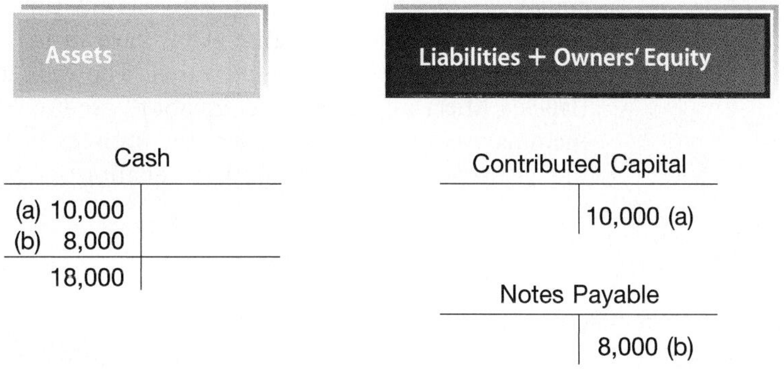

The addition of $8,000 to the cash account is represented by an additional debit entry. The combined effect of the two transactions is apparent after adding the two debit entries.

A third transaction (c), payment of $12,000 for equipment, is illustrated in Exhibit 21. The payment decreases Cash and is recorded as a credit to the cash account. The balance of the account decreases to a debit balance of $6,000. Equipment increases by $12,000, as represented by the debit to that account. Asset accounts normally have debit balances. Liability and owners' equity accounts normally have credit balances. Keep in mind that expenses are decreases in owners' equity and normally have debit balances.

Exhibit 21 illustrates the advantages of a debit and credit system of recording transactions when transactions are recorded manually. Because increases in accounts are separated from decreases, it is simpler to calculate balances than if increases and decreases are recorded in one column. Remember that for most of our history, computers, calculators, and other electronic devices were not available. Account balances had to be determined using basic rules of math. Debits and credits facilitated that process.

Observe from Exhibit 21 that each transaction involves recording debits and credits of equal magnitude. Also note that the accounting equation remains in balance after

EXHIBIT 21
Recording a Decrease in an Asset Account

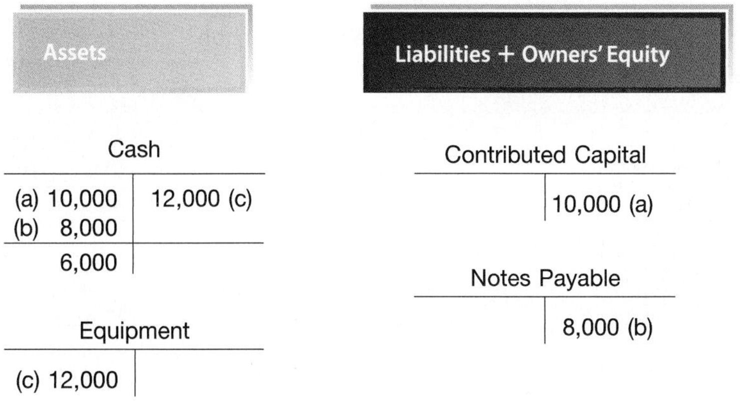

each transaction. In Exhibit 21, total assets of $18,000 ($6,000 + $12,000) equals total liabilities and owners' equity ($10,000 + $8,000).

An alternative to the T-account approach is the traditional journal format. **The journal is a book (or computer file) in which transactions are recorded individually.** The journal provides for each transaction to be recorded using debits and credits without having to set up T-accounts. T-accounts are useful for simple transactions but become unwieldy when many transactions are being recorded.

Transactions considered in this chapter can be recorded using the traditional journal format as shown in Exhibit 22. The first transaction records cash received by Favorite Cookie Company from the owners. Observe that the total amount of debits equals the total amount of credits. Debits are listed first, and credits are indented to the right. Cash is debited because assets have increased. Contributed Capital is credited because owners' equity has increased. The cells to the right side of the transaction (labeled Effect on Accounting Equation) are not part of the journal entry. We include them as a reminder of the effect the transaction has on the equation. We abbreviate the elements of the accounting equation as follows: A = Assets, L = Liabilities,

EXHIBIT 22 Journal Representation of Financing Transaction

Journal

Date	Accounts	Debits	Credits
Jan. 2	Cash	10,000	
	Contributed Capital		10,000

Effect on Accounting Equation

A	=	L +	OE	
			CC +	RE
+10,000				
			+10,000	

EXHIBIT 23 Journal Representation of Investing Transaction

Journal

Date	Accounts	Debits	Credits
Jan. 6	Equipment	25,000	
	Cash		3,000
	Notes Payable		22,000

Effect on Accounting Equation

A	=	L +	OE	
			CC +	RE
+25,000				
−3,000				
		+22,000		

EXHIBIT 24 Journal Representation of Sales Transaction

Journal

Date	Accounts	Debits	Credits
Jan. 31	Cash	11,400	
	Sales Revenue		11,400
Jan. 31	Cost of Goods Sold	6,080	
	Merchandise Inventory		6,080

Effect on Accounting Equation

A	=	L +	OE	
			CC +	RE
+11,400				
				+11,400
				−6,080
−6,080				

OE = Owners' Equity, CC = Contributed Capital, and RE = Retained Earnings. Refer to Exhibit 5 for comparison.

The purchase of a delivery van on January 6 by Favorite Cookie Company is shown in Exhibit 23. The purchase increased Equipment, decreased Cash, and increased Notes Payable. Observe that negative signs are not used with debits and credits because the credit to an asset or expense or the debit to a liability, owners' equity, or revenue identifies the amount as a decrease in the account balance.

As a final example, Exhibit 24 provides the journal entries for the sale of goods from Exhibit 9. Cash and Sales Revenue increase, thus increasing both assets and owners' equity. Cost of Goods Sold and Merchandise Inventory decrease when goods are sold. Since Cost of Goods Sold is an expense, owners' equity decreases. The decrease in inventory reduces assets.

Thinking Beyond the Question

HOW DO WE KNOW HOW WELL OUR BUSINESS IS DOING?

At the beginning of the chapter we asked how a business can determine how well it is performing. This chapter has described the key elements of a basic accounting system. Accounts are used to record business activities. Account balances are summarized at the end of a fiscal period, and those balances are used to prepare financial statements. Those statements help owners, creditors, and other stakeholders understand the resources available to a company, how the resources were financed, how they were used in the business, how much profit the business earned, and the events that affected the company's cash during the period.

The procedures described in this chapter may appear mechanical. Some of them are. However, sometimes judgments have to be made about when certain events should be recorded. Assuming you are making the accounting decisions for a company, what information do you think would tell you when revenues have been earned and expenses have been incurred? What events would be important for determining when to recognize revenues and expenses?

Self-Study Problem Solutions

SSP2-1

Accounts	Assets	=	Liabilities	+	Owners' Equity
Beginning Amounts	0	=	0	+	0
Cash	220,000				
Notes Payable			120,000		
Contributed Capital					100,000
Equipment	160,000				
Cash	−160,000				
Building	400,000				
Cash	−40,000				
Notes Payable			360,000		
Ending Amounts	580,000	=	480,000	+	100,000

SSP2-2

		Assets		=	Liabilities	+	Owners' Equity	
Date	Accounts	Cash	Other Assets				Contributed Capital	Retained Earnings
	Beginning Amounts	0	+0	=	0		+0	+0
Jan. 3	Cash Contributed Capital	40,000					40,000	
Jan. 5	Cash Notes Payable	25,000			25,000			
Jan. 8	Equipment Cash	−35,000	35,000					
Jan. 10	Merchandise Inventory Cash	−20,000	20,000					
Jan. 11	Supplies Expense Cash	−2,000						−2,000
Jan. 15	Cash Sales Revenue	12,000						12,000
Jan. 15	Cost of Goods Sold Merchandise Inventory		−8,000					−8,000
Jan. 22	Cash Sales Revenue	9,000						9,000
Jan. 22	Cost of Goods Sold Merchandise Inventory		−6,000					−6,000
Jan. 31	Wages Expense Cash	−3,000						−3,000
Jan. 31	Utilities Expense Cash	−800						−800
	Ending Amounts	25,200	+41,000	=	25,000	+	40,000	+1,200

SSP2-3 A.

Philistine Co.
Income Statement
For the Month Ended August 31, 2007

Sales revenue	$ 520,000
Cost of goods sold	(300,000)
Other expenses	(140,000)
Net income	$ 80,000

B.

Retained earnings, August 1	$ 0
Net income	80,000
Less: Payments to owners	30,000
Retained earnings, August 31	$50,000

C.

Philistine Co. Balance Sheet At August 31, 2007	
Assets	
Cash	$ 25,000
Merchandise inventory	200,000
Equipment	425,000
Total assets	$650,000
Liabilities and Owners' Equity	
Notes payable	$350,000
Investment by owners	250,000
Retained earnings	50,000
Total liabilities and owners' equity	$650,000

D. Return on Assets = $80,000 ÷ $650,000 = 12.3%

Define *Terms and Concepts Defined in This Chapter*

account (46)
assets (46)
balance sheet (56)
business activities (45)
cash (47)
contributed capital (47)
cost of goods sold (52)
credits (60)
debits (60)
expense (50)
financial statements (54)
financing activities (46)
fiscal period (54)
income statement (54)
interest (45)
investing activities (48)
liabilities (46)
merchandise inventory (51)
net income (55)
notes payable (47)
operating activities (50)
owners' equity (45)
principal (45)
retained earnings (51)
return on assets (ROA) (58)
revenue (50)
sales revenue (52)
statement of cash flows (56)
transactions (46)

Review *Summary of Important Concepts*

1. Accounting provides information about business activities.
   a. Accounting is an information system for measuring, recording, reporting, and analyzing business activities.
   b. Financing activities provide financial resources for a company from creditors and owners. Claims to resources by creditors and owners are recorded in liability and owners' equity accounts.
   c. The accounting equation, Assets = Liabilities + Owners' Equity, provides a basis for recording transactions.
   d. Accounting measures business activities by the cash value of resources transferred or consumed in a transaction.
   e. Investing activities involve acquiring and disposing of long-term assets.
   f. Operating activities involve acquiring and selling goods and services. Revenues identify the amount of goods and services sold to customers. Expenses identify the amount of resources consumed in acquiring and selling goods and services. Profit or net income for a fiscal period is the revenue earned during the period minus expenses incurred during the period.

2. Accounting reports business activities in the form of financial statements.
   a. An income statement reports revenues, expenses, and net income for a fiscal period as a measure of operating results.

(Continued)

b. A balance sheet reports the assets controlled by a company and the claims to those assets by creditors and owners at a particular time, usually the end of a fiscal period.
c. A statement of cash flows reports the events that resulted in cash being received or paid by a company during a fiscal period.
d. Accounting measures and reports the results of the company's transformation of resources into goods and services for sale to customers.

3. Financial analysis involves the interpretation and use of accounting information to make business decisions.
   a. Analysis involves the comparison of accounting numbers with other numbers and comparison among companies or time periods.
   b. Financial ratios compare one financial statement number with another. Return on assets is one ratio used to evaluate a company's performance.

Questions

Q2-1 *Obj. 1* Joan Hoyt is considering opening a small retail store to sell knives and other kitchen utensils. She has a small amount of money to invest and wants to maintain as much control over the business as she can. She has asked you to help her decide how to finance her business. Describe the primary issues you would suggest Joan to consider.

Q2-2 *Obj. 1* Hardly Moving and Storage Corporation needs an additional $1,000,000 in financing to build new facilities. How might Hardly get the money? What issues should company management consider in deciding on the type of financing to use?

Q2-3 *Obj. 1* Jerrilyn has invested $5,000 in shares of the stock of Ambitious Enterprises, Inc. From the corporation's perspective, was this a financing activity, an investing activity, or an operating activity? Why?

Q2-4 *Obj. 2* Discuss the effect on the accounting equation if a company accurately reports its assets, yet understates its liabilities.

Q2-5 *Obj. 2* How are liabilities and owners' equity similar?

Q2-6 *Obj. 2* Explain why the accounting equation must balance after each transaction.

Q2-7 *Objs. 3, 4* Is purchasing merchandise inventory considered an investing or operating activity? Explain.

Q2-8 *Obj. 4* If owners contribute resources to a company, Owners' Equity increases. If a company records Sales Revenue, Owner's Equity also increases. How are Contributed Capital and Sales Revenue dissimilar?

Q2-9 *Obj. 4* While reviewing a company's balance sheet, John observed the Retained Earnings account with a balance of $850,000. "Wow," he thought. "That's a lot of cash!" Has John correctly interpreted the company's financial information? Explain.

Q2-10 *Obj. 5* Think of a company that operates in the same city as the college you are attending. With that company in mind, identify two examples each of assets, liabilities, owners' equity, revenues, and expenses that the company is likely to report on its financial statements.

Q2-11 *Obj. 5* Assume you are reviewing a balance sheet that has assets listed on the left side and liabilities and owners' equity on the right side. What question or questions can you answer by looking at the information on the left side of the balance sheet? What question or questions can you answer by looking at the information on the right side of the balance sheet?

Q2-12 *Obj. 5* What types of information are reported, respectively, on the balance sheet, income statement, and the statement of cash flows? Be specific.

Q2-13 *Obj. 2* A balance sheet identifies assets and claims to assets. Typically, who has claims on a company's assets?

Q2-14 *Obj. 5* Both the income statement and the statement of cash flows provide information about operating activities during a fiscal period. Why are both statements included in a company's financial report? How can decision makers use information in each statement?

Q2-15 *Obj. 5* Why are account balances summarized into financial statements? Why don't companies simply distribute a list of year-end account balances?

Exercises

E2-1 Write a short definition for each of the terms listed in the *Terms and Concepts Defined in This Chapter* section.

E2-2 *Objs. 1, 3, 4* Leonetta Garcetti owns and manages a large construction company. This morning she is faced with the following issues.

1. The office manager just submitted his resignation and the search for a replacement must be organized.
2. A loan officer from the company's bank just phoned saying that the company's application for a $400,000 loan has been approved.
3. Bids from several vendors have been received regarding installation of a new computerized information system. One proposal must be selected.
4. Because the new bank loan has been approved, two short-term loans can be paid off.
5. Old office furniture is awaiting disposal.
6. A long-time customer is unhappy with the firm's latest architectural drawings for a new shopping center complex.
7. A new construction crane is being purchased.
8. An investor has approached Leonetta offering to purchase 20% of her company in exchange for cash.
9. The firm is considering the purchase of exclusive regional rights to a patented construction process.
10. One of the company's customers is behind on scheduled payments. The amounts are large and Leonetta must decide whether to suspend construction on the project involved.

Identify each of the issues above as involving a financing activity, an investing activity, or an operating activity.

E2-3 *Objs. 1, 3, 4* For each of the following items, identify which part of the transformation process is involved. Use *F* to indicate a financing activity, *I* to indicate an investing activity, or *O* to indicate an operating activity.

a. ____ New manufacturing equipment was purchased for installation in the factory.
b. ____ Three new salespersons were hired.
c. ____ A loan was obtained from a local bank.
d. ____ A $500 down payment on goods sold was received from a customer.
e. ____ The Human Resources department hired three new employees.
f. ____ The company's worn-out delivery truck was sold to the junk yard for $400.
g. ____ The owner contributed more cash to the business.
h. ____ Refunds totaling $450 were given to several customers.
i. ____ Goods were shipped to a customer in a neighboring state.
j. ____ The remaining balance of a loan was repaid in full.

E2-4 *Obj. 2* Popovich Company had the following transactions during June.

June	1	$15,000 of merchandise inventory was purchased with cash.
	15	Sold merchandise for $60,000 cash. The merchandise had cost Popovich $28,000.
	23	Borrowed $250,000 from a bank.
	25	Paid $2,000 for supplies used in June.
	28	June wages of $5,000 were paid.
	30	$100,000 of equipment was purchased using cash.
	30	Paid $6,000 for utilities consumed in June.

Indicate the amount of cash, other assets, liabilities, and/or owners' equity that would result from each transaction by completing the table provided on the next page.

(Continued)

		Assets		=	Liabilities	+	Owners' Equity	
Date	Accounts	Cash	Other Assets				Contributed Capital	Retained Earnings
June 1	Beginning Amounts	$40,000	+60,000	=	30,000	+	50,000	+20,000
	Ending Amounts							

E2-5 *Objs. 1, 3, 4* Identify each transaction in E2-4 as financing, investing, or operating.

E2-6 *Obj. 2* Perez Company had the following selected transactions during the month of May. Show how the financial effects of each transaction would be recorded using the following format. The first transaction has been completed as an example.

Juanita Perez invested $10,000 in the company on May 1.

		Assets		=	Liabilities	+	Owners' Equity	
Date	Accounts	Cash	Other Assets				Contributed Capital	Retained Earnings
	Beginning Amounts	70,000	+90,000	=	60,000	+	60,000	+40,000
May 1	Cash	10,000						
	Contributed Capital						10,000	

May 5 Sold goods for $35,000 cash. The goods had cost $14,000.
10 Purchased merchandise inventory for $45,000 cash.
15 Paid back part of a bank loan, $2,000 (decrease Notes Payable).
22 Purchased equipment for $4,000 using cash.
31 Paid the utility company for services consumed, $800.
31 Paid $7,500 wages for labor services consumed.

E2-7 *Objs. 1, 3, 4* Identify each transaction in E2-6 as financing, investing, or operating.

E2-8 *Obj. 2* The Fashion Statement Inc. distributes perfumes and cosmetics. The following account changes were made in the company's accounting records during March. For each item, describe the transaction that caused the changes. The first item has been completed as an example.

a. Cash increased $18,000; Contributed Capital increased $18,000.
The owners invested $18,000 in the company.
b. Equipment increased $12,000; Cash decreased $12,000.
c. Cash decreased $8,500; Notes Payable decreased $8,500.
d. Supplies inventory increased $13,500; Cash decreased $13,500.
e. Merchandise Inventory decreased $10,000; Cost of Goods Sold increased $10,000.
f. Cash increased $23,500; Sales Revenue increased $23,500.
g. Supplies Expense increased $3,000; Supplies inventory decreased $3,000.

E2-9 *Objs. 2, 5* Amelio has operated a one-person law firm for many years. During the first week of February, the following events occurred in his business.

Feb. 2	Collected $1,800 from a client for legal work performed.
3	February's office rent of $1,200 was paid to the landlord.
4	A $300 payment was made on a loan previously obtained from a local bank.
4	The monthly subscription to *Lawyer's Monthly* magazine (a Miscellaneous Expense) was paid: $35.
5	Collected $4,250 for legal services performed.
5	Purchased a computer for $3,200 using cash.
6	Wages were paid to the office staff totaling $525.
6	Office supplies of $128 were purchased for cash and were consumed.

Show how the events above would be recorded using the format demonstrated in the chapter. Beginning account balances were as follows: Cash $5,000, Liabilities $1,500, Contributed Capital $3,000, and Retained Earnings $500. Prepare an income statement for the first week of February.

E2-10
Objs. 1,3, 4

Identify each transaction in E2-9 as financing, investing, or operating.

E2-11
Obj. 2

Balance sheet accounts for Dale's Delightful Florist Shoppe at the end of a recent fiscal year are listed below. Prepare a schedule demonstrating that assets = liabilities + owner's equity for the company.

Supplies Inventory	$ 4,350
Buildings	79,500
Cash	1,500
Equipment	12,750
Flowers and Plants	26,000
Notes Payable	57,500
Proprietor's Capital	66,600

E2-12
Obj. 2

Harmony Cabot opened a music store in a local mall, selling CDs. She invested $80,000 in the business and borrowed $140,000 from a local bank. The following additional events occurred during April, the first month of operations:

a. Paid cash for equipment costing $45,150.
b. Purchased an inventory of CDs for $129,600 in cash.
c. Sold one-third of the CDs for a cash sales price of $85,000.
d. Paid expenses as follows:

Employee wages	$12,300
Rent	15,500
Utilities	4,800
Postage	650
Insurance	1,290

Record the transactions using the format shown in the chapter.

E2-13
Obj. 4

Chang Pottery Works began November with a Retained Earnings balance of $95,000. During November the company earned $15,000 and returned $4,000 to the owners. Prepare a schedule that reports the beginning balance, changes, and ending balance of retained earnings.

E2-14
Obj. 5

The following events occurred during December for Christmas Cookie Company:

a. Purchased and consumed $60,000 of flour, sugar, and other ingredients for cookies sold.
b. Paid $97,500 for December wages.
c. Paid $24,000 for utilities consumed in December.
d. Sold $234,000 of cookies and received cash.

Prepare an income statement for Christmas Cookie Company.

E2-15 *Obj. 5*

Wheatgerm Healthfoods reported the following information:

Proceeds from issuance of notes payable	$13,057
Additions to plant and equipment	5,379
Proceeds from owners	30,957
Proceeds from sales of plant and equipment	1,986
Payments of debt	80,323

Calculate the net cash flow from (a) financing and (b) investing activities for Wheatgerm.

E2-16 *Obj. 5*

Darden Bottling Company has the following information available for the first six months of the year:

Cash collected from customers	$270,000
Cash paid for merchandise inventory	83,500
Cash paid for utilities	25,000
Cash paid for insurance	23,000
Cash paid for equipment	76,500
Cash paid to employees	58,000
Cash paid for postage	7,500
Cash paid to owners	5,000
Cash received from sale of old equipment	18,500

Determine the cash flow from operating activities for the six-month period.

E2-17 *Obj. 5*

Listed below are typical accounts or titles that appear on financial statements. For each item, identify the financial statement(s) on which it appears.

Wages expense
Cost of goods sold
Sales revenue
Merchandise inventory
Net income
Retained earnings
Contributed capital
Rent expense
Cash
Notes payable

E2-18 *Obj. 5*

After six months of operation, Brothers' Lawn Service had the following revenue and expense account balances:

Supplies expense	$ 4,000
Wages expense	6,000
Service revenue	12,300
Utilities expense	500
Rent expense	1,000

Prepare an income statement for Brothers' Lawn Service for the first six months of operation that ended June 30.

E2-19 *Obj. 5*

On June 30, 2007, Brothers' Lawn Service had the following account balances:

Cash	$3,000
Notes payable	1,000
Contributed capital	6,700
Retained earnings	800
Supplies inventory	500
Equipment	5,000

Prepare a balance sheet for Brothers' Lawn Service.

E2-20 *Obj. 2, appendix* Record each transaction described in E2-4, using the debit and credit format illustrated in the appendix.

E2-21 *Obj. 2, appendix* Record each transaction described in E2-6, using the debit and credit format illustrated in the appendix.

E2-22 *Obj. 2, appendix* Record each transaction described in E2-9, using the debit and credit format illustrated in the appendix.

E2-23 *Obj. 2, appendix* Record each transaction described in E2-12, using the debit and credit format illustrated in the appendix.

Problems

P2-1 *Obj. 2*

RECORDING TRANSACTIONS

Surf-The-Net.com had the following events occur during October:

1. Paid $5,800 for utilities.
2. Made cash sales to customers that totaled $89,460. The merchandise had cost Surf-The-Net.com $60,000
3. Paid $28,600 for new equipment.
4. Repaid $4,900 that was borrowed from a bank.
5. Borrowed $65,000 from local bank.
6. Paid $59,430 to employees for salaries.
7. Paid $11,900 for maintenance and repair.
8. Received $48,600 from investors.
9. Paid $3,750 for supplies that were used.

Required

A. Record transactions 1–9 using the format illustrated in the chapter.
B. What issues must a manager consider before making a financing decision or investing decision?

P2-2 *Objs. 1, 3, 4*

CLASSIFYING ACTIVITIES AS OPERATING, INVESTING, OR FINANCING

Refer to the information provided in P2-1.

Required Identify each transaction in P2-1 as a financing, investing, or operating activity.

P2-3 *Obj. 2*

THE ACCOUNTING EQUATION

Apollo Corporation reported the following accounts and balances in its financial statements:

Cash	$10,000
Merchandise Inventory	30,000
Equipment	45,000
Notes Payable	20,000
Contributed Capital	35,000
Retained Earnings	30,000

Required Arrange the accounts and balances into the accounting equation as shown below.

Assets = Liabilities + Equity

P2-4 RECORDING TRANSACTIONS
Objs. 2, 5

Davidson Enterprises had the following transactions during its first month of business, June 2007.

June	1	Lynne Davidson set up a bank account in the business name and deposited $7,000 of her personal funds to it.
	2	June's rent of $525 per month for a store-front location was paid in cash.
	7	Goods for resale costing $5,000 were purchased using cash.
	12	Paid advertising costs of $800 for the firm's Gala Grand Opening.
	26	Goods costing $4,500 were sold during June for $7,500 in cash.
	30	Workers were paid $850 and the utility company was paid $228 for June services.

Required

A. Use the format illustrated below to show how these transactions would be recorded.
B. Prepare an income statement that reports the firm's profit during June.
C. Prepare a balance sheet that reports the firm's assets, liabilities, and equity at June 30.

		Assets		=	Liabilities	+	Owners' Equity	
Date	Accounts	Cash	Other Assets				Contributed Capital	Retained Earnings
	Beginning Amounts	0	+0	=	0	+	0	+0

P2-5 CLASSIFYING TRANSACTIONS AS FINANCING, INVESTING, OR OPERATING
Objs. 1, 3, 4

Refer to the information provided in P2-4.

Required Identify each transaction in P2-4 as financing, investing, or operating.

P2-6 RECORDING TRANSACTIONS
Obj. 2

Carmen Bay Company markets a variety of souvenirs to tourists on the beach. Students are paid 20 percent of the sales price to sell the wares up and down the beach and are paid daily. The company was formed only recently and given approval by the local city council to operate. The following events are the first in the company's short history:

1. The company was formed when Carmen Bay contributed $3,000 to the firm.
2. A local bank loaned the firm $4,000 in exchange for the firm's one-year note payable.
3. Merchandise costing $3,500 was purchased with cash.
4. Goods costing $825 were sold to tourists for a total of $2,500 in cash, and the students were paid their commissions.
5. A payment of $1,500 was made to the local bank on the note payable.
6. Carmen Bay withdrew $750 cash for personal use (Hint: reduce retained earnings).

Assume the company uses the following set of accounts:

Cash	Notes Payable
Cost of Sales	Merchandise Inventory
Sales	Contributed Capital
Retained Earnings	Commissions Expense

Required Determine how each event affects the company, and record the events using the format shown below.

		Assets		=	Liabilities	+	Owners' Equity	
Date	**Accounts**	**Cash**	**Other Assets**				**Contributed Capital**	**Retained Earnings**
	Beginning Amounts	0	+0	=	0	+	0	+0

P2-7 RECORDING TRANSACTIONS

Objs. 2, 5

Randi had a hard time finding a summer job when she went home from college, so she decided to go into business for herself mowing lawns. She had the following business activities during the month of June.

June 1 Used $300 of her own money and borrowed $450 from her father to start the business.
2 Rented a used pickup truck from an uncle for $85 per month. Paid for the first month's use.
3 Rented a lawnmower ($75 per month), an edger ($50 per month), and a wheelbarrow ($10 per month) at an equipment rental store. Paid the first month's rental fees in full.
16 During the first two weeks, performed $650 of lawn-mowing services. Customers paid in cash. Paid out $67 for gas, oil, and other supplies.
18 Paid $70 for a newspaper advertisement that had appeared earlier in the month.
30 During the last half of the month, performed $507 of lawn-mowing services and collected the cash.
30 Paid out $105 for gas, oil, and other supplies.
30 Paid back one-half of the amount she had borrowed from her father plus $5 for interest.

Randi knew from taking an accounting class at college that the following accounts would be needed to keep track of her business activities.

Cash	Equipment Rental Expense
Note Payable—Dad	Contributed Capital
Service Revenue	Retained Earnings
Gas and Oil Expense	Advertising Expense

Required

A. Show how each event would be entered into the accounting system.
B. Prepare an income statement for Randi's Lawn-mowing Service for the month of June.
C. Prepare a balance sheet as of June 30.
D. Did Randi make a smart decision when she started her own business? What factors might be considered in making that evaluation?

P2-8 RECONSTRUCTING EVENTS FROM INFORMATION IN THE ACCOUNTING DATABASE

Obj. 2

Jill Jones has just established a security alarm maintenance service. She charges $20 per hour per person and is paid by check upon completion of the job. Her expenses are rather low—usually only supplies and transportation. Following are the entries to the accounting system that were made for the first seven transactions of the company.

		Assets		=	Liabilities	+	Owners' Equity	
Date	**Accounts**	**Cash**	**Other Assets**				**Contributed Capital**	**Retained Earnings**
1	Cash	5,000						
	Contributed Capital						5,000	
2	Supplies Inventory		300					
	Cash	−300						
3	Cash	4,200						
	Service Revenues							4,200
4	Utilities Expense							−450
	Cash	−450						
5	Transportation Expense							−500
	Cash	−500						
6	Insurance Expense							−700
	Cash	−700						
7	Retained Earnings							−1,300
	Cash	−1,300						
	Ending Amounts	5,950	+300	=			5,000	+1,250

Required

A. For each transaction, describe the event that caused the entry to be made.
B. How much income (or loss) did the company earn?

P2-9 UNDERSTANDING INFORMATION IN THE ACCOUNTING INFORMATION SYSTEM
Obj. 2

Jacqueline owns and operates a specialty cosmetics manufacturing firm. Distribution is primarily through boutique shops in regional shopping centers, although some items are sold directly through a network of beauty consultants. Raw materials consist of various lotions, potions, fragrances, oils, and powders. The transactions that occurred during the month of March were entered into the accounting system as follows.

		Assets		=	Liabilities	+	Owners' Equity	
Date	**Accounts**	**Cash**	**Other Assets**				**Contributed Capital**	**Retained Earnings**
Mar. 1	Cash	10,000						
	Contributed Capital						10,000	
Mar. 3	Cash	7,000						
	Notes Payable				7,000			
Mar. 5	Merchandise Inventory		8,100					
	Cash	−8,100						
Mar. 18	Cash	15,250						
	Sales Revenue							15,250
	Cost of Goods Sold							−7,500
	Merchandise Inventory		−7,500					
Mar. 18	Wages Expense							−650
	Cash	−650						
Mar. 23	Notes Payable				−2,500			
	Cash	−2,500						
Mar. 31	Retained Earnings							−2,000
	Cash	−2,000						
	Ending Amounts	19,000	+600	=	4,500	+	10,000	+5,100

Required

A. Describe each of the firm's transactions. Specify as much detail about each transaction as you can.

B. Assume an income statement and balance sheet are prepared immediately after the last transaction.
   1. What amount of net income would be reported?
   2. What total amount of owners' equity would be reported on the balance sheet?

P2-10 RECONSTRUCTING EVENTS FROM THE FINANCIAL STATEMENTS
Obj. 2

Costantino Company just started in business. The first seven transactions have been entered into and processed by the company's computerized accounting information system. To be sure the accounting system is operating properly, Jim Costantino, the owner, has printed out the financial statements as produced by the accounting system after seven transactions.

Assets:		**Liabilities and Equity:**	
Cash	$22,850	Payable to bank	$ 6,285
Equipment	11,000	Payable for equipment	11,000
		Owner investment	15,000
		Retained earnings	1,565
Total assets	$33,850	Total liabilities and equity	$33,850

Revenues	$ 2,250
Expenses:	
Rent	(400)
Wages	(250)
Internet service	(35)
Net income	$ 1,565

Required Identify the seven transactions and as much detail about each transaction as you can.

P2-11 RECORDING TRANSACTIONS AND PREPARING FINANCIAL STATEMENTS
Objs. 2, 5

Assume that you began a small business in May 2007 by (1) investing $10,000 and (2) borrowing $30,000 from a bank. You (3) purchased equipment for $25,000 cash and (4) purchased merchandise for $12,000 using cash. During the first month of operations, your company (5) sold merchandise for $27,000 in cash. (6) The cost of merchandise sold during the month was $10,000. You (7) repaid $300 of the amount borrowed from the bank. You (8) withdrew $800 from the business for personal use. The name of your business is Sand Dune Trading Company.

Required

A. Record transactions 1–8 using the format illustrated in the chapter.

B. Prepare an income statement for May 2007, the first month of operations.

C. Prepare a balance sheet at the end of the first month.

P2-12 IDENTIFYING FINANCIAL STATEMENTS
Obj. 5

Refer to the information about financial statements below.

1. The statement provides information about resources consumed during an accounting period.
2. The statement is dated as of a specific point in time.
3. The amounts that are owed to other organizations or individuals are reported.
4. The total amount of capital that has been contributed to the organization is reported.
5. The cash used for investing activities is reported.
6. Information is reported regarding the rewards that have been earned from serving customers during the accounting period just ended.

(Continued)

7. The cash received from financing activities is reported.
8. The statement is not as of a specific date, but covers a period of time.
9. The statement contains information about the financial obligations that were made to acquire resources.
10. The statement reports cash inflows and outflows.

Required For each item above, indicate the financial statement for which the information is true. Use *I* to indicate income statement, *B* to indicate balance sheet, *C* to indicate cash flow statement. If an item is not true for any of the three financial statements, indicate with an *N*.

P2-13 SUMMARIZING THE RESULTS OF FINANCIAL ACTIVITIES

Obj. 5

The accounting staff at Moonbeam Enterprises prepares monthly financial statements. At the end of April 2007 the company had the following account balances:

Land	$45,000
Notes payable	33,000
Merchandise inventory	12,480
Buildings	50,000
Cash	10,360
Contributed capital	38,770
Retained earnings, April 30	46,070
Cost of goods sold	15,050
Sales revenue	26,000
Supplies expense	1,300
Income tax expense	1,060
Wage expense	1,500
Insurance expense	550
Interest expense	900

Required Prepare an income statement and balance sheet in good form. For each statement, use a three-line heading on the statement that includes (a) the name of the company, (b) the name of the statement, and (c) the appropriate time period or date.

P2-14 RECORDING TRANSACTIONS

Obj. 2

Larrisa Enterprises Inc. owns and operates a chain of mini-mart stores in a popular summer resort area. Business is highly seasonal with about 80% of annual sales occurring during June, July, and August. Shown below are transactions that occurred during the first week of June.

June 3	Merchandise costing $120,000 was purchased from a supplier using cash.
4	Dividends of $25,000 were distributed to owners for their own personal use. (Hint: Dividends reduce Retained Earnings.)
5	Goods costing $112,000 were sold to customers for $140,000 cash.
5	Advertising was run in local newspapers during the first week. The bill, for $9,000, was paid on June 5.
6	Electricity, water, natural gas, and Internet charges totaling $450 were paid in cash.
6	Display equipment was purchased for $15,000 cash.
7	Employees were paid a total of $12,900 for all work performed through the end of the first week of June.

Required Show how the events above would be entered into the accounting system using the format demonstrated in the chapter. Beginning balances are provided below.

		Assets		=	Liabilities	+	Owners' Equity	
Date	Accounts	Cash	Other Assets				Contributed Capital	Retained Earnings
	Beginning Amounts	90,000	150,000		80,000		60,000	100,000

P2-15 *Objs. 1, 3, 4*

CLASSIFYING TRANSACTIONS AS FINANCING, INVESTING, OR OPERATING ACTIVITIES

Refer to the information provided in P2-14.

Required Identify each transaction in P2-14 as a financing, investing, or operating activity.

P2-16 *Obj. 5*

PREPARING A STATEMENT OF CASH FLOWS

Crimson Florist had the following cash flows for the month of July.

Cash paid for wages	$ 4,500
Cash paid for supplies	3,000
Cash received from sales to customers	15,000
Cash paid for equipment	7,000
Cash received from owners	13,000
Cash paid for utilities	2,700
Cash received from creditors	9,000

The cash balance on July 1 was $3,300.

Required

A. Prepare a statement of cash flows for Crimson Florist.
B. What is the purpose of the statement of cash flows?

P2-17 *Obj. 5*

PREPARING A STATEMENT OF CASH FLOWS

During January, The College Shop had the following cash flows:

Cash paid for merchandise	$ 4,000
Cash paid for rent	5,300
Cash received from sales to customers	13,000
Cash paid for utilities	200
Cash received from owners	9,000
Cash paid for equipment	7,000
Cash paid for insurance	2,500
Cash received from a bank loan	10,500
Cash paid for wages	1,200

The beginning cash balance was $4,000.

Required Prepare a statement of cash flows for The College Shop.

P2-18 *Obj. 5*

FINANCIAL ANALYSIS

Holiday Travel Store is a retailer that sells merchandise at a family campground. The company's most recent income statement and balance sheet are presented below.

Holiday Travel Store Income Statement For the Year Ended December 31, 2007	
Sales revenue	$80,000
Cost of goods sold	(42,000)
Wages expense	(18,500)
Supplies expense	(3,500)
Utilities expense	(4,000)
Rent expense	(8,000)
Net income	$ 4,000

Holiday Travel Store Balance Sheet December 31, 2007	
Assets	
Cash	$ 1,100
Merchandise inventory	7,500
Equipment	22,000
Total assets	$30,600
Liabilities and Owners' Equity	
Notes payable	$15,500
Contributed capital	10,000
Retained earnings	5,100
Total liabilities and owners' equity	$30,600

(Continued)

Required

A. Calculate Holiday Travel Store's return on assets.
B. Explain what the ratio means.
C. What kinds of changes might the owners make if the return on assets is not acceptable?

P2-19 RECORDING TRANSACTIONS USING THE DEBIT AND CREDIT FORMAT

Obj. 2, Appendix

Refer to the information provided in P2-1.

Required For each transaction described in P2-1, record the transaction using the debit and credit format illustrated in the appendix.

P2-20 RECORDING TRANSACTIONS USING THE DEBIT AND CREDIT FORMAT

Obj. 2, Appendix

Refer to the information provided in P2-6.

Required For each transaction described in P2-6, record the transaction using the debit and credit format illustrated in the appendix.

P2-21 RECORDING TRANSACTIONS USING THE DEBIT AND CREDIT FORMAT

Obj. 2, Appendix

Refer to the information provided in P2-7.

Required For each transaction described in P2-7, record the transaction using the debit and credit format illustrated in the appendix.

P2-22 RECORDING TRANSACTIONS USING THE DEBIT AND CREDIT FORMAT

Obj. 2, Appendix

Refer to the information provided in P2-11.

Required For each transaction described in P2-11, record the transaction using the debit and credit format illustrated in the appendix.

P2-23 EXCEL IN ACTION

Millie and Milo Wermz are the owners of The Book Wermz. The business is operated as a corporation. The Wermz invested $100,000 in the company when they started it in 1996. This investment represents the company's stockholders' equity. The company's account balances on September 30, 2007—the end of the fiscal year—were: Cash $4,238.72, Inventory of Books $235,892.35, Supplies $2,343.28, Equipment $43,297.00, Notes Payable $123,452.88, Investment by Owners $100,000, and Retained Earnings $62,318.47.

Summary transactions for The Book Wermz for October 2007 included:

Cash sales	$38,246.50
Cost of goods sold	27,318.93

Required Use a spreadsheet to keep track of account balances for The Book Wermz. Enter the titles of accounts in Row 1. Use column A for dates. Enter account balances for September 30, 2007 in Row 2. A partial spreadsheet is illustrated on the following page as an example:

	A	B	C
1	Date	Cash	Inventory
2	9/30/07	4,238.72	235,892.35

Use the Format menu to adjust cell formats as needed to wrap text for long titles. Use the comma button to format dollar amounts. See instructions from Chapter 1 if you need help with formatting. Include columns for Sales and for Cost of Goods Sold. The beginning balances for these two accounts will be $0.

In Row 3, enter the sales transaction for October, and in Row 4 enter the cost of goods sold transaction. Use 10/31/07 as dates for these transactions. Using the illustration of closing the accounts in this chapter, close the revenue and expense accounts for October in Row 5. In Row 6, calculate the account balance for each account at October 31, 2007. Use the Sum function [=Sum(B2:B5)] or button Σ for this purpose. Note that =Sum(B2:B5) performs the same operation as =B2+B3+B4+B5. The ending balances for revenue and expense accounts should be $0 after these accounts have been closed.

Beginning in Row 9, prepare a balance sheet and income statement for The Book Wermz for October 2007. Use the format illustrated in Exhibits 13 and 14 in this chapter. You may need to make some of the columns in the spreadsheet wider to accommodate captions. Format cells with the currency format so that they display $, as shown in Exhibits 13 and 14. You can use the Currency $ and Comma , buttons for this purpose. Cells containing totals should be formatted to contain double underlines. Use the Borders button for this purpose.

Use cell references in the financial statements to identify amounts for each account. For example: **Cash** =B6

Also, use the Sum function or button to calculate totals in the balance sheet and income statement. You should be able to change any of the numbers in the transactions at the top of the spreadsheet and have the financial statements change automatically in response to the new amounts.

P2-24 MULTIPLE-CHOICE OVERVIEW OF THE CHAPTER

1. Which of the following is a financing activity?
   a. A manufacturing company purchases supplies.
   b. A retail company borrows $40,000 from a bank.
   c. A manufacturing company acquires a new building.
   d. A service organization pays the monthly utility bill.

2. If a company borrows cash from a bank, the effect on the accounting equation is as follows:
   a. Assets increase, Liabilities increase
   b. Assets decrease, Liabilities increase
   c. Assets increase, Liabilities decrease
   d. Assets decrease, Liabilities decrease

3. The balance sheet describes a company's assets. Financial resources to acquire these assets are obtained from
   a. investing activities.
   b. financing activities and revenues earned.
   c. investing activities and expenses paid during a fiscal period.
   d. none of the above.

4. Which of the following is an investing activity?
   a. A manufacturer borrows from creditors.
   b. A service firm pays a return to its stockholders.
   c. A retailer sells goods to a not-for-profit agency at cost.
   d. A government agency purchases a new mainframe computer system.

5. Which of the following is *not* an operating activity?
   a. Merchandise is sold to customers.
   b. Utility bills are paid.

(Continued)

c. Merchandise is shipped to customers.
d. Equipment is purchased for use in manufacturing.

6. Return on assets represents
   a. cash that is returned to investors.
   b. merchandise that is returned by customers.
   c. the ratio of income to total assets.
   d. the ratio of merchandise returned by customers to sales.

7. Accounting information is

	Needed by Managers for Internal Decision Making	Needed by Managers for Persons Outside the Firm
a.	Yes	Yes
b.	Yes	No
c.	No	Yes
d.	No	No

8. Liability and owners' equity accounts usually arise from which type of activities?
   a. Investing activities
   b. Financing activities
   c. Operating activities
   d. Manufacturing activities

9. Expresso Delivery Service purchased a new delivery truck for $21,000 by making a $4,000 cash payment and giving a $17,000 note payable to the seller. How were each of the following affected when this event was recorded in the firm's accounting information system?

	Assets	Liabilities
a.	Increased	Increased
b.	No change	Increased
c.	Increased	Decreased
d.	Decreased	Increased

10. The statement of cash flows for the Halyard Exploration Company reported the following:

Cash paid for equipment	$ 300,000
Cash paid to employees	400,000
Cash paid to owners	150,000
Cash paid to suppliers	560,000
Cash received from customers	1,200,000

What were Halyard's net cash flows from operating, investing, and financing activities?

	Operating	Investing	Financing
a.	$240,000	($300,000)	($150,000)
b.	$500,000	($860,000)	$200,000
c.	$640,000	($860,000)	$200,000
d.	$240,000	($860,000)	$200,000

11. When an investor contributes cash to a business, the transaction is recorded as follows:

	Debit	Credit
a.	Cash	Retained Earnings
b.	Cash	Contributed Capital
c.	Contributed Capital	Cash
d.	Retained Earnings	Cash

Cases

C2-1 DESIGNING AN ACCOUNTING INFORMATION SYSTEM

Obj. 2

For about a year, Frank Poppa has been operating a hot dog stand in the parking lot of a major discount retailer in a suburban area. The stand appears to be a pushcart but is actually a small trailer that is towed from home each day. Frank cleverly designed the stand to include storage compartments, napkins, and the like. What started out as a "weekend gig" to pick up a few extra bucks has turned into a full-time occupation. Frank soon found that on a hot summer day, he could easily take in more than $1,000 from sales of a full line of fancy hot dogs and cold sodas.

About four months ago, Frank decided to expand to more locations. He found that large discount retailers were quite happy to provide him adequate space near the front door because customers enjoyed the convenience and the stand helped build traffic for the retailer. Frank formed Poppa's Dogs Company and negotiated contracts with several retailers to provide pushcart operations outside their stores. The contracts generally call for Poppa's Dogs to pay a location fee to the retailer plus 3% of the pushcart's sales.

Frank plans to be very careful when hiring the people necessary to operate the five new pushcart locations. He is confident that he can assess good moral character and avoid hiring anyone who would take advantage of him. Frank will have to spend about $3,000 for each new pushcart and related equipment. In addition, he will have to finance an inventory of hot dogs, condiments, and sodas for each location. A local bank has agreed to provide financing.

Until now, Frank has maintained an informal accounting system consisting of an envelope full of receipts and his personal checking account. The system has served him well enough so far, but he is finding that more and more he is getting his personal financial activities confused with those of his business. Frank is positive that the business is profitable because he seems to have more money left at the end of the month than he did when he was working full time as an auto mechanic. He has decided he needs a better accounting system and has decided to consult with a CPA he knows to see what she might recommend.

Required What information does Frank's current accounting system provide him? What additional information should Frank want from an improved accounting system? Make recommendations to Frank regarding how he can improve his accounting system and identify a chart (list) of accounts that you would expect to find in Frank's new accounting system. For each account, identify whether it is an asset, liability, owner's equity, revenue, or expense.

C2-2 FINANCING, INVESTING, AND OPERATING ACTIVITIES AS PART OF THE TRANSFORMATION PROCESS

Objs. 1, 3, 4

Environmental Housing Company designs and builds log homes. Financing is provided by owners and creditors, primarily banks. The company owns buildings and equipment it uses in the management, design, transportation, and construction process. It purchases logs and other building materials from other companies. These materials are shipped by the sellers. Homes are designed for customers. Logs are cut to the dimensions called for in a design and shipped to the customer's building site with other materials for assembly. Environmental Housing employs design engineers, construction and assembly workers, maintenance personnel, and marketing and service personnel, in addition to its management and office staff. The company is in charge of the construction process until the home is completed and ready for occupancy. The company gives warranties for one year after completion. The warranties state the completed home is free of defects from materials or construction.

Required List decisions involving the acquisition, use, or disposal of resources that Environmental Housing's managers would make at each stage (financing, investing, and operating) of the transformation process.

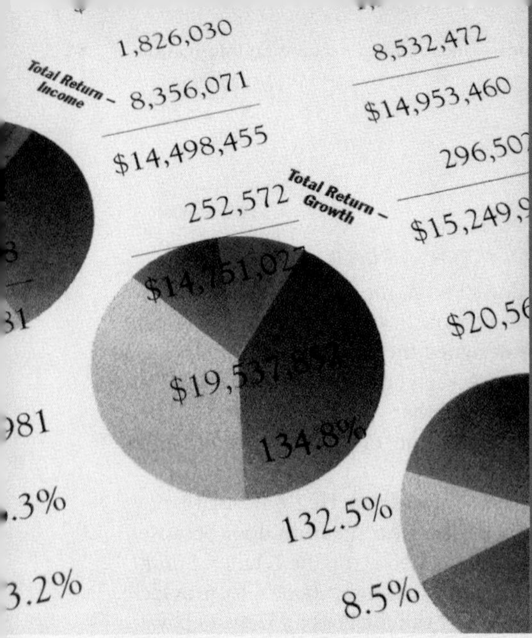

Measuring Revenues and Expenses

3

HOW DO WE KNOW HOW MUCH PROFIT OUR BUSINESS HAS EARNED?

With their accountant's help, Maria and Stan set up an accounting system for recording the business activities of Favorite Cookie Company. They prepared financial statements for January from information recorded in their accounting system. However, certain types of transactions were not considered in preparing those statements. A business requires an accounting system that ensures that all revenues and expenses are recorded in the appropriate fiscal period.

Food for Thought

If you were running a business, how would you know when to record revenues and expenses? It's easy to keep track of cash when your business receives it at the time goods are sold or services are provided. What would you do if your goods are transferred or services are provided to customers in one fiscal period and cash is received in a different period? You might consume resources in one fiscal period but pay for those resources in a different period. When should you recognize the expense? Now that they understand some basic accounting procedures, Maria and Stan discuss the appropriate recognition of revenues and expenses with their accountant, Ellen.

Stan: *We recorded transactions and prepared financial statements for January, but it seems like we haven't included all the business activities that occurred during January. We owe interest on our loan to the bank, and we used equipment we purchased in January without recording any expense.*

Ellen: *You're correct. We created a basic accounting system for recording transactions in January. Now we need to expand that system to include all transactions that should be recorded each month.*

Maria: *Does it really matter that much if we don't include everything in the appropriate month?*

Ellen: *Businesses are required to record revenues and expenses in the fiscal period in which revenues are earned and expenses incurred. Careful identification of the proper amount of revenues and expenses is important to provide accurate and reliable information about your company's performance. If you fail to do so, you may report misleading information. That could cause you to make bad decisions and it may affect decisions by creditors and other stakeholders.*

Stan: *How can we know if we have recorded all the transactions we need to record each month?*

Ellen: *You need to follow the proper accounting rules and procedures. Once you identify the kinds of events that need to be recorded each month, following these rules and procedures will help make sure your financial statements are accurate and reliable. Let's look at these rules and procedures and learn how to apply them to your company.*

Objectives

Once you have completed this chapter, you should be able to:

1. Explain the concept of accrual accounting and why it is used.
2. Record revenue transactions using accrual accounting.
3. Record expense transactions using accrual accounting.
4. Identify and record adjusting entries at the end of a fiscal period.
5. Prepare closing entries and financial statements at the end of a fiscal period.
6. Identify steps in the accounting cycle.

ACCRUAL ACCOUNTING

Objective 1
Explain the concept of accrual accounting and why it is used.

Almost all of the transactions we examined in Chapter 2 involved receipt or payment of cash. Cash often is received from customers at the time goods are sold. Cash often is paid when equipment, merchandise inventory, and supplies are purchased. These transactions involve increasing or decreasing the cash account and recording an offsetting amount to the revenue or expense account that explains the cause of the increase or decrease in cash.

In many cases a company earns revenue or incurs expenses in a fiscal period other than the one in which cash is received or paid. Consider the following examples for Favorite Cookie Company for the first three months of operation:

- Money was borrowed in January, but repayment of principal was not made until later.
- Interest was incurred on debt in January and February, but the interest was not paid until March.
- Goods were sold to customers on credit in February, but cash was not received until March.
- Employees worked in February and earned wages, but the wages were paid in March.
- Customers ordered goods in February and paid cash at the time of the order, but the goods were not delivered to the customers until March.
- Rent was paid on a building in February for use of the building in February, March, and April.

These types of transactions are common for most companies. To accommodate these types of events, businesses use a form of accounting known as accrual accounting. *Accrual accounting* **is a form of accounting in which revenues are recognized when they are earned and expenses are recognized when they are incurred.** To recognize revenues and expenses means to record them as accounting transactions. Normally, revenues are earned when goods are transferred or when services are provided. Expenses are incurred when resources are consumed in the processes of acquiring and selling goods and services. Accrual accounting focuses on business activities to determine when to record revenues and expenses.

A company does not have to receive or pay cash at the time revenues or expenses are recorded. However, the accounting process is more complicated when revenues or expenses are recorded in one period and cash is received or paid in another. Let's consider some examples for Favorite Cookie Company.

REVENUE TRANSACTIONS

Objective 2

Record revenue transactions using accrual accounting.

On February 12, 2007, Favorite Cookie Company sold boxes of cookies to a customer for $600 on credit. The boxes cost Favorite Cookie Company $400. The customer paid for the goods on March 10, 2007. Because the revenue was earned in February, Favorite Cookie Company must recognize the revenue in February. The transaction to record the sale would be as follows:

		Assets		=	Liabilities	+	Owners' Equity	
Date	**Accounts**	**Cash**	**Other Assets**				**Contributed Capital**	**Retained Earnings**
Feb. 12	Accounts Receivable		600					
	Sales Revenue							600
Feb. 12	Cost of Goods Sold							−400
	Merchandise Inventory		−400					

Neither of these transactions involves cash. Cash was not received from the customer at the time of the sale. Cash was not paid by Favorite Cookie Company for the merchandise at the time of sale, either. The company was selling merchandise that it had already purchased.

Accounts Receivable **is an asset account that increases when goods are sold on credit.** It represents an amount a customer owes to a company. Revenue is recognized because the goods have been transferred to the customer. Favorite Cookie Company has done the work necessary to earn revenue, and accrual accounting requires revenue to be recognized when it is earned.

The sale transaction is linked to a second transaction that occurs on March 10. When the customer pays for the goods, Favorite Cookie Company records the following:

		Assets		=	Liabilities	+	Owners' Equity	
Date	**Accounts**	**Cash**	**Other Assets**				**Contributed Capital**	**Retained Earnings**
Mar. 10	Cash	600						
	Accounts Receivable		−600					

Cash increases because it has been received from the customer. Accounts Receivable decreases because the customer has fulfilled the obligation to pay for the goods sold in February. **Revenue is not recognized at the time cash is received because it has already been recognized when goods were sold.** Because the sale occurs at one time and cash is received at a different time, two transactions are needed to record the sale and cash receipt. Accounts Receivable provides a means of linking the two transactions. It records the amount the customer owes the company until the customer pays for the goods. Exhibit 1 describes the effect of the transactions on the Cash, Accounts Receivable, and Sales Revenue accounts.

Accounts Receivable increases at the time of sale in February. The amount the customer owes is decreased when the customer pays cash in March, reducing the Accounts Receivable balance for this sale to zero. The net result of the two transactions is the same as if the customer had paid cash for the goods. However, two transactions are necessary

EXHIBIT 1
Linking Revenue and Cash through Accounts Receivable

Date	Cash	Accounts Receivable	Sales Revenue
Feb. 12		600	600
Mar. 10	600	−600	
Net result	600	0	600

to achieve this result. The first transaction is important because Maria and Stan and other decision makers are interested in when a company sells goods. All of the sales that occur in February should appear on Favorite Cookie Company's income statement for February. The income statement provides information about business activities that occurred during a particular fiscal period. If a company waited until cash was received from customers to record revenues, it would appear that the business sold the goods in the period when cash was received. Instead, accrual accounting ensures that decision makers have information about sales activities for the period in which the sales occurred. In addition, recording accounts receivable provides information about the amount owed by customers that a company expects to collect in a future fiscal period.

Sometimes a company receives cash from a customer before a sale is made. For example, Favorite Cookie Company received an order from a customer on February 24, 2007, for more goods than the company had in its inventory. Maria and Stan agreed to fill the order for the customer but required the customer to pay for the goods at the time of the order. The customer paid $3,000 on February 24, and Favorite Cookie Company ordered the goods from its supplier. The goods were delivered to the customer on March 3.

The payment transaction would be recorded as follows:

		Assets		=	Liabilities	+	Owners' Equity	
Date	Accounts	Cash	Other Assets				Contributed Capital	Retained Earnings
Feb. 24	Cash	3,000						
	Unearned Revenue				3,000			

Cash increases by the amount received from the customer. Revenue has not been earned, however, because goods have not been transferred to the customer. Instead, Favorite Cookie Company has incurred a liability as represented by the Unearned Revenue account. ***Unearned Revenue*** **is a liability account that results when a company receives cash from a customer for goods or services to be provided in the future.** The liability results from the obligation Favorite Cookie Company has to order the goods and provide them to the customer. If the company fails to complete the obligation, it will be required to refund the $3,000 to the customer.

The sales transaction is recorded on March 3 when goods are transferred to the customer:

		Assets		=	Liabilities	+	Owners' Equity	
Date	Accounts	Cash	Other Assets				Contributed Capital	Retained Earnings
Mar. 3	Unearned Revenue				−3,000			
	Sales Revenue							3,000
Mar. 3	Cost of Goods Sold							−2,000
	Merchandise Inventory		−2,000					

EXHIBIT 2
Linking Cash and Revenue through Unearned Revenue

Date	Cash	Unearned Revenue	Sales Revenue
Feb. 24	3,000	3,000	
Mar. 3		−3,000	3,000
Net result	3,000	0	3,000

Once the goods are transferred to the customer on March 3, the obligation has been fulfilled and the liability is eliminated. **In most sales transactions, Sales Revenue is recognized when the goods are transferred to the customer.** The cost of the merchandise to Favorite Cookie Company of $2,000 is also recognized when the goods are transferred to the customer. Again, this process results in revenue being recognized in the period in which it is earned rather than when cash is received. Expenses are recognized when resources are consumed. Exhibit 2 illustrates the effects of these activities on the company's accounts.

Unearned Revenue is an account used to link the receipt of cash in February with the revenue earned in March. This time, cash was received before revenue was recognized. Like Accounts Receivable, amounts are added or subtracted from Unearned Revenue as needed to ensure the proper timing of revenue recognition. The net result of these transactions is the same as if goods were sold for cash.

Transactions in which cash is received before revenue is earned are common for some types of companies. Examples include airlines, magazine publishers, and communications companies. Passengers often purchase airline tickets prior to their flights. At the time of the purchase, the airline records unearned revenue. When the passenger uses the ticket, the airline eliminates the unearned revenue and records passenger revenue. Similarly, subscribers often pay for magazine subscriptions before receiving the issues. At the time of purchase, the magazine records unearned revenue. As issues are published and mailed to subscribers, the amount of unearned revenue is reduced and subscription revenue is recognized. As an example, **Time Warner**, owner of *Time*, *Fortune*, and other magazines, reported unearned revenues of $1.175 billion for the fiscal year ended December 31, 2003.

Learning Note - Account titles vary in practice. For example, Unearned Revenue might appear as Customer Deposits, Air Traffic Liability, Prepaid Subscriptions, or Deferred Revenues.

To summarize, companies recognize revenues in the period in which they are earned. Typically, the earnings process is considered complete at the time goods are transferred to customers or services are provided to customers. Exhibit 3 illustrates the relationship between revenue recognition and cash inflow.

Three possibilities exist concerning the relationship. In all three possibilities, revenue is recognized when it is earned. Cash may be received at the time revenue is earned. In this situation, Revenue and Cash are the only accounts necessary for the transaction. If revenue is earned before cash is received, the revenue is accrued. **Accrued revenue is**

EXHIBIT 3
Revenue Recognition and Cash Flows

Timing Effect	First Period	Second Period	Linking Account
No Accrual or Deferral Needed	Revenue Earned Cash Received		None
Accrued Revenue	Revenue Earned	Cash Received	Accounts Receivable
Deferred Revenue	Cash Received	Revenue Earned	Unearned Revenue

revenue recognized prior to the receipt of cash. In this situation, Accounts Receivable is used to connect Revenue and Cash. If cash is received before revenue is earned, the revenue is deferred. *Deferred revenue* **is revenue recognized after cash has been received.** Unearned Revenue is used to connect Cash and Revenue.

EXPENSE TRANSACTIONS

Objective 3
Record expense transactions using accrual accounting.

In addition to recognizing expenses at the time cash is paid, expenses may also be accrued or deferred. *Accrued expenses* **result when expenses are recognized prior to the payment of cash.** *Deferred expenses* **result when expenses are recognized after the payment of cash.**

For example, assume Favorite Cookie Company purchases $400 of supplies on February 16, 2007. The supplies are not consumed at the time they are purchased. Instead of paying cash for the supplies, the company purchases them on credit, agreeing to pay the supplier by March 16. On March 15, 2007, Favorite Cookie Company sends a check to the supplier. Favorite Cookie Company should record this purchase of supplies as follows:

		Assets		=	Liabilities	+	Owners' Equity	
Date	Accounts	Cash	Other Assets				Contributed Capital	Retained Earnings
Feb. 16	Supplies		400					
	Accounts Payable				400			

This transaction records the supplies as an asset and the amount owed the supplier as a liability. *Accounts Payable* **is a liability account that identifies an obligation to pay suppliers in the near future.**

When Favorite Cookie Company uses the supplies, it records an expense. Suppose that the supplies have been consumed by the end of February. The company would record this amount as:

		Assets		=	Liabilities	+	Owners' Equity	
Date	Accounts	Cash	Other Assets				Contributed Capital	Retained Earnings
Feb. 28	Supplies Expense							−400
	Supplies		−400					

This transaction records the expense in the fiscal period in which resources were consumed.

Another transaction is necessary to record payment for the supplies. If Favorite Cookie Company sends a check to the supplier on March 15, it would record:

		Assets		=	Liabilities	+	Owners' Equity	
Date	Accounts	Cash	Other Assets				Contributed Capital	Retained Earnings
Mar. 15	Accounts Payable				−400			
	Cash	−400						

EXHIBIT 4
Linking Expense and Cash through Accounts Payable

Date	Cash	Supplies	Accounts Payable	Supplies Expense
Feb. 16		400	400	
Feb. 28		−400		−400
Mar. 15	−400		−400	
Net result	−400	0	0	−400

Learning Note - In Chapter 2, we recorded the purchase of supplies as an expense at the time the supplies were acquired because the supplies were used in January. In theory, it is preferable to record the purchase as an asset and then expense the supplies when they are used. Practically, however, it does not matter whether the supplies are recorded as an asset initially if all of the supplies are consumed in the same fiscal period as they were acquired. Either way, the amount will be an expense by the end of the fiscal period.

An expense is not recorded at the time the payment is made because the supplies were consumed in February. Exhibit 4 illustrates the use of the Accounts Payable account to link expenses recognized in one period with cash paid in a subsequent period. The net result of these transactions is the same as if cash had been paid for supplies at the time they were consumed. The transaction was recorded initially to the supplies account. Since the supplies were consumed in February, the transaction could have been recorded initially to supplies expense.

Expenses also may be recognized after cash is paid. For example, assume Favorite Cookie Company pays $600 for rent for use of a building on February 26. However, the rent is for March. The payment would be recorded as follows:

		Assets		=	Liabilities	+	Owners' Equity	
Date	**Accounts**	**Cash**	**Other Assets**				**Contributed Capital**	**Retained Earnings**
Feb. 26	Prepaid Rent		600					
	Cash	−600						

Learning Note - Accounts Payable is an example of a general category of liabilities known as accrued liabilities. Accrued liabilities record the obligation to make payments for expenses that have been incurred or for assets that have been acquired but for which payment has not been made. Other examples of accrued liabilities include Wages Payable, Interest Payable, and Income Taxes Payable.

The February transaction records the payment for rent. Prepaid Rent is an example of a prepaid expense account. **A *Prepaid Expense* is an asset account that identifies a resource that has been paid for but not used.** The purchase is an asset because a resource has been acquired that will be used in the future. The March transaction records use of the resource. The expense should be recognized in March, when the resource is consumed, rather than in February when cash is paid. The expense has been deferred from the time of the payment to March, when the building is used. By the end of March the rental service has been consumed and the expense would be recorded as follows:

		Assets		=	Liabilities	+	Owners' Equity	
Date	**Accounts**	**Cash**	**Other Assets**				**Contributed Capital**	**Retained Earnings**
Mar. 31	Rent Expense							−600
	Prepaid Rent		−600					

Exhibit 5 illustrates the use of the prepaid rent account to link cash paid in one period with expense recognized in a subsequent period. Prepaid Rent increases when cash is paid for next month's rent and decreases when the rent is consumed.

EXHIBIT 5
Linking Expense and Cash through Prepaid Rent

Date	Cash	Prepaid Rent	Rent Expense
Feb. 26	−600	600	
Mar. 31		−600	−600
Net result	−600	0	−600

In summary, accrual accounting records expenses when resources are consumed, not necessarily when cash is paid for those resources. Exhibit 6 illustrates the relationship between expense recognition and cash outflow.

EXHIBIT 6
Expense Recognition and Cash Flows

Timing Effect	First Period	Second Period	Linking Account
No Accrual or Deferral Needed	Expense Incurred Cash Paid		None
Accrued Expense	Expense Incurred	Cash Paid	Accounts Payable
Deferred Expense	Cash Paid	Expense Incurred	Prepaid Expense

Three possibilities exist concerning the relationship. In all three possibilities, expense is recognized when it is incurred. Cash may be paid at the time expense is incurred. In this situation, Expense and Cash are the only accounts necessary for the transaction. If expense is incurred before cash is paid, the expense is accrued. That is, it is recognized prior to the payment of cash. In this situation, Accounts Payable is used to connect Expense and Cash. If cash is paid before expense is incurred, the expense is deferred. That is, it is recognized after the cash is paid. Prepaid Expense is used to connect Cash and Expense.

By recording revenues when earned and expenses when incurred, a company matches resources consumed by business activities with revenues created by those activities. Consequently, net income (revenues minus expenses) measures business activity for a fiscal period. It is not a measure of how much cash a company received or paid. An important concept in accounting is the *matching principle*, **which requires companies to recognize the expenses used to generate revenue in the same accounting period in which the revenues are recognized.**

An important responsibility of accountants is to make decisions about when revenues and expenses should be recognized. They examine a company's business activities and use appropriate accounting rules to ensure the proper recording of revenue and expense transactions in the fiscal period in which those transactions occur.

Self-Study Problem #1

The following events occurred for Kirkland Co. in January and February:

1. Goods priced at $5,000 were sold on credit on January 15.
2. The cost of the goods sold in transaction 1 was $3,000.
3. Cash of $400 was received on January 23 for goods that will be transferred to customers in February.
4. Cash of $750 was paid on January 25 for supplies that will be used in February.
5. By January 31, employees had earned wages of $2,500 that will be paid in February.
6. On February 3, cash of $2,500 was paid to employees for wages earned in January.
7. On February 6, cash was collected from customers for the sales on January 15.
8. On February 8, goods were transferred to customers that had been paid for on January 23.
9. By February 28, the supplies purchased on January 25 had been consumed.

Required Record all transactions associated with these events in the order in which they occurred.

The solution to Self-Study Problem 1 appears at the end of the chapter.

ADJUSTING ACCOUNT BALANCES

Objective 4
Identify and record adjusting entries at the end of a fiscal period.

Some revenues and many expenses are associated with the passage of time. Rent, insurance, and equipment are resources that are purchased in one period and used during future periods. Wages relate to specific periods in which employees work, whether or not they are paid during those periods. Interest on debt accumulates over time. Revenues associated with some services, such as repair and maintenance contracts, also may be earned over time.

These activities often result in an expense or revenue that must be recognized for a fiscal period even though no specific event occurs to create the expense or revenue other than the passage of time. In these situations, a company must adjust its accounts at the end of a fiscal period to record the expenses and revenues that should be recognized for that period.

Let's consider some examples of adjustments for Favorite Cookie Company. Suppose in mid-February, Favorite Cookie Company decided to move to a new building on March 1. The rent for the new offices is $600 a month. On February 24 rent is paid for March and April. The transaction for February would be:

		Assets		=	Liabilities	+	Owners' Equity	
Date	**Accounts**	**Cash**	**Other Assets**				**Contributed Capital**	**Retained Earnings**
Feb. 24	Prepaid Rent		1,200					
	Cash	−1,200						

The transaction involves payment of rent for two months. The Prepaid Rent account is an asset that identifies the resource available for future use. At the end of March and April, Favorite Cookie Company must record Rent Expense for each month:

		Assets		=	Liabilities	+	Owners' Equity	
Date	Accounts	Cash	Other Assets				Contributed Capital	Retained Earnings
Mar. 31	Rent Expense							−600
	Prepaid Rent		−600					
Apr. 30	Rent Expense							−600
	Prepaid Rent		−600					

The accounting entries for March and April are adjusting entries. **An *adjusting entry* is a transaction recorded in the accounting system to ensure the correct account balances are reported for a particular fiscal period.** Usually, adjusting entries are made at the end of the fiscal period.

Another example of adjusting entries for Favorite Cookie Company involves interest. As indicated in Chapter 2, the company borrowed $30,000 ($8,000 + $22,000) in January. The bank charges $200 of interest each month but permits the interest to be paid the day after the end of each quarter. Accordingly, Favorite Cookie Company's first interest payment is not due until April 1, 2007. Nevertheless, interest expense accrues each month and should be recognized in the fiscal period in which it is incurred. Favorite Cookie Company would record the following adjusting entries at the end of January, February, and March:

		Assets		=	Liabilities	+	Owners' Equity	
Date	Accounts	Cash	Other Assets				Contributed Capital	Retained Earnings
Jan. 31	Interest Expense							−200
	Interest Payable				200			
Feb. 28	Interest Expense							−200
	Interest Payable				200			
Mar. 31	Interest Expense							−200
	Interest Payable				200			

An expense is recorded each month for the interest incurred on the loan. A liability is recorded as well because the interest is not being paid until the end of March. Consequently, an obligation exists for the unpaid interest. **Every adjusting entry, like the three above, includes at least one balance sheet and at least one income statement account.** Adjusting entries always involve recognition of a revenue or expense during a fiscal period.

Another transaction at the beginning of April records payment of the liability that accumulated over the three months. This entry is not an adjusting entry; it is a payment of an obligation when it becomes due. The payment is recorded as follows:

		Assets		=	Liabilities	+	Owners' Equity	
Date	Accounts	Cash	Other Assets				Contributed Capital	Retained Earnings
Apr. 1	Interest Payable				−600			
	Cash	−600						

Another example of adjustments involves the use of equipment. Favorite Cookie Company purchased equipment in January for $31,000 ($6,000 + $25,000). The equipment was recorded as an asset at that time. However, equipment and other physical assets usually wear out over time and eventually need to be replaced. Because resources are consumed over a number of fiscal periods, the usage should be recognized as an expense of each of the periods that benefits from that use. *Depreciation* **is the allocation of the cost of assets to the fiscal periods that benefit from the assets' use.** Favorite Cookie Company expenses its equipment at the rate of $520 per month. Consequently, it would record the following adjustments at the end of January and February:

		Assets		=	Liabilities	+	Owners' Equity	
Date	Accounts	Cash	Other Assets				Contributed Capital	Retained Earnings
Jan. 31	Depreciation Expense							−520
	Accumulated Depreciation		−520					
Feb. 28	Depreciation Expense							−520
	Accumulated Depreciation		−520					

Depreciation Expense identifies the estimated amount of the asset consumed. *Accumulated Depreciation* **is a contra-asset account used to identify the total amount of depreciation recorded for a company's assets.** It is subtracted from the related asset accounts on the company's balance sheet, and therefore is known as a contra account. **A** *contra account* **is an account that offsets another account.**

To understand Accumulated Depreciation, consider the effect the adjusting entries would have on the Accumulated Depreciation account. At the end of January, the account will have a balance of −$520, depreciation for January. At the end of February, the account will have a balance of −$1,040, depreciation for January and February.

Favorite Cookie Company's balance sheet for January and February will report the following:

	January	February
Equipment, at cost	$31,000	$31,000
Less: accumulated depreciation	520	1,040
Equipment, net of depreciation	$30,480	$29,960

The cost of the equipment continues to be reported at its cost of $31,000. The amount of accumulated depreciation increases each month, and the net amount of equipment reported each month decreases at the rate of $520 per month. We examine how depreciation amounts are determined in a later chapter.

The process of recording and reporting depreciation is necessary to make sure a company reports the appropriate expense each fiscal period. The use of Accumulated Depreciation provides useful information to decision makers. Examination of the balance sheet data for Favorite Cookie Company provides Maria and Stan with information about the cost of equipment and about how long the equipment has been used. Creditors and other external users of the company's financial statements might be especially interested in this information. They may want to know if a company's assets are replaced on a regular basis and if plans are being made for replacement as assets age.

Companies record transactions throughout each fiscal period. Accountants determine necessary adjustments for a company and develop and maintain information systems that allow them to determine interest, depreciation, and other expenses and revenues accurately. They adjust accounts at the end of each fiscal period prior to preparing financial statements. The next section considers the final steps in preparing these statements.

Self-Study Problem #2

The following events occurred for Davis Co. during 2007:

1. On September 27, the company paid rent for the following three months of $1,500 per month.
2. The company incurs interest expense of $800 per month. Interest is paid quarterly with the most recent payment being made in September.
3. The company purchased equipment for $200,000 on January 2, 2007. The equipment is depreciated at the rate of $4,000 per month.
4. The company paid $12,000 for property insurance on January 4, 2007. The insurance is for the 12 months ended December 31, 2007.

Required Record the adjusting entries associated with these events for October.

The solution to Self-Study Problem 2 appears at the end of the chapter.

LEDGER ACCOUNTS

Transactions, like those in this and the preceding chapter, are initially recorded by a company in a journal. **A *journal* is a chronological record of a company's transactions.** The format we have used in this chapter to record transactions is an example of a particular journal format. Each transaction is recorded according to the date the transaction occurred. The accounts affected by the transaction are listed along with the amounts associated with each account. Most companies use a computerized accounting system. Journal entries are recorded on a computer using a format that provides a place for each account to be identified and the amount to be entered. Regardless of the format, journal entries provide for a means of entering transactions in an accounting system.

Once transactions have been entered into a journal, the effects of transactions on particular accounts need to be transferred to those accounts. **A *ledger* is a file in which each of a company's accounts and the balances of those accounts are maintained.** A record is maintained for each account. Each time a transaction is recorded, the effects of that transaction are transferred to the ledger. ***Posting* is the process of transferring transactions to specific accounts in a company's ledger.** Exhibit 7 illustrates this process.

EXHIBIT 7 Posting Transactions to the Ledger

Journal

		Assets		=	Liabilities	+	Owners' Equity	
Date	**Accounts**	**Cash**	**Other Assets**				**Contributed Capital**	**Retained Earnings**
Jan. 31	Depreciation Expense							−520
	Accumulated Depreciation		−520					
Feb. 28	Depreciation Expense							−520
	Accumulated Depreciation		−520					

Ledger

Accumulated Depreciation

Date	Amount	Balance
Jan. 31	−520	−520
Feb. 28	−520	−1,040

Initially a transaction is recorded using the journal format. The transaction is then posted to the ledger accounts affected by the transaction. The balance of the account is updated to show the effect of the transaction. Thus, after transactions have been posted, the ledger provides a current record of the balance of each of a company's accounts. These balances are the primary source of data for preparing a company's financial statements.

The primary ledger a company uses to record its account balances is referred to as the *general ledger.* Companies often use other special ledgers to maintain information about specific types of account balances. For example, each customer who has purchased goods from a company on credit would be listed in the company's accounts receivable ledger. The accounts in the special ledger are referred to as subsidiary accounts. Subsidiary accounts are accounts of a specific type that are associated with a control account in the general ledger. The total of the balances of all of the subsidiary accounts of a specific type is equal to the balance of the general ledger control account. To illustrate, assume Favorite Cookie Company sells goods on credit to three stores: Hopkins' Grocery, Lori's Market, and Samson's Foods. Favorite Cookie Company maintains a subsidiary accounts receivable account for each store. The amounts owed by each of these stores at the end of February is the subsidiary account balance. The total of these amounts is the balance of accounts receivable for Favorite Cookie Company.

Subsidiary Accounts Receivable:	
Hopkins' Grocery	$1,300
Lori's Market	600
Samson's Foods	900
Accounts Receivable Control	$2,800

The subsidiary accounts are used to keep track of amounts owed by each customer. The control account balance is the amount reported in the company's financial statements.

CLOSING ENTRIES AND FINANCIAL STATEMENTS

Objective 5
Prepare closing entries and financial statements at the end of a fiscal period.

At the end of each month, Maria and Stan, with the help of their accountant, prepare financial statements for Favorite Cookie Company. The financial statements report a company's business activities to help managers, creditors, and other stakeholders make decisions.

Summary of Account Balances

To illustrate this process, we begin with a review of all the transactions for Favorite Cookie Company for January. These are presented in Exhibit 8 and include the adjusting entries for interest expense and depreciation expense described in this chapter.

Next we examine a summary of general ledger account balances for Favorite Cookie Company at the end of January. Exhibit 9, on page 96, provides balances for each of the company's general ledger accounts at January 31. The amounts shown are those from Exhibit 12 in Chapter 2, adjusted for interest and depreciation, as described in this chapter.

A purpose of the summary is to make sure that the accounting equation is in balance prior to preparing the financial statements. We can determine that the equation is in balance by reference to Exhibit 9 because:

Assets = Liabilities + Owners' Equity
$42,700 = $30,200 + $12,500

EXHIBIT 8 Transactions for Favorite Cookie Company for January

		Assets		=	Liabilities	+	Owners' Equity	
Date	**Accounts**	**Cash**	**Other Assets**				**Contributed Capital**	**Retained Earnings**
	Beginning Amounts	0	+0	=	0	+	0	+0
Jan. 2	Cash	10,000						
	Contributed Capital						10,000	
Jan. 3	Cash	8,000						
	Notes Payable				8,000			
Jan. 5	Equipment		6,000					
	Cash	−6,000						
Jan. 6	Equipment		25,000					
	Cash	−3,000						
	Notes Payable				22,000			
Jan. 6	Supplies Expense							−300
	Cash	−300						
Jan. 7	Merchandise Inventory		7,200					
	Cash	−7,200						
Jan. 8	Rent Expense							−600
	Cash	−600						
Jan. 31	Cash	11,400						
	Sales Revenue							11,400
Jan. 31	Cost of Goods Sold							−6,080
	Merchandise Inventory		−6,080					
Jan. 31	Wages Expense							−1,000
	Cash	−1,000						
Jan. 31	Utilities Expense							−200
	Cash	−200						
Jan. 31	Interest Expense							−200
	Interest Payable				200			
Jan. 31	Depreciation Expense							−520
	Accumulated Depreciation		−520					
	Ending Amounts	11,100	+31,600	=	30,200	+	10,000	+2,500

Income Statement

Balances of revenue and expense accounts appear in Favorite Cookie Company's Income Statement for January. Exhibit 10, on page 96, provides this statement. As discussed in Chapter 2, the income statement reports results of operating activities for a particular fiscal period. The statement shows that Favorite Cookie Company earned $2,500 of profit in January. This amount is less than that reported in Chapter 2 because of the adjusting entries that were considered in this chapter.

Closing Entries

An intermediate step in preparing financial statements is closing the revenue and expense account balances. Before preparing a balance sheet, the company's accountant closes Favorite Cookie Company's revenue and expense account balances at the end of February. Closing these accounts transfers the balances in these accounts to Retained Earnings. Exhibit 11, on page 97, provides the closing entries for January.

The closing process includes two transactions. In the first, revenue accounts are transferred to Retained Earnings. The closing transaction leaves the revenue account with a zero balance by subtracting the amount of revenue earned during the month from the Sales Revenue account and transferring the balance to Retained Earnings.

EXHIBIT 9
Summary of Account Balances for Favorite Cookie Company at January 31

Favorite Cookie Company
Account Balances
January 31, 2007

Account	Balance
Assets:	
Cash	11,100
Merchandise Inventory	1,120
Equipment	31,000
Accumulated Depreciation	(520)
Total Assets	**42,700**
Liabilities:	
Interest Payable	200
Notes Payable	30,000
Total Liabilities	**30,200**
Owners' Equity:	
Contributed Capital	10,000
Sales Revenue	11,400
Cost of Goods Sold	(6,080)
Wages Expense	(1,000)
Rent Expense	(600)
Depreciation Expense	(520)
Supplies Expense	(300)
Utilities Expense	(200)
Interest Expense	(200)
Total Owners' Equity	**12,500**

EXHIBIT 10
Income Statement for Favorite Cookie Company

Favorite Cookie Company
Income Statement
For the Month Ended
January 31, 2007

Sales revenue	$11,400
Cost of goods sold	(6,080)
Wages expense	(1,000)
Rent expense	(600)
Depreciation expense	(520)
Supplies expense	(300)
Utilities expense	(200)
Interest expense	(200)
Net income	$ 2,500

In the second transaction in Exhibit 11, expense account balances are transferred to Retained Earnings. The balances of these accounts also are zero after they are transferred to Retained Earnings.

If revenues are greater than expenses for the period, Retained Earnings increases. If revenues are less than expenses, Retained Earnings decreases. Remember that Retained Earnings is an accumulation of a company's profits. If profits are earned during a fiscal period, Retained Earnings increases. If losses are incurred during a fiscal period because revenues are less than expenses, Retained Earnings decreases.

Exhibit 12 illustrates the effect of closing entries on ledger account balances. Each account contains the balance of that account prior to the closing entry. ***Closing entries* reset the balances of each revenue and expense account to zero and transfer these balances to Retained Earnings.**

EXHIBIT 11 Closing Entries for January for Favorite Cookie Company

		Assets		=	Liabilities	+	Owners' Equity	
Date	**Accounts**	**Cash**	**Other Assets**				**Contributed Capital**	**Retained Earnings**
Jan. 31	Retained Earnings							11,400
	Sales Revenue							−11,400
Jan. 31	Retained Earnings							−8,900
	Cost of Goods Sold							6,080
	Wages Expense							1,000
	Rent Expense							600
	Depreciation Expense							520
	Supplies Expense							300
	Utilities Expense							200
	Interest Expense							200

EXHIBIT 12

Effect of Closing Entries on Revenue and Expense Account Balances

Ledger

Retained Earnings

Date	Amount	Balance
		0
Jan. 31	11,400	11,400
Jan. 31	−8,900	2,500

Sales Revenue

Date	Amount	Balance
		11,400
Jan. 31	−11,400	0

Cost of Goods Sold

Date	Amount	Balance
		−6,080
Jan. 31	6,080	0

Wages Expense

Date	Amount	Balance
		−1,000
Jan. 31	1,000	0

Rent Expense

Date	Amount	Balance
		−600
Jan. 31	600	0

Depreciation Expense

Date	Amount	Balance
		−520
Jan. 31	520	0

Supplies Expense

Date	Amount	Balance
		−300
Jan. 31	300	0

Utilities Expense

Date	Amount	Balance
		−200
Jan. 31	200	0

Interest Expense

Date	Amount	Balance
		−200
Jan. 31	200	0

The closing entries zero out the revenue and expense account balances at the end of a fiscal period. Consequently, the next fiscal period begins with zero balances and accumulates revenues and expenses for the new fiscal period. The closing process also transfers the amount of net income for a fiscal period to Retained Earnings. Keep in mind that revenues and expenses are subcategories of owners' equity. The closing process transfers amounts from the income statement accounts to owners' equity on the balance sheet so that the accounting equation (Assets = Liabilities + Owners' Equity) balances at the end of a fiscal period.

Because revenue and expense accounts are zeroed-out at the end of a fiscal period, they are referred to as temporary accounts. They are used during a fiscal period to collect the results of operating activities. These results are transferred to Retained Earnings at the end of the period. Retained Earnings and other balance sheet accounts are referred to as permanent accounts because their balances continue to accumulate from period to period.

Payments to Owners

Another transaction that affects the balance of Retained Earnings is a payment by a company to its owners. For example, if Maria and Stan decide to withdraw $500 from Favorite Cookie Company at the end of January, the transaction would be recorded like this:

		Assets		=	Liabilities	+	Owners' Equity	
Date	**Accounts**	**Cash**	**Other Assets**				**Contributed Capital**	**Retained Earnings**
Jan. 31	Retained Earnings							−500
	Cash	−500						

The retained earnings account accumulates profits earned by a company for its owners. The owners may choose to leave the profits in the company or withdraw some of them for personal use. Amounts withdrawn reduce Retained Earnings. The balances of Retained Earnings and Cash for Favorite Cookie Company after the withdrawal would be as follows:

Ledger

Retained Earnings		
Date	**Amount**	**Balance**
		2,500
Jan. 31	−500	2,000

Cash		
Date	**Amount**	**Balance**
		11,100
Jan. 31	−500	10,600

Post-Closing Account Balances

Let's look at the effects of the closing and withdrawal entries by preparing a summary of account balances after these entries have been posted to ledger accounts. Exhibit 13 provides a post-closing summary for Favorite Cookie Company at the end of January. At this point, the revenue and expense accounts have zero balances.

Balance Sheet

The balance sheet can now be prepared from the post-closing account balances. Exhibit 14 provides the balance sheet for Favorite Cookie Company at January 31, 2007. Observe that the amounts in the balance sheet for January 31 are those in the post-closing summary from Exhibit 13.

EXHIBIT 13
Post-Closing Summary of Account Balances for Favorite Cookie Company

Favorite Cookie Company
Post-Closing Summary of Account Balances
January 31, 2007

Account	Balance
Assets:	
Cash	10,600
Merchandise Inventory	1,120
Equipment	31,000
Accumulated Depreciation	(520)
Total Assets	**42,200**
Liabilities:	
Interest Payable	200
Notes Payable	30,000
Total Liabilities	**30,200**
Owners' Equity:	
Contributed Capital	10,000
Retained Earnings	2,000
Sales Revenue	0
Cost of Goods Sold	0
Wages Expense	0
Supplies Expense	0
Rent Expense	0
Depreciation Expense	0
Utilities Expense	0
Interest Expense	0
Total Owners' Equity	**12,000**

EXHIBIT 14
January 31 Balance Sheet for Favorite Cookie Company

Favorite Cookie Company
Balance Sheet
At January 31, 2007

Assets	
Cash	$10,600
Merchandise inventory	1,120
Equipment	31,000
Accumulated depreciation	(520)
Total assets	$42,200
Liabilities and Owners' Equity	
Interest payable	$ 200
Notes payable	30,000
Total liabilities	$30,200
Contribution by owners	10,000
Retained earnings	2,000
Total liabilities and owners' equity	$42,200

Along with the income statement, the balance sheet helps users determine how well the company performed during January. From the income statement, users can determine the major sources of revenue and expense. From the balance sheet, they can determine the assets controlled by the company and claims to those resources by creditors and owners. When statements for additional months become available, decision makers can compare the statements to determine whether the company is performing better or worse over time. Users can determine how much change there is in assets, liabilities, and owners' equity from one month to the next.

EXHIBIT 15
A Statement of Cash Flows

Favorite Cookie Company Statement of Cash Flows For the Month Ended January 31, 2007		
Operating Activities		
Received from customers	$11,400	
Paid for merchandise	(7,200)	
Paid for wages	(1,000)	
Paid for rent	(600)	
Paid for supplies	(300)	
Paid for utilities	(200)	
Net cash flow from operating activities		$ 2,100
Investing Activities		
Paid for equipment		(31,000)
Financing Activities		
Received from creditors	$30,000	
Received from owners	10,000	
Paid to owners	(500)	
Net cash flow from financing activities		39,500
Net cash flow for January		$ 10,600
Cash balance, January 1		0
Cash balance, January 31		$ 10,600

Statement of Cash Flows

A third financial statement, the statement of cash flows, also should be prepared. The adjusting transactions described in this chapter are associated with revenue and expense recognition, not with cash flows. Therefore, the statement of cash flows at the end of January is almost identical to the one in Chapter 2. Exhibit 15 includes the effect of the payment of $500 cash to owners. This payment is a financing activity.

SUMMARY OF ACCOUNTING CYCLE

Objective 6
Identify steps in the accounting cycle.

The procedures we have examined in this chapter are often referred to as the accounting cycle. **The *accounting cycle* is the process of recording, summarizing, and reporting accounting information.** As we have discussed in this chapter, the cycle consists of eight steps, as illustrated in Exhibit 16.

Once the accounting cycle is completed for one fiscal period, the accounting records are ready to begin recording transactions for the next fiscal period. As noted in Chapter 2, a fiscal period can be any time period for which managers want accounting information. Most companies prepare financial statements monthly and combine these to prepare statements for quarterly and annual periods.

ACCOUNTING AND ETHICS

The accounting system described in this chapter provides a way for Maria and Stan to monitor their business activities and to make decisions about their company's performance. Also, it provides a means for them to communicate with creditors about the performance of their company. An accounting system with adequate controls to ensure reliable information is expected by stakeholders of most companies and is a legal requirement for companies that sell shares of stock to the public and for many other companies that are regulated by state and local authorities.

These requirements are intended to protect owners, creditors, and other stakeholders from receiving inaccurate or improperly prepared financial information. A good accounting system helps ensure that all transactions are recorded properly and that stakeholders

EXHIBIT 16
Steps in the Accounting Cycle

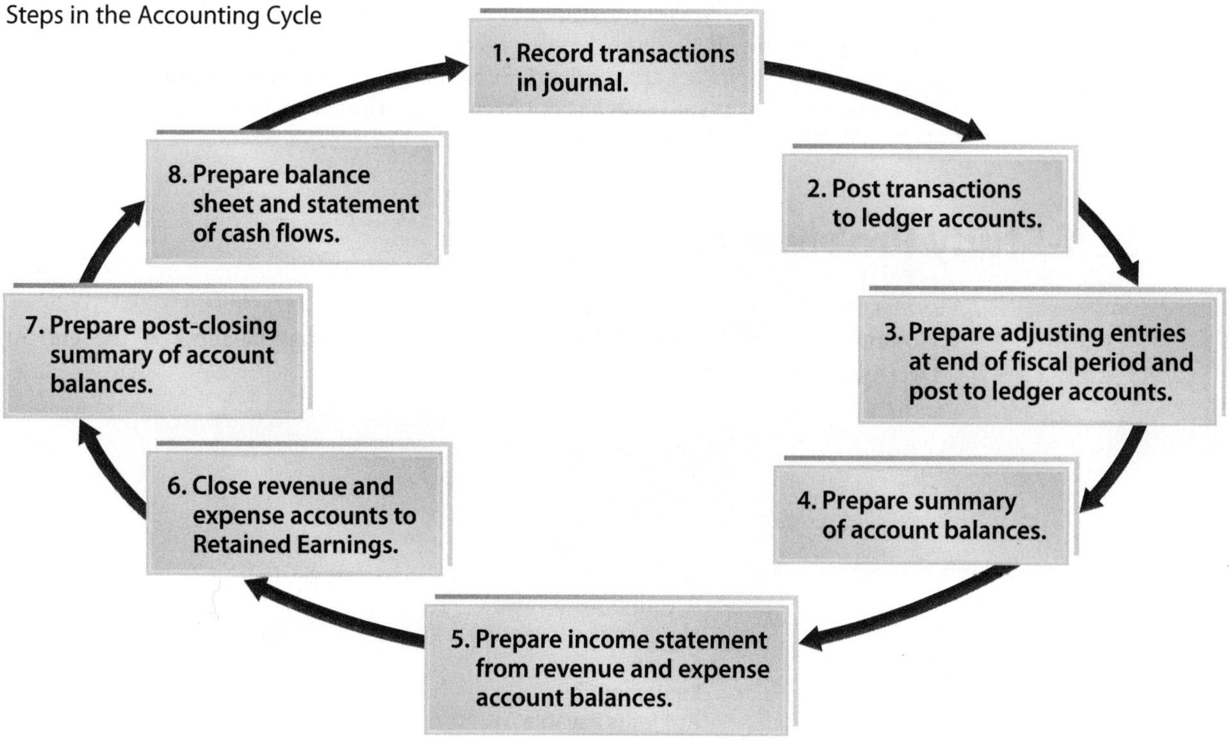

receive information that describes a business's activities on a timely basis. Most businesses are expected to comply with generally accepted accounting principles (GAAP) in preparing financial accounting information. GAAP require the use of the accrual rules and procedures described in this chapter. Making sure that a company's accounting procedures conform with GAAP and creating an accounting system that records and reports all transactions in the appropriate fiscal periods is a major responsibility of a company's management. Failure to understand and implement appropriate accounting procedures is, itself, unethical. Management is responsible for proper use of a company's resources and for proper reporting of its business activities. Managers who fail to take these responsibilities seriously leave a company vulnerable to improper behavior, such as fraud and theft, that reduces the value of the company for its owners and other stakeholders.

Unethical behavior may occur in businesses because appropriate accounting controls are not in place or are not enforced. For example, an employee sells goods to a customer but does not record the sale and pockets the cash. This behavior leads to incorrect accounting information. Sales Revenue, Cost of Goods Sold, Merchandise Inventory, and Cash are all misstated in this example. In general, unethical behavior by employees and managers leads to misstated accounting information. Protecting a company's

CASE IN POINT

http://ingram.swlearning.com

Visit Enron's home page to learn more about the company.

Economic Effects of Poor Accounting Practices

The failure of Enron Corporation's management to properly account for and report its business activities resulted in an understatement of the company's liabilities and an overstatement of profits. When the company's bad accounting practices became apparent in October 2001, creditors were unwilling to lend additional money to the company and investors tried to dump their stock. The value of Enron's stock dropped rapidly, resulting in losses of millions of dollars for owners. Many of Enron's owners were employees of the company who had invested in the company's stock as part of their retirement plans. Many employees lost their jobs and their retirement savings as a result of these events.

accounting records and assets is an important management task. Procedures should be in place to make it difficult for employees at all levels of the organization to engage in unethical behavior. For example, cash registers and scanning devices help ensure that sales made by employees are recorded. Supervisors should compare sales records with cash receipts to make sure cash has not been stolen. **Good accounting is the first line of defense against unethical behavior in business.**

Self-Study Problem #3

Howard Co. provided the following summary of account balances at the end of December 2007.

Howard Co. Summary of Account Balances December 31, 2007	
Account	**Balance**
Cash	37,450
Accounts Receivable	2,300
Merchandise Inventory	140,000
Supplies	30,000
Equipment	75,000
Accounts Payable	2,000
Notes Payable	200,000
Investment by Owners	65,000
Retained Earnings	15,000
Sales Revenue	20,000
Cost of Goods Sold	(13,000)
Wages Expense	(2,000)
Depreciation Expense	(750)
Interest Expense	(1,500)

Required Prepare closing entries and a post-closing summary of account balances for Howard Co.

The solution to Self-Study Problem 3 appears at the end of the chapter.

THINKING BEYOND THE QUESTION

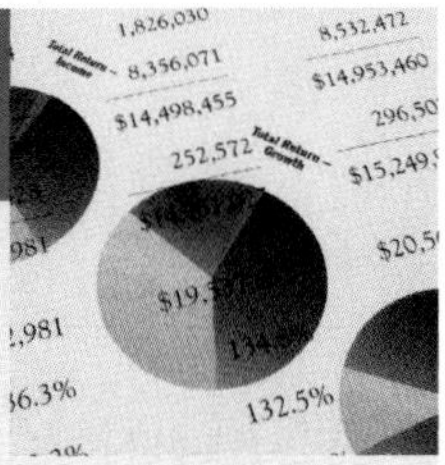

HOW DO WE KNOW HOW MUCH PROFIT OUR BUSINESS HAS EARNED?

At the beginning of the chapter we asked how you can know how much profit a company has earned. This chapter described the rules and procedures of accrual accounting. The rules specify when revenues and expenses should be recognized. The procedures help ensure that all revenues and expenses of a fiscal period have been recorded and reported. Understanding accrued and deferred revenues and expenses and adjusting and closing entries help ensure that the proper amount of profit is reported each fiscal period and that other accounting information is correct.

These rules may seem relatively simple. For example, it may be easy to identify when goods are transferred to customers. However, that may not always be the case. Suppose you agree to provide services to a customer over several fiscal periods. You negotiate a price with the customer that covers all of the services to be provided. How much revenue would

Self-Study Problem Solutions

SSP3-1

		Assets		=	Liabilities	+	Owners' Equity	
Date	Accounts	Cash	Other Assets				Contributed Capital	Retained Earnings
Jan. 15	Accounts Receivable		5,000					
	Sales Revenue							5,000
Jan. 15	Cost of Goods Sold							−3,000
	Merchandise Inventory		−3,000					
Jan. 23	Cash	400						
	Unearned Revenue				400			
Jan. 25	Supplies		750					
	Cash	−750						
Jan. 31	Wages Expense							−2,500
	Wages Payable				2,500			
Feb. 3	Wages Payable				−2,500			
	Cash	−2,500						
Feb. 6	Cash	5,000						
	Accounts Receivable		−5,000					
Feb. 8	Unearned Revenue				−400			
	Sales Revenue							400
Feb. 28	Supplies Expense							−750
	Supplies		−750					

SSP3-2

		Assets		=	Liabilities	+	Owners' Equity	
Date	Accounts	Cash	Other Assets				Contributed Capital	Retained Earnings
Oct. 31	Rent Expense							−1,500
	Prepaid Rent		−1,500					
Oct. 31	Interest Expense							−800
	Interest Payable				800			
Oct. 31	Depreciation Expense							−4,000
	Accumulated Depreciation		−4,000					
Oct. 31	Insurance Expense							−1,000
	Prepaid Insurance		−1,000					

SSP3-3

		Assets		=	Liabilities	+	Owners' Equity	
Date	Accounts	Cash	Other Assets				Contributed Capital	Retained Earnings
Dec. 31	Retained Earnings							20,000
	Sales Revenue							−20,000
Dec. 31	Retained Earnings							−17,250
	Cost of Goods Sold							13,000
	Wages Expense							2,000
	Depreciation Expense							750
	Interest Expense							1,500

Howard Co. Post-Closing Summary of Account Balances December 31, 2007	
Account	**Balance**
Assets:	
Cash	37,450
Accounts Receivable	2,300
Merchandise Inventory	140,000
Supplies	30,000
Equipment	75,000
Total Assets	**284,750**
Liabilities:	
Accounts Payable	2,000
Notes Payable	200,000
Total Liabilities	**202,000**
Owners' Equity:	
Investment by Owners	65,000
Retained Earnings	17,750
Sales Revenue	0
Cost of Goods Sold	0
Wages Expense	0
Depreciation Expense	0
Interest Expense	0
Total Owners' Equity	**82,750**

Define *Terms and Concepts Defined in This Chapter*

accounting cycle (100)
accounts payable (87)
accounts receivable (84)
accrual accounting (83)
accrued expense (87)
accrued liabilities (88)
accrued revenue (86)
accumulated depreciation (92)
adjusting entry (91)
closing entries (96)
contra account (92)
deferred expense (87)
deferred revenue (87)
depreciation (92)
general ledger (94)
journal (93)
ledger (93)
matching principle (89)
posting (93)
prepaid expense (88)
unearned revenue (85)

Review Summary of Important Concepts

1. Accrual accounting requires companies to recognize revenues in the fiscal period in which they are earned and to recognize expenses in the period incurred.
2. Accrual accounting requires the use of accounts such as Accounts Receivable and Unearned Revenue to link Cash received in one period with revenues earned in another period.
3. Accrual accounting requires the use of accounts such as Accounts Payable and Prepaid Expenses to link Cash paid in one period with expenses incurred in another period.
4. Adjusting entries record revenues and expenses that occur because of the passage of time to ensure that these revenues and expenses are recognized in the appropriate fiscal period.
5. At the end of a fiscal period, a company closes its revenues and expense accounts to transfer these account balances to retained earnings. The balance sheet reports retained earnings after the accounts have been closed.
6. The accounting cycle is the process of recording transactions, preparing summaries of account balances, closing accounts, and preparing financial statements.

Questions

Q3-1 *Obj. 1* Why isn't cash basis accounting the preferred method of reporting on the economic consequences of an organization's activities?

Q3-2 *Obj. 1* A friend observes that "in the long run, accrual and cash flow measurements equal out to the same amount. It's only in the short run that they differ." Do you agree or disagree? Explain.

Q3-3 *Obj. 1* How is it possible that a company could be very profitable yet be forced to go out of business because it cannot pay its bills?

Q3-4 *Obj. 2* How does Accounts Receivable "link" Revenue and Cash?

Q3-5 *Obj. 2* Where does the account Unearned Revenue appear in the financial statements? How does Unearned Revenue link Cash with Sales Revenue?

Q3-6 *Obj. 2* Accrued revenue and deferred revenue are both accrual concepts. Explain the order in which cash is received and revenue is recognized for each concept.

Q3-7 *Obj. 3* On May 31, a company paid $900 rent for June to its landlord. Would you recommend that this expenditure be presented in the end-of-May financial statements as an asset (Prepaid Rent) or as an expense (Rent Expense)? Why?

Q3-8 *Obj. 3* Quick Computer Company just spent $35,000 of its cash to purchase merchandise for later resale to customers. Would you agree that since $35,000 of cash has been used up, a $35,000 expense has been incurred in this transaction? Why or why not?

Q3-9 *Obj. 4* What is the difference between a subsidiary account and a control account?

Q3-10 *Obj. 4* Why are control account balances reported in external financial statements while subsidiary account balances are not? Are subsidiary account balances useful to anyone? Who?

Q3-11 *Obj. 4* The textbook lists depreciation as an example of a period cost that often must be updated in the accounting records at the end of a fiscal period. What other examples of period costs that must be updated at period-end can you identify? Why is it necessary to update these items?

Q3-12 *Obj. 5* A friend observes that "one of the most useful pieces of information found on a balance sheet is the current market value of assets such as buildings and land." Do you agree or disagree? Why?

Q3-13 *Obj. 5* Explain why accountants prepare a trial balance prior to preparing the financial statements.

Q3-14 *Obj. 5* Why do accountants close revenue and expense accounts prior to preparing the financial statements?

Q3-15 *Obj. 5* Is a payment to owners considered an expense? Explain.

Q3-16 *Obj. 6* Why are good accounting practices the first line of defense against unethical behavior in business?

Q3-17 *Obj. 6* Why is an accounting system with adequate controls a legal requirement for companies that sell shares of stock to the public?

Q3-18 *Obj. 6* Accountants prepare a post-closing trial balance as one step of the accounting cycle. Which types of accounts have non-zero balances? Which types of accounts have zero balances?

Exercises

E3-1 Write a short definition for each of the terms listed in the *Terms and Concepts Defined in This Chapter* section.

E3-2 *Obj. 1* Jon Harland is a wheat farmer. He owns farm equipment and buildings that cost $600,000 when purchased several years ago. He owes a local bank $425,000 for loans used to purchase these assets. In 2007, Jon sold $650,000 of wheat he raised during the year. He incurred operating costs of $585,000 to produce the wheat. This amount included $33,750 of interest on the bank loans and $52,500 of depreciation on the plant assets. In addition, Jon repaid $40,000 of the outstanding loan balance. The sales and all operating costs, except depreciation, were for cash. How much net income did Jon earn in 2007? What was his net cash flow for the year? Explain the difference.

E3-3 *Obj. 1* Jeni Arrington drives for a large moving company. The company contacts Jeni when it has a job for her and furnishes a truck for her use. Jeni picks up the truck, drives to the customer's home, and loads, transports, and delivers the customer's belongings. She returns the truck to the company and receives her pay. Jeni is paid $4.50 per mile for the job. She is responsible for paying for her own gas, food, and lodging. Also, she must hire any helpers she needs to load and unload the truck. Jeni traveled 2,400 miles on a recent job that was completed on June 30. She paid $500 for gas, $116 for food, $204 for lodging, and $100 for helpers. Jeni expects to receive payment on July 5. How much did Jeni earn for the job? How much cash did Jeni spend while providing the service? Why is there a difference in cash flow and net income?

E3-4 *Obj. 2* The Hardware Shoppe sold $222,500 of goods during September. It collected $75,000 from these sales plus $165,000 from sales of prior months. Complete the following table:

	Cash Flow for September	Cash Flow in Future	Sales Revenue for September
Cash from prior sales	?		
Cash from September sales	?	?	?
Total cash received in September	?		

E3-5 *Objs. 2, 3, 4* The Bike Shop has the following information available on December 31, the last day of the company's fiscal year. Each item involves an adjusting entry that must be made before financial statements can be prepared and the books closed for the year. Show how these adjusting entries would be entered into the accounting system.

1. A $40,000 note payable, incurring 9% interest, has been outstanding for the entire year. The note payable was properly recorded when it arose, but no entries regarding this event have been made since.
2. A $12,000 check was received on November 2 from a tenant that subleases part of the company's headquarters building. The amount was in payment of rent for November, December, and January. When the check was received, Cash was increased and Rent Revenue was increased. (Hint: Use a liability account titled Unearned Rent.)
3. On April 1 of the current year, the company purchased a two-year fire insurance policy for $8,400. When the policy was purchased, Cash was decreased and Prepaid Insurance was increased for the entire amount.
4. Wear and tear on the buildings and machinery for the year is estimated to be $48,000.

E3-6 *Objs. 2, 3* Record each transaction of Rose's Flower Shop.

a. Purchased merchandise for sale on October 1 for $3,600, to be paid by October 30.
b. Sold merchandise for $900 cash on October 3. The merchandise cost Rose's $270.
c. Sold merchandise for $1,800 on credit on October 6. The merchandise cost Rose's $590.
d. Ordered $2,150 of merchandise on October 7 from a supplier.
e. $400 of the merchandise purchased on October 1 spoiled on October 9 and had to be trashed, resulting in spoilage expense.
f. Paid $1,800 on October 10 to suppliers for merchandise purchased on October 1.
g. Received $1,200 on October 16 from customers for sales on October 6.

E3-7 *Obj. 4* Complete the following table. Each column represents a different company. All receivables are collected in the year following sale.

	Company A	Company B	Company C
Cash received from customers during 2007	$300,000	$625,000	?
Sales revenue for 2007	$352,500	$580,000	$260,000
Accounts receivable at beginning of 2007	$31,000	?	$35,000
Accounts receivable at end of 2007	?	$85,000	$53,000

E3-8 *Obj. 4* The following information is available for The Corner Pharmacy Inc. at December 31, the end of the fiscal year. It requires that adjusting entries be identified and entered into the accounting system. Unless specifically noted, none of this information has been previously entered into the accounting system. If the information below were ignored, net income for the year would be $72,400.

1. Employees are owed $7,600 for wages they have earned but will not receive until the next regular payroll distribution in five days.
2. A physical count reveals that there is $4,000 of office supplies remaining on hand at the end of the period. The company started the year with $3,500 of office supplies recorded in the Office Supplies Inventory account. During the year, $14,000 of office supplies was purchased, paid for, and charged to Office Supplies Expense.
3. The basement of the building is rented out to another firm and used for storage. At year end, the $2,500 rent for the month of December had not yet been collected.
4. At the end of the year, the company has long-term assets on which $11,000 of depreciation must be recorded.
5. Earlier in the year, a bank loan was obtained and recorded in the accounting system. Since then, interest of $5,700 has been incurred on that loan but it has not yet been recorded or paid.

(a) Using the spreadsheet format, show how this information would be entered into the accounting system. (b) After considering the effects of all five adjusting entries, what is the proper amount of net income that should be reported for the year?

E3-9 *Objs. 2, 3* Silberman Company transactions are listed below. Indicate the amount of revenue, expense, and cash flow that results from each. Use the format provided, and place the appropriate amount in each section of the table. Use a separate table for each transaction.

a. $5,000 of supplies were purchased in August for cash. $1,500 of the supplies were consumed in August, and $2,500 were consumed in September.
b. $15,000 of merchandise was sold in September. $6,000 of the sales were on credit.
c. Merchandise that cost Silberman $7,500 was sold in September. Silberman had paid $5,000 for the merchandise in August. The rest was paid for in September.
d. $50,000 was borrowed in August. $2,500 will be repaid each month for 20 months beginning in September. (Ignore interest.)
e. $25,000 of equipment was purchased and paid for in August. $500 of the equipment's revenue-generating ability was consumed in September; the remainder will be consumed in the future.

	Past	September	Future	Total
Revenues				
Expenses				
Cash received				
Cash paid				

E3-10 *Obj. 3* The Get Well Medical Clinic paid $50,000 in wages during June. Of this, $5,800 was for wages earned in May. An additional $4,200 of wages was owed to employees for services provided in June. These wages will be paid in July. Complete the following table:

	Cash Flow for June	Cash Flow in July	Wages Expense for June
Cash paid for prior wages	?		
Cash paid for June wages	?	?	?
Total cash paid in June for wages	?		

E3-11 *Obj. 3* George Carver borrowed $150,000 on January 1 to open a peanut processing plant. Interest on the loan is $3,750 each quarter. The first interest payment will be made on March 31. Complete the following table:

	January	February	March	Total for Quarter
Cash paid for interest	?	?	?	?
Interest expense	?	?	?	?

E3-12 *Obj. 3* Rapid Recovery Company manufactures prescription drugs. On January 1, 2007, the company purchased new equipment for $600,000 in cash. The company will depreciate the equipment over a 3-year period at $200,000 each year. Complete the following table:

	2007	2008	2009	Total for 3 Years
Cash paid for equipment	?	?	?	?
Depreciation expense	?	?	?	?

Explain the difference between cash flows each year and the amount of depreciation expense recorded.

E3-13 *Obj. 3* Tasaka Company manufactures oriental rugs. It pays utility bills at the end of the month in which services are received. The company received the following bills for April, May, and June, respectively: $850, $1,025, $1,150. Complete the following table:

	April	May	June	Total for 3 Months
Cash paid for utilities	?	?	?	?
Utilities expense	?	?	?	?

When are cash and accrual basis measures different? When are they the same?

E3-14 *Obj. 4* Each of the following independent situations relates to information available on the last day of the year. Each involves an adjustment that must be made to the accounting system before financial statements can be prepared. Show the effects of each adjusting entry on the accounting system.

a. A $15,000 note payable, incurring 8% interest, has been outstanding the entire year. The note payable was properly recorded when it arose.
b. A $3,000 check was received 2 months ago from a tenant that subleases part of a building. The amount was for 6 months' rent beginning the day the check was received. When received, the entire amount of the check was recorded in a liability account titled Unearned Rent.
c. Exactly halfway through the year just ended, the company purchased a 2-year fire insurance policy for $8,000. When the policy was purchased, the entire amount was recorded in the Prepaid Insurance account.
d. Wear and tear on the buildings and machinery for the year is estimated to be $35,000.

E3-15 *Obj. 4* On August 30, 2007, Goya Co. purchased $20,000 of canvas material from a supplier, Ramirez, Inc., on credit. The material is cut into smaller pieces for sale to customers. Prior to the purchase, Goya's merchandise inventory account had a balance of $135,000 and its accounts payable account had a balance of $17,000. Answer each of the following questions: (a) What subsidiary accounts are affected by the purchase and how are they affected? (b) What control accounts are affected and how are they affected? (c) If Goya Co. prepared a balance sheet immediately after recording the purchase, how would the balance sheet report the information associated with the purchase event?

E3-16 *Obj. 4* On December 31, 2007, the Rift Music Store reported net income of $1,200 and the following account balances.

Cash	$1,425
Accounts receivable	2,300
Prepaid insurance	1,200
Equipment & furnishings	3,200
Less: Accumulated depreciation	(500)
Accounts payable	1,300
Wages payable	1,520
Owners' equity (includes Net Income of $1,200)	4,805

After this information was prepared, the bookkeeper discovered that he had forgotten to make two necessary adjusting entries for the year and, therefore, they were not reflected in the balances shown. Information concerning the two missing adjusting entries follows:

a. The prepaid insurance involves a 3-year fire insurance policy that was purchased (and went into effect) on January 1, 2007. By the end of the year, a portion of the insurance policy had been used up.
b. The wages payable does not include the wages that were owed at year-end to two workers who had been temporarily assigned to work off the premises. This amount totaled $375.

(Continued)

Using the following schedule, determine the correct year-end amount of (1) total assets, (2) total liabilities, (3) owners' equity, and (4) net income.

	Assets	Liabilities	Equity	Net Income
Year-end amounts before correction				
Adjusting entry (a):				
Adjusting entry (b):				
Year-end corrected amounts	$	$	$	$

E3-17 *Obj. 5* On December 31, 2007, Bert's Farm Store had the following account balances in its accounting system. All year-end adjustments had been entered, but the books had not yet been closed.

Bert's Farm Store
Account Balances Before Closing
December 31, 2007

Account	Balance	Account	Balance
Cash	$ 700	Sales Revenue	$2,200
Merchandise	2,800	Cost of Goods Sold	900
Supplies	925	Wages Expense	400
Prepaid Insurance	450	Utilities Expense	150
Equipment	3,550	Depreciation Expense	50
Accumulated Depreciation	1,750	Insurance Expense	100
Interest Payable	150	Supplies Expense	150
Notes Payable	2,000	Interest Expense	100
Owners' Equity	4,175		

a. What is the purpose of closing the books?
b. Prepare all necessary closing entries.
c. After closing, what is the amount of owners' equity that will be reported on the balance sheet?

E3-18 *Obj. 5* Constantino Company presented the following general ledger account balances for the month ended December 31, 2007.

Assets:	
Cash	20,600
Accounts Receivable	2,250
Equipment	11,000
Total Assets	**33,850**
Liabilities:	
Wages Payable	250
Payable to Internet Service	35
Notes Payable	17,000
Total Liabilities	**17,285**
Owners' Equity:	
Contributed Capital	13,000
Retained Earnings	1,000
Service Revenue	3,315
Rent Expense	(400)
Wages Expense	(315)
Internet Service Expense	(35)
Total Owners' Equity	**16,565**

a. Close the books for Constantino Company.
b. Prepare a post-closing summary of account balances similar to Exhibit 13.

E3-19 *Obj. 5* Play Again Sports had the following general ledger balances at December 31, 2007:

Assets:	
Cash	10,500
Accounts Receivable	25,000
Inventory	47,000
Prepaid Insurance	5,000
Equipment	300,000
Accumulated Depreciation	(80,000)
Total Assets	**307,500**
Liabilities:	
Accounts Payable	31,000
Notes Payable	130,000
Total Liabilities	**161,000**
Owners' Equity:	
Contributed Capital	84,500
Retained Earnings	45,000
Sales Revenue	290,000
Cost of Goods Sold	(128,000)
Insurance Expense	(5,000)
Wages Expense	(72,000)
Utilities Expense	(40,000)
Interest Expense	(8,000)
Depreciation Expense	(20,000)
Total Owners' Equity	**146,500**

a. Prepare the entry to close the revenue and expense accounts at the end of the year.
b. Prepare a post-closing summary similar to Exhibit 13.

E3-20 *Obj. 5* The accounting staff at Taiwan Manufacturing have prepared the following summary of account balances at year end. The balances include all transactions for the fiscal year except for closing entries.

Account	Balance	Account	Balance
Cash	$ 1,850	Sales Revenue	$7,600
Merchandise	8,435	Cost of Goods Sold	2,840
Supplies	2,955	Wages Expense	1,015
Prepaid Insurance	1,375	Utilities Expense	550
Equipment	9,650	Depreciation Expense	660
Accumulated Depreciation	4,100	Insurance Expense	495
Interest Payable	425	Supplies Expense	525
Notes Payable	7,000	Interest Expense	300
Owners' Equity	11,525		

a. What is the purpose of closing the books?
b. Prepare all necessary closing entries.
c. After all closing entries are entered into the accounting system, what will be the amount of owners' equity reported on the balance sheet?

Problems

P3-1 *Obj. 1* **EXPLAINING THE DIFFERENCE BETWEEN CASH AND ACCRUAL ACCOUNTING**

The accounting department at Klinger Realty sent the financial reports, as shown on the next page, to Robin Garrison, general manager. Attached was a note indicating that both sets of data are based on the same set of events, which occurred during the quarter just completed. Robin

(Continued)

was only recently promoted to this position and is not very knowledgeable about accounting information.

After reviewing this report, Robin was somewhat disturbed because she always had thought accounting was an exact process. How, she wondered, can there be two different results from the same set of facts? Furthermore, how could they be so different? Which one is the "true" or "correct" report?

Klinger Realty
Results of Operating Activities
Third Quarter 2007

	Cash Basis		Accrual Basis	
Cash receipts/revenues:				
Sales commissions	$300,000		$400,000	
Property management	210,000		165,000	
Total		$510,000		$565,000
Cash payments/expenses:				
Office employee wages	$ (53,000)		$ (48,000)	
Advertising	(10,000)		(90,000)	
Office supplies	0		(3,400)	
Depreciation—office equipment	0		(1,800)	
Rent	(6,000)		(6,000)	
Sales staff commissions	(150,000)		(200,000)	
Property managers' salaries	(116,000)		(90,000)	
Total		(335,000)		(439,200)
Net cash flow		$175,000		
Net income				$125,800

Required Assume that you are called in to advise Ms. Garrison. Write a memo to her explaining why there can be two measures of operating results and why they differ.

P3-2 ETHICS AND ACCOUNTING MEASUREMENT
Obj. 1

Hardy Rock is proprietor of a jewelry store. In January, he applied for a bank loan and was asked to submit an income statement for the past year, ending in December. Near the end of the prior year, Hardy had purchased merchandise for resale that cost him $60,000. He still owed $45,000 for this merchandise at year end. Half of the merchandise was sold during the Christmas holidays for $75,000. Customers owed Hardy $50,000 for these purchases at year end. Hardy included these transactions as part of his financial statements as follows:

Added to revenues	$75,000
Added to expenses	7,500
Added to net income	$67,500

Hardy reasoned that because he had sold half the merchandise in December, he should report it as revenue, though he had not received all of the cash from customers. Also, he reasoned that because he had paid $15,000 for the merchandise by year end and had sold half of the merchandise, he should report $7,500 of this amount as cost of goods sold.

Required What problems do you see with Hardy's reasoning? Is there an ethical problem with Hardy's treatment of these transactions? What should the effect of these transactions have been on net income?

P3-3 REVENUE RECOGNITION AND ACCRUAL ACCOUNTING
Obj. 2

U.S. Political Consultants has been in existence for many years. During the month of November, the following events occurred:

1. The owners contributed an additional $6,500 to the business to finance an expansion of operations.
2. Consulting services totaling $11,000 were performed on credit during November and billed to customers.
3. A loan in the amount of $25,000 was obtained from a wealthy campaign contributor.
4. Expenses in the amount of $6,000 were incurred during the month. One-third had been paid for by month end.
5. Cash of $18,500 was collected from customers for whom services had been performed during September and October.
6. Services totaling $4,500 were performed for customers who had paid in the previous month for the services.

Required U.S. uses accrual basis accounting. For which of the events above should revenue be recorded in November? In each case, how much revenue should be recorded? If an event does not involve revenue, specify why not.

P3-4 HOW UNEARNED REVENUE LINKS CASH AND SALES REVENUE

Obj. 2

On March 15, the Spinnaker Company received $4,500 in cash from a customer who ordered a custom sail for her racing yacht. The company completed the sail and delivered it on April 30. The Spinnaker Company incurred costs of $3,000 in making the sail. Assume the company recorded the manufacturing costs in the Merchandise Inventory account.

Required

A. Record the transaction on March 15.
B. Record the transaction on April 30.
C. Prepare a table similar to Exhibit 2 that illustrates how Unearned Revenue links Cash with Sales Revenue.

P3-5 HOW PREPAID INSURANCE LINKS CASH AND INSURANCE EXPENSE

Obj. 3

On January 1, Taylor Manufacturing Company purchased a 12-month insurance policy for $3,600 and recorded it as Prepaid Insurance. On December 31, the bookkeeper observed the prepaid insurance account had a $3,600 balance representing the insurance purchased on January 1.

Required

A. Record the insurance purchase on January 1.
B. Prepare the entry required to record insurance expense for the year appropriately.
C. Prepare a table similar to Exhibit 5 that illustrates how Prepaid Insurance links Insurance Expense and Cash.

P3-6 EXPENSE RECOGNITION AND ACCRUAL ACCOUNTING

Obj. 3

The local chapter of Helping Hands, a social service organization, had the following economic events occur during the month of May:

1. A luncheon honoring volunteers was held at a cost of $950. By month end the bill hadn't been received or paid.
2. New letterhead and envelopes were printed at a cost of $625 and paid for. The new items will not be used, however, until the old supply is exhausted sometime in June.
3. The executive director was paid her usual salary of $3,800 during May.
4. Prizes, ribbons, and awards for events upcoming in July were delivered by the supplier, who charged $10,175. The amount was paid in cash.
5. The electric bill for April totaled $163 and was paid in full.
6. Radio, TV, and newspaper advertising related to a special fund-raising campaign ran during May. The $7,550 cost had been paid in April.

(Continued)

Required Helping Hands uses accrual basis accounting. For which of the events above should an expense be recorded in May? In each case, how much expense should be recorded? If an event does not involve an expense, specify why not.

P3-7 CONVERTING NET INCOME TO CASH FLOW

Objs. 1, 2, 3

Latin American Importers reports the following accrual basis information for a recent month.

Total revenue from sales to customers	$95,000
Total expenses	71,000
Net income	$24,000

In addition, the following account information is known:

	Accounts Receivable	Accounts Payable
Beginning of month balance	$10,000	$18,000
End of month balance	20,000	11,000

Required Determine (a) the amount of cash collected from customers during the month, (b) the amount of cash paid out for expenses during the month, and (c) the net cash flow for the month.

P3-8 CONVERTING NET CASH FLOW TO NET INCOME

Objs. 1, 2, 3

Carlyle Company reported the following cash flow information at the end of its first year in business:

Cash received from customers	$235,000
Cash paid out to suppliers of inventory	(55,000)
Cash paid out to employees	(77,500)
Cash paid out for advertising	(13,000)
Cash paid out for taxes	(30,000)
Net cash flow for the year	$ 59,500

Also known at year end was the following:

Amounts not yet collected from customers	$80,000
Amounts owed to suppliers	12,000
Wages owed to employees	18,000
Additional taxes still owed	20,000
Amount remaining in inventory	0

Required Prepare an accrual basis income statement for the company's first year in business.

P3-9 ETHICS AND ACCOUNTING MEASUREMENT

Objs. 1, 2, 3

Tinker, Evers, and Chance are partners in a sports equipment megastore. Tinker keeps the accounting records for the partnership because he is skilled in accounting and the other partners are not. The partners have agreed that they will share equally in the company's profits (or losses) at the end of each year. For fiscal 2007, the first year of operations, the company sold $7,600,000 of merchandise. Of this amount, $1,400,000 was still owed to the company by customers at year end. The company purchased and paid for merchandise costing $4,300,000 during 2007; $1,000,000 of this merchandise remained in inventory at year end. The company purchased and paid for $1,400,000 of equipment during the year. The equipment should have a useful life of 7 years. Thus depreciation expenses would be $200,000 each year. Other expenses amounted to $650,000, all paid for in cash. Tinker has prepared the following income statement and distribution of profits for 2007:

Tinker, Evers, and Chance Income Statement For Year 2007		
Revenues		$6,200,000
Expenses:		
Merchandise	$4,300,000	
Equipment	1,400,000	
Other	650,000	
Total expenses		6,350,000
Net loss		$ 150,000
Distribution of net loss:		
Reduction in owners' capital:		
Tinker		$ 50,000
Evers		50,000
Chance		50,000
Total distribution of net loss		$ 150,000

Evers and Chance are mystified by these results because they thought the company had been performing above their expectations. Tinker assured his partners that his numbers were correct. Tinker has offered to buy out his partners, explaining that "he got 'em into this and should do the right thing." Of course, the other partners will lose half of their original investment if they sell.

Required

A. What problems do you see with Tinker's financial report?
B. Advise the other partners as to whether they should sell out. To support your advice, prepare a revised income statement incorporating any changes you think appropriate to support a prudent decision.

P3-10 ACCRUAL VERSUS CASH FLOW

Objs. 2, 3, 4

The Water Fun Store is a retailer of water sports products for backyard swimming pools. During August, the firm had the following operating activities:

Date		Event
Aug.	1	Bought $5,000 of goods for resale from Pinetree Wholesalers on credit.
	5	Paid $450 to the local newspaper for advertising that ran during July.
	6	Paid $975 rent for the month of August.
	9	Sold goods to customers for $7,350 on credit. These goods had cost the firm $3,600.
	10	Paid $3,000 to Pinetree Wholesalers in partial payment for goods purchased August 1.
	11	Collected $5,350 from goods sold on August 9.
	13	Bought $9,200 of goods for resale from Stanley Company. Paid cash.
	16	Paid employees for their work so far in August, $1,050.
	19	Sold goods to customers on credit for $6,350. These goods had cost the firm $2,400.
	25	Collected $3,700 from the sales made on August 19.
	29	Paid $975 rent for the month of September.
	31	Employees had earned an additional $1,200 of wages but would not be paid until September 1.

Required

A. Prepare a report of net cash flow from operating activities.
B. Prepare an accrual basis income statement.
C. Which statement documents a more realistic or complete picture of August's activity? Why?

P3-11 DETERMINING TRANSACTIONS FROM CHANGES IN FINANCIAL STATEMENTS
Objs. 2, 3, 4

The Park Security Inc. is a private enterprise that contracts services to a midwestern state. At October 1, the beginning of its fiscal year, the organization had the following balance sheet.

Park Security, Inc.
Balance Sheet
at October 1

Assets:		Liabilities and Owners' Equity:	
Cash	$ 43,725	Accounts payable	$ 28,350
Supplies	65,700	Bonds payable	470,000
Equipment	350,000	Owners' investment	1,050,000
Building	1,400,000	Retained earnings	863,575
Accumulated depreciation	(100,000)		
Land	652,500		
Total	$2,411,925	Total	$2,411,925

During the month of October, a number of economic events occurred and were entered into the accounting system. At the end of October, the company prepared the following financial statements.

Park Security, Inc.
Financial Statements

Balance Sheet (at Oct. 31)

Assets:		Liabilities and Owners' Equity:	
Cash	$ 3,725	Accounts payable	$ 28,350
Supplies	26,500	Bonds payable	0
Equipment	350,000	Owners' investment	1,050,000
Building	1,400,000	Retained earnings	1,245,475
Accumulated depreciation	(108,900)		
Land	652,500		
Total	$2,323,825	Total	$2,323,825

Income Statement (for Oct.)

Revenues	$840,000
Expenses:	
Supplies	39,200
Depreciation	8,900
Wages	410,000
Net income	$381,900

Required

A. Identify the transactions that occurred during October.
B. Prepare a schedule that explains the changes in cash balance during October.

P3-12 UNDERSTANDING GOING CONCERN AND ACCOUNTING MEASUREMENT
Objs. 2, 3, 4

On March 1, Carl Caldwell started Caldwell Furniture Repair Company. He invested $2,000 of his own money, borrowed $16,000 from his father-in-law at 9% annual interest, and obtained an additional $3,000, 12% loan from Maxibank. He purchased $15,000 of tools and equipment (some new, some used) and bought $5,200 of supplies such as paints, resins, and glue, all for cash. He rented a shop at a local business park by paying $3,600 in advance for the months of March, April, and May. During March he performed repairs totaling $7,600 and used up $2,400 of supplies. Of the repair services performed, 75% were paid for in cash by the end of the month and the balance was expected to be collected in April. Carl estimated that wear and tear on the equipment and tools during March was $250. On March 31, he owed $332 to the electric company and $78 to the water company for services consumed. Also on that date, he paid interest totaling $150 on the two loans.

Required

A. Prepare an income statement for Caldwell Furniture Repair for the month of March.
B. Prepare a separate schedule that explains the changes in cash balance during March.
C. Is the transformation cycle complete or incomplete at the end of March? Explain your answer.

P3-13 ACCRUAL VERSUS CASH FLOW

Objs. 2, 3, 4

Consider each of the five independent situations below.

1. Asia Tea Company purchased a 3-month property insurance policy on March 1 at a cost of $3,600. The insurance became effective immediately although payment was due and paid 45 days later.
2. On February 1, Big Bang Chemical Company signed a contract with a customer. Big Bang agreed to deliver each month, for 3 months, goods priced at $7,500. The first delivery was made on April 1. The customer paid $22,500 for these goods on May 15.
3. Turning Tire Company borrowed $15,000 from a bank on February 1. Terms of repayment are that $1,000 of the principal amount must be repaid on the first day of each following month. In addition, interest at 2% per month on the unpaid balance must accompany each payment.
4. Bureaucrats Inc. consumes large amounts of office supplies. On February 1, a $10,000 order of supplies was received and paid for. Sixty percent of these supplies were used in March and the rest were used in April. On April 20, a $12,000 order of office supplies was received. The invoice for these goods was paid in May. Thirty percent of these goods were consumed in May and the rest were consumed in June.
5. Sales at the High-Price Furniture Store totaled $45,000 for the month of February. Of this amount, 20% was cash sales, 40% was collected during March, 30% during April, and 10% during May.

Required

A. Determine the proper amount of revenue, expense, and cash flow that should be entered into the accounting system during each month shown. Use the format shown below. The first event is completed as an example.
B. What does this information suggest to you about the pattern in which accrual-based measures are recognized versus cash-based measures?
C. What does this suggest to you about a manager's need for both accrual information and cash flow information?

Event	Revenue, Expense, or Cash Flow?	Month of February	Month of March	Month of April	Month of May	Month of June
1.	Expense Cash Flow	-0- -0-	$1,200 -0-	$1,200 3,600	$1,200 -0-	-0- -0-
2.						
3.						
4.						
5.						

P3-14 PREPARING FINANCIAL STATEMENTS AND MAKING DECISIONS

Objs. 2, 3, 4

The Desert Harbor Inn has been in business for more than 100 years but was recently renovated. On January 1, 2007, the balance sheet of the company was as shown on the next page.

(Continued)

During 2007, the inn earned $165,000 from room rentals and another $35,000 from parking, the gift shop, and other guest services. Of this amount, $187,000 was received in cash by year end; $13,000 was still collectible from credit card companies and one very reliable corporate account. Expenses incurred during the year included staff wages, $49,000; utilities, $10,400; supplies used, $4,300; depreciation on furniture and fixtures, $1,500; depreciation on the building, $3,500; interest on note payable, $4,700; cost of goods sold by gift shop, $11,000; and other miscellaneous expenses of $3,300.

Except for depreciation, supplies consumed, and $890 of wages still owed to employees, all expenses were paid for in cash. Other cash payments included $800 for purchase of supplies and $35,000 paid on the principal of the note payable. Owners withdrew $45,000 from the business for living expenses during the year.

Desert Harbor Inn
Balance Sheet
January 1, 2007

Assets		Liabilities and Owners' Equity	
Cash	$ 4,900	Notes payable	$ 56,500
Supplies on hand	8,800	Investment by owners	60,000
Furniture and equipment	25,000	Retained earnings	19,200
Buildings	95,000		
Accumulated depreciation	(10,000)		
Land	12,000		
Total	$135,700	Total	$135,700

Required

A. Prepare year-end financial statements for the company for 2007. Include an income statement, statement of cash flows, and a balance sheet.

B. From a financial perspective, does this company appear to be one that you would like to own? Why or why not?

P3-15 IDENTIFYING PROBLEMS IN FINANCIAL REPORTING

Objs. 2, 3, 4

Alma Zorditch started an Internet company and has computed the first year's profit as shown below. She is distressed. She thought the business had been going fairly well but does not know how she can live on the meager profit the company has earned. She is considering going out of business. Alma doesn't have any formal training in accounting but once took a 4-hour seminar on the subject. That seminar impressed on her the importance of keeping detailed and accurate records. All the numbers reported below are accurate, but there may be other problems that you can identify.

Zorditch.com
Profits I Made the First Year

Revenue:		
Cash collected from customers	$173,400	
Accounts receivable at year end	18,200	
Total revenue		$191,600
Expenses:		
Money I contributed to start the firm	$ 15,000	
Purchase of office furnishings & equipment	28,500	
Purchase of office supplies	1,560	
Rent on the office space	13,000	
Loan from the bank	50,000	
Wages paid to employees	36,200	
Advertising and promotion	24,280	
Miscellaneous	11,300	
Total expenses		179,840
Profit		$ 11,760

After talking with Alma, you discover the following additional information.

1. When purchased, the office furnishings and equipment have an expected useful life of 5 years. That estimate still appears reasonable.
2. All office supplies have been used up.
3. The rent amount includes $1,000 rent paid in advance for the first month of Year 2.
4. Half of the advertising and promotion amount is for a campaign that will begin 3 months from now.

Required

A. Study the information given and prepare a new income statement making all changes you believe are appropriate.
B. Wherever your report differs from Alma's, justify the change you have made.
C. Based on your revised income statement, what advice would you have for Alma? List two or three specific suggestions.

P3-16 ADJUSTING ENTRIES AND CLOSING ENTRIES: EFFECTS ON FINANCIAL STATEMENTS

Objs. 4, 5

The Flash Pan Company manufactures cooking products. On August 1, 2007, the company borrowed $125,000 from creditors. Semiannual interest payments of $7,500 are to be made to creditors beginning January 31, 2008. On July 1, 2007, the company purchased a 1-year insurance policy for $10,000 and recorded it as prepaid insurance. On January 1, 2007, the company purchased equipment for $50,000. The equipment has an expected life of 4 years. On October 1, 2007, the company rented some of its unused warehouse space to another company. The other company agreed to pay $15,000 for each 6-month period. The first payment would be made on April 1, 2008. Balance sheet and income statement information reported by Flash for the fiscal year ended December 31, 2007 included:

Assets	$625,000
Liabilities	250,000
Owners' equity	337,500
Revenues	150,000
Expenses	112,500
Net income	37,500

The balance sheet did not balance but it was distributed anyway. Later, it was discovered that the company's accounting staff had failed to record any adjusting entries at the end of 2007 for interest, insurance, depreciation, or rent. In addition, no closing entries had been made.

Required

A. Record the adjusting entries that should have been made at year end 2007.
B. Explain why the balance sheet did not balance and whether this was caused by the failure to record adjusting entries or the failure to record closing entries.
C. Identify the corrected amounts for the balance sheet and income statement. Show your work.

P3-17 END-OF-PERIOD ADJUSTMENTS AND CLOSING

Objs. 4, 5

At December 31, 2007, the accountant at Puget Sounds, a recording studio, has entered all the firm's transactions into the accounting system and is beginning the end-of-period process. He asks your help in identifying the necessary adjusting entries. In the first column on page 120, the accountant has listed the company's account balances before considering adjustments. In addition, he has provided other information that may cause you to recommend that certain adjusting entries be made.

1. $4,350 of wages earned by employees during December have not been recorded or paid.
2. The prepaid insurance is for a 3-year policy purchased on the first day of the year just ending.
3. Unearned revenues are for contracts for the use of studio facilities. $12,000 of this amount has been earned by December 31.
4. A count at year-end shows that $10,050 of supplies remain on hand.

(Continued)

5. The note payable was issued on October 1, 2007. Interest accumulates in the amount of $3,000 per month. Interest has not yet been recorded for December.
6. Depreciation on equipment is $1,500 per month. Depreciation on buildings is $600 per month. No depreciation has yet been recorded for the quarter (3 months) just ended.

	Account Balance Before Adjustment	Adjustments	Account Balance After Adjustment
Cash	$ 52,500		
Accounts receivable	35,250		
Supplies	19,200		
Prepaid insurance	4,050		
Equipment	468,000		
Accumulated depreciation—equipment	(129,000)		
Buildings	649,500		
Accumulated depreciation—buildings	(85,500)		
Land	58,500		
Total assets	**$1,072,500**		
Unearned revenues	$ 36,000		
Accounts payable	27,900		
Interest payable	6,000		
Wages payable	0	(1) +4,350	4,350
Notes payable	420,000		
Common stock	300,000		
Retained earnings *(a)*	224,100		
Total liabilities & stockholders' equity	**$1,014,000**		
Rent revenues	$ 100,500		
Wages expense	(36,000)	(1) −4,350	(40,350)
Supplies expense	0		
Insurance expense	0		
Interest expense	(6,000)		
Depreciation expense	0		
Net income	**$ 58,500**		
(a) Net income has not been added for the current year.			

Required

A. Identify any adjustments you believe necessary and enter their effects in the adjustments column of the table above. Code each adjustment with the number to which it relates. The first item is completed for you as an example.
B. Record the proper ending amount for each account in the final column.
C. On the table you have completed, why doesn't the total of all asset accounts equal the total of all liability and equity accounts?
D. What additional step(s) needs to be performed before financial statements can be prepared? Explain how this will solve the imbalance identified in part (C) above.
E. By what amount (and percentage) would net income have been misstated if no adjusting entries had been recorded by this company?

P3-18 TYPES AND TREATMENT OF ACCOUNTS

Obj. 5

Encanto Properties, Inc., uses the accounts listed below.

A. Prepaid Insurance
B. Retained Earnings
C. Accumulated Depreciation
D. Wages Expense

E. Commissions Revenue
F. Interest Payable
G. Supplies
H. Insurance Expense
I. Unearned Rent
J. Prepaid Advertising
K. Notes Payable
L. Cost of Goods Sold
M. Machinery
N. Owners' Capital
O. Accounts Receivable
P. Bonds Payable
Q. Supplies Expense
R. Depreciation Expense

Required (a) For each account above, indicate whether it is an asset, liability, owners' equity, revenue, or expense account. (b) Indicate whether the account is closed at the end of the fiscal year.

P3-19 ETHICAL ISSUES IN AN ACCOUNTING SYSTEM

Obj. 6

Mary Spikes works for Hard Rock Candy Company. She enters customer orders in the company's accounting system. The orders are written on prepared forms by the company's sales representatives (reps). The company employs ten sales reps, who work different territories. The reps are paid on a commission basis for sales made during the preceding month. Sales reports prepared by the accounting department supervisor are used to determine the commissions. Sales reps drop off the forms with the accounting supervisor each week. The supervisor then delivers the forms to Mary. She enters the orders in a computer and prints out a sales report and sales invoices for each customer. These are picked up by the supervisor, who delivers them to payroll and to shipping. The result of entering the orders in the accounting system is to increase accounts receivable and to increase sales revenue.

Mary has discovered an interesting regularity in some of the orders. One of the sales reps always reports abnormally high orders from a particular customer. A few days after the end of each month, the rep submits a cancelation form for the customer to eliminate a large portion of the customer's order. The supervisor directs Mary to record the cancelation by reducing accounts receivable for the customer and recording an increase in an operating expense account. Mary doesn't know much about accounting. When she asked her supervisor about this procedure, she was told that it was standard for this customer and not to worry about it.

Mary is suspicious, however, and has considered discussing the matter with the vice president of finance. But she is concerned she may simply be making waves that will alienate her supervisor.

Required Mary has sought your advice, as a friend, about this matter. What would you recommend to Mary? What problems do you see in Hard Rock's accounting system? How might these problems be solved?

P3-20 DESCRIBING PROCESSES IN AN ACCOUNTING SYSTEM

Obj. 6

Flora Wiser is the daughter of the owner of Wiser Florist Company. She recently completed college with a major in biology and has taken the job of assistant manager. Her primary duties involve purchasing inventory from suppliers. Flora has little understanding of accounting, and you have been asked to help her become familiar with the company's accounting system and how the system processes information.

Required Write a memo to Flora describing the purpose of an accounting system. Describe each of the basic processes that occur within financial accounting systems and how these processes accomplish the purpose of the system.

P3-21 EXCEL IN ACTION

The problem in Chapter 2 provided account balances for The Book Wermz on September 30, 2007, the end of the company's fiscal year: Cash $4,238.72, Inventory of Books $235,892.35, Supplies $2,343.28, Equipment $43,297.00, Notes Payable $123,452.88, Investment by Owners $100,000, and Retained Earnings $62,318.47. Chapter 2 also listed summary transactions for October 2007:

Cash sales	$38,246.50
Cost of goods sold	27,318.93

(Continued)

The Equipment account balance of $43,297.00 is net of accumulated depreciation of $12,353.00. Therefore, the Equipment balance before considering the effect of depreciation is $55,650.00.

Other transactions for the month ended October 31, 2007, include:

Cash paid for books purchased	$18,243.27
Cash paid for supplies	1,750.92
Cost of supplies used in October	2,129.48
Employee wages earned and paid in October	3,620.83
Employee wages earned in October but unpaid	527.12
Cash paid for portion of Notes Payable	1,122.77
Cash paid for interest incurred on Notes Payable	823.02
Cash paid for October rent	1,534.86
Depreciation on equipment for October	721.62

In addition, The Book Wermz held classes on book binding for local civic organizations in October. The organizations agreed to a $500 fee for these services but did not make the payment in October.

Required Add the transactions described above to those created in Chapter 2. Additional rows should be added to the spreadsheet for the transactions. Additional columns also will be needed for accounts not included in Chapter 2. The following accounts should be included in the spreadsheet in the order indicated: Cash, Accounts Receivable, Supplies, Inventory, Equipment, Accumulated Depreciation, Wages Payable, Notes Payable, Investment by Owners, Retained Earnings, Sales, Service Revenues, Cost of Goods Sold, Supplies Expense, Wages Expense, Rent Expense, Depreciation Expense, and Interest Expense. The beginning balance of all new accounts except Accumulated Depreciation is $0. The beginning balance of the Accumulated Depreciation account is $12,353 (note this is a negative amount because it is a contra account), and the beginning balance of the Equipment account should be changed to $55,650 (to permit Accumulated Depreciation to be included as a separate account). Column sums should be recalculated to determine totals at October 31. Make sure to close the revenue and expense accounts to Retained Earnings. Use October 31 as the date for all transactions.

Update the balance sheet and income statement by including the effects of the transactions recorded for October. Use cell references in the financial statements to identify amounts for each account. Add captions to identify each statement. The statements should include the name of the company on the top line. The next line should identify the financial statement as a balance sheet or income statement. The third line should identify the date (October 31, 2007 for the balance sheet) or period (for October 2007 for the income statement). List total revenues and total expenses as subtotals on the income statement. Use underlines to separate the subtotals from other numbers. The Borders button can be used for this purpose.

P3-22 MULTIPLE-CHOICE OVERVIEW OF THE CHAPTER

1. The primary difference between control accounts and subsidiary accounts is that
   a. control accounts appear on the balance sheet but subsidiary accounts appear on the income statement.
   b. subsidiary accounts provide detailed information; control accounts provide summary information.
   c. control account balances are reported on the financial statements but subsidiary accounts appear only in the general ledger.
   d. subsidiary accounts are necessary in a manual accounting system but not in a computerized system.

2. At the beginning of the year, Lagos Importers had $750 of office supplies on hand. During the year, an additional $3,250 of supplies were purchased and recorded in Office Supplies Inventory. At year end, $900 of supplies remained on hand. Just prior to preparing the year-end adjusting entry, the balance in the Office Supplies Inventory account was $1,200. Which of the following is a true statement about the necessary adjusting entry?
   a. An asset account must be decreased by $300.
   b. An asset account must be decreased by $3,250.

c. An expense account must be increased by $1,200.
d. An expense account must be increased by $900.

3. The balance of the merchandise inventory account increased by $3,000 during February. Which of the following statements can be made as a result of this information?
   a. Credit sales for the month were $3,000 greater than cash received from customers.
   b. Purchases of inventory for the month were $3,000 less than the cost of merchandise sold for the month.
   c. Purchases of inventory for the month were $3,000 greater than the cost of merchandise sold for the month.
   d. Merchandise purchased for the month totaled $3,000.

4. Which of the following accounts should always have a zero balance after all closing entries are completed?
   a. Interest Expense
   b. Interest Payable
   c. Prepaid Interest
   d. Accounts Payable

5. Tempel Manufacturing uses accrual accounting. Each of the following events occurred during the month of February. Which one of them should be recorded as a revenue or expense for the month of February?
   a. Sales of $30,000 were made on credit. They will be collected during March.
   b. Collections of $10,000 were made from sales that occurred during January.
   c. Materials costing $18,000 were purchased and paid for. It is expected that they will be used during March.
   d. A bill in the amount of $8,600 was received from a supplier for goods purchased during January. It was paid immediately.

6. Zinsli Company uses the accrual basis of accounting. Each of the following events occurred during July. Which one of them should be reported as an expense for July?
   a. Office supplies costing $800 were used up. They had been purchased and paid for during April.
   b. A new delivery truck was purchased on the last day of July. It was not put into use until August.
   c. On the third day of the month, $8,000 was paid to employees for hours worked during the month of June.
   d. Near the end of the month, August's rent of $1,500 was paid in advance.

7. The following information is available for two companies for the year 2007:

	Company A Cash Operating Statement For the Year 2007	**Company B Accrual Income Statement For the Year 2007**
Receipts/Revenues	$50,000	$55,000
Payments/Expenses	38,000	31,000
Net Cash/Net Income	$12,000	$24,000

   Which of the following statements can be determined from the information provided?
   a. Company B collected more cash from customers during 2007 than did Company A.
   b. Company B was profitable during 2007, whereas Company A may have been profitable.
   c. Company B was twice as profitable as Company A.
   d. Company A consumed more total resources during 2007 than did Company B.

(Continued)

8. Are the following accounts a liability?

	Depreciation Expense	Accounts Receivable
a.	Yes	Yes
b.	Yes	No
c.	No	Yes
d.	No	No

9. Using accrual-basis measurement, expenses should be recognized when
   a. a business owner recognizes that the firm is generating too much profit.
   b. resources are used rather than when they are paid for.
   c. cash is paid for resources.
   d. sufficient revenue is earned to offset the expenses.

10. Match the account name to the financial statement on which it is reported.

	Accumulated Depreciation	Depreciation Expense
a.	Statement of stockholder's equity	Balance sheet
b.	Balance sheet	Balance sheet
c.	Income statement	Balance sheet
d.	Balance sheet	Income statement

Cases

C3-1 ETHICAL ISSUES INVOLVING REVENUE RECOGNITION
Obj. 4

Flash Newton is national sales director at Bright & Shiny Toothpaste Company. The firm manufactures and distributes a full line of premium-priced personal care products sold through a carefully selected set of distributors nationwide. The popularity and profit margins of the Bright & Shiny product line make distributorships very profitable and there is intense competition when one becomes available.

Flash, and the regional sales directors working for him, are compensated by a base salary and a significant bonus tied to percentage increases in yearly sales. Because of an impending recession, sales have been mostly flat during the first three quarters of the year. On October 3, Flash convened a national sales meeting with representatives of all distributors. At that meeting, he presented the distributors with Bright & Shiny's newest sales plan. All distributors would be required to buy, during the 4th quarter, up to 2 years' worth of inventory of the firm's products. Further, the prices charged on these special purchases would be 10% greater than usual. Any distributors not agreeing to the proposal would automatically lose their distributorship. Because most distributors are not expected to have cash readily available to pay for these additional purchases under the usual 30-day credit terms, Bright & Shiny will allow up to 12 months to pay.

The new policy has been a huge success and by year end, total orders and shipments to distributors are up by 12% over the previous year. Bright & Shiny recorded all shipments as revenue even though some distributors were told by lower-level managers that they could return unsold products. Because many distributors could not handle the large shipments in their usual storage facilities, many orders have been shipped to third-party warehouses for storage at Bright & Shiny's expense. At Flash's suggestion, and to obtain maximum benefit of this new sales program, the company held the books open for a few days after December 31 to obtain and ship additional orders.

Required Identify and explain any problems you see with the sales plan. If you were Bright & Shiny's CEO, which aspects of the sales plan would you have approved and which would you have denied? Why?

C3-2 EVALUATING THE RESULTS OF AN ORGANIZATION'S TRANSFORMATION PROCESS
Objs. 1, 4, 5

Softech.com is an Internet wholesaler of a variety of commercial software applications. On January 1, 2007, the company's balance sheet appeared as follows (all amounts are in thousands of dollars):

Softech.com
Balance Sheet
January 1, 2007

Assets		**Liabilities & Stockholders' Equity**	
Cash	$ 4,240	Wages payable	$ 640
Accounts receivable	6,800	Capital stock (owner's investment)	33,000
Inventory	15,200	Retained earnings	13,600
Buildings & equipment	16,780		
Accumulated depreciation	(4,780)		
Land (for plant expansion)	9,000		
Total assets	$47,240	Total liabilities and stockholders' equity	$47,240

During the first quarter of the current year (January, February, March), the following events occurred.

A. New office furniture costing $500 was purchased on the last day of March. This was to be used in a new sales office that was scheduled to open April 1. The office furniture was paid for in cash.

B. Wages and salaries totaling $3,200 were paid. Of this amount, 20% was to liquidate wages payable that arose in the fourth quarter of the previous year. The company has a policy of not making wage or salary advances to employees.

C. All accounts receivable outstanding at January 1 were collected.

D. The company's advertising agency billed the firm $1,000 for a campaign that had run during the current quarter. The company is planning to pay the bill during April.

E. Sales totaling $18,000 were made to customers. Of these sales, 60% was collected during the first quarter, and the balance is expected to be collected during the next quarter. The goods that were sold had cost the company $13,000 when they were purchased.

F. Dividends were declared and paid to stockholders in the amount of $1,500.

G. Inventory (software programs) costing $10,500 was purchased, of which 10% was paid for by the end of the quarter.

H. A 3-year, $4,000, 12% loan was obtained from a local bank on the last day of the quarter.

I. New shares of stock were sold by the company for $2,000 in cash.

J. A new 3-year lease agreement was signed and executed. The lease required that a $900 monthly rental be paid in advance for the first 2 quarters of the current year. (Total paid is $5,400 = $900 $\times$ 6 months.)

K. The accountants calculated that depreciation totaling $350 should be recorded for the quarter for the firm's buildings and equipment.

L. The land that had been held for plant expansion was sold for $9,000.

Required Prepare any summary documents you believe might help management (or interested external parties) better understand the effectiveness or efficiency of the firm's first quarter transformation process. Did the company have a satisfactory first quarter?

Comprehensive Review

CR3-1 FINANCIAL STATEMENT PREPARATION AND CLOSING PROCESS

Summary account balances for Favorite Cookie Company at the end of February are presented on the next page. The summary includes all transactions for February, not just those described in this chapter. In particular, additional sales transactions have been included.

Favorite Cookie Company
Account Balances
February 28, 2007

Account	Balance
Assets:	
Cash	7,740
Accounts Receivable	4,100
Merchandise Inventories	7,520
Supplies	60
Prepaid Rent	1,200
Equipment	31,000
Accumulated Depreciation	(1,040)
Total Assets	**50,580**
Liabilities:	
Accounts Payable	1,400
Unearned Revenue	3,000
Interest Payable	400
Notes Payable	30,000
Total Liabilities	**34,800**
Owners' Equity:	
Contribution by Owners	10,000
Retained Earnings	3,000
Sales Revenue	17,160
Cost of Goods Sold	(11,440)
Wages Expense	(1,000)
Rent Expense	(600)
Depreciation Expense	(520)
Supplies Expense	(400)
Utilities Expense	(220)
Interest Expense	(200)
Total Owners' Equity	**15,780**

Required Use the account balances to (a) prepare an income statement for February, (b) close the revenue and expense accounts (show journal transactions and ledger accounts), (c) prepare a post-closing summary of account balances, and (d) prepare a balance sheet.

CR3-2 ACCOUNTING CYCLE

Orlando Co. reported the following account balances for its 2007 fiscal year, prior to the transactions described below.

Accounts Payable	$ 6,100
Accounts Receivable	8,000
Accumulated Depreciation	36,500
Cash	5,000
Contributed Capital	80,000
Cost of Goods Sold	115,000
Depreciation Expense	3,700
Interest Expense	6,300
Interest Payable	900
Merchandise Inventory	57,000
Notes Payable, Long-Term	76,400
Prepaid Rent	1,800
Property and Equipment	183,000
Rent Expense	16,000
Retained Earnings	37,200
Sales Revenue	198,000

Supplies	$ 3,600
Supplies Expense	5,900
Wages Expense	42,000
Wages Payable	2,200

The following events occurred during October, the last month of the company's fiscal year, that have not been recorded:

A. Sold $8,400 of goods for credit. The cost of the goods sold was $4,300.
B. Collected $7,600 from customers for prior credit sales.
C. Purchased $3,200 of supplies on credit.
D. Paid $2,100 to suppliers for supplies purchased earlier on credit.
E. Paid $1,800 for rent for future months.
F. Paid $4,300 for wages. $600 of this amount was for wages earned in September; the remainder was for wages earned in October.
G. Paid $900 for interest incurred in a prior month.

In addition, the following adjustments are needed at the end of October:

H. Used $700 of supplies that were purchased previously.
I. Incurred $800 of wages during October that will be paid in November.
J. Incurred $1,000 of interest during October that will be paid in November.
K. Depreciation for October was $570.

Required: (a) Record the transactions and adjustments for October, (b) close the appropriate accounts at the end of October, (c) prepare a summary (trial balance) of accounts at the end of October showing pre- and post-closing amounts, and (d) prepare an income statement for the fiscal year and a balance sheet at October 31, 2007.

© PHOTODISC/GETTY IMAGES

Reporting Earnings and Financial Position

4

HOW DO WE REPORT EARNINGS AND FINANCIAL POSITION TO STOCKHOLDERS?

Previous chapters described business activities of Favorite Cookie Company and the system the company used to account for those activities. As the business grew during 2007, Maria and Stan needed additional financial resources to take advantage of opportunities to sell more of their product. In September, they decided to issue shares of stock in their company to other individuals. Cash received from issuing the stock was used to acquire additional equipment, particularly delivery vans, and to increase the amount of inventory the company could purchase. Because the company has external investors (stockholders who are not managers of the company), it must report its business activities in conformance with generally accepted accounting principles to ensure these stockholders are properly informed of the company's earnings and financial position.

Food for Thought

Assume you own shares of stock in Favorite Cookie Company. What information about the company is important to you? As the company prepares to report accounting information to you and its other owners at the end of its 2007 fiscal year, what information must it include in its income statement and balance sheet? What information do corporations report, especially about their earnings and stockholders' equity, that other companies do not? Is there any information about the company that does not have to be disclosed?

Maria and Stan have arranged to meet with their accountant, Ellen, to discuss these issues.

Maria: *We have prepared monthly financial statements for our use in managing the company. I suspect that those statements are not adequate for reporting to our other stockholders.*

Ellen: *That's correct. The statements you have been preparing are fine for internal use and contain correct information. However, formal financial statements for external users need to follow a somewhat different format than those you have been using.*

Stan: *Does this mean we have to redo our accounting system and learn a new way of accounting for our company?*

Ellen: *No. Your accounting system is fine. You just need to modify the format of your statements to organize the information a bit differently, and you need to include more information about earnings and stockholders' equity than you have been reporting.*

Maria: *Will these changes be hard for us to make?*

Ellen: *No. You will need to understand how information is classified in formal financial statements and how corporations report such matters as earnings per share and changes in stockholders' equity. Now that you understand the basic content of financial statements and how business activities are reported in these statements, you shouldn't have much trouble preparing statements for your stockholders.*

Objectives

Once you have completed this chapter, you should be able to:

1. Identify the primary financial statements issued by businesses.
2. Explain information presented on a company's income statement.
3. Explain information presented on a company's balance sheet.
4. Explain information presented on a company's statement of stockholders' equity.
5. Identify some of the primary limitations of financial statements.

THE PURPOSE OF FINANCIAL STATEMENTS

Objective 1
Identify the primary financial statements issued by businesses.

Accounting information may serve general and specific purposes. Financial statements are the primary means organizations use to report general-purpose accounting information to external decision makers. Most business organizations prepare three financial statements:

1. An income statement
2. A balance sheet
3. A statement of cash flows

Many corporations also prepare a statement of stockholders' equity because of the variety and complexity of their ownership transactions. This chapter examines the purpose and content of the income statement, the balance sheet, and the statement of stockholders' equity. Chapter 5 examines the statement of cash flows. Information contained in financial statements and in the notes accompanying the statements is the primary focus of financial accounting. Specific-purpose accounting reports and other information used by internal decision makers are subjects of managerial accounting.

The form and content of financial statements evolved throughout the twentieth century and continue to change to meet user needs. Financial statements are used by internal and external decision makers. The format and content of the statements used by managers to make financing, investing, and operating decisions often follow those of statements prepared for external users. Statements for internal use, however, may be prepared in any form and with any content desired by management.

For many years the balance sheet was the primary financial statement reported to external users. It was designed to meet the needs of creditors, who wanted information about resources and claims to these resources. The income statement developed to meet the needs of corporate investors, who wanted information about earnings. Earnings information is useful for evaluating management decisions that affect payments to stockholders and stock values. The statement of stockholders' equity describes transactions affecting stock and the amount and use of retained earnings. The statement of cash flows, which is a more recent addition to external reports, provides information that enables creditors, investors, and other users to assess a company's ability to meet its cash requirements.

Financial statements for general-purpose external reporting normally are prepared according to generally accepted accounting principles (GAAP). As noted previously, GAAP are accounting and reporting standards established by authoritative agencies and monitored and enforced by the federal government. GAAP specify the format and content of the statements, though they permit managers to choose among alternative methods of reporting some transactions. The establishment and enforcement of accounting standards are discussed in Chapter 6.

An income statement (sometimes called an earnings statement, a statement of operations, or a profit and loss (P&L) statement) reports a company's revenues and expenses for a fiscal period. The income statement presents operating results on an accrual basis. It measures the amount of goods and services provided to customers during a fiscal period and resources consumed in providing those goods and services. Revenues and expenses result from the sale and consumption of resources for a fiscal period. Therefore, the income statement reports the results of operating activities for a particular period, such as a month, quarter, or fiscal year.

A balance sheet reports the balances of the asset, liability, and owners' equity accounts at a particular date. Other names for the balance sheet are statement of financial position and statement of financial condition. These names are good descriptions of the statement because it reports the amount of resources available to an organization at a particular date and the sources of financing used to acquire those resources. In combination, the resources and financing are the financial position, or condition, of the organization at the report date.

A *statement of stockholders' equity* **reports changes in a corporation's owners' equity for a fiscal period.** Owners of corporations are known as stockholders or shareholders because they acquire ownership by purchasing shares of stock issued by the corporation. Each share of stock represents an equal share of ownership in a corporation. The primary changes in stockholders' equity result from profits earned during a period, from dividends paid to owners, and from the sale or repurchase of stock by a corporation. *Dividends* **are distributions of cash or stock by a corporation to its stockholders.** The statement of stockholders' equity links the income statement to the balance sheet because it describes how much net income was reinvested as part of retained earnings.

THE INCOME STATEMENT

Objective 2
Explain information presented on a company's income statement.

The income statement reports the revenues, expenses, and net income for a fiscal period. Exhibit 1 provides the income statement of Favorite Cookie Company for the year ended December 31, 2007. The income statement reports revenues and expenses that are measured on an accrual basis. Revenues indicate the sales price of goods and services sold during a fiscal period. They do not indicate how much cash was received from the sales during that period. Expenses identify the cost of resources consumed in producing and selling goods and services sold during a fiscal period. They do not identify how much cash was paid for resources during that period. **Net income is not cash.** As a first step in understanding Exhibit 1, observe the general format of the statement. Unlike the statements we described in Chapters 2 and 3 that simply listed revenues and expenses,

EXHIBIT 1
A Corporate Income Statement

Favorite Cookie Company Income Statement For the Year Ended December 31, 2007	
Sales revenue	$ 686,400
Cost of goods sold	(457,600)
Gross profit	$ 228,800
Selling, general and administrative expenses	(148,300)
Operating income	$ 80,500
Interest expense	(4,800)
Pretax income	$ 75,700
Income taxes	(22,710)
Net income	$ 52,990
Earnings per share	$ 13.25*
Average number of common shares	4,000

*rounded

the income statements prepared by most companies are divided into several sections. The following paragraphs describe the sections commonly found on income statements.

Gross Profit

The income statement reports *gross profit*, **the difference between the selling price of goods or services sold to customers during a period and the cost of the goods or services sold.** For a merchandising company, the cost of goods sold is the cost of the merchandise inventory sold during a period. For a manufacturing company, cost of goods sold includes the dollar amounts of materials, labor, and other resources that are consumed directly in producing the goods sold during a period. These costs are **product costs**. Product costs are recorded as an asset (Inventory) until goods are sold. Then the costs are matched against the revenues generated from the sale by recording an expense (Cost of Goods Sold) during the same fiscal period as the sale.

Cost of services sold, rather than cost of goods sold, is important for service companies. **The** *cost of services sold* **is the cost of material, labor, and other resources consumed directly in producing services sold during a period.** For example, in a hospital, the cost of nursing is a cost of services. This cost cannot be held as inventory and, therefore, is expensed in the period in which the services are provided.

Gross profit is a measure of how much a company earned directly from the sale of its products during a fiscal period. Every company would like to earn a large gross profit by selling its products at a much higher price than their cost. Competition prevents most companies from being able to do so. Companies must price their products at amounts their customers are willing to pay, which is determined in part by prices of other similar products that customers could buy from other companies. Favorite Cookie Company cannot sell its cookies at a price that is much higher than that of other companies that sell similar cookies. Therefore, Favorite Cookie Company has to purchase the goods it sells at a cost that allows it to earn a reasonable gross profit. The amount of gross profit a company can earn depends on the kinds of products it sells and the markets in which it operates. Some markets are more competitive than others. For example, many competing companies sell computers, but not many sell the operating systems for computers.

Operating Income

The second section of an income statement lists operating expenses other than cost of goods sold or cost of services sold. *Operating expenses* **are costs of resources consumed as part of operating activities during a fiscal period and that are not directly associated with specific goods or services.** Most operating expenses are **period costs** because they are recognized in the fiscal period in which they occur. Operating expenses include selling, general, and administrative expenses incurred during a period.

Corporations usually do not identify specific operating expenses in detail. Salaries for managers and their support staffs who are not involved directly in producing goods and the cost of resources used by managers are operating expenses. These expenses include depreciation, taxes, and insurance on office buildings and equipment, and the costs of supplies and utilities consumed in operating these facilities. Operating expenses also include marketing and product development costs. GAAP require most marketing and selling costs and research and development costs incurred during a fiscal period to be reported as operating expenses of the period in which they occur. Because identifying how much of these costs is associated with benefits of future periods is difficult, GAAP require that these amounts be expensed to avoid an overstatement of profits during the current fiscal period.

The excess of gross profit over operating expenses is *operating income*. If operating expenses are greater than gross profit, the result is a loss from operations. Operating income is a measure of how much a company earned from its basic business activities. A company is in the business of acquiring and selling products. Cost of goods sold and other operating expenses include the cost of acquiring and making its products available to customers. Sales revenues, sometimes referred to as operating revenues, are the total prices of the goods sold during a fiscal period. Therefore, operating income is a measure of how much a company made from selling its products, after considering normal and recurring expenses of doing business.

Other Revenues and Expenses

Revenues and expenses may occur that are not directly related to a company's primary operating activities. These are considered **nonoperating** items and are reported separately on the income statement following operating income. The item listed in this category most often is interest expense. Borrowing money is frequently necessary for an organization's operations; however, except for financial institutions, it is not part of most businesses' primary operating activities. Accordingly, other expenses and revenues are reported on the income statement after operating income. This separate listing distinguishes them from revenues and expenses that result from a business's primary operating activities.

Income Taxes

Most corporations pay income taxes on their earnings. The amount of income tax expense is determined by applying tax rates required by current tax laws and regulations to the income earned by a company during a fiscal period. Exhibit 1 reports that Favorite Cookie Company incurred income taxes of 30% on its pretax income ($22,710 = $75,700 × 0.30).

Learning Note - Not all U.S. corporations pay income taxes on profits. Certain small corporations, known as Subchapter S corporations in the tax laws, are treated like partnerships for tax purposes. Each stockholder is taxed on his or her share of the corporation's profits.

As noted in Chapter 1, direct taxation of income is one of the disadvantages of corporations. Proprietorships and partnerships do not pay income taxes on their profits directly. Instead, those profits are treated as personal income of the owners. Owners pay income tax on a proprietorship's profits or on their share of the profits of a partnership as part of personal taxes.

Net Income

Net income, or net earnings, is the amount of profit earned by a company during a fiscal period. It represents an increase in owners' or stockholders' equity, and it can be either distributed to owners or reinvested in the company. Distributions to owners, such as dividends, are not an expense. They are a deduction from retained earnings when a transfer is made to owners of a portion of a company's earnings. Undistributed earnings are included in retained earnings on a company's balance sheet.

Learning Note - It is important to note that cash dividends and cash withdrawals are paid out of cash. Therefore, a company must have sufficient cash available before it can pay dividends or before owners can withdraw money. Remember that net income does not guarantee that a company will have favorable cash flows during a period.

Earnings Per Share

GAAP require that corporate income statements prepared for distribution to stockholders and other external users present earnings per share as part of the statement. *Earnings per share* **is a measure of the earnings performance of each share of common stock during a fiscal period.** *Common stock* **is the stock that conveys primary ownership rights in a corporation.** We examine other types of stock in a later chapter. In general, earnings per share is computed by dividing net income by the average number of shares of common stock outstanding during a fiscal period. By multiplying earnings per share times the number of shares they own, stockholders can identify the amount of profit or loss associated with their individual investments.

The average number of common shares is based on the number of shares a company has outstanding, weighted by the portion of the fiscal period the stock is outstanding. To illustrate, assume Favorite Cookie Company was formed on January 1, 2007 as a corporation by issuing 1,000 shares of stock to Maria and Stan (500 shares each). Then, on September 1, 2007, the company issued an additional 9,000 shares of stock to other stockholders. Consequently, the company had 1,000 shares outstanding for 8 months (January through August) and 10,000 shares outstanding for 4 months (September through December).

The **average number of shares outstanding** was:

$$4{,}000 \text{ shares} = (1{,}000 \text{ shares} \times 8/12) + (10{,}000 \text{ shares} \times 4/12)$$

Earnings per share for Favorite Cookie Company was computed as follows:

$$\$13.25^{*} \text{ earnings per share} = \frac{\$52{,}990 \text{ net income}}{4{,}000 \text{ average common shares}}$$

*rounded

Other Reporting Issues

Income statements of actual companies vary in format and terminology from that presented in Exhibit 1. Though it is not possible to present all the possibilities that you may encounter in practice, certain issues are common for most corporate reports. These are apparent from a review of an actual corporate income statement. Exhibit 2 provides the income statement for **Publix Super Markets, Inc.,** from its 2004 annual report. First note that the title of Publix's statement is labeled "consolidated statements of earnings." Most large corporations include a number of companies owned by the corporation. **The controlling corporation is referred to as the *parent* and the companies owned or controlled by the parent are its *subsidiaries. Consolidated financial statements* include the activities of the parent and its subsidiaries as though they were one company.** Thus, Publix's income statement reports profits for the entire corporation, including all subsidiaries it owns.

EXHIBIT 2 Income Statement for Publix Super Markets

Publix Super Markets, Inc.
Consolidated Statements of Earnings
Years Ended December 25, 2004, December 27, 2003 and December 28, 2002

(Amounts are in thousands, except shares outstanding and per share amounts)

	2004	2003	2002
Revenues:			
Sales	$ 18,554,486	16,760,749	15,851,301
Other operating income	131,885	126,120	121,296
Total revenues	18,686,371	16,886,869	15,972,597
Costs and expenses:			
Cost of merchandise sold	13,577,740	12,275,132	11,621,762
Operating and administrative expenses	3,869,791	3,613,759	3,381,244
Total costs and expenses	17,447,531	15,888,891	15,003,006
Operating profit	1,238,840	997,978	969,591
Investment income, net	35,311	21,926	16,477
Other income, net	20,860	27,185	16,762
Earnings before income tax expense	1,295,011	1,047,089	1,002,830
Income tax expense	475,628	386,156	370,426
Net earnings	$ 819,383	660,933	632,404
Weighted average number of common shares outstanding	176,775,733	184,112,742	194,466,212
Basic and diluted earnings per common share based on weighted average shares outstanding	$ 4.64	3.59	3.25

Most corporations, like Publix, report income statements for three fiscal years. Publix's fiscal year ends with the Saturday closest to the end of December. Three years of data permit readers to evaluate how company performance has changed in recent years. Also observe that amounts, except per share amounts, are in thousands of dollars. Thus, revenues for 2004 were greater than $18.6 billion. *Total revenue* **is the amount earned from selling goods and services.**

The items presented in a company's income statement vary depending on the type of company. Any items that are uncommon and that are important relative to the total income of the company should be reported as a separate income statement item. For example, Publix reports store cost of merchandise sold and operating and administrative expenses as separate operating expenses.

Items appearing after income from operations (operating profit) represent revenues and expenses that are not part of a company's primary operating activities. Investment income is a non-operating item because it is not part of a company's primary operating activities. Interest expense and interest income are common non-operating items on many companies' income statements.

For some corporations, earnings per share is complicated because the company has issued financial instruments, such as long-term liabilities, that can be exchanged for shares of common stock or that might result in the issuance of additional shares if certain conditions are met. If issued, the additional shares of common stock would reduce earnings per share. These companies, like Publix, report **basic and diluted earnings per share**. Basic earnings per share (as described above) is calculated without considering the effect of the additional shares that could be issued. Diluted earnings per share is adjusted for the effects of additional shares that could be issued. Diluted earnings per share is never greater than basic earnings per share. It is a more conservative measure of earnings per share during a period than is basic earnings per share. Publix reported the same amount for basic and diluted earnings per share.

Learning Note - You should become familiar with the variety of terms that are used by companies in their financial statements. "Net earnings" is often substituted for "net income" for example. Real companies do not follow textbook formats in presenting their statements. As you increase your understanding of the basic content of these statements, you will be able to determine the meaning of terms used by most companies.

Self-Study Problem #1

An income statement for **Procter & Gamble** for a recent fiscal year is provided below.

Consolidated Statements of Earnings

	Year ended June 30
Amounts in millions except per share amounts	**2004**
Net Sales	$51,407
Cost of products sold	25,076
Selling, general and administrative expense	16,504
Operating Income	9,827
Interest expense	629
Other non-operating income, net	152
Earnings Before Income Taxes	9,350
Income taxes	2,869
Net Earnings	$6,481
Basic Net Earnings Per Common Share*	$2.46
Diluted Net Earnings Per Common Share*	$2.32
Dividends Per Common Share*	$0.93

***Restated for two-for-one stock split effective May 21, 2004.**

Required Use this statement to answer the following questions:

1. How much revenue did P&G earn from operating activities?
2. How much gross profit did P&G earn?
3. How much expense did P&G incur for non-operating activities?
4. Approximately how many shares of stock did P&G have outstanding?
5. What were P&G's total product costs?
6. How much net income did P&G earn?
7. How much cash did P&G receive from its operating activities during the year?

The solution to Self-Study Problem 1 appears at the end of the chapter.

THE BALANCE SHEET

Objective 3
Explain information presented on a company's balance sheet.

A balance sheet reports the asset, liability, and owners' equity account balances for a company at the end of a fiscal period. Exhibit 3 provides a balance sheet for Favorite Cookie Company for the year ended December 31, 2007.

Recall that the total amount of assets reported on the balance sheet at the end of a fiscal period must be equal to the total amount of liabilities and owners' equity. This relationship, assets = liabilities + owners' equity, is the fundamental balance sheet equation.

Exhibit 3 provides a **classified** balance sheet in which assets and liabilities are separated by type. The primary sections of the balance sheet are described in the following paragraphs.

EXHIBIT 3
A Corporate Balance Sheet

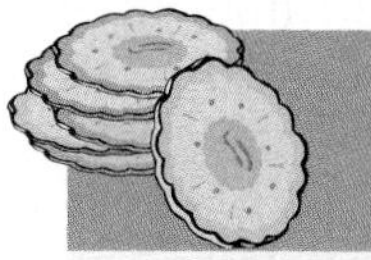

Favorite Cookie Company
Balance Sheet
At December 31, 2007

Assets	
Current assets:	
Cash	$ 10,680
Accounts receivable	8,570
Merchandise inventory	23,600
Supplies	690
Prepaid rent	2,000
Total current assets	$ 45,540
Property and equipment, at cost	215,660
Accumulated depreciation	(25,500)
Total assets	$235,700
Liabilities and Stockholders' Equity	
Current liabilities:	
Accounts payable	$ 9,610
Unearned revenue	4,250
Interest payable	650
Notes payable, current portion	5,000
Total current liabilities	$ 19,510
Notes payable, long-term	73,200
Total liabilities	$ 92,710
Stockholders' equity:	
Common stock, 10,000 shares issued	$100,000
Retained earnings	42,990
Total stockholders' equity	$142,990
Total liabilities and stockholders' equity	$235,700

*Learning Note - An organization's **operating cycle** is the period from the time cash is used to acquire or produce goods until these goods are sold and cash is received. The operating cycles of most organizations are less than 12 months. A fiscal year is the primary reporting period for these companies. Occasionally, a company's operating cycle is longer than 12 months. In such cases, which are rare, current assets are defined as those that a company expects to convert to cash or consume during the next operating cycle.*

Current Assets

GAAP require companies to report their current assets separately from their long-term assets. *Current assets* **are cash or other resources that management expects to convert to cash or consume during the next fiscal year.** Some current assets are liquid assets. *Liquid assets* **are resources that can be converted to cash in a relatively short period.** Cash equivalents include securities that are easily converted to cash and that have a short maturity, usually less than three months. In addition to cash and equivalents, current assets include (1) accounts receivable for which a company expects to receive cash during the next fiscal year, (2) inventory a company expects to sell during the next fiscal year, and (3) resources a company expects to consume during the next fiscal year, such as supplies and prepaid insurance, generally referred to as prepaid expenses.

Property and Equipment

Property and equipment, **often called** *fixed assets* **or** *plant assets*, **are long-term, tangible assets that are used in a company's operations.** Unlike inventory, these assets are not intended for resale. U.S. GAAP require fixed assets, other than land, to be depreciated over their estimated useful lives. Depreciation allocates the cost of these assets to the fiscal periods that benefit from their use as a means of matching expenses with revenues. The net value of fixed assets is the cost of the assets minus accumulated depreciation.

Land is not depreciated because it is not used up. Natural resources, such as petroleum, minerals, or timber, are accounted for separately from land and other property assets. The costs of these assets are allocated to expense over the periods that are expected to benefit from the use of the assets. **The process of allocating the cost of natural resources to expenses is known as** ***depletion*.** We examine depletion in Chapter 11.

Liabilities

GAAP require companies to report their current liabilities separately from their long-term liabilities. *Current liabilities* **are those obligations that management expects to fulfill during the next fiscal year.** *Long-term liabilities* **are those obligations not classified as current liabilities.**

Current liabilities include amounts owed by a company that will be paid during the coming fiscal year. Accounts, wages, interest, and income taxes payable all fit in this category. Unearned revenues that will be earned during the coming fiscal year also are classified as current liabilities.

The portion of long-term debt that will become due and be paid during the next year is a current liability. Exhibit 3 identifies this amount as "Notes payable, current portion." For example, assume Favorite Cookie Co. issued $80,000 in long-term notes payable during 2007. The notes are to be repaid in annual installments of $5,000. Therefore, $5,000 of the notes would be reported as a current liability on a balance sheet prepared at December 31, 2007. The unpaid balance would be reported as a long-term liability. From Exhibit 3 you can determine that $1,800 ($80,000 borrowed less $5,000 current portion and $73,200 long-term portion) of the notes was repaid in 2007, the year of issue.

The difference between current assets and current liabilities is known as *working capital*. Because current assets include those assets that are likely to produce cash inflows for a company and current liabilities include those liabilities that are likely to produce cash outflows, working capital is a measure of a company's liquidity. A company with a large amount of working capital should have little difficulty meeting its short-term obligations. Favorite Cookie Company reports $26,030 ($45,540 of current assets − $19,510 of current liabilities) of working capital in 2007.

Working capital often is reported as a ratio. **The ratio of current assets to current liabilities is the *working capital ratio* or *current ratio*.** Favorite Cookie Company's current ratio for 2007 is 2.33 ($45,540 ÷ $19,510).

Stockholders' Equity

Stockholders' equity includes (1) amounts paid by owners to a corporation for the purchase of shares of stock and (2) retained earnings, profits reinvested in the corporation. Common stock, as noted earlier, conveys basic ownership rights in a corporation. We examine other types of stock in Chapter 9.

OTHER BALANCE SHEET CONTENT

Like the income statement, the balance sheet may appear in a variety of formats. Companies may use reporting rules that differ from those previously described. Some types of companies—many utilities, for example—report fixed assets prior to current assets and report stockholders' equity prior to liabilities. Companies in the United States often use formats that differ from those used in other countries. The items included on a balance sheet depend on the activities of a company.

Exhibit 4 provides the balance sheet from Publix's 2004 annual report. Publix's balance sheet is **comparative** because it contains information for more than one year. Also, it is consolidated because it includes all the companies owned by the parent corporation.

Other Current Assets

In addition to current assets we considered earlier, Publix reports short-term investments and deferred taxes. **Short-term investments** are stocks or debt of other companies owned by Publix that it expects to sell in the near future. **Deferred income taxes** listed as current assets are prepaid taxes. These are taxes that the company has paid but that are associated with income tax expense of the coming fiscal period. The deferred taxes will be written off to income tax expense in a future period.

Publix reports its accounts receivable (trade receivables) net of allowances. The allowances are **estimated uncollectible accounts**. (These are sometimes referred to as **allowance for doubtful accounts** or **allowance for bad debts**.) When companies sell goods on credit, thus creating accounts receivable, it is likely that some customers will be unable to pay for their purchases. Companies are required by GAAP to estimate the amount of uncollectible receivables each fiscal period and to subtract that amount from their gross accounts receivable. The amount reported on the balance sheet for accounts receivable is the gross amount (total accounts receivable) minus the expected uncollectible amount (allowance). The net amount is the amount the company expects to collect from customers. We examine receivables in more detail in Chapter 13.

Other Long-Term Assets

In addition to property and equipment, long-term assets may include noncurrent receivables; fixed assets held for sale; prepaid expenses not expected to be consumed in

EXHIBIT 4 Balance Sheet for Publix Super Markets

Publix Super Markets, Inc. Consolidated Balance Sheets December 25, 2004 and December 27, 2003		
(Amounts are in thousands except par value and share amounts)		
ASSETS	**2004**	**2003**
Current assets:		
Cash and cash equivalents	$ 370,288	277,072
Short-term investments	101,718	16,661
Trade receivables	289,455	241,101
Merchandise inventories	1,054,183	981,456
Deferred tax assets	71,934	55,479
Prepaid expenses	11,804	9,778
Total current assets	1,899,382	1,581,547
Long-term investments	918,443	380,852
Other noncurrent assets	18,372	1,119
Property, plant and equipment:		
Land	159,023	174,283
Buildings and improvements	1,096,776	1,108,605
Furniture, fixtures and equipment	3,160,507	2,936,339
Leasehold improvements	912,689	833,569
Construction in progress	72,765	88,015
	5,401,760	5,140,811
Less accumulated depreciation	2,273,686	1,953,612
Net property, plant and equipment	3,128,074	3,187,199
	$5,964,271	5,150,717
LIABILITIES AND STOCKHOLDERS' EQUITY		
Current liabilities:		
Accounts payable	$ 762,655	724,228
Accrued expenses:		
Contribution to retirement plans	290,136	244,848
Self-insurance reserves	115,010	123,462
Salaries and wages	90,069	76,050
Other	187,451	190,510
Total accrued expenses	682,666	634,870
Federal and state income taxes	232,478	12,508
Total current liabilities	1,677,799	1,371,606
Deferred tax liabilities, net	313,073	284,458
Self-insurance reserves	240,821	202,737
Accrued postretirement benefit cost	68,101	67,960
Other noncurrent liabilities	78,761	54,646
Total liabilities	2,378,555	1,981,407
STOCKHOLDERS' EQUITY		
Common stock of $1 par value. Authorized 300,000,000 shares; issued and outstanding 172,591,732 shares in 2004 and 178,369,413 shares in 2003	172,592	178,369
Additional paid-in capital	630,983	494,154
Retained earnings	2,779,592	2,492,759
	3,583,167	3,165,282
Accumulated other comprehensive earnings	2,549	4,028
Total stockholders' equity	3,585,716	3,169,310
Commitments and contingencies	—	—
	$5,964,271	5,150,717

the next fiscal year; long-term legal rights such as patents, trademarks, and copyrights; additions to leased assets (leasehold improvements); construction in progress; and long-term investments. These types of assets may be listed on the balance sheet under separate headings if they constitute a significant portion of a company's assets. Otherwise, they often are listed simply as Other Assets.

Long-term legal rights resulting from the ownership of patents, copyrights, trademarks, and similar items are known as ***intangible assets*****,** in contrast to tangible assets such as property and equipment.

Long-term investments **occur when a company lends money to or purchases stock issued by other organizations and does not intend to sell those investments in the coming fiscal year.** Companies often invest in other companies to share in their earnings or to obtain access to resources, management skills, technology, and markets available to other companies. If management expects to hold these investments beyond the next fiscal year, they are classified as long-term investments. We examine accounting for each of these assets in later chapters.

Other Current Liabilities

The current liabilities listed on Publix's balance sheet are similar to those we have discussed for Favorite Cookie Company. The titles used for these liabilities are different, however. Accrued expenses is simply another name for liabilities such as wages payable and rent payable. One of the challenges of reading financial statements is becoming familiar with the wide variety of labels companies use. **A careful review of notes to the financial statements sometimes is important to understand the items reported by a company in those statements.**

Other Long-Term Liabilities

Publix reports deferred taxes, postretirement benefits, and self-insurance reserves. When **deferred taxes** are reported as a long-term liability, they represent income tax expenses that have not been paid and will not be paid during the coming year. Deferred taxes occur because of timing differences between when corporations recognize revenues and expenses for tax purposes and when those revenues and expenses are recognized for financial reporting purposes. If pretax income on a company's income statement exceeds its taxable income for tax purposes, a portion of the income tax expense a company recognizes will not be paid until some future fiscal period. Postretirement benefits are obligations for health care and similar benefits a company provides its employees after they retire. Self-insurance reserves are amounts a company has identified to cover losses associated with normal business operations. Rather than purchasing insurance from another company, Publix has elected to cover these losses through its own coverage.

Stockholders' Equity and Comprehensive Income

Like Favorite Cookie Company, Publix reports common stock and retained earnings. The number of shares of common stock authorized is the maximum number of shares the company could issue under its current charter. The number of shares issued (172.6 million in 2004) is the total number of shares that the company has sold to stockholders.

In addition to net income reported on the income statement, companies must report other comprehensive income. *Comprehensive income* **is the change in a company's owners' equity during a period that is the result of all nonowner transactions and activities.** Comprehensive income includes profits resulting from normal operating activities. It includes any event that changes owners' equity except those arising from dealings with the company's own stockholders. Accordingly, it excludes events such as selling stock or paying dividends. Comprehensive income also includes some activities that are not reported on the income statement.

Three items that are not included in net income are included as part of **other comprehensive income**. These are (a) gains or losses from holding certain marketable securities, (b) certain gains or losses from foreign currency effects on foreign subsidiaries, and (c) certain changes in the minimum liability for employee pensions. These items are reported as part of other comprehensive income that is included in stockholders' equity. Gains and losses from holding marketable securities are discussed in Chapter 11.

INTERNATIONAL

Foreign currency transactions occur when a corporation operates in other countries or owns subsidiaries outside the United States. These international activities involve currencies other than U.S. dollars. To prepare financial statements that are stated in U.S. dollars, those activities have to be translated from foreign currency amounts using exchange rates that are appropriate for the transaction. In some cases, U.S. currency must be exchanged for foreign currency or vice versa. Gains or losses can occur from changes in exchange rates. Gains or losses associated with foreign currency translations and exchanges are reported as part of other comprehensive income.

Changes in employee pension liabilities occur when estimates change about the amount a company can earn on assets it has invested to cover these liabilities or when other estimates change that affect the amount employees will receive in pension payments. These changes result in gains or losses that are reported as part of other comprehensive income.

Keep in mind that financial statements of actual companies can be complex because of the many types of business activities in which companies are involved. Understanding basic concepts of assets, liabilities, and owners' equity will help you interpret this information.

Self-Study Problem #2

Listed below are account balances, cash receipts and payments, and other data for Lewy Pasture, Inc., a company that distributes pharmaceutical supplies, for the fiscal year ended October 31, 2007.

Accounts payable	$ 22,000
Accounts receivable	11,000
Accumulated depreciation	164,000
Buildings	412,000
Cash	16,000
Common stock	300,000
Cost of goods sold	146,000
Dividends (declared and paid)	17,000
Equipment	245,000
General and administrative expenses	96,000
Goodwill	13,000
Income tax expense	14,000
Income tax payable	6,000
Interest expense	25,000
Interest payable	14,000
Land	35,000
Long-term investments	35,000
Merchandise inventory	62,000
Notes payable, current portion	10,000
Notes payable, long-term	278,000
Prepaid insurance	7,000
Retained earnings, October 31, 2006	25,000
Sales revenue	357,000
Selling expenses	47,000
Supplies	13,000
Wages payable	18,000

The average number of shares of common stock outstanding during the year was 10,000.

Required From the data presented on the previous page, determine the amount of each of the following items for Lewy Pasture's financial statements:

1. Gross profit
2. Income from operations
3. Net income
4. Earnings per share
5. Current assets
6. Land, buildings, and equipment
7. Other assets
8. Total assets
9. Current liabilities
10. Total liabilities
11. Retained earnings, October 31, 2007
12. Total stockholders' equity
13. Total liabilities and stockholders' equity

The solution to Self-Study Problem 2 appears at the end of the chapter.

THE STATEMENT OF STOCKHOLDERS' EQUITY

Objective 4
Explain information presented on a company's statement of stockholders' equity.

The statement of stockholders' equity provides information about changes in owners' equity for a corporation during a fiscal period. Exhibit 5 provides an example of this statement for Publix. Though Publix, like other corporations, presents three years of data for this statement in its annual report, only one year is included in Exhibit 5.

Exhibit 5 describes changes in the amount of stock, retained earnings, and comprehensive income during the 2004 fiscal year. The amount of stock issued changes when a company issues additional shares to stockholders or repurchases shares. Repurchased shares may be reissued at a later date, or they may be retired, as indicated in Exhibit 5.

EXHIBIT 5 Changes in Corporate Equity

Publix Super Markets, Inc.
Consolidated Statement of Stockholders' Equity (Excerpts)
Year Ended December 25, 2004

(Amounts are in thousands)

	Common Stock	Additional Paid-in Capital	Retained Earnings	Accumulated Other Comprehensive Earnings	Total Stock-holders' Equity
Balances at December 27, 2003	$178,369	494,154	2,492,759	4,028	3,169,310
Comprehensive earnings for the year	—	—	819,383	(1,479)	817,904
Cash dividends, $.45 per share	—	—	(80,764)	—	(80,764)
Contribution of shares to retirement plan	2,506	133,243	—	—	135,749
Sale of shares to stockholders	71	3,586	—	—	3,657
Retirement of shares	(8,354)	—	(451,786)	—	(460,140)
Balances at December 25, 2004	$172,592	630,983	2,779,592	2,549	3,585,716

Note: Adjustments have been made to the original to simplify the presentation.

The beginning and ending balances in the statement of stockholders' equity correspond with the balances in the stockholders' equity section of the company's balance sheet (Exhibit 4).

Retained earnings increased by the amount of net income earned in 2004. Retained earnings decreased by the amount of dividends paid or promised (declared) during the fiscal year. Dividends are not reported on the income statement because they are not expenses. They are a distribution of net income to owners. **Dividends are a reduction in retained earnings and are reported on the statement of stockholders' equity.**

Accumulated other comprehensive income increases (or decreases) by the amount of other comprehensive income reported during a fiscal period. The ending balance also is reported on the balance sheet as part of stockholders' equity; see Exhibit 4.

The ending balances on the statement of stockholders' equity are the amounts reported on the corporation's balance sheet for the same date. Compare the ending balances in each column of Exhibit 5 with the amounts in Exhibit 4. The statement of stockholders' equity describes the events that changed Publix's stockholders' equity during its 2004 fiscal year.

USE OF FINANCIAL STATEMENTS

Financial statements are a primary source of accounting information for external decision makers. External users analyze statements to evaluate the ability of an organization to use its resources effectively and efficiently. By comparing changes in assets, liabilities, earnings, and cash flows over time, users form expectations about return and risk. Comparisons across companies help determine which companies are being managed effectively and provide the best investment opportunities.

Later chapters of this book describe methods of analyzing and interpreting financial statements. The remainder of this chapter considers attributes of financial statements that decision makers should understand when interpreting them.

Interrelationships among Financial Statements

Taken as a whole, financial statements describe business activities that changed the financial condition of a company from the beginning to the end of a fiscal period. Information on the income statement and statement of cash flows explains changes in balance sheet accounts during a period.

The summary information presented in financial statements does not always provide sufficient detail to explain the change in every balance sheet account. Access to individual account balances would be necessary to provide a complete explanation. Nevertheless, the relationships among the financial statements are important. Balance sheets for the beginning and ending of a fiscal period reveal changes in a company's resources and finances. The company's income statement and statement of cash flows reveal major events that caused these changes. **The relationship among financial statements in which the numbers on one statement explain numbers on other statements is called** ***articulation.*** You should remember that a company's financial statements are not independent of each other. They work together to explain the events that changed the company's financial condition.

Limitations of Financial Statements

Objective 5
Identify some of the primary limitations of financial statements.

In spite of the abundant information financial statements provide, their usefulness is limited by certain constraints of the reporting process. Some of these limitations include:

1. Use of estimates and allocations
2. Use of historical costs

3. Omission of transactions
4. Omission of resources and costs
5. Delay in providing information

These constraints result primarily from costs associated with reporting financial information. Information is a resource, and it is costly to provide. Its value is determined by the benefits derived by those who use the information. For information to be valuable, its cost must be less than the benefits it provides to users. Therefore, the amount and type of reported information are constrained by costs and benefits.

The following paragraphs consider these limitations. Users should keep these limitations in mind when interpreting financial statement information.

Use of Estimates and Allocations. **Many of the numbers reported in financial statements result from estimates and allocations.** For example, depreciation is the allocation of asset costs to expenses over the estimated lives of the assets. These estimates often are not exact because the amount of the asset consumed in a particular fiscal period is difficult to determine. Decisions about when to recognize revenues and expenses frequently require management judgment. These subjective decisions and estimates mean that accounting numbers are not as precise as they might appear.

Use of Historical Costs. **Financial statements report primarily the historical cost of assets and liabilities.** ***Historical cost*** **is the purchase or exchange price of an asset or liability at the time it is acquired or incurred.** The recorded values are not adjusted for changes in the purchasing power of money or for changes in the current value of the assets or liabilities. The purchasing power of money changes over time because of inflation; for example, a dollar in 2007 buys less than a dollar bought in 1987. The current value of an asset is the amount at which that asset, in its current condition, could be bought or sold at the present time.

INTERNATIONAL

Certain assets and liabilities, particularly financial securities such as investments in stocks, are reported at market value in the United States. We will examine these reporting rules in a later chapter. Some countries, such as the United Kingdom and the Netherlands, permit plant assets and other items to be reported using current values. In these countries, assets and liabilities are restated to approximate their market values at the end of a fiscal period.

Omission of Transactions. Financial statements include the primary transactions that occur as part of a company's business activities. Nevertheless, **there is no guarantee that all important transactions are fully reported in a company's financial statements.** Some transactions do not result from specific exchanges. They result when revenues or expenses are allocated to fiscal periods. Accountants and managers sometimes disagree about when certain activities should be recognized. Also, they may disagree about the amount that should be reported in the financial statements for these activities. The accounting profession has debated extensively issues such as how to recognize the costs of employee retirement benefits. Today, companies report certain liabilities, assets, and expenses associated with these items that were not reported 10 years ago. Undoubtedly, other issues will arise that will alter information reported in the financial statements.

The importance of information changes over time. Companies develop new financing and compensation arrangements. Reporting rules for these arrangements may not be covered by existing GAAP. If the arrangements become common and new reporting rules would increase the benefits of information for users, GAAP may be created for transactions involving these new arrangements. GAAP are dynamic. They change as the needs of users and economic activities of organizations change.

Omission of Resources and Costs. **Certain types of resources and costs are not reported in financial statements.** The value of employees is not an asset listed on most balance sheets. Nevertheless, a well-trained and stable workforce and skilled managers may be the resource that adds the most to the value of many companies. Without skilled labor and management, the remaining resources of a company often would have little value. Financial statements do not report these human resources. They are not owned by a company, and their values are difficult and costly to determine. A major portion of the value of many companies derives from their research and development activities, which create new and improved products. The costs of these efforts are expensed when they are incurred each fiscal period even though they may have a major effect on the future earnings of a company. Such costs are expensed because of difficulty in identifying the timing and amount of future benefits a company will receive from these efforts. Nevertheless, the economic value of a company differs from the amount reported on its financial statements because of these measurement limitations.

Delay in Providing Information. **Financial statement information is not always timely.** Annual financial statements may lag actual events by a year or more; even monthly statements may lag events by several weeks. While such delays may not be a problem for certain types of decisions, they may be critical for others. Users often need more timely sources. Managers, in particular, may need information on an ongoing basis to make effective decisions. Traditional financial statements are only one type of accounting information. Because financial statements are costly to produce and distribute, external reporting is limited to distinct fiscal periods. In addition to annual financial reports, major corporations provide quarterly reports to stockholders. As information technology reduces the cost of reporting, more frequent reporting to external users may become feasible.

Though a variety of problems impair their usefulness, financial statements continue to be a primary source of information for managers and external users about a company's activities. But these problems mean that considerable care is needed to understand accounting information and to use it correctly in making decisions.

Self-Study Problem #3

A series of financial statement items is listed below.

Accounts payable	Notes payable
Accounts receivable	Patents
Buildings	Prepaid insurance
Common stock	Retained earnings
Cost of goods sold	Sales revenue
Depreciation expense	Stock issued
Dividends	Stock repurchased
Interest expense	Supplies
Interest payable	Wages expense
Merchandise	Wages payable

Required For each account, indicate the financial statement (income statement, balance sheet, or statement of stockholders' equity) on which the account would appear.

The solution to Self-Study Problem 3 appears at the end of the chapter.

THINKING BEYOND THE QUESTION

HOW DO WE REPORT EARNINGS AND FINANCIAL POSITION TO STOCKHOLDERS?

This chapter describes important rules for corporations and other businesses when they report financial information to external users. We considered the need for separating ordinary revenues and expenses from those, such as interest revenue or expense, that are secondary to a business's primary purpose. Corporations report corporate taxes and earnings per share as part of their income statements. Balance sheets should distinguish between current and long-term assets and liabilities and should report details about common stock issued by a corporation. Changes in stockholders' equity should be described in the statement of stockholders' equity.

Why is it important for businesses to follow specific rules and use common formats in reporting their business activities? What would be the consequences for businesses and the economy if individual companies were permitted to select their own reporting rules?

Self-Study Problem Solutions

SSP-1 (Answers in millions except numbers of shares)

1. Revenue from operations	\$51,407
2. Gross profit (51,407 − 25,076)	\$26,331
3. Interest expense	\$629
4. Number of shares outstanding (\$6,481 net income ÷ \$2.46 basic earnings per share) = 2,635 million shares	
5. Total product costs	\$25,076
6. Net income	\$6,481
7. Net cash from operations cannot be determined from the income statement.	

SSP-2

1. Gross profit:	
Sales revenue	\$357,000
Cost of goods sold	146,000
Gross profit	\$211,000
2. Income from operations:	
Gross profit	\$211,000
General and administrative expenses	96,000
Selling expenses	47,000
Income from operations	\$ 68,000
3. Net income:	
Income from operations	\$ 68,000
Interest expense	25,000
Income tax expense	14,000
Net income	\$ 29,000
4. Earnings per share:	
Net income ÷ shares of common stock (\$29,000 ÷ 10,000) = \$2.90	
5. Current assets:	
Cash	\$ 16,000
Accounts receivable	11,000
Merchandise inventory	62,000
Supplies	13,000
Prepaid insurance	7,000
Current assets	\$109,000

6. Land, buildings, and equipment:

Land	$ 35,000
Buildings	412,000
Equipment	245,000
Accumulated depreciation	(164,000)
Land, buildings, and equipment	$528,000

7. Other assets:

Long-term investments	$ 35,000
Goodwill	13,000
Other assets	$ 48,000

8. Total assets:

Current assets	$109,000
Land, buildings, and equipment	528,000
Other assets	48,000
Total assets	$685,000

9. Current liabilities:

Accounts payable	$ 22,000
Wages payable	18,000
Interest payable	14,000
Income tax payable	6,000
Notes payable, current portion	10,000
Current liabilities	$ 70,000

10. Total liabilities:

Current liabilities	$ 70,000
Notes payable, long-term	278,000
Total liabilities	$348,000

11. Retained earnings, October 31, 2007:

Retained earnings, October 31, 2006	$ 25,000
Net income	29,000
Dividends	(17,000)
Retained earnings, October 31, 2007	$ 37,000

12. Total stockholders' equity:

Common stock	$300,000
Retained earnings	37,000
Stockholders' equity	$337,000

13. Total liabilities and stockholders' equity:

Total liabilities	$348,000
Stockholders' equity	337,000
Total liabilities and stockholders' equity	$685,000

SSP-3

Item	Financial Statement
Accounts payable	Balance sheet
Accounts receivable	Balance sheet
Buildings	Balance sheet
Common stock	Balance sheet and statement of stockholders' equity
Cost of goods sold	Income statement
Depreciation expense	Income statement
Dividends	Statement of stockholders' equity
Interest expense	Income statement
Interest payable	Balance sheet
Merchandise	Balance sheet
Notes payable	Balance sheet
Patents	Balance sheet

Prepaid insurance	Balance sheet
Retained earnings	Balance sheet and statement of stockholders' equity
Sales revenue	Income statement
Stock issued	Statement of stockholders' equity
Stock repurchased	Statement of stockholders' equity
Supplies	Balance sheet
Wages expense	Income statement
Wages payable	Balance sheet

Define *Terms and Concepts Defined in This Chapter*

articulation (142)
common stock (132)
comprehensive income (139)
consolidated financial statements (133)
cost of services sold (131)
current assets (136)
current liabilities (136)
current ratio (137)
depletion (136)
dividends (130)
earnings per share (132)
fixed assets (136)
gross profit (131)
historical cost (143)
intangible assets (139)
liquid assets (136)
long-term investments (139)
long-term liabilities (136)
operating expenses (131)
operating income (131)
parent (133)
plant assets (136)
property and equipment (136)
statement of stockholders' equity (130)
subsidiaries (133)
total revenue (134)
working capital (137)
working capital ratio (137)

Review *Summary of Important Concepts*

1. Financial statements report business activities.
   a. Financial statements include the balance sheet, the income statement, the statement of cash flows, and the statement of stockholders' equity.
   b. The income statement reports on the accrual basis the results of a company's operations for a fiscal period. It reports information about the creation and consumption of resources in producing and selling goods and services.
   c. A balance sheet identifies asset, liability, and owners' equity account balances at the end of a fiscal period. Balance sheets classify accounts into current and long-term asset and liability categories. Comparative balance sheets report account balances for more than one fiscal period.
   d. The statement of stockholders' equity describes the results of transactions that have changed the amount of stockholders' equity of a corporation during a fiscal period.
2. The interrelated financial statements, as a set, describe the financial effects of business activities of a company from the beginning to the end of a fiscal period.
3. Consolidated financial statements report the economic activities of a parent and its subsidiaries as though they were one business entity.
4. Financial statements have limitations that affect the usefulness of the information the statements report. These limitations include the need for estimates of financial results, the use of historical costs for representing asset values, and incomplete measures for some resources or transactions that might affect a company's value.

Questions

Q4-1 *Obj. 1* Are dividends an expense? Sometimes? Always? Never? Explain.

Q4-2 *Obj. 1* Identify three questions that can be answered by reviewing a firm's income statement but that cannot be answered by reviewing the firm's balance sheet or statement of stockholders' equity. Be specific.

Q4-3 *Obj. 1* Identify three questions that can be answered by reviewing a firm's balance sheet but that cannot be answered by reviewing the firm's income statement or statement of stockholders' equity. Be specific.

Q4-4 *Obj. 2* Why are there so many different sections of information on an income statement?

Q4-5 *Obj. 2* Why does a parent company prepare consolidated financial statements?

Q4-6 *Obj. 2* A friend says, "The income statement doesn't reveal anything about the amount of cash that was received from sales during a fiscal period." Do you agree with this statement? Why or why not?

Q4-7 *Obj. 3* Explain the difference between a classified balance sheet and a comparative balance sheet.

Q4-8 *Obj. 3* Assume you are reviewing a balance sheet that has assets listed on the left side and liabilities and owners' equity on the right side. What question or questions are answered by looking at the information on the left side of the balance sheet? What question or questions are answered by looking at the information on the right side of the balance sheet?

Q4-9 *Obj. 4* If all of the stockholders' equity accounts are reported on the balance sheet, why is the statement of stockholders' equity necessary?

Q4-10 *Obj. 4* The statement of stockholders' equity can be thought of as a bridge between the income statement and the balance sheet? Why?

Q4-11 *Obj. 4* What does the term *articulation* mean as applied to accounting and financial reporting?

Q4-12 *Objs. 2, 3, 4* How do the purpose of the income statement, the purpose of the balance sheet, and the purpose of the statement of stockholders' equity differ?

Q4-13 *Obj. 5* Why is the use of historical cost information a limitation of financial statements?

Q4-14 *Obj. 5* It is often said that measuring performance for a fiscal period requires periodic measurement and the use of estimates and approximations. Do you agree that this is true? Why or why not?

Exercises

E4-1 Write a short definition for each of the terms listed in the *Terms and Concepts Defined in this Chapter* section.

E4-2 *Obj. 1* A list of information contained in financial statements is provided below. For each item, indicate which financial statement provides the information.

a. Changes in a corporation's stockholders' equity for a fiscal period
b. The dollar amount of resources available at a particular date

c. The amount of credit sales not yet collected
d. Accrual-based operating results for a fiscal period
e. The cost of resources consumed in producing revenues for a period
f. The sources of finances used to acquire resources
g. The effect of issuing stock on the amount of contributed capital during a period
h. The amount of profit earned during a period
i. Revenues generated during a fiscal period

E4-3 *Obj. 1* For each of the items listed below, indicate the financial statement (or statements) for which the information is true. Use *I* to indicate income statement, *B* to indicate balance sheet, and *SE* to indicate statement of stockholders' equity. If the item below is not true for any of the three financial statements, indicate with an *N*.

1. The statement provides information about resources consumed during an accounting period.
2. The portion of profits that were distributed to owners of the firm is disclosed.
3. The current market value of the firm's resources is reported.
4. The statement is dated as of a specific point in time.
5. The amounts that are owed to other organizations or individuals are reported.
6. The total amount of capital that has been contributed to the organization is reported.
7. The amount of capital that has been contributed to the organization during the accounting period just ended is reported.
8. Information is reported regarding the rewards that have been earned from serving customers during the accounting period just ended.
9. The statement is not as of a specific date, but covers a period of time.
10. Reports information that has been developed on the accrual basis.
11. The statement contains information about the financial sacrifices that were made to acquire resources.
12. The statement contains information concerning contributed capital.
13. The statement contains information concerning the results of operating activities.
14. The amount of stock sold during the accounting period just ended is disclosed.
15. The information provided links two other statements.

E4-4 *Obj. 2* Alex didn't study very hard when he took accounting because he thought he wouldn't ever use it on the job at Valentine Company. Yesterday, after preparing all end-of-the-month adjusting entries, both of the company's accounting staff became ill. The company owner, knowing that Alex had taken accounting as part of his college major, asked him to finish the job by preparing

Valentine Company Income Statement at September 30, 2007	
Sales revenue	$ 48,500
Wages expense	11,369
Operating income	**$37,131**
Operating expenses:	
Advertising	3,133
Cost of goods sold	30,070
Insurance	670
Interest expense	240
Utilities	1,250
Gross profit	**$ 1,768**
Depreciation expense	282
Pretax income	**$ 1,486**
Income tax expense	519
Net income	$ 967

(Continued)

the financial statements. The owner needs the statements tomorrow to present to her banker. Alex isn't sure that his income statement is prepared properly.

Alex is confident that each revenue account and expense account balance is correct because those were determined by the accounting staff. He is unsure, however, that he has organized them properly on the income statement. Therefore, he is unsure about the summary amounts listed in bold-faced print on the statement.

Rearrange the accounts into proper income statement format. Be sure to date the statement correctly.

E4-5 *Obj. 2* Downhill Inc. sells, rents, and services ski equipment. Information about the company's financial performance for a recent fiscal period is provided below.

Average shares outstanding	20,000
Cost of goods sold	$36,000
Debt outstanding	65,000
General and administrative expenses	12,000
Income tax expense	20,000
Interest expense	7,500
Payments to owners	30,000
Rental revenue	50,000
Sales revenue	81,000
Selling expense	28,000
Service revenue	23,000

From the information provided, compute the following amounts for the period:

a. Gross profit
b. Operating expenses
c. Income from operations
d. Pretax income
e. Net income
f. Earnings per share

E4-6 *Obj. 2* Flowers by Freddie presented the income statement below for its most recent fiscal year. The items have been numbered for convenience in analysis.

(1) Sales revenue	$371,923
(2) Cost of goods sold	201,668
(3) Gross profit	$170,255
(4) Operating expenses	72,853
(5) Operating income	$ 97,402
(6) Other revenues	538
(7) Other expenses	(13,227)
(8) Pretax income	$ 84,713
(9) Income taxes	29,650
(10) Net income	$ 55,063

Answer the following questions. Be specific. Give examples to clarify.

a. What is the difference between the revenue listed in item 1 and that listed in item 6?
b. What does item 3 represent, and why is it important?
c. What do items 2, 4, and 7 have in common?
d. How are items 2, 4, and 7 different from one another?
e. How is item 9 similar to items 2, 4, and 7?
f. Why do you think items 2, 4, 7, and 9 are listed separately on an income statement rather than being lumped together as one item?

E4-7 *Obj. 2* An income statement for **Continental Airlines, Inc.**, for a recent fiscal year is provided below.

Continental Airlines, Inc. Consolidated Statements of Operations	
Year Ended December 31, 2004	
(In millions, except per share data)	
OPERATING REVENUE:	
Passenger	$8,984
Cargo, mail and other	760
	9,744
OPERATING EXPENSES:	
Wages, salaries and related costs	2,819
Aircraft fuel and related taxes	1,587
ExpressJet capacity purchase, net	1,351
Aircraft rentals	891
Landing fees and other rentals	646
Commissions, booking fees, credit card fees and other distribution costs	552
Maintenance, materials and repairs	414
Depreciation and amortization	414
Passenger servicing	306
Special charges	121
Other	872
	9,973
OPERATING INCOME (LOSS)	(229)
NONOPERATING INCOME (EXPENSE):	
Interest expense	(389)
Interest capitalized	14
Interest income	29
Income from affiliates	118
Other, net	17
	(211)
INCOME (LOSS) BEFORE INCOME TAXES AND MINORITY INTEREST	(440)
INCOME TAX BENEFIT	77
NET INCOME (LOSS)	$ (363)

Note: Slight modifications have been made to the statement to simplify the presentation.

Use this income statement to answer the following questions:

a. What was Continental's primary source of revenue?
b. What percentage of Continental's revenue came from this source?
c. What were its largest expenses?
d. How much revenue did Continental earn from transporting passengers?
e. How much revenue did it earn from operating activities other than transporting passengers?
f. How much revenue did it earn from nonoperating activities?
g. How much operating income did Continental earn (or lose)?
h. How much expense did it incur for nonoperating activities?
i. How much profit or loss did Continental report during the fiscal year?

E4-8 *Obj. 2* A recent income statement for Harley-Davidson is provided below.

Harley-Davidson, Inc. Consolidated Statements of Income Years ended December 31, 2004, 2003 and 2002	2004	2003	2002
(In thousands, except per share amounts)			
Net revenue	$5,015,190	$4,624,274	$4,090,970
Cost of goods sold	3,115,655	2,958,708	2,673,129
Gross profit	1,899,535	1,665,566	1,417,841
Financial services income	305,262	279,459	211,500
Financial services expense	116,662	111,586	107,273
Operating income from financial services	188,600	167,873	104,227
Selling, administrative and engineering expense	726,644	684,175	639,366
Income from operations	1,361,491	1,149,264	882,702
Investment income, net	23,101	23,088	16,541
Other, net	(5,106)	(6,317)	(13,416)
Income before provision for income taxes	1,379,486	1,166,035	885,827
Provision for income taxes	489,720	405,107	305,610
Net income	$ 889,766	$ 760,928	$ 580,217
Basic earnings per common share	$ 3.02	$ 2.52	$ 1.92
Diluted earnings per common share	$ 3.00	$ 2.50	$ 1.90
Cash dividends per common share	$ .405	$ .195	$ .135

Use this financial statement to answer the following questions for 2004:

a. How much revenue did Harley-Davidson earn from selling motorcycles?
b. How much revenue did it earn from providing financial services?
c. How much revenue did it earn from nonoperating activities?
d. What amount of gross profit did Harley-Davidson earn? Express your answer in both dollars and as a percentage of net revenue.
e. Approximately how many shares of stock did Harley-Davidson have outstanding during the year?
f. How much income from operations did Harley-Davidson earn during the year? Express your answer in both dollars and as a percentage of total revenues (net revenue from the sale of motorcycles plus financial services income).
g. Can the amount of cash Harley-Davidson received from its operating activities during the year be determined from the income statement? If so, what is the amount? If not, why not?

E4-9 *Obj. 2* SuperQuick Computer Corporation reported the following income statement for a recent quarter.

Consolidated Statement of Income For the Quarter Ended December 31, 2007	
Sales	$719,150
Cost of sales	549,313
	169,837
Research and development costs	16,900
Selling, general, and administrative expense	83,771
Other income and expense, net	7,685
	108,356
Income before income taxes	61,481
Provision for income taxes	15,451
Net income	$ 46,030
Earnings per share	$0.93

Assume that Other Income and Expense are nonoperating.

a. What was the company's gross profit for the quarter?
b. What was the amount of the company's product costs expensed during the quarter?
c. What was the amount of its operating expenses?
d. What was the amount of its operating income?
e. What was the amount of its nonoperating income or expense?

E4-10 *Obj. 2* BioTek's 2007 annual report included the following income statement information.

(In millions, except earnings per share)

Year Ended June 30	**2005**	**2006**	**2007**
Revenue	$8,671	$11,358	**$14,484**
Operating expenses:			
Cost of revenue	1,188	1,085	**1,197**
Research and development	1,432	1,925	**2,502**
Acquired in-process technology	0	0	**296**
Sales and marketing	2,657	2,856	**3,412**
General and administrative	316	362	**433**
Other expenses	19	259	**230**
Total operating expenses	5,612	6,487	**8,070**
Operating income	3,059	4,871	**6,414**
Interest income	320	443	**703**
Income before income taxes	3,379	5,314	**7,117**
Provision for income taxes	1,184	1,860	**2,627**
Net income	$2,195	$ 3,454	**$ 4,490**
Earnings per share	$0.86	$1.32	**$1.67**

Ratios often are used to assess changes in financial statement information over time. Use Bio-Tek's income statements to answer the following questions. Express your answers as percentages.

a. What was the ratio of net income to net revenues each year?
b. What was the ratio of cost of revenues (cost of goods sold) to net revenues each year?
c. What was the ratio of operating expenses to net revenues each year?
d. What was the percentage change in net income between 2005 and 2006 and between 2006 and 2007? (Hint: Divide the increase in net income from one year to the next by the net income for the earlier year.)
e. Did Bio-Tek's operating results improve between 2005 and 2007? Explain your answer.

E4-11 *Obj. 3* Listed below are selected account balances for Hemmingway Company for June 30.

Accounts payable	$ 95,300	Merchandise inventory	$390,000
Accounts receivable	78,100	Notes payable, current portion	50,000
Accumulated depreciation	318,000	Notes payable, long-term	571,300
Buildings	750,000	Prepaid insurance	38,000
Cash	34,500	Retained earnings	279,000
Contributed capital	700,000	Supplies on hand	52,000
Cost of goods sold	840,000	Trademarks	45,000
Equipment	450,000	Wages expense	375,000
Interest payable	38,000	Wages payable	36,000
Land	250,000		

Determine each of the following amounts. (Hint: Not all items will be used.)

a. Current assets
b. Current liabilities
c. Property, plant, and equipment
d. Total assets
e. Long-term liabilities

(Continued)

f. Total liabilities
g. Stockholders' equity
h. Total liabilities and stockholders' equity
i. Working capital

E4-12 *Obj. 3* Advances Unlimited reported the following information at January 31.

Accounts payable	$ 275
Accounts receivable	1,057
Accrued expenses (current)	348
Cash and equivalents	351
Contributed capital	319
Deferred income taxes (liabilities)	275
Income taxes payable (current)	93
Inventories	759
Long-term debt	650
Other current assets	109
Other current liabilities	46
Other long-term assets	248
Other long-term liabilities	61
Property and equipment, net of depreciation	1,667
Retained earnings, net of adjustments	2,124

Accrued expenses are current liabilities. Deferred income taxes are long-term liabilities.

Use the information provided to prepare a balance sheet for Advances Unlimited in good form.

E4-13 *Obj. 3* The accounting staff at Marvelous Enterprises prepares monthly financial statements. At the end of April, the company's ledger accounts have the following balances. All adjusting entries have been made and the next step is to prepare the financial statements. The company has 18,200 shares of stock outstanding.

Accounts payable	$17,000	Land	$45,000
Accounts receivable	14,700	Long-term notes payable	33,000
Accumulated depreciation	13,100	Merchandise inventory	12,480
Buildings	50,000	Notes payable, current portion	14,200
Cash	10,360	Patents	3,300
Contributed capital	38,770	Prepaid insurance	1,100
Copyrights and trademarks	5,000	Retained earnings, March 31	8,400
Cost of goods sold	15,050	Sales revenue	26,000
Depreciation expense	1,100	Supplies	3,570
Dividends declared	1,200	Supplies expense	1,300
Income tax expense	1,060	Wage expense	1,500
Insurance expense	550	Wages payable	17,700
Interest expense	900		

Prepare a classified balance sheet in proper format. (Show land separately.) Use a three-line heading on the statement that includes (1) the name of the company, (2) the name of the statement, and (3) the appropriate date. Explain how you determined the April 30 balance in Retained Earnings.

E4-14 *Obj. 3* Jenny didn't study very hard when she took accounting because she thought she would never use it on the job at Tech-Noid Company. Yesterday, after preparing all end-of-the-month adjusting entries, the company's accountant became ill. The company asked Jenny to finish the job by preparing the financial statements. The owner needs the statements tomorrow to present to his banker. Jenny is having trouble getting the balance sheet to balance.

Tech-Noid Company Balance Sheet January 31, 2007			
Assets		**Liabilities and Stockholders' Equity**	
Current assets:		**Current liabilities:**	
Inventory	$1,121	Accounts payable	$ 231
Interest payable	100	Accounts receivable	691
Land	2,200	Wages payable	636
Noncurrent assets:		**Long-term liabilities:**	
Buildings and equipment	4,990	7%, 10-year note payable	2,000
Retained earnings	1,398	Accumulated depreciation	531
		Stockholders' equity:	
		Contributed capital	4,230
		Cash	124
Total assets	$9,809	Total liabilities and equity	$8,443

a. Help Jenny by making a list of the five account categories that are printed in bold-face type on the balance sheet. Leave three lines between each category listed. For each category, write the names of Tech-Noid's accounts that should be reported under it on the balance sheet.

b. Determine the correct balance sheet amounts for:

1. total current assets
2. total noncurrent assets
3. total assets
4. total current liabilities
5. total long-term liabilities
6. total stockholders' equity
7. total liabilities and equity

E4-15 *Objs. 2, 3* Listed below are account balances and other data for Hands & Eyes, Inc., a company that sells crafts and decorative supplies, for the fiscal year ended December 31, 2007.

Accounts payable	$ 41,000	Interest payable	$ 31,000
Accounts receivable	29,000	Land	65,000
Accumulated depreciation	180,000	Long-term investments	46,000
Buildings	430,000	Merchandise inventory	79,000
Cash	35,000	Notes payable, current portion	25,000
Contributed capital	315,000	Notes payable, long-term	307,000
Cost of goods sold	130,000	Prepaid insurance	22,000
Dividends (declared and paid)	22,000	Retained earnings,	
Equipment	262,000	Dec. 31, 2006	19,000
General and administrative		Sales revenue	373,000
expenses	98,000	Selling expenses	34,000
Income tax expense	8,000	Supplies	25,000
Income tax payable	22,000	Trademarks	31,000
Interest expense	33,000	Wages payable	36,000
Shares of common stock outstanding:	20,000		

From the data presented above, determine the amount of each of the items that follow. (Hint: Pretax income for the year 2007 = $78,000.)

1. Gross profit
2. Operating income
3. Net income
4. Earnings per share
5. Current assets
6. Property, plant, and equipment
7. Other assets
8. Total assets
9. Current liabilities
10. Working capital and working capital ratio
11. Total liabilities
12. Retained earnings, December 31, 2007
13. Total stockholders' equity
14. Total liabilities and stockholders' equity

E4-16 *Objs. 2, 3, 4* Listed below are typical accounts or titles that appear on financial statements. For each item, identify the financial statement(s) on which it appears.

a. Loss on sale of equipment
b. Taxes payable
c. Trademark
d. Accumulated other comprehensive income
e. Current assets
f. Investments
g. Rental revenue
h. Gross profit
i. Earnings per share
j. Accumulated depreciation
k. Net income
l. Minority interest
m. Contributed capital
n. Operating income
o. Common stock issued during year

E4-17 *Objs. 2, 3, 4* A list of financial statement items is given below.

1. Accounts receivable
2. Rent payable
3. Retained earnings
4. Cost of sales
5. Prepaid rent
6. Supplies expense
7. Equipment
8. Dividends
9. Depreciation expense
10. Copyrights
11. Accrued liabilities
12. Wages payable
13. Land
14. Notes payable
15. Service revenue
16. Inventory
17. Advertising expense
18. Common stock

Use the format shown below.

a. For each account, indicate the financial statement on which the account would appear.
b. Identify the information provided by the account. The first item is completed as an example:

Item	*Financial Statement*	*Information Provided*
1. Accounts receivable	Balance sheet	Cash to be received in the future from prior sales

E4-18 *Obj. 4* Listed below are financial statements for the Sunflower Company.

Income Statement For the Year Ended December 31, 2007	
Sales revenue	$ 20,000
Cost of sales	(12,000)
Gross profit	$ 8,000
Operating expenses	(4,000)
Selling and administrative expenses	(3,000)
Net income	$ 1,000

Statement of Stockholders' Equity
For the Year Ended December 31, 2007

	Contributed Capital	Retained Earnings	Total
Balance at December 31, 2006	$5,000	$13,000	$18,000
Common stock issued	2,000		2,000
Net income		1,000	1,000
Dividends		(4,000)	(4,000)
Balance at December 31, 2007	$7,000	$10,000	$17,000

Balance Sheet
as of December 31, 2007

Assets:		Liabilities and Stockholders' Equity	
Cash	$ 9,000	Accounts payable	$ 5,000
Accounts receivable	3,000	Notes payable	8,000
Inventory	2,000	Common stock	7,000
Land	16,000	Retained earnings	10,000
Total	$30,000	Total	$30,000

a. Describe what is meant by the term *articulation.*
b. What evidence of articulation is there in this set of financial statements?

E4-19 *Obj. 4*

Crane Pool Corporation reported the following selected information for its 2007 fiscal year.

Contributed capital at June 30, 2006	$ 657
Retained earnings at June 30, 2006	1,536
Dividends	222
Net income	953
Common stock issued	243

Use this information to prepare a statement of stockholders' equity for Crane Pool for the year ended June 30, 2007.

E4-20 *Objs. 2, 4*

Use the information provided in Exercise 4-13.

a. Prepare an income statement following the format shown in Exhibit 1. (List expenses separately.)
b. Prepare a statement of stockholders' equity in good form.

(Hint: There was no change in contributed capital during the month.) For each statement, use a three-line heading on the statement that includes (1) the name of the company, (2) the name of the statement, and (3) the appropriate time period or date.

Problems

P4-1 *Obj. 1*

IDENTIFYING THE PURPOSE OF FINANCIAL STATEMENTS

Assume you are a financial manager with a U.S. corporation. A. Suliman is a recently employed manager in the Middle Eastern division of your corporation and a visitor to the United States. He has little familiarity with financial reporting practices in the United States. Your boss has given you the responsibility of explaining financial reports to Mr. Suliman.

Required Write a short report describing each of the four basic corporate financial statements for Suliman. Make sure you are clear about the purpose of each statement and its contents. Also, consider the information these statements provide about a company's resources.

P4-2 ETHICAL ISSUES IN FINANCIAL REPORTING

Obj. 1

Flower Childs is a regional sales manager for Green-Grow, Inc., a producer of garden supplies. The company's fiscal year ends on April 30. In mid-April, Flower is contacted by the president of Green-Grow. He indicates that the company is facing a financial problem. Two years ago, the company borrowed heavily from several banks to buy a competing company and to increase production of its primary products: insecticides and fertilizers. As a part of the loan agreement, Green-Grow must maintain a working capital ratio of 1.5 to 1 and earn a net income of at least $2 per share. If the company fails to meet these requirements, as reflected in its annual financial statements, the banks can restrict future credit for the company or require early payment of its loans, potentially forcing the company into bankruptcy.

The president explains that this fiscal year has been a difficult one for Green-Grow. Sales have slipped because of increased competition, and the rising prices of chemicals have increased the company's production costs. The company is in danger of not meeting the loan requirements. The company could be forced to make drastic cuts or to liquidate its assets. The president informs Flower that her job could be in danger. The president asks her to help with the problem by dating all sales invoices that clear her office during the first half of May as though the sales had been made in April. May is a month of heavy sales volume for the company as retail stores stock up for the coming season. The president believes that the added sales would be sufficient to get the company past the loan problem. He explains that this procedure will be used only this one time. By next year, the company will be in better shape because of new products it is developing. Also, he reminds Flower that her bonus for the year will be higher because of the additional sales that will be recorded for April. He points out that the company is fundamentally in sound financial shape, and that he would hate to see its future jeopardized by a minor bookkeeping problem. He is asking for the cooperation of all of the regional sales managers. He argues that the stockholders, employees, and managers will all be better off if the sales are predated. He wants Flower's assurance that she will cooperate.

Required

A. What effect will predating the sales have on Green-Grow's balance sheet, income statement, and statement of cash flows? Be specific about which accounts will be affected and why.
B. How will this practice solve the company's problem with the banks?
C. What would be the appropriate behavior for the company president under the circumstances the company is facing?
D. What would be the appropriate behavior for Flower?

P4-3 IDENTIFYING AND CORRECTING ERRORS IN AN INCOME STATEMENT

Obj. 2

Just after preparing the adjusting entries for the year, the long-time controller at Parrot Company took a leave of absence. Her inexperienced assistant did his best to prepare financial statements from the information the controller had left behind. He had particular difficulty with the income statement.

The item labeled sales expense is the sum of the amounts charged customers during the year for goods and services provided.

Income Statement December 31, 2007		
Sales expense		$260,722
Cost of goods sold		102,690
Net profit		$158,032
Operating expenses:		
Wages	$59,780	
Utilities	9,002	
Interest	14,420	
Depreciation	13,510	
Total operating expense		97,712
Operating income		$ 60,320
Advertising expense		9,968
Pretax income		$ 50,352
Income tax expense		13,150
Net income		$ 63,502
Earnings per share of common stock ($64,502 ÷ 15,000 shares)		$4.30

Required

A. Identify and list the errors in the income statement.
B. Prepare a corrected income statement.

P4-4 INTERPRETING AN INCOME STATEMENT

Obj. 2

Microsoft Corporation's 2004 annual report included the following income statement information.

Microsoft Corporation
Income Statements

(In millions, except earnings per share)			
Year Ended June 30	**2002**	**2003**	**2004**
Revenue	$28,365	$32,187	**$36,835**
Operating expenses:			
Cost of revenue	5,699	6,059	**6,716**
Research and development	6,299	6,595	**7,779**
Sales and marketing	6,252	7,562	**8,309**
General and administrative	1,843	2,426	**4,997**
Total operating expenses	20,093	22,642	**27,801**
Operating income	8,272	9,545	**9,034**
Losses on equity investees and other	(92)	(68)	**(25)**
Investment income/(loss)	(305)	1,577	**3,187**
Income before income taxes	7,875	11,054	**12,196**
Provision for income taxes	2,520	3,523	**4,028**
Net income	$ 5,355	$ 7,531	**$ 8,168**
Earnings per share:			
Basic	$ 0.50	$ 0.70	**$ 0.76**
Diluted	$ 0.48	$ 0.69	**$ 0.75**
Weighted average shares outstanding:			
Basic	10,811	10,723	**10,803**
Diluted	11,106	10,882	**10,894**

Required Ratios often are used to assess changes in financial statement information over time. Use Microsoft's income statements to answer the following questions. Express your answers as percentages.

A. What was the ratio of net income to revenue each year?
B. What was the ratio of cost of revenue (cost of goods sold) to revenue each year?
C. What was the ratio of operating expenses to revenue each year?
D. What was the percentage change in net income between 2002 and 2003, and between 2003 and 2004? (Hint: Divide the increase in net income from 2002 and 2003 by the net income for 2002.)
E. Did Microsoft's operating results improve between 2002 and 2003? Between 2003 and 2004? Explain your answers.

P4-5 COMPREHENSIVE INCOME

Objs. 2, 3, 4

The Lo Company imports and sells Chinese furniture in the United States. Its new accountant has been assigned the task of preparing the income statement. She knows that the FASB is now requiring that certain unrealized gains and losses be reported as part of comprehensive income. She has the following information available for the year just ended.

1. Loss on cumulative effect of change of depreciation method, net of tax	$ 840
2. Gain from disposal of discontinued operations, net of tax	3,500
3. Cost of goods sold	180,000
4. Revenue received in advance	2,500
5. Work in process inventory	135,000
6. Interest expense	4,000
7. Provision for income tax	11,700
8. Sale of treasury stock at a price greater than cost	5,050

(Continued)

9. Sales revenue	$250,000
10. Unrealized gain on increase of market value of investment	1,240
11. Sale of stock to investors	60,300
12. General and administrative expense	27,000
13. Gain on retirement of debt	4,200
14. Unrealized loss on foreign currency translation (regarding foreign subsidiary)	3,600
15. Cash received from customers	75,000
16. Dividends paid to shareholders	8,000

Required

A. From the information given above, decide which items should appear in the income statement, which would appear on a separate statement of comprehensive income, and which would not appear on either. If an item does not appear on either statement, indicate where it would be found. Also indicate which are transactions with owners.

B. Using the information above, prepare an income statement and a separate statement of comprehensive income.

P4-6 READING AND INTERPRETING A BALANCE SHEET

Obj. 3

A recent balance sheet for **Walt Disney Company** is provided below.

Walt Disney Company
Consolidated Balance Sheets

(In millions, except per share data)

September 30	2004	2003
ASSETS		
Current Assets		
Cash and cash equivalents	$ 2,042	$ 1,583
Receivables	4,558	4,238
Inventories	775	703
Television costs (current)	484	568
Other assets	1,510	1,222
Total current assets	9,369	8,314
Film and television costs	5,938	6,205
Investments	1,292	1,849
Parks, resorts and other property, at cost		
Attractions, buildings and equipment	28,147	21,472
Accumulated depreciation	(11,665)	(8,794)
	16,482	12,678
Intangible assets, net	19,781	19,752
Other assets	1,040	1,190
Total assets	$53,902	$49,988
LIABILITIES AND STOCKHOLDERS' EQUITY		
Current Liabilities		
Accounts payable and other accrued liabilities	$ 5,623	$ 5,044
Current portion of borrowings	4,093	2,457
Unearned royalties and other advances	1,343	1,168
Total current liabilities	11,059	8,669
Borrowings	9,395	10,643
Other noncurrent liabilities	6,569	6,457
Minority interests	798	428
Stockholders' Equity		
Common stock	12,447	12,154
Retained earnings	15,732	13,817
Adjustments	(2,098)	(2,180)
Total stockholders' equity	26,081	23,791
Total liabilities and stockholders' equity	$53,902	$49,988

Note: Slight modifications have been made to the format of the statement to simplify the presentation.

Required Respond to the following questions.

A. Do you agree that Disney's balance sheet is both classified and comparative? Explain why or why not.
B. At year-end 2004, what percentage of total assets was composed of current assets? Had this percentage increased or decreased since year-end 2003?
C. What was Disney's amount of working capital at year-end 2004? Did it change significantly from year-end 2003?
D. Compute the working capital ratio at year-end 2004 and year-end 2003. Did it improve or deteriorate between 2003 and 2004?
E. Film and television costs is the amount paid to produce movies or television shows. Explain why it appears in two places on the balance sheet.
F. What were the amounts of total assets, total liabilities, and stockholders' equity at year-end 2004 and year-end 2003?
G. Did Disney's overall financial position improve between 2003 and 2004? Explain.

P4-7 IDENTIFYING AND CORRECTING ERRORS IN A BALANCE SHEET

Obj. 3

Ceramics Inc. reported the following balance sheet for the year 2007.

Balance Sheet For the year ending December 31, 2007	
Assets:	
Cash	$ 2,000
Accounts payable	500
Inventory	900
Equipment	1,000
Land	1,500
Total assets	$ 6,000
Liabilities:	
Accounts receivable	$ 3,000
Accrued liabilities	1,000
Total liabilities	$ 4,000
Stockholders' equity:	
Common stock	1,800
Retained earnings	5,100
Total stockholders' equity	$ 6,900
Total liabilities and stockholders' equity	$10,900

Required

A. Identify and list the errors in the balance sheet above.
B. Prepare a corrected balance sheet.

P4-8 INTERPRETING AN INCOME STATEMENT

Obj. 2

A recent Consolidated Statement of Income for the **Coca-Cola Company** and Subsidiaries is presented at the top of the following page.

Required

A. What is the amount of cost of goods sold for 2004, 2003, and 2002? What kinds of costs are included in cost of goods sold?
B. What does gross profit represent? Calculate gross profit as a percentage of net operating revenues for each year. What do you observe?
C. How does gross profit differ from operating income?
D. Was Coca-Cola more profitable in 2004 than in 2003? Explain.

(Continued)

Consolidated Statements of Income
The Coca-Cola Company and Subsidiaries

Year Ended December 31 *(In millions except per share data)*	**2004**	**2003**	**2002**
NET OPERATING REVENUES	**$21,962**	$21,044	$19,564
Cost of goods sold	**7,638**	7,762	7,105
GROSS PROFIT	**14,324**	13,282	12,459
Selling, general and administrative expenses	**8,146**	7,488	7,001
Other operating charges	**480**	573	—
OPERATING INCOME	**5,698**	5,221	5,458
Interest income	**157**	176	209
Interest expense	**196**	178	199
Equity income—net	**621**	406	384
Other income (loss)—net	**(82)**	(138)	(353)
Gains on issuances of stock by equity investees	**24**	8	—
INCOME BEFORE INCOME TAXES AND CUMULATIVE EFFECT OF ACCOUNTING CHANGE	**6,222**	5,495	5,499
Income taxes	**1,375**	1,148	1,523
NET INCOME BEFORE CUMULATIVE EFFECT OF ACCOUNTING CHANGE	**4,847**	4,347	3,976
Cumulative effect of accounting change for SFAS No. 142, net of income taxes:			
Company operations	**—**	—	(367)
Equity investees	**—**	—	(559)
NET INCOME	**$ 4,847**	$ 4,347	$ 3,050
BASIC NET INCOME PER SHARE:			
Before accounting change	**$ 2.00**	$ 1.77	$ 1.60
Cumulative effect of accounting change	**—**	—	(0.37)
	$ 2.00	$ 1.77	$ 1.23
DILUTED NET INCOME PER SHARE:			
Before accounting change	**$ 2.00**	$ 1.77	$ 1.60
Cumulative effect of accounting change	**—**	—	(0.37)
	$ 2.00	$ 1.77	$ 1.23
AVERAGE SHARES OUTSTANDING	**2,426**	2,459	2,478
Effect of dilutive securities	**3**	3	5
AVERAGE SHARES OUTSTANDING ASSUMING DILUTION	**2,429**	2,462	2,483

Note: Slight modifications have been made to the statement to simplify the presentation.

P4-9 UNDERSTANDING WORKING CAPITAL AND LONG-TERM DEBT

Obj. 3 A recent Consolidated Balance Sheet for the Coca-Cola Company and Subsidiaries is presented on the following page.

Required

A. Was Coca-Cola a larger or smaller company in 2004 than in 2003? Explain.
B. What was the total amount of long-term debt? Explain why Coca-Cola classifies long-term debt into two categories.
C. What was working capital?
D. How much working capital did Coca-Cola report in 2004 and 2003? What conclusions can you make as a result of your calculations?

Consolidated Balance Sheets
The Coca-Cola Company and Subsidiaries

December 31	**2004**	**2003**
(In millions)		
ASSETS		
CURRENT		
Cash and cash equivalents	**$ 6,707**	$ 3,362
Marketable securities	**61**	120
	6,768	3,482
Trade accounts receivable, less allowances of $69 in 2004 and $61 in 2003	**2,171**	2,091
Inventories	**1,420**	1,252
Prepaid expenses and other assets	**1,735**	1,571
TOTAL CURRENT ASSETS	**12,094**	8,396
INVESTMENTS AND OTHER ASSETS		
Equity method investments:		
Coca-Cola Enterprises Inc.	**1,569**	1,260
Coca-Cola Hellenic Bottling Company S.A.	**1,067**	941
Coca-Cola FEMSA, S.A. de C.V.	**792**	674
Coca-Cola Amatil Limited	**736**	652
Other, principally bottling companies	**1,733**	1,697
Cost method investments, principally bottling companies	**355**	314
Other assets	**3,054**	3,322
	9,306	8,860
PROPERTY, PLANT AND EQUIPMENT		
Land	**479**	419
Buildings and improvements	**2,853**	2,615
Machinery and equipment	**6,337**	6,159
Containers	**480**	429
	10,149	9,622
Less allowances for depreciation	**4,058**	3,525
	6,091	6,097
TRADEMARKS WITH INDEFINITE LIVES	**2,037**	1,979
GOODWILL	**1,097**	1,029
OTHER INTANGIBLE ASSETS	**702**	981
TOTAL ASSETS	**$31,327**	$27,342
LIABILITIES AND SHAREOWNERS' EQUITY		
CURRENT		
Accounts payable and accrued expenses	**$ 4,283**	$ 4,058
Loans and notes payable	**4,531**	2,583
Current maturities of long-term debt	**1,490**	323
Accrued income taxes	**667**	922
TOTAL CURRENT LIABILITIES	**10,971**	7,886
LONG-TERM DEBT	**1,157**	2,517
OTHER LIABILITIES	**2,814**	2,512
DEFERRED INCOME TAXES	**450**	337
SHAREOWNERS' EQUITY		
Common stock, $0.25 par value Authorized: 5,600,000,000 shares; Issued: 3,500,489,544 shares in 2004 and 3,494,799,258 shares in 2003	**875**	874
Capital surplus	**4,928**	4,395
Reinvested earnings	**29,105**	26,687
Accumulated other comprehensive income (loss)	**(1,348)**	(1,995)
	33,560	29,961
Less treasury stock, at cost (1,091,150,977 shares in 2004; 1,053,267,474 shares in 2003)	**(17,625)**	(15,871)
	15,935	14,090
TOTAL LIABILITIES AND SHAREOWNERS' EQUITY	**$31,327**	$27,342

P4-10 USING THE BALANCE SHEET TO DETERMINE ASSET COMPOSITION
Obj. 3

Recent Balance Sheets for **Microsoft Corporation** are presented below.

Microsoft Corporation
Balance Sheets
(In millions)

June 30	2003	2004
Assets		
Current assets:		
Cash and equivalents	$ 6,438	$15,982
Short-term investments	42,610	44,610
Total cash and short-term investments	49,048	60,592
Accounts receivable, net	5,196	5,890
Inventories	640	421
Deferred income taxes	2,506	2,097
Other	1,583	1,566
Total current assets	58,973	70,566
Property and equipment, net	2,223	2,326
Equity and other investments	13,692	12,210
Goodwill	3,128	3,115
Intangible assets, net	384	569
Other long-term assets	3,332	3,603
Total assets	$81,732	$92,389
Liabilities and stockholders' equity		
Current liabilities:		
Accounts payable	$ 1,573	$ 1,717
Accrued compensation	1,416	1,339
Income taxes	2,044	3,478
Short-term unearned revenue	7,225	6,514
Other	1,716	1,921
Total current liabilities	13,974	14,969
Long-term unearned revenue	1,790	1,663
Other long-term liabilities	1,056	932
Stockholders' equity:		
Common stock and paid-in capital—shares authorized 24,000; shares issued and outstanding 10,771 and 10,862	49,234	56,396
Retained earnings, including accumulated other comprehensive income of $1,840 and $1,119	15,678	18,429
Total stockholders' equity	64,912	74,825
Total liabilities and stockholders' equity	$81,732	$92,389

Required

A. Microsoft reports property and equipment, net on the balance sheet. Calculate property and equipment as a percentage of total assets for 2003 and 2004.
B. Microsoft reports cash and short-term investments as a current asset. Calculate cash and short-term investments as a percentage of total assets.
C. Comment on your analysis from Requirements A and B.
D. Calculate the working capital ratio for 2003 and 2004. Discuss your results.

P4-11 PREPARING FINANCIAL STATEMENTS
Objs. 2, 3

Argyle Company has the following account balances at December 31, 2007. During the year, Argyle had 10,000 shares of stock outstanding.

Argyle Company Account Balances at December 31, 2007	
Account	**Balance**
Cash	$ 4,650
Accounts receivable	16,350
Inventory	30,500
Supplies	7,700
Prepaid insurance	3,550
Equipment	42,500
Accumulated depreciation—equipment	17,500
Buildings	170,000
Accumulated depreciation—buildings	105,000
Land	10,000
Patents	3,000
Accounts payable	18,250
Wages payable	3,450
Interest payable	1,700
Income taxes payable	4,050
Notes payable, current portion	2,500
Notes payable, long-term	37,500
Owners' investment	25,000
Retained earnings, December 31, 2006	60,150
Dividends	15,000
Sales revenue	130,000
Cost of goods sold	62,500
Wages expense	16,000
Utilities expense	2,000
Depreciation expense	1,050
Insurance expense	1,500
Supplies expense	2,300
Interest expense	3,650
Advertising expense	1,450
Patent expense	400
Income tax expense	11,000

Required

A. Prepare an income statement in good form based on Argyle Company's account balances.

B. Prepare a classified balance sheet as of December 31, 2007. Include appropriate headings and subheadings.

P4-12 PREPARING FINANCIAL STATEMENTS

Objs. 2, 3

The following account balances are provided for Rustic Company at December 31, 2007. Revenues and expense accounts cover the fiscal year ending on that date. All numbers are dollars except shares outstanding.

Account	**Amount**
Accounts payable	$ 14,000
Accounts receivable	18,000
Accumulated depreciation	30,000
Cash	6,000
Common stock, par value	20,000
Cost of goods sold	35,000
Current portion of long-term debt	2,000
Income taxes	6,000
Interest expense	4,000
Interest payable	500
Inventory	34,000

(Continued)

Long-term debt	$ 40,000
Net income	12,000
Paid-in capital in excess of par	30,000
Patents and trademarks	4,000
Prepaid insurance	2,500
Property, plant and equipment, cost	150,000
Retained earnings	78,000
Sales revenues	110,000
Selling, general, and administrative expenses	65,000
Service revenues	12,000
Supplies	3,000
Wages payable	3,000
Shares outstanding	20,000

Required

A. Prepare an income statement in good form for Rustic Company.
B. Prepare a classified balance sheet.

P4-13 INFORMATION IN THE STATEMENT OF STOCKHOLDERS' EQUITY

Obj. 4 A recent annual report for **Wal-Mart Stores, Inc.,** and its subsidiaries is provided below.

Wal-Mart Stores, Inc.
Consolidated Statements of Shareholders' Equity

(Amounts in millions)	Number of shares	Common stock	Capital in excess of par value	Retained earnings	Other accumulated comprehensive income	Total
Balance January 31, 2001	4,470	$447	$1,660	$29,984	$(684)	$31,407
Comprehensive Income						
Net income				6,592		6,592
Other accumulated comprehensive income					(584)	(584)
Total Comprehensive Income						**6008**
Cash dividends ($0.28 per share)				(1,249)		(1,249)
Purchase of Company stock	(24)	(2)	(62)	(1,150)		(1,214)
Stock options exercised and other	7		240			240
Balance January 31, 2002	4,453	$ 445	$1,838	$34,177	$(1,268)	$35,192
Comprehensive Income						
Net income				7,955		7,955
Other accumulated comprehensive income					759	759
Total Comprehensive Income						**8,714**
Cash dividends ($0.30 per share)				(1,328)		(1,328)
Purchase of Company stock	(63)	(5)	(150)	(3,228)		(3,383)
Stock options exercised and other	5		266			266
Balance January 31, 2003	4,395	440	1,954	37,576	(509)	39,461
Comprehensive Income						
Net income				9,054		9,054
Other accumulated comprehensive income					1,360	1,360
Total Comprehensive Income						**10,414**
Cash dividends ($0.28 per share)				(1,569)		(1,569)
Purchase of Company stock	(92)	(9)	(182)	(4,855)		(5,046)
Stock options exercised and other	8		363			363
Balance January 31, 2004	**4,311**	**$431**	**$2,135**	**$40,206**	**$ 851**	**$43,623**

Note: Slight modifications have been made to the statement for purposes of simplifying the presentation.

Required From the information provided, answer the following questions:

A. What was the total amount of contributed capital as of January 31, 2001?
B. Did total contributed capital increase or decrease between January 31, 2001 and January 31, 2004? By what amount?
C. How much profit has been distributed to owners in cash during the three years covered by this statement?
D. Has stockholders' equity increased or decreased over the three years and what was the main reason?
E. Compute the ratio of cash dividends to net income for each year. Did the portion of profits paid out in dividends each year increase, decrease, or stay about the same?
F. Compute the percentage change in net income between 2002 and 2003, and between 2003 and 2004. (Hint: Divide the increase in net income from 2002 to 2003 by the net income for 2002.) Do you believe this is an encouraging sign or a discouraging sign?
G. Compute the percentage change in dividends between 2002 and 2003, and between 2003 and 2004. Is the rate of dividend increase greater or smaller than the rate of profit increase?

P4-14 UNDERSTANDING STOCKHOLDERS' EQUITY

Obj. 4 Recent stockholders' equity statements for Microsoft are presented below.

Microsoft Corporation
Stockholders' Equity Statements

(In millions)			
Year Ended June 30	**2002**	**2003**	**2004**
Common stock and paid-in capital			
Balance, beginning of period	$34,950	$41,845	**$49,234**
Common stock issued	1,655	2,966	**2,815**
Common stock repurchased	(676)	(691)	**(416)**
Other, net	5,916	5,114	**4,763**
Balance, end of period	41,845	49,234	**56,396**
Balance, beginning of period	$13,837	$12,997	**$15,678**
Net income	5,355	7,531	**8,168**
Other comprehensive income:			
Net gains/(losses) on derivative instruments	(91)	(102)	**101**
Net unrealized investments gains/(losses)	5	1,243	**(873)**
Translation adjustments and other	82	116	**51**
Comprehensive income	5,351	8,788	**7,447**
Common stock dividend	—	(857)	**(1,729)**
Common stock repurchased	(6,191)	(5,250)	**(2,967)**
Balance, end of period	12,997	15,678	**18,429**
Total stockholders' equity	$54,842	$64,912	**$74,825**

Note: Slight modifications have been made to the statement to simplify the presentation.

Required

A. What was the amount of common stock and paid-in capital at June 30, 2002, 2003, and 2004?
B. Does Microsoft pay dividends on common stock?

(Continued)

C. How can you explain the increase in common stock and paid-in capital over the three-year period?
D. Without consulting Microsoft's Statement of Income, can we determine net income reported in 2002, 2003, and 2004? Why or why not?
E. Microsoft's Stockholders' Equity Statements report common stock repurchased. Why do you think a company would repurchase its own shares? If the shares are later reissued at a higher price, do you think Microsoft should report a gain on shares reissued?

P4-15 USING INTERRELATIONSHIPS AMONG FINANCIAL STATEMENTS

Objs. 2, 3, 4

Corey Issacson is an investor in Stone Cold Enterprises. Last week he received the company's most recent financial statements but some of the numbers were smudged and unreadable. Each of the unreadable numbers is represented with a letter as shown below and at the top of the following page.

Stone Cold Enterprises
Comparative Balance Sheet
December 31, 2006 and 2007

(In thousands)	December 31, 2007	December 31, 2006
Assets		
Cash	$ 2,940	$ 1,020
Accounts receivable	1,850	1,225
Merchandise	2,855	1,000
Prepaid insurance	(a)	3,000
Property, plant and equipment	25,000	(b)
Accumulated depreciation	(c)	(6,250)
Other assets	8,400	3,000
Total assets	$35,545	$ (d)
Liabilities and equity:		
Accounts payable	$ 1,580	$ 950
Wages payable	125	700
Rent payable	500	500
Long-term notes payable (8%)	12,000	12,000
Common stock	(e)	(f)
Retained earnings	(g)	10,845
Total liabilities and equity	$ (h)	$ (i)

Stone Cold Enterprises
Statement of Stockholders' Equity
Year Ended December 31, 2007

	Common Stock	Retained Earnings	Total
Balance, December 31, 2006	$3,000	$ (j)	$ (k)
Issued common stock	(l)		(m)
Net income		14,495	14,495
Dividends paid		(9,000)	(9,000)
Balance, December 31, 2007	$5,000	$ (n)	$21,340

Stone Cold Enterprises Income Statement Year Ended December 31, 2007		
Sales revenue		$103,000
Cost of goods sold		66,000
Gross profit		$ 37,000
Operating expenses:		
Wages	$5,490	
Interest	(o)	
Rent	(p)	
Insurance	1,000	
Depreciation	1,250	
Total operating expenses		(q)
Pretax income		$ (r)
Income taxes (35%)		(s)
Net income		$ (t)

Additional information:

1. No items of plant, property and equipment were purchased or sold during the year.
2. The prepaid insurance account represents the remaining portion of a four-year policy purchased on January 1, 2006.
3. The rent payable account at year end (both years) represents December's rent that had not yet been paid.

Required Use your knowledge regarding the interrelationships among financial statements to determine each of the missing amounts.

P4-16 PREPARING FINANCIAL STATEMENTS

Objs. 2, 3, 4

ABC Inc. has the following account balances at December 31, 2007.

Accounts payable	$17,080	Income tax expense	$ 1,300
Accounts receivable	9,400	Land	50,000
Accumulated depreciation	26,100	Notes payable	30,000
Buildings	60,000	Retained earnings, December 31, 2006	17,000
Cash	20,880		
Contributed capital	31,000	Sales revenue	26,000
Cost of goods sold	15,600	Supplies	7,500
Depreciation expense	2,200	Wages expense	3,000
Dividends paid	1,200	Wages payable	23,900

During the year 2007, the company issued $6,000 of new common stock.

Required From this information, prepare (A) an income statement, (B) a statement of stockholders' equity, and (C) a classified balance sheet. (D) Show how the three financial statements articulate. (Note: In parts (A), (B), and (C), include appropriate headings and subheadings in the financial statements that you prepare.)

P4-17 UNDERSTANDING THE INFORMATION IN FINANCIAL STATEMENTS

Objs. 2, 3, 4

Today is April 1 and Dale has just received the annual report of Clam Chowder Company, in which he owns stock. Displayed on the following page are the comparative balance sheet and income statement that have drawn his attention.

(Continued)

Balance Sheet	Dec. 31, 2007	Dec. 31, 2006
Cash	$ 1,244	$ 1,512
Accounts receivable	6,914	5,886
Inventory	11,211	9,099
Buildings and equipment	49,900	46,500
Accumulated depreciation	(5,319)	(2,497)
Land	22,000	22,000
Total assets	$85,950	$82,500
Accounts payable	$ 2,313	$ 1,988
Interest payable	-0-	2,563
Wages payable	7,364	6,327
7%, 10-year note payable	20,000	20,000
Contributed capital	42,300	42,300
Retained capital	13,973	9,322
Total liabilities and equity	$85,950	$82,500

Income Statement	For Year 2007
Sales revenue	$485,000
Cost of goods sold	300,700
Gross profit	184,300
Operating expenses:	
Advertising	31,330
Depreciation	2,822
Utilities	19,200
Wages	113,698
Operating income	17,250
Interest expense	2,400
Pretax income	14,850
Income tax expense	5,200
Net income	$ 9,650
Earnings per share	$ 3.86

After reviewing this information, Dale makes the following comments.

1. I'm surprised that the value of the company's land has not increased. Prices have been increasing rapidly in the area the company is located.
2. I'm sure that I received a dividend from this company, but they don't report that they paid any.
3. I don't see how the company's cash balance could have declined when it took in $485,000 in cash from sales to customers.
4. I see that the value of the buildings and equipment declined by $2,822. That seems about right.
5. I don't understand why the company's highly trained workforce is not listed as an asset. It is one of the most important resources that the company has.
6. One thing I really like about this company is the up-to-the-minute financial reports it provides.
7. It's good to see that the value of the inventory has increased since last year.

Required

A. Help Dale better understand these financial statements by responding to each of his comments. Explain whether you agree or disagree with each comment and why.
B. Did the company declare and pay cash dividends during the year just ended? If so, what total amount was distributed?
C. Approximately how many shares of stock does the company have outstanding?

P4-18 THE TRANSFORMATION PROCESS AS REPORTED IN FINANCIAL STATEMENTS

Objs. 2, 3, 4

Far East Specialties is an import company, financed primarily by stockholders and bank loans. It imports handmade goods from Central and East Asia to the United States, where they are sold to retail stores. The company's buyers contract with small companies for goods, which the buyers ship to a central location in the United States. The goods are inventoried and then redistributed as orders are received from retailers. The company receives a bill from the manufacturers along with the goods it receives. Payment is made each month. Bills are sent to retailers along with orders. Most retailers pay their bills each month, as well. It can be several months from the time goods are shipped to the United States until cash is received from retailers.

Required

A. Explain how the various aspects of Far East Specialties' transformation process are reported in its financial statements. That is, consider the events just described and identify where information about each event is reported in the financial statements. In particular, consider the relationship the company has with its investors, suppliers, and customers.

B. Why is it important that time, and the timing of events, be considered in reporting accounting information?

P4-19 LIMITATIONS ON FINANCIAL STATEMENTS

Obj. 5 Markus O'Realius is considering the purchase of Caesar Company. The potential seller has provided Markus with a copy of the business's financial statements for the last three years. The financial statements reveal total assets of $350,000 and total liabilities of $150,000. The seller is asking $300,000 for the business. Markus believes that the business is worth only about $200,000, the amount of owners' equity reported on the balance sheet. He has asked your assistance in determining a price to offer for the business.

Required Write a memo to Markus explaining why he should not interpret the balance sheet as an accurate measure of the value of the business. Describe limitations of financial statements that might mean that the market value of the business was higher (or lower) than the financial statement amounts.

P4-20 LIMITATIONS OF FINANCIAL STATEMENTS

Obj. 5 Limits Ltd. had the following financial statements for the fiscal year ending December 31, 2007 (the statement of stockholders' equity and the statement of cash flows are not shown).

Limits Ltd. Income Statement For the Year Ending December 31, 2007		
Sales revenue		$20,000
Operating expenses:		
Cost of sales	$1,000	
Wages expense	800	
Advertising expense	100	
Depreciation expense	300	
Research and development expense	300	
Total operating expense		2,500
Operating income		$17,500
Other expenses:		
Interest expense		500
Income before taxes		$17,000
Income tax		5,100
Net income		$11,900

Limits Ltd. Balance Sheet as of December 31, 2007			
Assets		*Liabilities and stockholders' equity*	
Current assets:		Current liabilities:	
Cash	$ 2,300	Accounts payable	$ 3,000
Accounts receivable	8,000	Wages payable	7,600
Inventory	15,000	Interest payable	900
Total current assets	$25,300	Total current liabilities	$11,500
Property, plant and equipment:		Notes payable, long-term	9,000
Equipment	21,000	Total liabilities	$20,500
Accumulated depreciation	(8,000)	Stockholders' equity:	
Buildings	90,000	Owners' investment	$ 9,700
Accumulated depreciation	(85,000)	Retained earnings	13,100
PP&E	$18,000	Total stockholders' equity	$22,800
		Total liabilities and	
Total assets	$43,300	stockholders' equity	$43,300

(Continued)

Required The text lists several limitations of financial statements. Using the financial statements given here, identify as many examples of limitations or items that relate to limitations of financial statements as you can.

P4-21 EXCEL IN ACTION

Listed below are account balances and other data for The Book Wermz at the close of November 30, 2007. Revenue and expense account balances are for the month of November. All amounts are dollars except shares of common stock. The Book Wermz operates as a corporation.

Accounts payable	$ 6,131.77
Accounts receivable	375.00
Accumulated depreciation	13,891.82
Cash	12,307.99
Contributed capital	100,000.00
Cost of goods sold	30,937.32
Depreciation expense	817.20
Dividends paid	1,500.00
Equipment	57,650.00
Income tax expense	897.45
Interest expense	932.03
Inventory	235,255.06
Notes payable, current portion	1,122.77
Notes payable, long-term	120,084.57
Rent expense	1,738.15
Sales	43,312.25
Service revenues	1,566.23
Shares of common stock	1,000
Supplies	2,130.12
Supplies expense	2,411.53
Wages expense	4,697.35
Wages payable	1,150.68

Required Use the account balances to produce an income statement, a statement of stockholders' equity, and a balance sheet for The Book Wermz in a spreadsheet. The financial statements should follow the examples illustrated in Chapter 4. The balance sheet should contain columns for November and October. October 31 balances should be obtained from data provided in the Chapter 3 spreadsheet problem.

Enter account titles in column A. Use columns B, C, and D as necessary for amounts. Use the Borders button to produce single and double lines by selecting the cell to be formatted, using the button down arrow to select the proper line type, and clicking on the button. Use the Indent button to indent titles and captions as needed by selecting the cell and clicking on the button. Use the Comma and Currency buttons to format amounts by selecting the cell and clicking on the appropriate buttons. The Comma button also formats numbers so that negative amounts appear in parentheses. The first and last amounts in a column of numbers should include dollar signs as illustrated in the chapter. Set column widths by placing the cursor at the right edge of a column header so the Change Width cursor appears. Then click and drag the column to the right or left as needed. Use functions to sum subtotals and totals, =SUM(B5:B8) for example, so the spreadsheet will automatically recalculate any changes in account numbers. To merge adjacent cells for titles, select the cells to be merged and click on the Merge Cells button. Put titles in bold type by selecting the cell containing the title and clicking on the Bold Type button **B**.

Suppose sales for November had been $45,000 and the cash balance at November 30 had been $13,995.74. How much net income would the company report for November? How much total assets and stockholders' equity would it report at November 30?

P4-22 MULTIPLE-CHOICE OVERVIEW OF THE CHAPTER

1. Which of the following is *not* a statement you would expect to find in a corporate annual report?
   a. Statement of financial position
   b. Statement of earnings

c. Statement of stockholders' equity
d. Statement of accounts receivable

2. The following information was reported on the income statement of Wagon Wheel Company.

Sales revenues	$450,000
Cost of goods sold	200,000
Selling, general, and administrative expenses	150,000
Interest expense	30,000

Wagon Wheel's gross profit and operating income would be

	Gross profit	**Operating income**
a.	$300,000	$70,000
b.	$250,000	$70,000
c.	$250,000	$100,000
d.	$100,000	$70,000

3. Which of the following is a *false* statement regarding the statement of stockholders' equity?
   a. It lists changes in contributed capital and retained earnings for a fiscal period.
   b. It contains information about net income and dividends for a fiscal period.
   c. It reports the net change in stockholders' equity for a fiscal period.
   d. It reports increases or decreases in stocks and bonds for a fiscal period.

4. The following assets appear on the balance sheet for Astroid Company:

Accounts receivable	$ 50,000
Accumulated depreciation	160,000
Cash	20,000
Intangible assets	60,000
Inventory	100,000
Plant assets	400,000

The amount of current assets reported by Astroid is
   a. $170,000.
   b. $150,000.
   c. $230,000.
   d. $470,000.

5. A balance sheet that provides information for more than one fiscal period is:
   a. a classified balance sheet.
   b. a comparative balance sheet.
   c. a consolidated balance sheet.
   d. a combined balance sheet.

6. Working capital is the amount of
   a. cash and cash equivalents available to a company at the end of a fiscal period.
   b. long-term investments available at the end of a fiscal period less long-term debt at the end of the period.
   c. current assets available at the end of a fiscal period less current liabilities at the end of the period.
   d. total assets available at the end of a period that can be converted to cash.

7. Orange Bowl Company reported plant assets for the latest fiscal year of $5 million, net of accumulated depreciation. From this information, which of the following is an accurate statement about the company?
   a. The book value of the company's plant assets at the end of the fiscal year was $5 million.
   b. The company would have to pay $5 million to replace its assets if they were replaced at the end of the fiscal year.
   c. The amount the company would receive if it sold its plant assets at the end of the fiscal year would be $5 million.
   d. The amount the company paid for the plant assets it controlled at the end of the fiscal year was $5 million.

(Continued)

8. A consolidated financial statement is one in which
   a. more than one year's financial data is included.
   b. the personal financial activities of the owner are combined with those of the company.
   c. the income statement and the balance sheet are combined into a single statement.
   d. the financial information of multiple corporations is reported as if they were a single firm.

9. Which of the following is *false*?
   a. Financial statement information is not always presented in a timely manner.
   b. The purpose of a balance sheet is to report the market value of assets and liabilities.
   c. Certain types of resources and costs are not reported in financial statements.
   d. Many of the numbers reported in financial statements result from estimates and allocations.

10. Where on an income statement would you expect to find administrative salaries expense?
   a. just after cost of goods sold
   b. grouped with other operating expenses
   c. as part of cost of goods sold
   d. following income taxes

Cases

C4-1 EVALUATING THE TRANSFORMATION PROCESS

Objs. 1, 5

Italiano Pizza Company has just completed its first month in business. The owners, Charla and Maria, had previously worked for a major pizza chain but were convinced that they could offer a better product in a better atmosphere. They knew the importance of accurate financial records and hired a bookkeeper. Yesterday, the bookkeeper hand-delivered financial statements to the owners and announced her resignation. You have been retained by Charla and Maria to interpret the following financial information and explain its significance.

Italiano Pizza Company
Financial Statements
After One Month in Business

Balance sheet accounts				**Income statement accounts**	
Assets:		Liabilities + Owners' Equity:		Revenues	$ 4,000
Cash	$ 2,240	Wages payable	$ 180	Expenses:	
Food products	980	Advertising payable	400	Store rent	800
Supplies	1,000	Loan from bank	6,800	Food products	1,475
Prepaid rent	2,400	Owners' investment	4,340	Wages	990
Equipment	5,150			Advertising	1,430
Accumulated				Interest	40
depreciation	(50)			Supplies	375
Total	$11,720	Total	$11,720	Depreciation	50
				Net loss	$(1,160)

Required

A. Discuss whether the information provided could be helpful to the owners and, if so, describe how. If not, describe why not.
B. Identify at least 10 events that occurred as part of the transformation process during the firm's first month in business. For each event, identify the amount of cash involved. (Note: Charla and Maria established the company with a cash investment.)
C. Did Charla and Maria make a good judgment when they decided to get into this business? Would you recommend that they continue with the pizza business or

discontinue it? What additional information would be helpful to you in making such a recommendation?

C4-2 THE FINANCIAL STATEMENTS OF GENERAL MILLS, INC.

Objs. 2, 3, 4

Selected information from **General Mills'** 2004 annual report and 10K is provided in Appendix A at the end of the text.

Required

A. Answer the following questions about the General Mills Consolidated Statements of Earnings:
   1. General Mills recorded sales of $11 billion. Is this the amount of cash collected? Explain.
   2. Sales increased each year from 2002 to 2004. Compute the percentage increase for each year.
   3. What was the largest expense for General Mills? Compute this expense as a percentage of sales for each of the three years. Was there a trend?
   4. Compare the net income figures for three years. What do you observe?
   5. Explain why a company's stock price generally is influenced by the amount of net income.
   6. General Mills paid dividends in 2004, 2003, and in 2002, yet the corresponding total dividend payments do not appear as expenses on the income statement. Why not?

B. Answer the following questions about the General Mills Consolidated Balance Sheets:
   1. Why does a company have assets?
   2. What is the total amount of assets at the end of 2004?
   3. What two groups have contributed assets to General Mills and have claims on the company's assets?

C. The consolidated statement of stockholders' equity identifies comprehensive income. Briefly explain the concept of comprehensive income. What kinds of activities are included in comprehensive income?

Reporting Cash Flows

5

HOW IS CASH FLOW INFORMATION DETERMINED AND REPORTED TO EXTERNAL USERS?

Chapter 4 examined the reporting of operating results and financial position to stockholders and other external users. Corporations and other companies also report information about their cash flows for a fiscal period to external users. The statement of cash flows identifies the cash created by and used for operating, investing, and financing activities. Stan and Maria realize it is important for their company to provide information about how much cash is generated from business activities and how this cash was used. In addition to helping them, as managing owners of the firm, this information helps external stockholders and other decision makers determine whether a company is likely to grow and to meet its financial obligations.

Food for Thought

As a stockholder of Favorite Cookie Company, what information about cash flows do you need to make decisions about your investment? How do companies determine how much cash they received and paid during a fiscal period? Knowing they need to provide key cash flow information to stockholders and others, Maria and Stan have arranged to meet with their accountant, Ellen, to discuss these issues.

Stan: *We prepared an income statement, balance sheet, and statement of stockholders' equity for our stockholders. I understand we also need to report cash flow information.*

Ellen: *Yes, the statement of cash flows is an important part of your total financial report. This statement requires you to look carefully at your business activities to identify activities that created cash and those that used it.*

Maria: *We know how much cash the company had at the end of the year. Many of our transactions during the year involved cash. Do we have to look at all of these transactions to prepare the statement of cash flows?*

Ellen: *No. You can summarize your cash flows without looking at individual transactions. Most of the information for the statement can be obtained from the income statement and balance sheets you have already prepared.*

Stan: *Those statements don't include much cash information. How can they tell us anything about cash flows?*

Ellen: *The income statement contains information about the results of operating activities measured using the accrual basis. Timing differences between when revenues and expenses were recognized and when cash was received and paid are reported on the balance sheets for this fiscal year end and the prior one. Preparing the statement of cash flows is largely a matter of adjusting income statement numbers for these timing differences and looking at other activities that increased or decreased balance sheet amounts during the year.*

Maria: *That sounds complicated.*

Ellen: *It requires a good understanding of accrual accounting and working systematically with the income statement and balance sheet numbers. Once you learn how the statement is prepared, you'll have a good understanding of how accrual and cash flow information is related. Also, you will see how valuable cash flow information can be for understanding your company.*

Objectives

Once you have completed this chapter, you should be able to:

1. Explain information reported on a statement of cash flows using the direct format.
2. Explain information reported on a statement of cash flows using the indirect format.
3. Interpret cash flow information as a basis for analyzing financial performance.

THE STATEMENT OF CASH FLOWS

The purpose of the statement of cash flows is to identify the primary activities of a fiscal period that resulted in cash inflows and outflows for a company. The statement describes the cash flow results of financing, investing, and operating activities for a company for a fiscal period, and it explains the change in a company's cash balance during the period. GAAP permit the statement of cash flows to be presented in either of two formats: direct or indirect. The two formats differ only with respect to the presentation of operating activities.

THE DIRECT FORMAT

Objective 1

Explain information reported on a statement of cash flows using the direct format.

Some companies, especially smaller companies, use the direct format to present the statement of cash flows. Most large corporations use the indirect format. Exhibit 1 provides an example of the cash flow statement for Favorite Cookie Company using the direct format.

The direct format of the statement of cash flows presents each major source and use of cash. The statement of cash flows is divided into three sections corresponding to the three primary types of business activities: operating, investing, and financing.

The source of data for the direct format of the statement of cash flows is the transactions that affect the cash account. The operating cash flow section of the statement includes those transactions that affected cash and were associated with operating activities: sales to customers, purchases of merchandise, wages, and other operating activities. GAAP require that interest payments be included in the operating activities section of the statement of cash flows because interest expense is reported on the income statement. Thus, **operating cash flows are the cash equivalent of the accrual results reported on the income statement.** That is, they represent a cash-basis income statement for the fiscal period.

The investing activities section includes cash transactions associated with the purchase or sale of long-term assets. The financing activities section includes cash transactions associated with debt (short- or long-term) and owners' equity, including payments to owners.

The direct format of the statement of cash flows lists the direct effects of transactions that affect the cash account during a period. It answers the question, "Where did cash come from and where did cash go?" Therefore, it is an explanation of business activities that resulted in an increase or decrease in cash. In total, these activities explain the change in a company's cash account balance for a fiscal period. Because 2007 was Favorite Cookie Company's first year of operations, the beginning cash balance was $0. The company's ending cash balance was equal to the net increase in cash for 2007, $10,680. The net increase (or decrease) in cash for a fiscal period is the sum of net cash flow from operating, investing, and financing activities.

EXHIBIT 1
Statement of Cash Flows, Direct Format

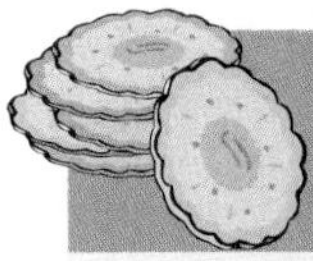

Favorite Cookie Company
Statement of Cash Flows
For the Year Ended December 31, 2007

Operating Activities	
Receipts: Collections from customers	$ 682,080
Payments:	
For inventory	(471,590)
To employees	(70,800)
For rent	(24,000)
For utilities	(4,500)
For supplies	(15,990)
For insurance	(3,700)
For advertising	(6,500)
For interest	(4,150)
For income tax	(22,710)
Net cash flow from operating activities	58,140
Investing Activities	
Payments for purchase of equipment	(216,000)
Receipts from sale of equipment	340
Net cash flow for investing activities	(215,660)
Financing Activities	
Receipts from sale of common stock	100,000
Payment of dividends	(10,000)
Receipts from borrowing	80,000
Repayments of debt	(1,800)
Net cash flow from financing activities	168,200
Net increase in cash	10,680
Cash balance, December 31, 2006	0
Cash balance, December 31, 2007	$ 10,680

Operating Activities

Operating activities are transactions involving the acquisition or production of goods and services and the sale and distribution of these goods and services to customers. Cash flow from operating activities identifies cash received from the sale of goods and services. Also, it identifies cash paid for resources used to provide goods and services. An important relationship exists between the income statement and the operating activities section of the statement of cash flows—both are based on the same set of activities. On the income statement, operating activities are measured on an accrual basis. On the cash flow statement, these activities are measured on a cash basis. These amounts can be compared to determine timing differences between accrual basis recognition of revenues and expenses and cash flows for the period.

To understand how the cash flow numbers in Exhibit 1 were computed, we need to refer to the income statement and balance sheet from Chapter 4. These are reproduced in Exhibit 2.

Selling, general and administrative expenses are as follows:

Wages	$ 70,800
Utilities	4,500
Insurance	3,700
Advertising	6,500
Depreciation	25,500
Rent	22,000
Supplies	15,300
Total	$148,300

EXHIBIT 2

Income Statement and Balance Sheet for Favorite Cookie Company

Favorite Cookie Company Income Statement For the Year Ended December 31, 2007	
Sales revenue	$ 686,400
Cost of goods sold	(457,600)
Gross profit	228,800
Selling, general and administrative expenses	(148,300)
Operating income	80,500
Interest expense	(4,800)
Pretax income	75,700
Income taxes	(22,710)
Net income	$ 52,990

Favorite Cookie Company Balance Sheet At December 31, 2007	
Assets	
Current assets:	
Cash	$ 10,680
Accounts receivable	8,570
Merchandise inventory	23,600
Supplies	690
Prepaid rent	2,000
Total current assets	45,540
Property and equipment, at cost	215,660
Accumulated depreciation	(25,500)
Total assets	$235,700
Liabilities and Stockholders' Equity	
Current liabilities:	
Accounts payable	$ 9,610
Unearned revenue	4,250
Interest payable	650
Notes payable, current portion	5,000
Total current liabilities	19,510
Notes payable, long-term	73,200
Total liabilities	92,710
Stockholders' equity:	
Common stock, 10,000 shares issued	100,000
Retained earnings	42,990
Total stockholders' equity	142,990
Total liabilities and stockholders' equity	$235,700

Of these items, wages, utilities, insurance, and advertising were paid in cash. Observe that there are no noncash assets or liabilities (prepaid insurance or wages payable, for example) on the balance sheet associated with these items. **Depreciation expense does not require the payment of cash.** Rent and supplies expenses were not completely paid in cash because prepaid rent and supplies are reported on the balance sheet. Income tax also was paid in cash. Again, observe that there are no noncash assets or liabilities associated with income taxes, such as income taxes payable. There are noncash assets and liabilities associated with sales revenue, cost of goods sold, and interest expense. These assets and liabilities result from timing differences between when revenues and expenses are recognized and when cash is received or paid. Therefore, they must be adjusted to determine cash flows. Exhibit 3 explains the calculation of operating cash flows from the data in Exhibit 2.

EXHIBIT 3 Calculation of Operating Cash Flows for Direct Method

Accounts	Accrual	Adjustment	Cash Flow	Explanation
a. Sales Revenue	$686,400			Accrual
Less: Accounts Receivable		$ (8,570)		Sales for which cash not received
Add: Unearned Revenue		4,250		Cash received but not yet earned
Cash Collected from Customers			$682,080	Cash flow
b. Cost of Goods Sold	(457,600)			Accrual
Add: Merchandise Inventory		(23,600)		Cash paid but goods not sold
Less: Accounts Payable		9,610		Goods purchased but cash not paid
Cash Paid for Merchandise			(471,590)	Cash flow
c. Wages	(70,800)			Cash paid equals accrual amount
Utilities	(4,500)			Cash paid equals accrual amount
Insurance	(3,700)			Cash paid equals accrual amount
Advertising	(6,500)			Cash paid equals accrual amount
Income Taxes	(22,710)			Cash paid equals accrual amount
Cash Paid for Other Operating Items			(108,210)	Cash paid equals accrual amount
d. Rent Expense	(22,000)			Accrual
Prepaid Rent		(2,000)		Cash paid but not expensed
Cash Paid for Rent			(24,000)	Cash flow
e. Supplies Expense	(15,300)			Accrual
Supplies		(690)		Cash paid but not expensed
Cash Paid for Supplies			(15,990)	Cash flow
f. Interest Expense	(4,800)			Accrual
Interest Payable		650		Cash not paid in 2004
Cash Paid for Interest			(4,150)	Cash flow
g. Depreciation Expense	(25,500)		0	Accrual
		25,500		Cash not paid
			0	Cash flow
Net Income	$ 52,990			
Net Cash Flow from Operating			$ 58,140	

To determine cash collected from customers (a), revenue is adjusted for cash not received (because it is still owed) and for cash received that has not been earned. To determine cash paid for merchandise (b), cost of goods sold is adjusted for cash paid for merchandise that has not been sold and for amounts owed suppliers. It is important in these computations that expenses and cash outflows are shown as negative amounts.

Other operating cash flows are either accrued expenses that were paid in cash, as those in (c), or expenses that require adjustment, as with rent, supplies, and interest. To determine cash paid for rent (d), rent expense is adjusted for cash paid for rent of future periods. To determine cash paid for supplies (e), supplies expense is adjusted for supplies that have been purchased but that have not been used. To determine cash paid for interest (f), interest expense is adjusted for interest that has not been paid.

Depreciation and amortization expenses (g) are tied to operating activities but are not cash flow items. When the direct format is used, these expenses are not listed in the statement of cash flows.

Investing Activities

Investing activities involve acquisition or sale of long-term assets and financial investments during a fiscal period. As noted above, depreciation and amortization expenses are not part of investing activities. Cash flow for investing activities occurs when fixed assets are purchased or sold, not when these assets are depreciated.

Calculation of investing cash flow in Exhibit 1 is straightforward. Favorite Cookie Company purchased $216,000 of equipment for cash in 2007. It sold equipment for $340 in cash. Investing cash flow is simply the amount paid for long-term assets minus the amount received from selling these assets.

Some transactions affect investing and financing activities without affecting cash directly. For example, suppose a company borrows $300,000 from a bank to purchase a building. The transaction increases Buildings and Notes Payable but does not have a direct effect on Cash. GAAP require that such transactions be reported. Most of these events are reported as though they were cash transactions: cash received from borrowing and then paid for property and equipment.

Financing Activities

Financing activities are transactions between a company and its owners or creditors. The financing activities section reports only the cash flow effects of transactions associated with borrowing or repaying debt and investments by owners. Cash flows result when debt is issued or repaid and when stock is issued or repurchased. Payment of dividends or other cash distributions to owners also are financing activities.

The calculation of financing cash flow for Favorite Cookie Company is straightforward. The company received $100,000 from issuing common stock and paid $10,000 of dividends to stockholders. It received $80,000 of cash from borrowing and paid back $1,800 of the amount borrowed. (It is important to remember the repayment of debt is the repayment of the amount actually borrowed, not the payment of interest on the borrowed money. As noted above, the payment of interest is an operating activity.)

GAAP require a schedule to reconcile cash flows from operating activities with net income when the direct format is used. This schedule is similar to the presentation of the statement of cash flows using the indirect format described in the next section of this chapter.

Self-Study Problem #1

Listed below are cash activities for Jerome Inc. for a recent fiscal period. Jerome's cash balance at the beginning of the period was $16,350.

Paid for dividends	$ 2,500
Paid to employees	4,000
Paid for utilities	2,200
Paid for equipment	13,500
Received from sale of stock	100,000
Paid for supplies	1,800
Paid for inventory	8,400
Received from customers	14,750
Paid for debt repayment	35,000
Received from sale of land	20,000
Paid for building	75,000

Required Use these activities to prepare a statement of cash flows for Jerome Inc. using the direct format. What were Jerome's primary sources and uses of cash for the period?

The solution to Self-Study Problem 1 appears at the end of the chapter.

THE INDIRECT FORMAT

Objective 2

Explain information reported on a statement of cash flows using the indirect format.

The direct format of the statement of cash flows identifies the sources of cash received and the purposes for which cash is paid during a period. Thus, operating activities identify cash received from customers and paid to suppliers, employees, and so on. In practice, however, this format is rarely used by major corporations.

Instead, nearly all major corporations use the indirect format for reporting the statement of cash flows. **The differences between the direct and indirect formats are in the operating activities section only.** The indirect format reconciles net income on an accrual basis with cash flow from operating activities on a cash basis. It answers the question, "Why was cash flow from operations different from net income?" Consequently, operating cash flows are presented as the indirect result of changes in current assets, current liabilities, and other accounts.

Exhibit 4 provides the statement of cash flows for Favorite Cookie Company using the indirect method. In this method, the operating activities section begins with net income. This is the amount reported on the company's income statement (see Exhibit 2). The indirect format begins with the results of operating activities reported on an accrual basis (net income) and adjusts this amount to arrive at the amount that explains the results of operating activities on a cash basis (net cash flow from operating activities). Adjustments are made for activities that had a different effect on net income than they had on cash flow. Observe that **the net cash flows in each section (operating, investing, and financing) are the same as those reported using the direct method** in Exhibit 1. In fact, the investing and financing sections are identical in the two methods.

The operating activities section looks quite different, however. To understand this method, refer to Exhibit 3. The adjustments column of the exhibit identifies the differences between the accrual amounts from the income statement and the cash

EXHIBIT 4

Indirect Format of Statement of Cash Flows

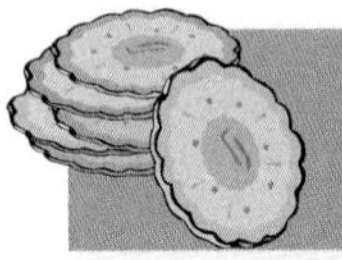

Favorite Cookie Company Statement of Cash Flows For the Year Ended December 31, 2007	
Operating Activities	
Net income	$ 52,990
Depreciation expense	25,500
Increase in accounts receivable	(8,570)
Increase in merchandise inventory	(23,600)
Increase in supplies	(690)
Increase in prepaid rent	(2,000)
Increase in accounts payable	9,610
Increase in unearned revenue	4,250
Increase in interest payable	650
Net cash flow from operating activities	58,140
Investing Activities	
Payments for purchase of equipment	(216,000)
Receipts from sale of equipment	340
Net cash flow for investing activities	(215,660)
Financing Activities	
Receipts from sale of common stock	100,000
Payment of dividends	(10,000)
Receipts from borrowing	80,000
Repayment of debt	(1,800)
Net cash flow from financing activities	168,200
Net increase in cash	10,680
Cash balance, December 31, 2006	0
Cash balance, December 31, 2007	$ 10,680

flow amounts. Starting with net income, we can simply list these adjustments to compute cash flow from operating activities. The indirect method does just that. It starts with the accrual amount (net income) and lists the adjustments necessary to determine cash flow from operating activities.

Though the determination of the adjustments may seem somewhat complicated, they are actually fairly simple. They consist of subtracting any revenues that did not result in cash inflow or adding any expenses that did not require cash outflow. Most adjustments are associated with current assets and current liabilities, with the exclusion of financial resources such as cash and investments.

When current assests increase during a fiscal period, one of two things has occurred:

- Revenue was earned but cash was not received—resulting in an increase in accounts receivable. That is, cash inflows from revenues were less than revenues recorded. Or,
- Cash was paid for resources that have not been expensed—resulting in an increase in inventory or prepaid expenses. That is, cash outflows for resources were greater than recorded expenses.

In either case, net cash flow is less than net income. Therefore, **increases in current assets are subtracted from net income to calculate operating cash flow.**

When current assets decrease, the opposite has occurred, either:

- Cash has been received from customers that was not earned this period—resulting in a decrease in accounts receivable. That is, cash inflows from revenues were greater than revenues recorded. Or,
- Resources have been used that were not paid for this period—resulting in a decrease in inventory or prepaid expenses. That is, cash outflows for resources were less than recorded expenses.

In either case, net cash flow is greater than net income. Therefore, **decreases in current assets are added to net income to calculate operating cash flow.**

When current liabilities increase, either:

- Cash has been received from customers but has not been earned—resulting in an increase in unearned revenue. That is, cash inflows from revenues were greater than revenues recorded. Or,
- Resources have been used but payment has not been made—resulting in an increase in accounts payable. That is, cash outflows for resources were less than recorded expenses.

In either case, net cash flow is greater than net income. Therefore, **increases in current liabilities are added to net income to calculate operating cash flow.**

When current liabilities decrease during a fiscal period, one of two things has occurred:

- Revenue was earned but cash was received in a previous period—resulting in a decrease in unearned revenue. That is, cash inflows from revenues were less than revenues recorded. Or,
- Cash was paid for resources that were expensed in a previous period—resulting in a decrease in accounts payable. That is, cash outflows for resources were greater than recorded expenses.

In either case, net cash flow is less than net income. Therefore, **decreases in current liabilities are subtracted from net income to calculate operating cash flow.**

Exhibit 5 summarizes these rules. The rules apply to changes in current asset and current liability accounts during a fiscal period. Because 2007 was the first year of operations for Favorite Cookie Company, the beginning balances of all current asset and current liability accounts was zero. Consequently, the changes in these accounts were equal to the ending balances. When working with a company that has beginning and ending balances, it is necessary to compute the change in current asset and current liability balances and use these in the calculations in Exhibit 2. Also keep in mind that some current asset and

EXHIBIT 5
Rules for Adjusting Net Income to Calculate Operating Cash Flow

Event	Rule
Increase in Current Assets	Subtract from Net Income
Decrease in Current Assets	Add to Net Income
Increase in Current Liabilities	Add to Net Income
Decrease in Current Liabilities	Subtract from Net Income
Noncash Expenses	Add to Net Income

current liability accounts, such as short-term investments and short-term debt (including the current portion of notes payable), are not associated with operating activities. These accounts are associated with financial resources and involve investing activities (for assets) or financing activities (for liabilities). Finally, some revenue and expense items, depreciation and amortization expenses in particular, do not require cash payments. Therefore, they are always added to net income to calculate operating cash flow.

Exhibit 6 provides the statement of cash flows for **Procter & Gamble** from the company's 2004 annual report. Though the statement contains more items than that for

EXHIBIT 6 Indirect Format of Statement of Cash Flows

Consolidated Statements of Cash Flows
The Procter & Gamble Company and Subsidiaries
Years ended June 30

(Amounts in millions)	**2004**	2003	2002
Cash and Cash Equivalents, Beginning of Year	**$5,912**	$3,427	$2,306
Operating Activities			
Net earnings	**6,481**	5,186	4,352
Depreciation and amortization	**1,733**	1,703	1,693
Deferred income taxes	**415**	63	389
Change in accounts receivable	**(159)**	163	96
Change in inventories	**56**	(56)	159
Change in accounts payable, accrued and other liabilities	**625**	936	684
Change in other operating assets and liabilities	**(88)**	178	(98)
Other	**299**	527	467
Total Operating Activities	**9,362**	8,700	7,742
Investing Activities			
Capital expenditures	**(2,024)**	(1,482)	(1,679)
Proceeds from asset sales	**230**	143	227
Acquisitions	**(7,476)**	(61)	(5,471)
Change in investment securities	**(121)**	(107)	88
Total Investing Activities	**(9,391)**	(1,507)	(6,835)
Financing Activities			
Dividends to shareholders	**(2,539)**	(2,246)	(2,095)
Change in short-term debt	**4,911**	(2,052)	1,394
Additions to long-term debt	**1,963**	1,230	1,690
Reductions of long-term debt	**(1,188)**	(1,060)	(461)
Proceeds from the exercise of stock options	**555**	269	237
Treasury purchases	**(4,070)**	(1,236)	(568)
Total Financing Activities	**(368)**	(5,095)	197
Effect of Exchange Rate Changes on Cash and Cash Equivalents	**(46)**	387	17
Change in Cash and Cash Equivalents	**(443)**	2,485	1,121
Cash and Cash Equivalents, End of Year	**$5,469**	$5,912	$3,427
Supplemental Disclosure			
Cash payments for:			
Interest	**$ 630**	$ 538	$ 629
Income taxes	**1,634**	1,703	941

Favorite Cookie Company, the interpretation is similar. For each operating cash flow adjustment, a note identifies why the amount was added (or subtracted). All of these items identify either revenues for which cash was not received, cash received that was not earned, expenses for which cash was not paid, or cash paid for which expenses were not incurred. In short, all are timing differences between when revenue or expense was recognized and when cash was received or paid.

Exhibit 6 indicates that Procter & Gamble's operating cash flow ($9.362 billion in 2004) is consistently higher than its net income ($6.481 billion in 2004). This difference is explained by depreciation expense, which reduces net income but does not require cash payments; by deferred taxes, which reduce net income but have not been paid; and by changes in current assets and liabilities, particularly the increase in accounts payable and other liabilities. Increases in payables are common for companies that are increasing in size, as has been the case with Procter & Gamble.

The investing activities in Exhibit 6 demonstrate that Procter & Gamble has been growing. It has acquired additional assets (capital expenditures of $2.024 billion in 2004) and has made large acquisitions of other businesses (acquisitions of $7.476 billion in 2004). The investing activities have been paid for primarily by operating cash flows. Procter & Gamble's financing activities involved paying dividends ($2.539 billion in 2004) and repurchasing shares of its own stock (Treasury purchases of $4.070 billion in 2004). It also had some increase in debt, particularly short-term debt ($4.911 billion in 2004).

Procter & Gamble's cash balance did not change substantially during 2004. The net change in cash is not particularly important for most companies. The primary issue of concern is whether a company is generating sufficient cash flows to meet its operating needs and to take advantage of growth opportunities. Procter & Gamble demonstrates strong cash flows.

Many companies, including Procter & Gamble, provide supplemental disclosures on their cash flow statements. The amounts of interest and income taxes paid often are presented after the cash balance. Other cash items also may be presented if a company believes the information may be useful to investors and other stakeholders.

Self-Study Problem #2

The following information appears on the income statement and balance sheet of Bryson Co. for a recent fiscal period.

Net income	$16,540
Depreciation and amortization expense	3,560
Increase in accounts receivable	2,500
Decrease in merchandise	3,200
Increase in supplies	430
Increase in accounts payable	660
Decrease in wages payable	375
Increase in interest payable	280
Decrease in income tax payable	700

Required Use the information provided to prepare the operating activities section of the statement of cash flows for Bryson Co. using the indirect format.

The solution to Self-Study Problem 2 appears at the end of the chapter.

INTERPRETING CASH FLOWS

Objective 3
Interpret cash flow information as a basis for analyzing financial performance.

Understanding a company's cash flows and the reasons for the cash flows is critical to investors, managers, and other decision makers. To survive and prosper, a company must create sufficient cash flows to pay its bills, repay its debt, and provide a reasonable return to its owners. The statement of cash flows provides important information for evaluating past decisions and future prospects.

A company's net income and operating cash flow are seldom equal. A major difference between the two amounts is Depreciation and Amortization Expense. This expense reduces net income but does not require the use of cash. As shown in Exhibit 6, much of the difference between Procter & Gamble's net income and its operating cash flows is due to its depreciation and amortization expense. Other differences are explained by changes in current asset and current liability accounts. Changes in these accounts can provide useful information about a company's operations. Increases in current assets (Accounts Receivable and Inventory) and increases in Accounts Payable are common for companies that exhibit increases in net income. Higher sales lead to more receivables and require larger amounts of inventories. Payables also increase because of the increased demand for inventories. Increases in operating cash flows over time and large operating cash flows relative to net income (as seen in Exhibit 6) usually indicate good financial performance.

The amount of cash flow from operating activities normally is approximately equal to the amount of cash flow from (for) investing activities plus the amount of cash flow from (for) financing activities. A company depends on its operating activities to meet most of its cash flow needs. In the long run, operating cash flows must be sufficient to meet the cash needs of a company. If net operating cash flows are negative, a company is normally facing serious financial problems. In the short run, the company may be able to borrow cash or sell long-term assets to generate cash. But in the long run, it will be unable to stay in business using these methods. Creditors will refuse to lend money to a company that cannot create operating cash flows to ensure repayment of the debt. Also, the company will run out of assets that it can sell and still stay in business. Accordingly, negative operating cash flows combined with cash inflows from investing activities (from selling assets) and cash inflows from financing activities (from borrowing) is clearly a negative sign.

A company that is performing well normally creates net cash flow from operating activities. This excess cash can be used for expansion (to buy additional assets) or for financing purposes (to repay debt, repurchase stock, or pay dividends to stockholders). Accordingly, a combination of positive net cash flows from operating activities and negative cash flows for investing activities normally is a sign of good performance **and growth**. A growing company usually is increasing in value. As the company expands by purchasing more assets, it has the ability to produce and sell more products, which may result in additional profitability and increased operating cash flows. Observe that Procter & Gamble is using most of its operating cash flows for investing purposes. The company is acquiring additional assets each year.

If a company creates more cash from operating activities than it can use for investing purposes, it normally will use the cash to repay debt or to make payments to stockholders. If these payments are large, they may be an indication that the company is performing well but does not have a lot of good investing opportunities.

A company with a lot of good investing opportunities may borrow money or sell stock to provide additional cash to take advantage of these opportunities. Thus, cash inflow from financing activities is a positive sign if a company is using this cash to purchase additional assets (for investing activities). Cash inflow from financing activities is a bad sign if the cash is used for operating activities. This may indicate that the company cannot create enough cash from its operations to meet ongoing needs.

The cash flow information presented in Exhibit 6 suggests that Procter & Gamble was performing well during the three years reported. Operating cash flows were large and generally increasing, and cash was being invested in additional assets. The company was not experiencing any difficulty in repaying debt or in meeting any of its cash flow needs.

EXHIBIT 7
Cash Flow Patterns and the Financial Health of a Company

Operating Cash Flows	Investing Cash Flows	Financing Cash Flows	Normal Interpretation
+	−	+	The company is prosperous and growing. Financing cash flow is used to take advantage of growth opportunities.
−	+	+	The company is facing serious financial problems. It is selling assets and using financing activities to meet current cash needs.
+	+ or −	−	The company is prosperous but may not have a lot of good growth opportunities. It is using operating cash to pay off debt and pay stockholders.
+ or −	+	−	The company may be facing a current cash flow problem. It is selling assets to supplement current cash flows to cover its financing needs. This is especially a problem if the company is short of cash to repay debt.

Exhibit 7 summarizes the types of information provided by a cash flow statement. Other cash flow combinations are possible, but these are the most common and the most likely to provide a clear indication of how well a company is performing.

The amount of change in a company's cash balance usually is not of major importance. This change usually is small, and a small increase or decrease does not signal financial problems or strengths. In particular, you should not assume that a net decrease in cash is an indication of a major financial problem for a company. You should **focus instead on changes in operating, investing, and financing cash flows.**

CASE IN POINT

http://ingram.swlearning.com

Visit United Airlines' home page to learn more about the company.

Cash Flow Problems

Many companies in the airlines industry have faced financial problems in recent years. Some of these problems were created by the tragic events of September 11, 2001, which resulted in a dramatic decline in passenger miles. Additional problems were caused by the general economic downturn of the early years of the decade, increasing fuel costs, and competition from low-cost airlines.

The following information was reported by United Airlines in its 2003 annual report:

(In millions) Year Ended December 31	2003	2002	2001
Net earnings (loss)	$(2,808)	$(3,212)	$(2,145)
Cash flows from (for) operating activities	1,001	(1,139)	(160)
Cash flows from (for) investing activities	271	71	(1,969)
Cash flows from (for) financing activities	(336)	266	2,138

United reported losses each year. Operating cash flows were negative in 2001 and especially in 2002. They became positive in 2003, largely because of efforts to downsize and sell assets. Note that cash flow from investing activities was positive in 2002 and 2003, resulting from a sell-off of assets. The company borrowed heavily in 2001 to provide needed cash. Overall, United's earnings and cash flows are typical of a company facing financial problems.

Self-Study Problem #3

A statement of cash flows is provided below for Sound Bytes Company.

Sound Bytes Company Statement of Cash Flows For the Year Ended December 31, 2007	
Operating Activities	
Net income	$ 40,698
Adjusted for:	
Increase in accounts receivable	(23,034)
Increase in merchandise	(36,780)
Increase in accounts payable	22,479
Increase in prepaid expenses	(12,340)
Decrease in other payables	(3,982)
Depreciation and amortization	35,612
Net cash flow from operating activities	22,653
Investing Activities	
Sale of plant assets	86,511
Financing Activities	
Repayment of debt	(115,240)
Net decrease in cash	(6,076)
Cash balance, December 31, 2006	15,495
Cash balance, December 31, 2007	$ 9,419

Required Use the statement to answer the following questions.

A. How much cash flow did the company create from its operating activities?

B. What are the primary explanations for the difference between the company's net income and operating cash flow?

C. How did the company use its cash flows?

D. How well does the company appear to be performing based on its cash flow information?

The solution to Self-Study Problem 3 appears at the end of the chapter.

THINKING BEYOND THE QUESTION

HOW IS CASH FLOW INFORMATION DETERMINED AND REPORTED TO EXTERNAL USERS?

This chapter examined the opening question by describing two methods of preparing the statement of cash flows. Both methods use income statement and balance sheet amounts to determine cash flows. It is important to understand the relationships among the statements to obtain a complete picture of a business.

Is it possible for a profitable business to fail? What do you think are the primary causes of business failure? How are a company's financial statements useful for identifying financial problems that may lead to failure? What role does the statement of cash flows play in decision making by investors and creditors?

Self-Study Problem Solutions

SSP5-1

Jerome, Inc. Statement of Cash Flows	
Operating Activities	
Received from customers	$ 14,750
Paid for merchandise	(8,400)
Paid to employees	(4,000)
Paid for utilities	(2,200)
Paid for supplies	(1,800)
Net cash flow for operating activities	(1,650)
Investing Activities	
Received from sale of land	$ 20,000
Paid for building	(75,000)
Paid for equipment	(13,500)
Net cash flow for investing activities	(68,500)
Financing Activities	
Received from sale of stock	$100,000
Paid for debt repayment	(35,000)
Paid for dividends	(2,500)
Net cash flow from financing activities	62,500
Net decrease in cash	(7,650)
Cash balance at beginning of period	16,350
Cash balance at end of period	$ 8,700

The company's primary sources of cash were from selling stock, selling land, and from sales of goods to customers. Its primary uses of cash were the purchase of a building and equipment and the repayment of debt.

SSP5-2

Bryson Co. Statement of Cash Flows	
Operating Activities	
Net income	$16,540
Adjustments to reconcile net income to cash flows:	
Depreciation and amortization expense	3,560
Increase in accounts receivable	(2,500)
Decrease in merchandise	3,200
Increase in supplies	(430)
Increase in accounts payable	660
Decrease in wages payable	(375)
Increase in interest payable	280
Decrease in income tax payable	(700)
Net increase in operating cash flows	$20,235

SSP5-3 A. Net cash flow from operating activities was $22,653.

B. Primary explanations of the differences are increases in current assets (merchandise and receivables), an increase in accounts payable, and depreciation and amortization expense.

C. Cash flows from operating and investing activities were used to repay debt.

D. The company does not appear to be performing very well. Its operating cash flows were much less than its net income. The increase in merchandise and receivables and the increase in payables suggest that the company was not selling the inventory it was acquiring, was having difficulty collecting from its customers, and was having difficulty paying its suppliers. Selling plant assets to meet current cash needs is also a sign of poor financial performance. The company apparently needed more cash than it could create from its operating activities to meet its obligations. It was forced to sell assets to raise cash. In the long run, a company cannot survive by selling assets to repay debt.

Review *Summary of Important Concepts*

1. The statement of cash flows reports the cash inflows and outflows associated with the operating, investing, and financing activities of a company for a fiscal period. The statement may be presented in a direct or indirect format.
   a. The direct format lists cash activities associated with operating activities for a fiscal period.
   b. The indirect format reports cash flow from operating activities by adjusting net income for operating activities that did not generate or use cash during a fiscal period. These adjustments consist of revenues or expenses (such as depreciation) that did not have a cash effect and changes in current asset and current liability accounts.

2. Cash flow information is important to decision makers.
   a. Information about the sources and uses of cash indicates a company's ability to meet its payment obligations now and in the future.
   b. Cash flow information, along with information on the income statement and balance sheet, provides insight into a company's operating, investing, and financing activities.

Questions

Q5-1 *Obj. 1* What question is the direct format of the statement of cash flows designed to answer?

Q5-2 *Objs. 1, 2* If a company acquires machinery in exchange for a long-term note payable, both a financing activity and an investing activity have taken place. Explain how this is true.

Q5-3 *Objs. 1, 2* If long-term assets are acquired in exchange for shares of stock, no cash is involved. Will this transaction be reported on the statement of cash flows? If not, why not? If so, how?

Q5-4 *Objs. 1, 2* The direct format and indirect format relate only to the operating activities section of the statement of cash flows. Regarding the investing and financing activities sections, are they presented in a direct-type format or an indirect-type format?

Q5-5 *Objs. 1, 2* Why does the cash effect of interest appear as an operating activity, rather than a financing or investing activity?

Q5-6 *Obj. 2* Explain why depreciation expense and amortization expense are added back to net income in the determination of cash flows from operations when the indirect format is used.

Q5-7 *Obj. 2* In indirect format, why is an increase in accounts receivable subtracted from net income in computing cash flow from operations?

Q5-8 *Obj. 2* What question is the indirect format of the statement of cash flows designed to answer? Explain.

Q5-9 *Obj. 3* Why would one usually expect a growing company to have negative cash flow from investing activities?

Q5-10 *Obj. 3* Why is it a bad sign if cash flow from operations is consistently negative?

Q5-11 *Obj. 3* Why is it a bad sign if cash flow from investing activities is consistently positive?

Q5-12 *Obj. 3* Assume a company consistently produces net cash inflow from operations. To what uses might this cash inflow be applied?

Q5-13 *Obj. 3* Assume a company consistently reports a net cash outflow from financing activities. What does this suggest about the company?

Q5-14 *Obj. 3* Upon studying its statement of cash flows, you note that over the last three years a firm has consistently reported negative cash flow from operating activities, positive cash flow from investing activities, and negative cash flow from financing activities. What does this combination of cash flows suggest to you about the firm?

Q5-15 *Obj. 3* Explain how a company can have a net loss for a fiscal period but have a net increase in cash from operating activities.

Q5-16 *Obj. 3* A company operating in a mature industry with few opportunities for growth or expansion will generally report negative cash flow from financing activities. Why? Where might this cash be going?

Exercises

E5-1 *Obj. 1* The following information reflects cash flow and other activities of Better Vision Eyeglass Company for three months ended March 31.

Paid for equipment	$42,000	Paid to suppliers	$39,000
Paid for income taxes	3,000	Depreciation expense	13,000
Paid for insurance	200	Received from customers	87,500
Paid for interest	450	Received from issuing long-term debt	23,000
Paid for utilities	790	Received from sale of land	19,500
Paid for advertising	300	Paid to employees	18,000
Paid to owners	12,000		

Use this information to answer the following questions:

a. What was net cash flow from operating activities for the period?
b. What was net cash flow from financing activities for the period?
c. What was the net cash flow from investing activities for the period?
d. What was the net change in cash for the period?

E5-2 *Obj. 1* For each of the items listed below, identify whether the item would appear on the statement of cash flows (direct format) as part of the computation of cash flow from operating activities, investing activities, financing activities, or would not appear at all. Also, indicate whether the item is added or subtracted in computing cash flow using the direct method of preparing the statement of cash flows.

a. Purchase of plant assets
b. Cash paid to suppliers
c. Cash collected from customers
d. Payment of long-term debt
e. Net income
f. Depreciation expense
g. Payment of dividends
h. Issuing stock
i. Cash paid to employees
j. Cash paid for income taxes
k. Disposal of plant assets

E5-3 *Obj. 1* Northridge Company has the following information available for the first six months of the year.

Cash collected from customers	$247,000
Cash paid to suppliers	81,400
Cash paid for utilities	18,200
Cash paid for insurance	23,000
Cash paid for equipment	75,000
Cash paid to employees	60,400
Cash paid for interest	9,000
Cash paid for dividends	7,000
Cash received from disposal of equipment	18,500

Determine the cash flow from operating activities for the six-month period.

E5-4 *Obj. 1* Bay View Company reported the following information at the end of its most recent fiscal year.

Cash paid for fire insurance	$ 5,000
Cash paid for dividends	22,600
Cash paid to suppliers of inventory	119,850
Cash paid for interest	3,750
Cash collected from customers	187,200
Cash received from disposal of equipment	38,000
Cash paid for utilities	9,400
Cash paid to employees	31,500
Cash paid for equipment	65,100

Determine each of the following amounts. Show your work neatly and clearly.

a. Net cash flow from operating activities (direct format)
b. Net cash flow from financing activities
c. Net cash flow from investing activities

E5-5 *Obj. 1* Eden Healthfoods reported the following information.

Proceeds from issuance of long-term debt	$13,057
Additions to plant and equipment	5,500
Proceeds from sales of businesses	30,957
Proceeds from sales of plant and equipment	1,986
Payments of debt	83,000

Calculate the net cash flow from (a) financing and (b) investing activities for Eden.

E5-6 *Objs. 1, 2* All of the following statements apply to the statement of cash flows covering a given period. If a statement applies only to the direct format, write *D* in the space allowed. If a statement applies only to the indirect format, write *I* in the space allowed. If a statement applies to both formats, write *B* in the space allowed.

__________ a. The amount of cash received from customers is listed.
__________ b. A purpose of the statement is to reconcile the amount of cash generated by operating activities to the amount of net income generated by operating activities.
__________ c. The amount by which cash receipts from customers differed from sales is reported.
__________ d. Certain revenues and expenses that did not generate or consume cash are listed.
__________ e. The amount of net income is listed on the face of the statement.
__________ f. The amount of cash paid to suppliers of inventory is included.
__________ g. The amount of cash paid for taxes is reported.
__________ h. The amount of cash raised from selling bonds to investors is listed on the face of the statement.
__________ i. The purpose of the statement is to reveal the amount of cash received from or paid out for specific operating activities.
__________ j. The amount of cash paid to acquire land and buildings is included.

E5-7 *Objs. 1, 2* Each of the items found below might appear on a statement of cash flows.

	Statement Section	Statement Format	Added or Subtracted?
1. Decrease in taxes payable			
2. Cash paid to suppliers of inventory			
3. Dividends declared and paid			
4. Depreciation expense			
5. Sale of stock			
6. Increase in accounts receivable			
7. Cash collected from customers			
8. Purchase of plant assets			
9. Payments on long-term debt			
10. Cash paid for taxes			
11. Increase in wages payable			
12. Purchase of treasury stock			

For each item, indicate answers as shown.

a. Would it appear on the statement of cash flows under the operating activities (*O*), investing activities (*I*), or financing activities (*F*) section?
b. Would it appear in the direct format (*D*), indirect format (*I*), or in both formats (*B*)?
c. Would it be added (+) or subtracted (−) in computing cash flow?

E5-8 *Obj. 2* For each item in the following list, identify whether it would appear on the statement of cash flows (indirect format) as part of the computation of cash flow from operating activities, cash flow from investing activities, or cash flow from financing activities. Also, indicate whether the item is added or subtracted in computing cash flow using the indirect method of preparing the statement of cash flows.

a. Purchase of plant assets
b. Increase in accounts payable
c. Decrease in accounts receivable
d. Payment of long-term debt
e. Net income
f. Depreciation expense
g. Payment of dividends
h. Issuing stock
i. Increase in inventory
j. Decrease in taxes payable
k. Disposal of plant assets

E5-9 *Obj. 2* The following information is available for Sentry Company for the first month of the year.

Revenues	$17,000
Expenses	8,000
Increase in accounts receivable	800
Decrease in inventory	1,200
Decrease in supplies	400
Increase in accounts payable	1,050
Decrease in wages payable	900
Depreciation expense	1,100
Patent expense	250

Determine the cash flow from operating activities for the month.

E5-10 *Obj. 2* Use the information provided in each of the following independent situations to answer the questions. For each situation, briefly explain the reasoning behind each of your calculations.

a. Cash paid to suppliers for merchandise during a period was $37,500. Accounts payable decreased during the period by $3,000. Inventory increased during the period by $3,500. What was the cost of goods sold for the period?
b. Interest paid during a period was $4,000. Interest payable decreased during the period by $1,200. What was the interest expense for the period?
c. Cash flow from operations for a period was $28,000. Current assets decreased during the period by $6,000. Current liabilities decreased during the period by $2,000. What was net income for the period?
d. Cash collected from customers for a fiscal period was $27,000. Accounts receivable increased during the period by $3,000. What was sales revenue for the period?

E5-11 *Obj. 2* Use the information provided in each of the following independent situations to answer the questions. For each situation, briefly explain the reasoning behind each of your calculations.

a. Net cash flow from operations for a period was $30,000. Noncash revenues for the period were $11,000. Noncash expenses for the period were $13,200. What was net income for the period?
b. Wages expense for a period was $69,000. Wages payable increased during the period by $10,500. How much cash was paid to employees during the period?
c. Cash collected from customers for a fiscal period was $224,500. Sales revenue for the period was $241,000. Accounts receivable at the beginning of the period was $36,000. What was the balance in accounts receivable at the end of the period?
d. Net income for a period was $45,000. Current assets increased during the period by $7,500. Current liabilities increased during the period by $10,000. How much was cash flow from operations for the period?

E5-12 *Obj. 2* Changes in account balances are shown in the following chart. For each item, where appropriate, indicate the adjustment that would be made to net income in the operating cash flow section of a cash flow statement using the indirect method and the reason for the adjustment. Item *a* is provided as an example.

Account Balance	Adjustment and Reason
a. Accounts receivable increased $10,000	Subtract $10,000 from net income because cash collected from customers was $10,000 less than sales for the period.
b. Accounts payable increased $7,500	
c. Inventory decreased $50,000	
d. Notes payable increased $100,000	
e. Equipment decreased $80,000	
f. Prepaid insurance decreased $22,000	
g. Wages payable decreased $8,000	
h. Unearned revenue increased $13,000	

E5-13 *Obj. 2* The following information was reported by **The Boeing Company** in its 2004 annual report (in millions of dollars).

Decrease in inventories	$ 611
Increase in prepaid expenses	4,355
Depreciation and amortization	1,412
Increase in accounts payable	862
Increase in accounts receivable	241
Increase in income taxes payable	1,086
Net earnings	3,458
Other additions to net income	625

What was Boeing's cash flow from operating activities for the fiscal year?

E5-14 *Obj. 2* Martha Rosenbloom holds stock in several major corporations. Each year she receives a copy of the companies' annual reports. She looks at the pictures, reads the discussion by management, and examines some of the primary financial statement numbers. She has a pretty good understanding of some of the financial statement information. She tells her friends that she doesn't know how to make heads or tails of the statement of cash flows, however. She doesn't understand how depreciation and changes in current assets and liabilities have anything to do with cash. A mutual friend, Arthur Doyle, has found out that you are taking accounting and asks you to help Martha. Write Martha a letter explaining the cash flow from operating activities section of the statement of cash flows found in most annual reports. Martha's address is 945 Oak Lane, Anytown, USA.

E5-15 *Obj. 2* Great Wall Travel Company had the following adjustments to net income when computing its cash flow from operations for the year just ended.

Net income		$315,000
Add: Adjustments		
(1) Depreciation	$13,000	
(2) Increase in accounts receivable	(2,500)	
(3) Increase in inventory	(3,000)	
(4) Decrease in accounts payable	(1,700)	5,800
Cash flow from operations		$320,800

a. Explain why it is generally necessary to make additions to and subtractions from net income when computing cash flow from operations in the indirect format.

b. For each adjustment (labeled 1 through 4), explain why that specific adjustment was necessary to determine cash flow from operations.

E5-16 *Obj. 3* At year-end, the following manufacturing companies reported cash flows as shown below.

	Co. A	Co. B	Co. C
Cash flow from operating activities	$ 6,480	$ 15,200	$ 2,304
Cash flow from (for) investing activities	(5,508)	457	938
Cash flow from (for) financing activities	(834)	(13,600)	(2,307)

Respond to each of the following questions.

a. Which company had the largest amount of cash flow from operating activities? Which had the smallest?

b. Would you generally expect cash flow associated with investing activities to be negative? Why or why not?

c. In what ways does Co. A appear to be different from the other two companies? What do these differences suggest about the companies?

E5-17 *Obj. 3* Consider the pattern in following selected year-end data for Landsdowne Company.

Year	1	2	3	4	5	6
Cash flow from operating activities	$20,000	$25,000	$18,000	$12,000	$ 6,000	$ 2,000
Receivables	35,000	37,000	42,000	45,000	50,000	53,000
Inventory	70,000	76,000	80,000	84,000	86,000	90,000
Payables	24,000	28,000	32,000	46,000	57,000	66,000
Net income	50,000	53,000	55,000	59,000	63,000	55,000

Provide an explanation for the changes over the six-year period. Year 6 is the most recent year. What difficulties do you believe the company is facing?

E5-18 *Obj. 3* Sommer Company has experienced the following results over the past three years.

Year	1	2	3
(In thousands)			
Net income (loss)	$ 2,000	$(10,000)	$ (8,000)
Depreciation and amortization	(9,000)	(11,000)	(14,000)
Net cash flow from operating activities	13,000	15,000	18,000
Net expenditures for plant assets	9,000	6,000	5,000

The price of Sommer's common stock has declined steadily over the three-year period. At the end of year 3, it is trading at $10 per share. Early in year 4, Bottom Fischer, who specializes in taking over poorly performing businesses, has offered shareholders of Sommer $18 per share for their stock. Why would Fischer be willing to pay such an amount? What does he see in the company that suggests value?

E5-19 *Obj. 3* Rockman Associates has reported the following selected account balances on its most recent balance sheet.

Account and balance	Anticipated future event and cash flow
a. Accounts receivable, $12,000	$12,000 of cash should be received from customers during the next fiscal year. This will appear in the operating activities section.
b. Prepaid insurance, $22,000	
c. Merchandise, $50,000	
d. Treasury stock, $33,000	
e. Accounts payable, $6,500	
f. Machinery, $92,000	
g. Notes payable, long-term, $88,000	
h. Unearned revenue, $10,000	
i. Taxes payable, $7,800	
j. Retained earnings, $56,000	

For each item, describe the anticipated future event and cash flow (if any) that is expected to occur and in which section of a future statement of cash flows it will appear. The first item is completed as an example.

Problems

P5-1 *Obj. 1* **PREPARING A STATEMENT OF CASH FLOWS (DIRECT FORMAT)**

San Garza Properties has been in business for many years. On December 31, 2006, the firm's cash balance was $9,121. During January of 2007, the 14 events on the following page were recorded in the company's accounting system.

Required Prepare a statement of cash flows for the month of January 2007. Use good form and the direct format.

		Assets		=	Liabilities	+	Owners' Equity	
Date	**Accounts**	**Cash**	**Other Assets**				**Contributed Capital**	**Retained Earnings**
1	Cash	18,000						
	Bank Loan Payable				18,000			
2	Rent Expense							−3,000
	Cash	−3,000						
3	Office Furniture		5,500					
	Cash	−5,500						
4	Merchandise		9,000					
	Accounts Payable				9,000			
5	Cash	10,000						
	Common Stock						10,000	
6	Advertising Expense							−2,200
	Cash	−2,200						
7	Accounts Receivable		18,000					
	Sales Revenue							18,000
8	Merchandise		−7,500					
	Cost of Goods Sold							−7,500
9	Cash	8,100						
	Accounts Receivable		−8,100					
10	Accounts Payable				−7,000			
	Cash	−7,000						
11	Computer Equipment		4,800					
	Cash	−4,800						
12	Wages Expense							−1,400
	Wages Payable				1,400			
13	Dividends							−2,000
	Cash	−2,000						
14	Bank Loan Payable				−5,000			
	Interest Expense							−135
	Cash	−5,135						

P5-2 PREPARING THE STATEMENT OF CASH FLOWS (DIRECT FORMAT)
Obj. 1

Planet Accessories Company reported the following balance sheet and income statement at year-end 2007. In addition, dividends totaling $1,000 were paid.

Balance Sheets at December 31	**2007**	**2006**
Cash	$ 826	$ 553
Accounts receivable	8,950	8,000
Inventories	11,600	10,100
Prepaid insurance	400	300
Property, plant and equipment	8,750	3,735
Less: Accumulated depreciation	(2,900)	(1,900)
Land	5,850	4,850
Total assets	$33,476	$25,638
Rent payable	$ 3,750	$ 4,000
Wages payable	1,750	1,400
Loan payable, long-term	9,200	5,200
Common stock, $1 par value	5,400	4,400
Retained earnings	17,950	12,212
Treasury stock	(4,574)	(1,574)
Total liabilities and shareholders' equity	$33,476	$25,638

Income Statement for 2007	
Sales revenue	$135,800
Cost of goods sold	54,300
Gross profit	81,500
Operating expenses:	
Advertising	17,029
Depreciation	1,000
Insurance	4,800
Rent	14,255
Wages	33,400
Operating income	11,016
Interest expense	650
Income before taxes	10,366
Taxes	3,628
Net income	$ 6,738

Required

A. Assume the company uses the direct format to prepare its statement of cash flows. What amounts would be reported on the 2007 statement of cash flows for each of the following?
   1. Cash collections from customers (Hint: Inspect Sales Revenue and the change in Accounts Receivable.)
   2. Cash paid to suppliers of inventory (Hint: Assume all purchases were made for cash.)
   3. Cash paid for insurance (Hint: Inspect the insurance expense account and the change in the prepaid insurance account.)
   4. Cash paid for rent (Hint: Inspect Rent Expense and the change in Rent Payable.)
   5. Cash paid for depreciation
   6. Cash paid for wages

B. What items and amounts would be reported under cash flow from investing activities? (Hint: Inspect the changes in long-term asset accounts.)

C. What items and amounts would be reported under cash flow from financing activities? (Hint: Inspect the changes in long-term liability and stockholders' equity accounts.)

D. Prepare a statement of cash flows using the direct format.

P5-3 RECONCILING NET INCOME AND CASH FLOW FROM OPERATIONS

Obj. 2

For the fiscal year just completed, Dollar Sine Enterprises had the following summary information available concerning operating activities. The company had no investing or financing activities this year.

Sales of merchandise to customers on credit	$307,400
Sales of merchandise to customers for cash	88,250
Cost of merchandise sold on credit	200,000
Cost of merchandise sold for cash	57,400
Purchases of merchandise from suppliers on credit	233,700
Purchases of merchandise from suppliers for cash	48,100
Collections from customers on accounts receivable	321,000
Cash payments to suppliers on accounts payable	293,600
Operating expenses (all paid in cash)	93,500

Required

A. Determine the amount of:
   1. net income for the year.
   2. cash flow from operations for the year (direct format).

B. Indicate the direction and amounts by which each of these accounts changed during the year.
   1. Accounts receivable
   2. Merchandise inventory
   3. Accounts payable

C. Using your results above, prepare the operating activities section of the statement of cash flows (indirect format).

P5-4 PREPARING A STATEMENT OF CASH FLOWS (INDIRECT FORMAT)

Obj. 2

Reuben Corporation has completed its comparative balance sheet and income statement, shown at the top of the following page, at year-end 2007.

Additional information:

1. A payment of $8,250 was made on the loan principal during the year.
2. Just before year-end, a dividend was distributed to stockholders.
3. A parcel of land was acquired early in the year.
4. New shares of common stock were sold during the year.

Required Prepare a statement of cash flows in good form using the indirect format.

Comparative Balance Sheet	December 31, 2007	2006
Cash	$ 4,400	$ 3,550
Accounts receivable	4,100	5,300
Inventory	5,700	4,100
Prepaid advertising	900	1,200
Buildings and furnishings	20,000	20,000
Accumulated depreciation	(6,000)	(5,000)
Land	14,000	10,000
Total assets	$43,100	$39,150
Rent payable	$ 2,800	$ 2,600
Taxes payable	1,600	2,000
Wages payable	2,000	900
Loan payable, long-term	14,000	22,250
Common stock	16,000	10,000
Retained earnings	6,700	1,400
Total liabilities and equity	$43,100	$39,150

Income Statement for 2007	
Sales revenue	$355,000
Cost of goods sold	241,400
Gross profit	113,600
Operating expenses:	
Advertising	8,300
Depreciation	1,000
Insurance	3,500
Rent	31,200
Wages	57,380
Operating income	12,220
Interest expense	1,450
Income before tax	10,770
Taxes	3,770
Net income	$ 7,000

P5-5 PREPARING THE STATEMENT OF CASH FLOWS (INDIRECT FORMAT)

Obj. 2

Refer to the financial statement information in Problem P5-2 and use it to complete the requirements below.

Required

A. Assume the company uses the indirect format to prepare its statement of cash flows. What amounts would be reported on the 2007 statement of cash flows for each of the following?
   1. Net income
   2. Adjustment for depreciation expense
   3. Adjustment for accounts receivable
   4. Adjustment for inventories
   5. Adjustment for prepaid insurance
   6. Adjustment for rent payable
   7. Adjustment for wages payable

B. What items and amounts would be reported under cash flow from investing activities? (Hint: Inspect the changes in long-term asset accounts.)

C. What items and amounts would be reported under cash flow from financing activities? (Hint: Inspect the changes in long-term liability and stockholders' equity accounts.)

D. Prepare a statement of cash flows using the indirect format.

P5-6 INTERPRETING CASH FLOWS

Obj. 3

Located in Milwaukee, Wisconsin, **Harley-Davidson Inc.** has been a manufacturer of motorcycles for over one hundred years. On the following pages are the Consolidated Statements of Cash Flows and Consolidated Statements of Income for the years ended 2004, 2003, and 2002.

Required Use the financial statements shown on the following pages to respond to the questions below.

1. Can you find evidence in the financial statements to indicate the company has sources of income other than from manufacturing and selling motorcycles?
2. What trends do you observe when examining the company's sales and earnings?
3. What is the primary source of cash from operating activities over the three years shown in the 2004 statements?
4. What are the company's major uses of cash?
5. Based on your assessment of the earnings and cash flows of Harley-Davidson, what are your conclusions about its financial strength?

Harley-Davidson, Inc.
Consolidated Statements of Cash Flows
Years ended December 31, 2004, 2003 and 2002
(In thousands)

	2004	2003	2002
Cash flows from operating activities:			
Net income	$ 889,766	$ 760,928	$ 580,217
Adjustments to reconcile net income to net cash provided by operating activities:			
Depreciation	214,112	196,918	175,778
Provision for long-term employee benefits	62,806	76,422	57,124
Provision for finance credit losses	3,070	4,076	6,167
Gain on current year securitizations	(58,302)	(82,221)	(56,139)
Net change in wholesale finance receivables	(154,124)	(154,788)	(140,107)
Contributions to pension plans	—	(192,000)	(153,636)
Tax benefit from the exercise of stock options	51,476	13,805	14,452
Deferred income taxes	(41,513)	42,105	38,560
Other	27,301	16,051	7,057
Net changes in current assets and current liabilities	(24,866)	(18,644)	16,089
Total adjustments	79,960	(98,276)	(34,655)
Net cash provided by operating activities	969,726	662,652	545,562
Cash flows from investing activities:			
Capital expenditures	(213,550)	(227,230)	(323,866)
Finance receivables acquired or originated	(2,394,644)	(2,090,201)	(1,731,169)
Finance receivables collected	274,670	252,705	230,153
Proceeds from securitizations	1,847,895	1,724,060	1,246,262
Collection of retained securitization interests	125,732	118,113	89,970
Purchase of marketable securities	(1,091,326)	(1,538,548)	(1,508,285)
Sales and redemptions of marketable securities	742,284	1,145,000	1,253,719
Purchase of remaining interest in joint venture	(9,500)	—	—
Other, net	10,689	9,690	22,813
Net cash used in investing activities	(707,750)	(606,411)	(720,403)
Cash flows from financing activities:			
Proceeds from issuance of medium term notes	—	399,953	—
Net increase (decrease) finance credit facilities and commercial paper	305,047	(175,835)	165,528
Dividends paid	(119,232)	(58,986)	(41,457)
Purchase of common stock for treasury	(564,132)	(103,880)	(56,814)
Issuance of common stock under employee stock option plans	62,171	19,378	12,679
Net cash (used) provided by financing activities	(316,146)	80,630	79,936
Net increase (decrease) in cash and cash equivalents	(54,170)	136,871	(94,905)
Cash and cash equivalents:			
At beginning of year	329,329	192,458	287,363
At end of year	$ 275,159	$ 329,329	$ 192,458

Harley-Davidson, Inc.
Consolidated Statements of Income
Years ended December 31, 2004, 2003 and 2002
(In thousands, except per share amounts)

	2004	2003	2002
Net revenue	$5,015,190	$4,624,274	$4,090,970
Cost of goods sold	3,115,655	2,958,708	2,673,129
Gross profit	1,899,535	1,665,566	1,417,841
Financial services income	305,262	279,459	211,500
Financial services expense	116,662	111,586	107,273
Operating income from financial services	188,600	167,873	104,227
Selling, administrative and engineering expense	726,644	684,175	639,366
Income from operations	1,361,491	1,149,264	882,702
Investment income, net	23,101	23,088	16,541
Other, net	(5,106)	(6,317)	(13,416)
Income before provision for income taxes	1,379,486	1,166,035	885,827
Provision for income taxes	489,720	405,107	305,610
Net income	$ 889,766	$ 760,928	$ 580,217
Basic earnings per common share	$ 3.02	$ 2.52	$ 1.92
Diluted earnings per common share	$ 3.00	$ 2.50	$ 1.90
Cash dividends per common share	$ 0.405	$ 0.195	$ 0.135

P5-7 *Obj. 3* **ERRORS IN REPORTING CASH FLOW FROM OPERATING ACTIVITIES**

Starkovich Architects Inc. uses the direct format to prepare the statement of cash flows. At year-end 2007, the following comparative balance sheet and abbreviated income statement were available as shown.

	December 31			
Comparative Balance Sheet	**2007**	**2006**	**Income Statement for 2007**	
Cash	$ 3,400	$ 2,750	Service revenue	$ 73,000
Accounts receivable	5,800	4,300	Commission revenue	42,100
Inventory	4,700	5,100	Advertising expense	(13,400)
Land	10,000	10,000	Rent expense	(24,000)
Total assets	$23,900	$22,150	Wages expense	(42,600)
			Taxes expense	(12,000)
Rent payable	$ 2,500	$ 2,900	Net income	$ 23,100
Taxes payable	1,600	1,600		
Wages payable	3,200	1,050		
Common stock	15,000	15,000		
Retained earnings	1,600	1,600		
Total liabilities and equity	$23,900	$22,150		

From this information, the accounting staff prepared the operating activities section of the statement of cash flows shown below using the direct format.

Starkovich Architects, Inc.
Operating Activities (Direct Format)
Year Ending December 31, 2007

Operating Activities	
Cash received from customers	$115,100
Cash paid for advertising	(13,400)
Cash paid for rent	(23,600)
Cash paid for wages	(40,450)
Cash paid for taxes	(11,000)
Cash provided by operating activities	$ 26,650

(Continued)

Required

A. What evidence can you identify to suggest that certain items are misstated in the computation of cash flow from operating activities? For each item that you believe is misstated, specify why you know this. (You may assume that the income statement and balance sheets are correct as presented.)

B. Prepare a revised computation of cash flow from operating activities incorporating the necessary changes.

P5-8 DEPRECIATION AND CASH FLOW

Obj. 3

A colleague is about to make a presentation to the management group regarding a $2 million capital investment proposal. She is quite sure that the management group will press her to identify a new source of financing to support the proposed investment. She shows you the operating activities section of the company's most recent statement of cash flows. (Amounts are in thousands of dollars.)

Operating Activities	
Net Income	$ 84,597
Depreciation expense	10,501
Decrease in accounts receivable	4,157
Increase in wages payable	2,924
	$102,179

Your colleague is aware that there are a variety of methods acceptable under GAAP by which depreciation expense can be computed. Further, she knows that the company currently uses a very conservative method that results in low depreciation expense, especially in the early years of an asset's life. Your colleague is going to suggest that the firm use a more aggressive depreciation policy that will result in higher depreciation expense for the next several years. Says she, "The higher depreciation expense will generate more cash from operating activities. According to the cash flow statement here, adding back greater depreciation expense will result in more cash provided by operating activities. See?" Assume it's quite reasonable that the firm use a more aggressive depreciation method.

Required

A. What format is this company using to prepare the statement of cash flows?

B. Do you agree with your colleague's thinking? Why or why not?

C. Construct a numerical example to prove your argument.

P5-9 INTERRELATIONSHIPS AMONG FINANCIAL STATEMENTS

Objs. 2, 3

AutoZone is one of the largest retailers of automotive parts and accessories in the United States with over 3,500 stores in the United States and Mexico. The company is listed on the New York Stock Exchange (NYSE: AZO). AutoZone offers its products to the "do-it-yourself" automotive market segment. Presented on the following page is the cash flow statement from the company's 2004 annual report.

Required Answer the following questions.

A. Which reporting format does AutoZone use for the statement of cash flows?

B. Compare the three-year trends of sales and net income. Are these trends encouraging? Why or why not?

C. How does the pattern of cash flow from operations match up with the trends of net income and sales for the most recent three years?

D. During the most recent year shown, determine whether the following balance sheet accounts increased or decreased.
   1. Cash and cash equivalents
   2. Accounts receivable and prepaid expenses
   3. Merchandise inventory
   4. Accounts payable and accrued expenses

E. What has been the major use of cash from investing activities during the three years?

F. What has been the major use of cash from financing activities during the three years?

AutoZone
Consolidated Statements of Cash Flows

(In thousands)	August 28, 2004 (52 Weeks)	Year Ended August 30, 2003 (52 Weeks)	August 31, 2002 (53 Weeks)
Cash flows from operating activities:			
Net income	**$ 566,202**	$ 517,604	$ 428,148
Adjustments to reconcile net income to net cash provided by operating activities:			
Depreciation and amortization of property and equipment	**106,891**	109,748	118,255
Amortization of debt origination fees	**4,230**	7,334	2,283
Income tax benefit realized from exercise of options	**24,339**	37,402	42,159
Gains from warranty negotiations	**(42,094)**	(8,695)	—
Changes in operating assets and liabilities:			
Deferred income taxes	**44,498**	65,701	28,483
Accounts receivable and prepaid expenses	**(26,101)**	(27,468)	(12,879)
Merchandise inventories	**(119,539)**	(135,732)	(168,150)
Accounts payable and accrued expenses	**60,154**	176,702	282,408
Income taxes payable	**32,118**	(3,460)	13,743
Other, net	**(12,319)**	(18,329)	1,720
Net cash provided by operating activities	**638,379**	720,807	736,170
Cash flows from investing activities:			
Capital expenditures	**(184,870)**	(182,242)	(117,239)
Acquisition	**(11,441)**	—	—
Proceeds from sale of business	—	—	25,723
Proceeds from disposal of capital assets	**2,590**	14,443	25,094
Notes receivable from officers	—	—	1,911
Net cash used in investing activities	**(193,721)**	(167,799)	(64,511)
Cash flows from financing activities:			
Net change in commercial paper	**254,400**	44,800	(162,247)
Proceeds from issuance of debt	**500,000**	500,000	150,000
Repayment of debt	**(431,995)**	(215,000)	(15,000)
Net proceeds from sale of common stock	**33,552**	45,303	55,676
Purchase of treasury stock	**(848,102)**	(891,095)	(698,983)
Settlement of interest rate hedge instruments	**32,166**	(28,524)	—
Other	**(929)**	14,304	(4,814)
Net cash used in financing activities	**(460,908)**	(530,212)	(675,368)
Net increase (decrease) in cash and cash equivalents	**(16,250)**	22,796	(3,709)
Cash and cash equivalents at beginning of year	**93,102**	70,306	74,015
Cash and cash equivalents at end of year	**$ 76,852**	$ 93,102	$ 70,306
Supplemental cash flow information:			
Interest paid, net of interest cost capitalized	**$ 77,871**	$ 77,533	$ 77,935
Income taxes paid	**$ 237,010**	$ 215,760	$ 178,417

(Continued)

AutoZone
Consolidated Statements of Income

(In thousands, except per share data)	August 28, 2004 (52 Weeks)	Year Ended August 30, 2003 (52 Weeks)	August 31, 2002 (53 Weeks)
Net sales	**$ 5,637,025**	$ 5,457,123	$ 5,325,510
Cost of sales, including warehouse and delivery expenses	**2,880,446**	2,942,114	2,950,123
Operating, selling, general and administrative expenses	**1,757,873**	1,597,212	1,604,379
Operating profit	**998,706**	917,797	771,008
Interest expense, net	**92,804**	84,790	79,860
Income before income taxes	**905,902**	833,007	691,148
Income taxes	**339,700**	315,403	263,000
Net income	**$ 566,202**	$ 517,604	$ 428,148
Weighted average shares for basic earnings per share	**84,993**	94,906	104,446
Effect of dilutive stock equivalents	**1,357**	2,057	2,665
Adjusted weighted average shares for diluted earnings per share	**86,350**	96,963	107,111
Basic earnings per share	**$ 6.66**	$ 5.45	$ 4.10
Diluted earnings per share	**$ 6.56**	$ 5.34	$ 4.00

P5-10 EVALUATING INFORMATION FROM A STATEMENT OF CASH FLOWS

Obj. 3

Circuit City is one of the nation's largest retailers of brand-name consumer electronics and major appliances. Its headquarters are in Richmond, Virginia. The company's comparative statements of cash flows from a recent annual report are shown on the next page.

Required Answer the following questions.

A. For the three years shown, compare the trend in net income to the trend in cash provided by operations.

B. What were the most significant reasons that cash provided by operations was negative for fiscal 2004?

C. Inspect the information shown under investing activities. Also note the amount of depreciation and amortization reported under operating activities. Does this company's long-term asset base appear to be expanding, shrinking, or staying about the same size? Explain your answer.

Circuit City Stores, Inc.
Consolidated Statements of Cash Flows

(Amounts in thousands)	Years Ended February 29 or 28 2004	2003	2002
Operating Activities:			
Net (loss) earnings	**$ (89,269)**	$ 82,263	$ 199,930
Adjustments to reconcile net (loss) earnings to net cash (used in) provided by operating activities of continuing operations:			
Net loss (earnings) from discontinued operations	**88,482**	(87,572)	(132,374)
Depreciation and amortization	**197,969**	157,469	134,371
Stock option expense	**24,184**	30,823	25,184
Amortization of restricted stock awards	**13,395**	20,828	15,678
Loss on dispositions of property and equipment	**7,500**	15,659	13,735
Provision for deferred income taxes	**(35,618)**	(18,664)	19,558
Changes in operating assets and liabilities:			
(Increase) decrease in accounts receivable, net	**(13,654)**	6,229	41,191
Increase in retained interests in securitized receivables	**(186,537)**	(92,888)	(12,256)
(Increase) decrease in merchandise inventory	**(107,520)**	(175,493)	176,284
(Increase) decrease in prepaid expenses and other current assets	**(20,452)**	21,081	16,071
Decrease (increase) in other assets	**10,150**	(27,898)	(2,359)
(Decrease) increase in accounts payable	**(84,066)**	(55,818)	202,289
Increase (decrease) in accrued expenses and other current liabilities and accrued income taxes	**35,232**	(59,485)	118,064
Increase in accrued straight-line rent and other liabilities	**28,528**	19,407	71,188
Net Cash (Used in) Provided By Operating Activities of Continuing Operations	**(131,676)**	(164,059)	886,554
Investing Activities:			
Purchases of property and equipment	**(175,769)**	(150,757)	(172,580)
Proceeds from sales of property and equipment	**46,590**	60,838	88,461
Net Cash Used in Investing Activities of Continuing Operations	**(129,179)**	(89,919)	(84,119)
Financing Activities:			
(Payments on) proceeds from short-term debt, net	—	(397)	184
Principal payments on long-term debt	**(1,458)**	(24,865)	(19,788)
Repurchase and retirement of common stock	**(84,353)**	—	—
Issuances of Circuit City common stock, net	**11,391**	8,901	17,920
Issuances of CarMax Group common stock, net	—	298	(1,958)
Proceeds from CarMax Group stock offering, net	—	—	139,546
Dividends paid	**(14,660)**	(14,687)	(14,556)
Net Cash (Used in) Provided by Financing Activities of Continuing Operations	**(89,080)**	(30,750)	121,348
Cash Provided by (Used in) Discontinued Operations:			
Bankcard Operation	**248,736**	(94,533)	(87,125)
Carmax Operation	—	26,185	(2,904)
Divx Operation	—	(10,500)	(22,837)
(Decrease) increase in cash and cash equivalents	**(101,199)**	(363,576)	810,917
Cash and cash equivalents at beginning of year	**884,670**	1,248,246	437,329
Cash and cash equivalents at end of year	**$783,471**	$ 884,670	$1,248,246
Supplemental Disclosures of Cash Flow Information			
Cash paid (received) during the year for:			
Interest	**$ 2,999**	$ 1,824	$ 2,340
Income taxes	**$ 36,324**	$ 107,946	$ (44,926)
Non-cash operating, investing and financing activities:			
Asset acquired from variable interest entity	**$ 12,600**	$ —	$ —
Liability assumed from variable interest entity	**$ 12,600**	$ —	$ —
Reduction of liability related to the discontinued Divx operation	**$ 2,315**	$ —	$ —

P5-11 EVALUATING INCOME AND CASH FLOWS

Objs. 2, 3 Selected financial statement information is reported below for Office Decor Company. All amounts are in thousands.

For the Year Ended December 31, 2007	
Sales revenue	$11,200
Cost of goods sold	6,400
Operating expenses	2,800
Net income	2,000
Dividends paid	1,000

December 31	2007	2006
Cash	$ 1,340	$1,940
Accounts receivable	4,600	2,200
Inventories	9,400	5,000
Accounts payable	3,800	2,600
Notes payable	10,000	6,000

Required Prepare a statement of cash flows (indirect format) for Office Decor, assuming that all important cash flow activities are reflected in the information provided above. Examine the financial information presented for Office Decor Company. What financial problems do you see? What are some potential causes of these problems?

P5-12 INTERPRETING A CASH FLOW STATEMENT

Obj. 3 The 2004 consolidated statement of cash flows of **McDonald's Corporation** is presented below.

McDonald's Corporation
Consolidated Statement of Cash Flows

(In millions)	Years ended December 31, 2004	2003	2002
Operating Activities			
Net income	**$ 2,278.5**	$ 1,471.4	$ 893.5
Adjustments to reconcile to cash provided by operations			
Cumulative effect of accounting changes		36.8	98.6
Depreciation and amortization	**1,201.0**	1,148.2	1,050.8
Deferred income taxes	**(171.9)**	181.4	(44.6)
Changes in working capital items			
Accounts receivable	**(35.9)**	64.0	1.6
Inventories, prepaid expenses and other current assets	**(14.9)**	(30.2)	(38.1)
Accounts payable	**86.7**	(77.6)	(11.2)
Income taxes	**84.2**	23.5	139.0
Other accrued liabilities	**70.2**	(170.7)	309.0
Other (including noncash portion of impairment and other charges)	**405.7**	622.0	491.5
Cash provided by operations	**3,903.6**	3,268.8	2,890.1
Investing Activities			
Property and equipment expenditures	**(1,419.3)**	(1,307.4)	(2,003.8)
Purchases of restaurant businesses	**(149.7)**	(375.8)	(548.4)
Sales of restaurant businesses and property	**306.3**	390.6	369.5
Other	**(120.4)**	(77.0)	(283.9)
Cash used for investing activities	**(1,383.1)**	(1,369.6)	(2,466.6)

	2004	2003	2002
Financing Activities			
Net short-term borrowings (repayments)	**$ 35.9**	$ (533.5)	$ (606.8)
Long-term financing issuances	**225.6**	398.1	1,502.6
Long-term financing repayments	**(1,077.0)**	(756.2)	(750.3)
Treasury stock purchases	**(621.0)**	(391.0)	(670.2)
Common stock dividends	**(695.0)**	(503.5)	(297.4)
Proceeds from stock option exercises	**580.5**	171.2	195.0
Other	**(82.5)**	(121.9)	115.9
Cash used for financing activities	**(1,633.5)**	(1,736.8)	(511.2)
Cash and equivalents increase (decrease)	**887.0**	162.4	(87.7)
Cash and equivalents at beginning of year	**492.8**	330.4	418.1
Cash and equivalents at end of year	**$ 1,379.8**	$ 492.8	$ 330.4
Supplemental cash flow disclosures			
Interest paid	**$ 370.2**	$ 426.9	$ 359.7
Income taxes paid	**1,017.6**	608.5	572.2

Required Use the information from the consolidated statement of cash flows to answer the following questions.

A. What was the amount of change in McDonald's cash and cash equivalents for 2004?
B. What were the primary sources of cash for the company?
C. What were the primary uses of cash?
D. Why were depreciation and amortization added to net income in computing cash flow from operations?
E. Why were increases in accounts receivable subtracted from net income in computing cash flow from operating activities?
F. Why were property and equipment expenditures listed as investing activities?
G. How much new long-term debt was issued during the year? How much long-term debt was paid off?
H. Does the company appear to be facing a cash flow problem? Explain your answer.

P5-13 INTERPRETING CASH FLOWS

Obj. 3 The operating activities section of Bernstein Company's cash flow statement is reported below.

(In millions)	2007	2006	2005
Net income	$ 391	$ 455	$467
Depreciation and amortization	258	247	223
Special and nonrecurring items	(3)	0	0
Changes in current assets and liabilities:			
Accounts receivable	(220)	(102)	(66)
Inventories	(112)	(73)	(45)
Accounts payable	15	(22)	19
Income taxes	6	(7)	30
Other accrued expenses	(17)	26	11
Cash flow provided by operations	$ 318	$ 524	$639

Required What does this information reveal about why cash flow from operations has decreased by 50% over the three-year period? Be specific and explain the basis for your conclusions.

P5-14 INTERPRETING THE CASH FLOW STATEMENT

Obj. 3 **Best Buy Company, Inc.**, a retailer of consumer electronics headquartered in Minnesota, recently reported the following cash flow from operating activities and income statement.

(Continued)

Cash Flow from Operating Activities

(In millions)	February 28, 2004
Operating Activities	
Net Earnings	$ 705
Loss from discontinued operations	95
Earnings from continuing operations	800
Adjustments to reconcile net earnings to net cash:	
Depreciation and amortization	405
Increase in accounts receivable	(27)
Increase in inventories	(507)
Increase in other assets	(22)
Increase in accounts payable	318
Increase in accrued expenses and other	447
Net cash provided by operating activities	$1,414

Income Statement

(In millions)	February 28, 2004
Revenues	$24,547
Cost of goods sold	18,350
Gross profit	6,197
Selling, general, and administrative expenses	4,893
Interest expense, net	8
Earnings from continuing operations before income tax expense	1,296
Income tax expense	496
Earnings from continuing operations	800
Loss from discontinued operations (net of tax)	95
Net earnings	$ 705

Required Use the information from the financial statements to answer each of the following questions.

A. How much cash did Best Buy collect from customers in the fiscal year ended February 28, 2004?
B. How much cash did Best Buy pay out for inventory in the fiscal year ended February 28, 2004?
C. How much cash did Best Buy pay out for selling, general, and administrative expenses in the fiscal year ended February 28, 2004? The changes in Other Assets and in Accrued Expenses and Other are related to selling, general and administrative expenses.

P5-15 COMPARING CASH FLOWS

Obj. 3

Summarized cash flow information is shown on the following page for two computer industry firms: **Dell Inc.,** based in Round Rock, Texas, and **Apple Computer**, headquartered in Cupertino, California.

	Dell	Apple Computer
(In millions)	**Year ended 1/28/2005**	**Year ended 9/25/2004**
Net income	$3,043	$ 276
Adjustments:		
Depreciation and amortization	334	150
(Increase) decrease in accounts receivable	(779)	(8)
(Increase) decrease in inventories	(132)	(45)
(Increase) decrease in other assets	(698)	(215)
Increase (decrease) in payables	3,240	297
Other adjustments	302	479
Net cash provided by operating activities	5,310	934
Net cash provided by (used in) investing activities	(2,317)	(1,488)
Net cash provided by (used in) financing activities	(3,128)	127
Effect of exchange rates on cash equivalents	565	
Net change in cash	430	(427)

Required Write a short report comparing the financial performance of the two companies. In what important ways were the results for both companies similar? In what important ways were the results different?

P5-16 INTERPRETING CASH FLOWS

Obj. 3

Required Identify whether each of the following statements is true or false. Explain your answers. Write in complete sentences. Computations may be used as part of your explanation.

A. When a company prepares a cash flow statement using the indirect method, it adds depreciation expense to net income because depreciation is a source of cash during a fiscal period.
B. Alpha Company reported an increase in Accounts Receivable of $2 million during 2007. As a result, Alpha's cash flow from operating activities was $2 million less than its operating revenues.
C. Beta Company purchased $40 million of merchandise inventory during 2007. Beta's accounts payable increased from $5 million to $8 million during the year. Beta's cash flow statement (indirect method) would report an adjustment to net income of −$3 million.
D. Delta Company reported cost of goods sold of $27 million for 2007. Its merchandise inventory increased by $8 million during the year. If all inventory purchased was paid for in cash, then Delta's cash payments to suppliers of inventory during the year were $35 million.
E. Gamma Company reported the following:

Net cash flow for operating activities	$80
Net cash flow from investing activities	35
Net cash flow from financing activities	50
Net change in cash	$ 5

From this information, it appears that Gamma is facing financial problems.

P5-17 THE DIFFERENTIAL EFFECT OF TRANSACTIONS ON NET INCOME AND CASH FLOW

Obj. 3

During March, each of the following events occurred at Frolic Park, Inc.

(Continued)

Event	Type of Activity	Effect on March's Net Income	Effect on March's Cash Flow
1. Sold $18,000 of goods on credit to customers. Received a 25% down payment with the balance on account.			
2. Paid $500 cash for office supplies that will be used during April.			
3. Received $3,000 from a customer in full payment of her account balance.			
4. Borrowed $80,000 from a local bank to be repaid in monthly installments plus interest starting in April.			
5. Paid rent on the office space ($1,200 per month) for the months of February, March, and April.			
6. Distributed monthly paychecks to employees totaling $13,300. 30% was for work performed in February and the balance for work performed in March.			
7. Purchased new Internet server equipment at a cost of $50,000.			
8. Purchased a 3-year fire insurance policy at a total cost of $10,800. Its coverage began on March 1.			
9. Purchased merchandise from suppliers on credit at a cost of $70,000.			
10. Collected $22,000 from customers in payment of their accounts. 80% of this amount was from sales recorded in February and the balance was from March sales.			
11. Collected four months' rent in advance (at $700 per month) from a tenant who will move in on April 1.			
12. Paid $45,000 to suppliers in partial payment for goods purchased in #9 above.			
13. Sold $33,000 of merchandise to customers on credit.			
14. Sold an investment in stocks and bonds for $28,000; the same amount that had been paid for it. A 3-year, 9% note receivable was accepted in full payment.			
Totals for March			

Required

A. Identify whether each transaction is an operating, investing, or financing activity.
B. For each event, identify the effect it had on March's net income and on March's cash flow from operations.
C. What does this problem suggest to you about the hazards of trying to manage an organization with accrual-basis accounting information only? Discuss.

P5-18 COMPARING CASH FLOW STATEMENTS AMONG FIRMS

Obj. 3

Sheik, Speer, and Love are three companies in similar industries. Five years of summarized cash flow data are available for each firm. Year 5 is the most recent.

	Year 5	Year 4	Year 3	Year 2	Year 1
Sheik Company:					
Operating activities	$ 30	$ 31	$ 28	$ 26	$ 28
Investing activities	3	1	6	5	4
Financing activities	(31)	(28)	(33)	(30)	(32)
Speer Company:					
Operating activities	(15)	(3)	7	14	26
Investing activities	8	4	(9)	(17)	(35)
Financing activities	6	0	3	4	11
Love Company:					
Operating activities	9	6	3	2	(1)
Investing activities	(13)	(12)	(11)	(10)	(10)
Financing activities	8	7	8	10	9

Study the information carefully. What clues can you find in the information concerning what is (or has been) going on with each firm? Do their business histories appear similar or dissimilar? Does the situation of one or more firms appear more favorable than one or more of the others?

Required For each firm, describe and discuss what you have learned from reviewing its summarized cash flow information.

P5-19 INTERPRETING THE CASH FLOW STATEMENT

Obj. 3

Embarcadero Company's most recent statement of cash flows is shown below.

Embarcadero Company Consolidated Statement of Cash Flows For the Year Ended December 31, 2007	
Operating activities	
Net loss	$(682)
Adjustments to reconcile NI to cash flows:	
Depreciation and amortization	592
Noncash gains and losses, net	(136)
Changes in:	
Accounts receivable	172
Inventories	110
Other current assets	(24)
Accounts payable	98
Other current liabilities	148
Cash provided by operations	278
Investing activities	
Investments and acquisitions	(424)
Capital expenditures	(42)
Sales of investments	206
Cash used by investing activities	(260)
Financing activities	
Increase in long-term debt	1,014
Repurchase of common stock	(740)
Dividends paid	(402)
Cash provided by financing activities	(128)
Decrease in cash	$(110)

Required Use Embarcadero's statement of cash flows to answer the following questions.

A. What was the primary source of cash inflow for the company?
B. Why was the company able to report a net cash inflow from operations when it incurred a net loss for the period?
C. What were the primary uses of cash during the period?
D. Did Receivables, Inventories, and Accounts Payable increase or decrease during the year?
E. If revenues (as reported on the income statement) were $3,960 for the year, how much cash was collected from customers during the year?

P5-20 INTERRELATIONSHIPS AMONG THE INCOME STATEMENT, BALANCE SHEET, AND STATEMENT OF CASH FLOW

Objs. 2, 3

Frontera Corporation reported the following income statement and comparative balance sheet for the year ended December 31, 2007.

(Continued)

Income Statement (for the Year Ended December 31, 2007) *(In thousands)*	
Sales revenue	$6,930
Cost of goods sold	3,660
Gross profit on sales	3,270
Operating expenses:	
Wages	855
Depreciation	102
Rent	546
Advertising	1,224
Operating income	543
Other revenues and expenses:	
Interest revenue	84
Interest expense	(24)
Income before taxes	603
Income tax expense	210
Net income	$ 393

Balance Sheet (at December 31)	2007	2006
Assets:		
Cash	$ 482	$ 318
Accounts receivable	246	189
Inventory	471	483
Prepaid advertising	54	21
Total current assets	1,253	1,011
Buildings and equipment	2,811	1,974
Accumulated depreciation	(922)	(820)
Land	350	300
Investments, long-term	250	400
Total assets	$3,742	$2,865
Liabilities and stockholders' equity:		
Rent payable	$ 450	$ 478
Wages payable	32	24
Total current liabilities	482	502
Notes payable, long-term	1,150	750
Common stock	1,400	1,100
Retained earnings	710	513
Total liabilities and equity	$3,742	$2,865

Frontera Corporation used the indirect format to prepare the statement of cash flows, but it has been misplaced and is not available.

Required Use your knowledge of financial statements to answer each of the questions that follow. For each item you list as part of your answer, describe fully why the item appears on the statement of cash flows.

A. Which line items from the income statement will also be found in the operating activities section of the statement of cash flows?
B. Which line items from the balance sheet contain information that will be reflected in the operating activities section?
C. Which line items from the income statement will also be found in the investing activities section?

D. Which line items from the balance sheet contain information that will be reflected in the investing activities section?
E. Which line items from the income statement will also be found in the financing activities section?
F. Which line items from the balance sheet contain information that will be reflected in the financing activities section?

P5-21 EVALUATING INCOME AND CASH FLOWS

Obj. 3

Selected financial statement information is reported below for Beltway Distributors Inc.

For the Fiscal Year Ended January 30, 2007 *(In thousands)*		
Sales revenue	$35,400	
Cost of goods sold	22,700	
Operating expenses (except depreciation)	4,500	
Depreciation expense	2,900	
Net income	5,300	
Dividends declared and paid	5,000	
For January 30	**2007**	**2006**
Cash	$ 2,050	$ 1,950
Accounts receivable	8,600	13,400
Inventories	23,500	27,100
Accounts payable	8,600	8,800
Bank loan payable	18,700	30,000

Required

A. Prepare a statement of cash flows (indirect format) for Beltway Distributors, assuming that all important cash flow activities are reflected in the information provided.
B. Assume this has been the pattern of cash flows for several years. What does this imply about the firm's business situation?

P5-22 EXCEL IN ACTION

The following information is available for The Book Wermz for November 2007. All numbers are dollar amounts.

Cash balance, November 30	$12,307.99
Cash balance, October 31	15,389.55
Cash paid for debt repayment	1,122.77
Cash paid for dividends	1,500.00
Cash paid for equipment	2,000.00
Cash paid for interest	932.03
Cash paid for merchandise	33,243.92
Cash paid for rent	1,738.15
Cash paid for supplies	2,576.93
Cash paid for taxes	897.45
Cash paid for wages	4,073.79
Cash received from customers	45,003.48
Decrease in accounts receivable	125.00
Depreciation expense	817.20
Increase in accounts payable	6,131.77
Increase in inventory	8,438.37
Increase in supplies	165.40
Increase in wages payable	623.56
Net income	2,447.45

(Continued)

Required Use the data provided to prepare a statement of cash flows for The Book Wermz for November using a spreadsheet. Prepare the statement using both the direct and indirect formats. Show cash outflows as negative amounts. Use the appropriate formatting buttons to include commas and dollar signs as needed. Use the Merge Cells and Bold buttons to position and format titles. The captions for the direct format statement should appear in column A and the amounts should appear in column B. The captions for the indirect format should appear in column D and the amounts should appear in column E. Use functions to sum subtotals and totals, such as =SUM(B5:B8), so that changes to any of the amounts being totaled will be automatically recalculated.

Suppose net income had been $2,600 and the amount of cash received from customers had been $45,156.03. What would operating cash flow have been?

P5-23 MULTIPLE-CHOICE OVERVIEW OF THE CHAPTER

1. The primary difference between a statement of cash flows prepared in direct format and one prepared in indirect format is
   a. in how net cash flow from operations is computed.
   b. that the indirect approach always results in higher net cash flow.
   c. in how net cash flow from investing activities is reported.
   d. that the beginning-of-the-year cash balance is included in direct format but not in indirect.

2. The statement of cash flows for the Halyard Exploration Company reported the following:

Cash paid for equipment	$ 300,000
Cash paid to employees	400,000
Cash paid to owners	150,000
Cash paid to suppliers	560,000
Cash received from creditors	200,000
Cash received from customers	1,200,000

What were Halyard's net cash flows from operating, investing, and financing activities?

	Operating	Investing	Financing
a.	$240,000	($300,000)	$ 50,000
b.	$500,000	($860,000)	$200,000
c.	$640,000	($860,000)	$200,000
d.	$240,000	($860,000)	$200,000

3. Haddad Company is a well-established, growing company. Which categories of activities would you generally expect to generate positive cash flows?
   a. Operating activities only
   b. Financing activities only
   c. Investing activities only
   d. Both operating activities and financing activities
   e. Both financing activities and investing activities

4. A statement of cash flows has been prepared in the indirect format. Depreciation expense has been added back to net income because depreciation is
   a. not really an expense and to list it as such understates profitability.
   b. an investing activity and should be reported in that section.
   c. a source of cash for the company.
   d. a noncash expense.

5. Zeff Company reports positive operating cash flows, near zero investing cash flows, and negative financing cash flows. This may indicate that the company
   a. is raising new capital to purchase long-term assets for expansion.
   b. does not have many good growth opportunities.
   c. has severe cash flow problems caused by too-rapid growth.
   d. is unable to provide goods and services that customers want.

6. A statement of cash flows prepared using the indirect format would report an increase in Accounts Receivable as
   a. an addition to cash flow from financing activities.
   b. a subtraction from cash flow from financing activities.
   c. an addition to net income in computing cash flow from operating activities.
   d. a subtraction from net income in computing cash flow from operating activities.

7. Flag Ship Company reported depreciation and amortization expense of $300,000 for the latest fiscal year. The depreciation and amortization expense
   a. increased cash flow for the year $300,000.
   b. decreased cash flow for the year $300,000.
   c. had no effect on cash flow for the year.
   d. had an effect on cash flow if assets were purchased during the year.

8. Rust Iron Company purchased a three-month insurance policy on March 1, 2007. The company paid $3,000 for the policy. The amount of insurance expense and cash outflow the company should report for March would be

	Insurance Expense	Cash Outflow
a.	$3,000	$3,000
b.	3,000	1,000
c.	1,000	3,000
d.	1,000	1,000

9. Micro Fish Company recognized $10,000 of interest expense in 2007. The balance of the company's interest payable account decreased $2,000. The amount of cash paid by the company for interest in 2007 was
   a. $10,000.
   b. $12,000.
   c. $2,000.
   d. $8,000.

10. Operating activities are reflected on a company's balance sheet primarily in
    a. plant assets.
    b. current assets and liabilities.
    c. income from operations.
    d. cash flow from operating activities.

Cases

C5-1 GENERAL MILLS, INC., STATEMENT OF CASH FLOWS

Objs. 2, 3

Selected information from **General Mills**' 2004 annual report and 10K is provided in Appendix A at the end of the text.

Required Answer the following questions about the General Mills Consolidated Statement of Cash Flows.

A. What are the three categories of cash flows shown on the company's cash flow statement?
B. Compare the net income figure to the amount of net cash provided by operating activities for each of the three years. What do you observe?
C. Has the net cash provided by operating activities been large enough to meet the net investing cash outflow? Explain where the difference came from (or went).
D. Compare the dividend payments to the income amounts for the current year. (Note: You may find it helpful to calculate the dividend payout ratio, which is the total dividends for the period ÷ net income for the period. This ratio is explained further in Ch. 10.)

C5-2 ANALYSIS OF CORPORATE FINANCIAL STATEMENTS

Obj. 3

Selected information from **General Mills**' 2004 annual report and 10K is provided in Appendix A at the end of the text. Examine these statements and answer the following questions.

(Continued)

Required

A. What were General Mills' major operating activities during 2004? What were the major differences between the accrual and cash flow effects of these activities?
B. What were the company's returns on total assets (net income ÷ total assets) for 2004 and 2003? Did the return improve or deteriorate from 2003?
C. If you owned 10,000 of the company's common stock, what would be your claim on the company's earnings for 2004? Was this a larger or smaller claim than you would have had for 2003?
D. What were the company's major sources of cash for 2004? In general, what did the company do with the cash it received?
E. What were the major financing activities during 2004? In general, how would you describe the company's financing activities overall during the last three years?
F. As of the end of 2004, what were the company's most important reported assets? What other resources may be important to the company that are not reported on its balance sheet?

C5-3 INTERPRETING CASH FLOWS

Obj. 3

Selected information from **General Mills**' 2004 annual report and 10K is provided in Appendix A at the end of the text.

Required Prepare a short report analyzing each of the following issues.

A. What were the accrual and cash basis results of operating activities for 2004? Explain any major differences between the two results.
B. Inspect the balance sheet to identify which current assets and liabilities increased and decreased during 2004. What was the amount of cash collected from customers during 2004?
C. What have been the relative amounts and trends in net income and cash flow from operating activities over the 2002–2004 period? What accounts for the differences you observe?
D. How would you assess the company's financial performance for 2004?

C5-4 COMPARING DIRECT FORMAT AND INDIRECT FORMAT STATEMENTS OF CASH FLOW

Objs. 1, 2, 3

Rowe Furniture, located in Elliston, Virginia, produces upholstered furniture. The company's 2004 statement of cash flows is presented below. Most companies use the indirect format for reporting cash flows; however, Rowe Furniture uses the direct format.

Rowe Furniture
Consolidated Statements of Cash Flows

		Year Ended	
	11/28/04 (52 weeks)	11/30/03 (52 weeks)	12/1/02 (52 weeks)
(In thousands)			
Increase (Decrease) in Cash			
Cash flows from operating activities:			
Cash received from customers	$298,887	$300,659	$336,853
Cash paid to suppliers and employees	(288,268)	(287,266)	(317,217)
Income taxes received (paid), net	(1,418)	1,352	2,839
Interest paid	(3,343)	(5,225)	(4,028)
Interest received	102	225	347
Other receipts—net	1,714	942	1,340
Net cash and cash equivalents provided by operating activities	7,674	10,687	20,134

	11/28/04	11/30/03	12/1/02
Cash flows from investing activities:			
Payments received on notes receivable	$ 100	$ 100	$ 125
Increase in cash surrender value	(131)	(121)	(150)
Proceeds from life insurance policies	370	—	—
Proceeds from sale of Mitchell Gold	—	39,573	—
Capital expenditures	(3,790)	(3,995)	(3,323)
Payments under earn-out and related obligations	—	(15,759)	—
Net cash (used in) provided by investing activities	(3,451)	19,798	(3,348)
Cash flows from financing activities:			
Restricted cash released from (deposited to) collateral for letters of credit	470	(96)	(1,938)
Net borrowings (repayments) under line of credit	—	—	(9,368)
Draws under revolving loans	8,798	12,570	3,994
Proceeds from issuance of long-term debt	—	—	39,442
Repayments under revolving loans	(8,272)	(20,751)	(10,244)
Payments to reduce long-term debt	(3,240)	(18,759)	(47,874)
Payments to reduce loans on cash surrender value	(306)	(16)	—
Proceeds from issuance of common stock	210	3	38
Purchase of treasury stock	(31)	(2)	(19)
Net cash used in financing activities	(2,371)	(27,051)	(25,969)
Net increase (decrease) in cash and cash equivalents	1,852	3,434	(9,183)
Cash at beginning of year	3,708	274	9,457
Cash at end of year	$ 5,560	$ 3,708	$ 274

Rowe Furniture
Reconciliation of Net Earnings to Net Cash Provided by (Used in) Operating Activities

		Year Ended	
(In thousands)	11/28/04 (52 weeks)	11/30/03 (52 weeks)	12/1/02 (52 weeks)
Net earnings	$1,032	$ 2,546	$ 2,020
Adjustments to reconcile net earnings to net cash provided by operating activities, net of disposition of business:			
Pre-tax loss on disposition of Mitchell Gold assets	—	1,011	—
Depreciation and amortization	6,559	7,213	8,889
Provision for deferred compensation	335	170	218
Payments made for deferred compensation	(306)	(241)	(2,802)
Deferred income taxes	(807)	577	1,031
Provision for losses on accounts receivable	107	376	262
Loss on disposition of assets	55	—	640
Change in operating assets and liabilities net of effects of disposition of business:			
Decrease (increase) in accounts receivable	2,900	(1,627)	(956)
Decrease (increase) in inventories	(5,394)	(1,644)	3,863
Decrease (increase) in prepaid expenses and other	(2,789)	272	(2,120)
Decrease (increase) in other miscellaneous assets	(420)	1,051	1,381
Increase (decrease) in accounts payable	4,635	(1,238)	(1,881)
Increase (decrease) in income taxes payable	3	1,070	3,978
Increase (decrease) in accrued expenses	980	(1,926)	2,287
Increase (decrease) in customer deposits	784	3,077	3,324
Total adjustments	6,642	8,141	18,114
Net cash provided by operating activities	$7,674	$10,687	$20,134

Required Study the **Rowe Furniture** cash flow statement and the **McDonald's** cash flow statement shown in Problem 5-12 and answer the following questions.

A. What are the similarities and differences in format of the two cash flow statements?
B. Note the reconciliation of net income to net cash provided by operating activities that appears at the bottom of the direct format statement. What information does it provide? Does this reconciliation look familiar?
C. Which statement format do you believe presents more understandable information? Why?

Comprehensive Review

CR5-1 PREPARING FINANCIAL STATEMENTS

Alice Springs Merchandise is a retail company that sells general household products. Account balances for the company's fiscal years ended January 31, 2006 and 2007, are provided below. Changes in balance sheet account balances also are provided. Additional information for the 2007 fiscal year includes the following:

- The company paid $38,802 for additional property and equipment and received cash from the sale of equipment of $1,967.
- Amounts borrowed or repaid are equal to changes in Notes Payable, Current and changes in Notes Payable, Long-Term.
- The change in Common Stock is the amount of stock issued or repurchased during the year.
- The balance of Retained Earnings includes the effects of net income and dividends.

Required From the information provided, prepare the following in good form.

A. An income statement containing separate columns for 2006 and 2007.
B. A balance sheet containing separate columns for 2006 and 2007.
C. A schedule like Exhibit 3 in this chapter (page 180) that includes the adjustments necessary to calculate operating cash flow. The adjustments should be the changes in the appropriate account balances.
D. A statement of cash flows for 2007 using the direct method.
E. A statement of cash flows for 2007 using the indirect method.

	2007	2006	Change
Sales Revenue	$ 589,351	$ 530,666	
Cost of Goods Sold	(359,504)	(328,343)	
Wages Expense	(123,764)	(117,136)	
Rent Expense	(30,116)	(28,052)	
Depreciation Expense	(24,871)	(22,628)	
Supplies Expense	(13,555)	(10,751)	
Cash	63,168	57,845	5,323
Accounts Receivable	48,386	43,106	5,280
Merchandise Inventory	130,247	117,202	13,045
Prepaid Rent	2,530	2,314	216
Supplies	1,129	952	177
Property and Equipment	365,398	328,563	36,835
Accumulated Depreciation	(43,848)	(18,977)	(24,871)
Accounts Payable	25,953	23,674	2,279
Wages Payable	10,272	9,500	772
Unearned Revenue	12,966	11,675	1,291
Notes Payable, Current	47,249	44,249	3,000
Notes Payable, Long-Term	214,838	222,467	(7,629)
Common Stock	102,629	95,581	7,048
Retained Earnings	153,103	123,859	29,244
Dividends Paid	8,297	5,250	

© PHOTODISC/GETTY IMAGES

Full and Fair Reporting

6

HOW DO WE ENSURE THAT REPORTS TO EXTERNAL USERS FAIRLY PRESENT BUSINESS ACTIVITIES?

Previous chapters examined how businesses collect and record information about their activities and report this information in the form of financial statements. Maintaining a reliable accounting system and reporting information that fairly presents a company's business activities is an important task. Because stockholders and other external users rely on a corporation's managers to provide this information, the financial reporting process is regulated. Corporations and other businesses must conform with regulations and standards that describe accounting procedures, the content and format of financial statements, and other information that must accompany those statements.

Maria and Stan, like other managers, must ensure that their corporation conforms with these requirements. Maintaining an accounting system and producing financial statements is not sufficient. Maria and Stan must be aware of the requirements that ensure that businesses fairly present their activities and make sure they conform with those requirements.

Food for Thought

As a stockholder, what information, in addition to financial statements, do you and other external users need to understand the business activities of Favorite Cookie Company? How can you be sure information provided by the business is accurate and reliable? Maria and Stan are discussing these issues with Ellen, their accountant.

Maria: *I've noticed that many corporations produce elaborate annual reports for their stockholders. Is this something we need to do for Favorite Cookie Company?*

Ellen: *Providing financial statements is not all you have to do to report to your stockholders. An annual report that contains those statements is necessary. It does not have to be elaborate, but it does have to contain certain information.*

Stan: *Our financial statements describe our business activities. Why aren't these adequate?*

Ellen: *You need to help your stockholders understand the information in your statements. You must discuss and analyze the financial statement information to identify activities that are key to understanding the performance of your company. And, you must provide disclosures about assumptions you made and methods you used in preparing the statements. In some cases, the statements may not fully inform users about your activities. You may need to provide details about some of your business activities.*

Maria: *Once we prepare all this information, do we simply have it printed and mail it to our stockholders?*

Ellen: *Before you send any financial information to external users for your fiscal year, you must have that information audited.*

Stan: *Who do we get to do the audit?*

Ellen: *The audit must be performed by an independent Certified Public Accountant. The CPA must be someone who is not employed by your company and who has no financial ties to your company. I'll help you identify someone for the job. First, let's examine the broader picture of corporate financial reporting and the regulations that govern that activity.*

Objectives

Once you have completed this chapter, you should be able to:

1. Explain the purpose of accounting regulation.
2. Describe how accounting standards are established in the United States.
3. Explain the purpose of the Financial Accounting Standards Board's conceptual framework.
4. Identify supplementary information to the financial statements in a corporate annual report.
5. Describe the purpose of internal controls and types of controls that should be evident in business organizations.

THE PURPOSE OF ACCOUNTING REGULATION

Objective 1
Explain the purpose of accounting regulation.

Decision makers who are not managers of a business have limited access to information about the business. These external users rely on financial reports for much of the information they need to make decisions. Stockholders and creditors use accounting information to decide whether to purchase or sell stock and whether to make loans to a company. Suppliers also make decisions about whether to sell goods and provide services to a business on credit. Government authorities use accounting information to determine taxes owed by businesses and whether companies have met legal requirements and regulations. Even customers and employees may use accounting information to determine the financial viability of a company from which they purchase goods and services or for which they work.

Accounting regulations protect the interests of external decision makers by ensuring that information for evaluating the performance and financial condition of a business is available and that the information is prepared according to specific guidelines. These guidelines provide assurance that the information is reliable and comparable over time and across companies.

Though many accounting regulations apply to any business that provides financial reports to external users, they are particularly applicable to publicly traded corporations. These are businesses whose stock can be bought and sold in stock markets. Because owners of these businesses are not involved in their day-to-day operations, they have special information needs. Shareholders of most corporations do not manage the companies in which they invest. They elect members of a corporation's board of directors, who then hire professional managers to run the corporation. Investors can own part of a corporation or parts of many corporations without having to participate in the day-to-day decisions of running those companies. Many Americans own stock in corporations through personal investments and retirement plans, but they are not required to commit large amounts of their individual time to these businesses.

Corporations have continuous lives apart from those of their owners. If a proprietor or partner dies or sells her or his share of a business, the business ceases to exist as a legal entity. The new owner of the business must reestablish the business as a new legal entity. Most corporations, however, continue unchanged if current owners sell their stock. Thus, while proprietorships and partnerships are separate accounting entities from their owners, most are not separate legal entities. They have no legal identity apart from their owners. Most corporations *are* separate accounting and legal entities.

The purchaser of a corporation's stock needs assurance that the shares are reasonably priced and represent a legitimate business. To ensure access to capital markets, corporations prepare accounting information in conformity with generally accepted accounting principles (GAAP). Accounting regulations assure investors of the financial integrity of a corporation. Compliance with these regulations is costly. Large corporations maintain large staffs to handle financial reporting requirements and pay large fees to independent auditors who report on the reliability of financial information reported to external users.

Sources of Accounting Regulation

http://ingram.swlearning.com

Visit the NYSE's home page to learn more about the organization.

Accounting regulation involves both government and private organizations. The first significant regulation of accounting and financial reporting in the United States was provided by the New York Stock Exchange (NYSE). The NYSE was formed in 1792 to facilitate the growing trade in corporate stocks. By the early 1900s the exchange required listed companies to provide accounting information to their stockholders. Listing requirements have changed over time. Today, corporations listed on exchanges must conform with GAAP and government regulations for the sale of securities.

Adoption of the 16th Amendment to the U.S. Constitution in 1913 permitted federal taxation of individual and corporate income. Taxation of income is not possible without rules and reporting requirements that determine how income will be computed. Consequently, the U.S. government and state governments have an interest in ensuring that businesses comply with accounting standards.

The early 1900s was a period of intense corporate activity. Many corporations were created, and many individuals invested in stock. During the 1920s the average price of corporate shares increased dramatically for many companies. That growth ended abruptly in late 1929, when stock prices plummeted to levels below those of the early 1920s. Many stockholders lost their life savings, and many companies were forced out of business. The collapse of the stock market in 1929 resulted in a demand for increased regulation of corporate financial reporting. Many people believed a cause of the collapse was a lack of sufficient information about corporate activities and a lack of government oversight of the stock markets.

http://ingram.swlearning.com

Visit the SEC's home page to learn more about the organization.

In response to these concerns, the U.S. Congress passed the *Securities Act of 1933*. This legislation **required most corporations to file registration statements before selling stock to investors.** As a part of these statements, corporations were required to provide financial reports containing balance sheets and income statements. Additional legislation, the *Securities Exchange Act of 1934,* **required corporations to provide annual financial reports to stockholders.** The legislation also required that these reports be audited by independent accountants. The 1934 act also created the *Securities and Exchange Commission (SEC)*, a federal agency that reports to Congress. The SEC **was given responsibility for overseeing external financial reporting by publicly traded corporations.**

Currently, the SEC requires publicly traded corporations to publish annual and quarterly financial reports. In addition, annual and quarterly registration statements must be filed by corporations with the SEC. Annual registration statements filed by corporations with the SEC are known as Form 10-K reports. They are required by Section 10-K of the 1934 act. Quarterly statements are known as 10-Q reports.

During the twentieth century, financial accounting has become a highly regulated and formalized process. Publicly traded corporations must provide audited financial reports to stockholders. The managers and auditors of companies who fail to provide this information, or who do so fraudulently, are subject to civil and criminal prosecution. The SEC reviews corporate reports to ensure they conform with GAAP. The SEC can require corporations that do not conform with GAAP to restate their financial statements. Under extreme circumstances, the SEC can halt the trading of a company's stock. If it believes a corporation's managers have attempted to mislead stockholders by their reports, the SEC can refer the matter to the Justice Department for criminal and civil proceedings. An announcement that the SEC is opening an investigation of a company's accounting practices often has a major impact on the company's stock price. Evidence of improper accounting practices is a major cause of lawsuits by investors against corporate managers and their auditors.

Case In Point

http://ingram.swlearning.com

Visit Enron's home page to learn more about the company.

The Effect of an SEC Investigation

In October 2001, Enron Corporation announced that it was being investigated by the SEC for its accounting and reporting practices. On the day of the announcement, its stock price dropped 20%.

USA Today reported that, on October 22, Enron's stock closed at $20.65 per share, a drop of $5.40 or 21%. That effectively decreased the company's market capitalization by $4.1 billion, which was the NYSE's largest percentage loser that day. The stock price actually fell below $20 per share at one point during the day. Enron's stock had not traded that low for almost four years.

Enron's stock had experienced very heavy losses throughout the prior week. The closing price on October 22 reflected a 75% drop for the year to date. This was very different from the same time during 2000 when the stock price rose by 87%.*

The Rise and Fall of Enron's Stock Price

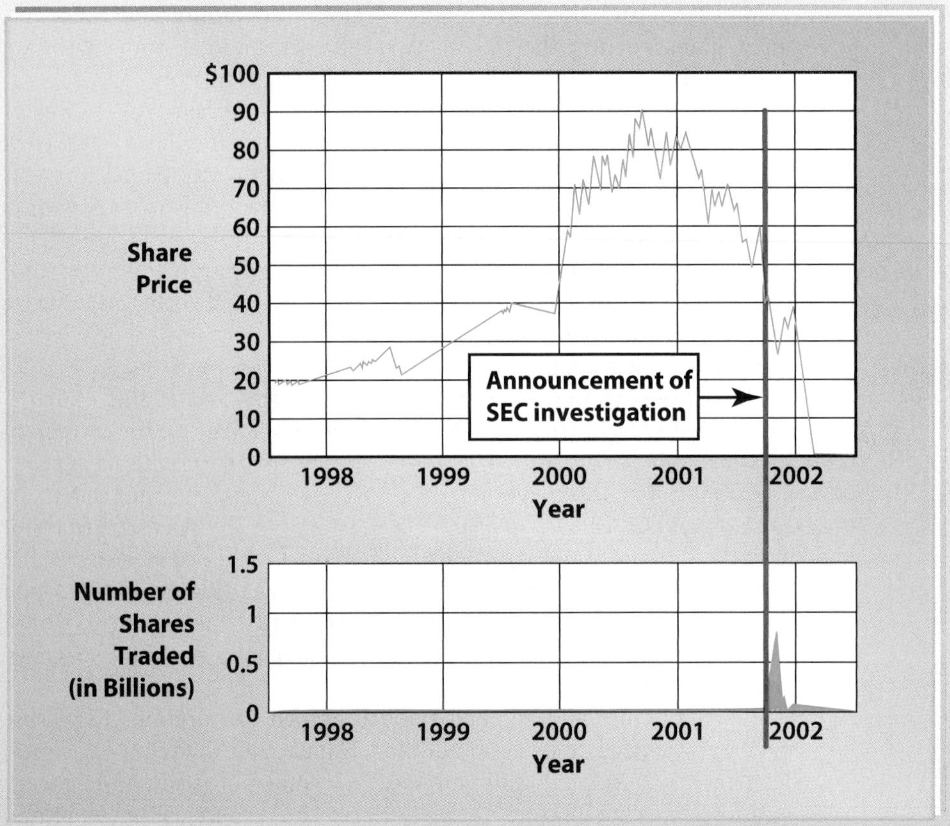

The decline in stock price was one of the major causes of Enron's bankruptcy and the primary cause of lawsuits against the company by its stockholders. The restatement resulted in a reduction in Enron's stockholders' equity of approximately $1.2 billion resulting from a write-down of earnings from 1997 through 2000. In addition, the company's reported debt increased by over $600 million.†

***Source: *USA Today*, 10/22/01, www.usatoday.com/money/energy/2001-10-22-enron.htm.**
†Source: www.enron.com/corp/pressroom/releases/2001/ene/78-SECReleaseLtr.html.

The failure of corporations to report fairly their activities to stockholders is a major concern in a capitalistic economy. The stock markets are a primary mechanism for the allocation of financial resources. Society benefits when resources are allocated to the most efficient and effective companies. Misleading information can result in markets allocating resources to companies that are not efficient or effective. When investors become aware that information is misleading, they may suffer losses as many investors attempt to sell their shares.

These problems can lead to a crisis of confidence in the markets if investors are unsure of whom they can trust and whether they are being treated fairly. Improper and inadequate reporting affect everyone. The economy suffers because resources are not being properly allocated. The decrease in economic activity has a ripple effect that leads to decreased sales and profits for other companies, loss of jobs for employees, and loss of taxes for government organizations.

http://ingram.swlearning.com

See the Sarbanes-Oxley home page to learn more about this Act.

Sarbanes-Oxley Act of 2002. Concern for the effects of misstated financial statements by Enron, WorldCom, and other companies on the confidence of investors in financial markets in the United States resulted in legislation to provide additional oversight of accounting and auditing practices. The Sarbanes-Oxley Act (SOX) was passed by Congress in 2002. The act, along with subsequent regulations, affected the responsibilities of auditors, boards of directors, and corporate managers with respect to financial reporting. Also, the act established the Public Companies Accounting Oversight Board (PCAOB) that is now responsible for oversight of financial statement audits of publicly-traded corporations and the establishment of auditing standards in the United States.

The primary purpose of SOX was to increase investor confidence in the financial reports provided by corporations. To achieve this purpose, the act established the PCAOB to oversee external auditing and corporate governance issues that potentially affect the reliability of financial reports of publicly-traded corporations. Further, SOX increased the responsibilities of corporate managers for producing reliable financial reports and specified restrictions on the activities of external auditors to increase their independence from their audit clients.

Though there are many provisions in the legislation and subsequent regulations, three issues are of primary importance for accounting. These involve the financial reporting responsibilities of the PCAOB, corporations (including their boards of directors and managers), and external auditors.

http://ingram.swlearning.com

Visit the PCAOB's home page to learn more about the organization.

Responsibilities of the Public Companies Accounting Oversight Board The PCAOB reports to the Securities and Exchange Commission (SEC), which appoints members of the Board. The Board has five full-time members. The Board establishes auditing standards for external audits of publicly-traded companies and oversees the accounting firms that provide these audits. Accounting firms that provide external audits of companies that report to the SEC must register with the PCAOB and report to the PCAOB information about their audit clients, audit fees, and the services provided to clients. As part of its oversight responsibilities for accounting firms, the PCAOB issues standards for accounting firms that provide guidance concerning the auditing methods, auditor ethics and independence; supervision, hiring, and development of audit personnel; and client acceptance and continuation. Also, the PCAOB is responsible for inspecting auditing firms to ensure their compliance with SOX regulations and professional auditing standards.

The PCAOB is responsible for investigating potential violations of SOX regulations, the Board's rules, and professional accounting standards. The Board may impose sanctions on accounting firms, including suspension from auditing public companies and civil penalties. The Board may refer these matters to the SEC and the Department of Justice for further legal action if it believes such action is needed.

Responsibilities of Corporate Management The Sarbanes-Oxley Act affects corporations that are required to report financial information to the SEC. Section 302 of the act requires a certification from the chief executive officer (CEO) and chief financial officer (CFO) along with their financial reports. The officers certify that the financial reports comply with requirements of the Securities Exchange Act of 1934 and contain information that fairly presents, in all material respects, the financial condition and results of operations of the issuer. A company's balance sheet reports its financial condition, and its income statement and statement of cash flows report its results of operations. Consequently, the CEO and CFO are required to confirm that the corporation's financial statements reliably represent its economic activities. These provisions affect a company's annual report (10-K) and quarterly reports (10-Q) that must be filed with the SEC. The penalty for falsely certifying the financial statements is a fine of up to $5 million and imprisonment for up to 20 years.

The certification reports signed by the CEO and CFO must state that:

- they have reviewed the financial reports
- the reports are not misleading
- the reports fairly present the company's financial condition and results of operations
- the officers are responsible (1) for establishing and maintaining an adequate system of internal controls sufficient to ensure reliable financial reporting and (2) for assessing the effectiveness of those controls
- the officers have disclosed to the company's audit committee and external auditors (1) significant deficiencies in the company's controls identified in their assessment and any significant changes in the controls and (2) any fraud involving management or employees who have a significant role with respect to internal controls.

SOX also effectively mandates that corporations create audit committees as part of their boards of directors. Members of the audit committee must be independent of corporate management, meaning that managers of a corporation cannot serve on the audit committee. The audit committee is responsible for selection, compensation, and oversight of the corporation's external auditor. Thus, the audit committee, rather than corporate management, is the primary contact for a corporation's external auditor. The audit committee must include a member who is a financial expert. A financial expert is defined as someone who has an understanding of generally accepted accounting principles, internal controls, financial statements, and audit committees and who has experience preparing, auditing, analyzing, or evaluating financial statements.

A corporation's financial reports must disclose all material off-balance sheet transactions and activities that have a material effect on the corporation's current or future financial condition. Off-balance sheet items usually involve obligations that do not fit the definition of liabilities that must be reported on the balance sheet. Corporations also must disclose on a rapid and current basis material changes in their financial conditions and operations.

A corporation also must disclose whether it has a code of ethics for its top managers. Among other things, a code of ethics should promote honest behavior, accurate and timely disclosure of financial information, and compliance with laws and regulations. A corporation is required to make its code of ethics available to the public.

Responsibilities of External Auditors A corporation's external auditor must provide timely information to the audit committee about important accounting practices and policies adopted by corporate management and any discussion between the auditor and management about alternative practices or policies. Any disagreements between the auditor and management about these matters also must be disclosed to the audit committee.

SOX prohibits external auditors from providing certain services to a client corporation. These include:

- bookkeeping or other services relating to the accounting records or financial statements of the audit client
- financial information systems design and implementation
- appraisal or evaluation services, fairness opinions or contribution-in-kind reports

- actuarial services
- internal audit outsourcing services
- management functions or human resources
- broker or dealer, investment advisor, or investment banking services
- legal services and expert services unrelated to the audit
- any other service that the accounting board (PCAOB) determines, by regulation, is impermissible

The audit committee must approve of any services provided by the external auditor, particularly those that are not directly related to the financial audit. These services must be disclosed in reports to the SEC.

Section 404 of the act requires that the auditor must attest to and report on management's assessment of a corporation's internal controls. The auditor is responsible for examining the client firm's internal control system and verifying that the system provides reasonable assurance of reliable financial reporting. The auditor expresses an opinion concerning management's assertions about its internal control system. This opinion is based on the results of the auditor's assessment and appears in a report that accompanies the company's audited financial statements.

The external auditor must be independent of management in *fact* and *appearance*. As part of this requirement, SOX mandates that the CEO, CFO, and chief accounting officer cannot have been employed by the company's external auditor during the one-year period preceding the audit. It is not uncommon for employees of audit firms to take positions with client corporations. SOX limits the ability of corporations to hire employees from their external audit firms.

The Sarbanes-Oxley Act has had profound effects on financial accounting and auditing practices. Some provisions of the act and related regulations are still being implemented, and we will undoubtedly see revisions and additions to some of these provisions. The extent to which these provisions are successful in increasing the reliability of financial reporting remains to be seen. However, there is no question that the way that boards of directors, corporate managers, and external auditors approach their responsibilities has changed and that greater efforts are being made to ensure that timely and accurate financial information is provided to investors.

Accounting regulations are important because they provide standards for determining whether corporations are reporting their activities fairly to stockholders. The next section examines the processes and organizations associated with establishing accounting standards.

Self-Study Problem #1

Abe Milton is the owner and sole proprietor of Honest Abe's Used Cars. Abe needs a loan to help finance an expansion of his business. You are the loan manager of a local bank where Abe has applied for a loan. The loan application requires financial statements, which Abe has supplied. You asked Abe whether the statements were prepared according to GAAP and whether they have been independently verified. Abe says he doesn't know anything about GAAP and that he does not permit anyone else to examine his financial information because he is afraid competitors will find out how well he is doing. He notes, however, that he is "Honest" Abe and that the financial statements are accurate.

Required Briefly explain to Abe why GAAP is important and why moral hazard is an issue of concern in making a loan decision.

CREATING ACCOUNTING STANDARDS

Objective 2
Describe how accounting standards are established in the United States.

This section considers organizations responsible for setting accounting standards in the United States and the organization that coordinates accounting standards among many of the world's most developed countries.

The Securities and Exchange Commission is authorized by law to establish and enforce accounting standards in the United States. From time to time, the SEC uses that authority to issue standards on matters it considers to be important and in need of authoritative guidance. For the most part, however, the SEC has delegated the setting of accounting standards to private (nongovernment) organizations. The United States differs from most other countries in this respect. In most countries, accounting standards are set by the country's central government.

Standard-Setting Organizations

INTERNATIONAL

Several organizations are responsible for establishing accounting standards in the United States. Different organizations set standards for businesses and other nongovernmental organizations than the ones that establish standards for governments. In addition, an international organization exists for coordinating standards across countries and for establishing standards that are used in some countries.

Learning Note - Accounting standards are established by the government in most countries. These standards are part of the nation's laws and are the responsibility of government agencies.

http://ingram.swlearning.com
Visit the FASB's home page to learn more about the organization.

The *Financial Accounting Standards Board (FASB)* **has been the primary organization for setting accounting standards for businesses in the United States since 1973.** The FASB has seven full-time members and is privately funded. It is not a government organization. The FASB also sets accounting and financial reporting standards for nonprofit organizations other than governmental units. It is headquartered in Norwalk, Connecticut. The FASB employs a research staff to study accounting problems. It periodically issues *Statements of Financial Accounting Standards,* which are authoritative guidelines for accounting and financial reporting in the United States.

http://ingram.swlearning.com
Visit the GASB's and the GAO's home page to learn more about the organization.

The *Governmental Accounting Standards Board (GASB)* **sets accounting standards for state and local governmental units.** Like the FASB, the GASB is a private rather than a governmental organization. The GASB also is headquartered in Norwalk, Connecticut, and shares staff and facilities with the FASB. The federal government is not subject to FASB or GASB standards but establishes its own accounting rules. The *General Accounting Office (GAO)* **is the primary federal government agency that oversees accounting in the federal government.**

http://ingram.swlearning.com
Visit the IASB's home page to learn more about the organization.

The regulation of financial accounting and reporting is an international activity. Considerable diversity exists in accounting standards among nations. The International Accounting Standards Committee (IASC) was created in 1973 as an international effort to study accounting issues and to reduce the diversity of standards. The IASC was reconstituted as the *International Accounting Standards Board (IASB)* in 2001. The IASB **recommends accounting standards that it believes are appropriate for a broad range of global activities involving companies in many nations.** The IASB describes itself on its website as follows:

INTERNATIONAL

> . . . [A]n independent, privately-funded accounting standard setter based in London, UK. Board Members come from nine countries and have a variety of functional backgrounds. The Board is committed to developing, in the public interest, a single set of high quality, understandable and enforceable global accounting standards that require transparent and comparable information in general purpose financial statements. In addition, the Board cooperates with

national accounting standard setters to achieve convergence in accounting standards around the world.

Accounting standards are important to protect the interests of investors, managers, and the general public. Therefore, the standards must be perceived as being reasonable and responsive to the needs of different constituents. Arbitrary and unnecessary standards do not serve the needs of society. For these reasons, accounting standards are established through a political process. This process gives interested parties an opportunity to express their opinions and to provide information that may have a bearing on prospective standards. The fact that accounting standards are referred to as generally accepted accounting principles is not accidental. To serve the needs of society, accounting standards must be accepted by those who are affected by them.

Learning Note - The IASB has issued accounting standards that identify preferred accounting methods. Many countries have adopted these standards for accounting and financial reporting.

The Standard-Setting Process

The process used by the FASB to create accounting standards is typical of that used by other organizations, such as the GASB and the IASB. The process consists of the following steps:

1. Accounting issues are identified and evaluated for consideration.
2. A discussion memorandum is issued and responses are solicited.
3. Public hearings are held.
4. An exposure draft is issued and responses are solicited.
5. Additional public hearings are held as needed.
6. A standard is issued.
7. Existing standards are reviewed and modified as needed.

Accounting issues may be identified by accounting professionals, managers, investors, or the FASB staff. The staff evaluates the issues, and the board determines those issues that appear to be important enough to address.

A ***discussion memorandum*** **is a document that identifies accounting issues and alternative approaches to resolving the issues.** All interested parties are encouraged to respond to a discussion memorandum. The board develops a proposed standard after reviewing responses to a discussion memorandum and issues its proposal in the form of an exposure draft. **An** ***exposure draft*** **is a document that describes a proposed accounting standard.** It identifies requirements that may be contained in an actual standard. Responses again are solicited, and public hearings sometimes are held.

Once the board reviews responses to an exposure draft, it may modify and reissue the exposure draft or issue a standard. **An accounting standard is an official pronouncement establishing acceptable accounting procedures or financial report content. FASB standards are known as** ***Statements of Financial Accounting Standards.*** To issue a standard, at least five of the seven members of the board must agree to it. Once a standard has been issued, it becomes part of GAAP. Standards can be reviewed at any time to determine if they are serving their intended purposes and can be modified or replaced if they are found to be ineffective.

The FASB's Conceptual Framework

Objective 3
Explain the purpose of the Financial Accounting Standards Board's conceptual framework.

The conceptual framework was developed by the FASB in the late 1970s and early 1980s to provide guidance in the development of accounting standards. **The** ***FASB conceptual framework*** **is a set of objectives, principles, and definitions to guide the development of new accounting standards.**

The FASB conceptual framework includes four major components:

1. Objectives of financial reporting
2. Qualitative characteristics of accounting information

3. Elements of financial statements
4. Recognition and measurement in financial statements

Objectives of financial reporting provide an overall purpose for financial reports. The purpose of financial reports is to provide information useful to current and potential investors, creditors, and other users. Financial reports should help these decision makers assess the amounts, timing, and uncertainty of prospective cash flows. Financial reports should also provide information about resources, claims to resources, and changes in resources for business organizations.

Qualitative characteristics are attributes that make accounting information useful. **Understandability** and **usefulness** for decision making are the most important characteristics. **Relevance** and **reliability** are considered to be the two primary qualities that result in accounting information being useful. **To be relevant, information should be timely and have predictive or feedback value. To be reliable, information should faithfully represent economic events and should be verifiable and neutral.** Information about an organization is more valuable when it can be compared with information from other organizations and when it is prepared using consistent methods over time.

Elements of financial statements provide definitions of the primary classes of items contained in financial statements. Elements include assets, liabilities, equity, investments by owners, distributions to owners, revenues, expenses, gains, and losses.

Recognition and measurement criteria identify information that should be contained in financial statements. The primary financial statements are described in the conceptual framework, along with the items that should be contained in each statement.

Learning Note - The accounting systems of most organizations report periodically the estimated results of financing, investing, and operating activities. Such periodic measurement is needed to ensure the timely reporting of financial information that is needed for effective decision making.

DISCLOSURE AND FAIR REPRESENTATION

Objective 4
Identify supplementary information to the financial statements in a corporate annual report.

In addition to establishing acceptable accounting procedures and methods and guidelines for the format and content of financial statements, GAAP require companies to include information in addition to their financial statements in annual reports to stockholders. This information includes management's discussion and analysis of the company's business activities and disclosures about methods used in determining accounting information and details about those activities that are not evident in the financial statements.

Corporate annual reports usually include the following:

- a letter from the president or chief executive officer of the company
- a description of the company's products and business activities
- a summary of selected business data
- a discussion by management of the company's performance
- financial statements
- notes to the financial statements
- a statement of management responsibility for the financial statements
- an audit report

The president's letter and the description of a company's products and business are not part of the financial section of a company's annual report. Management has a fair amount of discretion in what to include in these sections. The president's letter often

EXHIBIT 1 Procter & Gamble's Financial Summary (Unaudited)

	2004	2003	2002	2001	2000
Net Sales	**$51,407**	$43,377	$40,238	$39,244	$39,951
Operating Income	**9,827**	7,853	6,678	4,736	5,954
Net Earnings	**6,481**	5,186	4,352	2,922	3,542
Net Earnings Margin	**12.6%**	12.0%	10.8%	7.4%	8.9%
Basic Net Earnings Per Common Share	**$ 2.46**	$ 1.95	$ 1.63	$ 1.08	$ 1.30
Diluted Net Earnings Per Common Share	**2.32**	1.85	1.54	1.03	1.23
Dividends Per Common Share	**0.93**	0.82	0.76	0.70	0.64
Restructuring Program Charges	**$ —**	$ 751	$ 958	$ 1,850	$ 814
Research and Development Expense	**1,802**	1,665	1,601	1,769	1,899
Advertising Expense	**5,504**	4,373	3,773	3,612	3,793
Total Assets	**57,048**	43,706	40,776	34,387	34,366
Capital Expenditures	**2,024**	1,482	1,679	2,486	3,018
Long-Term Debt	**12,554**	11,475	11,201	9,792	9,012
Shareholders' Equity	**17,278**	16,186	13,706	12,010	12,287

Source: Procter & Gamble 2004 annual report.

summarizes the company's financial performance for the year. As long as information contained in the letter is consistent with that reported in the financial section, it is not subject to accounting regulation.

The following paragraphs describe the financial section items contained in an annual report, with the exception of financial statements that were examined in Chapters 4 and 5. Appendix A of this book contains the financial section of General Mills' 2004 annual report. You may wish to refer to the appendix for a better idea of the contents of each item in the financial section.

Summary Business Data

Financial and nonfinancial data often are included for various periods beyond those covered by the primary financial statements. For example, Exhibit 1 provides a five-year summary reported in Procter & Gamble's annual report.

The summary data reported in Exhibit 1 is useful for determining trends in Procter & Gamble's business activities. The data indicate a steady growth in sales, income, and asset over the five years. The company has grown substantially over this period in most categories.

Management's Discussion and Analysis

Corporate annual reports should include discussion and analysis of the company's financial performance. This section, known as *management's discussion and analysis (MD&A),* **explains important events and changes in performance during the years presented in the financial statements.**

Typical issues considered in the MD&A include the following:

- a comparison of operating results among the data provided in the company's income statement
- liquidity and cash flows as indicated by cash and short-term investments and the statement of cash flows
- major business risks

- financial risks such as foreign currency exchange rates, equity security prices, and interest rate changes on debt securities
- changes in accounting methods used by the company
- subsequent events

EXHIBIT 2
Management's Discussion and Analysis from a Corporate Report

The purpose of this discussion is to provide an understanding of our financial results and condition by focusing on changes in certain key items from year to year. Management's Discussion and Analysis (MD&A) starts with an overview of the Company, followed by a review of results of operations and financial condition. Lastly, we provide insight to our significant accounting policies and estimates, and some other information you may find useful.

Overview

Our business is focused on providing branded products of superior quality and value to improve the lives of the world's consumers. We believe this will lead to leadership sales, profits and value creation, allowing employees, shareholders and the communities in which we operate to prosper.

Strategic Focus

We are focused on strategies that we believe are right for the long-term health of the Company and that will increase returns for our shareholders. Our long-term financial targets include:

- Sales growth of 4% to 6% excluding the impact of changes in foreign exchange rates from year-over-year comparisons. On average, we expect approximately 2% of our growth to come from market growth; 1% to 3% of our growth to come from the combination of market share growth, expansion to new geographies and new business creation; and the remaining 1% to come from smaller, tactical acquisitions to access markets or round out our current business portfolios.
- Earnings-per-share growth of 10% or better.
- Free cash flow productivity greater than 90% (defined as the ratio of operating cash flow less capital expenditures divided by net earnings).

In order to achieve these targets, we have focused Procter & Gamble's core strengths of branding, innovation, go-to-market capability and scale against the following growth areas:

- Drive our core businesses of Baby Care, Fabric Care, Feminine Care and Hair Care into stronger global leadership positions.
- Grow our leading brands in our biggest markets and with our largest customers.
- Invest in faster-growing businesses with higher gross margins that are less asset-intensive, primarily in the Health Care and Beauty Care segments.
- Build on opportunities in select developing markets and with lower income consumers.

Summary of 2004 Results

For the fiscal year ended June 30, 2004, our sales, earnings and free cash flow grew above our long-term targets.

- Every business segment and, within the MDO, every geographic region posted volume growth.
- We increased our overall market share, with share growth in categories representing approximately 70% of the Company's net sales. We increased market share in each of our core businesses of Baby Care, Fabric Care, Feminine Care and Hair Care.
- Net sales increased 19%, including the impact of the Wella acquisition that was completed in September 2003. Organic sales increased 8%.
- Net earnings increased 25% behind higher volume and the completion of the Company's restructuring program, which reduced earnings by $538 million in 2003.
- Operating cash flows were $9.36 billion. Free cash flow productivity was 113%.

Source: Procter & Gamble 2004 annual report.

Exhibit 2 provides excerpts from the MD&A section of Procter & Gamble's 2004 annual report. This section of the annual report provides a summary of business activities for the fiscal year. The information in Exhibit 2 is a small portion of the total section provided in the annual report. It summarizes the purpose of the MD&A, provides an overview of the company and its strategy, and summarizes key results of the 2004 fiscal year.

Notes to the Financial Statements

Notes to the financial statements are important for helping readers interpret the statements. They describe how some of the numbers were computed and provide additional information about items reported in the statements. Exhibit 3 contains example notes from the 2004 annual report of Procter & Gamble. These notes identify when certain revenues and expenses were recognized and the amounts of certain expenses that were not reported individually in the financial statements. We will examine other notes in future chapters as we examine specific accounting and reporting issues.

EXHIBIT 3
Excerpts from Notes to Consolidated Financial Statements

Note 1 Summary of Significant Accounting Policies

Nature of Operations
The Procter & Gamble Company's (the Company) business is focused on providing consumer branded products of superior quality and value. The Company markets approximately 300 consumer products in more than 160 countries around the world. Our products are sold primarily through retail operations including mass merchandisers, grocery stores, membership club stores and drug stores.

Basis of Presentation
The Consolidated Financial Statements include The Procter & Gamble Company and its controlled subsidiaries. Intercompany transactions are eliminated in consolidation. Investments in certain companies over which the Company exerts significant influence, but does not control the financial and operating decisions, are accounted for as equity method investments.

Use of Estimates
Preparation of financial statements in conformity with accounting principles generally accepted in the United States of America (U.S. GAAP) requires management to make estimates and assumptions that affect the amounts reported in the Consolidated Financial Statements and accompanying disclosures. These estimates are based on management's best knowledge of current events and actions the Company may undertake in the future. Estimates are used in accounting for, among other items, consumer and trade promotion accruals, pensions, post-employment benefits, stock options, useful lives for depreciation and amortization, future cash flows associated with impairment testing for goodwill and long-lived assets, deferred tax assets, potential income tax assessments and contingencies. Actual results may ultimately differ from estimates, although management does not believe such changes would materially affect the financial statements in any individual year.

Revenue Recognition
Sales are recognized when revenue is realized or realizable and has been earned. Most revenue transactions represent sales of inventory, and the revenue recorded includes shipping and handling costs, which generally are included in the list price to the customer. The Company's policy is to recognize revenue when title to the product, ownership and risk of loss transfer to the customer, which generally is on the date of shipment. A provision for payment discounts and product return allowances is recorded as a reduction of sales in the same period that the revenue is recognized.

Notes to the financial statements provide information about how amounts reported in the financial statements were determined and provide more detailed information about some income statement items. Exhibit 3 contains only a few of these notes. They describe such matters as the company's typical operations, consolidated financial statements, the use of estimates, and when revenue is recognized. Other notes provide similar information about other financial statement items. These notes are intended to assist readers in understanding and interpreting the information reported in the financial statements. They are an important part of the financial statement presentation and should be included when audited financial statements are presented.

The Auditors' Report

The auditors' report is an important item accompanying a company's financial statements. Auditors issue an audit report upon completion of their audit work. **An *audit* involves a detailed, systematic investigation of a company's accounting records and procedures for the purpose of determining the reliability of financial reports.** The auditor attempts to verify that the numbers and disclosures made by management in its financial reports are consistent with the company's actual financial position, operating results, and cash flows. Records, operating procedures, contracts, resources, and management policies and decisions are examined to provide evidence of the fairness of financial report information. Auditors determine if control procedures to ensure the integrity of accounting information exist and are being used. They compare the information in financial reports with information from prior years and other sources to confirm the fairness of the reports.

Attestation **occurs when an auditor affirms the fairness of financial statements and other information.** The audit report, or audit opinion, provides public notice of the auditors' belief about the fairness of the accompanying financial information. Exhibit 4 provides the auditors' report from Procter & Gamble's annual report.

The auditors' report is addressed to the board of directors and shareholders of the company. Normally, an audit is performed on behalf of the shareholders and other external parties. Audits may be requested for special purposes also—for example, to secure a bank loan or as part of merger negotiations. In such a case, the auditors' report would be addressed to the intended users.

The audit report states the auditor's opinion. Most audit reports provide an **unqualified opinion**. Such an opinion states that the auditor believes that the financial statements fairly present the company's actual economic events for the period covered by the audited statements. Fair presentation means that the financial statements are prepared in conformity with GAAP and are free from material omissions and misstatements. An unqualified opinion means that the auditor has not stated any qualifying (limiting) conditions or exceptions in the opinion. If the financial statements do not fully conform to GAAP or if serious concerns exist as to the ability of a company to continue as a going concern, the auditor lists qualifications to the opinion that the reader should consider in interpreting the financial information.

The auditors' report identifies the statements and fiscal periods covered by the audit. A typical audit will cover all the primary financial statements: income statement, balance sheet, and statement of cash flows. The audit normally covers the most recent three years of operations. For most large corporations, the audited financial statements are the consolidated statements of the parent and its subsidiaries.

The auditors' report describes the responsibilities of auditors and management. Management is responsible for preparing the statements. Auditors are responsible for competently using the technology available to them to confirm (or disconfirm) the assertions of management made in its financial statements and related disclosures.

The report summarizes the audit process. ***Auditing standards*** **include procedures used in conducting an audit to help auditors form an opinion about the fairness of the audited statements.** Auditing standards are developed in the United States by the Public Companies Accounting Oversight Board. Failure to conform to auditing standards in an independent audit is a major violation of a CPA's responsibilities.

EXHIBIT 4
Independent Auditors' Report

Deloitte

REPORT OF INDEPENDENT REGISTERED PUBLIC ACCOUNTING FIRM

To the Board of Directors and Shareholders of The Procter & Gamble Company:

We have audited the accompanying consolidated balance sheets of The Procter & Gamble Company and subsidiaries (the "Company") as of June 30, 2004 and 2003 and the related consolidated statements of earnings, shareholders' equity and cash flows for each of the three years in the period ended June 30, 2004. These financial statements are the responsibility of the Company's management. Our responsibility is to express an opinion on these financial statements based on our audits.

We conducted our audits in accordance with standards of the Public Company Accounting Oversight Board (United States). Those standards require that we plan and perform the audits to obtain reasonable assurance about whether the financial statements are free of material misstatement. An audit includes examining, on a test basis, evidence supporting the amounts and disclosures in the financial statements. An audit also includes assessing the accounting principles used and significant estimates made by management, as well as evaluating the overall financial statement presentation. We believe that our audits provide a reasonable basis for our opinion.

In our opinion, such consolidated financial statements present fairly, in all material respects, the financial position of the Company at June 30, 2004 and 2003 and the results of its operations and cash flows for each of the three years in the period ended June 30, 2004, in conformity with accounting principles generally accepted in the United States of America.

Deloitte + Touche LLP

Deloitte & Touche LLP
Cincinnati, Ohio

August 6, 2004

From evidence collected from applying auditing standards, auditors assert that the financial statements are free of material misstatement. Materiality is a criterion for establishing the importance of a potential misstatement in audited financial statements. Financial statements contain estimates and allocations that depend on management judgment. In addition to finding errors in accounting records, auditors may disagree with managers about their estimates and allocations. Unless these errors and disagreements are material (important) to the overall amounts reported on the financial statements, however, auditors are not required to take action on these issues.

Auditors examine accounting records on a "test basis." Auditors do not examine 100% of a company's transactions. Instead, they use sampling techniques to select representative transactions. By verifying these transactions, auditors form an opinion about the financial statements as a whole. Sampling is necessary because the cost of auditing all of a company's records would be prohibitive.

Learning Note - Unless information is found that raises doubts about a company's ability to continue operating in the future, it is assumed to be a going concern. This means the company is an organization with an indefinite life that is sufficiently long that, over time, all currently incomplete transactions will be completed.

Auditors' reports must be signed by the public accounting firm that performed the audit, thus indicating its responsibility. The date of the auditors' report is the date on which all audit work was completed for the periods covered by the report. The auditor is responsible for disclosing any material information that might affect a decision maker's interpretation of the financial statements through the date of the audit report.

INTERNATIONAL

Learning Note - Auditors' reports for foreign corporations differ from those for U.S. corporations. Different countries establish their own auditing and accounting standards. The format of the auditors' report depends on the auditing standards of the country in which a company has its principal operations.

The auditor certifies that financial statements present fairly a company's business activities. The audit is not a guarantee that a company will be successful. If a company is not performing well, the financial statements should reveal the company's problems. It is up to stockholders to interpret the statements and assess the company's performance. Good information should lead to informed decisions about whether to invest in a company or not. Good information does not mean a company is doing well or that investors are likely to earn high returns. The audit certifies the quality of financial information, not the quality of management or the ability of management to make good business decisions.

Report of Management Responsibilities

In addition to the auditors' report, the annual report usually contains a statement of management responsibilities. Exhibit 5 contains a typical statement of management responsibilities.

Management is responsible for preparing financial statements and related information that fairly reports the business activities of a corporation. This information should be prepared in conformity with GAAP. Management is also responsible for developing and implementing a system of internal controls. *Internal controls* **are procedures a company uses to protect its assets and ensure the accuracy of its accounting information.** The next section of this chapter describes internal controls in more detail.

A corporation's board of directors should establish an audit committee. The committee should be made up of members of the board who are not part of the corporation's

EXHIBIT 5
Report of Management Responsibilities

The management of Favorite Cookie Company is responsible for the preparation and integrity of the financial statements included in this Annual Report to Shareholders. The financial statements have been prepared in conformity with accounting principles generally accepted in the United States of America and include amounts based on management's best judgment where necessary. Financial information included elsewhere in this Annual Report is consistent with these financial statements.

Management maintains a system of internal controls and procedures designed to provide reasonable assurance that transactions are executed in accordance with proper authorization, that transactions are properly recorded in the Company's records, that assets are safeguarded and that accountability for assets is maintained. The concept of reasonable assurance is based on the recognition that the cost of maintaining our system of internal accounting controls should not exceed benefits expected to be derived from the system. Internal controls and procedures are periodically reviewed and revised, when appropriate, due to changing circumstances and requirements.

Independent auditors are appointed by the Company's Board of Directors and ratified by the Company's shareholders to audit the financial statements in accordance with auditing standards generally accepted in the United States of America and to independently assess the fair presentation of the Company's financial position, results of operations and cash flows. Their report appears in this Annual Report.

The Audit Committee, all of whose members are outside directors, is responsible for monitoring the Company's accounting and reporting practices. The Audit Committee meets periodically with management and the independent auditors to ensure that each is properly discharging its responsibilities. The independent auditors have full and free access to the Committee without the presence of management to discuss the results of their audits, the adequacy of internal accounting controls and the quality of financial reporting.

EXHIBIT 6
CEO's Financial Statement Certification

Pursuant to 18 U.S.C. Section 1350, as adopted pursuant to Section 906 of the Sarbanes-Oxley Act of 2002, the undersigned officer of The Procter & Gamble Company (the "Company") certifies to his knowledge that:

(1) The Annual Report on Form 10-K of the Company for the year ended June 30, 2004 fully complies with the requirements of Section 13(a) or 15(d) of the Securities Exchange Act of 1934; and
(2) The information contained in that Form 10-K fairly presents, in all material respects, the financial conditions and results of operations of the Company.

A.G. LAFLEY

(A.G. Lafley)
Chairman of the Board,
President and Chief Executive

September 7, 2004

Date

management. The audit committee is responsible for receiving information from the independent auditors and from those in the corporation who implement and evaluate internal controls. Accounting and auditing problems should be reported to the audit committee. The committee can discuss problems with management and can take steps to correct the problems if necessary.

As a result of the Sarbanes-Oxley Act, the chief executive officer and chief financial officer of a company must certify the accuracy of the company's financial statements. That report appears in a company's 10-K report to the SEC. An example from Procter & Gamble's 10-K appears in Exhibit 6.

Self-Study Problem #2

Listed below are statements about auditing:

A. An independent audit guarantees the accuracy of financial information.
B. An auditor does not have to examine all of an audited company's transactions to certify the reliability of the company's financial statements.
C. An auditor must follow auditing standards in performing an audit.
D. An auditor is responsible only for the period covered by the financial statements audited when preparing an audit report.

Required Identify each statement as true or false and explain your reasoning.

INTERNAL CONTROLS

Objective 5
Describe the purpose of internal controls and types of controls that should be evident in business organizations.

An essential requirement of any accounting system is that it provide accurate data. Incorrect data are not useful and can lead to poor decisions. Consequently, controls are important in a company to help ensure that data are accurate. Incorrect data can result from errors in recording data or from events that affect a company's assets. For example, if Favorite Cookie Company purchased inventory at a cost of $1,200, it would be incorrect to record the amount owed the supplier as $1,150. It is correct to record an increase in Accounts Payable and Merchandise Inventory of $1,200. However, if the merchandise is stolen from the company, the accounting data are in error because they are not consistent with the amount of the asset actually available to the company. Accordingly, a company uses a system of internal controls both to protect assets and to ensure accuracy of accounting information.

Management Philosophy

A strong system of internal controls begins with a management philosophy that encourages appropriate security and behavior in a company. If top management takes a lax attitude about these matters, it is unlikely that it will develop and enforce an effective system. Accordingly, top management should develop policies and ensure that these are communicated throughout the company. It should also ensure that procedures are developed to monitor and enforce control policies. If Maria and Stan want their company's employees to act with integrity, they must establish a tone of ethical conduct by acting with integrity themselves and by creating and enforcing policies and procedures that require ethical behavior in conducting business activities.

Part of management philosophy should involve developing rewards and incentives that encourage employees to take appropriate actions. For example, a bonus system that places too much emphasis on sales quotas could encourage employees to create false sales, to predate sales orders, and to make credit sales to risky customers. A good system of rewards will encourage employees to focus on the value and ongoing success of a company.

Business Ethics

Management should create a code of ethics and other documents that establish company policy and inform employees of acceptable and expected behavior. These policies should consider the relationship between a company and its customers, employees, suppliers, stockholders, and community. As an example, Exhibit 7 summarizes the contents of **United Technologies Corporation**'s Code of Ethics.

http://ingram.swlearning.com

Visit the FCPA's home page to learn more about the Foreign Corrupt Practices Act.

A major purpose of internal controls is to ensure compliance with laws and regulations. If a company fails to comply with laws, it can be subject to civil and criminal penalties resulting in significant losses. Antitrust laws prohibit collaboration among competitor companies that leads to unfair pricing or trade practices. Companies that sell similar products in the same markets cannot collude to set prices or limit competition. The Foreign Corrupt Practices Act prohibits companies from offering or accepting bribes or other payments to obtain business or influence the behavior of customers or government authorities.

Ethical behavior involves treating individuals and companies fairly and providing full disclosure of information that might affect their decisions. Moral hazard is a potential problem in dealing with customers, suppliers, employees, and others who interact with a company. The company often has access to information that is not available to external stakeholders. Full disclosure is often a remedy for moral hazard. In the long run, fair treatment and disclosure will create a reputation for a company that will lead to financial benefits.

Computer System Controls

Many internal controls should be built into computer information systems. These **controls protect a company's information resources from unauthorized access, improper use, and destruction.** System controls determine who can gain access to various parts of a company's database. Users should have **appropriate identification and passwords** to log onto networks or to use network resources. Users typically are assigned to groups based on the type of work they perform. For example, data entry personnel in the sales division are permitted access to those files in the database that need to be updated when customers submit orders. They should not have access to other data in the system that they do not need in the course of their work.

System controls also manage databases to prevent several users from trying to update particular records at the same time. While one user is accessing a record or file, other users are locked out so that conflicting or incomplete changes cannot be made.

EXHIBIT 7
Ethical Issues Associated with Corporate Conduct

Relationships between the Company and:	Important Issues:
Customers	• Quality and safety of products • Honesty in dealings • Avoid conflicts of interest • Protection of confidential information • Comply with Foreign Corrupt Practices Act
Employees	• Equal opportunity in hiring, compensation, and treatment • Privacy of information about employees • Treatment with dignity and respect • Provide a safe and healthy work environment • Provide opportunity for development
Suppliers	• Fair competition
Stockholders	• Provide superior returns • Protect and improve investment value • Protect assets • Accurate accounting information and disclosure of business activities
Competitors	• Fairness • Comply with antitrust laws
Communities	• Responsible corporate citizenship • Abide by laws • Participate in civic affairs • Support through corporate philanthropy • Comply with laws concerning political donations • Comply with export laws • Protect environment

Source: www.utc.com.

Other controls **check data for errors** to make sure that data entered in a system are reasonable and appropriate. For example, a system may refuse to prepare a check for an amount larger than $1,000. This control prevents a clerk from accidentally writing large checks by mistyping data or omitting a decimal. **Automatic numbering** should be used to identify transactions and source documents such as sales orders, invoices, and purchase orders. Each transaction or document is assigned a number that follows a preset sequence. Consequently, each item can be tracked and missing items can be identified. Using automatic numbering makes it more difficult for employees to create fictitious transactions or falsify data by recording transactions and then deleting them from the system. Missing numbers are easily identified, and those responsible for deleting the numbered items can be held responsible.

Many other controls can be built into computer systems. Examples include the use of software and hardware to make it difficult for unauthorized users to break into computer networks and databases. The software and hardware also can monitor systems to detect attempts to gain unauthorized access.

Duplicate copies of databases often are maintained so that if one database system fails, the other is available for use. **Backup systems and data** are necessary to prevent data from being lost if a database system fails and to permit a company to continue to operate even if it has computer problems. Databases are backed up on a regular basis. Data are copied to tape or other permanent storage devices so they can be retrieved in case of a major problem with the active database. These backup data are stored in locations away from where the working database is maintained.

Complete computer systems must be protected. Many companies maintain centralized computer information system facilities. These facilities must be protected from destruction by natural disasters (fire, flood, earthquake) and from those who might attempt to destroy a company's systems (terrorists, disgruntled employees, competitors). An important control is a **disaster recovery plan** that a company can rely on to get its computer systems back into working order in case of a major disaster. Such a plan usually requires access to facilities, hardware, and software at locations other than those normally used.

Human Resources Controls

Many internal controls focus on a company's human resources. Important controls involve **hiring qualified employees** who have the appropriate skills for a particular job. **Background checks** can identify employees who have a history of improper behavior. A **good training program** can ensure that employees develop and maintain the skills needed for their jobs.

An important control involves **segregation of duties** so that an employee does not have access to resources and information that would make it easy for the employee to misuse those resources. For example, an employee should not have access both to a resource and to the accounting for that resource. If an employee has control over merchandise, supplies, or cash, that employee should not have control over records showing the amount of the resources received or transferred. Computer programmers and systems developers should not have access to actual operations of computer systems. Developers create the systems and can use them to create improper transactions that can transfer cash or other resources to improper persons. Developers can also destroy systems by creating programs to erase data or corrupt program logic. Disgruntled employees can be a major risk to an organization, especially if they understand and have access to a company's computer system.

Employees should understand their responsibilities and authority. They should know what they are permitted to do in their jobs and what they are not permitted to do. They should clearly understand lines of authority in a company. **Employees should be supervised** and inappropriate behavior should be reported and addressed.

Physical Controls

Safeguarding assets often involves controlling physical access. Merchandise and materials can be secured in warehouses or display cases. Merchandise can be tagged electronically to make shoplifting or theft difficult. Surveillance equipment can monitor important resources. Cash registers, vaults, and safety deposit boxes secure financial resources.

Conclusion

A strong system of internal controls is essential for protecting any information system. Though not all controls relate directly to how information is processed, the integrity of accounting information depends on controls that protect data and the systems used to process those data. An internal control system is an important part of an accounting information system. Without internal controls, users could not rely on accounting information as an accurate description of a company's economic activities.

THE RESPONSIBILITIES OF ACCOUNTANTS

Throughout this chapter we have considered various regulatory functions associated with accounting. Accountants and the accounting profession have primary responsibility for these functions. Accountants work to prepare **financial information** contained in companies' annual reports. They **manage the information systems** used to record and report this information. They help other managers **interpret information** reported by the accounting system and make sure the information is reliable and conforms with GAAP and legal requirements.

Accountants serve on organizations like the FASB and SEC that **establish and monitor accounting standards**. They research accounting issues, prepare standards, and research company financial reporting practices. Independent CPAs **audit business financial reports** to ensure that they fairly present the companies' business activities. The audit is an important tool in maintaining strong capital markets. If managers fail in their responsibilities to report fairly to external users, independent audits are a major line of defense to prevent misleading information from reaching investors. Consequently, auditors are held to a high standard of professional responsibility and integrity. Audit failure is a major source of concern for the SEC and society in general. CPAs and the audit firms in which they work are required to maintain current professional knowledge and are reviewed on a regular basis to make sure their practices are consistent with current standards.

In addition to working as external auditors, accountants also work as **internal auditors**. Internal auditors work for businesses and are responsible for developing and monitoring internal control systems and for auditing a company's divisions for compliance with accounting rules, company policies, and legal requirements. They also may evaluate the performance of a division or company to improve efficiency and effectiveness.

Self-Study Problem #3

Deborah Stinger works in the systems development department of a major company. She helped develop the company's computerized accounting system. Occasionally, she fills in for one of the operators in the accounts payable department. This operator is responsible for processing checks to suppliers for purchases made by the company. While filling in, Deborah created an account of a fictitious company, just to see if the system could be tricked into writing checks for nonexistent purchases. She added data to the company's file and entered some phony purchases. The computer wrote the checks, and they were mailed to a post office box Deborah opened. Over the last few years, Deborah has written over $80,000 in checks to her fictitious company.

Required Identify some internal control deficiencies in the accounting system that have allowed Deborah to embezzle money from her company.

THINKING BEYOND THE QUESTION

HOW DO WE ENSURE THAT REPORTS TO EXTERNAL USERS FAIRLY PRESENT BUSINESS ACTIVITIES?

Full and fair reporting involves reliable financial statements that accurately report a company's business activities. Information to describe, interpret, and extend that information also is important. Audits and internal controls also help ensure full and fair reporting. To what extent should full and fair reporting protect external users from poor management decisions? Does full and fair reporting guarantee that stakeholders will not suffer losses from their contractual relations with a business? Why or why not?

Self-Study Problem Solutions

SSP6-1 GAAP are guidelines for the preparation of financial statements and other accounting information. They are important because they provide standards for the content and format of financial reports. How earnings and other accounting information are measured is important for determining the reliability and usefulness of the information. If each company chose its own accounting rules, it could select those rules that made the company appear successful.

Moral hazard results when a person, like Abe, has incentives to behave in ways that can be harmful to others, such as creditors, who have a financial stake in the person's activities. To get a loan, Abe has an incentive to make his company appear financially strong. If he fails to repay the loan, the bank will lose money. Reliable financial information is a means of controlling moral hazard so that the bank can make a decision based on an accurate view of the company's business activities. GAAP help ensure that financial information is reliable.

SSP6-2

A. False. An independent audit provides reasonable assurance about the reliability of audited financial information. Auditors rely on information provided by management and on evidence collected from a sample of a company's transactions.

B. True. The cost of examining all of a company's transactions is usually too high. Auditors examine a representative sample of transactions.

C. True. Auditing standards are procedures that auditors must follow in performing an audit to help ensure the audit has been performed properly.

D. False. The auditor is responsible for making sure a company notifies readers of its financial reports of any events occurring between the end of the period covered by the financial statements and the date of the audit report that would have a material effect on the interpretation of the financial statements.

SSP6-3 Internal control deficiencies include access to the accounting system by an employee who should not have access. Limitations on physical access, passwords, and employee identification numbers should have prevented Deborah from gaining access to the system. Deborah should not have authority to use the system. Another deficiency was the failure to separate systems development from computer operations personnel. Deborah was able to embezzle funds because she understood the computer programs that created accounting files. Computer operators normally do not have sufficient knowledge of the system to manipulate it in this manner. An additional deficiency was the failure of the system to verify transactions or compare amounts from one part of the system to another. For example, use of sequentially numbered purchase orders should make it difficult for an employee to create fictitious data without the system identifying a problem.

Define *Terms and Concepts Defined in This Chapter*

Review Summary of Important Concepts

1. Accounting regulations are important to protect the interests of external users of accounting information who have limited access to business information. GAAP help ensure that reliable information is available to control moral hazard on the part of corporate managers.

2. Several events and organizations are important for the development of accounting regulations in the United States.
   a. The first regulations were established by the New York Stock Exchange.
   b. The Securities Act of 1933 and the Securities and Exchange Act of 1934 are major laws that affect accounting and financial reporting in the United States.
   c. The Sarbanes-Oxley Act of 2002 created the Public Companies Accounting Oversight Board to oversee and set auditing standards and required CEOs and CFOs to certify a company's financial statements.

3. Several organizations play a role in setting and enforcing accounting standards.
   a. The SEC has the authority to establish and enforce accounting standards in the United States.
   b. The FASB is a private-sector organization that is largely responsible for setting accounting standards in the United States.
   c. The GASB is a private-sector organization that establishes accounting standards for state and local governments in the United States.
   d. The IASB is a private-sector organization that helps develop global accounting standards.

4. Accounting standards are set through a process of public discussion that permits those affected by standards to have input into the standard-setting process.

5. The FASB's conceptual framework provides guidance for the development of financial accounting standards for business organizations.

6. Annual reports contain information supplemental to financial statements that is important for understanding and interpreting those statements.
   a. Supplemental financial disclosures provide information about business activities and for periods other than those covered by the primary financial statements.
   b. Notes to the financial statements provide additional information about business activities and explain methods used in preparing financial statements.
   c. The auditors' report describes the audit and expresses an opinion as to whether the financial statements are a fair presentation of a company's business activities in conformity with GAAP.
   d. The report of management's responsibilities identifies responsibilities of managers for financial statements and internal controls and describes a company's audit committee.

7. Internal controls are designed to protect a company's assets and ensure the reliability of its accounting information.
   a. Management is responsible for establishing an environment of integrity in which internal controls are important.
   b. Management should establish a code of ethics and inform employees of expected and appropriate behavior.
   c. Computer controls are important for protecting a company's data and computer systems.
   d. Human resource controls are designed to control the behavior of employees and managers and to provide expectations about appropriate behavior.
   e. Physical controls are designed to protect assets and to limit access to important resources.

8. Accountants and the accounting profession are responsible for development and enforcement of accounting regulations.

Questions

Q6-1 *Obj. 1* Other than business managers, who relies on financial reports to make decisions?

Q6-2 *Obj. 1* Compliance with regulations is costly. Why are public companies required to comply with GAAP?

Q6-3 *Obj. 1* Congress passed the Sarbanes-Oxley (SOX) Act in the wake of several high-profile corporate accounting frauds. What is the goal of SOX? What provisions of the act help ensure the goal is achieved?

Q6-4 *Obj. 1* SOX requires that corporations create audit committees as part of their boards of directors. What is the purpose of an audit committee?

Q6-5 *Obj. 2* Why does the FASB issue a discussion memorandum prior to releasing an exposure draft of a new pronouncement?

Q6-6 *Obj. 2* The SEC is authorized by law to establish and enforce accounting standards in the United States. Why are most accounting standards used by businesses issued by the FASB?

Q6-7 *Obj. 3* What are the elements of financial statements, according to the FASB's conceptual framework? Where would an investor find these elements?

Q6-8 *Obj. 3* One of the major components of the FASB conceptual framework is the objectives of financial reporting. What are the objectives of financial reporting?

Q6-9 *Obj. 4* A friend has been reviewing the annual report of a firm in which he has invested. He says, "I'm worried because the auditors gave an unqualified opinion on the financial statements. You'd think a big company like this would have auditors that were qualified." Clear up your friend's misunderstanding.

Q6-10 *Obj. 4* What is the purpose of notes to financial statements? If a firm does a good job presenting its financial statements, why are notes necessary?

Q6-11 *Obj. 4* What is an audit and why is it important?

Q6-12 *Obj. 5* Why is it necessary for managers and other decision makers to understand how accounting information is developed and reported? Shouldn't it just be management's job to manage and the accountant's job to account? Explain.

Q6-13 *Obj. 5* What are the two primary purposes of internal controls?

Q6-14 *Obj. 5* Explain why internal controls are important to a computerized management information system and identify several such controls that are commonly used.

Q6-15 *Obj. 5* Why is management philosophy an important internal control issue?

Q6-16 *Obj. 5* Identify some human resource controls that can be used in a company and explain why they are important.

Q6-17 *Obj. 5* Identify some physical controls that can be used in a company and explain why they are important.

Exercises

E6-1 *Objs. 1–5* Write a short definition for each of the terms listed in the *Terms and Concepts Defined in This Chapter* section.

E6-2 *Obj. 1* Three major developments in the history of accounting involved the development of the New York Stock Exchange, the 16th Amendment to the U.S. Constitution, and the events subsequent to the stock market crash of 1929. Explain briefly the significance of each of these events for contemporary accounting.

E6-3 *Obj. 1* Identify the major reporting requirements associated with each of the following:

a. Securities Act of 1933
b. Securities and Exchange Act of 1934
c. 10-K report
d. 10-Q report

E6-4 *Obj. 2* Identify each of the following:

a. The private sector organization currently responsible for setting financial accounting standards in the United States.
b. The private sector organization currently responsible for setting state and local governmental accounting standards in the United States.
c. The organization that exists to influence the development of international accounting standards.
d. The federal agency that oversees accounting at the federal government.
e. The organization responsible for the enforcement of financial accounting standards in the United States.

E6-5 *Obj. 2* How would you react to the following statement? "Accounting standards impose costs on corporations and their managers to protect the interests of investors."

E6-6 *Obj. 2* What is meant by the term "generally accepted accounting principles"? What is the significance of the phrase "generally accepted"?

E6-7 *Obj. 3* What is the purpose of the qualitative characteristics of financial reports? What are the primary qualitative characteristics as defined by the FASB?

E6-8 *Obj. 3* What is the FASB's conceptual framework?

E6-9 *Obj. 4* Identify each of the sections of an auditors' report and explain its purpose.

E6-10 *Obj. 4* Corporate annual reports include a discussion and analysis of the company's financial performance. What is the purpose of this discussion?

E6-11 *Obj. 4* **General Mills Corporation** had sales of $11 billion in fiscal year 2004 from Betty Crocker, Pillsbury, Wheaties, Cheerios, Pop Secret popcorn, and other products. The company reported total assets of more than $18 billion. Inspect the General Mills' balance sheet found in Appendix A at the back of this book. (a) Does it seem strange to you that such a big company is able to report all of its assets using only nine different accounts? How is this possible? (b) Why is this done? (c) Would this level of detail meet the needs of the general manager of the Pillsbury division, or the managers in other divisions of the company? Discuss.

E6-12 *Obj. 4* Quick Transport Company owns a large fleet of trucks that move freight throughout the country. Some of these trucks cost hundreds of thousands of dollars and are operated for 15 years or more before being replaced. The company issues long-term debt to pay for most of its equipment. The company's fiscal year ends on June 30. For each fiscal year, the company prepares financial reports that include estimates of its results of operations for the year. How do the operations of Quick illustrate the periodic measurement and going concern principles of accounting?

E6-13 *Obj. 4* Bill's grandparents have been buying shares of stock for his college education fund since the day he was born. Yesterday, Bill received the annual report of Thompson Consolidated Shoulderpads, Inc., and is telling you about it. Bill says:

> "I feel really good about the company because its financial statements were prepared and audited by a well-known national accounting firm. Not only that, but the firm received

(Continued)

an unqualified audit report. This means that the auditor checked out all the company's transactions and that the company is healthy. Since the auditors think the company is doing well, I think I'll invest some of my summer job savings in it."

How would you respond to your friend? Do you believe he has a good understanding of what information is conveyed by an auditors' report? Discuss.

E6-14 *Obj. 5* What is the role of an accountant who works for a business organization?

E6-15 *Obj. 5* Selma Fromm is a recent graduate in accounting. She has taken a position with Hand Writer Company. The company has three divisions that manufacture three products: pencils, pens, and colored markers. Financial information for the most recent fiscal period for each division includes the following:

	Pencils	Pens	Markers
Division revenues	$200,000	$ 300,000	$100,000
Division expenses	140,000	160,000	60,000
Division assets	600,000	1,000,000	200,000

One of Selma's regular duties is to prepare an analysis of the performance of each division. Prepare an analysis of division performance from the information provided. Which of the divisions appears to be most profitable? Is this responsibility typical of the tasks often performed by accountants who work for business organizations? Explain.

E6-16 *Obj. 5* What is the purpose of internal auditing? Why is it important to an organization?

E6-17 *Obj. 5* List and briefly describe the primary internal control procedures discussed in the chapter.

E6-18 *Obj. 5* What is the role of an independent CPA?

E6-19 *Obj. 5* Mag's Pie Shop is a rapidly growing baker and distributor of specialty pies for festive occasions. Mag's CPA adviser keeps recommending that Mag install better internal controls over the business. Specifically, the CPA recommends that Mag separate the company's recordkeeping function from the physical control of cash and other assets. The CPA also recommends that Mag use only preprinted and prenumbered forms for all business transactions.

a. What is the purpose of internal controls? Be specific.
b. For each internal control suggested by the CPA, give one example of an unsatisfactory situation or event that the control would prevent.

E6-20 *Obj. 5* Ima Crook is a sales clerk for Free Cash Company. Ima runs a cash register. Each day she obtains $200 from a supervisor and places the money in the cash register to make change. Customers bring goods to the sales counter, where Ima takes their money and writes out a sales slip using a form provided for this purpose. If requested by the customer, she writes out a separate slip for the customer. Ima works from 9 A.M. to 5 P.M. except for breaks and lunch when she is replaced by a coworker who runs the cash register for her. At 5 P.M. Ima takes all the cash from her cash register and puts it in an envelope along with the sales receipts and hands the envelope to a supervisor. Ima just bought a new $50,000 car and paid cash. What internal control problems exist in this situation? What can be done to solve the problems?

Problems

P6-1 *Obj. 1* **THE IMPORTANCE OF FINANCIAL ACCOUNTING STANDARDS**

Accounting and financial reporting is highly regulated in the United States. Standards specify the types of information to be reported and how accounting numbers are to be calculated. Listed on the following page are groups who benefit from these standards.

A. managers
B. stockholders
C. creditors
D. governmental authorities
E. employees

Required Explain why financial accounting standards are important to each of these groups.

P6-2 THE ROLE OF ACCOUNTING REGULATION

Obj. 1

On Wednesday, July 10, 2002, *The Wall Street Journal* reported the following headlines:

Securities Threat[1]
Bush Crackdown on Business Fraud Signals New Era
Stream of Corporate Scandals Causes Bipartisan Outrage; Return of Big Government?
Fiery Rhetoric on Wall Street

President Bush's tongue-lashing of big business marks a swing of the American political pendulum away from a quarter-century of bipartisan deference to capitalists. "We will use the full weight of the law to expose and root out corruption."

"Book-cooking" has eroded "the trust and the confidence that is absolutely vital to the function of our capital markets," Rep. Patrick Toomey, a Republican from Pennsylvania, said.

Required Discuss the role of accounting regulation. Why is trust vital to the function of our capital markets?

[1]*The Wall Street Journal*, Wednesday, July 10, 2002, Eastern Edition, p. A1.

P6-3 SERVICES PROHIBITED BY SARBANES-OXLEY (SOX)

Obj. 1

SOX prohibits external auditors from providing certain types of services to client corporations. Included in the list of prohibited services are the following:

- financial information systems design and implementation
- bookkeeping or other services relating to the accounting records for financial statements
- internal audit outsourcing services

Required What theme seems to be common across the list of prohibited services? Why do you think SOX specifically prohibits these services?

P6-4 CERTIFICATIONS REQUIRED BY SARBANES-OXLEY (SOX)

Objs. 1, 2

Sarbanes-Oxley requires a publicly traded company's CEO and CFO to make specific certifications as part of the company's annual report. Produced below is a certification from **Microsoft**'s 2004 Form 10-K filed with the SEC.

CERTIFICATIONS PURSUANT TO
SECTION 906 OF THE SARBANES-OXLEY ACT OF 2002
(18 U.S.C. § 1350)

In connection with the Annual Report of Microsoft Corporation, a Washington corporation (the "Company"), on Form 10-K for the year ended June 30, 2004, as filed with the Securities and Exchange Commission (the "Report"), Steven A. Ballmer, Chief Executive Officer of the Company and John G. Connors, Chief Financial Officer of the Company, respectively, do each hereby certify, pursuant to § 906 of the Sarbanes-Oxley Act of 2002 (18 U.S.C. § 1350), that to his knowledge:

(1) The Report fully complies with the requirements of section 13(a) or 15(d) of the Securities Exchange Act of 1934; and
(2) The information contained in the Report fairly presents, in all material respects, the financial condition and result of operations of the Company.

/s/ Steven A. Ballmer

Steven A. Ballmer
Chief Executive Officer
September 1, 2004

(Continued)

/s/ John G. Connors

John G. Connors
Chief Financial Officer
September 1, 2004

[A signed original of this written statement required by Section 906 has been provided to Microsoft Corporation and will be retained by Microsoft Corporation and furnished to the Securities and Exchange Commission or its staff upon request.]

Required Explain what the CEO and CFO are certifying. Why do you think SOX requires management to make this certification?

P6-5 SARBANES-OXLEY—ACHIEVING THE INTENDED EFFECT AT HEALTHSOUTH CORPORATION[1]

Obj. 1

Publicly traded corporations traditionally have included a statement of management responsibilities as part of the annual report. This statement typically used the following language:

> The company's management is responsible for the fairness and accuracy of the consolidated financial statements. The statements have been prepared in accordance with accounting principles that are generally accepted in the United States, using management's best estimates and judgments where appropriate.

In the wake of a series of high-profile public frauds, Congress passed the Sarbanes-Oxley Act. HealthSouth Corporation was one of the first companies tried under the new SOX legislation. Management was accused of overstating earnings by $2.6 billion from 1996 to 2002. The following is an excerpt from an article appearing in the *Birmingham Post* on February 5, 2005:

> Court testimony Friday showed the fraud at HealthSouth Corp. unraveled when a newly married executive returned from his honeymoon and said he could no longer live a life of deception.
>
> Weston Smith, [HealthSouth's] chief financial officer at the time, said in August 2002 he would quit rather than certify financial statements he knew were false . . . Smith had good reason not to sign the documents. When he returned from celebrating his marriage, the financial statements requiring his signature were the first bound by the Sarbanes-Oxley Act. . . .

Required If management had been responsible for the fairness and accuracy of the financial statements prior to SOX, explain why executives would have been more hesitant to sign statements they knew were fraudulent.

[1]The authors gratefully acknowledge the late Professor William Samson for his contributions to this problem.

P6-6 CERTIFICATIONS REQUIRED BY SARBANES-OXLEY (SOX)

Obj. 1

Sarbanes-Oxley requires certifications by management to be published with the company's annual report. Reproduced below are the certifications made by Steven Ballmer, CEO of Microsoft Corporation, as published in the company's June 30, 2004 Form 10-K.

CERTIFICATIONS

I, Steven A. Ballmer, certify that:

1. I have reviewed this annual report on Form 10-K of Microsoft Corporation;
2. Based on my knowledge, this report does not contain any untrue statement of a material fact or omit to state a material fact necessary to make the statements made, in light of the circumstances under which such statements were made, not misleading with respect to the period covered by this report;
3. Based on my knowledge, the financial statements, and other financial information included in this report, fairly present in all material respects the financial condition, results of operations and cash flows of the registrant as of, and for, the periods presented in this report;

4. The registrant's other certifying officer and I are responsible for establishing and maintaining disclosure controls and procedures (as defined in Exchange Act Rules 13a-15(e) and 15d-15(e)) for the registrant and have:
   a. Designed such disclosure controls and procedures, or caused such disclosure controls and procedures to be designed under our supervision, to ensure that material information relating to the registrant, including its consolidated subsidiaries, is made known to us by others within those entities, particularly during the period in which this report is being prepared;
   b. Evaluated the effectiveness of the registrant's disclosure controls and procedures and presented in this report our conclusions about the effectiveness of the disclosure controls and procedures, as of the end of the period covered by this report based on such evaluation; and
   c. Disclosed in this report any change in the registrant's internal control over financial reporting that occurred during the registrant's most recent fiscal quarter (the registrant's fourth fiscal quarter in the case of an annual report) that has materially affected, or is reasonably likely to materially affect, the registrant's internal control over financial reporting; and

5. The registrant's other certifying officer and I have disclosed, based on our most recent evaluation of internal control over financial reporting, to the registrant's auditors and the audit committee of registrant's board of directors (or persons performing the equivalent functions):
   a. All significant deficiencies and material weaknesses in the design or operation of internal control over financial reporting which are reasonably likely to adversely affect the registrant's ability to record, process, summarize and report financial information; and
   b. Any fraud, whether or not material, that involves management or other employees who have a significant role in the registrant's internal control over financial reporting.

September 1, 2004

/s/ Steven A. Ballmer

Steven A. Ballmer
Chief Executive Officer

Required

1. Read the certifications made by Steven Ballmer. Can you identify a theme that is common among the five certifications?
2. Why do you think a certification by management is necessary?

P6-7 SETTING ACCOUNTING STANDARDS

Obj. 2

Accounting standards are set in the United States in the private sector. Public hearings and written documents provide feedback during development of the standards. Opportunity is provided to those affected by standards to contribute information to standard-setting organizations such as the FASB.

Required List the major steps in the standard-setting process. Explain the purpose of each of the primary documents that results from the process.

P6-8 OBTAINING THE MOST RECENT INFORMATION ABOUT FASB ACTIVITIES

Obj. 2

http://ingram.swlearning.com

Access the FASB and IASB sites through the text's website.

Visit the FASB's website and prepare a report that summarizes the various types of information available on the site.

P6-9 OBTAINING THE MOST RECENT INFORMATION ABOUT IASB ACTIVITIES

Obj. 2

Visit the International Accounting Standards Board's website and prepare a report that summarizes the various types of information available on the site. Are there similarities between the processes of developing standards used by the IASB and the FASB? Explain.

P6-10 THE PURPOSE OF THE CONCEPTUAL FRAMEWORK

Obj. 3

The Financial Accounting Standards Board developed a conceptual framework to provide guidance in the development of financial accounting standards.

Required Identify the primary components of the conceptual framework for business organizations and explain the purpose of each component.

P6-11 THE CONCEPTUAL FRAMEWORK—QUALITATIVE CHARACTERISTICS

Obj. 3

Draw a diagram that describes the relationships among the qualitative characteristics as defined in the FASB conceptual framework. Explain your diagram.

P6-12 ETHICAL ISSUES IN AUDITING

Objs. 3, 4

Larry Clint is the president of Hometown Bank. The bank has several thousand depositors and makes loans to many local businesses and homeowners. Jenny Walters is a partner with a CPA firm hired to audit Hometown Bank. The financial statements the bank proposes to issue for the 2007 fiscal year include the following information.

Loans receivable	$4,000,000
Total assets	5,000,000
Net income	1,000,000

During the audit, Jenny discovers that many of the loans were made for real estate development. Because of economic problems in the region, much of this real estate remains unsold or vacant. The current market value of the property is considerably less than its cost. Several of the developers are experiencing financial problems, and it appears unlikely that the bank will recover its loans if they default. Jenny described this problem to Larry and proposed a write-down of the receivables to $2,800,000. The $1,200,000 write-down would be written off against earnings for 2007.

Larry is extremely upset by the proposal. He notes the write-down would result in a reported loss for the bank for 2007. Also, the bank would be in jeopardy of falling below the equity requirements imposed by the bank regulatory board to which the bank is accountable. He fears the board would impose major constraints on the bank's operations. Also, he fears depositors would lose confidence in the bank and withdraw their money, further compounding the bank's financial problems. He cites several economic forecasts indicating an impending improvement in the region's economy. Further, he notes the bank's demise would be a major economic blow to the local economy and could precipitate the bankruptcy of some of the bank's major customers.

Jenny acknowledges that Larry is correct in his perceptions of the possible outcomes of the write-down. Larry proposes an alternative to Jenny. The bank will write down the receivables by $300,000 for 2007. The remaining losses will be recognized over the next three years, assuming property values have not improved. Larry also tells Jenny that if she is unwilling to accept his proposal, he will fire her firm and hire new auditors. The bank has been a long-time client of Jenny's firm and is one of its major revenue producers. Jenny also recognizes Larry's proposal is not consistent with accounting principles.

Required What are the ethical problems Jenny faces? What action would you recommend she take?

P6-13 EVALUATING THE QUALITY OF FINANCIAL REPORTS

Objs. 3, 4

The following statements describe the annual report issued by Short Sheet Company for the fiscal year ended December 31, 2007.

A. The report was issued on October 1, 2008.
B. The balance sheet included management's estimates of the increased value of certain fixed assets during 2007.

C. Procedures used to calculate revenues and expenses were different for 2007 than for 2006 and earlier years.
D. Short's financial statements were audited by an accounting firm owned by the president's brother.
E. Some of the company's major liabilities were not included in the annual report.

Required For each statement, identify the qualitative characteristic that has been compromised.

P6-14 UNDERSTANDING THE AUDITORS' REPORT

Obj. 4

A standard auditors' report contains reference to each of the following:

A. Responsibility
B. Generally accepted auditing standards
C. Material misstatement and material respects
D. A test basis
E. Present fairly . . . in conformity with generally accepted accounting principles

Required Explain why each of these terms is important for understanding the auditors' report and the audit process.

P6-15 DISTINGUISHING AMONG TYPES OF ACCOUNTS

Obj. 4

Bonner Systems uses the following accounts when preparing its financial reports.

	Type of Account					Financial Statement	
	Asset	Liability	Equity	Revenue	Expense	Income Statement	Balance Sheet
1. Wages Payable							
2. Accounts Receivable							
3. Retained Earnings							
4. Buildings							
5. Supplies Used							
6. Inventory							
7. Sales (for cash)							
8. Accumulated Depreciation							
9. Loan from Bank							
10. Land							
11. Owners' Investment							
12. Supplies							
13. Sales (on credit)							
14. Bonds Payable							
15. Unearned Revenue							
16. Wages Earned by Employees							
17. Utilities Consumed							

Required

A. Place a mark in the appropriate column to indicate the type of account.
B. Place a mark in the appropriate column to indicate on which financial statement that account is reported.

P6-16 INTERPRETING INFORMATION REPORTED ON FINANCIAL STATEMENTS

Obj. 4

The two most recent monthly balance sheets of Apex Company are shown on the following page. Also shown is the most recent monthly income statement.

(Continued)

Balance Sheet	May 31	June 30		May 31	June 30
Assets:			Liabilities and Owners' Equity:		
Cash	$ 3,200	$ 1,300	Accounts payable	$ 2,300	$ 2,300
Accounts receivable	5,700	6,100	Wages payable	1,900	900
Equipment	26,300	26,300	Notes payable	48,600	39,600
Building	115,000	115,000	Owners' investment	43,000	48,000
Accumulated depreciation	(28,000)	(28,500)	Retained earnings	26,400	29,400
Total	$122,200	$120,200		$122,200	$120,200

Income Statement for June	
Service revenues	$7,900
Rent expense	(1,800)
Wages expense	(1,700)
Supplies expense	(700)
Depreciation expense	(500)
Interest expense	(200)
Net income	$3,000

Required From the financial statements presented, identify and record the transactions that occurred during June. Use the spreadsheet format shown below to record the transactions. One transaction is shown as an example.

		Assets		=	Liabilities	+	Owners' Equity	
	Accounts	Cash	Other Assets				Contributed Capital	Retained Earnings
	Beginning Amounts	3,200	+119,000	=	52,800	+	43,000	+26,400
1	Cash	+7,500						
	Accounts Receivable		+400					
	Service Revenues							+7,900

P6-17 LETTER TO THE SHAREHOLDERS

Obj. 4

Selected information from **General Mills'** 2004 annual report and 10K is provided in Appendix A at the end of the text. Read the letter addressed "to our shareholders" shown on page 2 of the annual report.

Required Comment on the following:

A. Who prepared the letter to the shareholders?
B. What is the overall tone of the letter?
C. What time periods are addressed in the letter (past, present, future)?
D. What are the accomplishments mentioned in the letter?

P6-18 MANAGEMENT'S DISCUSSION AND ANALYSIS OF FINANCIAL CONDITION AND RESULTS OF OPERATION

Obj. 4

Selected information from **General Mills'** 2004 annual report and 10K is provided in Appendix A at the end of the text. Read the Executive Overview section of Item 17, *Management's Discussion and Analysis of Financial Condition and Results of Operation*, on pages 9 and 10 of Form 10-K.

Required Comment on the following:

A. From reading the report, what can you learn about how General Mills is organized?
B. Management indicated earnings fell short of expectations in 2004. What were the three factors that caused the earnings shortfall?
C. How is management planning to deal with the higher costs of energy, labor, and other supply chain costs?

P6-19 EARNINGS RESTATEMENT AND STOCK PRICES

Objs. 3, 4, 5

In April 2001, the management of U.S. Aggregates, Inc., a producer of aggregates made of a combination of crushed stone, sand, and gravel, announced that the company would be restating its earnings for the first three quarters of 2000. After the announcement, the company's stock price per share dropped more than 75% from its high for the period affected by the company's restatement of earnings.

Postscript: While revising this textbook the authors learned that the company faced shareholder lawsuits following a restatement of its 2000 earnings. Staker & Parson Companies acquired the troubled company's assets for $140 million in June 2002.

Required

A. Did the company practice full and fair disclosure? Why did the stock price fall when investors learned that the company had produced financial information that was incorrect?
B. Do you believe misleading the investing public is an ethical issue? Explain.

P6-20 EVALUATING INTERNAL CONTROL PROCEDURES

Obj. 5

Consider each of the following situations.

A. Sales clerks in a retail store are assigned to a specific cash register. They are given a cash drawer containing $100 in change at the beginning of their shifts. They are required to record the amount of each purchase in the cash register. The cash register records an identification and price for each item purchased. Cash payments are collected from customers and placed in the cash drawer. A copy of the cash register sales slip is given to the customer. At the end of each shift, the employee takes the cash drawer and cash register tape to a supervisor who counts the cash, verifies the sales, and signs an approval form. The sales clerk also signs the form that identifies the amount of cash and amount of sales for the day.
B. A ticket seller at a movie theater is issued a cash drawer with $100 in change and a roll of prenumbered tickets when the theater opens each day. The seller collects cash from customers and issues the tickets. Each customer hands a ticket to a ticket taker who tears the ticket in half and gives half back to the customer. At the end of the day, the ticket seller returns the cash drawer and tickets to a supervisor.

Required For each situation, discuss why the procedures are used and how they provide effective internal control.

P6-21 EVALUATING INTERNAL CONTROL

Obj. 5

The Spring Valley Church is a small congregation with about 50 members. The church is financed by member donations. Most of these donations are collected during the Sunday morning service. Many of the donations are in cash. Other donations are by checks made payable to the church. Jay White has served as treasurer for the church since becoming a member a few years ago. The church accepted Jay's offer to serve as treasurer as an indication of his interest in being active in the church. Jay listed several previous experiences with financial matters on his resume as qualifying him for the position.

Once donations are collected each week, Jay takes the money to the church office where he counts it. He makes out a deposit slip and deposits the money in the church's account at a local bank. He records the deposit in the church's check register. He writes checks to pay the church's expenses. In some cases, he writes small checks to himself as reimbursement for incidental expenses he pays for the church. He opens bank statements received by the church each month and reconciles them with the church's check register. Jay prepares a monthly statement of cash received and disbursed that is distributed to members of the congregation.

The church always seems to be lacking sufficient financial resources. A recent meeting was held to discuss expansion of the church's building, but current finances seem to make expansion impossible. Some members don't understand why the church's financial condition appears to be so bleak, since they believe they are making large donations.

The church has asked you to help them evaluate their financial situation.

Required Evaluate the internal control problems of the Spring Valley Church. What explanation can be provided for the church's financial problems?

P6-22 INTERNAL CONTROLS FOR CASH SALES

Obj. 5

You and a friend have finished your Christmas shopping at the mall and have decided to relax and have lunch in a small restaurant in the food court. After selecting your entrees, you notice a sign on the cash register that reads "If you do not receive a receipt, your meal is free." Your friend is puzzled by the sign and asks you the purpose of giving away a free meal if a cashier forgets to give you a receipt.

Required Is the policy of providing a free meal if a receipt is not given a form of internal control? Why or why not?

P6-23 MULTIPLE-CHOICE OVERVIEW OF THE CHAPTER

1. To protect its assets and accounting information, a company should
   a. give one person sole responsibility for the accounting system.
   b. control access to its networks and databases.
   c. permit access to accounting records only by top managers.
   d. hire only employees with college degrees.

2. The purpose of an auditors' report is to show that
   a. a CPA has prepared the company's financial statements.
   b. all of the company's transactions have been inspected for accuracy.
   c. an independent party believes that the financial statements do not contain any significant errors.
   d. the company is healthy, profitable, and likely to remain that way into the foreseeable future.

3. An organization's plan and the procedures used to safeguard assets, ensure accurate information, promote efficiency, and encourage adherence to policies is its
   a. internal control system.
   b. cost accounting system.
   c. financial accounting system.
   d. management information system.

4. The Public Company Accounting Oversight Board (PCAOB)
   a. is responsible for issuing standards for accounting firms that provide guidance on a variety of audit-related matters.
   b. inspects auditing firms to ensure compliance with Sox regulations and professional auditing standards.
   c. reports to the Securities and Exchange Commission (SEC), which appoints members to the Board.
   d. all of the above.

5. The Securities and Exchange Act of 1934 established the
   a. FTC.
   b. SEC.
   c. FASB.
   d. GAO.

6. A 10-K report is
   a. a quarterly financial report for the SEC.
   b. a registration for a new stock issue with the SEC.
   c. an annual financial report for the SEC.
   d. a report of change in auditors for the SEC.

7. Financial accounting standards for businesses currently are established in the United States primarily by the
   a. Public Companies Accounting Oversight Board.
   b. Financial Accounting Standards Board.
   c. Securities and Exchange Commission.
   d. Accounting Principles Board.

8. The Sarbanes-Oxley Act of 2002 was passed to improve auditing and financial reporting in the United States after a number of high-profile accounting frauds occurred. Management must certify
   a. they have reviewed the financial reports.
   b. the reports are not misleading.
   c. the officers are responsible for establishing, maintaining, and assessing the effectiveness of internal controls.
   d. all of the above.

9. The Governmental Accounting Standards Board (GASB) sets standards for
   a. not-for-profit organizations.
   b. state and local governments.
   c. state and federal governments.
   d. the federal government.

10. The FASB releases the following document(s) as part of creating new standards.
   a. discussion memorandum
   b. exposure draft
   c. b only
   d. a and b

Cases

C6-1 GENERAL MILLS, INC. AUDIT REPORT

Obj. 4

Examine the auditors' report reproduced in Appendix A at the end of the text and answer the following questions.

Required

A. Who is General Mills' auditor? On what date did the auditor complete its audit work?
B. What was the auditor's responsibility with respect to the company's financial statements? What was the responsibility of management?
C. What kind of opinion did General Mills' auditors issue? Why is this opinion important to the company?

C6-2 GENERAL MILLS, INC. MANAGEMENT RESPONSIBILITIES AND AUDIT OPINION

Objs. 4, 5

Selected information from General Mills' 2004 annual report and 10K is provided in Appendix A at the end of the text.

Required Answer the following questions about the General Mills Report of Management Responsibilities and the Report of the Independent Public Accountants.

A. Who is responsible for the accounting numbers in the annual report?
B. What safeguards are in place to ensure the accuracy of the reported numbers?
C. Does the independent accountant state that the reported amounts are correct? What does the CPA assure?
D. Why does General Mills hire a CPA to audit the financial statements?

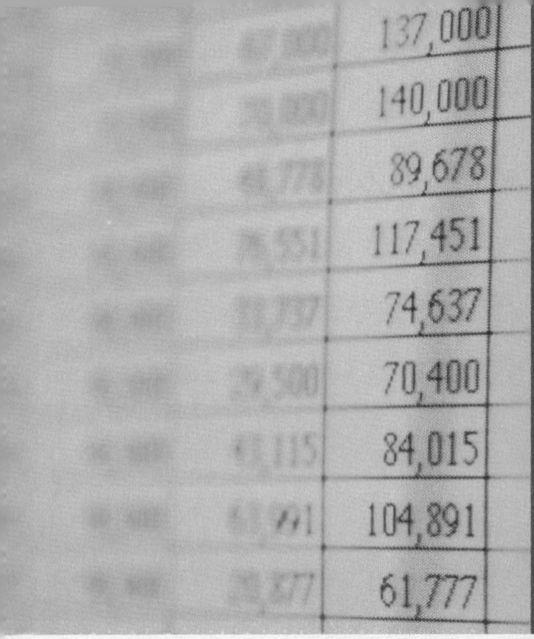

Computerized Accounting Systems

7

HOW DO WE IMPLEMENT A COMPUTERIZED ACCOUNTING SYSTEM?

As Favorite Cookie Company has grown and become more complex, a simple accounting system kept with pencil and paper has become increasingly inadequate. Large numbers of transactions, more customers and products, and more complex business activities mean that the company is likely to benefit from a computerized accounting system. Maria and Stan are now realizing that their manual system needs to be replaced by a computerized one.

Food for Thought

How does a computerized accounting system differ from a manual system? What issues must a company consider with regard to a computerized system? Maria and Stan discuss these questions with Ellen, their accountant.

Maria: *Recording transactions and preparing financial reports with our current accounting system is labor intensive and a bit slow. It takes us several hours a week to record transactions and prepare reports. Sometimes we are several days or even weeks behind in updating our accounts. Should we be looking at a computerized accounting system?*

Ellen: *Yes, there are a number of good systems on the market that are not expensive and that will meet your needs.*

Stan: *How different are these systems from what we have been using? Will a computerized system be difficult for us to learn?*

Ellen: *No, computerized systems use similar concepts to the manual approach you have been using. The computer will provide a means for you to record data. The main advantage of a computer system is that the system can do much of the work for you. Once data are recorded, the system automatically updates account balances and prepares financial statements.*

Maria: *That sounds easy. Are there problems with computer systems that we will need to avoid?*

Ellen: *You need to make sure the system is secure and that you have good backup procedures to protect your data in case the system fails. Let's look at some key issues that are important for understanding these systems.*

Objectives

Once you have completed this chapter, you should be able to:

1 Identify the primary components of a computerized accounting system.

2 Describe the components of a computerized accounting system used to process data and produce useful information.

3 Describe how data are processed in various modules of an accounting system.

4 Explain the use of relational databases to perform accounting functions.

5 Describe how a database system can be used to create a simple accounting system.

COMPONENTS OF A COMPUTERIZED ACCOUNTING SYSTEM

Objective 1
Identify the primary components of a computerized accounting system.

Many of the mechanical functions of an accounting system—posting to ledger accounts, updating account balances, and preparing schedules and reports from account balances—can be automated. Computers are capable of processing data through a series of steps to produce standard outputs such as reports. Consequently, certain accounting functions are automated in most companies.

Computerized accounting systems, even those for small companies like Favorite Cookie Company, are composed of modules. Each module provides a mechanism for recording and reporting specific types of business activities. Common modules are those associated with the most common business activities: sales and customer relations, purchasing and inventory management, production (for manufacturing companies), human resources, asset management, and financial management. A separate module is usually responsible for the general ledger and external financial reporting (GAAP-based financial statements) functions. Exhibit 1 illustrates an accounting system as a set of component modules.

EXHIBIT 1 Components of an Accounting Information System

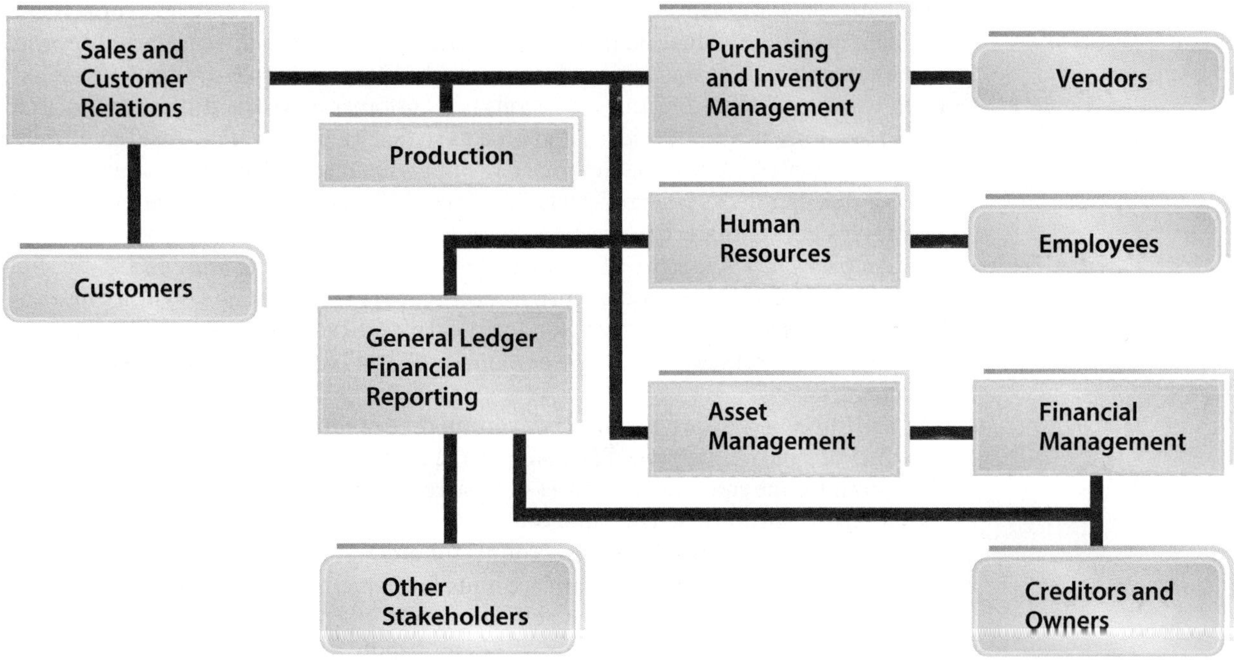

http://ingram.swlearning.com

Visit the home pages of these ERP developers and other computerized accounting systems to learn more about them.

All of the components in the system are linked so they share data with each other. Some businesses use one software application that integrates all of these functions. **Systems that integrate most of the business information functions as a basis for management decisions are referred to as** ***enterprise resource planning (ERP) systems.*** Many large companies have implemented these systems from ERP developers such as SAP® and Oracle®. Other companies may rely on software from different vendors for different components of their systems. Many smaller companies rely on software that handles most of the company's accounting functions. These systems lack the capabilities of larger systems but provide for most of the common accounting and financial reporting functions small businesses need. Thus, computerized accounting systems can be small basic systems such as QuickBooks®, MAS, Peachtree®, or Simply Accounting®; middle market systems such as Microsoft® Great Plains or ACCPAC®; or large-scale systems such as SAP and Oracle. Regardless of size, each of these systems is made up of component modules.

Each component in the information system has a particular role. This role depends on the stakeholders who interact with the component.

- The **sales module** receives sales order data from customers and maintains accounts receivable information.
- The **purchases and inventory management module** provides purchase order data to vendors. Vendors are those who supply specific products to a company. This module maintains accounts payable and inventory information.
- The **human resources module** maintains data about employees, including hours worked and wage rates. It is used for preparing payroll and payroll tax information.
- The **production module** tracks the flow of costs through the manufacturing process.
- The **asset management module** identifies long-term asset costs, their expected useful lives, and where these assets are located in a company.
- The **financial management module** keeps track of debt, repayment schedules, interest rates, and shareholder information.
- The **general ledger/financial reporting module** provides information for use by external stakeholders, including shareholders and government regulators.

The accounting process in a computerized system involves all modules. Each module maintains data for specific entities and activities. **The computerized system records financial data about individual items of importance to a company in** ***subsidiary accounts.*** These accounts include transactions for individual customers, suppliers, or products. Thus, when Favorite Cookie Company sells goods to a customer on credit, it uses the system to record customer and product identification data so that it can determine what was sold and to whom it was sold. A separate subsidiary account is maintained for each customer to keep track of that customer's sales and payments. **Records for all subsidiary accounts of a particular type are maintained in a subsidiary ledger.** A subsidiary accounts receivable ledger, for example, would consist of all the individual customer accounts, with data about purchases and payments for each customer. In a computerized accounting system, a subsidiary ledger is a file that provides records for a particular type of entity or activity. Thus, a customer file would contain data for the amount owed by that customer and when payment was due.

Control accounts **are summary accounts that maintain totals for all subsidiary accounts of a particular type.** For example, the balance of the accounts receivable control account is the sum of the balances of all accounts receivable subsidiary accounts for the company's customers. The same is true for inventory accounts for products a company sells and for accounts payable accounts for amounts owed to vendors.

A company maintains subsidiary accounts for management purposes. For example, Favorite Cookie Company must be able to respond when a specific customer inquires about his current account balance or wishes to dispute a billing statement. A company reports control account balances in financial statements to external users and in reports for higher level management decisions. Accordingly, account balances for both subsidiary and control accounts are updated on a regular basis. Control account balances are maintained in a company's general ledger. **Records for each control account are maintained in a company's *general ledger*.** The general ledger/financial reporting module keeps track of each control account and the balances in each account. The general ledger module uses these data to prepare general purpose financial statements for a company.

We examine modules in greater detail later in the chapter. First, we consider the processing of data in computerized systems.

DATA PROCESSING IN A COMPUTERIZED SYSTEM

Objective 2

Describe the components of a computerized accounting system used to process data and produce useful information.

Each component of an information system receives data, stores the data, processes the data to create useful information, and reports that information, as indicated in Exhibit 2.

Input originates in business activities and can come from a variety of sources. It may originate as paper documents, such as **sales orders** prepared by or for customers or **sales receipts** indicating the sale of goods to customers. Data must be entered into the computer system. Data entry may take place when clerical personnel transfer data by typing, or keying, information from paper documents to computer files. Increasingly, data are entered directly into computer systems. For example, many retail stores use scanners to read bar code data from products. The bar codes are linked to the company's inventory data so that sales prices, costs, and inventory amounts are recorded without data having to be keyed.

http://ingram.swlearning.com

Visit the online shopping sites of Amazon.com, Southwest Airlines, and Banana Republic.

Many companies provide web-based input systems that permit customers to place orders directly using the Internet. Companies like **Amazon.com**, **Southwest Airlines**, and **Banana Republic** provide for online shopping, reservations, and sales. Data entered by customers update company order and inventory files. Customers also can retrieve information about their orders from these systems.

Exhibit 3 provides a web page from Favorite Cookie Company's website. It provides options for online shopping such as selection of products and shipping information. Other

EXHIBIT 2 Data Processing in a Computerized Information System

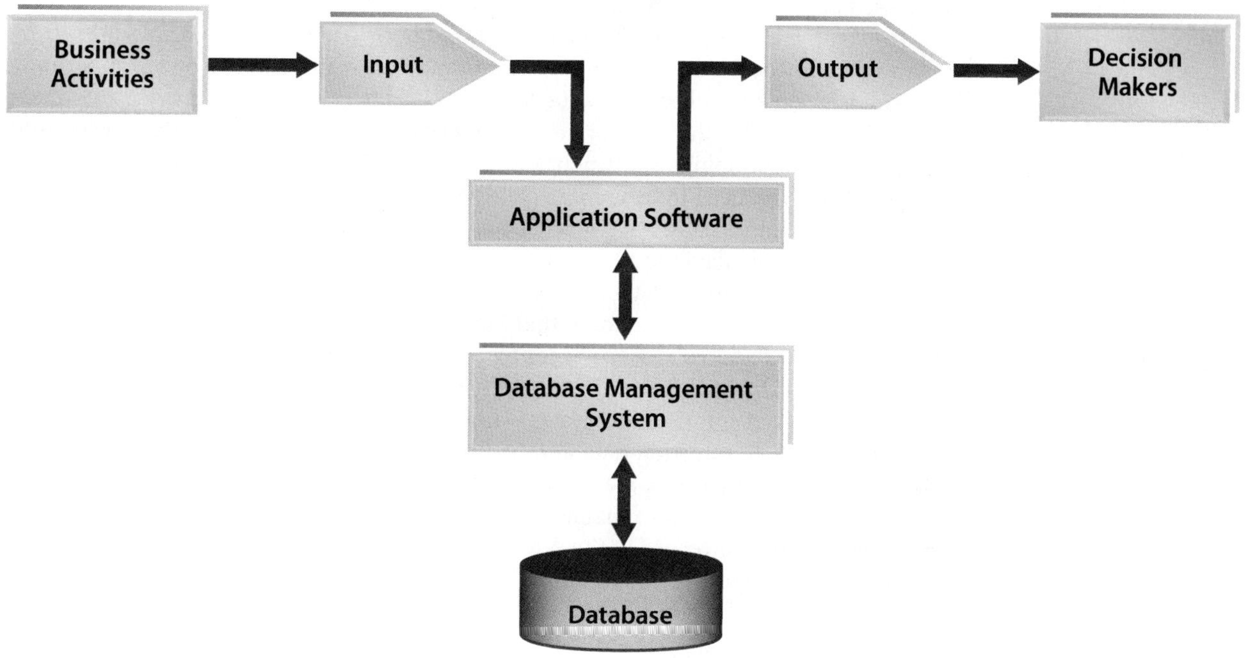

EXHIBIT 3
Example of Web-Based Input

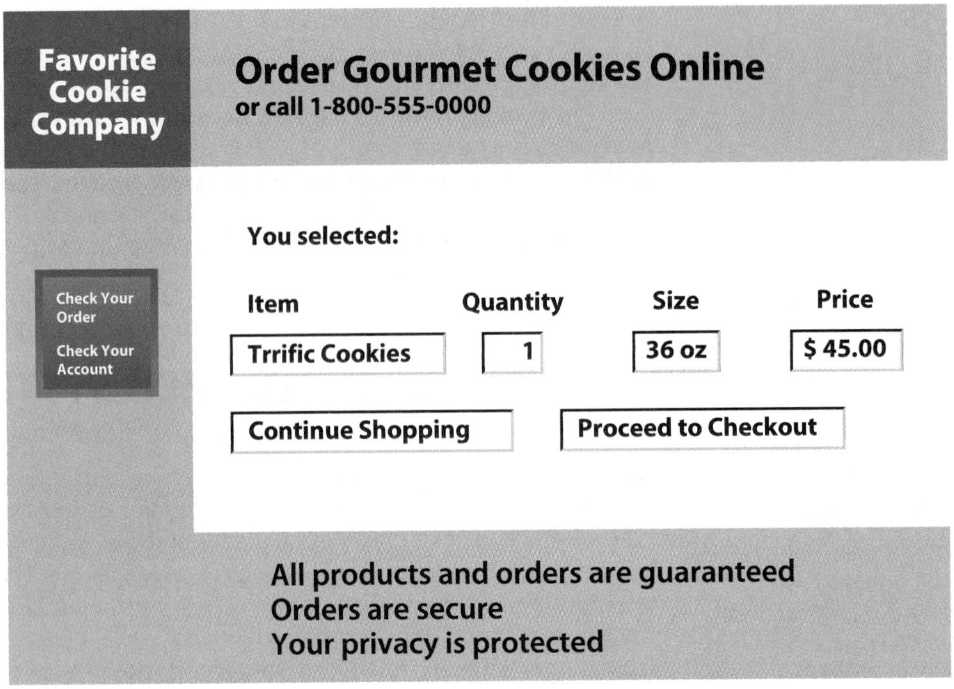

web pages provide for payment using a credit card. These pages are connected to Favorite Cookie's accounting system so that sales, inventory, and customer information can be updated automatically.

Using computer networks, such as the Internet, to make customer sales is referred to as ***E-business.*** Some E-business systems, like Favorite Cookie's, provide a means for a company to receive sales orders from customers. These systems are referred to as business-to-customer, or b2c, systems. Other systems permit companies to order goods from vendors and to track order information. These systems are referred to as business-to-business, or b2b, systems. In either system, customers do most of their own data entry. These data become the basis for recording sales, accounts receivable, cost of goods sold, and related transactions. Thus, many routine transactions are recorded and processed automatically without the seller having to take special steps.

Application software **includes the computer programs that permit data to be recorded and processed.** If a customer enters an order using a web browser, application software is needed to collect that data, to record it in the company's files, and to process the data to ensure that the appropriate actions occur. For example, a customer order must be recorded, the shipping department must be notified of the order so the goods can be shipped, a bill may need to be prepared and sent to the customer, and sales and accounts receivable accounts need to be updated. Application software automates these functions.

Databases store data used by various components of a system. Data are transferred by application software to databases. **A** ***database*** **is a set of computerized files in which company data are stored in a form that facilitates retrieval and updating of the data. A** ***database management system*** **controls database functions to ensure data are recorded properly and are accessed only by authorized users.**

Computerized information systems have many internal controls. These controls are important for protecting data and for helping to prevent errors. Controls, such as passwords, ensure that data are not accessed or modified by unauthorized personnel. Controls built into database management systems prevent more than one user from updating a particular record at the same time and make sure that all appropriate parts of a database are updated when a transaction is recorded.

Other controls require management action. For example, databases must be backed up on a regular basis so data will not be lost if a computer system fails or is destroyed.

A company also must have a plan in case its computer system is destroyed because of natural disaster, sabotage, or terrorism. Failure to provide backup systems can result in a company being unable to do business if its primary system is unusable.

Output from information systems often is in the form of reports. These reports may contain prescribed information and may be prepared automatically by a system. They may be print reports or electronic documents that are sent to users. Many output reports can be modified and retrieved as needed by users. For example, managers at Favorite Cookie Company need to know which customer accounts are overdue by more than 30 days. They need a report that gives them an up-to-date listing of grocery stores that are late in paying their accounts. Other managers need to know how much of each type of cookie the company sold in the last month. Database systems are useful because they allow users to query the database to obtain current information.

Regardless of which of the modules in a company's accounting system is involved, data flow through the system from inputs to outputs. How the data are processed depends on the module. Data flows are initiated by business activities, but they also stimulate these activities. For example, a customer order creates data that are processed by the system. Also, data about the order result in goods being shipped to the customer. Thus, business activities create data that are processed to create additional business activities.

Computerized systems rely on networks for processing data. **A *computer network* is a set of hardware devices that are linked so they can exchange data among themselves using software.** Exhibit 4 illustrates a computer network. Input devices, such as scanners, and client workstations allow data input as well as data access. A **client** is a computer or other network device that uses software to request services from other software. The services are provided by server software that resides on another computer, referred to as a **server**. Networks involve the cables that connect the clients and servers and the hardware and software needed to make the networks function properly. Most networks are client-server networks because they provide for the exchange of data between clients and servers.

Application software usually resides on one or more **application servers** on the network. Application servers are connected to **database servers**, which store and manage

EXHIBIT 4
A Computer Network

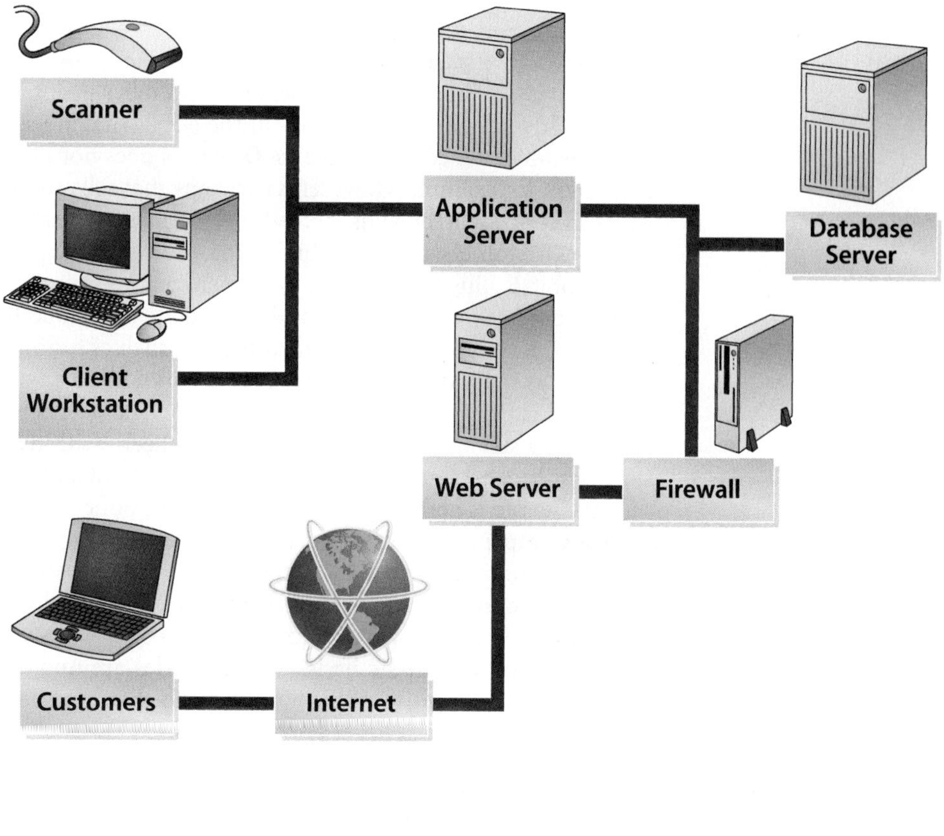

data. Companies engaged in E-business or that permit their employees to connect to their network from locations outside of the business often use web servers to provide the software needed to interact across the Internet. The Internet provides a network so that almost any computer can connect to a company to do business.

Networks pose security problems, especially when they are connected to the Internet. A **firewall** usually is special software running on a computer that makes it difficult for unauthorized users to gain access to a company's internal network. Data must pass through the firewall, where they are examined and filtered to determine whether they should be passed to the internal network. Firewalls can be placed at many locations in a network. Typically they are placed between devices that provide services to external users and the internal network to prevent unauthorized access to data and devices inside the firewall.

The next section examines various modules in a company's accounting system.

Self-Study Problem #1

Lavender's is a plant nursery that supplies specialty plants to other nurseries around the country. It also sells plants to customers from a retail store.

Required Describe the components of a computer network that Lavender's might use to run its business. Explain the purpose of each component.

ACCOUNTING SYSTEM MODULES

Objective 3
Describe how data are processed in various modules of an accounting system.

The following section examines each of several primary modules in an accounting system. Each module obtains, processes, and reports information for a particular type of business activity.

The Sales Module

Accounting systems are designed to meet information needs associated with business activities. These needs vary from company to company. For example, a retail company that sells goods directly to customers for cash relies primarily on point-of-sales systems that provide for collecting data about the goods that are sold and the amount received from customers. A company like **McDonald's** does not need to maintain data about its customers, for example. However, a company that sells goods using an order system, like Amazon.com, General Mills, or Southwest Airlines, must maintain customer data that identifies customers, addresses, billing information, and, perhaps, shipping information.

Exhibit 5 illustrates a sales and customer relations module for a company that receives orders from customers and sells goods on credit. To illustrate, Favorite Cookie Company permits its commercial customers, such as grocery stores, to submit orders by phone or by mail. When Fair-Price Foods submits a sales order, that order is received by the sales division at Favorite Cookie Company. The sales division checks to make sure the product is available. Also, the sales division checks with the credit department to make sure Fair-Price Foods has not exceeded its credit limit and that its payments are not overdue. If the sale is approved, the sales division notifies the shipping division at Favorite Cookie Company, which ships the cookies to the customer. The sales division also notifies the accounting department of the order. Accounting updates the customer file for the amount the customer owes. The transaction is recorded to sales revenue and accounts receivable. The general ledger accounts are posted either at the time the transaction is recorded or on a periodic basis. Inventory files are updated for the goods shipped to the customer. Accounting sends an **invoice** to the customer for the amount of the sale. The invoice notifies Fair-Price Foods of the amount owed and requests payment. When

EXHIBIT 5
A Sales Processing Module

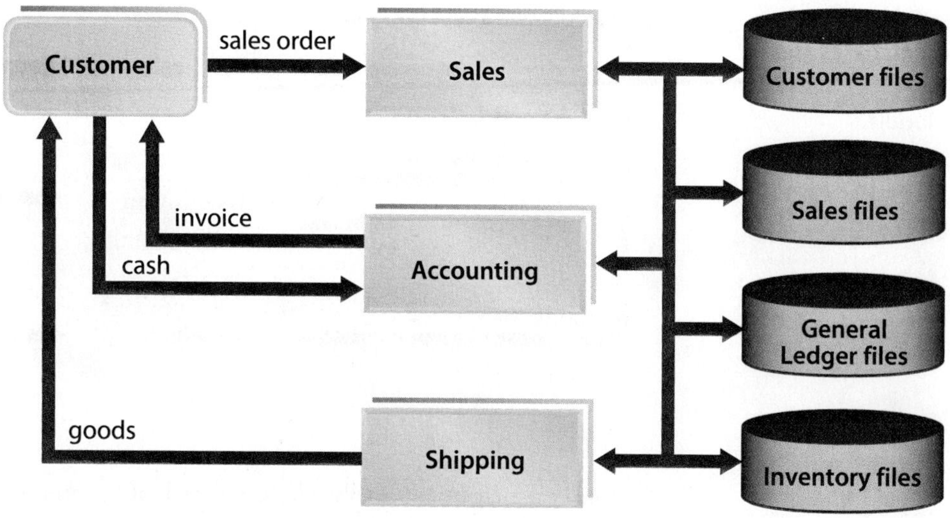

Fair-Price Foods pays for the order, the accounting department updates the customer's account and accounts receivable in the general ledger. The cash is transferred to a bank.

Good internal control requires that the personnel who account for the cash should not also have physical access to the cash. Therefore, these functions should be separated within the accounting department.

How much human intervention is needed in the processing of these data depends on the company and the sophistication of its computer systems. In many companies, the computer system handles most of these activities.

Sales, accounting, and shipping functions all are sources of data in the sales module. In addition, these functions also receive information from the system. An important part of this system is its ability to provide information to decision makers. The database files provide up-to-date data about sales activities. The sales department retrieves data about particular customers, such as what they purchased and how much they have purchased. These data guide decisions about advertising and promotion campaigns and about sales bonuses and commissions. Purchasing and production use this information to determine which products to purchase or produce and the amounts needed. The profitability of products and profits earned from sales to certain customers may help a company determine its strategy for which products or types of customers to emphasize. Customers who do not pay their accounts on a timely basis may be flagged to prevent future sales. A company can also use these data to evaluate performance. For example, a company may monitor how long it takes to process orders and ship goods. Unnecessary delays may help explain decreased sales or dissatisfied customers.

Accounting for transactions is an important part of each systems module. The sales department notifies accounting of a customer order. Shipping notifies accounting of goods shipped to customers. Accounting compares data from sales and shipping and bills the customer. **Accounts receivable and sales revenue transactions are recorded at the time goods are shipped to customers. Cash and accounts receivable transactions are recorded when cash is received.** These transactions update the general ledger account balances in the General Ledger files. However, they are a relatively small part of the overall data processing that occurs in the sales module. A considerable amount of data are collected and processed to keep track of customers, sales, shipments, inventory, receivables, and cash flow.

The Purchasing and Inventory Management Module

The purchasing and inventory management functions are responsible for the acquisition of merchandise and supplies. In a manufacturing company, these functions indicate when to acquire materials that are used in the products the company manufactures.

EXHIBIT 6
A Purchases and Inventory Management Module

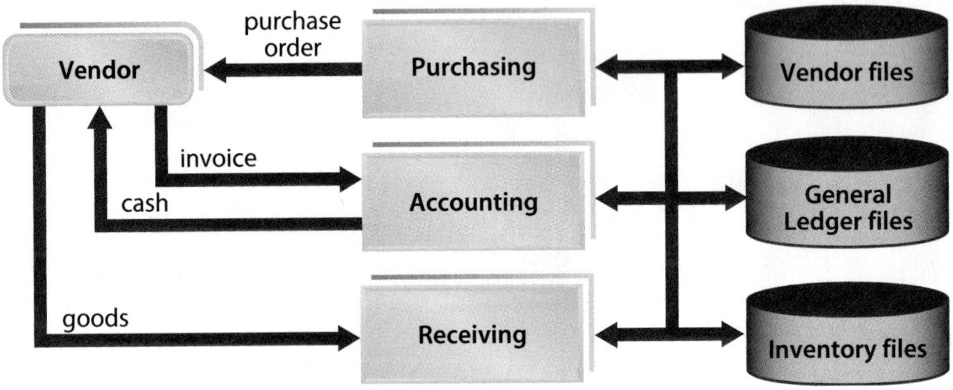

Inventory management involves keeping track of the amounts and locations of inventories and making sure these inventories are available when needed.

Exhibit 6 illustrates the purchasing and inventory management module. Purchasing is responsible for placing orders with vendors when additional merchandise or materials are needed. Vendor files identify approved vendors for each type of merchandise or material. Favorite Cookie Company purchases cookies from several bakeries. As additional cookies are needed to sell to grocery stores, orders are placed with the bakeries. Vendor files identify the names, locations, and contacts for each vendor. Also, they keep track of amounts owed to each vendor and when payments are due. Inventory files identify each type of cookie and the number of cases Favorite Cookie Company has available for sale. When inventory levels fall below a predetermined minimum, the purchasing department contacts a vendor and orders additional cookies. The receiving department receives cookies from the bakeries. The vendor sends a bill to the accounting department. Accounting compares the bill with information from the receiving department to verify that the goods were received. Once the billing information is verified, the vendor records are updated. Accounting also uses information from the receiving department to update inventory records to show the number of cases of each type of cookie available for sale.

When accounts payable become due to vendors, cash is transferred to the vendors in the form of checks or electronic transfers to the vendor bank accounts. Accounts payable and cash accounts are updated for these transfers.

The system permits appropriate personnel to determine the amount of each inventory item available, the cost of these items, and amounts owed to each vendor. In addition, the efficiency of vendors in responding to orders can be determined. Thus, the purchasing department may be interested in which vendors respond promptly and provide the best service in response to a company's orders.

Many vendors now permit their customers to place orders online. The purchaser can identify the items to be purchased and the cost of these items and submit an order directly to the vendor's computer system. The customer may also be able to connect to the vendor's system to determine product availability and when goods are expected to be shipped.

The interaction of a company and its suppliers is known as ***supply-chain management.*** Companies reduce purchasing and inventory costs by developing relationships with vendors to supply needed products promptly and efficiently. Many companies rely on close relationships with suppliers to make sure materials and merchandise are available when they are needed. If suppliers are reliable, the purchasing company can place orders and receive goods as they are needed rather than having to maintain large amounts of inventory. In addition, companies depend on their suppliers to provide inventory of the type and quality they need. Companies also work with suppliers to make sure they are getting the best deal possible on the goods they need.

If Favorite Cookie Company cannot get the cookies it needs from bakeries, if the quality of the cookies is not satisfactory, or if the costs are too high, it will not meet the needs of its customers.

EXHIBIT 7
A Human Resources Module

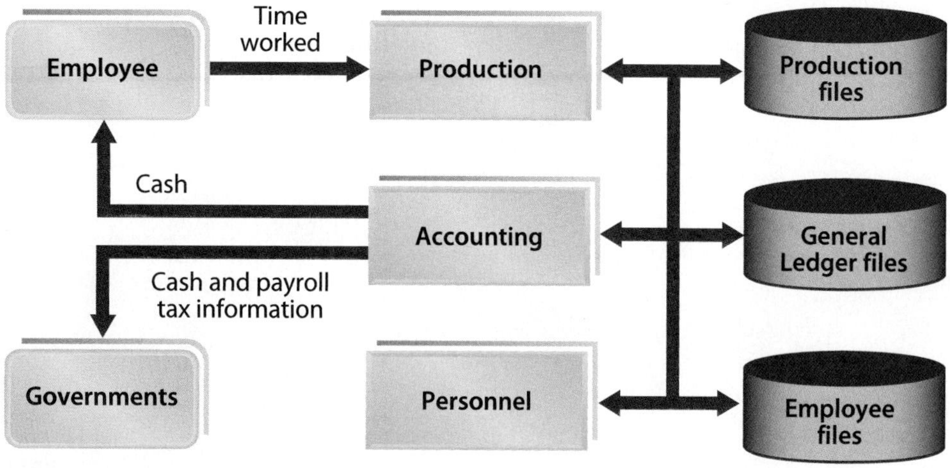

The Human Resources Module

The human resources function in a business is responsible for hiring and training employees. The data needed to account for employee activities involve employees' hours and their wages or salaries. How these data are obtained and processed depends on the type of company and the type of work employees perform.

Exhibit 7 illustrates the processing of employee wages for a manufacturing company, such as Parma's Bakery, one of Favorite Cookie Company's suppliers. Employees' hours are collected from time sheets or are entered automatically as employees log into computer systems to obtain data and perform tasks. The wage rate data are maintained by the personnel department. Accounting receives time data from the production division and wage rate information from personnel to determine how much each employee has earned each pay period.

Wage data are important for several activities. Amounts earned by and owed to each employee are in employee files. These data are used to process payroll information and to prepare paychecks or to transfer cash to employee bank accounts. Payroll taxes, such as income taxes, and benefits, such as retirement and health insurance, also usually are tied to amounts earned by employees. A company must keep track of taxes and other amounts associated with wages and provide information about these amounts to governments and other organizations. Payments also must be made to these organizations for payroll taxes and benefits.

Wage information also is important for determining production costs. Labor costs become part of the cost of manufacturing, as examined in the discussion of the production module in the next section. Amounts paid to employees and governments affect wages and taxes payable accounts and cash in a company's general ledger accounts.

The Production Module

Manufacturing companies carry out many complex activities and transactions. These companies may produce many different products, and each product may require numerous types of materials and processing activities. Many costs have to be recorded and many events have to be tracked by a manufacturing company's information system.

Exhibit 8 illustrates basic components of a production module. The manufacturing process usually responds to the actual or expected demand for a company's products. Sales orders or forecasts are inputs for the production planning and scheduling process. Planning and scheduling functions determine which products, how much of each, and when various products will be produced.

A special accounting function, known as **cost accounting**, keeps track of the costs of resources used in the manufacturing process. Materials, labor, and the costs of other resources used in producing goods must be identified and tracked throughout the

EXHIBIT 8
A Production Module

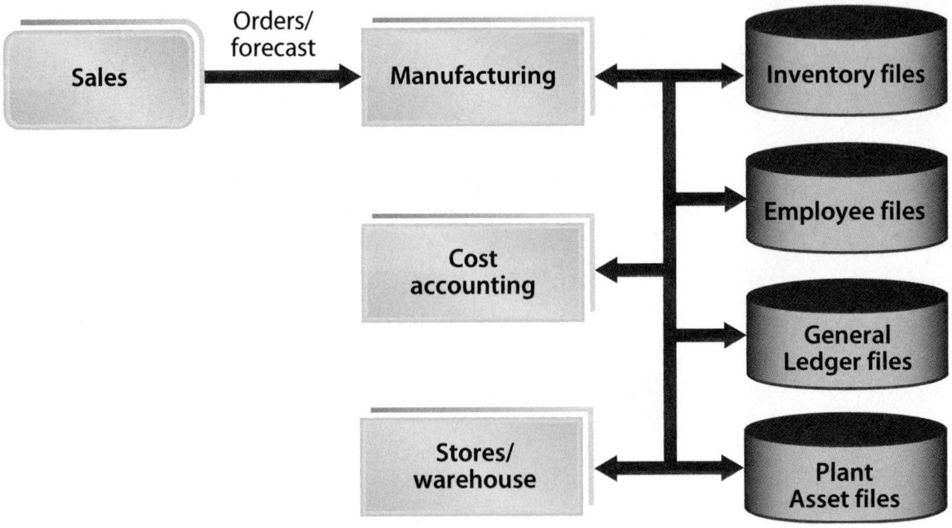

manufacturing process. Materials and supplies are obtained from stores (or the manufacturers' storage facilities) and placed into production. The costs of these materials must be identified in association with particular jobs or goods that are being produced. The wages earned by employees who work on these jobs or goods also must be identified. Other costs are associated with plant assets used in the production process, including utilities, insurance, and other resources used during a production period. Once goods are completed, they are shipped to customers or transferred to warehouses for storage until they are shipped.

Cost accounting identifies and records these costs. They are used to determine the costs of goods produced during a period or the cost of completing a particular order. These data become cost of goods sold once goods are completed and sold to customers. For example, Parma's Bakery keeps track of all the ingredients used in preparing an order for Favorite Cookie Company. Also, it keeps track of the labor costs associated with producing the cookies. These costs, along with other production costs, are used to identify Parma's cost for the goods prepared for Favorite Cookie Company. These costs are important for Parma to make sure it has earned a profit from the order.

Each module in an accounting system is responsible for data associated with certain business activities. As noted earlier, each module collects, records, and processes data and provides information to decision makers. The next section considers how a database system functions to provide these information services.

Self-Study Problem #2

Suppose you were in charge of production at Parma's Bakery.

Required What actions would you perform that would require you to interact with the company's computer system?

THE STRUCTURE OF ACCOUNTING SYSTEMS

Most computerized accounting systems are constructed as relational databases. **A *relational database* is a set of related files that are linked so that files can be updated and information can be retrieved from the files efficiently.**

EXHIBIT 9 Tables in a Relational Database

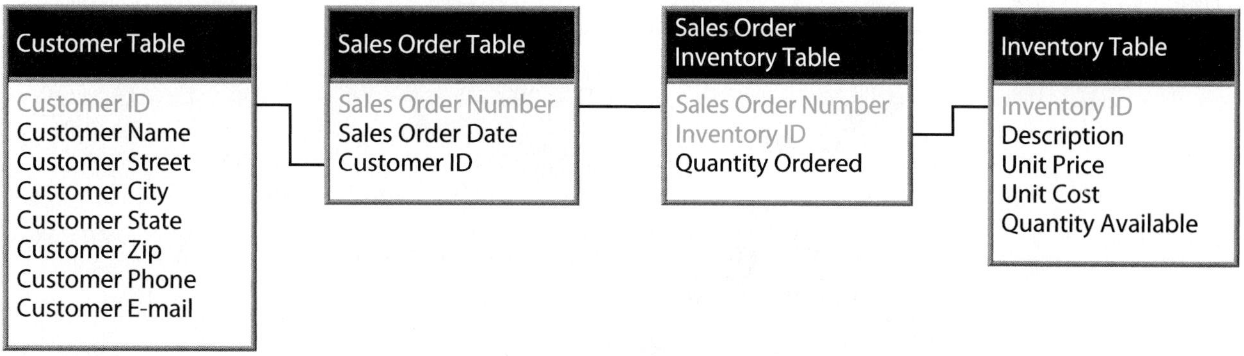

Objective 4
Explain the use of relational databases to perform accounting functions.

A relational database stores data in tables. **A *table* is a file that contains data represented as rows and columns.** Each column identifies a particular attribute of the entity or process described in the table. Each attribute in the table is referred to as a **field.** A customer table would include customer name and address attributes, for example. Each row in the table contains a record of data for a particular entity. Rows in a customer table would contain data for each customer, for example. Separate tables are used for specific types of entities (customers and products) and processes (sales orders and shipping). Each table contains one or more **primary keys** that uniquely identifies the entities or processes recorded in the rows of the table. These primary keys are used to connect the tables into relationships. The primary key in one table connects to the primary key or a **foreign key** in another table. A foreign key is a field that is a primary key in a different table.

Exhibit 9 illustrates the tables and relationships in a database. The boxes represent tables, identified by their captions at the top. Fields stored in each table are listed in the boxes. Fields in bold are primary keys. Lines connect the primary and foreign keys that form the relationships in the database.

The relationships permit a change to a field to affect each table containing that field. For example, when a sales order number is entered into the system, the Sales Order Number field is updated in the Sales Order and Sales Order Inventory tables. The relationships also permit a user to obtain data from more than one table. For instance, by using a particular sales order number, a user can obtain data from the Sales Order and Sales Order Inventory tables because these tables are linked by the sales order number. The sales order number can then be used to identify the customer and the items the customer has ordered.

Thus, a relational database is a network of information objects that permits efficient storage and retrieval of data. Knowing the relationships in the database, a user can retrieve any combination of fields to serve a particular decision need.

Individual tables in the database store data about a particular entity or activity. Exhibit 10 provides an example of a simple table. The top row identifies the attributes stored in the table. The remaining rows are records. The first column of each record identifies the sales order number that identifies that record. Records are listed sequentially by sales order number, which is the primary key for the table. Other fields identify other attributes associated with each sales order, such as the date and an identifier for the customer who placed the order.

Data are entered into a database using **forms.** Forms are computer screens that provide templates for entering data. Exhibit 11 provides an illustration of a simple form.

EXHIBIT 10
A Table in a Database

	Sales Order Number	Sales Order Date	Customer ID
▶	SO12473	04/12/07	CU3452
	SO12474	04/12/07	CU2490
	SO12745	04/13/07	CU2873

EXHIBIT 11
A Form for Data Entry

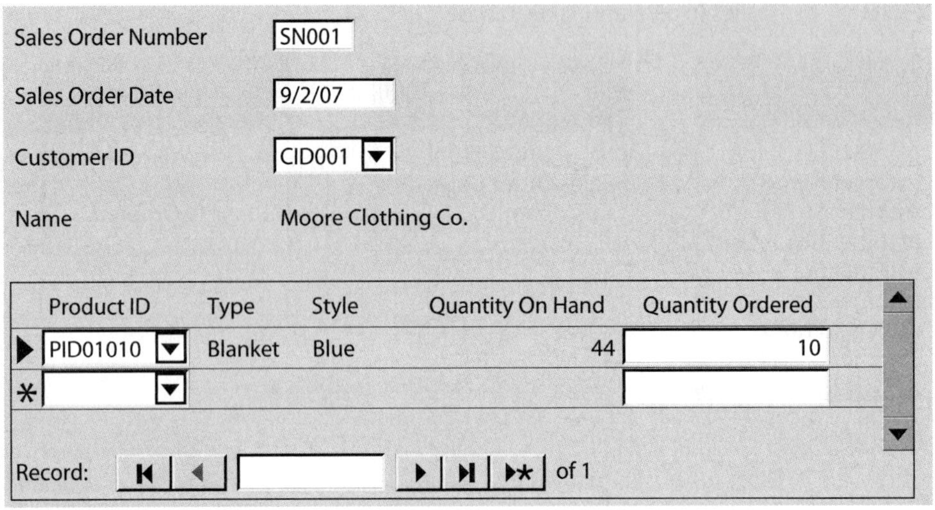

The form provides input areas where data are keyed into the system. Form fields are linked to attributes in tables in the database. Thus, when a new sales order number is entered in the form in Exhibit 11, data are added to the sales order table in the company's database.

As noted earlier, most data needed by a computerized system may be entered automatically through scanning devices. Customers enter data in forms when they place orders using web-based systems. However, most data needed in database systems are entered by company employees who are responsible for various data entry functions.

Each module of a computerized accounting system consists of tables and forms that collect and store data for the activities associated with that module. Individual tables often are part of more than one module. For example, an inventory table may be accessed by the sales module to determine product availability and price. It may be accessed by the purchasing module to update it for goods received from vendors.

The following section illustrates a database accounting system that is typical of real accounting systems, though it uses simple examples with limited transactions and examines only a small part of a total accounting system. The illustration is designed to help you see how accounting data are processed in a real system from data entry to storage and financial reporting.

AN ILLUSTRATION OF AN ACCOUNTING SYSTEM

Objective 5
Describe how a database system can be used to create a simple accounting system.

This section illustrates various components of a computerized accounting system. The illustration examines the sales module of Favorite Cookie Company's accounting system. Example transactions are provided for September 2007 to illustrate sales activities: receiving sales orders, shipping goods to customers, updating inventory files, invoicing customers, receiving cash, updating accounting records, and producing summary reports.

The electronic file used in this module is a Microsoft® Access database, which can be found in the CD that accompanies this text or which can be downloaded from ***http://ingram.swlearning.com***. Directions for use of the software are provided as part of the description that follows. To use the database, you must have a computer with a Microsoft® Windows® operating system and Access 2000 or a more recent version.

Access is application software built around a database system. It is inadequate for large-scale accounting applications but is useful for illustrating database systems. Unlike most business systems, all of the software runs on a workstation. Though it can be configured to run on a network with separate client and server components, it is easier to use and easier to understand when it is operated from a single computer.

Copying and Opening the Database

It is highly recommended that the database be copied to a hard disk before it is used. To copy the database, open Windows® Explorer and select the drive where the database is located. Click on FavoriteCookies.mdb and drag it to a folder. Release the mouse button, and the database will be copied. It is a good idea to make several copies of the database under different names (FavoriteCookies1.mdb, FavoriteCookies2.mdb, and so on). If the database is modified or accidentally corrupted, you still have an unmodified version for use.

Use one of the following options to open the database.

Option 1. Open Access by clicking Start, Programs, Microsoft Access. Once Access has opened, click File, Open Database. Double-click FavoriteCookies.mdb in the folder to which it was copied.

Option 2. Open Windows Explorer. Select the folder in which the database was copied. Double-click on FavoriteCookies.mdb.

Database files can become large when they are modified through use. It is a good idea to compact the database periodically. To compact the database, open it in Access, click Tools, Database Utilities, Compact Database. The database will be compacted automatically. Compacting removes unused space in the database. Running a database from a floppy disk requires frequent compacting.

Database Contents

A database consists of objects. Once you open FavoriteCookies.mdb database, these objects appear in various categories: tables, queries, forms, reports, macros, and modules. Examine these categories. **Tables** contain the data stored in the system. **Queries** are short programs that permit a user to obtain data from one or more tables. **Forms** provide a means for entering or reading data stored in the database. **Reports** provide summary information intended primarily to be printed. **Macros** are sequences of steps a user performs to complete a particular task. A macro runs a task without the user having to enter each keystroke separately. **Pages** provide a means of creating web documents for accessing a database. **Modules** are computer programs (written in Visual Basic) to provide higher level functions in the database. The Favorite Cookie Company database contains no macros or modules. Also, pages are not included in this illustration.

Tables

Tables are the key to understanding a database. Tables contain the data in the database. Other objects manipulate these data by adding new data, modifying existing data, deleting data, or retrieving data.

Begin by examining the tblProduct table. Click on the Tables tab in the Database window. Double-click on tblProduct or click on tblProduct and then click the Open button. Columns in the table identify categories (also known as fields or attributes) of data. The Product ID is a code that uniquely identifies each product. Name and Size describe the products. Unit Price and Unit Cost indicate the selling price and cost per unit. Quantity on Hand indicates the number of units available for sale. Units for Favorite Cookie Company are cases. Each case contains 20 bags of cookies that the grocery store sells individually. The stores must purchase the cookies in cases rather than as individual bags of cookies, however. Additional products could be added to the table by entering data in the bottom row. Existing data can be modified by entering the data in the appropriate cell. For example, if the unit price for PID0201 increased to $35.00, the new price could be entered in the Unit Price column for this product. Close the table by clicking the **X** box in the upper right corner of the table window. Do not click the **X** box in the Access window (top right of screen) or you will close the Access program. If you close Access by mistake, reopen it and the FavoriteCookies.mdb database.

Next examine the tblCustomer table. This table identifies Favorite Cookie Company's existing customers. Each customer is identified by a Customer ID. The table includes name and address data to identify where to ship goods and mail invoices. Close the table.

The tblProduct and tblCustomer tables are examples of master files. Master files contain data that are relatively stable and that may be updated periodically.

You can examine the relationships among all the tables in the database by clicking on the relationships button in the top row (toolbar) of buttons in the Database window. (This looks similar to Exhibit 9.) The relationship diagram that appears contains the tables and identifies the fields in each table. Lines in the diagram link the primary and foreign keys. Close the relationship window by clicking on the bottom X in the upper right corner of the screen.

Entering Transactions

You will have a chance to examine other database objects as you work through the process of entering transactions and producing information.

Sales Orders

Begin with a sales order. Open the tblSalesOrder table. Each order is identified by a Sales Order Number. The Order Date and Customer ID also are listed for each order. (This is similar to Exhibit 10.) The Customer ID connects each sales order to a specific customer. Close this table and open the tblSOProduct table. This table identifies the Sales Order Number, Product ID, and Quantity Ordered. This table connects to both the tblSalesOrder and tblProduct tables. Scroll down the table to the final row. Note the data for the last sales order. Once a new sales order is entered, new rows will appear in the tblSalesOrder and tblSOProduct tables. Close the table.

Personnel in the sales department would normally enter sales orders. To enter a transaction, click on the Forms tab of the Database window. Then open the frmSalesOrder form. Notice that the form identifies the Sales Order Number, Date, and Customer ID. (This is similar to Exhibit 11.) It also identifies customer name and address information and information about the products ordered. You can click on the Record selector arrow at the bottom of the form window to view existing orders. To enter a new order, click on the New Record selector arrow at the bottom of the form window. Two sets of arrows appear near the bottom of the form. Use the bottom set of arrows to move among the sales orders. Enter a new Sales Order Number, *SN010*, at the top of the form. You may wish to press the Caps Lock key when entering transaction data. Press the Tab key to go to the Sales Order Date box. Type *09/30/07* in the box. Click on the Customer ID selector arrow to see a list of customers. Click on CID003. The name of the customer appears on the form as confirmation of the customer's identity. Click on the Product ID selector arrow, and click on PID0201. The product Type, Style, and Quantity on Hand appear on the form. Tab to the Quantity Ordered box and enter *12*. Click on the second Product ID selector arrow, click on PID0202, tab to the Quantity Ordered box, and enter *9*. To save the order, you can click the new record selector arrow at the bottom of the form or close the form window.

To view the data entered for the order, open the tblSalesOrder and tblSOProduct tables, scroll to the last row, and observe the new data. Close each table after you view it.

You can view a summary of sales orders, including the one just entered, by selecting the Reports tab on the Database window and double-clicking on rptSalesOrders. A report appears listing the orders for September. To see the entire report you may need to enlarge the window and set the zoom control on the menu bar to 75% 75%. Sales orders are listed in the report by date. The order you just entered is listed at the bottom of the report. If you wish, print a copy of the report. Only transactions occurring in September 2007 are included in reports in this tutorial. Close the report when you have finished examining it.

Reports in the Favorite Cookie Company database are derived from queries. Queries obtain data from tables, manipulate these data in some cases to produce new data items, and store them temporarily. Click on the Queries tab to view the queries. Double-click on qrySalesOrders and view the data that appear in the rptSalesOrders report. Queries can be used to present data in table form when a formal report is not needed. Each of the reports described in this tutorial is associated with a query. Close the query.

Shipping Information

Once an order is received, personnel in the shipping department can review the order information. Review can take place on screen or from a printed copy of the sales order report. The shipping department then selects the goods and prepares them for shipment. Also, they update shipping records and prepare a shipping report.

To view shipping data, click on the Tables tab in the Database window and double-click on the tblShipping table. The table contains the Sales Order Number, Product ID, Date Shipped, and Quantity Shipped for each order shipped. The table also contains an Inventory Updated field. When a shipment is entered in this table, the Updated field is set to No, indicating that inventory records have not been updated. Observe that all the fields contain Yes in the tblShipping table, indicating that inventory records have been updated for all shipments. Close the table.

To enter a shipment, click on the Forms tab in the database window and double-click on the frmShipping form. This form indicates the Sales Order Number, customer information, and product information for each shipment. You can review previous entries by clicking on the selection arrow at the very bottom of the Form window ▶. To enter data for the sales order you just completed, click on the Last Record arrow at the bottom of the form window ▶|. The form will display the Sales Order Number of the order you just entered, SN010. The customer information also is displayed for this order. Click on the Product ID selection arrow and click on the product being shipped, PID0201. Press the Tab key and enter 09/30/07 for the shipping date. Press the Tab key again and enter 12 for quantity shipped. Click on the second Product ID selection arrow and repeat the process for the second item ordered (PID0202, 09/30/07, 9). Close the form to save the data.

You can view a report of shipments by clicking on the Reports tab of the Database window and double-clicking on rptShipping. You may need to expand the Report window and set the zoom to 75% to see the entire report. Use the Record selection arrows at the bottom of the Report window to view each page of the report. To see the most recent shipment, click on the Last Record selection arrow ▶|. A copy of the shipping report can be printed and enclosed with the goods shipped to the customer. A copy also may be sent to the billing department, or the shipping data may be viewed electronically by that department. Close the report.

Open the tblShipping table and scroll to the bottom of the table to view the data. Observe that the Inventory Updated field contains No for the items just shipped. It is important for the shipping personnel to update the inventory records so that the quantity of each product available is correct. Quantity available data are contained in the tblProducts table. Close the tblShipping table and open the tblProducts table. Note the Quantity on Hand for the products associated with the sales order you entered, PID0201 (29 units) and PID0202 (47 units). Close the table.

To update the inventory records, click on the Queries tab of the Database window and double-click on the qryUpdateShipments query. If you are asked if you want to run an update query, click the YES button. A dialog box appears asking for the sales order number associated with the records to be updated. Enter the number for the shipment, SN010, and click the OK and Yes buttons. The inventory records have now been updated. Verify the update by opening the tblProducts table and viewing the Quantity on Hand for PID0201 ($29 - 12 = 17$ units) and PID0202 ($47 - 9 = 38$ units). Also, if you examine the tblShipping table, you will find that the Inventory Updated field has been changed to Yes for the last shipment. The change to this field is an important control. Once inventory quantity has been updated for a particular Sales Order Number, it cannot be updated again. Close any tables you have open.

Receiving Goods

As goods are shipped, the quantity of goods available for sale decreases. The supply of goods must be increased periodically. In the case of Favorite Cookie Company, the increase occurs when goods are received at the warehouse from the supplier's manufacturing division. When goods are received, the receiving department places the goods in the appropriate location to be retrieved by shipping personnel. In addition, they update inventory records by completing the frmProductReceipt form. Click on the Forms tab of the Database window and double-click on frmProductReceipt to open this form. Review the form contents, then click on the New Record arrow ▸* at the bottom of the form window. Enter the following data in the form: Product Receipt Number, 10906; Product ID, PID0201; Receipt Date, 9/30/07; and Quantity Received, 25. Close the form.

The data entered in the form update the tblProductReceipt table. Open this table to see the items received. The Inventory Updated field is set to No for the most recent acquisition to indicate that the inventory records have not been updated for this receipt. Close the table.

To update the inventory records, click on the Queries tab of the Database window and double-click on the qryUpdateReceipts query. If you are asked if you want to run an update query, click the YES button. Enter the Product Receipt Number for the inventory item you entered in frmProductReceipt, 10906. Click the OK and Yes buttons and the inventory records are updated. To verify the update, open the tblProduct table and examine the Quantity On Hand value for PID0201 (17 + 25 = 42 units). Close the table. Open the tblProductReceipt table and confirm that the Inventory Updated field has changed to Yes. Close the table.

A report of available inventory is provided by rptInventory. Click on the Reports tab and double-click rptInventory. Each product is listed with quantity and cost data. The balance of the inventory account is the total cost for all products. Close the report.

Billing Customers

Once a shipment is made, the accounting department prepares a sales invoice to mail to the customer. The accounting department also creates the accounting transactions associated with the sale of goods to the customer. These transactions involve recording Sales and Accounts Receivable for the sales price of the goods shipped. In addition, Cost of Goods Sold and Inventory are adjusted for the cost of the goods shipped.

To view sales invoice data, click on the Tables tab of the Database window and double-click on the tblSalesInvoice table. This table contains Sales Invoice Number, Date, Sales Order Number, and Amount Billed associated with each invoice. Close the table.

Before preparing an invoice, the accounting department needs to determine the amount a customer owes. This information is found on the sales order and shipping reports. The Favorite Cookie Company database allows users to calculate the amount associated with each sales order. Click on the Queries tab and double-click on qrySalesAmount. Each sales order is listed with the amount owed. Close the query.

To prepare a sales invoice, click on the Forms tab of the Database window and double-click on frmSalesInvoice. You can review previously entered invoice data by clicking on the selection arrow at the bottom of the form. To enter a new sales invoice, click on the New Record arrow ▸* at the bottom of the form. Enter 10910 for the sales invoice number, 9/30/07 for the sales invoice date, and SN010 for the sales order number. Click the Tab key. Customer information appears on the form. Enter Amount Billed, 765. Do not enter the dollar sign. Close the form to save the data. You can verify that the data have been saved by clicking on the Tables tab of the Database window and double-clicking on the tblSalesInvoice table. Scroll down to view the last record in the table. Close the table.

View or print sales invoices from the rptSalesInvoice report on the Reports tab. Double-click on the report and scroll through the records to view each sales invoice. The last entry is the sales invoice you just prepared. Close the report.

Reporting Sales and Income

Once goods are shipped to customers, the accounting system updates Sales and Cost of Goods Sold. Obtain a list of sales from the rptSalesbyCustomer report. Double-click on the report. All sales for September are listed for each customer, including the most recent sale to customer CID003. Close the report.

A simple income statement is provided by rptIncomeStatement. The only income statement accounts included in this tutorial are Sales and Cost of Goods Sold. The simplified income statement lists these accounts, which have been updated for all transactions in September. Close the report.

Cash Receipts and Accounts Receivable

The last step in the revenue cycle is recording cash received from customers. The rptAccountsReceivable report lists the amounts sold to each customer, the cash received from these sales, and the amount the customer owes. Double-click on the report to view this information. Note the amount owed by customer CID001, $3,180. Close the report.

To record a cash receipt, open the frmCashReceipts form in the Forms tab. Use the Record selection arrow at the bottom of the form to scroll through the cash receipts. Go to record number 4. Observe that the sales order number and customer information appear on the form. Sales invoice number and cash receipts data do not appear because the cash has not been received. When a customer pays an invoice, a check is mailed to Favorite Cookie Company along with a copy of the sales invoice (the copy is known as a remittance advice). The accounting department receives the remittance advice and records the sales invoice number and amount of cash received. The check is deposited in a bank account.

To record a cash receipt for SN004, enter the sales invoice number associated with this sales order, 10904. Enter the cash receipt date, 9/30/07, and enter the cash receipt amount, 2280. Do not enter a dollar sign or comma. Close the form to update the records.

The tblCashReceipts table contains data on the amounts paid for each invoice. The rptAccountsReceivable report has been updated for the amount paid by customer CID001. Review the table and report to confirm that the cash receipt has been recorded. Close the table and report. Close the Access program.

Summary

Most companies use computerized accounting systems. These systems contain modules to handle the business activities that are accounted for in the system. Network components and database systems in accounting modules capture, store, and process data.

Self-Study Problem #3

The accounting system described in the last section of this chapter did not provide separate accounts for sales revenue and accounts receivable. Suppose you wanted to determine the accounts receivable for Favorite Cookie Company at the end of September.

Required Describe the steps you would go through to obtain the data necessary to determine accounts receivable for the company as reported in an accounts receivable report.

Thinking Beyond the Question

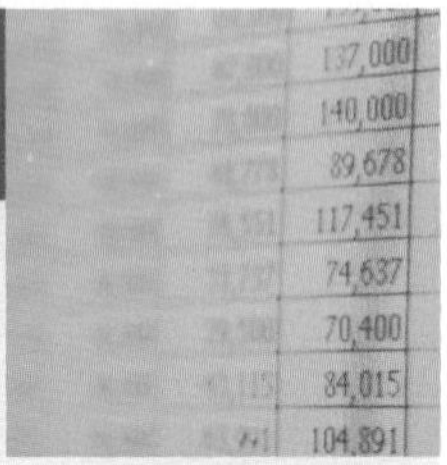

HOW DO WE IMPLEMENT A COMPUTERIZED ACCOUNTING SYSTEM?

Computerized accounting systems reduce the labor needed to record accounting information and prepare accounting reports. How can computerized systems also help managers, investors, and other stakeholders with their analysis and decision making tasks?

Self-Study Problem Solutions

SSP7-1 A client workstation and scanning device might be used to input data from local customers. A web server would be needed to provide access for web orders. An application server would provide the software needed to collect and process the data and convert data into reports. A database server would store data for customer orders, plant inventories, and shipments. A network would connect the servers and the client workstation and scanning device. An Internet connection would be needed to connect the web server to the Internet.

SSP7-2 To produce a product, such as cookies, you would need data about the materials needed to produce the product, availability of these materials, and production processes. You would need to schedule the production to make sure materials, labor, and equipment, such as mixers and ovens, are available. You would need information about sales orders so you know how much of each product to produce. Also, you would need to transfer goods from process to process as they are manufactured, and eventually you would need to transfer completed goods to shipping or to retail outlets. As you engage in these activities, you would need to update the company's information system so that the cost of goods produced could be determined.

SSP7-3 To determine accounts receivable, you would need to compare the amount shipped to each customer with the amount paid by the customer at a particular date. This comparison would require a query that retrieved data from several tables. The fields involved in this query are highlighted in the following diagram.

The Customer ID would be needed to identify each customer. All sales orders for each customer would need to be examined, using the Sales Order Number. Each sales order would be used to identify the product ordered, based on the Product ID, the cost per unit of each

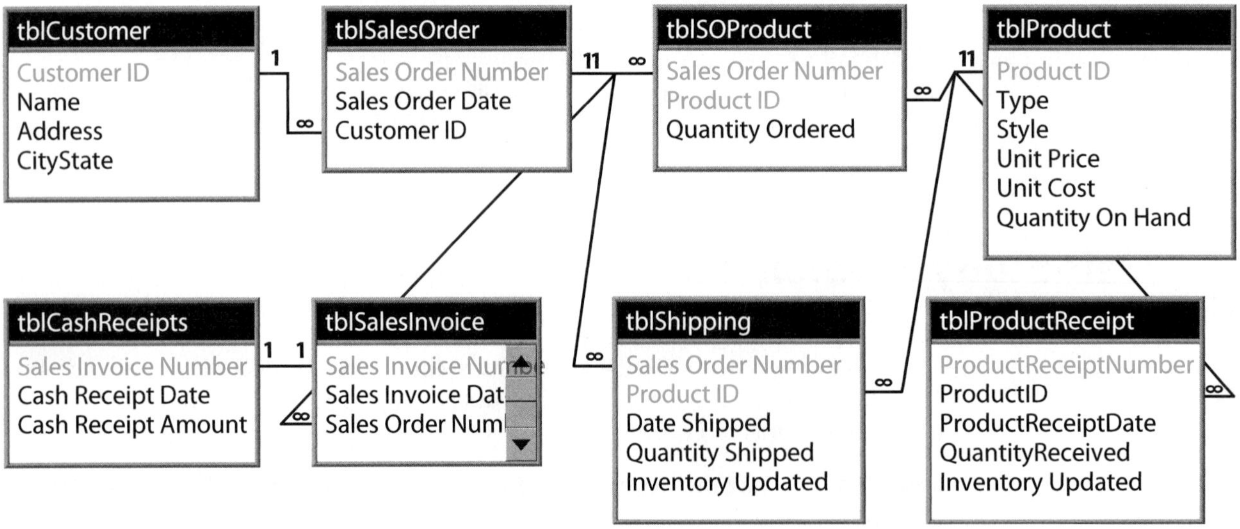

product (Unit Cost), and the Quantity Shipped. The total of unit cost times quantity shipped would determine the amount of each order for each customer. The Date Shipped field or the Sales Invoice Date would be used to establish the date of each receivable. The Cash Receipt Date and Cash Receipt Amount would determine when the customer made a payment. Comparing the total of the sales to each customer minus the total of cash received at a particular date would determine how much the customer owes at that date. A total of amounts owed for all customers would determine total accounts receivable.

Define *Terms and Concepts Defined in This Chapter*

application software (258)
computer network (259)
control accounts (256)
database (258)
database management system (258)
E-business (258)
enterprise resource planning (ERP) systems (255)
general ledger (257)
relational database (264)
subsidiary accounts (256)
supply-chain management (262)
table (265)

Review *Summary of Important Concepts*

1. Accounting systems contain modules. Each module handles data collection, processing, and reporting for a particular type of business activity, such as sales or purchasing.

2. Computer systems receive input from data entry sources, use application software to process the data, and store the data in databases. Database management systems control database operations as well as access to the database. Application software obtains data from the database and provides information as output to decision makers.

3. Accounting systems are implemented on computer networks. Client workstations and input devices, such as scanners, provide input to the system. Application servers, web servers, and database servers respond to client requests by processing and storing data, and by making information available to users.

4. The sales module receives customer orders, processes shipments, bills customers, and maintains data about customer purchases and receivables.

5. The purchasing and inventory management module is responsible for the acquisition of merchandise, materials, and supplies. It tracks available inventories, processes orders, and identifies goods received and on hand. It also determines amounts owed to vendors.

6. The human resources module maintains employee information, processes payroll, and monitors amounts owed to employees and to government agencies for payroll taxes.

7. The production module tracks the flow of costs from materials, labor, and other sources into the production process. It tracks these costs until goods are completed and shipped to customers. It may also assist managers with scheduling production jobs and monitoring the availability of materials for use in the production process.

8. Accounting systems usually are implemented as relational database systems. These systems contain tables that are linked through primary and foreign keys to facilitate the processing of data. Data are input in electronic forms. Queries allow users to access data and produce reports for decision makers.

Questions

Q7-1 *Obj. 1* Why are integrated business systems more efficient than using individual systems for different functions in a business?

Q7-2 *Obj. 3* Suppose a company sells to customers on-line. Customers are required to pay for their orders with credit cards at the time of the order. What primary activities would be required of the sales module to process and account for these orders?

Q7-3 *Obj. 3* The human resources module described in Exhibit 7 is for a manufacturing company. How would the module differ for a retail or service company?

Q7-4 *Obj. 2* What is a computer network? Why are they used by businesses to maintain accounting systems?

Q7-5 *Obj. 2* What is the purpose of a database management system?

Q7-6 *Obj. 3* Irmo Company's asset management module lists each piece of equipment the company has purchased, when it was purchased, its cost, its expected life, and its location in the company. Why would the company want this information?

Q7-7 *Obj. 3* Kreel Company's financial management module lists each loan the company has outstanding, when the money was borrowed, the amount borrowed, the interest rate, the dates payments were made, and the amounts of these payments. Why is this information important to the company?

Q7-8 *Obj. 3* What purposes does a retail company's purchasing module serve? What accounts and types of transactions are associated with this module?

Q7-9 *Obj. 3* What purposes does a service company's human resources module serve? What accounts and types of transactions are associated with this module?

Q7-10 *Obj. 3* Street Inc.'s financial management module lists each stockholder's name, address, the number of shares owned, and when the stock was purchased. How might the company use this information?

Q7-11 *Obj. 3* Why would the sales module of **Burger King** differ from the sales module of the mail order clothing company, **Lands' End**? What transactions would Lands' End record as part of its sales process that would differ from those of Burger King?

Q7-12 *Obj. 3* Why is it important for the accounting department of a company to receive data from sales and shipping? What internal control function is served by this process?

Q7-13 *Obj. 3* Why is it important for the accounting department of a company to receive data from purchasing and receiving? What internal control function is served by this process?

Exercises

E7-1 Write a short definition for each of the terms listed in the *Terms and Concepts Defined in this Chapter* section.

E7-2 *Objs. 1, 2, 3, 4, 5* Complete each sentence with the appropriate term.

1. Systems that integrate most of the business information functions are referred to as ______________.
2. Financial data about individual items of importance to a company are recorded in ______________.
3. Summary accounts that maintain totals for all subsidiary accounts of a particular type are called ______________.

4. A ____________ is an accounting record of each (control) account and the balance of each such account.
5. The use of computer networks, such as the Internet, to provide for customer sales is referred to as ____________.
6. A computer program that permits data to be recorded and processed is one kind of ____________.
7. A ____________ is a set of computerized files in which company data are stored in a form that facilitates retrieval and updating of the data.
8. A ____________ controls database functions to ensure data are recorded properly and can be accessed only by those authorized to record, update, or retrieve the data.
9. The interaction of a company and its suppliers is known as ____________.
10. A ____________ is a set of related files that are linked so the files can be updated and information can be retrieved from the files efficiently.

E7-3 *Objs. 1, 2, 3, 4, 5* Match each term with the appropriate definition.

a. application software
b. control accounts
c. database management system
d. database
e. E-business
f. enterprise resource planning (ERP) systems
g. general ledger
h. relational database
i. subsidiary accounts
j. supply-chain management

___ 1. A set of computerized files in which company data are stored in a form that facilitates retrieval and updating of the data
___ 2. A set of related files that are linked so the files can be updated and information can be retrieved from the files efficiently
___ 3. An accounting record of each (control) account and the balance of each such account
___ 4. Controls database functions to ensure data are recorded properly and can be accessed only by those authorized to record, update, or retrieve the data
___ 5. Includes the computer programs that permit data to be recorded and processed
___ 6. Type of account in which financial data about individual items of importance to a company are recorded
___ 7. Summary accounts that maintain totals for all subsidiary accounts of a particular type
___ 8. Systems that integrate most of the business information functions
___ 9. The interaction of a company and its suppliers
___ 10. Term that refers to the use of computer networks, such as the Internet, to provide for customer sales

E7-4 *Obj. 1* A friend is confused about entries to computerized accounting systems. She says, "I understand that there are both subsidiary accounts and control accounts, but why are the effects of individual transactions entered only into the subsidiary accounts? Doesn't this cause the subsidiary accounts and the control to report different information?" Explain the difference between a general ledger and a subsidiary ledger and the difference in how the information contained in each is used.

E7-5 *Obj. 2* **Lands' End, Inc.**, is a large, well-known mail-order retailer. Assume you logged onto its web site, ordered three pairs of shorts, and paid for them by credit card. Describe the business activities that would occur at Lands' End, including linkages to the accounting system, in handling your order.

E7-6 *Objs. 2, 3* Great Plains Manufacturing recently ordered 100 tons of raw materials including steel, aluminum, glass, and various plastics. Today, the goods were received via rail at the company's warehouse. Identify the documents that will be handled today (either by hand or electronically) and identify the specific and/or control accounts affected by this event.

E7-7 *Obj. 4* Modern accounting information systems often are maintained as relational databases. What is a relational database and what are the advantages of these database systems? Identify parts of a relational database and explain the purpose of each part.

E7-8 *Obj. 2* Computerized accounting systems create special control problems for an organization. Common control procedures used by organizations include the following:

a. Use of passwords to access terminals and programs
b. Limits placed on amounts that the computer will accept for various transactions

(Continued)

c. Backing up of data and programs regularly
d. Separation of design from operation of systems

Explain the purpose of each control procedure.

E7-9 *Obj. 4* Howard Company sells woolen goods and maintains its accounting system using a relational database. To prepare information about sales transactions, the company uses the following tables in its database. The fields that appear in each table are in brackets following the table.

- customers [customer ID, name, shipping address, phone number]
- sales orders [sales order number, customer ID, order date, product ID, order quantity]
- inventory [product ID, product name, quantity on hand, unit price]
- customer shipments [sales order number, shipping date]
- sales invoice [sales invoice number, sales order number, invoice date]
- cash receipts [sales invoice number, cash receipt amount, receipt date]

For each of the following events, identify the tables that would be needed to record the event.

1. Received an order from Jones & Sons for 12 blankets on November 3.
2. Shipped the blankets to Jones & Sons and billed the customer on November 6.
3. Received cash from Jones & Sons on December 5 for the purchase made on November 3.

E7-10 *Obj. 4* Refer to information provided in E7-9 as you answer the following questions.

1. If a manager for Howard Company wanted to query the company's database to obtain information about customer sales during November, which tables should she use to obtain the information? Explain why.
2. If the same manager wanted to query the database to obtain information about amounts owed by customers at the end of November, which tables should she use to obtain the information? Explain why.

E7-11 *Obj. 2* Computer networks in many organizations include client software, business management programs and databases on servers, and connections among the computers running these programs. For each of the following activities, identify the portions of the computer system that would be affected. Explain how the portions are affected.

1. Access to company data is requested
2. Records are updated
3. Data are transferred between a client and a server
4. New data for processing are entered
5. Data being used by another user are required
6. Data to print a report are obtained

E7-12 *Obj. 2* One Star Co. recently lost all of its customer and accounts receivable records. An irate customer walked into the company's sales office and took a sledge hammer to the company's computer. The company now has no basis for determining which customers owe it money or how much they owe. Identify control problems that permitted the loss to occur and controls that should have been in place to prevent the loss. Why is this an accounting problem?

Problems

P7-1 *Obj. 4* **PURPOSE OF RELATIONAL DATABASES**

Barbury Company sells machine parts to manufacturing companies. Parts usually are purchased to replace worn or broken parts. Most of Barbury's customers order goods by phone or through Internet connections from regional sales offices throughout North America. Sales are made on credit and are shipped immediately to avoid manufacturing delays at customer plants. Barbury uses a relational database for its accounting system.

Required Explain the purpose of a relational database and why it is useful to a company. Describe the parts of a relational database and identify specific examples of how these parts would be used by Barbury to obtain and fill customer orders.

P7-2 TABLES AND FORMS IN RELATIONAL DATABASES

Obj. 4 Exhibit 9 in this chapter provides examples of tables that might appear in a company's relational database. Exhibit 11 provides an example of a sales order form.

Required Using these exhibits as examples, explain the purpose of tables and forms in a relational database. Be specific about what the rows and columns in a table represent and how individual entities are identified in tables. Explain how forms are related to tables.

P7-3 COMPUTER NETWORKS

Obj. 2 You have just been hired as an account representative for a large financial institution. Your supervisor shows you to your desk that contains a workstation. She explains that the workstation is part of a wide-area network connecting all of the bank's offices through a client-server system. All of the bank's data are maintained in databases on servers and are accessed through a database management system. To obtain account information, you must log on to the network and use the bank's account service program on your workstation to retrieve data from the database.

Required What is the supervisor talking about? Explain the function of each part of the bank's computer network. Why do most companies use computer networks for their accounting systems?

P7-4 CONTROLLING NETWORKS

Obj. 2 Dora Company uses a client-server network for its accounting system. The company's database servers are kept at a central computer center. Users of the system access the company's database through workstations on their desks. Data are updated continuously throughout the day based on sales, production, billing, and other transactions recorded by users. Dora is a large company and its network connects offices in several states.

Required Identify four threats to the accounting system and accounting data that exist in Dora's network system that should be managed through internal controls. Identify an internal control that would be useful for dealing with each threat.

P7-5 WEB INTERFACES TO RELATIONAL DATABASES

Obj. 4 Visit Amazon's home page at ***http://ingram.swlearning.com*** to do this problem.

Required Identify the data items that are collected and processed by Amazon's web interface as part of selecting and placing an order for a book. How might these items be stored in a relational database? Identify potential tables and fields in the tables associated with these items.

P7-6 TABLES IN RELATIONAL DATABASES

Obj. 3 You have been assigned the responsibility of developing a purchasing module for a retail company.

Required Identify the tables that you think would be necessary as part of a relational database that will store data for the module. Identify the fields that will be important in each table and the primary and foreign keys that will link the tables together.

P7-7 APPLICATION SOFTWARE

Obj. 2 An Excel spreadsheet provides an example of an application program that can be used as a simple database.

Required Describe the applications that a spreadsheet can provide and how a spreadsheet could be used as a database. How do the application functions in the software differ from the database functions?

P7-8 DATABASE MANAGEMENT SYSTEMS

Obj. 2 Open an Access database like the Favorite Cookie Company database described in this chapter. Examine the Tools menu in the database window.

(Continued)

Required What database management functions are provided by the Tools menu options? Based on your examination, what are some of the primary purposes of a database management system?

P7-9 NETWORK COMPONENTS

Obj. 2

Trainor Company has decided to market its pet supplies on the Internet. It has developed a web site so that customers can identify products and order them online.

Required Describe a network configuration that Trainor might use to support its E-business activities.

P7-10 FIELDS IN A RELATIONAL DATABASE

Obj. 4

Linden Company sells more than 100 different types of nuts, bolts, and screws. Each product has an identification number and is described by its type, size, and material composition. Each product is purchased from one vendor.

Required Linden Company is developing a database system for its inventory. What fields would be important to include in the database for the inventory items? Why would these fields be important?

P7-11 RELATIONAL DATABASE DESIGN

Obj. 4

Niven Company manufactures and sells ornamental flamingoes. The flamingoes come in one color, pink, but come in three sizes, small, medium, and large. Customers order the products through the web by specifying the quantity of each product, and by providing a shipping address and credit card number. The credit card is verified and the customer's account is charged when the order is placed. Orders are rejected if the card cannot be charged.

Required Design a relational database system that Niven might use for its products and orders. Identify the tables, fields, and primary and foreign keys that would be part of the database.

P7-12 DIAGRAMMING A RELATIONAL DATABASE

Obj. 4

Plaxa Company developed a design for its order system that consisted of three tables. Tables and associated fields are listed below. The primary keys for each table are underlined.

Product Table [<u>Product ID</u>, Size, Price, Quantity Available]
Customer Table [<u>Customer ID</u>, Name, Address, City, State, Zip, email]
Order Table [<u>Customer ID</u>, <u>Product ID</u>, Order Date, Quantity Ordered]

Required Provide a relational diagram for the order system like that illustrated in Exhibit 9.

P7-13 DETERMINING REVENUE IN A RELATIONAL DATABASE SYSTEM

Obj. 4

Refer to P7-12. Plaxa ships its products on the same day orders are received.

Required Describe the process that Plaxa would use to determine the amount of sales it made during a particular period.

P7-14 MULTIPLE-CHOICE OVERVIEW OF THE CHAPTER

1. Which of the following statements does NOT describe an advantage of a computerized accounting system?
   a. Many accounting cycle steps are performed by the computer.
   b. It is easier to control than a manual system.
   c. It is faster than a manual system.
   d. Fewer opportunities for error exist than in a manual system.

2. Which of the following is NOT part of a computer network?
   a. transmitters
   b. clients
   c. servers
   d. databases

3. Data needed by a computerized accounting system may be entered
   a. automatically through scanning devices.
   b. by customers who enter data in forms when they place orders using web-based systems.
   c. by a company's employees.
   d. by all of the above.

4. An information system that integrates most of the business information functions of a company is known as an
   a. enterprise resource planning system.
   b. enterprise manufacturing relations system.
   c. enterprise resource module system.
   d. enterprise business planning system.

5. The part of a computer system that controls access to data and ensures reliability of processing in the system is the
   a. relational database.
   b. application software.
   c. database management system.
   d. control module.

6. The part of a client-server system that requests services from the system is the
   a. database server.
   b. application server.
   c. web server.
   d. client.

7. The Internet is an example of a
   a. client.
   b. network.
   c. server.
   d. database.

8. The module in an accounting system that is most concerned with vendors is the
   a. sales module.
   b. purchases module.
   c. human resources module.
   d. financial management module.

9. The field in a table that uniquely identifies records in the table is the
   a. primary key.
   b. foreign key.
   c. relation key.
   d. access key.

10. The part of a relational database system that permits users to define the information provided as output from the system is a
    a. form.
    b. table.
    c. query.
    d. report.

Case

C7-1 WORKING WITH A RELATIONAL DATABASE SYSTEM

Obj. 5 Favorite Cookie Company received an order from Fair-Price Foods on September 30, 2007 for seven boxes of Trrific Cookies, 24 oz. size.

Required Use the Favorite Cookie Company database to record the sale. Begin with the Sales Order form. Use 09/30/07 for all dates. Follow the example in the chapter for processing the order. Once the order has been recorded, complete the Shipping form and then the Sales Invoice form. Print the Sales Invoice for this sale.

Analysis and Interpretation of Financial Accounting Information

SECTION 2

The Time Value of Money 8

HOW MUCH WILL IT COST TO BORROW MONEY?

Maria and Stan have been successful in starting Favorite Cookie Company. The company has been profitable and is growing as more customers demand its products. Maria and Stan are now concerned about meeting the additional demand. They need to expand their operations, and they are considering producing their own products rather than purchasing them from other bakeries. Before they can expand, however, they must obtain additional financing for their company. The time value of money is an important concept that business owners need to understand before they borrow money.

Food for Thought

If you were going to borrow money, how much would you have to pay back over the life of the loan? How much would you have to pay each period? How much interest expense would you incur? Borrowing money always involves an investment by one entity, a bank for example, in another entity, such as Favorite Cookie Company. The amount repaid by the borrower includes interest in addition to the amount borrowed. Maria and Stan are considering borrowing from a local bank but have decided to discuss the loan with their accountant, Ellen, to determine how much the loan will cost.

Stan: *Ellen, Maria and I are considering expanding our business. To finance the expansion, we will need a loan. We are concerned about how much the debt will cost us and how much cash we will need to repay the principal and interest.*

Ellen: *You should be concerned about these issues. You should never borrow money without a clear idea of how much you will have to repay.*

Maria: *We know we'll have to repay the principal of the loan plus interest. We're not sure, however, how much the bank will require us to repay each period.*

Ellen: *To understand loan payments, you need to understand time value of money concepts. Interest computations can be complex, depending on when payments are made and whether you repay the loan in a single payment or in a series of payments. Let's review these concepts.*

Objectives

Once you have completed this chapter, you should be able to:

1. Define future and present value.
2. Determine the future value of a single amount invested at the present time.
3. Determine the future value of an annuity.
4. Determine the present value of a single amount to be received in the future.
5. Determine the present value of an annuity.
6. Determine investment values and interest expense or revenue for various periods.

FUTURE VALUE

Objective 1

Define future and present value.

Suppose a wealthy relative gives you $1,000 on January 1, 2007. You may use it as you like. What could you do with this money? One option is to spend it. You probably would have no difficulty identifying things you would like to buy. The total amount of goods you could purchase in January 2007 would be $1,000, the amount of money you have.

Suppose, however, that instead of spending the money immediately, you decide to invest it in a savings account at a local bank. The bank agrees to pay 5% interest on your savings account. Consequently, if you invest your money with the bank for a year, you will earn $50 interest ($1,000 principal invested × 5% interest rate).

Learning Note - Interest rates are stated as annual rates unless you are told otherwise. The amount of interest financial institutions pay on savings and for other investments usually is stated as an annual percentage rate.

The value of your investment in the future, at December 31, 2007, for example, is the future value of the investment. **The *future value* of an amount is the value of that amount at a particular time in the future.** The future value of $1,000 invested on January 1, 2007, at 5% interest is $1,050 on December 31, 2007. The amount invested is the present value of the investment. **The *present value* of an amount is the value of that amount on a particular date prior to the time the amount is paid or received.** The present value of $1,050 received on December 31, 2007, is $1,000 on January 1, 2007, assuming 5% interest is earned.

The future value of an investment is expected to be larger than its present value. The difference between future and present value of a single investment is the amount of interest earned by the investor. If you choose to invest in savings for a year, you are forgoing the option to buy goods you might like to have. The interest you earn on your savings is compensation for delaying your purchases to some time in the future.

In many situations, the relationship between future and present value is easily determined. The future value (FV) is the present value (PV) plus the interest earned (or expected) for the period of the investment. The interest earned is determined by the interest rate (R) paid on the investment. Therefore, we can express the relationship between future and present value as follows:

$$FV = PV(1 + R)$$

For example:

$$\$1{,}050 = \$1{,}000(1.05)$$

where 0.05 (5%) is the interest rate on the investment.

Compound Interest

Objective 2
Determine the future value of a single amount invested at the present time.

Suppose you decide to leave your money in the savings account for a second year, until December 31, 2008. How much would your investment be worth at that time? Assuming that you do not withdraw the interest earned for the first year ($50) and the bank continues to pay 5% interest, the value of your investment at the end of the second year would be as follows:

$$\$1{,}102.50 = \$1{,}050(1.05)$$

This amount is the future value on December 31, 2008, of the amount invested at the beginning of 2007. The earnings for the second year are higher than those for the first year because in the second year you earn interest both on the amount originally invested ($1,000) and on the amount earned in the first year ($50). Earning interest in one period on interest earned in an earlier period is known as **compound interest.** An investor earns compound interest any time an investment extends beyond one period and interest earned in prior periods is not withdrawn.

When compound interest is earned, computing the future value of an investment is more complicated. The simple equation previously described cannot be used. For example, the future value on December 31, 2008, of a $1,000 investment made on January 1, 2007, would be as follows:

$$\$1{,}102.50 = \$1{,}000(1.05)(1.05)$$

or:

$$\$1{,}102.50 = \$1{,}000(1.05)^2$$

We express the equation for computing the future value of an investment when interest is compounded like this:

$$FV = PV(1 + R)^t$$

where t is an exponent representing the number of periods of investment.

To illustrate, assume that you invest $500 for three years at 8% interest. How much would your investment be worth at the end of three years? This is another way of saying, What would be the future value of your investment at the end of three years? Compute the answer as follows:

$$\$629.86 = \$500(1.08)^3 = \$500(1.08)(1.08)(1.08)$$

Future value calculations of this type are relatively simple with a calculator that has an exponential function.

USING EXCEL

Spreadsheet programs also are commonly used for future value calculations. The future value of $500 that earns interest at 8% compounded for three years can be calculated by entering the following formula in a cell: =500*(1.08^3). The caret symbol (^) is used in Excel for exponents. The amount appearing in the cell is the future value ($629.86 in this example).

Tables also are available to assist with these calculations. Table 1 at the back of this text can be used for this purpose. This table contains the interest factors for computing future values for various interest rates and time periods. Remember, the interest factor is represented by $(1 + R)^t$ in the future value equation.

Excerpt from Table 1 Future Value of a Single Amount

	Interest Rate								
Period	0.01	0.02	0.03	0.04	0.05	0.06	0.07	**0.08**	0.09
1	1.01000	1.02000	1.03000	1.04000	1.05000	1.06000	1.07000	1.08000	1.09000
2	1.02010	1.04040	1.06090	1.08160	1.10250	1.12360	1.14490	1.16640	1.18810
3	1.03030	1.06121	1.09273	1.12486	1.15763	1.19102	1.22504	**1.25971**	1.29503

For example, the interest factor for 8% and three years in Table 1 is 1.25971. This number is equivalent to $(1.08)^3 = (1.08)(1.08)(1.08) = 1.25971$. The table provides the interest factor to simplify future value calculations. Thus, if you want to calculate the future value of $500 invested for three years at 8%, use the interest factor from Table 1:

$$\$629.86 = \$500 \times 1.25971$$

Using Table 1, compute the future value of a single amount as follows:

$$FV = PV \times IF \text{ (Table 1)}$$

where *FV* is the future value of the amount invested, *PV* is the present value (the amount invested), and *IF* is the interest factor from Table 1.

Learning Note - Future and present value calculations often contain rounding errors that depend on the number of decimal places included in computing interest factors. In this book, we round computations to the nearest cent or, for large amounts, to the nearest dollar.

The future value equation $[FV = PV(1 + R)^t]$ is useful for determining the future value of an investment. In addition to this information, you might want to determine the amount earned on an investment each period. For example, if you invested $500 for three years at 8% interest, how much interest would you earn each year? A table like the one shown in Exhibit 1 is useful for this purpose.

EXHIBIT 1 Interest Table for an Investment of $500 for Three Years at 8%

A Year	B Value at Beginning of Year	C Interest Earned (Column B × Interest Rate)	D Future Value at End of Year (Column B + Column C)
1	500.00	40.00	540.00
2	540.00	43.20	583.20
3	583.20	46.66	629.86
Total		129.86	

Column B shows the amount the investment is worth at the beginning of each year. Column C shows the amount of interest earned each year, and column D reports the amount the investment is worth at the end of each year. The total in column C is the total interest earned for three years. This table illustrates how the value of an investment grows over time as interest is earned and reinvested. A bank could use the same type of table to calculate the amount of interest expense incurred and the amount owed the investor in a savings account each period.

Objective 3
Determine the future value of an annuity.

Future Value of an Annuity

The future value calculations so far have been limited to determining the future value of a single investment, such as the future value of $1,000 invested on January 1, 2007. Now, consider a situation in which a series of investments is made. For example, suppose you invest $500 at the end of each year for three years. How much will your investments be worth at the end of three years if you earn 8% interest each year? This type of investment situation is known as an annuity. **An *annuity* is a series of equal amounts received or paid over a specified number of equal time periods.**

***Learning Note** - It is important to know* **when** *amounts are paid or received when working with annuities. An annuity in which amounts are paid or received at the* **end of each fiscal period** *is known as an ordinary annuity. An annuity in which amounts are paid or received at the* **beginning** *of each fiscal period is known as an annuity due. We limit our discussion to ordinary annuities, which are typical for most accounting transactions.*

Calculate the future value of these investments by computing the future value of the amount invested each year and adding all the amounts together.

End of Year 1	End of Year 2	End of Year 3	Future Value at End of Year 3	
Invested for 2 years $500 →			$ 583.20 =	$500 × 1.08^2
	Invested for 1 year $500 →		540.00 =	500 × 1.08^1
		Invested for 0 years →	500.00 =	500 × 1.08^0
	Future value of total investment		$1,623.20	
	Total amount invested over 2 years*		1,500.00	
	Interest earned over 2 years		$ 123.20	

**Though three payments are made, the period covered is only two years because the first payment is made at the end of year 1.*

***Learning Note** - Any amount raised to the zero power is 1. Therefore, $(1.08)^0 = 1$. Also, $(1.0)^0 = 1$, $(1.1)^0 = 1$, and $(200)^0 = 1$. Using an expression such as $500 × $(1.08)^0$ is the same as saying that $500 invested at any point in time is worth $500 at that point in time because no interest has been earned. Another way of saying the same thing is to say that the future value of any amount at zero periods in the future is that amount. The interest factor for any interest rate at zero periods in the future is 1.0.*

The $500 invested at the end of the first year is worth $583.20 at the end of the third year. The $500 invested at the end of the second year is worth $540.00 at the end of the third year, and the $500 invested at the end of the third year is worth $500.00 at the end of the third year. Thus, the future value of the total investment is the sum of these amounts, $1,623.20.

This calculation is the same as:

$$\$1{,}623.20 = \$500[(1.08)^0 + (1.08)^1 + (1.08)^2]$$

Therefore, we could use Table 1 to identify the interest factors for 8% and one and two periods.

Excerpt from Table 1 Future Value of a Single Amount

	Interest Rate								
Period	0.01	0.02	0.03	0.04	0.05	0.06	0.07	**0.08**	0.09
1	1.01000	1.02000	1.03000	1.04000	1.05000	1.06000	1.07000	**1.08000**	1.09000
2	1.02010	1.04040	1.06090	1.08160	1.10250	1.12360	1.14490	**1.16640**	1.18810
3	1.03030	1.06121	1.09273	1.12486	1.15763	1.19102	1.22504	1.25971	1.29503

The interest factor for zero periods is 1. Thus, the interest factor for the annuity is the sum of interest factors for zero, one, and two periods (3.2464 = 1.00 + 1.08 + 1.1664). Then, we multiply this interest factor times the amount invested each period to compute the future value of the annuity:

$$\$1{,}623.20 = \$500 \times 3.2464$$

Alternatively, tables are available that contain the interest factors for computing the future value of an annuity. Table 2 at the back of this book is this type of table. Using the table simplifies the calculation by providing the interest factor.

Excerpt from Table 2 Future Value of an Annuity

	Interest Rate								
Period	0.01	0.02	0.03	0.04	0.05	0.06	0.07	**0.08**	0.09
1	1.00000	1.00000	1.00000	1.00000	1.00000	1.00000	1.00000	1.00000	1.00000
2	2.01000	2.02000	2.03000	2.04000	2.05000	2.06000	2.07000	2.08000	2.09000
3	3.03010	3.06040	3.09090	3.12160	3.15250	3.18360	3.21490	**3.24640**	3.27810

USING EXCEL

We could use a spreadsheet and enter the amounts invested in a cell to calculate their future value: =(500*(1.08^2))+(500*1.08)+500. The first term in parentheses is the future value of $500 at the end of two periods. The second term in parentheses is the future value of $500 at the end of one period, and the last term is the final investment of $500. The amount appearing in the cell is the future value of the annuity ($1,623.20 in this example).

Spreadsheets also contain built-in functions for calculating the future value of an annuity. Locate these functions by clicking on the Function f_x button.

From the pop-up menu, select the type of function you want. The future value of an annuity (FV) function is in the Financial category.

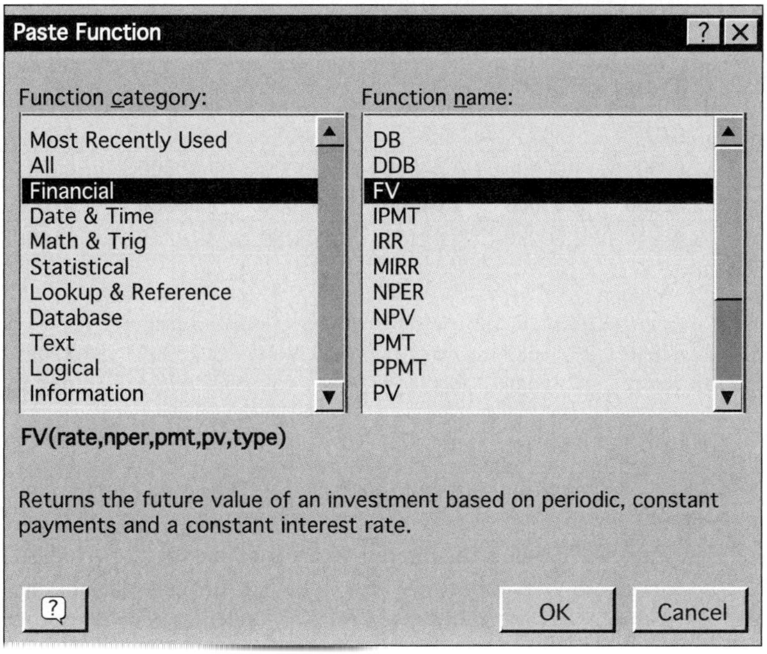

Click the OK button and the following box appears. Complete the box by entering the interest rate (Rate), number of periods for which investments will be made (Nper), and the amount invested (Pmt). The Pv and Type boxes can be left blank. Note that the amount invested is entered as a negative number because it is a cash outflow to the investor.

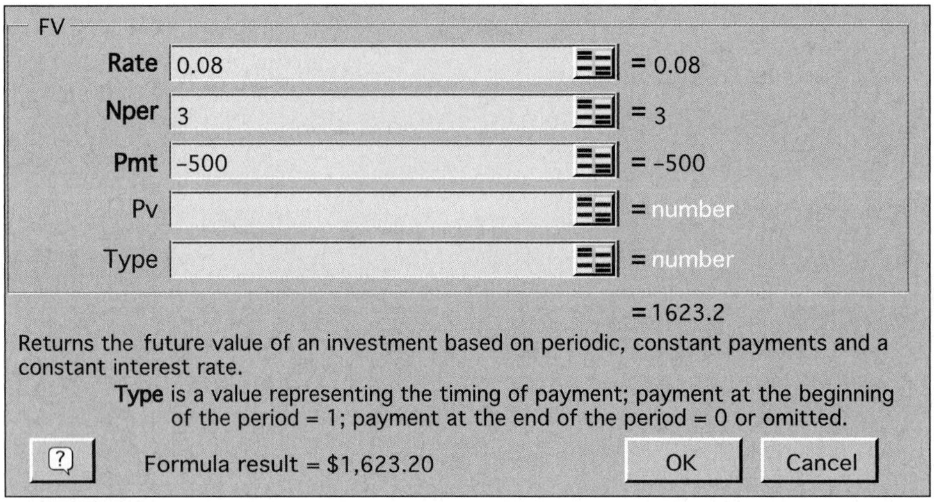

The amount appearing in the cell used to reference the FV function is the future value of the investment ($1,623.20 in this example). The function can be entered in the worksheet's cell directly by typing =FV(.08,3,−500). It is important that the values (known as arguments to a function) be entered in the cell in the correct order. The function for the future value of an annuity is =FV(Interest Rate, Number of Periods, Amount Invested).

Annuities are common in business activities. For example, suppose Favorite Cookie Company agrees to invest $5,000 for each of its employees in a retirement plan at the end of each year. If the investment earns 7% and an employee works 20 years before retiring, how much will be available when the employee retires? Using Table 2, we can calculate the future value of an annuity of $5,000 per year for 20 years.

Excerpt from Table 2 Future Value of an Annuity

	Interest Rate								
Period	0.01	0.02	0.03	0.04	0.05	0.06	**0.07**	0.08	0.09
1	1.00000	1.00000	1.00000	1.00000	1.00000	1.00000	1.00000	1.00000	1.00000
2	2.01000	2.02000	2.03000	2.04000	2.05000	2.06000	2.07000	2.08000	2.09000
3	3.03010	3.06040	3.09090	3.12160	3.15250	3.18360	3.21490	3.24640	3.27810
⋮	⋮	⋮	⋮	⋮	⋮	⋮	⋮	⋮	⋮
19	20.81090	22.84056	25.11687	27.67123	30.53900	33.75999	37.37896	41.44626	46.01846
20	22.01900	24.29737	26.87037	29.77808	33.06595	36.78559	**40.99549**	45.76196	51.16012

$$\$204{,}977 = \$5{,}000 \times 40.99549$$

where 40.99549 is the interest factor for 7% and 20 periods. The table is simply a labor-saving device to reduce the number of calculations for this type of problem. Alternatively, we could use a financial calculator or computer program that has future value functions.

USING EXCEL

The future value of the investment can be calculated in Excel by entering =FV(.07,20,−5000) in a cell.

Using Table 2, we compute the future value of an annuity as follows:

$$FVA = A \times IF \text{ (Table 2)}$$

where *FVA* is the future value of the annuity, *A* is the amount invested at the end of each period, and *IF* is the interest factor from Table 2.

In addition to determining the future value of an annuity, you might want to determine the amount earned each period. For example, if you invested $500 at the end of each year for three years at 8% interest, how much interest would you earn each year? A table like the one shown in Exhibit 2 is useful for this purpose.

EXHIBIT 2 Interest Table for an Annuity of $500 at End of Each Year for Three Years at 8%

A Year	B Value at Beginning of Year	C Interest Earned (Column B × Interest Rate)	D Amount Invested at End of Year	E Future Value at End of Year (Columns B + C + D)
1	0.00	0.00	500.00	500.00
2	500.00	40.00	500.00	1,040.00
3	1,040.00	83.20	500.00	1,623.20
Total		123.20	1,500.00	

Column B shows the amount the investment is worth at the beginning of each year before the contribution is made for that year. Column C contains the amount of interest earned for the year, and column D contains the amount invested at the end of each year. Column E reports the amount the investment is worth at the end of each year. The total in column C is the total interest earned for three years. Interest earned on the annuity is greater than that earned on a single investment of the same amount because the investment is growing each period by the additional amount invested as well as by the amount of interest earned.

Another question you might want to answer is, How much would you need to invest each period to accumulate a certain amount? For example, suppose you want to accumulate $1,000 over the next three years to take a trip to Mexico after you graduate from college. How much would you need to invest at the end of each year to accumulate $1,000 at the end of three years, assuming that you invest the same amount each year and can earn 6% on your investment?

We can answer this question using the future value of an annuity equation and Table 2.

$$FVA = A \times IF \text{ (Table 2)}$$
$$\$1{,}000 = A \times 3.18360$$
$$A = \$1{,}000 \div 3.18360$$
$$A = \$314.11$$

By investing $314.11 at the end of each year for three years, you can accumulate $1,000.

USING EXCEL

We can calculate the amount of the payment in Excel using the payment function (PMT). To determine the amount, enter =PMT(0.06,3,,1000) in a cell. The arguments of the function are PMT(Interest Rate, Number of Periods,, Future Value of the Annuity). Note that there are two commas following the number of periods because an argument has been omitted. We will use that argument in a future computation. The amount appearing in the cell where the function is entered is the amount of the annuity payment. It appears as a negative amount because it is a cash outflow to the investor.

Self-Study Problem #1

Harry Morgan recently graduated from college and started his first full-time job. He wants to accumulate enough money in the next five years to make a down payment on a house. He has $3,000 that he can invest at the beginning of the five-year period. His investment will earn 8% interest.

Required

A. How much would Harry's $3,000 investment be worth at the end of the five-year period? How much interest would he earn for the five years?

B. Independent of part (A), suppose the amount Harry needs for a down payment at the end of five years is $10,000. He wants to invest equal amounts at the end of each year for the next five years to accumulate the $10,000 he needs. How much would he need to invest each year, assuming that he earns 8% interest? How much would his investment be worth at the end of each year for the five-year period? How much would Harry invest over the five years? How much interest would he earn over the five years?

The solution to Self-Study Problem 1 appears at the end of the chapter.

PRESENT VALUE

Objective 4
Determine the present value of a single amount to be received in the future.

In many business activities, it is important to calculate the present value of an investment rather than the future value. In this section, you will learn how to calculate the present value of an investment from information about the future value. To illustrate, suppose a company offered to sell you an investment that pays $3,000 at the end of three years. You want to earn 8% return on your investment. How much would you be willing to pay for the investment?

To solve this problem, you should recognize that the $3,000 to be received at the end of three years is the future value of the investment. The amount you would pay for the investment at the beginning of the three-year period is the present value of the investment. Use the future value equation described earlier to solve the problem.

$$\text{FV} = \text{PV}(1 + \text{R})^t$$

$$\$3{,}000 = \text{PV}(1.08)^3$$

$$\text{PV} = \$3{,}000 \times \frac{1}{(1.08)^3} = \$3{,}000 \div 1.08^3$$

$$\text{PV} = \$2{,}381.50$$

Thus, the present value of the investment—the amount you would be willing to pay at the beginning of the three-year period—is $2,381.50.

We can also use Table 1 to solve the problem.

$$\begin{aligned} FV &= PV \times IF \text{ (Table 1)} \\ \$3{,}000 &= PV \times 1.25971 \\ PV &= \$3{,}000 \div 1.25971 \\ PV &= \$2{,}381.50 \end{aligned}$$

We can rewrite the future value equation as a present value equation.

$$PV = FV \times \frac{1}{(1 + R)^t}$$

USING EXCEL

The present value of the investment can be calculated in Excel by entering =3000*(1/(1.08^3)) in a cell. The amount appearing in the cell ($2,381.50 in this example) is the present value of the investment.

Tables are available that provide interest factors for computing the present value of an investment. Table 3 at the back of this book is an example of such a table. To illustrate, the interest factor for computing the present value of an investment of three periods at 8% is 0.79383 from Table 3.

Excerpt from Table 3 Present Value of a Single Amount

	Interest Rate								
Period	0.01	0.02	0.03	0.04	0.05	0.06	0.07	**0.08**	0.09
1	0.99010	0.98039	0.97087	0.96154	0.95238	0.94340	0.93458	0.92593	0.91743
2	0.98030	0.96117	0.94260	0.92456	0.90703	0.89000	0.87344	0.85734	0.84168
3	0.97059	0.94232	0.91514	0.88900	0.86384	0.83962	0.81630	**0.79383**	0.77218

The present value of an investment that pays $3,000 at the end of three years at 8%, then, is as follows:

$$\$2{,}381.49 = \$3{,}000 \times 0.79383$$

This is the same amount computed above, except for the effect of a rounding error. The interest factor for computing the present value of an investment is 1 divided by the interest factor for computing the future value of the same investment (same period and interest rate). Thus, 0.79383 in Table 3 for three periods at 8% equals 1 ÷ 1.25971 from Table 1 for three periods at 8%.

Using Table 3, we can compute the present value of a single payment as follows:

$$PV = FV \times IF \text{ (Table 3)}$$

where *PV* is the present value, *FV* is the future value (the payment made in the future), and *IF* is the interest factor from Table 3.

In addition to determining the present value of an investment, you might want to determine the amount earned each period. For example, if your investment paid $3,000 at the end of three years and earned 8% interest, how much interest would you earn each year? A table like the one shown in Exhibit 3 is helpful.

EXHIBIT 3 Interest Table for a Present Value of $2,381.49 for Three Years at 8%

A Year	B Present Value at Beginning of Year	C Interest Earned (Column B × Interest Rate)	D Value at End of Year (Column B + Column C)
1	2,381.49	190.52	2,572.01
2	2,572.01	205.76	2,777.77
3	2,777.77	222.23	3,000.00
Total		618.51	

Column B shows the amount the investment is worth at the beginning of each year. Column C shows the amount of interest earned each year, and column D reports the amount the investment is worth at the end of each year. The total in column C is the total interest earned for three years. Values in Exhibit 3 are calculated the same way as in Exhibit 1. The present value of the investment must be calculated before the table can be prepared. The amount computed for the future value at the end of the investment period should be the future value of the investment (see $3,000 in Exhibit 3).

Present Value of an Annuity

Objective 5
Determine the present value of an annuity.

The investment situation in the previous section assumed that a single amount was received at the end of an investment period. It is common for investments to pay an equal amount each period over an investment period. For example, assume that you could purchase an investment that would pay $1,000 at the end of each year for three years, and that you expect to earn a return of 8%. How much would you be willing to pay for the investment?

Calculate the present value of this annuity by calculating the present value of each payment and adding them together.

Present Value at Beginning of Year 1		Amount Received: End of Year 1	Amount Received: End of Year 2	Amount Received: End of Year 3
$ 925.93 = $1,000 ÷ $(1.08)^1$	←	$1,000		
857.34 = $1,000 ÷ $(1.08)^2$	←		$1,000	
793.83 = $1,000 ÷ $(1.08)^3$	←			$1,000
$ 2,577.10 Present value of total investment				

$ 3,000.00	Total amount received over 3 years
2,577.10	Present value of total investment
$ 422.90	Interest earned over 3 years

The first row in this calculation is the present value of $1,000 received at the end of the first year, the second row is the present value of $1,000 received at the end of the second year, and the third row is the present value of $1,000 received at the end of the third year.

Alternatively, we could use the interest factors from Table 3 for one, two, and three periods at 8% and add them together to determine the interest factor.

Excerpt from Table 3 Present Value of a Single Amount

	Interest Rate								
Period	0.01	0.02	0.03	0.04	0.05	0.06	0.07	**0.08**	0.09
1	0.99010	0.98039	0.97087	0.96154	0.95238	0.94340	0.93458	**0.92593**	0.91743
2	0.98030	0.96117	0.94260	0.92456	0.90703	0.89000	0.87344	**0.85734**	0.84168
3	0.97059	0.94232	0.91514	0.88900	0.86384	0.83962	0.81630	**0.79383**	0.77218

$2,577.10 = $1.000 × (0.92593 + 0.85734 + 0.79383)
$2,577.10 = $1.000 × 2.57710

USING EXCEL

Use the PV function in Excel to calculate the present value of an annuity. The function can be accessed by using the function button and completing the pop-up box or by entering the function directly in a cell. The present value of an annuity function is PV(Interest Rate, Number of Periods, Amount Invested each Period). Accordingly, we can enter =PV(0.08,3,−1000) in a cell. The amount appearing in the cell is the present value of the annuity ($2,577.10 in this example). Remember that the amount invested is entered as a negative value.

To avoid the need to add interest factors together, tables are available that provide this addition. Table 4 inside the back cover of this book is an example of this type of table. Notice that the interest factor in this table for an annuity of three periods at 8% is 2.57710, the sum of the interest factors for one, two, and three years from Table 3. Using this table, we can calculate the present value of an annuity as follows:

PVA = A × IF (Table 4)

where *PVA* is the present value of an annuity, *A* is the amount of the periodic payment of the annuity, and *IF* is the interest factor from Table 4.

Excerpt from Table 4 Present Value of an Annuity

	Interest Rate								
Period	0.01	0.02	0.03	0.04	0.05	0.06	0.07	**0.08**	0.09
1	0.99010	0.98039	0.97087	0.96154	0.95238	0.94340	0.93458	0.92593	0.91743
2	1.97040	1.94156	1.91347	1.88609	1.85941	1.83339	1.80802	1.78326	1.75911
3	2.94099	2.88388	2.82861	2.77509	2.72325	2.67301	2.62432	**2.57710**	2.53129

Again, in addition to determining the present value of an annuity, you might want to determine the amount earned each period. For example, if you purchased an investment that paid $1,000 each year for three years at 8% interest, how much interest would you earn each year? A table like the one shown in Exhibit 4 is useful for this purpose.

EXHIBIT 4 Interest Table for an Annuity of $1,000 Each Year for Three Years at 8%

A Year	B Present Value at Beginning of Year	C Interest Earned (Column B × Interest Rate)	D Total Amount Invested (Column B + Column C)	E Amount Paid at End of Year	F Value at End of Year (Column D – Column E)
1	2,577.10	206.17	2,783.27	1,000.00	1,783.27
2	1,783.27	142.66	1,925.93	1,000.00	925.93
3	925.93	74.07	1,000.00	1,000.00	0.00
Total		422.90		3,000.00	

This table is a bit more complicated than those presented earlier. The first step in preparing this table is to calculate the present value of the annuity. This amount ($2,577.10) is the present value at the beginning of the first year. Interest for the first year is earned on this amount, as shown in column C by multiplying the present value in column B by the interest rate (8%). Column D shows the amount of the investment after interest is earned for the period. It is the sum of columns B and C. However, an amount ($1,000) is paid out of the investment each year. The amount left in the investment at the end of the year (column F) then is the amount in column D minus the amount paid in column E. The amount in column F is what is available at the beginning of the next year before interest is earned for the year (column B).

Observe that the value of the investment decreases over time because the amount of the annuity ($1,000) is paid out each year. Once the final payment is made at the end of the life of the investment, the value of the investment is zero (year 3, column F).

Exhibit 4 describes the amount of interest earned, the amount paid, and the value for each period of an annuity. Note that the amount earned from the annuity over the three years is equal to the difference between the amount received over the life of the annuity and the present value of the annuity (the amount paid for the investment): $422.90 = $3,000 − $2,577.10.

Self-Study Problem #2

H. Greely has the option of buying either of two investments. One investment pays $5,000 at the end of four years. The other investment pays $1,000 at the end of each year for four years. Both investments earn 8% interest.

Required Which investment is worth more at the beginning of the four-year period? How much interest will Greely earn from each investment over the four-year period?

The solution to Self-Study Problem 2 appears at the end of the chapter.

LOAN PAYMENTS AND AMORTIZATION

Economic decisions frequently require the use of present value calculations. These calculations are used in a variety of transactions recorded in accounting systems. For example, assume that you want to buy a used car. You negotiate with a dealer to purchase a car for $5,000, which you arrange to borrow from a local bank. The bank charges 12%

Objective 6

Determine investment values and interest expense or revenue for various periods.

interest on the loan, which is to be repaid in two years in equal monthly payments. How much will your payments be each month? How much interest will you pay over the two years?

To answer these questions, you should recognize that this problem involves the present value of an annuity. The amount you borrow ($5,000) is the present value of the amount you will repay in equal installments. Because the repayment is in equal monthly installments, this investment is an annuity. In effect, the bank is investing $5,000 in you at the beginning of the two-year period in exchange for monthly payments that will earn 12% (annual) return for the bank.

When amounts are paid or received on less than an annual basis, the interest rate and number of periods must be adjusted for the shorter period. An annual rate of 12% is equivalent to a monthly rate of 1% (12% ÷ 12 months). Two years of monthly payments result in 24 monthly payments (12 × 2). Therefore, instead of an interest factor of 12% for 2 years, we should use an interest factor of 1% for 24 months. Interest is compounded monthly, and a portion of the loan principal is being repaid each month along with the interest.

We can use Table 4 to solve this problem:

http://ingram.swlearning.com

Calculate a loan schedule online.

$$\begin{aligned} \text{PVA} &= \text{A} \times \text{IF (Table 4)} \\ \$5{,}000 &= \text{A} \times 21.24339 \\ \text{A} &= \$5{,}000 \div 21.24339 \\ \text{A} &= \$235.37 \end{aligned}$$

Excerpt from Table 4 Present Value of an Annuity

	Interest Rate								
Period	**0.01**	0.02	0.03	0.04	0.05	0.06	0.07	0.08	0.09
1	0.99010	0.98039	0.97087	0.96154	0.95238	0.94340	0.93458	0.92593	0.91743
2	1.97040	1.94156	1.91347	1.88609	1.85941	1.83339	1.80802	1.78326	1.75911
3	2.94099	2.88388	2.82861	2.77509	2.72325	2.67301	2.62432	2.57710	2.53129
⋮	⋮	⋮	⋮	⋮	⋮	⋮	⋮	⋮	⋮
23	20.45582	18.29220	16.44361	14.85684	13.48857	12.30338	11.27219	10.37106	9.58021
24	**21.24339**	18.91393	16.93554	15.24696	13.79864	12.55036	11.46933	10.52876	9.70661

Thus, the answer to the first question (How much would you pay each month?) is $235.37. Remember that the interest rate used in this computation is 1% per month and the number of periods is 24 months. The interest rate must be adjusted for the period of the annuity. An annual rate of 12% is equivalent to a monthly rate of 1%.

USING EXCEL

Solve the problem using the payment function in Excel. Enter =PMT (.01,24,5000). The amount appearing in the cell is the amount of the annuity payment ($235.37 in this example). The arguments of the function are PMT(Interest Rate, Number of Periods, Present Value of the Annuity). Observe that this is the same function that we used to calculate the amount of payments for the future value of an annuity. The payment function is PMT(Interest Rate, Number of Periods, Present Value of Annuity, Future Value of Annuity). Either the third or fourth argument should be skipped depending on which value is being calculated. The third argument (Present Value of Annuity) is skipped if the last argument is included. In this case, an extra comma is needed after the second argument to indicate that the third argument has been omitted.

To determine how much interest you would incur on the loan, you need to prepare a table similar to the one in Exhibit 4. Exhibit 5 provides this information. This table usually is referred to as a loan amortization (or loan payment) table. It is a little different from Exhibit 4. A column has been added in Exhibit 5 to calculate the principal repaid each period, and the total investment column in Exhibit 4 has been omitted. Exhibits 4 and 5 contain essentially the same information. Formats of these tables vary in practice, but they all provide the same basic information.

EXHIBIT 5 Amortization Table for Automobile Loan of $5,000 for 24 Months at 1% per Month

A Month	B Present Value at Beginning of Month	C Interest Incurred (Column B × Interest Rate)	D Amount Paid	E Principal Paid (Column D – Column C)	F Value at End of Month (Column B – Column E)
1	5,000.00	50.00	235.37	185.37	4,814.63
2	4,814.63	48.15	235.37	187.22	4,627.41
3	4,627.41	46.27	235.37	189.10	4,438.31
⋮	⋮	⋮	⋮	⋮	⋮
23	463.70	4.64	235.37	230.73	232.97
24	232.97	2.33	235.30	232.97	0.00
Total		648.81	5,648.81		

This exhibit provides useful information about the loan. The total interest incurred over the life of the loan is $648.81. This amount equals the difference between the amount paid over the life of the loan ($5,648.81) and the amount borrowed ($5,000). The amount of interest incurred decreases each month (column C) because a portion of the loan principal is repaid each month (column E). Notice that the payment made each month ($235.37) repays a portion of the amount borrowed and pays the interest expense for the month. The amount of the loan repaid each month (column E) is the amount of the payment (column D) minus the interest expense for the month (column C). The amount owed decreases to zero over the 24 months. The final payment in month 24 (column D) is adjusted slightly because of rounding error. These characteristics are typical of many loan arrangements, especially consumer loans used to purchase autos, appliances and similar goods, and homes.

Interest $50.00 + **Principal $185.37** = **Total Payment $235.37**

The information in Exhibit 5 can be used to determine the transactions that the bank would record each month. It also can be used to determine transactions for the borrower (for example, if the borrower were a company concerned with this information).

Consider first the transactions that would be recorded by the bank for the first month of the loan, assuming the loan was made on April 1, 2007:

		Assets		=	Liabilities	+	Owners' Equity	
Date	Accounts	Cash	Other Assets				Contributed Capital	Retained Earnings
Apr. 1, 2007	Notes Receivable		5,000.00					
	Cash	−5,000.00						
Apr. 30, 2007	Cash	235.37						
	Notes Receivable		−185.37					
	Interest Revenue							50.00

The first transaction, at the beginning of the month (April 1), records the amount of the loan as a decrease in Cash and an increase in Notes Receivable. The second transaction, at the end of the month (April 30), records the amount received from the customer ($235.37) and the amount earned for the first month ($50.00). The balance in Notes Receivable ($4,814.63 = $5,000 − $185.37) is the amount owed to the bank by the customer at the end of the first month.

Similar transactions could be recorded by the customer:

		Assets		=	Liabilities	+	Owners' Equity	
Date	Accounts	Cash	Other Assets				Contributed Capital	Retained Earnings
Apr. 1, 2007	Cash	5,000.00						
	Notes Payable				5,000.00			
Apr. 30, 2007	Notes Payable				−185.37			
	Interest Expense							−50.00
	Cash	−235.37						

The first transaction records the amount received from the bank and the liability to the bank. The second transaction records the payment at the end of the first month. The amount paid reduces the liability to the bank and pays interest expense for the first month.

The bank records transactions for payments received each month over the life of the loan. The amount of principal paid and the amount of interest earned change each month. In the last month of the loan (March 2009), the bank would record the following:

		Assets		=	Liabilities	+	Owners' Equity	
Date	Accounts	Cash	Other Assets				Contributed Capital	Retained Earnings
Mar. 31, 2009	Cash	235.30						
	Notes Receivable		−232.97					
	Interest Revenue							2.33

After this transaction is recorded, the balance of Notes Receivable will be zero. The loan will have been paid off.

The customer also could record transactions each month. The amount of principal repaid and the interest expense incurred would change each month. The final payment would reduce the Notes Payable balance to zero.

UNEQUAL PAYMENTS

Investments do not always involve single amounts or annuities. For example, suppose Jill Johnson invested a portion of her salary at the end of each of four years. The amounts she invested in those years were \$700, \$800, \$900, and \$1,000, respectively. How much would her investments be worth at the end of the fourth year of investing if she earned 6% each year?

In this type of situation, each investment must be considered separately because the amounts invested are not the same each period.

Amount Invested at End of Year 1	End of Year 2	End of Year 3	End of Year 4		Future Value at End of Year 4
\$700 →					\$ 833.71
	\$800 →				898.88
		\$900 →			954.00
			\$1,000 →		1,000.00
				Total	\$3,686.59

The future value of the amounts can be determined using interest factors from Table 1.

FV	=	PV × IF (Table 1)
\$ 833.71	=	\$700 × 1.19102 (6%, 3 periods)
898.88	=	\$800 × 1.12360 (6%, 2 periods)
954.00	=	\$900 × 1.06000 (6%, 1 period)
1,000.00	=	\$1,000 × 1.00000 (6%, 0 period)
\$3,686.59		

Observe that the amount invested at the end of the first year (\$700) will be invested for three years, the amount invested at the end of the second year will be invested for two years, and so forth. Accordingly, the interest factor for the first investment is for three years, and the number of periods decreases by one for each successive investment.

Learning Note - A common mistake is to match investments with the incorrect period of investment. Consider how long an amount will be invested until the end of the investment period when computing future value, or until the beginning of the investment period when computing present value.

To continue the illustration, suppose you can purchase an investment that is expected to pay \$200, \$300, and \$400 at the end of the next three years. You expect the investment to earn 7% interest. How much should you pay for the investment?

You want to determine the present value of the amounts you expect to receive. The relevant period is from the time when the amount will be received to the beginning of the investment period. For example, the first amount (\$200) will be received at the end of one year; therefore, the relevant period is one year. The present value of the investment would be as follows:

Present Value at Beginning of Year 1	Amount Received: End of Year 1	End of Year 2	End of Year 3
$186.92 ←	$200		
262.03 ←		$300	
326.52 ←			$400
$775.47 Total			

The present value of the investment would be as follows:

$$
\begin{aligned}
PV &= FV \times IF \text{ (Table 3)} \\
\$186.92 &= \$200 \times 0.93458 \text{ (7\%, 1 period)} \\
262.03 &= \$300 \times 0.87344 \text{ (7\%, 2 periods)} \\
326.52 &= \$400 \times 0.81630 \text{ (7\%, 3 periods)} \\
\$775.47 &
\end{aligned}
$$

COMBINING SINGLE AMOUNTS AND ANNUITIES

In some cases an investment involves both a single amount and an annuity. For example, suppose you could purchase an investment that offered to pay $100 at the end of each year for 10 years and $1,000 at the end of the 10-year period. If you expect the investment to earn 8% interest, how much would you pay for the investment at the beginning of the 10-year period? To answer this question, compute the present value of the annuity and add the present value of the single amount.

$$
\begin{aligned}
PVA &= A \times IF \text{ (Table 4)} \\
\$671.01 &= \$100 \times 6.71008 \\
PV &= FV \times IF \text{ (Table 3)} \\
\$463.19 &= \$1{,}000 \times 0.46319
\end{aligned}
$$

Therefore, the amount you should pay is $1,134.20 = $671.01 + $463.19.

Any investment problem can be thought of as a single amount, a series of single amounts, an annuity, or a combination of these arrangements.

SUMMARY OF FUTURE AND PRESENT VALUE CONCEPTS

Future and present value consider timing differences between when cash is received or paid and the present period. They are based on the simple concept that a dollar received in the future is worth less than a dollar received at the present time. The difference between the two amounts depends on the rate of interest and the time period. Amounts invested today must increase in value to compensate the investor for forgoing the use of the amount invested. The higher the interest rate required from an investment, the greater the future value must be relative to the present value. The longer an investor must wait before receiving the future value, the larger the future value must be relative to the present value. Exhibit 6 illustrates the basic concepts of future and present value.

EXHIBIT 6
Future and Present Value Concepts

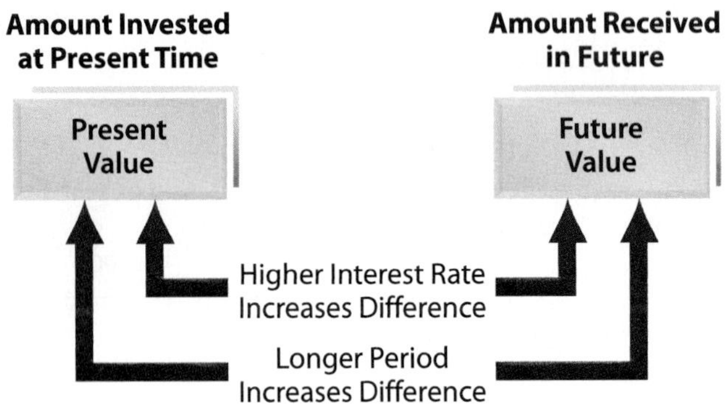

The interest rate an investment is expected to earn depends on the risk associated with the investment. The greater the uncertainty about the amount to be received from an investment, the higher the interest rate investors require before they will invest. Therefore, relatively safe investments, such as savings accounts, pay lower interest than relatively risky investments, such as corporate debt, where the chance of bankruptcy affects the amount an investor may receive. Similarly, the rate of interest a bank charges a customer for a loan depends on the customer's credit history as an indication of the probability that the customer will repay the amount borrowed, plus interest, when due.

Self-Study Problem #3

Required Calculate each of the following at the beginning of year one.

A. The present value of $100 received at the end of two years at 10%.

B. The present value of $100 received at the end of three years at 10%.

C. The present value of $100 received at the end of three years at 8%.

D. The present value of $100 received at the end of each year for three years at 10%.

E. The present value of $50 received at the end of one year, $100 received at the end of two years, and $150 received at the end of three years at 10%.

Use your answers to demonstrate the effect of time periods and interest rates on the difference between the future and present values of investments by comparing A and B, B and C, B and D, and D and E.

The solution to Self-Study Problem 3 appears at the end of the chapter.

THINKING BEYOND THE QUESTION

HOW MUCH WILL IT COST TO BORROW MONEY?

Most debt requires periodic payments of principal and interest. Consequently, debt often involves computations of annuities, particularly the present value of annuities. Determining the payment amount and the total cost of borrowing depends on the interest rate and the number of periods over which the debt is repaid.

As a borrower, you may be able to negotiate the number of periods over which debt is repaid. For example, you may be able to repay a loan over five or ten years. Often, agreeing to a shorter borrowing period means getting a loan with a lower interest rate. Why would that be true? What factors would encourage a lender to require a higher or lower rate of interest from a borrower? What kinds of information would a lender look for in the financial statements of a borrower like Favorite Cookie Company? Why? What financial information could help a borrower bargain for a lower rate or more money?

Self-Study Problem Solutions

SSP8-1 A. $FV = PV \times IF$ (Table 1)

$$FV = \$3{,}000 \times 1.46933$$
$$FV = \$4{,}407.99$$

The amount of interest earned would be \$1,407.99 = \$4,407.99 − \$3,000.

B. $FVA = A \times IF$ (Table 2)

$$\$10{,}000 = A \times 5.86660$$
$$A = \$1{,}704.56$$

Column E in the following interest table identifies the amount the investment is worth at the end of each year. The total of column D is the amount Harry invested over the five years. The total of column C is the amount of interest earned over the five years.

A	B	C	D	E
Year	**Value at Beginning of Year**	**Interest Earned (Column B × Interest Rate)**	**Amount Invested at End of Year**	**Future Value at End of Year (Columns B + C + D)**
1	0.00	0.00	1,704.56	1,704.56
2	1,704.56	136.36	1,704.56	3,545.48
3	3,545.48	283.64	1,704.56	5,533.68
4	5,533.68	442.69	1,704.56	7,680.93
5	7,680.93	614.48	1,704.56	9,999.97
Total		1,477.17	8,522.80	

SSP8-2 Option 1:

$$PV = FV \times IF \text{ (Table 3)}$$
$$\$3{,}675.15 = \$5{,}000 \times 0.73503$$
$$\text{Interest earned} = \$1{,}324.85 = \$5{,}000 - \$3{,}675.15$$

Option 2:

$$PVA = A \times IF \text{ (Table 4)}$$
$$\$3{,}312.13 = \$1{,}000 \times 3.31213$$
$$\text{Interest earned} = \$687.87 = \$4{,}000 \text{ (\$1,000 per year} \times \text{4 years)} - \$3{,}312.13$$

Option 1 is worth more, even though he will receive payments sooner from option 2.

SSP8-3 $PV = FV \times IF$

A. \$ 82.65 = \$100 × 0.82645 (Table 3)
B. \$ 75.13 = \$100 × 0.75131 (Table 3)
C. \$ 79.38 = \$100 × 0.79383 (Table 3)
D. \$248.69 = \$100 × 2.48685 (Table 4)
E. \$ 45.45 = \$50 × 0.90909
82.65 = \$100 × 0.82645
112.70 = \$150 × 0.75131
\$240.80

Comparison of A and B: The present value of an investment decreases relative to the future value as the time until the investment is received increases.

Comparison of B and C: The present value of an investment decreases relative to the future value as the interest rate increases. A higher interest rate results in a higher amount of interest being earned for investment B (\$21.07 = \$100 − \$75.13) than for investment C (\$20.62 = \$100 − \$79.38).

Comparison of B and D: The present value of an investment increases as the number of payments received increases. Thus, an annuity is more valuable than a single payment when each annuity payment is as large as the single payment.

Comparison of D and E: Both D and E pay $300 over three years. Investment D is worth more than investment E, however, because a larger amount is received sooner from D than from E.

Define Terms and Concepts Defined in This Chapter

annuity (286)
future value (283)
present value (283)

Review Summary of Important Concepts

1. The future value of an investment is the amount the investment will be worth at some particular time in the future.
   a. The future value of an investment equals the present value times an interest factor that depends on the rate of interest earned on the investment and the number of periods it is invested.
   b. The future value of an annuity is the future value of a series of equal amounts paid at equal intervals.

2. The present value of an investment is the amount the investment is worth at the beginning of an investment period.
   a. The present value of an investment equals the future value times an interest factor. The interest factor for the present value is the reciprocal of the interest factor for the future value: interest factor for PV = 1 ÷ interest factor for FV.
   b. The present value of an annuity is the present value of a series of equal amounts paid at equal intervals.

3. Loan payments are determined from the present value of the loan (the amount borrowed) and the interest factor (interest rate and time period).
   a. A loan amortization table is useful for determining the amount of interest incurred, the amount of principal repaid each period on the loan, and the amount owed at the end of each period.
   b. A loan amortization table provides a basis for transactions recorded by the borrower and lender.

4. Future and present value calculations may involve a series of unequal payments or a combination of an annuity and a single amount.

5. Three factors important for calculating any future or present value are the amount of the payments, the interest rate, and the time periods when payments are made.

Questions

Q8-1 *Obj. 1* A friend remarks, "I just got out of an accounting lecture about future value and present value. Frankly, I don't have a clue what the professor was talking about. And we have a quiz on Wednesday. Help!" Come to your friend's rescue. Clearly and concisely explain what is meant by the terms *future value* and *present value*.

Q8-2 *Obj. 1* What does this statement mean? "The future value of $1,000 is an amount greater than $1,000."

Q8-3 *Obj. 1* Why is the present value of $10,000 less than $10,000?

Q8-4 *Obj. 2* You are inspecting Table 1 at the back of this book. At the intersection of the 10% column and the 18-period row you find the following number: 5.55992. Interpret that number. What does it mean?

Q8-5 *Obj. 2* Freida invested $3,000 in an investment plan that guarantees 7% compound interest annually. The interest is deposited into the account at the end of each year. The account has now been open 30 years. As the years went by, were the earnings from interest in any given year larger than the year before, smaller than the year before, or the same as the year before? Explain the reason for your answer.

Q8-6 *Obj. 2* Why do the interest factors in Table 1 (at the back of this book) get larger and larger as you move from the upper left corner of the table to the lower right corner?

Q8-7 *Obj. 2* Your boss has asked you what the ending balance will be if he puts $8,000 into an investment earning 9% interest compounded annually. He plans to leave the money untouched for 29 years. Unfortunately, you only have your accounting textbook available to help you and you find that Table 1 (inside the front cover) only goes up through 25 periods. How can you solve this problem using only Table 1? What will be the ending amount in the account?

Q8-8 *Obj. 3* Kelly Walker places 5% of her salary each year into a company-sponsored 401k retirement plan. Assume her annual salary is $100,000 and deposits are made to the retirement plan at the end of each year. What will be the balance in her 401k account at the end of 25 years if she never receives a pay raise and the plan earns 11% per year?

Q8-9 *Obj. 3* You are inspecting Table 2 at the back of this book. At the intersection of the 6% column and the 13-period row you find the following number: 18.88214. Interpret that number. What does it mean?

Q8-10 *Obj. 4* Why do the interest factors in Table 3 (inside the back cover of this book) get smaller and smaller as you move from the upper left corner of the table to the lower right corner?

Q8-11 *Obj. 4* Your boss has asked you what amount she must invest today at 8% interest so that she will have $350,000 available to pay off a lump-sum debt that comes due in 32 years. In other words, what is the present value of $350,000 that must be paid in 32 years assuming an 8% rate? Unfortunately, you only have your accounting textbook available to help you and you find that Table 3 (inside the back cover) only goes up through 25 periods. How can you solve this problem using only Table 3? What is the present value?

Q8-12 *Obj. 5* Why do the interest factors in Table 4 (inside the back cover of this book) get smaller as you move from left to right, but larger as you move from top to bottom?

Q8-13 *Obj. 5* Jeraldo invested $4,100 into a financial instrument that promised to pay him $1,000 at the end of each year for the next five years. The salesperson explained that this would earn for him a 5% rate of return. At the end of five years, Jeraldo noticed that the dollar amount of his interest earnings had been smaller and smaller as the years went by. Explain why this happened.

Q8-14 *Obj. 6* Determine whether the rows in Tables 1 through 4 (at the back of your textbook) are labeled in years or in periods. Does it make a difference whether they are labeled in years or periods? Why?

Q8-15 *Obj. 6* Imelda is making equal-sized monthly payments of $288 on her car loan. She has only 18 payments left. Each month, the portion of her payment that goes to pay interest and the portion that goes to repay principal is different. Why? Is there any pattern to this change in portions? Explain why or why not.

Exercises

E8-1 Write a short definition for each of the terms listed in the *Terms and Concepts Defined in this Chapter* section.

E8-2 *Obj. 2* Assume that you borrow $25,000 on April 1, 2007, at an annual rate of 7%. How much will you owe on March 31, 2008 if you make no payments until that date? How much will you owe on March 31, 2009 if you make no payments until that date? If you pay the interest incurred for

(Continued)

the first year on March 31, 2008, how much will you owe on March 31, 2009 if you make no other payments until that date?

E8-3 *Obj. 2* Today is Gary's 40th birthday. He is experiencing a midlife crisis and is thinking about retirement for the first time. To supplement his expected retirement pension, he deposits $10,000 in an investment account guaranteed to return him 6% interest annually.

a. What balance will he have in this account on his 65th birthday?
b. How much interest will he earn between now and then?

E8-4 *Obj. 3* Paul G. is saving for a once-in-a-lifetime trip, to begin seven years from today. He plans to visit the South Pacific and Far East. Today he starts his savings plan; he will deposit $2,000 at the end of each of the next seven years into a 5% savings account.

a. What amount will he have in his account when he begins his trip?
b. What amount of the total will be from his own deposits and what amount will he have earned in interest?

E8-5 *Obj. 3* Optimism Inc. anticipates the need for factory expansion four years from today. The firm has determined that it will have the necessary funds for expansion if it puts $400,000 per year into a stock portfolio expected to earn 9% per year. Deposits will be made at the end of each year.

a. How much is the company planning to raise toward factory expansion with this plan?
b. What amount would the company expect to raise if it could invest $400,000 per year for seven years?
c. Why is the answer to part b more than twice as large as the answer to part a even though the length of the annuity is less than twice as long?

E8-6 *Obj. 3* Use an Excel spreadsheet and the FV function to determine the following:

a. The future value of a $2,000 annuity for 30 years at 8% compounded annually.
b. The future value of a $2,000 annuity for 30 years at 8% compounded semiannually.
c. The future value of a $2,000 annuity for 30 years at 8% compounded quarterly.
d. How much extra interest is earned on the annuity above simply by changing the compounding period from annually to quarterly?
e. How much extra interest would be earned by changing from annual compounding to daily compounding?
f. Louisa set up an individual retirement account (IRA account) on her 35th birthday. She contributed $2,000 to the account on each subsequent birthday through her 65th. The account earned 8% compounded annually. What amount of interest (in dollars) will she have earned on this investment?
g. Suppose she had started the IRA account 10 years earlier when she was 25 years old. How much additional interest would she have earned on this investment by age 65? (Hint: Her first payment into the account was on which birthday?)

E8-7 *Obj. 4* Assume you will receive $1,000 at the end of year 1. What is its present value at the beginning of year 1 if you expect an 8% rate of return? What is the present value if you expect a 9% return? 10%? What can you conclude about the effect of the rate of return on the present value of cash to be received in the future?

E8-8 *Obj. 4* What is the present value of $800 to be received at the end of one year if it must provide a return of 8%? What is the present value of $900 to be received at the end of one year? $1,500? What can you conclude about the effect of the amount expected to be received on its present value?

E8-9 *Obj. 4* What is the present value of $1,000 to be received at the end of one year if it must provide a return of 5%? What is the present value of $1,000 to be received at the end of two years? Three years? What can you conclude about the effect of time until receipt on the present value of future cash inflows?

E8-10 *Obj. 4* Assume that you received a loan on July 1, 2007. The lender charges annual interest at 6%. On June 30, 2012, you owe the lender $802.93. Assuming that you made no payments for principal or interest on the loan during the five years, how much did you borrow?

E8-11 *Obj. 5* You just won last night's lotto drawing for the $1,000,000 prize. It will be paid to you in 20 installments of $50,000 each. You will receive the first payment today and receive an additional

$50,000 payment at the end of each of the next 19 years. What is the present value of your winnings if 7 1/2% is the appropriate rate? Use an Excel spreadsheet and the PV function to determine the solution. (Hint: What is the present value of the amount you received today? How many periods long is the remaining annuity?)

E8-12 *Obj. 5* What is the present value of an annuity of $200 per year for five years if the required rate of return is 8%? What is the present value of the annuity if the required rate of return is 10%?

E8-13 *Obj. 5* A wealthy uncle has offered to give you either of two assets: (a) an asset that pays $500 at the end of three years or (b) an asset that pays $100 at the end of each year for five years. Assume that both assets earn a 7% annual rate of return. Which asset should you choose?

E8-14 *Obj. 5* Lincoln Corporation expanded recently by investing $100,000 in new business assets. This has increased annual operating cash inflows by $50,500 and annual operating cash outflows by $30,200. These increases are expected for a total of six years. At that time, these new assets will be obsolete and worthless. (Assume that operating cash inflows and outflows occur at the end of the year.)

a. If the corporation requires a return of 8% on its investments, was this a wise investment decision? Show calculations to prove your answer.
b. If you decide that the company has not met its investment goals, what minimum annual net cash inflow over the six-year period would give the desired rate of return?
c. Assuming that operating cash outflows do not change, what is the necessary increase in operating cash inflows that is needed to earn an 8% return?

E8-15 *Objs. 2, 5* Katina Washington is currently employed as a computer programmer by Megatel Company. Her dream, however, is to start her own computer software firm. To provide cash to start her own business in six years she will invest $10,000 today. She thinks the investment will earn a 12% annual return.

a. How much would Katina have in her account at the end of six years if she earns 12% on the investment? How much of this would be interest earned during the six years?
b. Assume, instead, that Katina has decided she needs $20,000 to begin business. She wants to invest equal amounts at the end of each year for the next six years to accumulate the $20,000 needed at that time.
   i. How much must be invested each year, assuming that it earns 12% interest?
   ii. How much will the investment be worth at the end of each of the next six years?
   iii. How much will Katina have put into the account over the six years?
   iv. How much interest will be earned over the six years?

E8-16 *Objs. 4, 5* I. M. Cansado is about to retire. He has a retirement account that allows two payment options. Under Option 1, he can choose to receive $140,000 at the end of six years. Under Option 2, he can choose to receive $20,000 at the end of each year for six years. An interest rate of 10% is applicable to both plans. (a) Which retirement plan has the highest present value at the beginning of the six-year period? (b) Which option would you recommend?

E8-17 *Objs. 2, 3, 4, 5* Complete the tables and answer the questions.

a.

Single Sum	Rate	Time	Compounding Frequency	Interest Factor	Future Value
$1,000	12%	2 years	Annual	______	______
$1,000	12%	2 years	Semiannual	______	______
$1,000	12%	2 years	Quarterly	______	______
$1,000	12%	2 years	Monthly	______	______

b. Summarize the effect of changing the compounding period on the future value of a single sum. Explain why this effect appears reasonable.
c. What effect do you think that changing the compounding period of an annuity would have on its future value? Explain why you think this.

(Continued)

d.

Single Sum	Rate	Time	Compounding Frequency	Interest Factor	Present Value
$1,000	12%	2 years	Annual	______	______
$1,000	12%	2 years	Semiannual	______	______
$1,000	12%	2 years	Quarterly	______	______
$1,000	12%	2 years	Monthly	______	______

e. Summarize the effect of changing the compounding period on the present value of a single sum. Explain why this effect appears reasonable.

f. What effect do you think that changing the compounding period of an annuity would have on its present value? Explain why you think this.

E8-18 *Obj. 6* An investment is expected to pay a return of $100 per year. The interest rate for the investment is 7%. What will the price of the investment be if it has a life of 5 years? 10 years? 20 years?

E8-19 *Obj. 6* What is the present value of an investment that pays $80 at the end of each year for 10 years and pays an additional $1,000 at the end of the tenth year if the required rate of return is 7%? 8%? 9%?

E8-20 *Obj. 6* An investment has a life of 10 years. The rate of return for the investment is 8%. What will the price of the investment be if it is expected to pay a return of $10 per year? $100 per year?

E8-21 *Obj. 6* What is the maximum amount a company should pay for production equipment that it expects will increase net income and cash flow by $300,000 per year for five years? The company requires a 12% return on its investment.

E8-22 *Obj. 6* Old Money Company borrowed $1 million from a bank on January 1, 2007. The loan is to be repaid in annual installments over a three-year period. The bank requires a 9% return.

a. What is the amount of Old Money's required payment to the bank each year?
b. How much interest expense will Old Money incur each year?
c. Show how this loan would be entered into Old Money's books on January 1, 2007.
d. Show how Old Money's first annual installment payment would be entered into its books. Use the format below for parts C and D.

		Assets		=	Liabilities	+	Owners' Equity	
Date	Accounts	Cash	Other Assets				Contributed Capital	Retained Earnings

E8-23 *Obj. 6* Nora Santos negotiated a three-year, 9%, $46,000 loan from her bank. It called for three equal-sized year-end payments.

a. Determine the amount of her payment each year (round to the nearest dollar).
b. Show how the loan, and each of the three payments, would be entered into her accounting system (round each amount to the nearest dollar). Use the format shown below.

		Assets		=	Liabilities	+	Owners' Equity	
Date	Accounts	Cash	Other Assets				Contributed Capital	Retained Earnings

E8-24
Objs. 4, 5, 6

a. Calculate each of the following:
   i. The present value of \$300 to be received at the end of three years if invested at 6%.
   ii. The present value of \$300 to be received at the end of four years if invested at 6%.
   iii. The present value of \$300 to be received at the end of four years if invested at 5%.
   iv. The present value of \$300 to be received at the end of each year for four years if invested at 6%.
   v. The present value of \$100 to be received at the end of one year, \$200 to be received at the end of two years, \$300 to be received at the end of three years, and \$600 to be received at the end of four years at 6%.

b. Inspect your results. What do they suggest to you about the effect of time periods and interest rates on the present value of amounts to be received in the future?

E8-25
Objs. 3, 5, 6

Use an Excel spreadsheet and the FV, PV, and PMT functions to determine the amount of each of the following. R = the annual interest rate and t = number of years. When there are multiple cash flows per year, the amount of the annuity shown below is the amount of each individual cash flow (not the total cash flow for the year). Round all answers to the nearest dollar.

a. Present value of a \$500 annuity when $R = 11\%$ compounded annually and $t = 18$
b. Future value of a \$2,400 annuity when $R = 5\%$ compounded annually and $t = 25$
c. Future value of a \$950 annuity when $R = 12.8\%$ compounded semiannually and $t = 15$
d. The annual annuity payment that will provide \$13,400 in eight years when $R = 9\%$ compounded annually
e. Present value of a \$10,000 annuity when $R = 8\%$ compounded quarterly and $t = 10$
f. Future value of a \$238 annuity when $R = 7\%$ compounded annually and $t = 16$
g. Present value of a \$1,000 annuity when $R = 6\frac{3}{8}\%$ compounded annually and $t = 3$
h. Present value of a \$700 annuity when $R = 10\%$ compounded semiannually and $t = 11$
i. The semiannual annuity payment that will pay off, over six years, a \$9,860 debt owed today if $R = 13\%$
j. Future value of a \$1 annuity when $R = 8\%$ compounded annually and $t = 200$

Problems

P8-1 **COMPUTING FUTURE VALUE**
Objs. 2, 3

Michael just graduated from college and has his first job. His salary is that of an entry-level employee, so he has to budget his money carefully. However, he does understand the need to save money for the future.

Required

A. Assume that he deposits \$600 at the end of each year for 10 years into an investment account earning 7%. He then stops making deposits and uses the money instead for house and car payments. How much will be in the investment account at the end of the 10-year period?
B. Assume Michael decides to keep the investment but does not make any additional contributions. How much will be in the account when he retires, after working for another 25 years?
C. Assume that Michael does not begin saving until he has worked for 20 years. If he plans to retire in 15 years from that time, how much would he have to invest at the end of each year, in an account earning 7%, to equal the balance in the account in part B?
D. Calculate the total amount of cash that Michael would pay in under parts A and B combined and the amount he would pay in under part C. Why is there a difference?

P8-2 **COMPUTING FUTURE VALUE**
Obj. 3

Stevie Gordon, age 40, is evaluating several supplemental retirement annuity plans offered by her employer. In general, all the plans call for Stevie to make annual contributions, some of which will be partially matched by the employer. The two plans drawing most of her attention are as follows. Plan 1 requires \$3,000 annual end-of-year contributions by Stevie; the employer will match 20% of Stevie's contribution each year; and the plan guarantees an 8% overall return. Plan 2 requires \$2,500 annual end-of-year contributions by Stevie; the employer will match 85% of Stevie's contribution; and the plan guarantees a 6% overall return.

(Continued)

Required Which option has the higher expected future value when Stevie reaches age 65? Which option would you recommend to Stevie? Why?

P8-3 THE POWER OF COMPOUND INTEREST
Obj. 3

Prudence and Margo are identical twins. Early on, it became clear that Prudence was a bit of a plodder whereas Margo was the fun-loving, carefree type. At age 15, both started working regularly after school. Prudence became a saver while Margo specialized in stimulating the economy with immediate purchases. Following her grumpy old grandfather's advice, Prudence began making annual contributions of $2,000 to an IRA (individual retirement account) on her 16th birthday. Margo's response to her grandfather's suggestion was "gimme a break."

Two strange events occurred, however, on their 23rd birthday. First, Prudence made her annual $2,000 IRA contribution, bringing her balance to $21,273.26. She never contributed again. Second, Margo promised to begin making $2,000 annual contributions to an IRA on her 26th birthday. She kept her promise and continued through her 65th birthday, which is today. Tomorrow, each will begin making withdrawals from their IRAs, which have been earning an 8% return.

Required

A. How much cash did Prudence contribute to her IRA over the years? How much cash did Margo contribute?
B. What is the balance in Prudence's IRA account today? (Hint: The interest factor for the future value of a single sum for 42 periods at 8% is 25.33948.)
C. What is the balance in Margo's IRA account today? (Hint: The interest factor for the future value of an ordinary annuity for 40 periods at 8% is 259.05652.)
D. Suppose Prudence had never stopped making contributions to her IRA. What would be her account balance today? (Hint: The interest factor for the future value of an ordinary annuity for 50 periods at 8% is 573.77016.)
E. What lesson does this suggest about the power of compound interest?

P8-4 USING TIME VALUE TECHNIQUES IN RETIREMENT PLANNING
Objs. 3, 4

Starla has decided to retire in 12 years. She has $44,400 available today and wants to invest the money to supplement her pension plan.

Required

A. Assume Starla wants to accumulate $100,000 by her retirement date. Will she achieve her goal if she invests $44,400 today and earns 7%?
B. If Starla invests a total of $44,400 through a series of 12 equal annual installments instead of a single amount, would Starla accumulate the desired $100,000? The first investment would be made one year from today. Show calculations and explain what you find.
C. If the amount accumulated in part A does not equal $100,000, approximately how many years would be required, assuming the same interest rate and equal annual deposits as above.

P8-5 COMPUTING PRESENT VALUE
Objs. 4, 5

Hal Green plans to choose one of three investments. Investment A pays $1,000 at the end of each year for four years. Investment B pays $4,500 at the end of four years. Investment C pays $600 at the end of each year for three years and pays $2,400 at the end of the fourth year. Hal requires a return of 8% on each of these investments.

Required Provide information to help Hal decide how much he should pay for each of these investments.

P8-6 ANNUITY DEPOSITS AT THE BEGINNING OF PERIODS VERSUS DEPOSITS AT THE END
Objs. 2, 3

Laura has decided to set up an IRA (Individual Retirement Account) in which she will make a deposit to her plan at the end of each year, beginning one year from today. She expects to earn 9% on her investment, over a period of 10 years.

Required

A. If she invests the maximum amount of $3,000 at the end of each of the 10 years, how much will she have accumulated after 10 years? How much of this will be interest?
B. Assume the same facts as stated previously, except that Laura plans to make her deposit for each of the 10 years beginning today. How much will she have accumulated 10 years from today? (Hint: You do not have a table in the text for this type of annuity. But you can compute the future value of each deposit separately and add the totals together.) How much of the ending account balance will be composed of interest?
C. Refer to the answers for parts A and B. Which one is larger? Why? Explain.

P8-7 USING TIME VALUE TO DETERMINE A COMPANY'S PENSION LIABILITY

Objs. 4, 5

Cellex Manufacturing is a family-owned company preparing its year-end 2007 financial statements. The firm will follow generally accepted accounting principles for the first time. Therefore, it is required to record, for the first time, a long-term liability for its employee pension plan. Employees who retire from the company will be paid $10,000 at the end of each year following retirement for five years. Below is the number of employees expected to receive benefits and their projected retirement dates:

1. Ten employees retiring at the end of 2011
2. Twenty employees retiring at the end of 2016
3. Thirty employees retiring at the end of 2021

Required

A. If all employees retire when scheduled and receive their full expected retirement benefits, what total amount of cash will this require?
B. If the applicable interest rate is 7%, what is the amount of the liability that should be recorded for 2007? (Hint: Calculate the solution in two steps. First, calculate the present value of a five-year annuity for each of the three employee groups. Second, calculate the present value of those three amounts based on the number of years until each annuity begins.)
C. Using the format presented in the chapter, show how the liability would be recorded in the accounting system.

P8-8 USING SPREADSHEET FUNCTIONS IN A CAR BUYING DECISION

Objs. 4, 5

Ricardo recently received a major promotion at work and a significant raise. He is shopping for a new car. He really likes large sport utility vehicles and has his eye on one priced at $35,000. He is not sure how to finance the vehicle, however. He has three choices.

1. The dealer has offered to finance the vehicle with zero down on a six-year, 14% loan.
2. A local bank will finance the vehicle for five years at 10% if he makes a 15% down payment.
3. His credit union will finance the vehicle for four years at 8% if he makes a 25% down payment.

Under all three options, equal-sized end-of-the-month payments are required. Ricardo has the cash available for a down payment but was hoping to use it for other purposes.

Required Use the Excel PMT function to help you answer the following questions.

A. For each financing alternative, identify the rate, number of periods, and amount that you must enter into the PMT function.
B. What is the size of the monthly payment under each alternative?
C. Based only on your answers to parts A and B, which option looks best to you?
D. What is the sum of the payments required under each financing option?
E. What total amount of interest will be paid under each financing option?
F. Based on the information available, which financing option would you recommend to Ricardo?

P8-9 REFINANCING DECISIONS
Obj. 6

The Taylors are considering refinancing the loan on their home. Currently, they have a 30-year loan with an 8% annual interest rate. The original loan was for $250,000, but over three years the Taylors have reduced the loan balance to $243,200. A local bank has offered them a 15-year loan with a 6.5% annual interest rate. The bank will charge a 1% fee of $2,432 ($0.01 \times \$243,200 = \$2,432$) to prepare the paperwork associated with the new loan. The fee will be added to the existing loan balance if the Taylors refinance.

Required

A. Using a spreadsheet program such as Excel, determine the Taylors' existing monthly payment. Next, multiply their payment times the number of months remaining on the loan to determine the total amount of payments remaining.
B. Determine the monthly payment if the Taylors refinance their loan.
C. What will be the total amount the Taylors will pay the bank over the life of the loan if they refinance?
D. What advice would you give the Taylors?

P8-10 REPAYING A NOTE
Obj. 6

Georgia Company borrowed $600,000 from a bank on May 1, 2007. The bank required a return of 12% on the loan. The loan is to be repaid over 12 months in equal installments. Georgia Company's fiscal year ends on December 31.

Required

A. Prepare an amortization table for the loan for the 12-month period.
B. How much interest expense would Georgia report on the loan for its 2007 fiscal year?
C. How much interest expense would it report for 2008?
D. What amount of liability would Georgia report for the loan at the end of 2007?
E. What amount would it report at the end of 2008?

P8-11 UNDERSTANDING AN AMORTIZATION TABLE
Obj. 6

On January 1, Waldman Enterprises purchased machinery on credit by signing a note payable for the full purchase price. The note payable called for interest to be paid on the unpaid balance and required three equal end-of-year payments. Waldman's accounting staff prepared the following amortization table related to the note:

Year	Balance at Beginning of Year	Interest Expense	End-of-Year Payment	Balance at End of Year
1	$2,577.10	$206.17	1,000.00	?
2	1,783.27	142.66	1,000.00	?
3	925.93	74.07	1,000.00	?

Required

A. What was the purchase price of the machinery?
B. What was the interest rate called for by the note?
C. By what amount was the principal balance of the note reduced during the first year?
D. What amount will be reported on Waldman's year 2 income statement regarding this note? What will it be labeled?
E. What amount will be reported on Waldman's year 3 statement of cash flows regarding this note?
F. What amount will be reported on Waldman's year 1 balance sheet regarding this note? In what section and under what title will it be reported?

P8-12 PREPARATION OF AN AMORTIZATION TABLE
Obj. 6

Becky is the owner of Brookstone Farm. On January 1, 2007, the beginning of the company's fiscal year, Becky borrowed $750,000 at 5% annual interest to purchase equipment. The loan is to be repaid over six years in equal annual installments. (Round each amount to the nearest dollar.)

Required

A. What is the amount of Becky's loan payment each year?
B. Prepare an amortization table for the loan.
C. What will be the amount of interest expense reported by Brookstone Farm for the loan in 2007 and in 2008?

P8-13 ENTERING LOAN DATA INTO THE ACCOUNTING SYSTEM

Obj. 6

Turn Buckle Company financed new equipment costing $50,000 with a five-year loan from a local bank. The bank charged 11% interest on the note. (Round each amount to the nearest dollar.)

Required

A. What would Turn Buckle's annual payments be to the bank each year, assuming that the note and interest are paid in equal annual installments?
B. How much interest expense would the company record for the first year of the note and for the second year?
C. Using the format presented in the chapter, show how the first and second year-end loan payments would be recorded in the accounting system.

P8-14 CALCULATION OF NOTES PAYABLE

Obj. 6

You have decided to purchase a car. You have found a clean used car that will cost you $8,500. You can finance your purchase through the dealer at an annual rate of 12% for 24 months. The dealer requires a down payment of $2,000.

Required

A. What will be the amount of your monthly payments?
B. How much will you pay the dealer over the life of the loan?
C. How much of this amount will be interest?
D. If you decide to pay off the loan at the end of the first year, how much will you owe the dealer?

P8-15 RECONSTRUCTING FACTS FROM PARTIAL INFORMATION

Obj. 6

Mezzelano Company was involved in a transaction in which a three-year note was exchanged. The note requires equal year-end payments. The accounting department prepared the following amortization table and sent you a copy. All amounts were rounded to the nearest dollar. Unfortunately, the copy machine malfunctioned, and none of the column headings are readable on your copy.

(i)	(ii)	(iii)	(iv)	(v)	(vi)
1	130,000	10,400	50,444	40,044	89,956
2	89,956	7,196	50,444	43,248	46,708
3	46,708	3,737	50,444	46,708	-0-

Required

A. Identify each of the missing column headings. Explain why each one must be as you identified it.
B. What is the principal amount of the note?
C. What is the interest rate of the note?
D. Is this an amortization table for a note receivable or a note payable? How can you tell? Discuss.
E. At the end of year 2, what amount from this table will be reported on the income statement?
F. At the end of year 2, what amount from this table will be reported on the balance sheet?
G. At the end of year 2, what total amount from this table will be reported on the statement of cash flows (direct approach)?

P8-16 COMBINING TWO ANNUITIES OF DIFFERENT SIZE

Obj. 6

The Faithful Servants Church has started a building fund. Annual end-of-year deposits of $4,000 will begin at the end of the current calendar year. The accumulating balance will earn 6% compound interest per year. The $4,000 deposits are expected to be made for eight years and then increased to $7,000 for four additional years.

Required

A. What balance will be in the fund immediately after the 12th deposit is made?
B. If no further deposits are made, and the balance is left to earn interest for 10 more years, what amount will be in the account?
C. What amount of interest revenue will be earned by the building fund up to the date of the 12th deposit?

P8-17 COMPUTING WITHDRAWALS FROM AN ANNUITY

Objs. 5, 6

Kwana Lovejoy received a cash gift of $30,000 from his grandfather exactly one year before he planned to start college. The gift was to be used to help pay Kwana's tuition and so it was deposited into an investment account earning 7% per year. The plan is for Kwana to withdraw equal annual amounts for each of four years so that at the end of that time, there will be a zero balance in the account and he will have completed his undergraduate degree.

Required

A. Given the above conditions, how much should Kwana withdraw at the beginning of each of his four college years?
B. What total amount of interest will the investment earn over the four years?
C. Assume that Kwana's grandfather agrees to allow him to withdraw a total of $12,000 at the beginning of his first year of college. (This will allow Kwana to pay his tuition and to buy a cheap used car.) What equal annual withdrawals can Kwana then make for the remaining three years of college?

P8-18 THE EFFECT OF INTEREST RATE ON COST OF AN INVESTMENT

Objs. 5, 6

Milo is considering an investment that will pay him $1,050 at the end of each year for seven years and then will pay a lump sum of $15,000 at the end of that time.

Required

A. If Milo requires his investments to earn 9% interest, what is the maximum amount he should pay for the investment at the beginning of the seven-year period?
B. Assume Milo requires his investment to earn 5% interest. What is the maximum amount he should pay for the investment described in part A?
C. Which investment will cost Milo the greater amount? Why is there a difference in the costs?

P8-19 USING SPREADSHEET FUNCTIONS IN A HOME-BUYING DECISION

Objs. 5, 6

Pauline is about to make an offer to buy a home. The list price is $235,000 but Pauline will make an offer of $209,500. She plans to make a $21,500 down payment with the balance financed with a 30-year mortgage at 8.4% annual interest. Pauline wonders what her monthly "principal and interest" payment would be under these circumstances. Use an Excel spreadsheet (and the PMT function) to help you answer the questions below.

Required

A. What is the interest rate that should be entered into the PMT function?
B. What is the number of periods that should be entered into the PMT function?
C. What is the amount that should be entered into the PMT function?
D. What is the amount of Pauline's monthly "principal and interest" payment?
E. When Pauline makes her first payment, what amount will go to pay interest and what amount will be repayment of principal? (Hint: What amount did she owe during the first month and what rate of interest did she incur during the month?)

F. Suppose Pauline decides to obtain a 15-year mortgage instead and that the annual rate is 8%. What will be the amount of her monthly payment?
G. How much interest will Pauline avoid paying if she takes the 15-year mortgage instead of the 30-year mortgage?

P8-20 ETHICS IN FINANCING ALTERNATIVES

Obj. 5 Bob and Lisa must replace their old car as soon as possible. They have found a new one that meets their needs and have negotiated a price of $24,500 with the dealer. The couple wishes to buy the car by making a down payment of $2,000 and borrowing the remaining $22,500. The dealer offered to finance their purchase with terms as follows:

Loan period	36 months
Annual interest rate	6%
Down payment	$2,000
Loan amount	$22,500
Monthly payment	$684.49

Bob and Lisa were shocked by the amount of the monthly payment. The dealer told them not to worry because he could adjust the terms of the loan to fit their budget. Bob and Lisa would agree to buy the car if the payment is no more than $500 per month.

The dealer disappeared for a while and returned bearing good news. By increasing the loan period to 60 months, the payment would be only $500 per month. The dealer presented the facts as follows:

Loan period	60 months
Annual interest rate	6%
Down payment	$2,000
Monthly payment	$500

Bob and Lisa were delighted. They found the perfect car that also fit their budget.

Required

A. Determine the sales price by calculating the present value of the payments using a spreadsheet program. [Hint, determine the present value of the *monthly* payments using a term of 60 periods (60 months = 5 years × 12 months) and the *monthly* interest rate by dividing the annual interest rate of 6% by 12 months (0.06 ÷ 12)].
B. Is the dealer's behavior ethical?
C. Many types of goods are sold by salespersons who explain that the monthly payment is *only* a certain amount each month. Explain how an understanding of present value techniques can help consumers determine whether such a sales pitch is a fair deal.

P8-21 EXCEL IN ACTION

In December 2007, Millie and Milo Wermz decided to purchase the property they had been renting for The Book Wermz. The cost of the building was $120,000 and the cost of the land was $60,000. A local bank agreed to lend $160,000 toward the purchase price in exchange for a mortgage on the property. The loan is to be repaid in equal monthly installments over 30 years beginning in January 2008. Interest on the loan is 8% and is fixed over the term of the loan.

Required

A. Determine the monthly payments on the loan using a spreadsheet. Enter the following captions in cells A1 to A4: Principal, Period, Interest Rate, Payment. In cell B1, enter "160000", the amount borrowed. In cell B2, calculate the number of months over which the loan will be repaid (=30*12). In cell B3, calculate the monthly interest rate on the loan (=0.08/12). In cell B4, use a function to calculate the payment amount. Click on the Function f_x button, select Financial from the Category list, and select PMT from the list of functions. Click the OK button. In the dialog box, enter B3 for rate, B2 for nper, and B1 for pv. (You can move the box by clicking and dragging it so that the data you entered in the spreadsheet are visible.) nper is the number of periods and pv is the present value of the loan (the amount borrowed). Leave the fv and type boxes blank, and

(Continued)

click on the OK button. Cell B4 contains the monthly payment amount as a negative number because it is a cash outflow. Make this number positive by clicking on cell B4 and changing the formula to read =PMT(B3,B2,B1)*(−1). You can make this change in the formula bar just above the column headers and then click the green checkmark.

Beginning in cell A6, prepare an amortization table for the first year of the loan. Enter captions in row 6 like those in Exhibit 5 of this chapter. Center the captions, use text wrapping, and make the captions bold.

Enter 1 through 12 in column A, beginning with cell A7.

In cell B7, reference the principal amount (=B1).

In cell C7, calculate the interest expense for the first month, the principal times the monthly interest rate (=B7*$B$3). Note that an absolute address should be provided for the interest rate ($B$3) because you will always reference this cell to determine the rate.

In cell D7, reference the amount paid (=$B$4). Again, use an absolute address.

In cell E7, calculate the principal paid (=C7–D7).

In cell F7, calculate the amount owed at the end of the month (=B7–E7).

In cell B8, reference the amount owed at the beginning of the second month (=F7).

Copy the contents of cells C7 through F7 to cells C8 through F8. Then copy the contents of cells B8 through F8 to the remaining rows to complete the monthly calculations.

In cell A19, enter "Total."

In cell C19, calculate the total interest expense for 2008 using the sum function.

In cell D19, calculate the total amount paid on the loan for 2008 using the sum function.

Format the numbers in the spreadsheet using the Comma button. Use single lines to separate captions from calculations in the amortization table. Use single lines before totals and double lines after totals.

B. How much does The Book Wermz owe the bank on December 31, 2008? What amount of interest expense is incurred the first year?

C. Suppose the Wermz's decided to repay the loan over 15 years instead of 30 years. What would be the monthly payment? Change the number of periods in cell B2 to 15 years (=15*12). What amount would be owed on December 31, 2008? What is the total interest incurred in the first year?

D. Suppose the interest rate charged by the bank was 9% over a 30-year repayment period. What effect would this rate have on the monthly payments and total interest for the first year?

P8-22 MULTIPLE-CHOICE OVERVIEW OF THE CHAPTER

1. For a given amount, interest rate, and number of years, which of the following will yield the highest number?
   a. Future value of a single sum
   b. Future value of an annuity
   c. Present value of a single sum
   d. Present value of an annuity

2. You have purchased an investment at a price of $1,500. It guarantees a 7% return, compounded annually, over its 10-year life. At the end of 10 years, your $1,500 will be returned to you plus all investment profit. Your investment revenue will be
   a. larger each year than the year before.
   b. smaller each year than the year before.
   c. equal each year to the year before.
   d. larger than the year before for the first five years and then smaller for the next five years.

3. The present value of an investment is $600. The investment earns a 7% annual rate of return. The investment consists of one payment made at the end of two years. The amount an investor should receive from the investment at the end of the second year would be
   a. $\$600 \div (1.07)^2$.
   b. $\$600 \times (1.07)^2$.
   c. $\$600 \times 1.07$.
   d. $\$600 \div 1.07$.

4. The present value of an investment that paid $500 at the end of three years and earned a 6% return would be
   a. $419.81.
   b. $471.70.
   c. $30.00.
   d. $470.00.

5. The present value of an investment that paid $100 at the end of each year for five years and earned a 6% return would be
   a. $470.00.
   b. $471.70.
   c. $373.63.
   d. $421.24.

6. A company borrowed $100,000 from a bank on July 1, 2007. The company made monthly payments of $5,235 on the note at the end of each month from July through December. Total interest expense on the note for this six-month period was $4,410. If this is the company's only note, what amount should the company report on its December 31, 2007 balance sheet for notes payable?
   a. $100,000
   b. $95,590
   c. $73,000
   d. $68,590

7. You are inspecting a present value table. As the interest rate increases, you should expect the table value to:
   a. increase.
   b. decrease.
   c. increase if it is a present value of a single sum table, but decrease if it is a present value of an annuity table.
   d. decrease if it is a present value of a single sum table, but increase if it is a present value of an annuity table.

8. A friend obtained a $7,500 car loan from a local bank at 9% interest. The loan requires 36 equal-sized monthly payments. The portion of the payment that goes to pay interest will
   a. increase each month.
   b. decrease each month.
   c. stay the same each month.
   d. decrease for the first 18 months and then increase during the last 18 months.

9. Clementine is part owner of a mining venture. A saver by nature, she puts part of her profits into a 6% savings account every other month. The first month she deposited $50. She has increased each of three subsequent deposits by $10. If she wants to forecast what the account balance will be after 10 months, she should use which of the following tables?
   a. Future value of a single sum
   b. Future value of an annuity
   c. Present value of a single sum
   d. Present value of an annuity

10. Assume that you borrowed $1,000 from a bank. The bank charges 12% interest and requires that the loan be repaid in 24 monthly installments. The interest expense you would incur for the first year would be:
    a. $120.
    b. more than $120.
    c. less than $120.
    d. less than interest expense for the second year.

Cases

C8-1 BORROWING COSTS

Obj. 6

Darren Driver is in the market for a new car. He has found a model he likes and has received prices from two dealers. The first dealer will charge $20,500 for the car. Darren will receive a rebate of $1,400 from the manufacturer, for a net price of $19,100. The dealer also will allow Darren $3,600 for his old car as a trade-in. The dealer will finance the purchase for four years at 12% per year. Interest and principal will be paid in four annual installments. The second dealer will charge $19,000 for the car after a $1,000 rebate. This dealer will allow $3,000 for the old car and will finance the purchase for four years at 10% per year, also payable in four annual installments.

Required Which is the better deal? Provide evidence to support your answer. (You are not required to prepare an amortization table.)

C8-2 PRINCIPAL AND INTEREST PAYMENTS

Obj. 6

Harold has decided to purchase a house. The price of the house is $80,000 after a down payment of $20,000. The bank will finance the purchase for 25 years at 9%. Alternatively, it will finance the house for 15 years at 8%. Under either option, the bank wants Harold to retire the loan by making a series of equal-sized year-end payments.

Required Evaluate the options for Harold. Write a memo to Harold (in good form) that explains how much total interest he will pay under each option and how much his total payments will be each year and over the life of the loan. Advise Harold about which choice he should take and the factors that are important in making the decision. (You do not have to prepare an amortization table.)

C8-3 EVALUATING CONTRACT PROPOSALS

Obj. 6

Fleet LaMont, a running back, was selected #1 in the recent draft of the National Football League. Fleet's agent and the team's general manager are locked in arduous negotiations. Each side has presented several proposals, but no agreement is in sight. All proposed contracts, except #6 below, are guaranteed. This means the contractual payments must be made even if Fleet is injured or cut from the team. Under contract proposal #6, all payments to Fleet may be cancelled by the team if Fleet is injured or cut. The average career in the NFL is less than four years. A brief summary of each proposal follows:

Contract Proposal	Sum of Cash Payments in Contract	Summary of Terms
1	$3,000,000	A three-year contract at $1 million per year payable quarterly starting on the date of signing the contract.
2	$4,000,000	A four-year contract at $1 million per year payable at the end of each completed year of the contract.
3	$2,900,000	A four-year contract with signing bonus of $900,000 (payable at signing) plus end-of-quarter salary payments of $125,000. The salary payments would begin three months after signing the contract.
4	$26,200,000	A three-year contract at $400,000 per year paid at each year-end plus a single $25 million payment to be paid 25 years after signing.
5	$2,500,000	A three-year contract with 2.5 million signing bonus and no salary payments.
6	$9,000,000	A six-year contract at $1,500,000 per year. Payable quarterly, cancelable if Fleet is injured or cut from the team.

Required Carefully evaluate each contract proposal. Fleet believes a 4% interest rate is appropriate for determining the present value of his contract offers. If you were Fleet, which contract would you accept? Write a memorandum to your agent explaining which contract you have chosen and the financial and nonfinancial reasons that support your decision. Be sure to include a discussion of why your choice is superior to each of the other alternatives.

© PHOTODISC/GETTY IMAGES

Financing Activities

9

WHAT ARE THE FUNDAMENTAL ACCOUNTING ISSUES ASSOCIATED WITH FINANCING ACTIVITIES?

As companies grow, they often need additional financial resources to pay for new assets. Successful companies frequently borrow from various sources and issue stock as a means of acquiring necessary financial resources. Maria and Stan have decided that it's time for Favorite Cookie Company to increase the size of its operations. Consequently, they need to understand various types of financing activities and how to account for these activities.

Food for Thought

What are the primary characteristics of debt and equity? How do these characteristics affect how we account for financing activities? Maria and Stan are considering these questions. The company has hired Ellen as a full-time accountant, and Maria and Stan are seeking her advice.

Stan: *To become a larger company, we need additional financing.*

Ellen: *Yes, and you need to understand how the financing will affect the company.*

Maria: *Financing provides additional money for us to use in the company.*

Ellen: *That's correct, but different types of financing involve different types of commitments and can affect your ability to control the company and make decisions in the future.*

Stan: *So, we need to understand how financing activities will affect our company.*

Ellen: *Yes, but first you need to understand some fundamental accounting issues associated with these activities.*

Maria: *We hired you to do that for us.*

Ellen: *True, but you need to understand these issues as well. They affect the company's cash flows and will affect your ability to raise additional funds in the future. To make decisions about how much debt and equity you want to issue, you need to understand how financing activities affect your company's balance sheet, income statement, and statement of cash flows.*

Objectives

Once you have completed this chapter, you should be able to:

1. Identify information that companies report about obligations to lenders and explain the transactions affecting long-term debt.
2. Describe appropriate accounting procedures for contingencies and commitments, including capital leases.
3. Identify information reported in the stockholders' equity section of a corporate balance sheet and distinguish contributed capital from retained earnings.
4. Explain transactions affecting stockholders' equity and describe how these transactions are reported in a company's financial statements.
5. Distinguish between preferred stock and common stock, and discuss why corporations may issue more than one type of stock.

TYPES OF OBLIGATIONS

Organizations engage in activities that obligate them to make future payments of cash or to provide goods or services. Most obligations are reported as liabilities on a company's balance sheet. Liabilities result from transactions with creditors, suppliers, customers, employees, and others.

An organization incurs debt when it borrows from creditors. For example, a company may borrow from a bank, another company, or an individual. The lender agrees to provide resources to the borrower. In exchange, the borrower signs a note (a contract), promising to repay the amount borrowed (the principal) plus interest.

In addition to contracting with creditors, organizations contract with suppliers, employees, and other providers of goods and services. Retail stores, for example, often acquire merchandise on credit from manufacturers and agree to pay for the goods in the near future. Companies also contract with their employees, exchanging wages for labor. Some compensation, such as retirement benefits, may be deferred to the future. Obligations to creditors, suppliers, and employees are all part of an organization's liabilities.

The term *liabilities* refers to an organization's obligations to deliver payments, goods, or services in the future. A liability links a past event (receiving something of value) and a future event (giving value back for what was received). **So, three attributes define a liability for an organization: (1) a present responsibility exists to transfer resources to another entity at some future time, (2) the organization cannot choose to avoid the transfer, and (3) the event creating the responsibility has already occurred.**[1]

Exhibit 1 presents the liabilities reported on the balance sheet of Favorite Cookie Company. The liabilities are like those of most companies. They include obligations to lenders (Notes Payable and Interest Payable), suppliers (Accounts Payable), employees (Wages Payable), and customers (Unearned Revenue).

Many of the liabilities reported by a company are associated with its operating activities. These liabilities result from transactions with suppliers, employees, and customers and involve resources used to produce and sell products. These obligations will be considered in a future chapter that examines operating activities. This chapter focuses on liabilities resulting from borrowing money from creditors.

[1] "Elements of Financial Statements," *FASB Statement of Financial Accounting Concepts*, no. 6 (1985).

EXHIBIT 1
Balance Sheet Presentation of Liabilities for Favorite Cookie Company

December 31,	2008	2007
Liabilities:		
Current liabilities:		
Accounts payable	$ 16,260	$ 9,610
Wages payable	3,590	
Unearned revenue	2,770	4,250
Interest payable	810	650
Notes payable, current portion	6,000	5,000
Total current liabilities	$ 29,430	$19,510
Notes payable, long-term	80,200	73,200
Total liabilities	$109,630	$92,710

DEBT OBLIGATIONS

Objective 1
Identify information that companies report about obligations to lenders and explain the transactions affecting long-term debt.

An organization's short-term and long-term borrowings are obligations to creditors. Typically, those obligations are a major portion of a company's liabilities. Debt is separated on a balance sheet into current- and long-term amounts (as in Exhibit 1).

Short-Term Debt

An organization has an obligation to repay short-term debt during the coming fiscal period. That debt consists of all obligations that mature during that time, including installments of long-term debt. For example, notes that will come due in 2008 are classified as current liabilities on the December 31, 2007 balance sheet.

Long-Term Debt

http://ingram.swlearning.com
Visit the text's web site to learn more about bonds.

Long-term debt includes **notes** and **bonds payable**. Notes and bonds payable are contracts between borrowers and creditors. In the contract, the borrower agrees to repay the amount borrowed at specified dates and agrees to pay specified amounts of interest.

A note usually is an agreement between a company and a financial institution that lends money to the company. A bond is debt in the form of a certificate in which the issuer (borrower) agrees to pay the maturity value of the bond at a predetermined date. Bonds often are marketable and are sold through brokers, like stock. Individuals, companies, and institutions can buy and sell bonds. Most corporate bonds have maturity values of $1,000 per bond. They can be sold to many individuals or organizations, permitting an issuer to borrow large amounts of money.

Some companies issue debt that is secured by specific assets, such as land, buildings, or equipment. These obligations are referred to as **secured debt** or **secured loans**. If a company does not have the cash to pay back secured debt when it comes due, the company must sell those assets pledged as security to pay the debt or transfer ownership of the assets to the creditor. Other types of debt are unsecured. For example, major corporations often issue **debentures**, which are unsecured bonds. If a company cannot repay this type of debt, it can be forced to liquidate (sell some or all of its noncash assets). In this situation, debentures and other unsecured debts are repaid from the sale of assets that are not pledged as security for secured debt. Therefore, secured debt typically is less risky than unsecured debt.

Debt can be issued with any maturity date. Most bonds mature in 10, 20, or 30 years from the date on which they are issued. In the notes of their financial reports, companies must disclose the maturity dates of their long-term debt and other relevant information.

CASE IN POINT

http://ingram.swlearning.com

Visit Procter & Gamble's home page to learn more about the company.

Disclosure of Long-Term Debt

The disclosure of long-term debt information communicates information that may be significant to a company's investors and creditors. Information about the expected debt payments for the next several years helps external entities determine the risk they may face if they lend the company money or buy its stock.

For example, **Procter & Gamble** reported the following information about its long-term debt in its 2004 annual report:

	June 30	
	2004	**2003**
Long-Term Debt		
6.60% USD note due December, 2004	**$ 1,000**	$ 1,000
4.00% USD note due April, 2005	**400**	400
5.75% EUR note due September, 2005	**1,827**	1,725
1.50% JPY note due December, 2005	**503**	459
3.50% CHF note due February, 2006	**240**	222
5.40% EUR note due August, 2006	**365**	—
4.75% USD note due June, 2007	**1,000**	1,000
6.13% USD note due May, 2008	**500**	500
4.30% USD note due August, 2008	**500**	500
3.50% USD note due December, 2008	**650**	—
6.88% USD note due September, 2009	**1,000**	1,000
2.00% JPY note due June, 2010	**458**	417
9.36% ESOP debentures due 2007–2021	**1,000**	1,000
4.85% USD note due December, 2015	**700**	—
8.00% USD note due September, 2024	**200**	200
6.45% USD note due January, 2026	**300**	300
6.25% GBP note due January, 2030	**906**	827
5.25% GBP note due January, 2033	**363**	331
5.50% USD note due February, 2034	**500**	—
Debt assumed by acquiring non-cash capital leases	**252**	146
All other long-term debt	**1,408**	2,541
Current portion of long-term debt	**(1,518)**	(1,093)
	12,554	11,475

Long-term weighted average interest rates were 4.0% and 3.7% as of June 30, 2004 and 2003, respectively, and included the effects of related interest rate swaps discussed in Note 7.

The fair value of the long-term debt was $13,168 and $12,396 at June 30, 2004 and 2003, respectively. Long-term debt maturities during the next five fiscal years are as follows: 2005—$1,518; 2006—$2,625; 2007—$1,433; 2008—$972; and 2009—$1,150. The Company has no material obligations that are secured.

Debt obligations have many different characteristics. Some require periodic interest and principal payments until the debt is repaid; others require principal repayment at the end of the debt's life. For example, most corporate bonds are repaid at the end of a fixed period, such as 10 years. But other bonds repay a portion of the principal each year over the life of the bond issue. Bond issues that require a portion of the bonds to be repaid each year are called **serial bonds**. They commonly are issued by governments.

A company can repurchase its own debt if it has enough cash and wants to reduce its liabilities. Or a company can repurchase its existing debt and replace (refinance) it with new debt. Refinancing becomes attractive when the general level of interest rates in the economy goes down. A company then can issue new debt at a lower rate of interest than its existing debt.

Some bonds require bondholders to resell the bonds to the issuing company at specific dates and prices if the issuer chooses to repurchase the bonds. **Callable bonds** are bonds that a company can reacquire after the bonds have been outstanding for a specific period. For example, a company might issue 30-year bonds that are callable after five years at 102% of maturity value. The 2% premium is compensation for calling the bonds.

When a company repurchases its debt, it may realize a gain or loss. For example, if debt is recorded on a company's books at $2,000,000, and the company repurchases the debt for $2,050,000, the company records a loss of $50,000. If, on the other hand, the repurchase price is less than the issuing price (book value) of the debt, the issuer would record a gain.

Learning Note - A gain increases net income, and a loss decreases it. The terms* gain *and* loss *are commonly used instead of* revenue *and* expense *for items that are not a primary part of a company's operating activities.

Debt Transactions

As an illustration of transactions involving issuing and repaying debt, assume that Favorite Cookie Company issued $20,000 of five-year bonds on January 1, 2008. The bonds pay $1,600 of interest (8% of $20,000) annually at the end of each year. The $20,000 is the amount the company will pay creditors at the end of the five-year period and is known as the **maturity value** or **face value** of the bonds. The annual interest paid on the debt (8%) is the **stated rate** of interest. Bonds often are sold to yield a return to creditors that is greater or less than the stated rate. For example, Favorite Cookie Company's bonds might be sold to give creditors a return of 9%. The actual rate of return earned by creditors is the **effective rate** of interest.

The effective rate of interest is determined by the amount creditors are willing to pay for the bonds and affects the amount of cash the company receives from its bonds when they are sold. A company may set the stated interest rate paid on debt it issues at any level it wishes. Suppose a company wants to borrow $100 for one year and agrees to pay $5 interest (5%) on the debt. A creditor agrees to loan $100 to the company but demands 8% interest. As shown in Exhibit 2, if the company agrees to this rate, the creditor can obtain an 8% return by lending the borrower $97.22 at the beginning of the year and receive $105 (the amount the borrower wants to pay) at the end of the year. The interest rate earned by the creditor is still 8% ($105 ÷ $97.22 = 1.08). In this alternative, the creditor **discounts** the amount of the loan (reduces the amount of the loan) by an amount sufficient to provide an 8% return.

EXHIBIT 2
Effective and Stated Rates of Interest

Rate borrower pays (stated rate)	5%
Rate lender demands (effective rate)	8%
Interest paid by borrower ($100 × 0.05)	$5.00
Amount lender pays borrower at beginning of year	$97.22
Amount borrower pays lender at end of year	$105.00
Interest earned by lender ($105.00 − $97.22)	$7.78
Interest rate earned by lender ($7.78 ÷ $97.22)	8%

This method is common for bonds and certain other types of debt issued by companies. The borrower determines the amount of interest paid, and creditors set the price

EXHIBIT 3
Example of the Relationship of Bond Cash Flows to Present Value

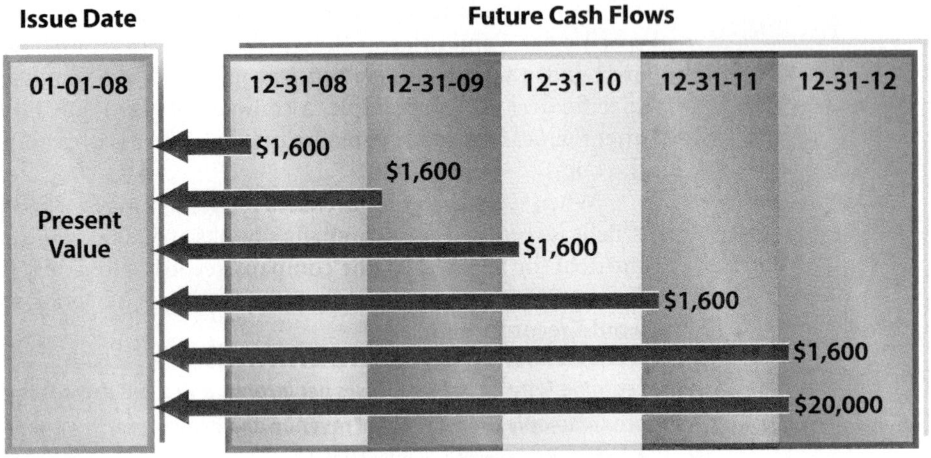

of the bonds to earn the interest rate they require. If a deal cannot be struck between the borrower and creditors, the borrower can look for other financing arrangements and the creditors can look for other investments.

To determine the amount received, we need to calculate the present value of the bonds, the amount they are worth at the time they are issued. The present value of a bond is the present value of the amounts the purchasers of the bonds (creditors) will receive over the life of the bonds. As illustrated in Exhibit 3, the purchasers of Favorite Cookie Company's bonds will receive five annual interest payments of $1,600 ($20,000 × 8%) plus $20,000 when the bonds mature. (See Chapter 8 for coverage of present value calculations.)

Therefore, the present value of the bonds is the present value of an annuity plus the present value of a single amount. We can use the present value tables (Table 3 and Table 4) to determine the present value of the bonds.

Let's assume the bonds will be sold to yield a 9% return to creditors. Therefore, we need to determine the present value of the interest that will be received by creditors plus the present value of the principal:

PV of bonds = PV of annuity + PV of single amount
PV of bonds = $1,600 × 3.88965 (5 periods, 9%) + $20,000 × 0.64993 (5 periods, 9%)
PV of bonds = $6,223 + $12,999
PV of bonds = $19,222

Thus, the amount Favorite Cookie Company will receive from selling the bonds is $19,222. Observe that the effective rate of interest (9%) is used to determine the interest factor for the present value calculation. Favorite Cookie Company receives *less than* maturity value for the bonds because the effective rate of interest (9%) on the bonds is higher than the stated rate (8%). When the effective rate is higher than the stated rate, bonds sell at a **discount**. Favorite Cookie Company's bonds sold at a discount of $778 ($20,000 − $19,222), or approximately 96% of maturity ($19,222 ÷ $20,000). When bonds sell at maturity value, they are said to sell at **par**. If they sell at less than maturity value, they are said to sell at a discount. The issue price often is stated as a percentage of par, such as 96% of par. If bonds sell at more than maturity value, they sell at a **premium**. We will consider a premium later in this section.

To determine transactions recorded for the bonds, we need to prepare an amortization table similar to that described in the previous chapter. Exhibit 4 provides an amortization table for Favorite Cookie Company's bonds.

EXHIBIT 4 Bond Amortization Table*

A Year	B Present Value at Beginning of Year	C Interest Incurred (Column B × Real Interest Rate)	D Amount Paid	E Amortization of Principal (Column C − Column D)	F Value at End of Year (Column B + Column E)
2008	19,222	1,730	1,600	130	19,352
2009	19,352	1,742	1,600	142	19,494
2010	19,494	1,754	1,600	154	19,648
2011	19,648	1,768	1,600	168	19,816
2012	19,816	1,783	1,600	183	20,000
Total		8,777	8,000	777	

USING EXCEL

Alternatively, we can use a spreadsheet to calculate the present value of the bonds. The annuity portion can be calculated using the PV function. In Excel, the function entered in a cell would be: =PV(0.09,5,−1600), where 0.09 is the effective interest rate, 5 is the number of periods, and −1600 is the amount of payment each period. Remember that the function uses a negative value for payments in computing the present value. This function returns a value of $6,223 (rounded to the nearest dollar) and is equivalent to the amount determined by using Table 4. The present value of the maturity value of $20,000 can be calculated in Excel by entering =20000/(1.09)^5, where 20000 is the maturity value, 1.09 is one plus the actual rate of interest, and 5 is the number of periods. This equation returns $12,999 (rounded to the nearest dollar), the same value as that calculated from Table 3. Adding the two values together ($6,223 + $12,999) results in the total present value of $19,222.

To prepare the table, we first determine the present value of the bonds. This amount is entered in column B for year 1. The interest expense on the bonds is the present value from column B times the real interest rate (9%). Consequently, the interest expense incurred by Favorite Cookie Company for the first year is $1,730 ($19,222 × 9%), shown in column C. The amount of interest Favorite Cookie Company pays each year is $1,600 (column D). The difference between the amount of interest expense (column C) and the amount of interest paid (column D) is the amortization of bond principal (column E). When bonds are issued at a discount, the amortization is added to the beginning-of-period present value to calculate the end-of-period value (column F). These calculations continue for each period. Observe that the value of the bonds at the end of the five-year period is their maturity value, the amount Favorite Cookie Company will repay in the fifth year.

The transactions associated with the bonds begin with their sale on January 1, 2008:

		Assets		=	Liabilities	+	Owners' Equity	
Date	Accounts	Cash	Other Assets				Contributed Capital	Retained Earnings
Jan. 1, 2008	Cash	19,222						
	Bonds Payable				19,222			

The amount of liability owed by Favorite Cookie Company when the bonds are issued is the amount received for the bonds.

At the end of the first year, Favorite Cookie Company records the interest paid and interest expense:

		Assets		=	Liabilities	+	Owners' Equity	
Date	Accounts	Cash	Other Assets				Contributed Capital	Retained Earnings
Dec. 31, 2008	Interest Expense							−1,730
	Bonds Payable				130			
	Cash	−1,600						

The difference between the cash paid and the interest expense is added to Bonds Payable when bonds are issued at a discount. The amount Favorite Cookie Company owes its creditors at the end of the first year is $19,352 ($19,222 + $130), as shown in Exhibit 4.

Favorite Cookie Company continues to record the interest payments and interest expense each year. In the fifth year, it records the final interest payment:

		Assets		=	Liabilities	+	Owners' Equity	
Date	Accounts	Cash	Other Assets				Contributed Capital	Retained Earnings
Dec. 31, 2012	Interest Expense							−1,783
	Bonds Payable				183			
	Cash	−1,600						

This transaction increases Bonds Payable to its maturity value of $20,000.

Then, Favorite Cookie Company pays creditors the maturity value of the bonds:

		Assets		=	Liabilities	+	Owners' Equity	
Date	Accounts	Cash	Other Assets				Contributed Capital	Retained Earnings
Dec. 31, 2012	Bonds Payable				−20,000			
	Cash	−20,000						

Over the life of the bonds, Favorite Cookie Company pays its creditors $28,000 ($20,000 maturity value + $8,000 interest payments). The amount the company received for the bonds was $19,222. Therefore, its total interest expense for the bonds was $8,778 ($28,000 − $19,222). This amount provided creditors with a 9% effective rate of return over the life of the bonds.

The information used in this example as a basis for transactions recorded by the issuer of debt also can be used for transactions involving the purchasers of the debt. If several creditors bought Favorite Cookie Company's bonds, the amounts recorded by each creditor would be a portion of the total. The totals for all the creditors would be the same as the amounts recorded by Favorite Cookie Company. Instead of recording interest expense and interest paid, the creditors would record interest revenue and interest

EXHIBIT 5 The Relationship between Effective and Stated Interest Rates

Interest Rate Comparison	Bonds Sell At	Relation between Interest and Amount Paid	Effect on Principal Each Period
Effective Rate > Stated Rate	Discount	Interest Expense > Amount Paid	Increase
Effective Rate = Stated Rate	Par	Interest Expense = Amount Paid	No Change
Effective Rate < Stated Rate	Premium	Interest Expense < Amount Paid	Decrease

received. Their cash outflow at the time of purchase would be $19,222, and the cash received at the end of the five-year period would be $20,000.

http://ingram.swlearning.com

Visit the text's web site to find out about getting online bond quote information.

When the effective rate of interest on debt is less than the stated rate, the debt is said to be issued at a **premium**. The borrower receives *more* for the bonds when they are sold than the maturity value of the bonds: The bonds sell at more than 100% of par. A premium *reduces* the interest expense on the debt each period. A portion of the amount paid by the borrower each period is a repayment of the amount borrowed, in addition to the payment of interest. The amount of principal amortized each period is *subtracted* from the beginning-of-period present value to calculate the end-of-period value in the amortization table. Self-Study Problem 1 illustrates transactions involving the sale of bonds at a premium.

If the effective and stated rates of interest are the same, bonds are sold at their maturity value (100% of par) and no premium or discount is recorded. Interest expense will equal interest paid each period. Exhibit 5 summarizes the relationships between effective and stated interest rates.

Self-Study Problem #1

Assume that instead of issuing its debt to yield an effective rate of 9%, Favorite Cookie Company issued the debt to yield an effective rate of 7%.

Required Using the information provided in the previous example as a guide:

A. Calculate the present value of the bonds at the time they are issued.

B. Prepare an amortization table.

C. Record transactions for Favorite Cookie Company for the first and fifth years.

The solution to Self-Study Problem 1 appears at the end of the chapter.

FINANCIAL REPORTING OF DEBT

A corporation's financial statements and accompanying notes provide much useful information. They help readers calculate the amount of debt a company has outstanding, and they also indicate changes in debt, the interest rates on debt, the interest expense during a given fiscal period, and current and future cash flows associated with existing debt and interest payments.

Exhibit 6 shows the items that would be reported on Favorite Cookie Company's financial statements at the end of each fiscal year during the life of the bonds described in the previous section. Amounts are from the amortization table in Exhibit 4.

The amount owed by Favorite Cookie Company to its creditors at the end of each year is reported on the balance sheet. At the end of the first three years, these amounts

EXHIBIT 6 Financial Statement Presentation of Debt Activities for Favorite Cookie Company

December 31,	2012	2011	2010	2009	2008
Balance sheet					
Liabilities:					
Current maturities of long-term debt	—	$19,816	—	—	—
Long-term debt	—	—	$19,648	$19,494	$ 19,352
Income statement					
Nonoperating expenses:					
Interest expense	$ 1,783	1,768	1,754	1,742	1,730
Statement of cash flows					
Cash flow from operating activities:					
Interest paid	(1,600)	(1,600)	(1,600)	(1,600)	(1,600)
Cash flow from financing activities:					
Long-term debt issued	—	—	—	—	19,222
Debt repaid	(20,000)	—	—	—	—

are reported as long-term debt. At the end of the fourth year, the amount owed is reported as a current liability because it will be repaid in the following fiscal year. At the end of the fifth year, the company reports no liability for these bonds because they have been repaid.

Interest expense, based on the effective rate of interest, is reported each year on the income statement. For most companies, interest expense is a nonoperating expense and is reported on the income statement after operating income.

The amount of interest paid is reported each year on the statement of cash flows as part of operating activities. If the indirect format of the statement is used, interest paid may not appear as a separate item on the statement of cash flows. In that case, the amount of interest paid usually is listed either at the bottom of the statement of cash flows (as supplemental data) or in the notes to the financial statements.

When debt is issued, the amount of cash received is reported on the statement of cash flows as cash from financing activities. When debt is repaid, the amount of cash paid is listed there as cash paid for financing activities.

OTHER OBLIGATIONS

Objective 2

Describe appropriate accounting procedures for contingencies and commitments, including capital leases.

Other types of obligations that involve financing activities also are reported on the balance sheet or in notes to the financial statements. Among those obligations are contingencies and commitments.

Contingencies

A *contingency* **is an existing condition that may result in an economic effect if a future event occurs.** GAAP require companies to report contingencies that could result in future obligations.

For most contingencies, a current obligation does not exist. If some future event occurs, however, an obligation might result. For example, suppose Favorite Cookie Company guarantees debt of one of its customers, Fair Price Foods. If Fair Price Foods is unable to make the loan payments, Favorite Cookie Company becomes liable for the payments. Favorite Cookie Company does not have a liability, however, unless Fair Price Foods is unable to pay.

Other common contingencies involve environmental costs and litigation. Government regulations in recent years have made companies contingently liable for costs associated with environmental cleanup and restoration if the companies are found not to have met regulatory requirements. Companies often face lawsuits associated with problems such as product defects and unfair treatment of employees. Until these suits are settled, a company is contingently liable for losses associated with the litigation.

Under certain circumstances, contingencies are reported as liabilities. **If a contingency probably will result in a loss, and the amount of the loss can be reasonably estimated, it should be included as a liability on a company's balance sheet.** Also, the amount of the expected loss is recognized on the income statement in computing net income.

CASE IN POINT

http://ingram.swlearning.com

Visit Procter & Gamble's home page to learn more about the company.

Disclosure of Contingencies

In its 2004 annual report, Procter & Gamble reported the following contingency:

Guarantees

In conjunction with certain transactions, primarily divestitures, the Company may provide routine indemnifications (e.g., retention of previously existing environmental, tax and employee liabilities) whose terms range in duration and often are not explicitly defined. Generally, the maximum obligation under such indemnifications is not explicitly stated and, as a result, the overall amount of these obligations cannot be reasonably estimated. Other than obligations recorded as liabilities at the time of divestiture, historically the Company has not made significant payments for these indemnifications. The Company believes that if it were to incur a loss in any of these matters, the loss would not have a material effect on the Company's financial condition or results of operations.

In certain situations, the Company guarantees loans for suppliers and customers. The total amount of guarantees issued under such arrangements is not material.

Source: Procter & Gamble's 2004 Annual Report.

Commitments

A *commitment* **is a promise to engage in some future activity that will have an economic effect.** Commitments usually involve agreements to purchase or sell something in the future. For instance, airlines place orders with airplane manufacturers several years prior to completion of the planes. These commitments will require the airlines to finance their purchases at some time in the future, but they are not liabilities until the airplanes have been manufactured and ownership is transferred to the airlines.

Leased assets are a common form of commitment. Certain leases, called **capital leases**, are financing arrangements and are examined in the next section. In addition to capital leases, companies use **operating leases** to obtain machinery, equipment, and other resources. Costs of operating leases are recorded as expenses in the period in which the leased assets are used. Liabilities are not recorded for operating leases. Some operating leases cannot be canceled, however, resulting in a commitment for future payments. The amount of future payments is reported in the notes to the financial statements. Companies typically report the amount they are committed to paying for operating leases in each of the next five years and the total amount of commitments that extend beyond five years. Disclosures like these help investors and other decision makers forecast future cash flows and profits.

CASE IN POINT

http://ingram.swlearning.com

Visit Procter & Gamble's home page to learn more about the company.

Disclosure of Lease Agreements

Procter & Gamble reported the following lease arrangements in its 2004 annual report:

Operating Leases

The Company leases certain property and equipment for varying periods under operating leases. Future minimum rental commitments under noncancellable operating leases are as follows: 2005—$186; 2006—$150; 2007—$134; 2008—$99; 2009—$86; and $265 thereafter. (Amounts in millions.)

Source: Procter & Gamble's 2004 Annual Report.

Capital Leases

Leases often provide a means of financing asset acquisitions. When a company leases a resource, usually buildings or equipment, for most of the useful life of the resource and controls the resource as though it had been purchased, the lease is treated as a capital lease. **Capital leases are recorded as liabilities, and the related leased resources are recorded as assets.**

http://ingram.swlearning.com

Visit the text's web site to find out more about leasing.

For example, suppose Favorite Cookie Company signs a lease on January 1, 2008 to acquire computer equipment. The lease is for three years, the assumed useful life of the equipment. The company agrees to pay $10,000 a year, including 8% interest. In effect, Favorite Cookie Company is purchasing the equipment and borrowing money from the lessor (the company that owns the equipment and leases it to Favorite Cookie Company) to finance the purchase.

To determine the amount of the lease obligation, we have to calculate the present value of the lease payments. We can make this calculation using the interest factor in Table 4 because the lease payments are an annuity. We use the interest factor for three periods at 8%:

$$\text{PVA} = \text{A} \times \text{IF (Table 4)}$$
$$\$25{,}771 = \$10{,}000 \times 2.57710$$

USING EXCEL

Alternatively, we can use the present value function in a spreadsheet. In Excel, we would enter the function =PV(0.08,3, −10000) to make this calculation. The amount returned is $25,771, rounded to the nearest dollar.

Favorite Cookie Company records the present value of lease payments as an asset and a liability:

		Assets		=	Liabilities	+	Owners' Equity	
Date	Accounts	Cash	Other Assets				Contributed Capital	Retained Earnings
Jan. 1, 2008	Leased Assets		25,771					
	Capital Lease Obligation				25,771			

EXHIBIT 7 Amortization Table for a Capital Lease

A Year	B Present Value at Beginning of Year	C Interest Incurred (Column B × Real Interest Rate)	D Amount Paid	E Amortization of Principal (Column C − Column D)	F Value at End of Year (Column B + Column E)
Dec. 31, 2008	25,771	2,062	10,000	(7,938)	17,833
Dec. 31, 2009	17,833	1,427	10,000	(8,573)	9,260
Dec. 31, 2010	9,260	740	10,000	(9,260)	0
Total		4,229	30,000	(25,771)	

Other transactions associated with the lease payments are like those for repayment of a loan. The amortization table in Exhibit 7 provides the necessary information.

This table is like that for a note that is repaid in equal installments, as described in Chapter 8. Observe that a portion of the principal is repaid each period, along with the interest.

Favorite Cookie Company records the payments and interest expense each period. For example, the transaction for the first year is:

		Assets		= Liabilities	+ Owners' Equity	
Date	**Accounts**	**Cash**	**Other Assets**		**Contributed Capital**	**Retained Earnings**
Dec. 31, 2008	Capital Lease Obligation			−7,938		
	Interest Expense					−2,062
	Cash	−10,000				

This transaction reduces the capital lease liability by the amount of principal paid. Over the course of the three years, the entire principal will be repaid. The amount of lease liability remaining at the end of the first year ($17,833 from Exhibit 7) is reported as a liability on Favorite Cookie Company's balance sheet at December 31, 2008.

From the perspective of the lessor, the $25,771 present value of the lease is the amount received for the equipment and is treated as sales revenue. Amounts received in excess of the present value are interest revenue. Therefore, the lessor would record $2,062 of interest revenue in the first year (see Exhibit 7).

STOCKHOLDERS' EQUITY

Objective 3
Identify information reported in the stockholders' equity section of a corporate balance sheet and distinguish contributed capital from retained earnings.

Liabilities are obligations that a company has a legal responsibility to meet. Creditors' claims against a company are enforceable by law. Stockholders' equity also represents claims against a company, claims by investors who own a corporation's stock. As long as a company is a going concern (is expected to continue to exist), those claims are met by the company's profits. Ordinarily, a company is not obligated to make payments to its stockholders or to repay them the amounts they have invested.

Profit is the value created from selling goods and services during a period in excess of the costs of resources consumed during that period. That excess value increases the value of stockholders' claims. When a company distributes its profit in the form of dividends or incurs a loss, the amount of stockholders' claims decreases.

EXHIBIT 8
Stockholders' Equity for Favorite Cookie Company

December 31,	2008	2007
Stockholders' equity:		
Common stock, $1 par value, 50,000 shares authorized, 20,000 and 10,000 shares issued	$ 20,000	$ 10,000
Paid-in capital in excess of par value	190,000	90,000
Retained earnings	130,417	42,990
Treasury stock, 1,000 shares at cost	(12,000)	0
Total stockholders' equity	$328,417	$142,990

The claims of creditors are honored before those of owners. In general, creditors' claims are met before cash or other assets are distributed to owners (stockholders). As a result, there is an important difference between liabilities and owners' equity, and liabilities and equity are separated on a company's balance sheet.

Exhibit 8 provides the owners' equity section of Favorite Cookie Company's balance sheet. Corporate owners' equity is referred to as **stockholders'** or **shareholders' equity** because owners hold shares of stock as an indication of their ownership.

http://ingram.swlearning.com

Visit the text's web site to find answers to frequently asked questions about the stock market.

The exhibit shows information about two main types of stockholders' equity: contributed capital and retained earnings. *Contributed capital* **is the direct investment made by stockholders in a corporation.** Contributed capital for Favorite Cookie Company consists of common stock and paid-in capital in excess of par value. **Retained earnings** is the accumulation of profits reinvested in a corporation. A third type of equity reported by many companies, including Favorite Cookie Company, is treasury stock. *Treasury stock* **is stock repurchased by a company from its stockholders.** The cost of treasury stock is deducted from stockholders' equity because it is an amount that a company has repaid to stockholders.

Companies often repurchase their stock to distribute it to employees as part of employee stock ownership plans and to provide bonuses and other compensation for managers and employees. Some companies repurchase stock to reduce the number of shares available in the market. Usually, fewer shares result in a higher stock price. Also, a company may repurchase its own shares to prevent another company from buying them. One company can take control of another company by buying its shares. Fewer shares outstanding makes it more difficult for another company to obtain a controlling interest.

Some corporations do not have treasury stock. All corporations have contributed capital and retained earnings. Retained earnings may be a negative amount, referred to as a deficit.

Contributed Capital

Corporations issue shares of stock in exchange for cash (and sometimes other resources, such as property). *Common stock*, **or** *capital stock*, **represents the ownership rights of investors in a corporation.** Each share of common stock represents an equal share in the ownership of a corporation. Owners of the shares have the right to vote on the activities of the corporation and to share in its earnings. For example, suppose a corporation has 100,000 shares of common stock outstanding. Someone who owns 10,000 shares controls 10% of the votes that can be cast on issues voted on by stockholders. That investor also has the right to 10% of the dividends paid to common stockholders.

U.S. corporations must be chartered by a state. **A** *charter* **is the legal right granted by a state that permits a corporation to exist.** The charter establishes a corporation as a legal entity. It also sets limits on the corporation's activities to protect owners and others who contract with the corporation. Among other things, a corporation's charter specifies the maximum number of shares of stock the corporation is authorized to issue. Favorite Cookie Company is authorized to issue up to 50,000 shares of common stock. At the end of 2008 it had issued 20,000 shares, and at the end of 2007 it had issued 10,000 shares (Exhibit 8).

Most shares of common stock are issued with a par value because states often require that corporate stock have a par value. **The *par value* of stock is the value assigned to each share by a corporation in its corporate charter.** A state may require that a corporation maintain an amount of equity equal to or greater than the par value of its stock. That equity cannot be transferred back to the owners unless the corporation liquidates its assets and goes out of business.

Originally, par value was designed to protect a corporation's creditors by making owners keep a certain level of investment in the corporation. This protection was important when the sale of stock and financial reporting were largely unregulated. With increased regulation and requirements for financial reporting, par value has lost much of its importance. In some states, charters do not require a par value. Stock issued without a par value is known as **no-par stock**. In states where charters do require a par value, that value often is set very low. A dollar per share, or less, is common.

Stock usually is sold at a price greater than par value. For example, the 20,000 shares of Favorite Cookie Company's common stock that had been issued by the end of 2008 were sold for $210,000 ($20,000 + $190,000 in Exhibit 8). Of this amount, $20,000 is reported as par value (20,000 shares × $1 par). The remainder of the amount the company received from selling its stock is reported as paid-in capital in excess of par value ($190,000).

***Paid-in capital in excess of par value* is the amount in excess of the stock's par value received by a corporation from the sale of its stock.** Corporate financial reports refer to this amount by many names: among them are paid-in capital, contributed capital in excess of par, proceeds in excess of par value, additional paid-in capital, surplus, and premium on capital stock.

Occasionally, a corporation establishes its own **stated value** for no-par stock. That value appears on the balance sheet in place of par value.

In addition to the number of shares authorized, a corporation reports the number of shares of stock issued (sold) to investors. **Issued shares** are shares that have been sold by a corporation to investors. **Outstanding shares** are shares currently held by investors. The difference (if any) between the number of shares issued and the number outstanding is the number of shares of treasury stock. Thus, at the end of 2008, Favorite Cookie Company had issued 20,000 shares, but only 19,000 shares were outstanding. The remaining 1,000 shares were owned by Favorite Cookie Company (Exhibit 8).

A company repurchases its own shares for various purposes. Many companies give these shares to managers or employees as additional compensation for their work for the company, especially if they or the company have performed well.

Retained Earnings

Retained earnings is profit reinvested in a corporation. Retained earnings also is referred to by a variety of names, such as reinvested earnings, profit retained in the business, or earnings reinvested in the business. The amount of retained earnings is the accumulated net income invested in corporate resources.

For example, assume the following information for Favorite Cookie Company for 2007 and 2008:

Year	Net Income	Dividends	Increase in Retained Earnings	Balance of Retained Earnings
2006				$ 0
2007	$ 52,990	$10,000	$42,990	42,990
2008	107,427	20,000	87,427	130,417

At the end of 2007, Favorite Cookie Company had retained earnings of $42,990. During 2007, the company earned net income of $52,990 and paid dividends of $10,000. Therefore, its retained earnings increased by $42,990 ($52,990 − $10,000). Each year, net income is added to retained earnings, and dividends are subtracted. A net loss would be subtracted from retained earnings.

There is an important difference between contributed capital and retained earnings. Retained earnings results from profits that could be used to pay dividends to stockholders. Dividends paid from retained earnings are a return to stockholders from a company's earnings. If dividends in excess of retained earnings are paid, this is a return of contributed capital. The company is repaying investors a portion of the amount they contributed to the company when they purchased the company's stock. Therefore, it is important to distinguish between contributed capital and retained earnings.

Self-Study Problem #2

Bovine Company, a dairy, began operations in January 2007. It issued 100,000 shares of $1 par value common stock. The stock sold for $5 per share. The company's charter permits it to issue 250,000 shares of stock. In 2008, the company repurchased 8,000 shares of stock at a cost of $7 per share. Bovine's net income and cash dividend payments have been as follows:

Year	Net Income	Dividends
2007	$ (60,000)	$ 0
2008	140,000	50,000
2009	220,000	100,000

Required Draft the stockholders' equity section of Bovine's balance sheet for the years ended December 31, 2008 and 2009.

The solution to Self-Study Problem 2 appears at the end of the chapter.

CHANGES IN STOCKHOLDERS' EQUITY

Objective 4
Explain transactions affecting stockholders' equity and describe how these transactions are reported in a company's financial statements.

The statement of stockholders' (or shareholders') equity describes events that changed the amount of stockholders' equity during a fiscal period. Exhibit 9 provides the statement of stockholders' equity for Favorite Cookie Company. Beginning and ending balances are the same as those reported in the company's balance sheet (Exhibit 8).

The format of the statement of stockholders' equity varies from corporation to corporation, but all statements list the events that changed stockholders' equity during the past fiscal year. Most corporations report this information for the most recent three fiscal years. Some companies report this information as a schedule in the notes section of their financial reports, rather than as a separate statement.

Exhibit 10 illustrates transactions that affect stockholders' equity for most companies.

EXHIBIT 9 Statement of Stockholders' Equity for Favorite Cookie Company

	Common Stock	Paid-In Capital	Retained Earnings	Treasury Stock	Total
December 31, 2007	$10,000	$ 90,000	$ 42,990	$ 0	$142,990
Net income			107,427		107,427
Dividends			(20,000)		(20,000)
Stock purchased				(12,000)	(12,000)
Stock issued	10,000	100,000			110,000
December 31, 2008	$20,000	$190,000	$130,417	$(12,000)	$328,417

EXHIBIT 10 Examples of Transactions That Affect Common Stockholders' Equity

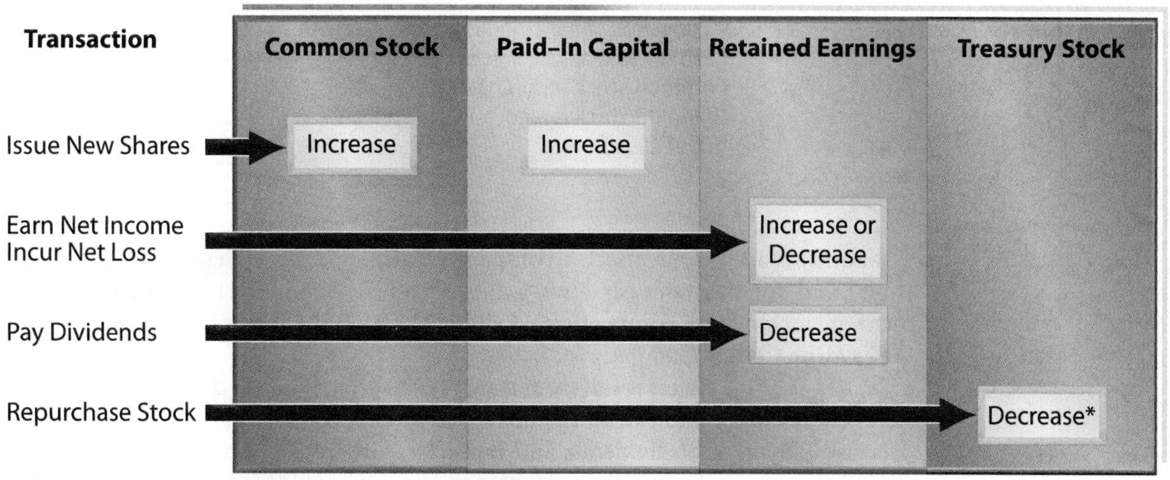

***An increase in treasury stock decreases stockholders' equity.**

Equity Transactions

The statement of stockholders' equity summarizes equity transactions for a fiscal period. From the information in Exhibit 9, we can reconstruct the transactions for 2008 for Favorite Cookie Company.

		Assets		=	Liabilities	+	Owners' Equity	
Date	Accounts	Cash	Other Assets				Contributed Capital	Retained Earnings
Dec. 31, 2008	Net Income*							−107,427
	Retained Earnings							107,427
Dec. 31, 2008	Retained Earnings							−20,000
	Cash	−20,000						
Dec. 31, 2008	Treasury Stock						−12,000	
	Cash	−12,000						
Dec. 31, 2008	Cash	110,000						
	Common Stock						10,000	
	Paid-In Capital						100,000	

***Individual revenue and expense accounts would be closed and the balances transferred to retained earnings. In total, these amounts are equal to net income. Transactions are assumed to have occurred on December 31.**

The first transaction transfers net income earned during 2008 to retained earnings. The second transaction deducts the amount of dividends paid during 2008 from retained earnings. The third transaction records the purchase of treasury stock, and the final transaction records the amount received from the sale of common stock. Note that, other than closing revenue and expense accounts to retained earnings, equity transactions normally do not involve revenues or expenses. **A company cannot earn profit from equity transactions.** When treasury stock is sold at a price higher than its cost, the incremental amount is added to Paid-In Capital. When treasury stock is sold at a price less than its cost, the amount is deducted from Paid-In Capital.

EXHIBIT 11
Equity Transaction Effects on Statement of Cash Flows for Favorite Cookie Company

Cash flow from financing activities:	
Cash dividends	$ (20,000)
Common stock repurchased	(12,000)
Common stock issued	110,000
Net cash flow	$ 78,000

Equity transactions affect a company's balance sheet, statement of stockholders' equity, and statement of cash flows. Exhibits 8 and 9 contain the balance sheet and statement of stockholders' equity effects. Exhibit 11 shows the statement of cash flow effects for Favorite Cookie Company for 2008.

The cash flow effects result from transactions affecting cash during the fiscal period. All of these effects result from financing activities and either increase (stock issued) or decrease (payment of dividends and repurchase of stock) cash. Cash flows associated with net income, which increases Retained Earnings, are reported as part of operating activities on the statement of cash flows.

Cash Dividends

http://ingram.swlearning.com

Visit the text's web site to find out which companies have declared dividends recently.

Several issues are important in recording cash dividend transactions. Cash dividends are paid only on shares outstanding. They are not paid on shares held in treasury; a company does not pay dividends to itself.

Three dates are important for dividend transactions. The *date of declaration* **for dividends is the date on which a corporation's board of directors announces that a dividend will be paid. The** *date of record* **for a dividend is the date used to determine those owners who will receive the dividend.** All registered owners on the date of record receive the dividend. The *date of payment* **for a dividend is the date on which the dividends are mailed to those receiving dividends.**

Dividends declared during a fiscal period are reported on the statement of stockholders' equity as a reduction in retained earnings. Dividends paid are reported on the corporation's statement of cash flows for that period. Those amounts are not always the same. For example, a company may declare a dividend near the end of its fiscal year but not pay the dividend until the following fiscal year. Dividends declared but not paid are reported as a current liability, Dividends Payable.

Issuing New Stock

When a company issues new shares of stock, each current stockholder normally has a right to purchase a portion of the new shares equal to the percentage of shares he or she owned prior to the sale. **The right to maintain the same percentage of ownership when new shares are issued is known as the** *preemptive right* **of stockholders.** This right prevents management from diluting the control (and wealth) of current owners by selling new shares to someone other than the current owners. Of course, current owners may choose not to purchase those shares.

When a company prepares to issue new shares, it normally issues stock rights to existing owners. *Stock rights* **authorize the recipient to purchase new shares.** The number of rights a stockholder receives depends on the number of shares the stockholder owns. Stock rights may be sold to others if the original recipient does not want to purchase the new shares.

Stock Dividends

Corporations sometimes issue stock dividends. *Stock dividends* **are shares of stock distributed by a company to its current stockholders without charge to the stockholders.** The effect of a stock dividend is to increase the number of shares of stock a company has outstanding and the number held by each stockholder. The increase in the number of shares held by each stockholder is in proportion to the number that stockholder owned before the distribution.

For example, assume that you owned 1,000 shares of Druid Company's stock on June 1, 2007, the date the company distributed a 5% stock dividend. You would receive 50 additional shares (1,000 shares × 5%). The total number of shares of common stock outstanding increased by 5% as a result of this distribution.

Unlike cash dividends, stock dividends do not decrease a company's cash. No cash is paid out. The amount of the stock dividend is subtracted from retained earnings and added to contributed capital. Therefore, the total amount of stockholders' equity does not change. The amount transferred is the market price of the stock at the time the dividend is declared.

Total Shares Outstanding	Stock Dividend	New Shares Issued	Market Value per Share	Effect on Balance Sheet
100,000	5%	5,000	$10	Contributed Capital* + $50,000
				Retained Earnings − $50,000

***This amount would be allocated to Common Stock for 5,000 shares × par value and to Paid-In Capital In Excess of Par for the remainder of the $50,000. If the stock is no-par, all $50,000 is applied to Common Stock.**

Sometimes corporations issue large stock dividends known as stock splits. **When a corporation declares a *stock split*, it issues a multiple of the number of shares of stock outstanding before the split.** For example, a company might issue two new shares for every one of its old shares.

A split does not change a company's total stockholders' equity. Usually, a company will reduce the par value of its common stock in proportion to the size of a stock split. Thus, if the par value is $1 per share before a 2-for-1 split, the par value will be $0.50 per share after the split. By changing the par value, the company keeps the same amount of contributed capital on its books after the split, and no account balances are altered.

2-for-1 Split	Total Shares Outstanding	Par Value per Share	Total Par Value
Before split	100,000	$1.00	$100,000
After split	200,000	$0.50	$100,000

If a company does not reduce its par value, an amount equal to the par value of the additional stock is transferred from retained earnings to contributed capital. The market value of a company's stock also adjusts to a stock split. For example, if stock was selling at $10 per share before a 2-for-1 split, it should sell at about $5 per share after the split. Companies often use stock splits to reduce the price of their stock to make it more attractive to investors who have to pay less to purchase the stock than prior to the split.

PREFERRED STOCK

Some corporations issue more than one class of stock. The classes usually have different voting and dividend rights. A corporation's annual report describes the different classes of stock issued by the company. In addition to common stock, many companies issue preferred stock.

Objective 5
Distinguish between preferred stock and common stock, and discuss why corporations may issue more than one type of stock.

***Preferred stock* is stock with a higher claim on dividends and assets than common stock.** Cash dividends must be paid to preferred stockholders before they can be paid to common stockholders. Also, preferred stockholders generally have a liquidation preference over common stockholders. That is, if a corporation has to liquidate its assets, preferred stockholders are repaid for their investments before common stockholders but after creditors. Preferred stock, therefore, is less risky as an investment than common stock but is more risky than bonds or other debt investments.

Preferred stockholders normally do not have voting rights in a corporation. They share in the profits of a corporation but not in decisions about the company's operations.

Preferred stock attracts investors who want to take less risk than that taken by common stockholders. If a company does well, holders of preferred stock receive a reasonable return on their investments and may be able to exchange their preferred shares for shares of common stock. If a company does poorly, preferred stockholders are likely to receive higher returns than common stockholders. Again, they have more protection against loss in case of liquidation.

Usually, a paid-in capital in excess of par value account is not reported for preferred stock. The stock often is issued at par value or has no par value. In some cases, a **liquidation value** or **dividend rate** is reported for preferred stock. A liquidation value is the amount stockholders would receive for each share if the company were to liquidate, assuming that sufficient cash were available after creditors had been paid to pay the full liquidation value. The dividend rate identifies the annual dividend paid on the stock as a percentage of the par value or liquidation value of the stock. For example, if preferred stock has a stated or par value of $10 per share and a dividend rate of 5%, the company would pay a cash dividend of $0.50 per share ($10 × 5%) each year to preferred stockholders.

Preferred stockholders receive cash dividends in the same way that common stockholders do. However, the amount of the dividend payment for the two types of stock often differs. Usually, preferred stockholders receive the stated dividend rate, while dividends to common stockholders depend on a company's profitability. When a company is highly profitable, it normally pays larger dividends to common stockholders than it does when it is less profitable. If it is unprofitable, it may skip dividends for the year.

Preferred stock often is **cumulative**. This means that any dividends not paid to preferred stockholders in prior years must be paid in the current year before any dividends can be paid to common stockholders. Most often, cash dividends are paid quarterly on both common and preferred stock, resulting in a cash outflow and reduction of retained earnings.

Dividends, whether on common or on preferred stock, are not an expense. They are a distribution of profits. Because preferred dividends are paid before common dividends, they reduce the amount of net income available for common stock dividends. **Net income available for common stockholders** is net income minus dividends on preferred stock.

Some companies issue **redeemable preferred stock**. This stock is repurchased by the issuing company at a particular time, usually within a few years after it is issued. Because it has a fixed life and does not have voting rights, redeemable preferred stock is not included as part of stockholders' equity. It is reported as a separate item between liabilities and equity on the balance sheet.

Companies may issue bonds or preferred stock that can be converted into shares of common stock. These securities are referred to as **convertible securities**. The number of shares of stock received in exchange for each bond or share of preferred stock is set at the time the convertible securities are sold.

Convertible bonds and preferred stock attract investors who want the greater protection of bonds or preferred stock but who also want the chance to share in a company's earnings if it is successful. Investors can convert their bonds or preferred stock into common stock if a company performs well. Because of this conversion feature, convertible bonds often pay a lower rate of interest and convertible preferred stock pays a lower dividend than do similar nonconvertible securities.

CASE IN POINT

http://ingram.swlearning.com

Visit Procter of Gamble's home page to learn more about the company.

Disclosure of Preferred Stock Information

Procter & Gamble reported stockholders' equity in its 2004 annual report as follows:

	2004	**2003**
Shareholders' Equity[1]		
Convertible Class A preferred stock, stated value $1 per share (600 shares authorized)	**1,526**	1,580
Non-Voting Class B preferred stock, stated value $1 per share (200 shares authorized)	—	—
Common stock, stated value $1 per share (5,000 shares authorized; shares outstanding: 2004—2,543.8, 2003—2,594.4)	**2,544**	2,594
Additional paid-in captial	**2,425**	1,634
Reserve for ESOP debt retirement	**(1,283)**	(1,308)
Accumulated other comprehensive income	**(1,545)**	(2,006)
Retained earnings	**13,611**	13,692
Total Shareholders' Equity	**17,278**	16,186
Total Liabilities and Shareholders' Equity	**$57,048**	$43,706

[1]Restated for two-for-one stock split effective May 21, 2004.

Source: Procter & Gamble's 2004 Annual Report.

INTERNATIONAL REPORTING OF FINANCING ACTIVITIES

INTERNATIONAL

Foreign corporations report debt and stockholders' equity much as U.S. corporations do. Most industrialized nations use similar reporting rules, though some big differences exist. Each nation sets its own accounting and reporting rules. Therefore, it is not always safe to assume that the amounts in a foreign company's statements mean the same as those in a U.S. company's statements.

Financial terms vary from country to country. For example, common stock may be known as share capital. Share premium may refer to paid-in capital in excess of par value. Earned surplus or profit and loss may be used instead of retained earnings. Reserve accounts also are common in many foreign countries. Such accounts identify portions of stockholders' equity that are restricted for a particular purpose and cannot be used to pay dividends.

***Learning Note** - If a foreign corporation has stock listed on U.S. stock exchanges, it normally issues annual financial reports that conform with U.S. GAAP. These companies may issue different annual reports to stockholders in their own countries, using different accounting rules.*

OTHER RELATED TOPICS

This section describes other related topics that may be observed for some companies.

Stock Options

Stock options are rights to purchase shares of a company's stock at a specified price. Options often are granted to employees and managers of a company as part of compensation. For example, assume that employees receive options to purchase 10,000 shares of their company's stock on January 2, 2007. The options permit employees to purchase shares at $50 per share on January 2, 2008. If the company does well in 2007 and the stock price rises above $50, employees will profit from using (exercising) their options. Options provide an incentive for employees to be productive and help a company's stock price to increase.

A company sometimes may sponsor an employee stock ownership plan (ESOP). The company makes shares of its stock available to the plan. The shares are distributed when employees earn them through service to the company. These shares are like treasury stock until they are earned by employees. A company's stockholders' equity, therefore, may include an item for employee compensation related to an ESOP that reduces its stockholders' equity.

Stock option plans can be complex. Many types of plans exist, and accounting for them varies according to plan type and terms. Stock option plans often bring tax benefits to corporations. The terms of stock option plans, therefore, often are determined by tax regulations.

Noncontrolling Interest

Noncontrolling interest, sometimes called minority interest, is the portion of a subsidiary company's equity owned by shareholders other than the parent corporation. For example, assume that Parent Company owns 80% of Subsidiary Company's stock. Subsidiary Company reports total stockholders' equity of $2 million for fiscal 2007. Therefore, the noncontrolling interest (20% $\times$ $2,000,000) is $400,000. Parent Company reports this amount as noncontrolling interest on its balance sheet.

Corporations report noncontrolling interest in different ways. Some report it as part of stockholders' equity, a portion of the corporation's total equity held by outside interests. Others report noncontrolling interest as a liability, a claim by outside interests against a portion of the corporation's resources. Most companies include noncontrolling interest as a separate category between liabilities and equity.

Appropriation of Retained Earnings

An appropriation of retained earnings transfers part of the retained earnings balance to a restricted retained earnings account. The restricted amount cannot be distributed as dividends. The new account title might be Retained Earnings—Appropriation for Plant Expansion, or something similar. Appropriations are rare among U.S. companies but sometimes are found in the financial statements of foreign companies.

Foreign Currency Adjustments

These adjustments to stockholders' equity are commonly made by multinational corporations. Multinationals are companies that operate in both foreign and domestic (U.S.) markets. Some of their operations are conducted in foreign currency—British pounds or Japanese yen, for example. When preparing financial statements in the United States, multinationals translate their foreign operations into U.S. dollars. Foreign currency translation is the process of converting the financial results of operations in a foreign currency into U.S. dollars for financial-reporting purposes.

A translation adjustment is the gain or loss that results when the operations of a company's foreign subsidiaries are translated from foreign to U.S. currency for reporting consolidated financial statements. These adjustments may result in gains or losses depending on whether the dollar has gained or lost value relative to other currencies. Translation adjustments are reported in the stockholders' equity section of the balance sheet as part of other comprehensive income. Gains are added in computing total stockholders' equity and losses are deducted.

Self-Study Problem #3

Required Use information from the accompanying financial statements of Lesco Inc. to answer the following questions:

A. What was Lesco's total contributed capital for 2007?

B. How many shares of common stock were outstanding at the end of 2007?

C. What dollar amount of treasury stock did Lesco hold at the end of 2007?

D. What dollar amount of stock did Lesco repurchase during 2007? How much did it issue?

E. What was the amount of dividends paid in 2007?

F. How much net cash flow came from financing activities associated with stockholders' equity during 2007, excluding the effect of net income? What were the sources of that cash flow?

G. How much net income came from financing activities associated with stockholders' equity during the current year?

Lesco Inc.
Balance Sheet (Excerpt)
December 31, 2007

Stockholders' Equity	
Common stock, $0.10 par value, 1,000,000 shares authorized, 700,000 shares issued	$ 70,000
Paid-in capital in excess of par value	810,240
Retained earnings	356,812
Treasury stock (30,000 shares at cost)	(42,296)
Total stockholders' equity	$1,194,756

Lesco Inc.
Statement of Stockholders' Equity
December 31, 2007

	Common Stock	Paid-In Capital	Retained Earnings	Treasury Stock	Total
December 31, 2006	$65,000	$747,196	$306,201	$(33,941)	$1,084,456
Net income			92,611		92,611
Dividends			(42,000)		(42,000)
Stock purchased				(8,355)	(8,355)
Stock issued	5,000	63,044			68,044
December 31, 2007	$70,000	$810,240	$356,812	$(42,296)	$1,194,756

The solution to Self-Study Problem 3 appears at the end of the chapter.

THINKING BEYOND THE QUESTION

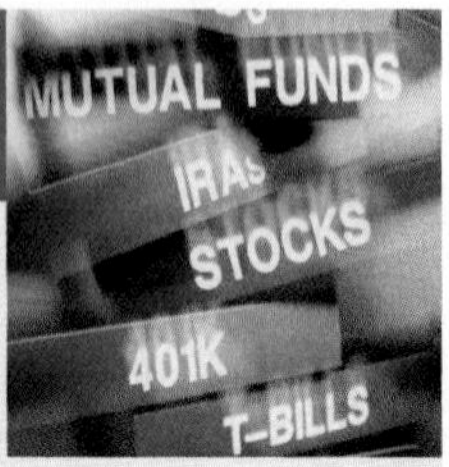

WHAT ARE THE FUNDAMENTAL ACCOUNTING ISSUES ASSOCIATED WITH FINANCING ACTIVITIES?

Financing activities for corporations involve issuing debt and stock. These activities provide financial resources for the corporation to grow. Debt has to be repaid along with interest. Stockholders expect dividends or increases in stock prices resulting from profits earned by the corporation. How do managers decide how much of their financing should come from debt and how much from equity? What effect does the mix of debt and equity have for a corporation's profits and risk?

Self-Study Problem Solutions

SSP9-1 A. Present value of bonds = PV of annuity (interest) + PV of maturity value

PV = \$1,600 × 4.10020 (Table 4, 5 periods, 7%) + \$20,000 × 0.71299 (Table 3, 5 periods, 7%)
PV = \$6,560 + \$14,260 = \$20,820

B.

A Year	B Present Value at Beginning of Year	C Interest Incurred (Column B × Real Interest Rate)	D Amount Paid	E Amortization of Principal (Column C − Column D)	F Value at End of Year (Column B + Column E)
2008	20,820	1,457	1,600	(143)	20,677
2009	20,677	1,447	1,600	(153)	20,524
2010	20,524	1,437	1,600	(163)	20,361
2011	20,361	1,425	1,600	(175)	20,186
2012	20,186	1,413	1,600	(187)	20,000
Total		7,179	8,000	(821)	

*Amounts include small rounding errors.

C. First year:

		Assets		=	Liabilities	+	Owners' Equity	
Date	**Accounts**	**Cash**	**Other Assets**				**Contributed Capital**	**Retained Earnings**
Jan. 1, 2008	Cash	20,820						
	Bonds Payable				20,820			
Dec. 31, 2008	Interest Expense							−1,457
	Bonds Payable				−143			
	Cash	−1,600						

Fifth year:

		Assets		=	Liabilities	+	Owners' Equity	
Date	**Accounts**	**Cash**	**Other Assets**				**Contributed Capital**	**Retained Earnings**
Dec. 31, 2012	Interest Expense							−1,413
	Bonds Payable				−187			
	Cash	−1,600						
Dec. 31, 2012	Bonds Payable				−20,000			
	Cash	−20,000						

SSP9-2

Bovine Company Stockholders' Equity		
December 31,	2009	2008
Common stock, $1 par value, 250,000 shares authorized, 100,000 shares issued	$100,000	$100,000
Paid-in capital in excess of par value	400,000	400,000
Retained earnings	150,000	30,000
Treasury stock, 8,000 shares at cost	(56,000)	0
Total stockholders' equity	$594,000	$530,000

SSP9-3 A. Contributed capital = $880,240 = $70,000 common stock + $810,240 paid-in capital in excess of par value

B. Shares outstanding = 670,000 = 700,000 issued − 30,000 treasury shares

C. Treasury stock = $42,296

D. Stock repurchased = $8,355; stock issued = $68,044

E. Dividends paid = $42,000

F. Cash flow:

Paid for dividends	$(42,000)
Purchase of stock	(8,355)
Sale of stock	68,044
Net cash flow	$ 17,689

G. Net income from financing activities = $0. Financing activities do not create net income.

Define Terms and Concepts Defined in This Chapter

capital stock (330)
charter (330)
commitment (327)
common stock (330)
contingency (326)
contributed capital (330)
date of declaration (334)
date of payment (334)
date of record (331)
paid-in capital in excess of par value (331)
par value (331)
preemptive right (334)
preferred stock (336)
stock dividends (334)
stock rights (334)
stock split (335)
treasury stock (330)

Review *Summary of Important Concepts*

1. Liabilities result from contractual relationships with lenders, suppliers, customers, employees, governments, and other parties.
2. Three attributes of a liability are (1) a present responsibility to repay (transfer resources) at some future time, (2) the binding nature of the agreement (to return resources), and (3) the occurrence of the original transfer of value at some time in the past.
3. Debt obligations include notes and bonds payable.
   a. Debt is recorded at its present value.
   b. Principal repaid and interest are recorded over the life of the debt.
   c. An amortization table is useful for determining amounts recorded and reported for debt obligations.
4. Other obligations include contingencies and commitments, including leases.
   a. Contingencies are possible future events that may result in obligations.
   b. Commitments are agreements to use or acquire resources in the future.
   c. Capital leases are financing arrangements that result in a company recording assets and liabilities for the present value of future lease payments.
5. Stockholders' equity includes contributed capital and retained earnings.
   a. Contributed capital includes the par (or stated) value of stock plus paid-in capital in excess of par (or stated) value. If stock has no par or stated value, the entire amount of contributed capital is reported as common or capital stock.
   b. Stock repurchased by a corporation from its stockholders is reported on the balance sheet as treasury stock.
6. Transactions affecting stockholders' equity include paying cash dividends, issuing stock, repurchasing stock, and those transactions that result in net income.
   a. The effects of these transactions are summarized in the statement of stockholders' equity.
   b. A company cannot create income through transactions involving its own stock.
   c. The main stockholders' equity transactions that affect cash flow are the issuance or repurchase of stock and the payment of cash dividends.
   d. Stock dividends increase the number of shares outstanding but do not change the total equity balance and do not affect cash.
7. Corporations may issue preferred stock in addition to common stock. Preferred stock has a higher claim to dividends and assets than common stock. Some preferred stock and some bonds that are issued are convertible; this feature permits the purchaser to exchange the securities for common stock.
8. Amounts reported in the financial statements of foreign corporations often are determined using rules that are different from those used in the United States. Terms used in these reports also may differ from those used in the United States.
9. Some companies engage in special financing arrangements or activities that affect their financial statements.
   a. A company sometimes grants employees or managers stock options that permit them to purchase the company's stock at a specified price.
   b. Noncontrolling interest is the portion of a parent company's subsidiary that is not owned by the parent.
   c. An appropriation of retained earnings separates a portion of retained earnings so that it cannot be used to pay dividends.
   d. A foreign currency adjustment is a gain or loss that results when a company translates foreign operations into U.S. dollars for financial reporting purposes.

Questions

Q9-1 *Obj. 1* Why is it useful to report short-term liabilities separately from long-term liabilities when preparing the balance sheet?

Q9-2 *Obj. 1* What are the differences among debentures, serial bonds, and callable bonds?

Q9-3 *Obj. 1* Distinguish between the stated rate and the effective rate. Under what circumstances are these rates the same? Under what circumstances are these rates different?

Q9-4 *Obj. 2* While studying for an accounting exam, a friend observes that a capital lease is merely a means of financing the acquisition of assets. Do you agree? Explain the basis for your answer. If you agree, describe the ways in which a capital lease is similar to other financing activities. If you disagree, describe the ways in which it is different.

Q9-5 *Obj. 2* What is a contingency, and how does it differ from a liability? Under what conditions should a contingency be reported as if it were a liability?

Q9-6 *Obj. 2* How is a commitment different from a contingency?

Q9-7 *Obj. 3* You and Bob are studying for an upcoming accounting exam. Bob says, "Contributed capital is basically the stockholders' equity of the company. It includes things like common stock, paid-in capital in excess of par, preferred stock, and retained earnings." Do you agree? Discuss.

Q9-8 *Obj. 1* A friend remarks that, as he understands it, most current liabilities appearing on the balance sheet arise from transactions involving operating activities. Do you agree? List three current liabilities that might appear on the balance sheet. For each one, explain the underlying transaction that must have occurred for that specific liability to arise. Indicate, for each liability, whether it is the result of an operating activity, a financing activity, or an investing activity.

Q9-9 *Obj. 3* Jane has just purchased, from Beach Club Inc., 5,000 shares of Beach Club's $10 par value common stock at a price of $40 per share. Explain how this event should be accounted for by Beach Club. Indicate which accounts will be involved and the amounts.

Q9-10 *Obj. 4* GAAP require that a firm disclose the details of changes to all stockholders' equity accounts. What are the two primary techniques that companies use to meet this obligation?

Q9-11 *Obj. 4* The text states that "a company cannot earn profit from equity transactions." Why might this be? If a company buys widgets at $10 and resells them at $13, there is a $3 profit. What's the difference if a company buys back some of its own stock for $25 per share and resells it at $28 per share? Why do you think that GAAP do not allow a profit (or loss) to be recorded on equity transactions?

Q9-12 *Obj. 4* Clearly distinguish among the following terms: date of declaration, date of record, and date of payment. Construct a realistic example in which you use these terms.

Q9-13 *Obj. 5* Preferred stock generally does not have voting rights and its holders, therefore, do not have a formal voice in company affairs. Why, then, is it said that preferred stock is a less risky investment than common stock?

Q9-14 *Obj. 5* If preferred stock generally has a dividend preference over common stock anyway, what is gained by holding preferred stock that is cumulative?

Q9-15 *Obj. 5* Preferred stock generally pays a larger return to investors than do bonds but a lesser return than earned by common stockholders. Why?

Q9-16 *Obj. 5* Clarify the differences among the following terms: contributed capital, common stock, capital stock, preferred stock, and treasury stock.

Exercises

E9-1 Write a short definition for each of the terms listed in the *Terms and Concepts Defined in this Chapter* section.

E9-2 *Obj. 1* Camden Company issued $1 million of five-year, 8% bonds on January 1, 2007. The bonds pay interest annually. How much did the bonds sell for under each of the following situations?

a. The bonds sold to yield a real rate of 9%.
b. The bonds sold to yield a real rate of 5%.
c. The bonds sold to yield a real rate of 8%.

E9-3 *Obj. 1* For each of the following independent situations, determine: (a) whether the bonds sold at face (maturity) value, at a premium (more than face value), or at a discount (less than face value), and (b) whether interest expense recognized each year for the bonds was less than, equal to, or greater than the amount of interest paid on the bonds.

a. Bonds with a stated rate of 8% were sold to yield an effective rate of 9%.
b. Bonds with a stated rate of 12% were sold to yield an effective rate of 9%.
c. Bonds with a stated rate of 9% were sold to yield an effective rate of 9%.

E9-4 *Obj. 1* Herbal Enterprises issued 10-year bonds with a face value of $10 million on October 1, 2007. The bonds pay interest at 7% annually. The bonds sold at 93.29% of face value to yield an effective rate of 8%.

a. How much interest expense should Herbal recognize on the bonds for the fiscal year ended September 30, 2008?
b. What amount of net liability would the company report for the bonds on its 2008 balance sheet?
c. How much total expense would the company recognize for the bonds over the 10 years they are outstanding?

E9-5 *Obj. 1* Today is the fiscal year end for the Benson Boat Company. The regular year-end interest payment on its 9% bonds payable was made earlier today. All necessary entries were recorded. Bonds Payable now has a balance of $186,400. The chief financial officer (CFO) has proposed buying back this debt in the open market later today for $175,000. The debt is not due for repayment for another seven years. Explain how this proposed action would affect this year's (a) income statement, (b) balance sheet, and (c) statement of cash flows. Be specific.

E9-6 *Obj. 1* Watercrest Company sold 20-year bonds having a face value of $400,000 at a price of $360,728. The bonds pay annual interest at 7% and were priced to yield an effective return of 8%. Using the format presented in this chapter, record the following:

a. The issuance of the bonds.
b. The first payment of interest.
c. The repayment of principal at maturity. Assume that the last payment of interest has already been made and recorded.

E9-7 *Obj. 1* The Digital Manufacturing Company issued $600,000 of six-year bonds on January 1, 2007. The bonds pay interest of 7% on the face value ($0.07 \times \$600{,}000 = \$42{,}000$). The bonds were sold to give creditors a return of 6%.

a. Calculate the present value of the bonds at the time they are issued.
b. Prepare an amortization table for the bonds.
c. Record Digital Manufacturing's bond transactions at January 1, 2007, December 31, 2007, and December 31, 2012.

E9-8 *Obj. 1* The Calvert Corporation plans to expand its operations. To obtain the necessary cash, $5 million of 6%, five-year bonds were issued on January 1, 2007. The bonds pay interest annually.

a. Assume Calvert Corporation issued the bonds to yield an effective rate of 7%. Calculate the selling price of the bonds and describe the interest rate conditions under which the bonds were sold.
b. Now, assume Calvert Corporation issued the bonds to yield an effective rate of 5%. Calculate the selling price of the bonds and describe the conditions under which the bonds were sold.
c. Without setting up an amortization table, calculate the total amount of interest expense over the life of the bonds in parts a and b above. How do they compare? Why?

E9-9
Obj. 2
The Medical Lake Clinic acquired diagnostic equipment via a five-year capital lease. Medical Lake Clinic promised to make five end-of-year lease payments of $5,200. Each payment is to include 9% interest. Using the format presented in this chapter, record:

a. The entry necessary at the beginning of the lease.
b. The entry necessary at the date of the first lease payment.

E9-10
Obj. 2
For each of the situations that follow, determine whether a liability should be reported on the balance sheet. If a liability should be reported, suggest an account name and indicate whether it should be reported as a current liability or as a long-term liability. If no liability should be reported, indicate why.

a. The last installment payment on a three-year note payable is due next month.
b. Specialized production machinery has been acquired under a capital lease.
c. A $14 million lawsuit has been filed by a customer who claims injury from one of the company's products.
d. The labor services of employees have been consumed but not paid for yet. Payment is not anticipated until the next regular payday in two weeks.
e. A 20-year issue of bonds has been outstanding for 19 years and is expected to be repaid in cash at its maturity date.
f. The company has signed a contract promising to buy $600,000 worth of merchandise during the coming year.

E9-11
Objs. 1, 2
Below are listed key word clues and descriptions. The key word clues relate to different features or aspects of debt. Match the letter of each clue to the most relevant description provided. Use each clue only once.

a. bond	e. contingency	i. liability	m. secured
b. callable	f. current	j. maturity value	n. serial
c. capital	g. debenture	k. nominal	
d. commitment	h. effective	l. operating	

_____ 1. Obligations expected to be discharged within one year
_____ 2. A financial instrument that promises to repay principal at maturity and to pay interest each period until then
_____ 3. An obligation to convey resources to another entity in the future
_____ 4. Debt that is backed up by specific assets of the debtor company
_____ 5. A bond backed only by the general creditworthiness of the issuing company
_____ 6. Bonds that can be reacquired at the request of the issuing company
_____ 7. The amount repaid to bondholders at the end of the bond's life
_____ 8. The rate of interest that determines the amount of cash sent to bondholders each period
_____ 9. Bonds that mature a portion at a time over the life of the issue
_____ 10. The actual (or real) rate of return earned by the holder of a bond
_____ 11. A type of lease that results in a liability being reported on the balance sheet
_____ 12. An existing condition that may result in an economic effect later
_____ 13. A promise to engage in some future economic activity
_____ 14. A lease that does not result in a liability being reported on the balance sheet

E9-12
Obj. 3
Nantuckett Company's charter allows it to sell 500,000 shares of $1 par value common stock. So far, the firm has sold 80,000 shares for a total of $760,000. Just yesterday, the company reacquired 1,000 shares from an unhappy shareholder at a price of $10 per share.

(Continued)

a. What is a charter and by whom is it issued?
b. What total amount of contributed capital should this company report in the stockholders' equity section of its balance sheet?
c. What was the average selling price of each share of common stock?
d. How many shares of stock are outstanding?
e. What balance should be reported in stockholders' equity for Common Stock?

E9-13
Obj. 3

The charter of Pelenova, Inc. states that it may issue up to one million shares of common stock. Over the life of the company, 255,000 shares have been sold to investors. Total profits over the life of the company have been $876,000, and exactly one-half of that amount has been paid out in dividends. As of today's balance sheet date, the company holds 13,000 shares that have been bought back from shareholders.

a. What is the number of authorized shares?
b. What is the number of issued shares?
c. What is the number of outstanding shares?

E9-14
Obj. 3

The Quick Chips Company, a fast-food manufacturer, began operations in January 2007. It issued 500,000 shares of $0.25 par value common stock. The stock sold for $20 per share. There are 600,000 shares authorized. In 2009, the company repurchased 15,000 shares of stock at a cost of $26 per share. Quick Chips's net income and cash dividend payments have been as follows:

Year	Net Income	Dividends
2007	$(100,000)	$ 0
2008	250,000	75,000
2009	400,000	150,000

Draft the stockholders' equity section of Quick Chips's balance sheet for the years ended December 31, 2008 and 2009.

E9-15
Obj. 4

Harbor Company reported net income of $1.7 million for the year ending December 31, 2007. On January 27, 2008, the board of directors met and decided that each of the firm's 400,000 outstanding common shares should receive a dividend of $0.65. The board voted to distribute the dividend on March 15 to those stockholders who owned the shares as of February 10.

a. Identify the date of declaration, the date of record, and the date of payment.
b. What percentage of net income was distributed in dividends?
c. Why do you suppose the company did not distribute 100% of net income as dividends? What else can companies do with profits?

E9-16
Obj. 4

On March 1, Yukon Company distributed a $2.00 cash dividend to each of its 60,000 outstanding shares of $3.00 par value common stock. On June 12, the company declared and issued a 5% stock dividend when the market price of the stock was $7 per share. On September 20, the company declared a 2-for-1 stock split and changed the par value accordingly. Describe how the company's year-end income statement, balance sheet, statement of cash flows, and statement of stockholders' equity will be affected by the

a. cash dividend,
b. stock dividend, and
c. stock split.

E9-17
Obj. 4

Fast Start Corporation manufactures automobile ignitions. Selected portions of the company's recent financial statements are given on the following page.

a. What was Fast Start's total contributed capital at year end?
b. How many shares of common stock were outstanding at year end?
c. What dollar amount of treasury stock did Fast Start hold at year end?
d. What dollar amount of treasury stock did Fast Start repurchase during the year? How much common stock did the company issue?
e. What was the amount of dividends paid during the year?
f. How much cash flow came from financing activities associated with shareholders' equity during the current year, excluding the effect of net income? What were the sources of that cash flow?
g. How much net income came from financing activities associated with stockholders' equity during the current year?

Fast Start Corporation
Balance Sheet (Excerpt)
December 31, 2007

Stockholders' Equity:	
Common stock, $0.50 par value, 2,000,000 shares authorized, 1,400,000 shares issued	$ 700,000
Paid-In capital in excess of par value	8,200,000
Retained earnings	4,600,000
Treasury stock (60,000 shares at cost)	(480,000)
Total stockholders' equity	$13,020,000

Fast Start Corporation
Statement of Stockholders' Equity
December 31, 2007
(in thousands)

	Common Stock	Paid-In Capital	Retained Earnings	Treasury Stock	Total
December 31, 2006	$650	$7,450	$4,035	$(260)	$11,875
Net income			900		900
Dividends			(335)		(335)
Stock purchased				(220)	(220)
Stock issued	50	750			800
December 31, 2007	$700	$8,200	$4,600	$(480)	$13,020

E9-18 *Objs. 4, 5* Study the partial statement of stockholders' equity below. The left-most column, which usually contains the explanations of events affecting stockholders' equity, is missing. You may assume that the first number in a column is the beginning balance and the last number is the ending balance.

Preferred Stock	Common Stock	Paid-In Capital	Retained Earnings	Treasury Stock	Total
$55,000	$20,000	$315,000	$182,183	$(7,212)	$564,971
			23,488[a]		23,488
			(8,500)[b]		(8,500)
				1,906[c]	1,906
	5,000[d]	85,000[e]			90,000
$55,000	$25,000	$400,000	$197,171	$(5,306)	$671,865

Using your knowledge of the statement of stockholders' equity, explain what underlying event caused each of the five items on the statement that is marked by a letter.

E9-19 *Obj. 5* San Diego Company has 4,000 shares of $100 par value, 7% cumulative preferred stock outstanding. In addition, the company has 10,000 shares of common stock outstanding. The company began operations and issued both classes of stock on January 1, 2007. The total amount of cash dividends declared and paid during each of the first four years of the company's life is shown on the following page. Complete the table by indicating the dollars of dividends that should be paid each year to each class of stock.

(Continued)

Year	Total Dividends Paid	Dividends to Preferred	Dividends to Common	Unpaid Dividends to Preferred
2007	$50,000			
2008	10,000			
2009	45,000			
2010	70,000			

E9-20
Objs. 3, 4, 5

Below are listed key word clues and descriptions. The key word clues relate to different features or aspects of equity. Match the letter of each key word clue to the most relevant description provided. Use each clue only once.

a. authorized	f. declaration	k. preemptive	p. split
b. charter	g. issued	l. preferred	q. stock
c. common	h. outstanding	m. record	r. treasury
d. contributed	i. par	n. redeemable	
e. cumulative	j. payment	o. retained	

_____ 1. Shares of a company's own stock that have been reacquired by the company
_____ 2. Capital resulting from direct investments made by stockholders in the company
_____ 3. Earnings that have not been distributed to owners as dividends
_____ 4. The voting stock in a corporation
_____ 5. The actual number of shares that have been sold or given to stockholders
_____ 6. The document granted by a state that gives a corporation the legal right to exist
_____ 7. An arbitrary value assigned to a share of stock (not a very meaningful value)
_____ 8. The maximum number of shares that a corporation is permitted to issue
_____ 9. Stock that receives a fixed dividend amount
_____ 10. The number of shares that are currently in the hands of stockholders
_____ 11. The date on which a corporation announces that a dividend will be paid
_____ 12. Preferred stock that will be repurchased by the issuing company at a fixed future date
_____ 13. A type of dividend in which new shares are distributed to existing stockholders
_____ 14. The privilege of existing stockholders to buy a prorata share of any new stock that is offered for sale
_____ 15. The date on which a dividend is distributed to stockholders
_____ 16. A very large stock dividend
_____ 17. A feature that encourages corporations to make up any previously omitted dividends on preferred stock
_____ 18. The date that determines who will receive a dividend that has been declared

E9-21
Objs. 4, 5

Sweetwater Company reports the following stockholders' equity section of the balance sheet.

Preferred stock, $50 par value, 8% cumulative	$ 2,500,000
Common stock, $2 par value	800,000
Paid-in capital in excess of par value, common stock	11,000,000
Retained earnings	4,894,000
Total	$19,194,000

a. How many preferred shares are outstanding?
b. How many common shares are outstanding?
c. At what average price was the common stock sold?
d. If the firm declares dividends totaling $376,000, what amount per share will be paid to the preferred stockholders and what amount per share will be paid to common stockholders? (Assume that there are no unpaid prior dividends on the preferred stock.)

Problems

P9-1 BOND AMORTIZATION TABLE
Obj. 1

On January 1, 2007, Holstein Enterprises issued bonds. Its accounting department prepared the amortization table below.

Year	Present Value at Beginning of Year	Interest Incurred	Amount Paid	Amortization of Principal	Value at End of Year
1	384,440	34,600	32,000	2,600	387,040
2	387,040	34,834	32,000	2,834	389,874
3	389,874	35,089	32,000	3,089	392,963
4	392,963	35,367	32,000	3,367	396,330
5	396,330	35,670	32,000	3,670	400,000
Total		175,560	160,000	15,560	

Required

A. What was the total face value of the bonds issued?
B. At what price were the bonds sold?
C. What is the stated rate, or nominal rate, of interest for these bonds?
D. What is the real, or effective, rate of interest for these bonds?
E. What amount will appear on the year 3 income statement related to these bonds?
F. What amount will appear on the year 4 balance sheet related to these bonds?
G. Explain the interrelationship among the three items reported in the last row of the table (the row labeled Total).

P9-2 BONDS AND THE ACCOUNTING SYSTEM
Obj. 1

Pattison Associates issued 4-year bonds with a face value of $300,000 to yield an effective rate of 6%. The bonds pay interest annually and were sold at a price of $310,394.

Required

A. What was the stated rate for these bonds?
B. Show what information would be entered into the accounting system regarding these bonds on the date of issue. Using the format presented in this chapter, record the entry necessary at issuance and at the first interest payment date, and the entry at the final interest payment date. (Hint: It may be helpful to prepare an amortization table.)

P9-3 ISSUANCE AND AMORTIZATION OF BONDS
Obj. 1

Sky King Company sold $9 million of four-year, 8% debentures on July 1, 2007. The bonds sold to yield a real rate of 7%. Interest is paid annually on June 30.

Required

A. Determine the price of the bonds.
B. Prepare an amortization schedule for the bonds.
C. Using the format presented in this chapter, record the entry to the accounting system that is necessary to recognize interest on the bonds at June 30, 2008.
D. Assume the bonds had been sold to yield a real rate of 9%. At what price would they have sold?

P9-4 ISSUANCE AND AMORTIZATION OF BONDS
Obj. 1

Plum Grove Company sold $10 million of four-year, 9% debentures on July 1, 2007. The bonds sold to yield an effective rate of 10%. Interest is paid annually on June 30.

(Continued)

Required

A. Determine the price of the bonds.
B. Prepare an amortization schedule for the bonds.
C. Using the format presented in this chapter, record the entry to the accounting system that is necessary to recognize interest on the bonds at June 30, 2008.
D. Assume the bonds had been sold to yield 8%. At what price would they have sold?

P9-5 ETHICAL ISSUES RELATED TO DEBT

Obj. 1

Ethan Jones is an investment broker. Recently he contacted potential investors and offered to sell them bonds that were paying an 8% annual rate of interest. He noted that the bonds were paying a much higher return than other investments and that similar bonds were selling at a real rate of 6% interest. The bonds had a 10-year maturity and paid interest semiannually. Several investors purchased the bonds because of the high rate of interest but later were concerned to learn that the maturity value of $1,000 per bond was considerably less than the $1,350 they had paid for each bond.

Required Compare the price of the bonds sold by Ethan to bonds yielding a real rate of 6%. What was the approximate real rate of return earned by the investors? Did they have a right to be concerned about their investments? Do you see any ethical problems with Ethan's sales pitch?

P9-6 CHOOSING BETWEEN FINANCING OPTIONS

Obj. 1

The management of Evening Star Financial plans to borrow $50,000 to carry out current operations. Two repayment options are available. The appropriate interest rate is 7%.

Option 1: The company may repay the amount borrowed by making four equal annual payments, the first one due in one year.
Option 2: The company may pay just the interest annually, and then pay the entire amount of $50,000 at the end of four years.

Required

A. Identify the amount of the annual payment required under Option 1 and the amount of the required annual interest payment under Option 2.
B. Identify the total cash outflows and the total interest expense incurred for the four years under each option.
C. Explain why there is a difference in the total cash outflow and total interest expense between the two plans.
D. Which plan would you recommend to the company?

P9-7 CHOOSING BETWEEN FINANCING OPTIONS

Obj. 1

Careful Electric Company is planning to purchase equipment for one of its generating plants. Dealer A has offered to sell the equipment at a total cost of $2 million, including installation. This dealer requires a 6% return and is willing to spread the payments over a 10-year period. Payments are to be made at the end of each year in equal installments.

Dealer B is asking $1.8 million for the same equipment and will charge an additional $50,000 for installation, to be paid when the equipment is delivered. Payments can be spread over 10 years, made at the end of each year. This dealer requires an 8% return.

Required

A. Calculate the amount of the annual payments required by each dealer. Round to nearest whole dollar.
B. Determine the projected total cash outflow under each option.
C. If Careful could pay cash for the new equipment, how much money (interest) would it save under each option?
D. Which option should be chosen?
E. Assume the equipment is acquired using the financing offered by Dealer A. How will the financing activities section of the statement of cash flows be affected by these transactions in the first year?

P9-8 ACQUIRING ASSETS VIA CAPITAL LEASE

Obj. 2

Jessica Johnson Logging Company is considering the acquisition of a new bulldozer. Big Dig Inc. has offered to lease the equipment to Johnson Company for all 12 years of its useful life at annual year-end lease payments of $24,500. Each payment will include 9% interest. At the end of 12 years of lease payments, Big Dig Inc. will allow Johnson to keep the bulldozer.

Required

A. At what amount should the bulldozer and lease obligation be recorded on Johnson's books at the date of acquisition?
B. Prepare an amortization table covering only the first four years of the lease.
C. Explain why a $24,500 lease payment doesn't cause the amount owed to decrease by $24,500.
D. Explain why Johnson's interest expense gets smaller for each successive year of the lease.
E. Using the format presented in this chapter, record the entry to capitalize the bulldozer and lease obligation on Johnson's books.
F. Using the format presented in this chapter, record the entry to recognize the first year-end lease payment.

P9-9 DETERMINING LEASE PAYMENTS

Obj. 2

Garcia Orchards & Processing Company has been taking bids for three new tractors. Goldbaum Equipment has made an offer to sell a qualifying model for $41,000 each. In addition, Goldbaum has offered to finance the transaction through a capital lease over the expected 15-year life of the tractors with no money down. No mention of the size of the required year-end lease payments has been made yet, but Garcia knows that Goldbaum will expect a 9% return on the lease arrangement.

Required If Garcia accepts this option:

A. What will be the size of each annual year-end lease payment?
B. What amount will Garcia capitalize on its balance sheet for the tractors and for the lease obligation? What does this amount represent?
C. Using the format presented in this chapter, record the entry to set up the lease on Garcia's books.
D. What total amount will Garcia pay over the life of the lease for financing? (Hint: You do not need to prepare an amortization table.)
E. Using the format presented in this chapter, record the entry necessary when Garcia makes the first lease payment.
F. When the second year's lease payment is recorded, will the amount of interest expense be larger or smaller than that for the first year? Explain.

P9-10 USING SPREADSHEET FUNCTIONS TO EVALUATE A LEASE PROPOSAL

Obj. 2

FencePost.com needs additional equipment to expand production capacity. A vendor has suggested a lease plan in which FencePost would make end-of-the-month payments for five years of $3,250. At that point the equipment would be worthless and discarded. The vendor expects to earn a return on this financing arrangement of 9.75% compounded annually. The chief financial officer at FencePost recognizes this arrangement would be accounted for as a capital lease.

Required

A. Use the PV function in an Excel spreadsheet to determine the amount at which the lease would be recorded in the accounting system. List the arguments you inserted into the formula.
B. Show how this transaction would be entered into the accounting system at inception of the lease.
C. Prepare an amortization table for the lease (first four months only).
D. Show the entry that must be made on the date of the first lease payment.
E. Explain how you can tell that the vendor earns a 9.75% rate of return on this transaction.

P9-11 USING SPREADSHEET FUNCTIONS TO EVALUATE A LEASE PROPOSAL

Obj. 2

Rampaging Technology Inc. is growing rapidly and is expanding its production capacity. An equipment supplier has suggested a lease plan based on a selling price of $350,000. Rampaging

(Continued)

would make five equal-size end-of-the-year payments and then own the machine. The supplier expects to earn a return on this financing arrangement of 11.35% compounded annually. Such a lease would be accounted for as a capital lease.

Required

A. Use the PMT function in an Excel spreadsheet to determine the amount of the annual payment that would be required. List the arguments you inserted into the formula.
B. Show how this transaction would be entered into the accounting system at inception of the lease.
C. Prepare an amortization table for the lease.
D. Explain why the annual interest expense decreases during each of the five years.
E. Show the entry that must be made on the date of the first lease payment.
F. Explain how you can tell that the vendor earns an 11.35% rate of return on this transaction.

P9-12 REPORTING CHANGES IN STOCKHOLDERS' EQUITY

Obj. 4

Below is shown the stockholders' equity section of Tulip Company's balance sheet at December 31, 2007.

Common stock, $2 par value, 5,400,000 shares authorized, 2,200,000 shares issued and outstanding	$ 4,400,000
Paid-in capital in excess of par value	30,800,000
Retained earnings	46,000,000
Total stockholders' equity	$81,200,000

All of the following occurred in year 2005 and were properly recorded.

1. The company purchased 30,000 shares of its own stock at $21 per share on January 2.
2. The company purchased 20,000 shares of the Sumo Corporation at $6 per share on February 14.
3. The company declared and issued a 10% stock dividend on March 2. The fair market value of the stock at that time was $25 per share.
4. The company declared and paid a cash dividend of $0.40 on its common stock on July 21.
5. The company reported a net loss of $5,200,000 on December 31.

Required

A. Prepare the stockholders' equity section as of December 31, 2008 after all the events described above have been properly accounted for.
B. Describe the effects on the financing section of the year 2008 statement of cash flows.

P9-13 STOCK SPLITS AND STOCK DIVIDENDS

Obj. 4

The Sunergy Corporation manufactures solar panels that provide electricity for businesses and homes. The company has been doing well for several years and so the board of directors has decided to declare a stock split in the amount of two shares for every share of stock held by shareholders. The split will be effective as of February 15, 2007.

Below is the stockholders' equity section of the Sunergy Corporation's balance sheet at December 31, 2006.

Common stock, $2 par, 600,000 shares authorized, 200,000 shares issued and outstanding	$ 400,000
Additional paid-in capital in excess of par	1,500,000
Retained earnings	3,600,000
Total	$5,500,000

Required

A. Prepare the stockholders' equity section for the Sunergy Corporation's balance sheet after the stock split. How many shares of stock will be issued to the shareholders? Assume the market value of the stock is $18 per share on February 15, 2007.
B. Assume that the Sunergy Corporation's board of directors decided to declare a 100% stock dividend instead of the split. Prepare the stockholders' equity section after the stock

dividend. How many shares of stock will be issued to the shareholders? (Note that for a large stock dividend—100% in this case—the dollar amount transferred from retained earnings to contributed capital will be the par value of the stock, instead of the market price.)

C. Compare the stockholders' equity sections after the split and after the dividend. How do they differ?

D. What should be the selling price of the stock after the split? After the dividend?

P9-14 THE STATEMENT OF STOCKHOLDERS' EQUITY AND OTHER FINANCIAL STATEMENTS

Objs. 3, 4

Olafson Electronics reported the following statement of stockholders' equity at the end of its 10th year in business.

Required For each of the five lettered items in the statement below, indicate where that same information will be found on one or more other financial statements. Be specific as to the statement(s) and the specific section of the statement(s).

	Preferred Stock	Common Stock	Paid-In Capital	Retained Earnings	Treasury Stock	Total
December 31, year 9	$21,000	$10,000	$188,000	$77,831	$(10,094)	$286,737
Net income				26,182[a]		26,182
Dividends				(14,300)[b]		(14,300)
Stock purchased					(1,263)[c]	(1,263)
Stock issued		4,000	75,000			79,000[d]
December 31, year 10	$21,000	$14,000[e]	$263,000	$89,713	$(11,357)	$376,356

P9-15 CONVERTIBLE PREFERRED STOCK

Obj. 5

The Neese Company has 4,000 shares of $5 par preferred stock outstanding. The stock originally had been issued for $12 per share. It is convertible into shares of common stock at the rate of three shares of $1 par common for every share of preferred. No cash would be paid by the converting shareholders. This convertible preferred stock pays a dividend of $0.50 per share per year.

Required

A. Assume there are 45,000 shares of common stock outstanding, originally issued at $30 per share, but having a current market value of $32 per share. The retained earnings account balance is $3,200,000. Prepare the stockholders' equity section of the balance sheet before conversion of any preferred stock.

B. Now, assume that all of the preferred stock is converted to common stock. Prepare the stockholders' equity section of the balance sheet. Compare and explain the totals in stockholders' equity before and after the conversion of the preferred stock.

C. Explain how the conversion of preferred stock into common stock will be reported in the financing section of the cash flow statement.

D. Assume that the Velasquez Corporation is similar to the Neese Company in many respects including the fact that it has $10 par value preferred stock outstanding. Velasquez pays a dividend of $1.60 per share per year on its preferred stock; the stock is not convertible to common. What do you think is the main reason for the difference in dividend rates between the two companies?

P9-16 UNDERSTANDING THE STOCKHOLDERS' EQUITY SECTION OF THE BALANCE SHEET

Objs. 3, 4, 5

Saigon Building Supply was organized and began operations on January 1, 2007. At December 31, 2008, it reported the following stockholders' equity section on its comparative balance sheet.

(Continued)

December 31,	2008	2007
Stockholders' equity		
8.5% preferred stock, $10 par value, 10,000 shares authorized and issued	*b*	*a*
Common stock, $2 par value, 300,000 shares authorized, 110,000 and 90,000 shares issued	*d*	*c*
Paid-in capital in excess of par value	*f*	*e*
Retained earnings	*h*	*g*
Treasury stock (4,500 and 3,100 shares at cost)	*j*	*i*
Total stockholders' equity	$1,411,750	$1,037,800

The company reported net income of $75,000 for calendar year 2007 and $125,000 for 2008. The firm's dividend policy is to pay out 10% of its profits each year in dividends. The date of payment is always April 1 of the following year. Treasury stock was acquired at a cost of $12 per share in 2007. At December 31, 2008, the average cost of treasury stock was $13.50 per share. The common shares sold during 2008 were sold at $14 each.

Required Replace each of the italicized letters with the correct numerical value.

P9-17 INTERPRETING THE STOCKHOLDERS' EQUITY SECTION OF THE BALANCE SHEET

Objs. 3, 4, 5

Hampton Inc. began operations on January 1, 2007. On December 31, 2008, it reported the following stockholders' equity section of its balance sheet.

December 31,	2008	2007
Stockholders' equity		
7% cumulative preferred stock, $100 par value	$ 300,000	$ 300,000
Common stock, $2 par value	150,000	120,000
Paid-in capital in excess of par value	830,000	620,000
Retained earnings	362,500	157,500
Treasury stock	(16,800)	(25,725)
Total stockholders' equity	$1,625,700	$1,171,775

The company has a policy of paying out 10% of its net income as cash dividends. The date of declaration is always 30 days after the end of the year, and the date of payment occurs 60 days after the end of the year. At year-end 2007, the average price of treasury stock was $10.50. At year-end 2008, the average price of treasury stock was $12.

Required

A. How many preferred shares have been issued as of year-end 2007 and 2008?
B. How many common shares have been issued as of year-end 2007? As of year-end 2008?
C. How many treasury shares are there at year-end 2007? At year-end 2008?
D. How many common shares are outstanding at year-end 2007? At year-end 2008?
E. What was the average price (at original issuance) of common stock as of year-end 2007?
F. What was the average selling price of the shares issued during 2008?
G. What was net income for 2007? For 2008?
H. What was the dividend per share paid to preferred stock on March 1, 2008?
I. What was the dividend per share paid to common stock on March 1, 2008?
J. What is the dividend per share that is scheduled to be paid to common stock on March 1, 2009? Why?

P9-18 INTERPRETING THE STOCKHOLDERS' EQUITY SECTION OF THE BALANCE SHEET

Objs. 3, 4, 5

Nakishima Industries reported the following stockholders' equity section of its balance sheet at December 31, 2008.

December 31,	2008	2007
Stockholders' equity		
8.5% cumulative preferred stock, $25 par value	$ 450,000	$ 375,000
Common stock, $5 par value	680,000	575,000
Paid-in capital in excess of par value, common	4,050,000	2,500,000
Retained earnings	9,400,300	7,300,800
Treasury stock	(1,970,050)	(1,510,000)
Total stockholders' equity	$12,610,250	$ 9,240,800

The company has paid cash dividends annually for 24 years. There are no dividends in arrears. The date of declaration is always March 1 and the amount of dividends declared is always 25% of prior year net income. Year 2007 net income was $2.0 million. At year-end 2008, the average cost of treasury stock was $31 per share. At year-end 2007, the average price of treasury stock was $25.

Required

A. How many preferred shares have been issued as of the end of 2008 and 2007?
B. How many common shares have been issued as of the end of 2008? As of year-end 2007?
C. How many treasury shares are there at year-end 2008 and at year-end 2007?
D. How many common shares are outstanding at year-end 2008 and at year-end 2007?
E. As of year-end 2008, what was the average price (at original issuance) of common stock?
F. What was the average selling price of the common shares issued during 2008?
G. What was net income for 2008?
H. What was the amount of the dividend per share paid to preferred stock during 2008?
I. What was the amount of the dividend per share paid to common stock during 2008? (Assume there were 54,600 common shares outstanding at the date of the 2008 dividend distribution.)
J. What is the dividend per share that is scheduled to be paid to common stock in 2009? (Assume there will be no change in the number of shares outstanding between December 31, 2008 and the distribution of dividends in 2009.)

P9-19 DETERMINING WHETHER A LIABILITY EXISTS

Objs. 1, 2, 3, 4, 5

Determine if a liability should be recorded in each of the following cases involving the Soft-Wear Manufacturing Company. If there is no liability, explain how the item should be recorded.

A. The company guarantees to repair or replace any of its products that are defective.
B. The company estimates that some customers will not pay for merchandise purchased on credit.
C. The company obtains an asset and signs a lease that extends for one-third of the useful life of the asset.
D. The company is being investigated for potential pollution problems by the Environmental Protection Agency. The company's engineers believe it is likely that the company will be held responsible for an expensive cleanup activity.
E. The company has issued bonds that are maturing at the end of the current month.
F. The company is being sued by an unhappy customer. The case has not yet come to court.
G. The company has declared a 20% stock dividend.
H. The company has declared a $0.25 cash dividend to be paid on all outstanding shares.
I. The preferred stock is cumulative and dividends have not been paid for three years.
J. The company has a noncontrolling interest of 3%.
K. The company has bonds outstanding that are convertible into common stock. The company's accountants believe that bond holders are likely to convert their bonds because the company has performed exceptionally well this year.
L. Stock options have been issued to the company's executives. The options have not yet been exercised.

P9-20 EXCEL IN ACTION

In March 2008, the Wermz's decided to expand their business. They purchased an existing chain of bookstores for a price of \$5 million. They financed their purchase by issuing \$3 million of common stock and by issuing \$2 million of 20-year bonds payable. Interest will be paid monthly beginning in April 2008. The stated rate of interest on the bonds is 9% (annual interest payments are 9% of \$2 million). The bonds were sold to earn a 9.25% interest rate (the actual annual rate of interest is 9.25%).

Required Use a spreadsheet to determine the present value of the bonds. Enter the captions (as shown in the example below) in cells A1 to A7.

In cell B1, enter the maturity value of the bonds.

In cell B2, calculate the amount of interest paid each month.

In cell B3, calculate the actual monthly interest rate.

In cell B4, calculate the number of months during which interest will be paid.

In cell B5, calculate the present value of the interest payments. Use the PV function (click on the Function button and select Financial and PV). Enter the rate (B3), number of periods (B4), and monthly payments (B2). The resulting value is negative because it is a cash outflow. Change the amount to a positive value by multiplying by (-1).

In cell B6, calculate the present value of the maturity value of the bonds. The calculation is based on the equation $PV = MV/(1+R)^t$, where *PV* is present value, *MV* is maturity value (B1), *R* is the actual interest rate (B3), and *t* is the number of periods until maturity (B4).

In cell B7, calculate the total maturity value of the bonds.

	A	B
1	Maturity	
2	Interest Payments	
3	Actual Interest Rate	
4	Periods	
5	Present Value of Interest	
6	Present Value of Principal	
7	Total Present Value	

Beginning in cell A9, prepare an amortization table for April through December 2008 for the bonds. Use Exhibit 4 in this chapter as an example. Use formulas for all spreadsheet calculations. (See the Continuous Problem in Chapter 8 if you need help.) How much interest expense will The Book Wermz incur on the bonds in 2008? How much interest will the company pay? How much liability will the company report for the bonds at the end of 2008?

Suppose the effective interest rate was 8.75%. What would be the present value of the bonds? How much interest expense would the company incur in 2008?

Suppose the effective interest rate was 9.0%. What would be the present value of the bonds? How much interest expense would the company incur in 2008?

P9-21 MULTIPLE-CHOICE OVERVIEW OF THE CHAPTER

1. Which of the following are attributes of a liability?

	Result from a Prior Transaction	Involve a Promise to Convey Resources in the Future
a.	Yes	Yes
b.	Yes	No
c.	No	Yes
d.	No	No

2. Which of the following should be reported on a year-end balance sheet under the heading of short-term debt?

	Wages Already Earned by Employees but Not Yet Paid	30-Year Debentures that Have Been Outstanding for 29 Years
a.	Yes	Yes
b.	Yes	No
c.	No	Yes
d.	No	No

3. A contingency is reported on the balance sheet as a liability if
   a. it arises from a potential claim regarding damage to the environment.
   b. a loss is probable and it can be reasonably estimated.
   c. a lawsuit has been filed.
   d. it involves a potential loss of a large amount of money.

4. The stockholders' equity section of Tarro Company's balance sheet includes the following selected information.

Common stock, $1 par, 15,000 shares authorized, 9,000 shares issued, 7,000 shares outstanding	?
Additional paid-in capital in excess of par value	$ 27,000
Retained earnings	14,000
Treasury stock	(20,000)

   What is the correct balance of the common stock account?
   a. $15,000
   b. $11,000
   c. $9,000
   d. $7,000

5. A stockholder who owns 5% of the common stock of a corporation has a right to each of the following except
   a. 5% of any dividends paid to common stockholders.
   b. to cast votes on matters brought to stockholders for a vote.
   c. to receive a dividend of 5% of net income for the current period.
   d. to purchase 5% of any additional common stock issued by the company.

6. A corporation had retained earnings of $400,000 at December 31, 2007. Net income for 2008 was $175,000, and the company paid a cash dividend of $75,000. Also, the company repurchased shares of its stock during the year at a total cost of $50,000. The balance of retained earnings at December 31, 2008, would be
   a. $450,000.
   b. $550,000.
   c. $575,000.
   d. $500,000.

7. A corporation issued a 10% stock dividend during its 2008 fiscal year. The market value of the stock was $20 per share at the time the dividend was issued. One million shares of stock were outstanding. The par value of the stock was $1 per share. Which of the following correctly identifies the effect on the financial statements of this transaction?

	Assets	Equity	Net Income
a.	Increase	Decrease	No effect
b.	No effect	Decrease	No effect
c.	No effect	No effect	No effect
d.	No effect	Decrease	Decrease

8. Which of the following is *not* a true statement about preferred stock?
   a. Preferred stockholders receive a current cash dividend before common stockholders do.
   b. Preferred stockholders must receive the stated dividend each year.
   c. Preferred stock generally does not have voting privileges.
   d. The cumulative feature serves to protect preferred stockholder interests.

(Continued)

9. The statement that "dividends are not an expense" is
   a. always true.
   b. never true.
   c. sometimes true.
   d. frequently true.

10. The presence of a foreign currency adjustment on the balance sheet means that
    a. the company owns at least one foreign subsidiary.
    b. the company's primary operations are located in a foreign country.
    c. shares of the company's stock have been sold to foreign investors.
    d. retained earnings of a foreign subsidiary have been appropriated.

Cases

C9-1 MAKING CREDIT DECISIONS

Objs. 1, 2, 3, 4

Suppose that you are an employee of the loan department of Metropolitan Bank, and one of your primary tasks is analyzing information provided by organizations applying for commercial loans. Most applicants are small businesses seeking additional capital to acquire long-term assets. Other applicants are seeking financing to acquire existing businesses. A typical applicant is Cleopatra Jones, who owns Cleopatra's, a women's clothing store. Ms. Jones has applied for a loan of $50,000 to finance an expansion of her business.

Required Identify the types of information you would need from Ms. Jones to help you make a loan decision. Explain why each type of information would be useful.

C9-2 INTERPRETING STOCKHOLDERS' EQUITY

Objs. 3, 4, 5

Selected disclosures from a consolidated balance sheet are shown below.

December 31,	2007	2006
(in millions)		
Total assets	**$3,759.7**	**$3,774.4**
Total liabilities	**$2,411.9**	**$2,652.3**
Stockholders' equity:		
Preferred stock	**785.1**	789.0
Common stock, shares issued:		
2007 = 171.2; 2006 = 162.6	**0.9**	0.8
Retained earnings (accumulated deficit)	**79.9**	(114.0)
Other capital	**481.9**	446.3
Total stockholders' equity	**$1,347.8**	$ 1,122.1
Total liabilities and stockholders' equity	**$3,759.7**	**$3,774.4**

A note to the financial statements reveals:

> The Company has 180,000,000 authorized shares of common stock. In February of 2005, the Certificate of Incorporation of the Company was amended to change the par value of the common stock from $4 per share to $0.01 per share.
>
> In 2006, the Company resumed payment of dividends on preferred stock, which had been suspended in February 2005. Preferred dividends of $53.9 million and $61.4 million were in arrears at December 31, 2007 and December 31, 2006, respectively.

Required Prepare a report that explains the following:

A. Of what economic significance is the par value of a company's stock? What is the significance of the decision to restate the par value of the stock? What is the advantage for the company?

B. What are the primary attributes of preferred stock? In what ways is preferred stock equity? In what ways is it debt? Why do companies issue preferred stock?
C. What effect does the suspension of dividends on the preferred stock have on the financial statements? What economic effect does it have on the company? If the preferred stock and dividends in arrears were reported as liabilities, what would be the effect on the company's balance sheet?
D. Assess the position of the company's common stockholders at the end of 2007.

C9-3 ANALYZING LIABILITIES AND STOCKHOLDERS' EQUITY

Objs. 1, 2, 3, 4, 5

Selected information from **General Mills**' 2004 annual report and 10K is provided in Appendix A at the end of the text.

Required Write a report that covers the following:

A. How important were liabilities as a source of financing for assets as of the end of fiscal 2004? What are some of the implications of this? Discuss.
B. What were the company's most significant liabilities at year-end 2004? Did the relative significance of certain liabilities change from the prior year? Describe any material changes.
C. Did financing activities concerning liabilities affect cash flows during 2004? Did financing activities concerning liabilities affect its net income in 2004? Identify any such effects.
D. Describe any significant changes in stockholders' equity that occurred between year-end 2001 and year-end 2004. For any significant changes, indicate what caused them to change.

© PHOTODISC/GETTY IMAGES

Analysis of Financing Activities

10

HOW DO WE FINANCE OUR BUSINESS?

Chapter 9 discussed financing activities, including accounting for debt and equity. Accounting involves more than determining amounts to report in financial statements. It involves the analysis of information about business activities to understand those activities and how they affect the performance and value of a business.

If Maria and Stan are going to increase the size of their business, they will need additional financing. They need to be aware of the effect that debt and equity have on a business's profitability and value. And they need to make financing decisions that increase company value and permit it to survive for the long run.

Maria, the company president, Stan, the vice president of operations, and Ellen, the vice president of finance of Favorite Cookie Company, sat in Maria's office discussing financial plans for their company. Maria and Stan formed the company to sell cookies produced from family recipes. Initially, the company purchased its products from bakeries because it did not have sufficient financial resources to buy the equipment and facilities it would need to manufacture its own products. As the company's products have become more popular, Maria and Stan have decided to expand their company. The volume of sales is sufficient to warrant acquiring production facilities. Ellen was hired recently as vice president of finance to help the company with its growth potential. They have met to discuss how to finance their company's expansion.

Food for Thought

What issues should managers consider when deciding on the amounts of debt and equity financing to use in a company? How should investors analyze a company's financial statements to assess managers' financing decisions and the effects of these decisions on profits and company value?

Maria: *I've noticed that different companies use different amounts of debt and equity financing. How can we determine the right amounts for our company?*

Ellen: *One issue we can look at is the effect that different forms of financing can have on the risk and return of owners and other stakeholders.*

Stan: *Can it really make that much of a difference?*

Ellen: *Yes. Many companies have a hard time surviving because they made financing decisions that were not right for the companies. There are good reasons that some companies use more debt than others. Let's take a look at some of these reasons.*

Objectives

Once you have completed this chapter, you should be able to:

1. Define capital structure, and explain why it is important to a company.
2. Explain when it is beneficial for a company to use financial leverage.
3. Explain why cash flows are important for a company's financing decisions.
4. Use financial statements to evaluate the financing activities of different companies.
5. Determine and explain the effect of financial leverage on a company's risk and return.
6. Use cash flow and liquidity measures to evaluate financing decisions.
7. Explain why financing activities are important for determining company value.

FINANCING DECISIONS

Maria, Stan, and Ellen know that if the company is properly managed, it will have a good chance of making a lot of money. They also knew of several companies like theirs, with promising futures, that failed within a few years because of poor financial management. They are determined not to make the same mistakes. Let's follow their conversation as they discuss their financing alternatives.

Stan continued the conversation. "The potential for our product is good. At our current growth rate, we should sell $3 million of product next year, and I believe sales will grow at a rate of 20% per year for the foreseeable future. We need $5 million to fund production facilities and to expand production and marketing activities. Of this amount, $4 million will go into plant assets."

Capital Structure Decisions

Objective 1
Define capital structure, and explain why it is important to a company.

Maria spoke next, "OK, we know we have great potential. We have a quality product that meets the needs of a large market. Our current concern is how do we finance our production costs? I think we might want to use as much debt as possible. A friend of mine from college is a manager with a company that uses well over 50% debt in its capital structure, and the company has been very successful. What do you think?"

Stan interrupted, "What do you mean by capital structure?"

"*Capital structure* **is the relative amounts of debt and equity used by a company to finance its assets,"** Ellen answered. "Those are our basic choices. Either we can borrow money, or we can issue stock. Some companies are successful using a lot of debt, but our situation is different. I think we should rely primarily on equity."

"I don't understand," Stan replied. "What difference does it make? We need $5 million. As long as we get it from someone, why should we care where it comes from? A dollar of debt will pay for just as many assets as a dollar of equity."

"Yes," answered Ellen, "but that's not the complete story. Let's look at some numbers. Exhibit 1 contains projected sales and operating income figures for the next three years based on Stan's estimates. Operating costs will be high relative to sales next year because of initial training and development costs and special marketing efforts to increase customer awareness of our product. Also, we will not be producing at full capacity until we get more of our product into customers' hands and they see how good it is."

"I still don't see the point," Stan observed.

Ellen responded, "Well, let's see what happens to our profits and stockholder returns depending on how we finance our operations. Exhibit 2 provides a simplified balance

EXHIBIT 1
Projected Sales and Income for Favorite Cookie Company

(In thousands)	Year 1	Year 2	Year 3
Sales	$3,000	$3,600	$4,320
Cost of goods sold	(1,800)	(2,160)	(2,592)
Operating expenses	(1,000)	(1,000)	(1,000)
Operating income	$ 200	$ 440	$ 728
Income taxes	(60)	(132)	(218)
Net income	$ 140	$ 308	$ 510

EXHIBIT 2
Projected Summary Balance Sheet for Favorite Cookie Company

(In thousands)	Year 1	Year 2	Year 3
Assets:			
Current assets	$1,000	$1,200	$1,440
Plant assets	4,000	4,000	4,000
Total assets	$5,000	$5,200	$5,440
Liabilities:			
Current liabilities	$ 800	$ 960	$1,152
Long-term debt	0	0	0
Total liabilities	$ 800	$ 960	$1,152
Stockholders' equity	4,200	4,240	4,288
Total liabilities and equity	$5,000	$5,200	$5,440

sheet for Favorite Cookie Company, assuming that we finance our company without any long-term debt. These numbers assume that we invest $4 million in plant assets and start with $1 million in current assets. Further, I assume that current assets will increase at the same rate as sales, 20% per year. Plant assets will be replaced each year as they wear out to maintain a constant investment, at least for the first few years. Also, I assume that we issue $4.2 million of stock and use current liabilities to fund the remainder of our assets. Some of our current assets, such as inventories, can be purchased on short-term credit from suppliers. Therefore, Accounts Payable and other current liabilities will provide a source of funding for a portion of current assets.

"Using this financing arrangement," Ellen continued, "our income statement will look like Exhibit 1, which does not include any interest expense. A useful measure of performance, in addition to net income, is return on equity. ***Return on equity (ROE)*** **is net income divided by stockholders' equity.** It measures net income relative to the amount invested by stockholders in a company, including retained earnings. Investors and financial analysts use return on equity to compare the performances of companies, either to compare one company with another or to compare a company's performance in one period with its performance in another period. From the data in Exhibits 1 and 2, we can compute Favorite Cookie Company's return on equity as shown in Exhibit 3.

"Exhibit 3 indicates that stockholders will earn 3.3 cents next year for each dollar they invest in Favorite Cookie Company," Ellen observed. "Three years from now, they will earn 11.9 cents for each dollar invested. Now let's see what happens if we include long-term debt in our capital structure."

EXHIBIT 3
Return on Equity (Net Income ÷ Stockholders' Equity) for Favorite Cookie Company

(In thousands)	Year 1	Year 2	Year 3
Net income	$ 140	$ 308	$ 510
Stockholders' equity	$4,200	$4,240	$4,288
Return on equity	3.3%	7.3%	11.9%

The Effect of Financial Leverage

Objective 2
Explain when it is beneficial for a company to use financial leverage.

"Let's look at the numbers," Ellen continued. "Exhibit 4 describes the results if we use \$2.5 million of liabilities and \$2.5 million of equity next year. This would give us an initial **debt-to-equity ratio** of 1.0 (\$2.5 million of liabilities ÷ \$2.5 million of equity) and a **debt-to-assets ratio** of 0.5 or 50% (\$2.5 million of liabilities ÷ \$5 million of assets). These ratios are used frequently as measures of capital structure; the higher the ratios, the more debt in a company's capital structure. It's not uncommon for some companies to have a debt-to-assets ratio of 70% or more, as you noted earlier, Maria. But in our case I think it is unwise.

"As you can see in Exhibit 4," Ellen continued, "net income would be lower each year because of interest expense on the long-term debt. I have assumed a 10% interest rate, which is about what debt would cost us. Our rate would be higher than that for established companies because of the risk associated with an unproven company like ours. Also, I have assumed that we will maintain a debt-to-equity ratio of 1.0 each year.

"While net income is lower each year, stockholders' equity also is lower, primarily because we will not need to issue as much stock to finance the company. Observe from Exhibit 4, however, that return on equity is lower in the first year if we use debt. In the second year, return on equity is about the same whether we use debt or not (compare with Exhibit 3). In the third year, as profits increase, return on equity is higher if we use debt than if we use only equity.

"Exhibit 5 provides a graph that helps explain the effect of using debt. The graph shows the amount of return on equity Favorite Cookie Company would report at various levels of sales revenues. Return on equity varies more when larger amounts of debt are used."

"This effect is known as financial leverage," Maria remarked. "*Financial leverage (FL)* **is the use of debt to increase a company's return on equity.** The more debt there is in a company's capital structure, the greater the financial leverage. As you can see from the graph, financial leverage magnifies return on equity. When return on equity is low, financial leverage makes it lower. When return on equity is high, financial leverage makes it higher.

EXHIBIT 4
Projected Financial Results for Favorite Cookie Company Based on a 1.0 Debt-to-Equity Ratio

(In thousands)	Year 1	Year 2	Year 3
Sales	\$3,000	\$3,600	\$4,320
Cost of goods sold	(1,800)	(2,160)	(2,592)
Operating expenses	(1,000)	(1,000)	(1,000)
Operating income	\$ 200	\$ 440	\$ 728
Interest expense	(170)	(164)	(157)
Pretax income	\$ 30	\$ 276	\$ 571
Income taxes	(9)	(83)	(171)
Net income	\$ 21	\$ 193	\$ 400
Assets:			
Current assets	\$1,000	\$1,200	\$1,440
Plant assets	4,000	4,000	4,000
Total assets	\$5,000	\$5,200	\$5,440
Liabilities:			
Current liabilities	\$ 800	\$ 960	\$1,152
Long-term debt	1,700	1,640	1,568
Total liabilities	\$2,500	\$2,600	\$2,720
Stockholders' equity	2,500	2,600	2,720
Total liabilities and equity	\$5,000	\$5,200	\$5,440
Return on equity	0.8%	7.4%	14.7%

EXHIBIT 5
The Effect of Financial Leverage on Return on Equity

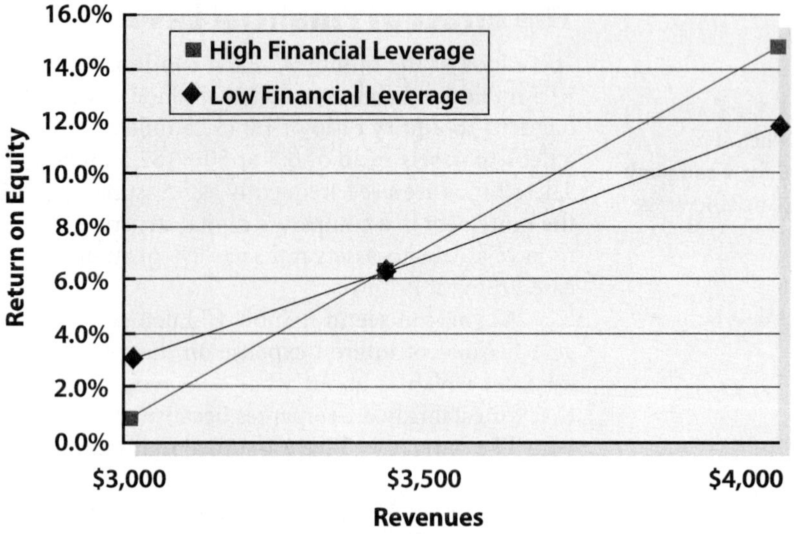

"The magnification effect of financial leverage can be thought of as a simple formula:

Return on Equity (ROE) = Return on Assets (ROA) × Financial Leverage (FL)

$$\frac{\text{Net Income}}{\text{Stockholders' Equity}} = \frac{\text{Net Income}}{\text{Total Assets}} \times \frac{\text{Total Assets}}{\text{Stockholders' Equity}}$$

As explained earlier in this chapter, net income divided by stockholders' equity is return on equity. Recall from Chapter 2 that net income divided by total assets is known as **return on assets (ROA)**. The formula for calculating **financial leverage (FL)** is **total assets divided by stockholders' equity**. If a company has a lot of debt, the ratio of total assets to stockholders' equity will be large.

"You can see the effect of leverage by looking at Favorite Cookie Company's numbers. In the first year, if we don't use any long-term debt, the formula would look like this:

$$\text{ROE} = \text{ROA} \times \text{FL}$$

$$\frac{\$140}{\$4{,}200} = \frac{\$140}{\$5{,}000} \times \frac{\$5{,}000}{\$4{,}200}$$

$$3.3\% = 2.8\% \times 1.19$$

The only leverage we would have would come from current liabilities.

"If we use $2.5 million of liabilities, the formula would show this:

$$\text{ROE} = \text{ROA} \times \text{FL}$$

$$\frac{\$21}{\$2{,}500} = \frac{\$21}{\$5{,}000} \times \frac{\$5{,}000}{\$2{,}500}$$

$$0.8\% = 0.4\% \times 2.0$$

"If we don't use any long-term debt, the magnification factor is about 1.2. If we use long-term debt, the magnification factor is 2.0. Though higher financial leverage works against us when our profits are low, it works for us in later years when we start making more profit."

"That's why I thought we should use a relatively large amount of debt," Maria continued. "We expect Favorite Cookie Company to earn a lot of money in the next few years. If we use a lot of debt, we can leverage those earnings to generate a high return on equity. This will make our company more valuable and probably will make us rich. Ellen's graph in Exhibit 5 demonstrates what will happen. In the third year, return on equity will be about 15% if we use long-term debt, but it will be only about 12% if we don't. I don't see why you want to avoid debt, Ellen."

Ellen replied, "If we could be sure of the numbers in Stan's estimates, I would agree that financial leverage would make Favorite Cookie Company more valuable. However, you have to remember that these numbers are only estimates, and that we are dealing with a relatively unknown product in a highly competitive market. Suppose we don't start out with sales of $3 million, and suppose sales don't grow at 20% per year. That financial leverage magnification factor will continue to work against us as long as our profits are low. We need to examine some other factors, as well. Let's take a break and continue our discussion later."

Self-Study Problem #1

Financial statement information is presented below for Andromeda Corporation, which manufactures airline-tracking equipment. Andromeda is considering a change in its capital structure. Management has proposed issuing $200 million of additional long-term debt. The long-term debt would be used to repurchase a portion of the company's common stock. This purchase would reduce the company's stockholders' equity by $200 million. The interest expense on the additional debt would be $14 million. The company's tax rate is 35% of pretax income.

(In millions)	2007
Sales	$982
Cost of goods sold	607
Operating expenses	294
Operating income	$ 81
Interest expense	(6)
Pretax income	$ 75
Income taxes	(26)
Net income	$ 49
Assets:	
Current assets	$277
Plant assets	555
Total assets	$832
Liabilities:	
Current liabilities	$212
Long-term debt	75
Total liabilities	$287
Stockholders' equity	545
Total liabilities and equity	$832

Required

A. Compute Andromeda's return on equity for 2007 as reported.

B. Compute what Andromeda's return on equity would have been in 2007 if the company had issued the additional debt and had repurchased common stock. You will need to recompute net income beginning with operating income. Also, recompute liabilities and equity on the balance sheet. Round to the nearest million dollars.

C. Based on these computations, would the change in capital structure be good for Andromeda's stockholders?

The solution to Self-Study Problem 1 appears at the end of the chapter.

EFFECTS OF FINANCING DECISIONS ON CASH FLOW AND LIQUIDITY

Objective 3
Explain why cash flows are important for a company's financing decisions.

Ellen continued the discussion after the break. "Also, consider our cash flows. We will have a lot of cash outflows next year to increase the size of the business. We will have to extend credit to some of our customers just to compete in this market. Consequently, some of our sales may not be collected for several months. At the same time, we will be paying for materials and labor to create our products.

"If we add interest payments to our cash demands, we could face cash flow problems, especially if sales are less than expected. If sales are lower than we anticipate, we can cut back on materials purchases and reduce labor costs, but we can't skip interest payments. If we can't make those payments and still have enough money to meet our normal operating needs, we'll be in serious trouble before we give our company time to prove itself. If we get into cash flow problems because of too much debt, we'll have trouble staying in business. We will have difficulty borrowing additional money because creditors already will be concerned about getting repaid for the original loan. We won't be in a good position to sell additional stock, either. Who will want to buy stock in a company that can't pay its debts?

"No, Maria, I really think our situation is too risky to use much debt. Our sales may be lower than expected, and our profits may be more volatile than we anticipate. Until we get the business on solid ground and know more about our market, I think we should stick with equity financing. At some time in the future, once we are more established and can be pretty sure of our profits and cash flows, we might consider using more financial leverage."

Dividend Decisions

Maria and Stan still were not completely satisfied. "What about dividends?" Stan asked. "I understand what you are saying about interest, but won't we have to pay dividends on the stock we sell? Investors aren't going to give us their money without expecting something in return. If we pay dividends, we'll be facing the same cash flow problems we would if we use debt."

"I don't think so," Ellen responded. "People who invest in new companies like ours know the risk they are taking. They invest for long-run profits and stock value, not for short-run dividends. If we convince the market of our growth potential and demonstrate good growth in the first few years, we will create good value for our stockholders.

"Dividend policy is an important financing decision for a company. Managers must decide how much cash dividend to pay each fiscal period. Dividend policies vary considerably among companies. Some companies, especially new ones like ours with good growth potential, do not pay dividends.

"Stockholders benefit from their investments in two ways. One way is by receiving dividends. The other way is by having the value of their stock increase over time. Favorite Cookie Company has great growth potential. If we invest the cash from our operating activities back in the company to create greater production and sales capacity and earn higher profits, our investors will be better off than if we pay dividends. If we can increase sales by 20% each year, the value of our stock is likely to climb at a much higher rate than if we pay cash dividends and grow more slowly because we don't have enough cash to invest. Exhibit 6 illustrates the dividends relative to investment of cash.

"Stockholders realize the value of growth. Many growth companies don't pay dividends or pay only low dividends. Companies like **Microsoft** and **Intel** have paid very few dividends, but they have made millions for their investors because of higher stock values. Of course, we have to deliver growth, not just promise it. If we don't pay dividends because we aren't creating enough profits and cash flows to make these payments, we'll be in trouble. But we would be in more trouble if we had a lot of interest to pay. Interest would decrease our profits and cash flows, compounding our problems. If we can't become profitable and grow at a reasonable rate, we won't be in business long, regardless of how we finance Favorite Cookie Company.

EXHIBIT 6
Stockholders Benefit from Dividends and from Investment of Cash in Productive Assets

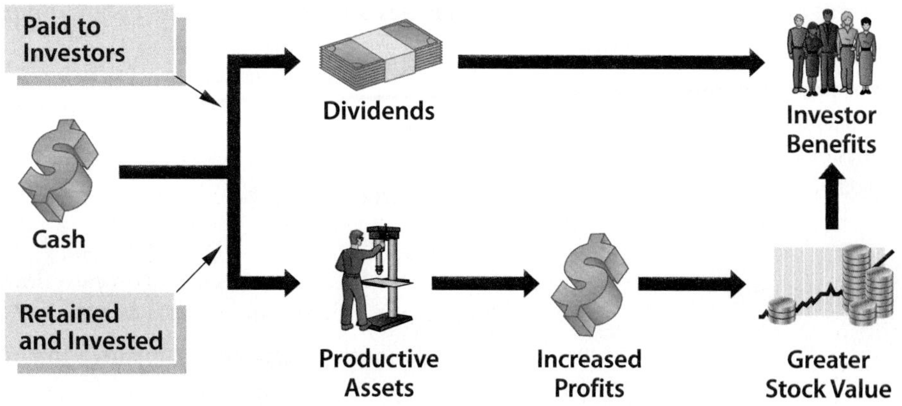

"Thus, dividends are not a concern. Stockholders won't expect them initially and will be satisfied as long as the price of their stock increases each year consistent with their expectations. Favorite Cookie Company will be a less risky company if we avoid much debt. Keep in mind that investors expect a higher return from a high-risk company than from a low-risk company. We are already a high-risk company because we are new and we are operating in a highly competitive market. Financial leverage would increase this risk even more and might scare away many investors. At a minimum, it would reduce the amount we will receive from selling stock. If we increase our risk, investors will bid the price of our stock down because they will be more uncertain about our ability to survive and generate future profits."

Other Financing Alternatives

"What about other alternatives?" Stan queried. "We could lease some of our plant assets. Wouldn't that be an alternative to equity financing?"

"Yes," Maria added, "and what about preferred stock? Could we use that rather than common stock for some of our financing needs?"

Ellen responded, "Leases wouldn't improve our situation very much. We would still have to make payments each period. Most of the leases would be long-term capital leases that are equivalent to debt. We would be making interest and principal payments just the way we would be paying other creditors. Leases would add to our risk and liquidity problems just like other forms of debt.

"We would also need to be careful with preferred stock. If we sell preferred, we probably will have to make dividend payments to the preferred stockholders. Also, our common stock will be a bit riskier because of the dividend and liquidation preferences of the preferred stock. If we are not as successful as we hope to be in the first few years, common stockholders stand to lose more money if we issue preferred stock than if we don't. If we can sell enough common stock to meet our financing needs and can get a reasonable price for our stock, I would not issue preferred stock. Let's use preferred stock as an alternative only if we can't meet all of our needs by issuing common."

Maria and Stan left the meeting feeling comfortable with Ellen's explanations. They had high expectations for their product, and they had faith in Ellen's understanding of financing activities.

INTERPRETATION OF FINANCING ACTIVITIES

The first part of this chapter examined the financing decisions of managers and the effects of these decisions on a company's financial statements. This section examines financial statement information provided by actual corporations. We use this information to demonstrate how investors and other decision makers can interpret the financing

Objective 4
Use financial statements to evaluate the financing activities of different companies.

activities of companies and make decisions about companies' risk, return, and value attributes.

In this section, we will use a five-step process to analyze accounting information for the purpose of evaluating financing activities.

1. Identify financing activities for one or more companies and fiscal periods.
2. Measure capital structure for the companies and periods.
3. Evaluate the effect of the companies' financing decisions on risk and return.
4. Evaluate the effect of financing decisions on cash flows and determine the ability of companies to make debt and interest payments.
5. Examine the relationship between a company's financing decisions and its value to stockholders.

Exhibit 7 provides selected financial statement information for **Microsoft** and **Procter & Gamble**. Both companies are large producers of consumer products.

A General Overview

Our analysis begins with a general overview of the two companies. In Exhibit 7, it appears that Microsoft is more profitable than Procter & Gamble. Net income for both companies is positive in both years. However, Microsoft's net income is considerably higher than Procter & Gamble's.

When comparing different companies, one must keep in mind that the sizes of the companies usually are different. For that reason, ratios are used to make the financial statement numbers comparable. For example, observe that Microsoft was larger than Procter & Gamble, based on the assets reported by each company. Accordingly, we should expect Microsoft's net income to be larger than Procter & Gamble's.

A common method for comparing the income of different companies is to compute **return on assets**, the ratio of net income to total assets. In 2004, Microsoft's return on

EXHIBIT 7 Selected Income Statement and Balance Sheet Information for Microsoft and Procter & Gamble

	Microsoft		*Procter & Gamble*	
(In millions)	2004	2003	2004	2003
Total revenues	$36,835	$32,187	$51,407	$43,377
Operating expenses	27,801	22,642	41,580	35,524
Income from operations	$ 9,034	$ 9,545	$ 9,827	$ 7,853
Nonoperating income (expense)	3,162	1,509	(477)	(323)
Income before taxes	$12,196	$11,054	$ 9,350	$ 7,530
Provision for income taxes	4,028	3,523	2,869	2,344
Net income	$ 8,168	$ 7,531	$ 6,481	$ 5,186
Assets:				
Total current assets	$70,566	$58,973	$17,115	$15,220
Long-term assets	21,823	22,759	39,933	28,486
Total assets	$92,389	$81,732	$57,048	$43,706
Liabilities and Equity:				
Total current liabilities	$14,969	$13,974	$22,147	$12,358
Total long-term liabilities	2,595	2,846	17,623	15,162
Total liabilities	$17,564	$16,820	$39,770	$27,520
Shareholders' Equity:				
Common stock	$56,396	$49,234	$ 4,969	$ 4,228
Retained earnings and other	18,429	15,678	12,309	11,958
Total shareholders' equity	$74,825	$64,912	$17,278	$16,186
Total liabilities and equity	$92,389	$81,732	$57,048	$43,706

assets was 8.8% ($8,168 ÷ $92,389), compared with Procter & Gamble's return on assets of 11.4% ($6,481 ÷ $57,048). In 2003, Microsoft's return on assets was 9.2% ($7,531 ÷ $81,732), compared with Procter & Gamble's 11.9% ($5,186 ÷ $43,706). Both companies were more profitable in 2003 than in 2004. However, Procter & Gamble was more profitable in both years than Microsoft.

Comparing Capital Structures

As a second step in our analysis of financing activities, we compare the capital structures of the two companies. We use ratios such as **debt to assets** and **assets to equity** for this purpose. These measures compare the amount of debt (debt to assets) or equity (assets to equity) a company uses to finance its assets with the company's total investment in assets. **A high debt-to-assets ratio or a high assets-to-equity ratio indicates that a company is using a lot of debt in its capital structure.**

We include all liabilities as part of debt. For 2004, Microsoft's debt-to-assets ratio was 19.0% ($17,564 ÷ $92,389), much lower than Procter & Gamble's debt-to-assets ratio of 69.7% ($39,770 ÷ $57,048).

Learning Note - Many ratios do not have standard definitions. Various decision makers and companies compute ratios differently. For example, debt to assets may include all liabilities in the numerator, or it may include only long-term debt. The denominator may use assets from the beginning of the year, from the end of the year, or an average for the year. Therefore, be careful in comparing companies. Make sure you understand how ratios were computed and make sure the ratios were computed the same way for each company.

Another measure of capital structure useful for comparing the effects of financing activities is **financial leverage**: the ratio of assets to stockholders' equity. For 2004, this ratio was 1.23 ($92,389 ÷ $74,825) for Microsoft and 3.30 ($57,048 ÷ $17,278) for Procter & Gamble. Though this ratio uses a different scale from the one used for the debt-to-assets ratio, it provides the same type of information. Note that a company that uses more debt in its capital structure has a higher debt-to-assets or assets-to-equity ratio than one that uses less debt.

THE EFFECT OF FINANCIAL LEVERAGE ON RISK AND RETURN

Objective 5

Determine and explain the effect of financial leverage on a company's risk and return.

A third step in our analysis is to determine the effect of financial leverage on the risk and return of our companies. A ratio commonly used for this purpose is **return on equity**: net income divided by stockholders' equity. This ratio is affected by a company's capital structure. The use of financial leverage (higher amounts of debt) magnifies a company's return on assets.

Return on Equity = Return on Assets × Financial Leverage

$$\frac{\text{Net Income}}{\text{Stockholders' Equity}} = \frac{\text{Net Income}}{\text{Total Assets}} \times \frac{\text{Total Assets}}{\text{Stockholders' Equity}}$$

For example, Microsoft's return on equity in 2004 was 10.9% ($8,168 ÷ $74,825). This amount is equal to Microsoft's return on assets times its asset to equity ratio: 10.9% = 8.8% × 1.23. Microsoft's financial leverage resulted in a return on equity that was larger than its return on assets. What do these numbers mean in practical terms? Think of them this way: If Microsoft had financed its assets using equity without any liabilities, its stockholders would have made 8.8 cents for each dollar they invested in Microsoft, including reinvested profits, in 2004. But, because Microsoft used debt in its capital structure, its stockholders made 10.9 cents for each dollar invested. Thus, **financial leverage works for stockholders when a company performs well.**

Financial leverage also worked for Procter & Gamble's stockholders because the company was profitable in both years. Return on equity was 37.5% ($6,481 ÷ $17,278) in 2004 and 32.0% ($5,186 ÷ $16,186) in 2003. In each year, return on equity was greater than return on assets because of financial leverage.

Observe that Procter & Gamble's return on equity was approximately three times as large as Microsoft's. Most of that difference results from Procter & Gamble's higher financial leverage, 3.30 for Procter & Gamble and 1.23 for Microsoft. By using much debt in its capital structure, Procter & Gamble has created additional profitability for its stockholders.

So, why did Microsoft use less financial leverage than Procter & Gamble? If financial leverage increases return on equity, why not use a lot of financial leverage? There is a cost to using a lot of debt in a company's capital structure. That cost is higher risk. Financial risk increases when a company uses a lot of debt because debt and interest must be paid whether or not a company is profitable and creates operating cash flows. Exhibit 8 illustrates the relationship between financial leverage and return on equity.

The return on assets lines identify positive and negative returns of 5%. As a company's financial leverage increases, its return on equity increases relative to its return on assets when return on assets is positive. But when return on assets is negative, return on equity decreases relative to return on assets as financial leverage increases. Accordingly, financial leverage increases uncertainty about the returns that stockholders will earn at a particular level of return on assets or for a particular amount of net income. Uncertainty increases as the volatility of return increases. Return on equity varies more (is more volatile) for higher amounts of financial leverage.

Therefore, companies trade off return for risk. Higher risk, in the form of higher financial leverage, has the potential to create higher returns. But it also has the potential to create lower returns if a company is not profitable. As an example, if Procter & Gamble had reported a net loss of $6,481 million in 2004 rather than a net income, its return on assets would have been −11.4% and its return on equity would have been −37.5%. **When a company's earnings are negative, the use of debt in the capital structure results in a lower return for stockholders than when debt is not used.**

EXHIBIT 8
The Effect of Financial Leverage on Risk and Return

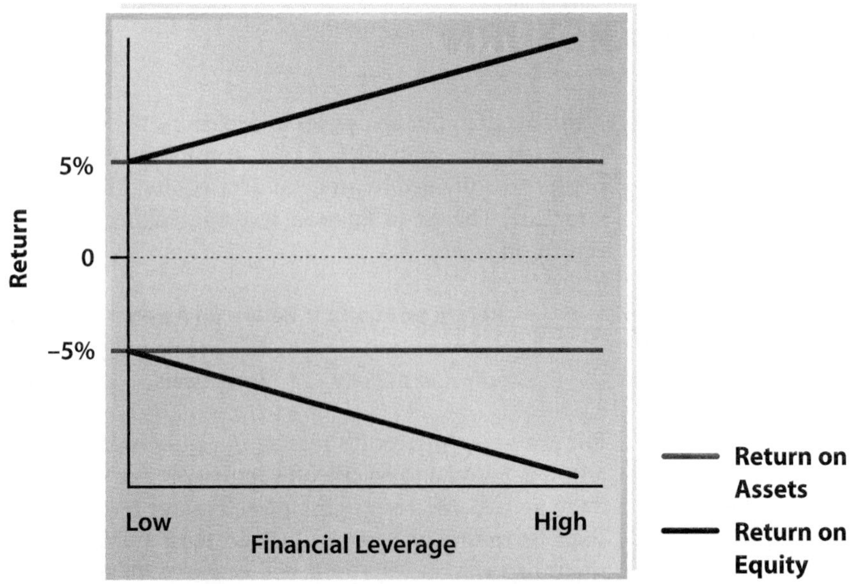

Self-Study Problem #2

Examine the information for Andromeda Company provided in Self-Study Problem 1. Suppose Andromeda's operating income in 2007 is $70 million, as summarized below.

(In millions)	2007
Operating income	$ 70
Interest expense	(6)
Pretax income	$ 64
Income taxes	(22)
Net income	$ 42
Assets:	
Total assets	$832
Liabilities:	
Current liabilities	$212
Long-term debt	75
Total liabilities	$287
Stockholders' equity	545
Total liabilities and equity	$832

Required

A. Compute return on equity for Andromeda as reported above.

B. Compute the return on equity as it would be if the company issued $100 million of long-term debt to repurchase stock. Additional interest expense would be $8 million, and the tax rate is 35%.

C. What effect would the additional debt have on Andromeda's risk and return?

The solution to Self-Study Problem 2 appears at the end of the chapter.

OTHER RISK CONSIDERATIONS

Objective 6
Use cash flow and liquidity measures to evaluate financing decisions.

The fourth step in the analysis of financing activities involves evaluating the ability of each company to make debt and interest payments. Creditors and stockholders are concerned about a company's ability to meet its obligations, including the payment of interest, as they become due. Debt ratios, such as the ratio of debt to total assets, provide information that is helpful in evaluating default risk. **Default risk** is the likelihood that a company will not be able to make debt or interest payments when they come due. As the amount of debt in a company's capital structure increases, the likelihood of default increases because principal and interest payments become larger.

Therefore, though financial leverage can increase a company's return on equity, the amount of financial leverage a company can use is limited by the amount of principal and interest the company can pay and still have enough cash to cover expenses, purchase new assets, and pay dividends. Also, as financial leverage increases, the interest rate demanded by creditors is likely to increase. Creditors demand higher returns as compensation for the higher default risk of a company's debt. Creditors may impose limitations on a company's ability to borrow additional money, require it to maintain a certain debt ratio, or limit its ability to pay dividends unless certain ratios are maintained.

These limitations are called **debt covenants**, and they protect the interests of creditors against a company becoming too risky or paying cash to stockholders when it has too much debt.

CASE IN POINT

http://ingram.swlearning.com

Visit Procter & Gamble's home page to learn more about the company.

Disclosure of Debt Covenants

A note in Procter & Gamble's 2004 annual report describes a covenant in the company's credit facilities, which are borrowing arrangements:

> *While not considered material to the overall financial condition of the Company, there is a covenant in the credit facilities stating the ratio of net debt to earnings before interest expense, income taxes, depreciation and amortization cannot exceed four at the time of a draw on the facility. As of June 30, we are comfortably below this level, with a ratio of approximately 1.3.*

Source: Procter & Gamble's 2004 annual report.

In addition to debt ratios, creditors consider cash flow and liquidity measures. **A commonly used liquidity measure is the *current ratio*: current assets divided by current liabilities. If this ratio is low, especially if it is less than one, or if it decreases substantially over time, the risk that a company may not be able to pay its current obligations increases.**

The current ratio for Microsoft in 2004 was 4.71 ($70,566 ÷ $14,969). In 2003, this ratio was 4.22 ($58,973 ÷ $13,974). Thus, Microsoft increased its current assets in 2004 and increased its current ratio. Procter & Gamble's current ratio decreased to 0.77 ($17,115 ÷ $22,147) in 2004 from 1.23 ($15,220 ÷ $12,358) in 2003. Note, Procter & Gamble's current ratio was lower than Microsoft's in 2004. That means Microsoft was in a better position to meet its current liability obligations than was Procter & Gamble.

Exhibit 9 provides selected cash flow information for Microsoft and Procter & Gamble. Both companies reported positive operating cash flows and negative investing cash flows. This pattern is common for many companies. Operating activities should provide a primary source of cash for a company. Cash created from selling goods and services can be used to expand a company's activities by investing the cash in additional long-term assets. Thus, both Microsoft and Procter & Gamble were growing as a result of reinvestment of cash flows into long-term assets.

Both Microsoft and Procter & Gamble generated large cash flows from their operating activities in 2004. In 2004, Microsoft's **operating cash flows to total assets** was 15.8% ($14,626 ÷ $92,389). Procter & Gamble's ratio was 16.4% ($9,362 ÷ $57,048).

EXHIBIT 9
Selected Cash Flow Information for Microsoft and Procter & Gamble

	Microsoft		Procter & Gamble	
(In millions)	2004	2003	2004	2003
Net operating cash flow	$14,626	$15,797	$ 9,362	$ 8,700
Net investing cash flow	(2,745)	(7,213)	(9,391)	(1,507)
Financing cash flow:				
From issuing debt			$ 6,874	$ (822)
From issuing stock	$ 2,748	$ 2,120	555	269
For purchase of stock	(3,383)	(6,486)	(4,070)	(1,236)
For payment of dividends	(1,729)	(857)	(2,539)	(2,246)
For payment of debt			(1,188)	(1,060)
Net financing cash flow	$ (2,364)	$ (5,223)	$ (368)	$(5,095)
Net change in cash	$ 9,517	$ 3,361	$ (397)	$ 2,098

Thus, both companies had large amounts of cash to invest. The ratio of **investing cash flow to total assets** was −3.0% (−$2,745 ÷ $92,389) for Microsoft and −16.5% (−$9,391 ÷ $57,048) for Procter & Gamble. Both companies were investing their cash in additional assets, indicating that the companies were growing.

Microsoft invested less cash in 2004 and in 2003 than it created from operating activities. Some of the additional cash was used to repurchase stock and to pay dividends (see Exhibit 9). The company appears to have been generating more cash than it could use in the short run. Procter & Gamble invested its operating cash flow in 2004 and issued sufficient debt to repurchase stock and pay dividends. Issuing debt to repurchase stock is a common way a company can increase its financial leverage.

Both companies paid dividends in 2004 and 2003. A measure of the relative size of dividend payments is the **dividend payout ratio**, the ratio of dividends to net income. Microsoft's dividend payout ratio for 2004 was 21.2% ($1,729 ÷ $8,168). Procter & Gamble's ratio was 39.2% ($2,539 ÷ $6,481).

Microsoft and Procter & Gamble were healthy companies in 2004. Both were profitable, generating operating cash flows, growing, and capable of paying relatively high amounts of dividends. Neither company was having any difficulty meeting its cash flow needs for repayment of debt or interest. Consequently, both companies had relatively low financial risk.

FINANCING ACTIVITIES AND COMPANY VALUE

Objective 7

Explain why financing activities are important for determining company value.

The final step in the evaluation of financing activities is assessing the relationship between financing decisions and company value. As we have seen from examining the financing activities of Microsoft and Procter & Gamble, financing activities affect a company's risk and return. Financial leverage can work for or against a company and its stockholders. When a company does well, financial leverage can be useful. Stockholders earn higher returns than they would if a company had no financial leverage. **When a company is not doing well, financial leverage is detrimental.** Stockholders earn lower returns. In addition, creditors face higher default risk, and a company has less cash to meet its other needs because it is forced to make interest and principal payments.

A measure of a company's value to investors is the **market-to-book-value** ratio. **Market value** is the price of a company's stock times the number of shares of stock outstanding. It is a measure of the total value placed on a company by the securities market. **Book value** is the amount of stockholders' equity reported by a company on its balance sheet.

Microsoft's market value in 2004 was $293 billion and its book value was $74.8 billion (Exhibit 7). Therefore, its market-to-book-value ratio was 3.92. In practical terms, this ratio says that every dollar invested in Microsoft by stockholders, including retained earnings, was worth $3.92 at the end of the 2004 fiscal year.

Procter & Gamble's market-to-book-value ratio was 7.06 in 2004. Procter & Gamble was worth $7.06 at the end of the 2004 fiscal year for each dollar invested by stockholders.

Financing activities affect company value. A company that is performing well can increase return to its stockholders by including debt in its capital structure. How much debt a company uses depends on several factors. In particular, a company with stable earnings and operating cash flows can afford more debt than one with unstable earnings and cash flows. If a company runs the risk of not performing well (because of volatile product markets or poor sales, for example), debt can increase the likelihood that the company will earn lower returns and be unable to pay its creditors. A company that is growing rapidly already has a large amount of risk associated with its growth activities. It is investing with the expectation that it will be able to earn high returns on its investment in the future. Maintaining low financial risk can be advantageous, at least until the company determines whether its investment strategy is working.

Company value also is affected by the purpose of financing activities. A company's value is likely to increase if it is using financing activities to acquire additional assets.

EXHIBIT 10
Summary of Ratios for Microsoft and Procter & Gamble

	Microsoft		Procter & Gamble	
	2004	2003	2004	2003
Return on assets	8.8%	9.2%	11.4%	11.9%
Debt to assets	19.0%	20.6%	69.7%	63.0%
Financial leverage (assets to equity)	1.24	1.26	3.30	2.70
Return on equity	10.9%	11.6%	37.5%	32.0%
Current ratio	4.71	4.22	0.77	1.23
Operating cash to assets	15.8%	19.3%	16.4%	19.9%
Investing cash to assets	−3.0%	−8.8%	−16.5%	−3.4%
Dividend payout	21.2%	11.4%	39.2%	43.3%
Market to book value	3.92	4.14	7.06	6.92

These assets help the company grow because it can use them to produce and sell more products and earn additional income from these sales. If debt or stock is issued because of operating cash flow problems, however, a company's value is likely to decrease.

Exhibit 10 provides a summary of the ratios for Microsoft and Procter & Gamble that have been presented in this chapter.

Self-Study Problem #3

Data are provided below for Alzona Company, a large trucking company.

Required

A. Compute the following ratios for each year: debt (long-term) to assets, assets to stockholders' equity, return on assets, return on equity, current, dividend payout, and market to book value.

B. Describe the company's financing activities for 2007 and evaluate the effect they had on the company's stockholders.

The solution to Self-Study Problem 3 appears at the end of the chapter.

(In millions)	2007	2006
Current assets	$ 433	$ 378
Total assets	1,237	1,065
Current liabilities	389	343
Long-term debt	422	404
Stockholders' equity	426	318
Operating income	151	127
Interest expense	(34)	(31)
Income taxes	(40)	(33)
Net income	77	63
Operating cash flows	113	102
Investing cash flows	(154)	(112)
Financing cash flows	60	8
Debt issued	30	20
Debt repurchased	(12)	(10)
Stock issued	50	25
Dividends paid	(20)	(16)
Market value	643	512

THINKING BEYOND THE QUESTION

HOW DO WE FINANCE OUR BUSINESS?

Financial decisions are critical for a company. It is important for a company to create value for its owners by earning a high return and by controlling its risk. Higher financial leverage can result in both high returns and high risk. Consequently, managers must examine the tradeoff and choose an amount of financial leverage that is appropriate for their company. That amount will be different for different companies. When is it appropriate for a company to have a large amount of financial leverage? What kinds of companies are likely to have high financial leverage? Why?

Self-Study Problem Solutions

SSP10-1 A. Return on equity = $49 ÷ $545 = 9.0%

B. Revised financial statement numbers:

(In millions)	2007	
Sales	$982	
Cost of goods sold	607	
Operating expenses	294	
Operating income	$ 81	
Interest expense	(20)	$6 from old debt + $14 from new
Pretax income	$ 61	
Income taxes	(21)	$61 × 0.35
Net income	$ 40	
Assets:		
Current assets	$277	
Plant assets	555	
Total assets	$832	
Liabilities:		
Current liabilities	$212	
Long-term debt	275	
Total liabilities	$487	
Stockholders' equity	345	
Total liabilities and equity	$832	

Return on equity = $40 ÷ $345 = 11.6%

C. Issuing additional debt reduces net income because of the additional interest expense. However, stockholder's equity is reduced as well because the additional debt was used to repurchase stock. Therefore, return on equity would be higher if the debt were issued (increasing from 9% to 11.6%). Based on this information, increasing financial leverage is a good decision for this company. Whether it will continue to be a good decision in the future depends on whether the company continues to be profitable.

SSP10-2 A. Return on equity (as reported) = \$42 ÷ \$545 = 7.7%

B. Financial statement effects of issuing \$100 million of debt:

(In millions)	2007	
Operating income	\$ 70	
Interest expense	(14)	\$6 from old debt + \$8 from new
Pretax income	\$ 56	
Income taxes	(20)	\$56 × 0.35
Net income	\$ 36	
Assets:		
Total assets	\$832	
Liabilities:		
Current liabilities	\$212	
Long-term debt	175	
Total liabilities	\$387	
Stockholders' equity	445	
Total liabilities and equity	\$832	
Return on equity = \$36 ÷ \$445 =	8.1%	

C. Higher financial leverage increases risk. If net income and return on assets are low, financial leverage reduces return on equity. If net income and return on assets are high, financial leverage increases return on equity. Consequently, financial leverage may increase or decrease return. It increases risk.

Andromeda's return on equity in 2007 increases from 7.7% to 8.1% when the additional debt is issued. However, uncertainty about future net income and return on equity increases because of the increase in financial leverage. If Andromeda can continue to earn a profit, the additional debt should result in a higher return on equity in the future than if the debt were not issued.

SSP10-3 A.

	2007	2006
Debt to assets	0.34 = \$422 ÷ \$1,237	0.38 = \$404 ÷ \$1,065
Assets to stockholders' equity	2.90 = \$1,237 ÷ \$426	3.35 = \$1,065 ÷ \$318
Return on assets	0.062 = \$77 ÷ \$1,237	0.059 = \$63 ÷ \$1,065
Return on equity	0.181 = \$77 ÷ \$426	0.198 = \$63 ÷ \$318
Current ratio	1.11 = \$433 ÷ \$389	1.10 = \$378 ÷ \$343
Dividend payout	0.260 = \$20 ÷ \$77	0.254 = \$16 ÷ \$63
Market to book value	1.51 = \$643 ÷ \$426	1.61 = \$512 ÷ \$318

B. Alzona's primary financing activities in 2007 consisted of issuing additional debt (\$18 million more than it repaid), issuing \$50 million of stock, and paying \$20 million of dividends. The company's performance was strong. Its net income and operating cash flows were positive and increased from 2006 to 2007. Additional financing activities were used to support investing activities. Additional assets were acquired in 2006 and 2007, indicating growth.

Alzona's financial leverage decreased during 2007. Therefore, though its return on assets increased from 2006 to 2007, its return on equity decreased. Thus, because the company was performing well, stockholders would have benefited from an increase in financial leverage. The decrease in financial leverage reduced stockholder return (return on equity). The lower return on equity was accompanied by a decrease in company value (market to book value). Both profitability and capital structure affect company value.

Define Terms and Concepts Defined in This Chapter

capital structure (361)
current ratio (372)
financial leverage (FL) (363)
return on equity (ROE) (362)

Review Summary of Important Concepts

1. Capital structure refers to the relative amounts of debt and equity used by a company to finance its assets.
   a. The use of larger amounts of debt reduces net income because of additional interest expense.
   b. The use of larger amounts of debt also reduces the amount of equity a company needs to finance its assets.
   c. Therefore, additional debt increases return on equity when a company is performing well, but decreases return on equity when the company is performing poorly.
   d. The amount of debt a company uses depends on its expectations about performance, the potential volatility of its performance, and the amount of risk it is prepared to take.

2. Debt increases a company's risk.
   a. Financial leverage magnifies a company's returns, making them potentially more volatile.
   b. Debt increases risk because of the potentially negative effect on stockholder return and the potential for default on debt and interest payments.
   c. Debt also affects liquidity and cash flow. Interest and debt payments require the use of cash. If a company does not have sufficient cash to meet these and other needs, it may be unable to make payments when they are due.

3. Dividend policy is another financing decision.
   a. The amount of cash dividends a company pays depends on the alternatives the company has for using its cash.
   b. If a company has good investment opportunities, stockholders may be better off leaving cash in the company and letting management invest it in additional assets.
   c. Stockholders benefit both from receiving dividends and from increases in stock value because of company profitability and growth.

4. Investors can use accounting information to understand a company's financing activities.
   a. Analysis begins with identifying financing activities and profitability for one or more periods or companies.
   b. The second step is measuring capital structure.
   c. The third step is evaluating the effect of financing decisions on risk and return.
   d. The fourth step is evaluating the effect of financing decisions on cash flows and determining the ability of a company to make debt and interest payments.
   e. The fifth step involves examining the relationship between a company's financing decisions and its market value.

5. Important ratios for analysis of financing activities of a company and for comparing the results of those activities between different companies:
   a. Return on equity (ROE): Net income divided by stockholders' equity (which is also equal to ROA times FL)—measures net income relative to the amount invested by the owners of the company. The owners' investment in the company includes not only contributed capital but also retained earnings.
   b. Debt-to-equity ratio: Total debt divided by total stockholders' equity—measures the company's capital structure in terms of the relationship between the company's obligations to its creditors and the investment by the owners.
   c. Debt-to-assets ratio: Total debt divided by total assets—measures the company's capital structures in terms of the proportion of total assets that are financed by debt.

d. Return on assets (ROA): Net income divided by total assets—measures the amount of return the company has earned from its assets.
e. Financial leverage (FL): Total assets divided by total stockholders' equity—measures how well the company has used debt to increase its return on equity.
f. Current ratio: Current assets divided by current liabilities—a liquidity measure of a company's ability to cover its current debts with its current assets.
g. Operating cash flow to total assets: Net operating cash flow divided by total assets—measures the portion of net cash inflow (outflow) that contributed to (depleted) total assets.
h. Investing cash flow to total assets: Net investing cash flow divided by total assets—measure the portion of net cash outflow (inflow) that was provided by (contributed to) total assets.
i. Dividend payout ratio: Total dividends divided by net income—measures the portion of net income that is paid to stockholders as dividends.
j. Market value: Total shares outstanding times the market value per share—measures the total value placed on the company by the securities market.
k. Book value: Total assets minus total liabilities—measures the amount of stockholders' equity on the balance sheet.
l. Market-to-book-value ratio: Market value of the entire company divided by the book value of the entire company.

Questions

Q10-1 *Obj. 1* What is capital structure? Why do the capital structures of companies vary?

Q10-2 *Obj. 1* Why is return on equity such a valuable measure to investors?

Q10-3 *Obj. 2* Company X and Company Y are both managed successfully by teams of highly respected executives. The firms operate in different industries. After careful analysis, you observe that Company X employs a very high level of financial leverage while Company Y employs almost none. How can both sets of executives be highly respected when their firms employ such different levels of financial leverage?

Q10-4 *Obj. 2* Why would stockholders tend to believe that return on equity is a more important measure of a company's performance than is return on assets?

Q10-5 *Obj. 3* Why does the use of financial leverage cause the current ratio to be lower than if no financial leverage was used?

Q10-6 *Obj. 3* Some companies, such as Tommy Hilfiger Corporation, have never paid a dividend and are unlikely to do so anytime soon. If an investment is never going to yield a dividend, why would anyone buy stock in such a company?

Q10-7 *Obj. 4* You are reviewing the balance sheets of Alpha Company and Beta Company. You observe that Alpha has $800,000 of long-term debt and that Beta has $4,000,000. Which company is more highly leveraged? If you need additional information to answer this question, identify what information you could use.

Q10-8 *Obj. 4* Beaumont Company has no current liabilities. Its only long-term debt is $20 million of bonds payable. The company's debt-to-assets ratio is 0.20 and its assets-to-equity ratio is 1.25. What is the company's debt-to-equity ratio?

Q10-9 *Obj. 5* Does the use of financial leverage always have a favorable impact on the firm and its owners? If not, explain the circumstances under which it would not be desirable to employ financial leverage.

Q10-10 *Obj. 5* How does the use of financial leverage affect the risk and return of a company?

Q10-11 *Obj. 6* When a company issues long-term debt, creditors often require the company to agree to certain restrictions on future activities. For example, a restriction may limit a company's debt-to-assets ratio and its dividend payout ratio. What is the purpose of these restrictions? How do they benefit creditors?

Q10-12 *Obj. 6* Evaluate the following statement: Companies that issue a lot of new debt and equity to create cash are usually in a bad financial condition.

Q10-13 *Obj. 6* Ernesto wants some advice. He heard that some companies pay out a large portion of their earnings as dividends to stockholders. Other companies pay few or no dividends. A friend told him that dividends affect the value of stock and that he should invest in stocks that pay high dividend rates. What advice would you give Ernesto about this matter?

Q10-14 *Obj. 7* Applause Company has a market to book ratio of 0.75 to 1. Bravo Company has a market-to-book-value ratio of 3.4 to 1. What information does the market-to-book-value ratio capture and what does this ratio tell you about the companies mentioned?

Q10-15 *Obj. 7* What relationship would you expect between financial leverage and the market-to-book-value ratio? Does a high value in one lead to a high value in the other? Or a low value in the other? Or do you think there is not necessarily a relationship? Explain your reasoning.

Exercises

E10-1 Write a short definition of each of the terms listed in the *Terms and Concepts Defined in This Chapter* section.

E10-2 *Obj. 1* Describe how each of the following transactions affects the capital structure of a company. Is there an effect on the short-term liability portion, the long-term liability portion, the equity portion, or is there no effect at all?

a. The issuance of common stock
b. The sale of bonds
c. The purchase of equipment for cash
d. The purchase of inventory on credit
e. The purchase of treasury stock
f. The borrowing of cash, with a two-year note, from a bank
g. The declaration of dividends to stockholders
h. The payment of dividends

E10-3 *Obj. 1* Given below is the most recent balance sheet of Carousel Company.

Carousel Company
Balance Sheet
At December 31, 2007

Assets		**Liabilities and Equity**	
Cash	$ 6,000	Accounts payable	$ 3,100
Accounts receivable	13,200	Wages payable	3,000
Prepaid rent	2,800	Bonds payable (due 2011)	33,000
Inventory	10,000	Common stock	17,000
Machinery	14,000	Retained earnings	17,400
Land	13,500	Treasury stock	(14,000)
Total assets	$59,500	Total liabilities and equity	$59,500

a. Describe the firm's capital structure.
b. How would the capital structure be different if the company had raised the needed capital by issuing additional stock instead of the bonds that are due in 2011?

E10-4 *Obj. 2* Why is return on equity commonly used along with net income to evaluate a company's performance? Assume that a company issued long-term bonds during a fiscal period, increasing its interest expense. The bonds were used to finance new plant assets. What effect would the financing and asset acquisition have on the company's financial leverage? What effect should the additional financing have on the company's risk and return?

E10-5 *Obj. 2* The following summary information is available regarding Robinson Sports Gear. The income statements are for the respective fiscal years, and the balance sheets are as of the end of each fiscal year.

Income Statements	**2008**	**2007**	**2006**
Net sales	$53	$48	$45
Cost of sales	31	28	27
Other expenses	15	15	15
Net income	$ 7	$ 5	$ 3

Balance Sheets	**2008**	**2007**	**2006**
Total current assets	$26	$13	$ 5
Total long-term assets	41	22	9
Total liabilities	12	8	2
Total stockholders' equity	$55	$27	$12

a. What does this income statement information suggest to you about this firm and its attractiveness as a potential investment?
b. Compute the return on equity for each of the three years.
c. How does the return on equity information change your initial conclusion about the attractiveness of this company as an investment?
d. What do your responses to parts a and c suggest to you about evaluating a company?

E10-6 *Obj. 2* A friend is studying for an accounting exam and exclaims, "I'm really confused by all this leverage stuff. What is leverage, anyway? How does it affect a company? And what has it got to do with the debt-to-equity ratio or debt-to-assets ratio? The professor keeps saying that a company with a low debt-to-equity ratio might want to increase its leverage. What's she talking about, anyway?" Write an explanation of these issues that your friend can use to study for his exam.

E10-7 *Obj. 2* At year end 2007, Istanbul Company had stockholders' equity of $18 million. Stockholders' equity at year end 2007 consisted of one million shares of common stock. For 2007, the company reported net income of $4 million. The company paid common dividends of $2 per share in 2007. Compute Istanbul's return on equity for 2007. What would this amount have been if the company had issued bonds at the beginning of 2007 and had used the proceeds to repurchase common stock, reducing stockholders' equity at the end of 2007 to $14,540,000? Assume net income decreased to $3.79 million as a result of additional interest expense, and dividends per share remained at $2 per share for common stock.

E10-8 *Obj. 2* Boswell Company expects net income of $5 million for 2008. Pretax earnings are projected to be $7 million. The company's average total assets during 2008 were $25 million. It had no liabilities or preferred stock. It had 1 million shares of common stock outstanding. Boswell is considering issuing $10 million of debentures to repurchase 300,000 shares of its common stock. If the debt had been outstanding in 2008, the company would have paid $900,000 in interest expense. Calculate the company's net income and return on equity for 2008 as reported and as they would have been if the debt had been issued. Assume average stockholders' equity of $15 million for computing return on equity with debt financing and that the tax rate is 28.6%.

E10-9 *Obj. 2* Kandahar Company had stockholders' equity of $100 million in 2007 and long-term debt of $10 million. It had 10 million shares of common stock outstanding. Its interest expense was $800,000, and its income tax rate was 30%. The company expects that its annual income before interest and taxes will run between $5 million and $15 million for the foreseeable future. The average is expected to be about $8 million. The company is considering issuing $25 million of additional debt to replace three million shares of its common stock. The additional debt would cost the company $3 million a year in interest. If you were asked by the company for advice on whether to issue the debt, what advice would you give?

E10-10 *Obj. 2* Linfield Company has assets of $200 million and long-term debt of $110 million. The debt consists primarily of callable debentures having interest rates ranging from 10% to 12%. (Callable debentures are bonds that a company can recall and pay off at any time it chooses.) Over the last couple of years, the general level of interest rates has decreased by about 2.5%. Linfield could issue new debt today at a rate of approximately 8%. Also, over the last two years, Linfield's stock price has increased about 30%. How might this information affect Linfield's management when it considers financing decisions for the future?

E10-11 *Objs. 2, 3* Selected information is provided below for **Georgia-Pacific Corporation** from its 2004 and 2003 annual reports:

(In millions)	2004	2003	2002
Interest expense	$ 701	$ 819	$ 827
Income tax expense (benefit)	297	109	(318)
Net income (loss)	623	254	(735)
Cash from operations	1,474	1,792	1,007
Total assets	23,072	24,405	24,629
Stockholders' equity	6,225	5,394	4,560

Evaluate the effect of the company's capital structure on its profitability, cash flow from operations, and risk for the three years presented.

E10-12 *Objs. 2, 3* Metro Flight Service reported net income of $8 million in 2008. Its average stockholders' equity of $22 million included preferred stock of $5 million that was outstanding throughout the year. The company paid dividends of $2 million on common stock and $400,000 on preferred stock. (a) Calculate the company's return on equity for 2008. (Note: When a company has preferred stock outstanding, the preferred dividends must be deducted from the numerator and preferred stock must be deducted from the denominator when computing returns on equity.) (b) Management is thinking of issuing $5 million of additional common stock to repurchase all of its preferred stock. Is the replacement of preferred stock with common stock a good idea in this case?

E10-13 *Obj. 3* Selected information from the year-end financial statements of Arabia Company is presented below. All amounts are in millions of dollars.

	2008	2007	2006	2005
Net income	$ 36	$ 38	$ 42	$ 44
Interest expense	6	8	6	8
Current assets	64	66	64	60
Current liabilities	56	48	36	30
Total liabilities	122	116	118	102
Stockholders' equity	400	382	376	340
Cash from operations	34	40	38	46

Management is considering the issuance of $200 million of new bonds that would pay 9% interest. Based on the information presented here, how do you believe the financial markets will respond to the proposed bond offering? Why?

E10-14 *Objs. 2, 4* For each of the events or transactions on the following page, indicate the effect on each ratio listed. Use *I* to indicate increase, *D* to indicate decrease, and *NE* to indicate no effect.

(Continued)

		Debt to Equity	Debt to Assets	Financial Leverage	Current Ratio
a.	Sold common stock to investors	____	____	____	____
b.	Borrowed cash from a bank on long-term note	____	____	____	____
c.	Paid cash dividends on stock	____	____	____	____
d.	Sold inventory for cash (at a small profit)	____	____	____	____
e.	Paid off loan in part b	____	____	____	____
f.	Bought stock of another company	____	____	____	____
g.	Purchased treasury stock	____	____	____	____

E10-15 *Obj. 4* **Intel Corporation** reported the following selected information in its 2004 annual report:

(In millions)	2004
Current Liabilities:	
Short-term debt	$ 201
Total current liabilities	8,006
Long-Term Liabilities:	
Long-term debt	703
Deferred income taxes	855
Stockholders' Equity:	
Common stock	6,143
Other	148
Retained earnings	32,288
Total stockholders' equity	38,579

Evaluate Intel's capital structure. Explain which amounts you would include in a computation of the company's debt-to-equity ratio and why.

E10-16 *Obj. 4* Selected information from the 2004 annual reports of **Eastman Chemical Company** and **Microsoft** is given below. All amounts are in millions.

	Eastman Chemical	Microsoft
Current assets	$1,768	$70,566
Total assets	5,872	92,389
Current liabilities	1,099	14,969
Long-term debt	2,061	0
Other long-term liability items	1,528	2,595
Total stockholders' equity	1,184	74,825
Net income	170	8,168

a. For each of the companies, compute the following values: (i) return on assets, (ii) total assets to total equity, (iii) return on equity, (iv) long-term debt-to-equity ratio, and (v) long-term debt-to-assets ratio.
b. Inspect the values you have computed for the items in a. What do these indicators tell you about financing strategy and financing decisions that have been made by the management of these two firms? Have the decisions been similar or different? How have these financing decisions affected returns to stockholders? Discuss.

E10-17 *Obj. 4*

Given below are selected data for **Wal-Mart** for the years ended January 31, 2004 and 2003:

	2004	2003
Long-term debt to equity	1.25	1.25
Long-term debt to assets	0.52	0.52
Return on equity	20.8%	20.2%
Return on assets	8.6%	8.4%
Financial leverage	2.41	2.40
Current ratio	0.92	0.95

Study the information above and discuss what the changes from 2003 to 2004 mean. What conclusion can you make about Wal-Mart's financing activities?

E10-18 *Obj. 4*

Assume the following summarized balance sheet information at December 31, 2007:

	Giffin Co.	Good Co.
Current assets	$35,000	$45,000
Long-term assets	65,000	55,000
Current liabilities	10,000	20,000
Long-term liabilities	60,000	10,000
Common stock, $10 par	25,000	60,000
Retained earnings	5,000	10,000
Operating income	40,000	40,000
Interest rate for long-term liabilities	10%	10%
Income tax rate	40%	40%

a. Describe how these two firms compare regarding the use of leverage.
b. Is the firm with the higher degree of leverage using it effectively? Discuss. Show any supporting computations clearly and neatly.

E10-19 *Obj. 5*

Given below is the most recent set of financial statements for BeanSprout Farms.

Balance Sheet at December 31, 2007

Assets:	
Cash	$ 6,000
Marketable securities	2,800
Accounts receivable	5,200
Inventory	5,000
Machinery, net	21,000
Land	10,500
Total assets	$50,500
Liabilities and Equity:	
Accounts payable	$ 3,100
Notes payable (due 2012)	12,000
Common stock ($1 par)	4,000
Paid-in capital	16,000
Retained earnings	15,400
Total liabilities and equity	$50,500

Income Statement for Year 2007

Sales revenue	$82,000	
Cost of sales	51,000	
Gross margin		$31,000
Expenses:		
Wages	$14,000	
Depreciation	2,000	
Interest	1,000	
Bad debts	3,000	20,000
Pretax income		$11,000
Taxes (30%)		3,300
Net income		$ 7,700

a. Calculate return on assets and return on equity.
b. Assume the company had $18,000 less of contributed capital and $18,000 more of long-term debt. Recalculate return on assets and return on equity.
c. Assume the company replaced all its long-term debt with equity capital. Recalculate return on assets and return on equity.

(Continued)

d. Discuss how financial leverage affects return on assets and return on equity as shown in the results on the previous page.

E10-20 *Objs. 3, 6* Information from the annual reports of two companies is provided below.

(In millions)	2004	2003	2002
General Mills			
Net income	$1,055	$ 917	$ 458
Dividends	413	406	358
Wal-Mart			
Net income	9,054	7,955	6,592
Dividends	1,569	1,328	1,249

What do the dividend policies indicate about future prospects for the two companies?

E10-21 *Obj. 7* Data from the 2004 annual reports of **J.C. Penney** and **Wal-Mart** are shown below. The objective of this assignment is to determine which company is more highly regarded by the financial markets.

	J.C. Penney	Wal-Mart
Common stockholders' equity (millions)	$4,856	$43,623
Common shares (millions)	271	4,311
Approximate market price per common share	$42	$55

a. In general, what information is revealed by computation of the market-to-book-value ratio?
b. Compute the market-to-book-value ratio for J.C. Penney and Wal-Mart.
c. What do you conclude from the results of the market-to-book-value ratios of the two companies?

E10-22 *Obj. 7* Data are provided below for Register Company, a large security company. All amounts are in millions of dollars.

	2008	2007
Current assets	$ 736	$ 643
Total assets	2,103	1,810
Current liabilities	541	475
Long-term debt	862	815
Stockholders' equity	700	520
Operating income	241	200
Interest expense	(58)	(53)
Income taxes	(68)	(56)
Net income	115	91
Operating cash flows	192	173
Investing cash flows	(262)	(190)
Financing cash flows	102	14
Debt issued	51	34
Debt repurchased	(20)	(17)
Stock issued	85	43
Dividends paid	(34)	(27)
Market value	1,093	870

a. Compute the following ratios for each year: debt (long-term) to assets, assets to stockholders' equity, return on assets, return on equity, current ratio, dividend payout, and market to book value.
b. Identify and describe the company's financing activities for 2008. Be specific.
c. Evaluate the effects the firm's financing activities had on the company's stockholders.

Problems

P10-1 CAPITAL STRUCTURE AND RETURN ON EQUITY

Obj. 2

Financial statement information is presented below for Platform Corporation, a manufacturer. Platform is considering a change in its capital structure. Management has proposed issuing $150 million of additional long-term debt. The long-term debt would be used to repurchase a portion of the company's common stock. This purchase would reduce the company's stockholders' equity by $150 million. The interest expense on the additional debt would be $9 million. The company's tax rate is 30% of pre-tax income.

Required

A. Compute Platform's return on equity for 2007 as reported.
B. Compute what Platform's return on equity would have been in 2007 if the company had issued the additional debt and had repurchased common stock before the year began. You will need to recompute net income beginning with operating income. Also, recompute liabilities and equity on the balance sheet. Round to the nearest million dollars.
C. Based on these computations, would the change in capital structure be good for Platform's stockholders? Explain your reasoning.

Income Statement Fiscal Year 2007 (In millions)	
Sales	$ 893
Cost of goods sold	(552)
Operating expenses	(267)
Operating income	74
Interest expense	(8)
Pretax income	66
Income taxes	(20)
Net income	$ 46

Balance Sheet At Year-end (In millions)	
Assets:	
Current assets	$252
Plant assets	505
Total assets	$757
Liabilities and Equity:	
Current liabilities	$197
Long-term debt	100
Total liabilities	297
Stockholders' equity	460
Total liabilities and stockholders' equity	$757

P10-2 OBSERVING CHANGES IN CAPITAL STRUCTURE FROM COMPARATIVE BALANCE SHEETS

Objs. 1, 2, 4

Shown below are comparative balance sheets for Claudia Company at December 31.

	2008	2007
Assets:		
Cash	$12,000	$ 7,400
Accounts receivable	16,200	8,100
Inventory	10,000	8,000
Prepaid rent	5,600	5,100
Machinery, net	28,000	30,000
Land	27,000	27,000
Total assets	$98,800	$85,600
Liabilities and Equity:		
Accounts payable	$ 6,200	$ 5,800
Wages payable	5,800	6,100
Bonds payable (long-term)	46,000	16,400
Common stock	34,000	34,000
Retained earnings	34,800	26,400
Treasury stock	(28,000)	(3,100)
Total liabilities and equity	$98,800	$85,600

Net income for 2008 was $8,400. In 2007, it was $7,300.

(Continued)

Required

A. Identify the changes in capital structure that occurred during fiscal 2008.
B. Compute the (long-term) debt-to-equity ratio and (long-term) debt-to-assets ratio for both 2007 and 2008.
C. What were the return on assets and return on equity in 2007?
D. What were the return on assets and return on equity in 2008?
E. What role did the changes in capital structure have on return on assets and return on equity in 2008?

P10-3 COMPARING CAPITAL STRUCTURES

Obj. 4

Financial information from the 2004 annual reports of two companies is provided below. **Intel Corporation** is a manufacturer of semiconductors (primarily computer microprocessors). **Pacific Gas & Electric** is a privately owned utility.

(In millions) Intel Corporation	2004	(In millions) Pacific Gas & Electric	2004
Current assets	$24,058	Current assets	$ 6,408
Plant assets, net	15,768	Plant assets, net	18,989
Other noncurrent assets	8,317	Other noncurrent assets	9,143
Total assets	48,143	Total assets	34,540
Current liabilities	8,006	Current liabilities	6,918
Long-term debt	703	Long-term debt	7,323
Other noncurrent liabilities	855	Other noncurrent liabilities	11,380
Preferred stock	0	Preferred stock	286
Stockholders' equity	38,579	Common stock equity	8,633

Required

A. Identify at least three measures that can be used to assess capital structure. Compute their values for these two companies. (Hint: Treat preferred stock as a liability.)
B. Compare and contrast the capital structures of the two companies.
C. Why might these differences in capital structure exist between the two companies?

P10-4 EVALUATING FINANCING ALTERNATIVES

Obj. 4

Information is provided below for the Baker Mountain Company.

(In thousands, except per share amounts)	2007
Operating income	$ 306,679
Interest expense	(55,528)
Income taxes (40%)	(100,460)
Net income	150,691
Earnings per share (144.6 million shares)	1.04
Total assets	3,297,390
Short-term borrowing	1,612
Current portion of long-term debt	247
Total current liabilities	635,320
Long-term debt	673,588
Deferred income taxes	150,460
Other long-term liabilities	51,178
Total stockholders' equity	1,689,209

Assume that during 2007, Baker Mountain Company had the opportunity to acquire additional assets at a price of $500 million. The additional assets were expected to increase the company's operating income by $80 million annually (to $386,679,000) for the foreseeable future. They could be financed either by selling stock or issuing debt.

Required Prepare a pro forma (projected) income statement for each financing alternative. Start with operating income. Compute pro forma return on assets and pro forma return on equity under each alternative. Discuss whether Baker Mountain should finance the acquisition with debt or stock. Assume that debt could be issued at a 7% interest rate.

P10-5 EVALUATING FINANCING ALTERNATIVES

Obj. 4

Given below are the balance sheet and income statement for fiscal 2007 for the Crossroads Company.

Balance Sheet	
Assets:	
Cash	$ 14,000
Inventory	42,000
Investments	11,000
Buildings (net)	47,000
Land	37,000
Total assets	$151,000
Liabilities and Equity:	
Accounts payable	$ 17,000
Notes payable	32,000
Common stock	61,000
Retained earnings	41,000
Total liabilities and equity	$151,000

Income Statement	
Sales revenue	$358,000
Cost of sales	227,000
Gross margin	$131,000
Interest expense	(5,000)
Other fixed expenses	(70,000)
Taxes (40%)	(22,400)
Net income	$ 33,600

Crossroads Company plans to purchase new productive equipment, for $200,000, that will increase the company's revenues by 20% during 2008. Management would like to maintain the company's current return on equity if at all possible. Crossroads can finance the purchase by selling stock or issuing long-term debt at 6% interest.

Required

A. Prepare a pro forma (projected) income statement for 2008 assuming the new equipment is financed through the issuance of new equity.
B. Prepare a pro forma (projected) income statement for 2008 assuming the new equipment is financed through the issuance of new long-term debt.
C. Assess the company's two options and make a recommendation for financing the new equipment that best matches management's objective. Can you think of any other alternatives that management might consider?

P10-6 ANALYZING FINANCING ACTIVITIES AND CAPITAL STRUCTURE

Obj. 4

Presented below is condensed and summary information from the financial statements of **Tommy Hilfiger Corporation.**

Tommy Hilfiger
Consolidated Balance Sheets
(In thousands)

	2004	2003
Assets:		
Current assets	$ 929,658	$ 915,532
Property and equipment net	233,020	248,290
Intangible assets	881,242	853,102
Other assets	9,486	11,227
Total assets	$2,053,406	$2,028,151
Liabilities and shareholders' equity:		
Current liabilities	$ 240,613	$ 404,922
Long-term debt	350,080	350,280
Other noncurrent liabilities	236,277	229,574
Shareholders' equity	1,226,436	1,043,375
Total liabilities and shareholders' equity	$2,053,406	$2,028,151
Number of common shares outstanding	91,307	90,579

(Continued)

Required

A. Analyze the capital structure of Tommy Hilfiger Corporation and discuss your findings.
B. Analyze Tommy Hilfiger's liquidity and discuss your findings. (Hint: Assume the average current ratio of companies in this industry is 1.84.)

P10-7 EVALUATING THE EFFECTS OF FINANCIAL LEVERAGE

Objs. 4, 5 Information is provided below from the 2004 annual report of **Pacific Gas & Electric.**

(In millions)	2004	2003
Operating income	$ 7,118	$ 2,343
Interest expense	797	1,147
Pretax income	6,286	1,249
Income taxes	2,466	458
Net income	4,504	420
Total assets	34,540	30,175
Total stockholders' equity	8,633	4,215
Long-term debt	7,323	3,314

The interest expense relates primarily to the long-term debt.

Required

A. Calculate the company's return on equity for 2004 and 2003.
B. How much did the company's financial leverage help or hurt the stockholders each year?
C. What would have happened to return on equity in these two years if, prior to 2003, the company had sold more common stock and used the proceeds to pay off debt?

P10-8 IDENTIFYING CAPITAL STRUCTURE CHOICES

Objs. 3, 5 You are a financial manager with a medium-sized company, Kangaroo Express. The company is owned and managed by the Marsupial family. Currently, 60% of the company's financing is composed of long-term notes, 20% is current liabilities, and the remainder consists of stock held by members of the Marsupial family. You have been asked to meet with the company's top management to discuss the company's capital structure and plans to raise capital for expansion.

Required Write a short report describing alternative types of financing Kangaroo Express might consider. Explain the risk and return implications of each alternative for the Marsupials.

P10-9 COMPARING CAPITAL STRUCTURES AND THE EFFECT OF LEVERAGE

Objs. 4, 5 Given below are summary financial statements for two companies.

	2008	2007	2006
Clipper Company:			
Total assets	$6,000	$5,500	$5,000
Total liabilities	3,273	4,014	3,750
Net income	300	200	100
Dividends	75	50	25
Battle Company:			
Total assets	$7,000	$6,000	$5,000
Total liabilities	5,333	4,286	3,333
Net income	300	200	100
Dividends	150	100	50

Required

A. Compute the debt-to-equity ratios for, and compare the capital structures of, the two companies.
B. Compute and compare the return on equity, return on assets, and financial leverage factors of the two companies.
C. Compute and compare the dividend payout ratios of the two companies.
D. After this analysis, which company would you prefer to invest in and why?

P10-10 EVALUATING THE EFFECT OF FINANCIAL LEVERAGE ON RISK

Obj. 5

Information is provided below for two companies, describing likely outcomes for the companies in various economic circumstances.

	Halyard Company			*Spinnaker Company*		
	Bad Year	Normal Year	Good Year	Bad Year	Normal Year	Good Year
Assets	$800	$800	$800	$800	$800	$800
Debt	200	200	200	600	600	600
Equity	600	600	600	200	200	200
Net income	(25)	75	175	(25)	75	175

Required

A. Calculate the following ratios for each company. Interpret the results of your calculations and explain what you conclude from the ratios.
   i. Debt-to-equity ratio
   ii. Debt-to-assets ratio
B. Calculate the following for each company under each economic circumstance.
   i. Return on assets
   ii. Financial leverage
   iii. Return on equity
C. Evaluate the effect of financial leverage on the risks of the two companies.

P10-11 EVALUATING THE EFFECT OF FINANCIAL LEVERAGE

Obj. 5

Information is provided below for two companies that have the same capital structure but different amounts of net income for the three years presented:

James Company:	2008	2007	2006
Assets	$3,000	$2,000	$1,000
Debt	1,800	1,200	600
Equity	1,200	800	400
Net income (loss)	1,000	500	250
Joyce Company:	**2008**	**2007**	**2006**
Assets	$3,000	$2,000	$1,000
Debt	1,800	1,200	600
Equity	1,200	800	400
Net income (loss)	(400)	(200)	300

Required

A. Calculate the following ratios for each company for each of the three years given:
   1. Debt-to-equity ratio
   2. Debt-to-assets ratio
   3. Return on assets
   4. Financial leverage
   5. Return on equity

(Continued)

B. Graph the results of the return on assets and return on equity calculations, putting the three years along the X (horizontal) axis and the percentages along the Y (vertical) axis. Discuss your conclusions.
C. For each company, reverse the amounts shown for debt and equity on the previous page. (For example, in 2008 both companies would have $1,200 of debt and $1,800 of equity.) Repeat the requirements for parts A and B. Discuss your conclusions and how they differ from the results you obtained in part B.

P10-12 ADDITIONAL DEBT, CAPITAL STRUCTURE, AND RETURN ON EQUITY
Obj. 5

Louisiana Company's fiscal year 2007 operating results and year-end balance sheet are as shown below.

Partial 2007 Income Statement (in millions)

Operating income	$122
Interest expense	(16)
Pretax income	106
Income taxes (30%)	(32)
Net income	$ 74

Year-end 2007 Balance Sheet

Total assets	$1,514
Liabilities:	
Current liabilities	$ 394
Long-term debt	200
Total liabilities	594
Stockholders' equity	920
Total liabilities and stockholders' equity	$1,514

Required

A. Compute return on equity for the company based on the information reported above.
B. Determine what the company's return on equity would have been in 2007 if, before the year began, the company had issued $225 million of additional long-term debt (at 8% interest) and had repurchased common stock. (Hint: You will need to recompute net income, liabilities, and stockholders' equity. Round financial statement amounts to the nearest million dollars.)
C. What effect would the additional debt have on the company's risk and return?

P10-13 ANALYZING PERFORMANCE AND THE EFFECT OF FINANCIAL LEVERAGE
Obj. 5

The financial statement information at the top of the following page is from the annual report of **Best Buy, Inc.**, a large retailer of electronics.

Required

A. Analyze the profit performance of Best Buy, Inc., and discuss your findings.
B. Analyze the effect of financial leverage on Best Buy, Inc., and discuss your findings.

Best Buy, Inc.
Consolidated Statements of Earnings
($ in millions, except per share amounts)

For the fiscal years ended	February 28, 2004	March 1, 2003	March 2, 2002
Revenue	$24,547	$20,946	$17,711
Cost of goods sold	18,350	15,710	13,941
Gross profit	6,197	5,236	3,770
Selling, general and administrative expenses	4,893	4,226	2,862
Operating income	1,304	1,010	908
Net interest income (expense)	(8)	4	18
Earnings from continuing operations before income tax	1,296	1,014	926
Income tax expense	496	392	356
Earnings from continuing operations	800	622	570
Loss from discontinued operations net of tax	(95)	(441)	—
Cumulative effect of change in accounting principle for goodwill, net of $24 tax	—	(40)	—
Cumulative effect of change in accounting principle for vendor allowances, net of $26 tax	—	(42)	—
Net earnings	$ 705	$ 99	$ 570

Note: Slight modifications have been made to simplify presentation of the financial statement.

In addition, the following information was presented on the company's balance sheets.

Total assets	$8,652	$7,694	$7,367
Stockholders' equity	3,422	2,730	2,521

P10-14 EVALUATING FINANCING CASH FLOWS

Objs. 3, 4, 6

Information is provided below from the 2004 annual report of **Johnson & Johnson:**

(In millions)	2004	2003
Cash flows from financing activities:		
Dividends to stockholders	$(3,251)	$(2,746)
Repurchase of common stock	(1,384)	(1,183)
Proceeds from short-term debt	514	3,062
Retirement of short-term debt	(1,291)	(4,134)
Proceeds from long-term debt	17	1,023
Retirement of long-term debt	(395)	(196)
Proceeds from the exercise of stock options	642	311
Net cash used by financing activities	$(5,148)	$(3,863)

Required Evaluate Johnson & Johnson's financial condition from the information provided. Do the financing activities indicate that the company is facing financial problems? Explain your thinking. What effect have these activities had on the company's capital structure?

P10-15 ANALYZING CREDIT-PAYING ABILITY

Objs. 3, 4, 6

Sunny Meadow Enterprises disclosed the following information in its 2007 annual report:

(In millions)	2007	2006
Net income (loss)	$ (31.0)	$ 58.6
Net cash flow from operating activities	6.8	144.2
Net cash flow from financing activities	135.8	(339.6)
Interest payments	65.9	81.4
Current portion of long-term debt	27.7	31.6
Total current liabilities	357.2	344.0
Total liabilities	1,384.3	1,210.9
Total current assets	695.9	626.3
Total assets	2,160.5	2,073.5

You are a financial analyst with a large investment company. Several clients are creditors and stockholders of the company. One client in particular, Wellington Smythe, has expressed concern about the company's recent net loss. He is concerned about the company's ability to meet its principal and interest payments and the effect of this on the company's stockholders.

Required Write a memo to Wellington explaining whether you think he should be concerned about the company's ability to meet its obligations and whether stockholders should be concerned about the company's performance. Use relevant information from the data presented above to support your explanations.

P10-16 ANALYZING CAPITAL STRUCTURE DECISIONS

Objs. 4, 5, 6

Companies are sometimes acquired by investors using a technique called a leveraged buyout (LBO). Selected information for a company both before and after such a transaction is given below. The information is typical of an LBO.

(In millions)	Year After the LBO	Year Before the LBO
Net income (loss)	$ (747)	$ 786
Operating income	1,334	1,498
Interest expense	1,909	318
Interest paid in cash	1,293	318
Cash provided by operations	1,687	1,901
Current maturities of long-term debt	1,711	105
Total current liabilities	3,269	2,680
Long-term debt	14,266	2,525
Stockholders' equity	804	3,925

Required

A. From the information for the years before and after the LBO, how would you define an LBO?
B. In the year after the LBO, how could Interest Expense exceed Interest Paid?
C. Is the company more risky or less risky after the LBO? Discuss.
D. After the LBO, net income was drastically reduced. Do you think the firm is in immediate danger? Discuss.

P10-17 EVALUATING FINANCING CASH FLOWS

Objs. 6, 7

Consider the following excerpts from the statement of cash flows for **Tommy Hilfiger Corporation** together with the information provided in Problem 10-6.

Tommy Hilfiger Corporation
Consolidated Statements of Cash Flows
For the fiscal year ended March 31

(In thousands)	2004	2003	2002
Cash flows from operating activities	$ 241,857	$ 230,105	$ 353,300
Cash flows from investing activities	$ (84,328)	$ (71,903)	$(301,984)
Cash flows from financing activities			
Proceeds from long-term debt	—	—	144,921
Payments on long-term debt	(152,051)	(74,234)	(155,538)
Proceeds from the exercise of stock options	8,190	7,177	7,997
Short-term bank borrowings (repayments), net	(19,946)	(57,566)	20,120
Net cash provided by (used in) financing activities	$(163,807)	$(124,623)	$ 17,500
Net (decrease) increase in cash	$ (6,278)	$ 33,579	$ 68,816
Cash and cash equivalents, beginning of period	420,826	387,247	318,431
Cash and cash equivalents, end of period	$ 414,548	$ 420,826	$ 387,247

In addition, Tommy Hilfiger Corporation provided the following information and quotation in the section of its annual report entitled "Market for Registrant's Common Equity And Related Matters."

	High	Low
Fiscal year ended March 31, 2004		
Fourth quarter	17.41	12.73
Fiscal year ended March 31, 2003		
Fourth quarter	7.44	5.61

"Tommy Hilfiger Corporation has not paid any cash dividends since its initial public offering (IPO) in 1992, and has no current plans to pay cash dividends."

Required

A. Describe and summarize the company's financing cash flows for the fiscal periods covered by the information provided.
B. Besides the quotation from the annual report, how else do you know that the company has not been paying dividends?
C. Compute the market to book value at the points in time for which you have the necessary information available in the problem. Describe any changes over that period that you observe.

P10-18 ETHICAL ISSUES IN FINANCING DECISIONS

Objs. 6, 7

Randy Slowpush is chief financial officer (CFO) for Endrun Financial Corp. Because the rapidly growing company wishes to maximize financial leverage, the company is in constant need of new debt capital. As CFO, Randy is famous for creative financing techniques by which the firm is able to raise money without reporting the debt on its own balance sheet. A common technique is to establish a partnership, partially owned by Randy, that borrows money to finance certain business ventures on behalf of Endrun Corp. Endrun secretly guarantees the loans by pledging to issue its own stock, if necessary, to repay the partnership loans.

Randy then negotiates contracts with Endrun, on behalf of the partnerships, to manage specified business activities for Endrun. Often he negotiates with Endrun employees who report to the CFO. In 2007, Randy earned $30 million from operating about 15 of these partnerships. Endrun benefits from this arrangement by keeping the debt off its books, which keeps its leverage ratios in an acceptable range, which keeps its interest rates low on the debt it does report. Stockholders and creditors are not aware of these arrangements.

Required Are these activities unethical? Why or why not?

P10-19 EVALUATING FINANCING CHOICES

Obj. 6

Aitken Company needs cash. The company has several hot new products and sales are growing rapidly. The controller has just presented CEO Jim Aitken the following balance sheet updated through today, saying, "we've got to raise $90,000 cash immediately."

Assets		**Liabilities**	
Cash	$ 11,200	Accounts payable	$ 18,550
Accounts receivable	15,000	Other short-term liabilities	39,550
Inventory	10,000	Long-term debt	100,000
Machinery, net	107,500	**Stockholders' equity**	
Buildings, net	253,600	Contributed capital	200,000
Land	80,000	Retained earnings	119,200
Total assets	$477,300	Total liabilities and equity	$477,300

The controller proposed three options to raise the $90,000: (1) obtain a short-term bank loan, (2) sell new shares of common stock, or (3) issue long-term bonds payable. She also presented the CEO with the following information about financial ratio benchmarks for companies in their industry.

Ratio	High	Average	Low
Current ratio	2.5	1.5	1.0
Long-term debt to equity	0.28	0.40	0.53
Long-term debt to assets	0.19	0.26	0.35
Assets to equity	1.3	1.7	2.0

Required

A. Compute today's value of the four ratios for which benchmarks are given.
B. Evaluate each value computed in part A with its industry benchmark. Which ratio values are strong? Which are weak?
C. Compute pro-forma (projected) ratio values under each of the three financing options. That is, for each option, what would be the new ratio values immediately after that option was implemented?
D. Evaluate your results from part C. Which financing option would best strengthen the company's financial position as measured by the four ratios considered? Explain.

P10-20 EXCEL IN ACTION

The Book Wermz issued common stock and bonds in March 2008. Following that, the company created projected income statement and balance sheet account balances for the fiscal year ended December 31, 2008 that appear below. Only selected balances are presented.

Operating income	$ 647,585
Total assets	5,623,107
Long-term debt	2,097,416
Stockholders' equity	3,370,241

Assume that interest expense is 9% of long-term debt and the company's income tax rate is 35%.

Required Enter the data shown above for The Book Wermz in columns A and B of a spreadsheet. Calculate interest expense, pretax income, income taxes, and net income for the company for 2008 using the assumptions provided. Then, calculate return on assets, financial leverage (Assets ÷ Stockholders' Equity), and return on equity. Place captions in column A and amounts in column B.

Copy the data from column B to column C. Assume that the company's long-term debt decreased by $1 million and its stockholders' equity increased by $1 million. Adjust these amounts in the spreadsheet. What effect would this change have on the company's return?

Copy the data from column C to column D. Assume that the company's long-term debt increased by $1 million and its stockholders' equity decreased by $1 million relative to the amounts in column B. Adjust these amounts in the spreadsheet. What effect would this change have on the company's return?

Suppose that the company's operating income for 2008 was $200,000. What effect would this change have on the company's return under each of the scenarios described above? Copy columns B, C, and D to columns E, F, and G and change the operating income in columns E, F, and G to $200,000.

Graph the relation between financial leverage and return on equity. Select the rows in which these two calculations appear on your spreadsheet. Click on the Chart Wizard button. Select XY (Scatter) as the chart type and click the Next button. Make sure the Rows button is checked in the Series field. Click the Next button. In the Titles tab, enter "Effect of Financial Leverage on Return" for the chart title. Enter "Financial Leverage" for the Value (X) axis, and "Return on Equity" for the Value (Y) axis. In the Legend tab, click the Show Legend box so the checkmark is removed. Click the Next button. Click on the As object in button and then the Finish button. You can resize the chart by clicking on it, clicking any of the small boxes around the edge of the chart and dragging the chart to the size and shape you want. You can move the entire chart by clicking on the chart (not one of the boxes) and dragging it to a new location. Various parts of the graph can be reformatted by clicking on the graph item with the right mouse button and selecting Format from the dialog box. For example, if you want to remove the shading from the plot area, click on the shaded area with the right mouse button, select Format Plot Area, and click on the None button in the Area category. You can change colors, fonts, axes, numbers of decimals, and other properties using this method.

What can you conclude about the relation between financial leverage and return on equity?

P10-21 MULTIPLE-CHOICE OVERVIEW OF THE CHAPTER

1. The way a company finances its assets and operating activities is its
   a. capital structure.
   b. financial leverage.
   c. return on equity.
   d. present value.

2. Honey Farms Company reported the following information.

Net sales	$ 85
Net income	10
Total assets	103
Total liabilities	41
Stockholders' equity	62

   Return on equity is
   a. 6.2%.
   b. 9.7%.
   c. 11.8%.
   d. 16.1%.

3. Financial leverage always
   a. increases profits.
   b. decreases profits.
   c. increases risk.
   d. decreases risk.

4. Which of the following ratios is an indicator of liquidity?
   a. Debt to assets
   b. Current assets to current liabilities
   c. Assets to equity
   d. Net income to equity

5. Financing with capital leases and financing with preferred stock are similar in that both
   a. require the payout of fixed amounts each period.
   b. increase the amount of net income available to common stockholders.
   c. increase the riskiness of the firm's common stock.
   d. cause cash flow from operations to be smaller than it otherwise would be.

(Continued)

6. At year end, J. J. Walker Company had total assets of $90,000 and total stockholders' equity of $50,000. The firm's return on assets was 12% for the year. What were net income and return on equity?

	Net Income	Return on Equity
a.	$4,800	9.6%
b.	$6,000	12.0%
c.	$10,800	21.6%
d.	$16,800	33.6%

7. Crispy Chips Inc. earned net income this past year of $100,000 on assets of $1.9 million and stockholders' equity of $1.2 million. To raise $500,000 of additional capital, Crispy can either issue long-term debt paying 9% interest or issue additional common stock. Use of the new capital should raise net income, before considering any new interest cost, by $68,000. To maximize return on equity, Crispy should
   a. not issue any new debt or equity.
   b. issue new equity only.
   c. issue new debt only.
   d. issue half in new equity and half in new debt.

8. High amounts of financial leverage are most common for companies with
   a. small proportions of plant assets and stable earnings.
   b. large proportions of plant assets and stable earnings.
   c. small proportions of plant assets and unstable earnings.
   d. large proportions of plant assets and unstable earnings.

9. Low dividend payout ratios are common for companies
   a. with low growth potential.
   b. in stable industries.
   c. with high growth potential.
   d. with stable earnings.

10. If a company is having difficulty paying interest and principal on its debt, creditors should be particularly concerned with
   a. its return on assets.
   b. its return on equity.
   c. its debt to equity ratio.
   d. its cash flows.

Cases

C10-1 EVALUATING CAPITAL STRUCTURE

Obj. 4 Selected information for Terabyte Technology Inc. is provided on the next page.

Required Write a short report describing Terabyte's capital structure. Consider changes in the company's capital structure in 2008, and identify the causes of these changes. Identify Terabyte's primary source of financing in 2008, and evaluate the company's financial condition at the end of 2008.

(In millions except per share amounts)	2008	2007
Earnings before interest and taxes	$ 742	$ 799
Interest expense	129	133
Earnings before income taxes	613	666
Income taxes	159	167
Net income	454	499
Net income per share	3.44	3.80
Average shares outstanding	131.9	131.3
Total current assets	4,487	4,452
Total assets	9,375	8,742
Total current liabilities	3,063	3,048
Long-term debt	954	792
Deferred income taxes	196	203
Other liabilities	532	442
Total stockholders' equity	4,630	4,257
Net cash provided by operations	1,358	1,307
Net cash used for investing activities	(1,232)	(1,443)
Net cash provided by financing activities:		
Increase (decrease) in notes payable and current portion of long-term debt	(143)	208
Increase in long-term debt	135	7
Issuance of common stock	19	55
Payment of dividends	(100)	(100)
Net cash provided by (used for) financing activities	(89)	170

C10-2 EVALUATING CAPITAL STRUCTURE DECISIONS

Objs. 4, 5

At year end 2007, the capital structure of Hard Luck Casino Inc. was as follows:

Current liabilities	$ 2,400,000
Long-term debt (9% bonds)	5,000,000
Preferred stock, $100 par	1,000,000
Common stock, no par value	15,000,000
Retained earnings	2,600,000
Total liabilities and equity	$26,000,000

During 2007, the company earned net income of $3 million. It paid the required preferred dividends of $80,000 and paid dividends to common stockholders of $750,000.

Required For each of the following independent scenarios, assume it occurred or was true during year 2007. Explain the effect the scenario would have had on the company's net income, return on assets, and return on equity for year 2007. What effect would you expect the event to have had on the riskiness of each type of security issued by Hard Luck Casino?

A. On January 2, 2007, the company issued $5 million of new common stock and used the proceeds to repurchase its bonds.
B. Because of new competition during 2007, the company's profits had been $1 million less than reported above.
C. On January 2, 2007, the company issued $8 million of new bonds to finance the purchase of additional plant assets. The bonds were issued at a market rate of 10%. The new assets produced $1.6 million of additional profits before considering the added interest cost.

C10-3 ANALYZING FINANCING DECISIONS

Objs. 4, 5, 6, 7 Sporty Footware Inc. reported the following financial information at year-end 2007:

Consolidated Statements of Operations
For the Year Ended December 31,

(In thousands, except per share amounts)	2007	2006	2005
Net revenue	$847,110	$661,688	$478,131
Cost of goods sold	447,524	344,884	258,419
Gross profit	$399,586	$316,804	$219,712
Selling, general, and administrative expenses	236,571	190,976	132,270
Income from operations	$163,015	$125,828	$ 87,442
Interest expense	(1,258)	(761)	(754)
Interest income	7,013	6,181	5,712
Income before income taxes	$168,770	$131,248	$ 92,400
Provision for income taxes	55,590	44,866	30,900
Net income	$113,180	$ 86,382	$ 61,500

Consolidated Balance Sheets (In thousands, except share data)	December 31, 2007	December 31, 2006
Assets:		
Current assets	$438,284	$332,353
Property and equipment, net	160,089	121,540
Other assets	19,637	9,192
Total assets	$618,010	$463,085
Liabilities and shareholders' equity:		
Current liabilities	$ 92,398	$ 61,686
Other liabilities	6,550	2,425
Long-term debt	—	1,510
Shareholders' equity*	519,062	397,464
Total liabilities and shareholders' equity	$618,010	$463,085
*Common shares outstanding	37,557,934	37,249,529

Consolidated Statements of Cash Flows
For the Year Ended December 31,

(In thousands)	2007	2006	2005
Cash flows from operating activities	$108,049	$ 62,635	$34,227
Cash flows from investing activities	$ (67,814)	$(83,960)	$21,520
Cash flows from financing activities			
Proceeds from the exercise of employee stock options	$ 5,685	$ 3,929	$13,027
Tax benefit from exercise of stock options	2,703	5,812	17,715
Short-term bank borrowings, net	—	(5,975)	5,700
Payments on long-term debt	(1,510)	(279)	(275)
Other	30	3	12
Net cash provided by financing activities	$ 6,908	$ 3,490	$36,179

Other information:

1. The company has a policy of not paying dividends.
2. Year-end stock prices were as follows:

   2007 = $61.50
   2006 = $59.13

Required Would you lend money to this firm? Would you buy its common stock? Why or why not? Conduct whatever analysis and evaluation you believe would be helpful to answer these questions. Support your answer by referencing your analysis.

Investing Activities

11

HOW DO WE ACCOUNT FOR INVESTING ACTIVITIES?

Long-term assets are necessary to support a company's operating activities. Facilities are needed to produce and sell products. Other long-term assets recognize the cost of intellectual property and other legal rights controlled by a company, as well as investments and other financial resources. As a company becomes larger, it invests in more assets and often requires more types of assets to support its business activities.

Maria, Stan, and Ellen are considering expanding Favorite Cookie Company. They are aware that they will need additional property and equipment for the company to produce and sell its products to a larger market.

Food for Thought

If you were advising the owners of Favorite Cookie Company, what kinds of long-term assets would you recommend they invest in and how should they account for those various assets? Are there any tax issues that might have an impact on the way they account for the new investments?

Stan has called a meeting with Maria and Ellen to talk about expansion plans. They begin their discussion of the assets the company will need by considering different types of assets and how to account for them.

Stan: *If we are going to produce and sell more of our products, we will need to acquire additional plant and equipment.*

Maria: *Are there other long-term assets that we will require?*

Ellen: *Other long-term assets may be useful. For example, we may want to protect some of our recipes and our brand name with patents and trademarks. We may need to make some financial investments to provide financial resources when we need them in the future.*

Stan: *Acquiring long-term assets is really just a matter of buying them and putting them to work, isn't it? These activities really don't have much effect on our profits, do they?*

Ellen: *How we depreciate our property and equipment will have an effect on profitability and the timing of our income tax payments. Other revenues and expenses can result from other activities, such as income earned from investments in marketable securities.*

Maria: *Perhaps we should examine these investing activities and how they can affect our financial statements before we make any more decisions.*

Objectives

Once you have completed this chapter, you should be able to:

1. Identify types of long-term assets, their purposes, and the measurement basis companies use to record their assets.
2. Apply appropriate measurement rules to the purchase, depreciation, and disposal of plant assets.
3. Apply appropriate measurement rules to the purchase and use of natural resources.
4. Apply appropriate measurement rules to the purchase, valuation, and sale of long-term and short-term investments.
5. Explain accounting issues associated with intangible and other long-term assets.
6. Summarize the effects of investing activities on a company's financial statements.

TYPES OF ASSETS

Objective 1

Identify types of long-term assets, their purposes, and the measurement basis companies use to record their assets.

Investing activities supply the resources that an organization needs to operate. Most of those resources are reported as assets, although some—for example, the value of management and employee skills—are not. On its balance sheet, a company reports those assets for which it can reasonably identify costs and that are important to its operations. Exhibit 1 provides the asset section of the balance sheet Favorite Cookie Company reported in its 2008 annual report. This exhibit is used as a basis for discussing the types of assets most corporations report.

Most companies divide their assets into two major categories: current and long-term. **Current assets are those that management expects to convert to cash or consume during the coming fiscal year.** Most current assets are created or used as part of a company's operating activities. The company uses those assets to produce and sell goods and services. Accounts receivable and inventories are examined in Chapter 13 when we consider operating activities. (Prepaid expenses were discussed in an earlier chapter.) Cash is created and used in all types of activities. We consider the effects of investing activities on cash in this chapter.

EXHIBIT 1

Balance Sheet Presentation of Assets for Favorite Cookie Company

December 31,	2008	2007
Assets		
Current assets:		
Cash	$ 17,510	$ 10,680
Accounts receivable	15,400	8,570
Merchandise inventory	75,920	23,600
Supplies	2,480	690
Prepaid rent	3,500	2,000
Total current assets	114,810	45,540
Long-term investments	4,000	0
Property and equipment, at cost	572,467	215,660
Accumulated depreciation	(53,630)	(25,500)
Property and equipment, net	518,837	190,160
Intangible assets	1,600	0
Other long-term assets	850	0
Total assets	$640,097	$235,700

Learning Note - In rare cases, a company's cycle of conversion, or operating cycle, is longer than a year. An ***operating cycle*** *is the period from the time cash is paid for inventory until the inventory is sold and converted back to cash. In these cases, the company uses the longer operating cycle, rather than the fiscal year, as a basis for determining its current assets.*

Long-term assets include assets a company uses to produce and sell its products. These assets **provide benefits to a company that extend beyond the coming fiscal year** or operating cycle. Long-term assets usually are divided into four categories, though some companies choose not to invest in all four categories.

Long-term investments are investments in financial securities. These securities are debt or equity issued by other companies or organizations.

Property, plant, and equipment includes investments in tangible assets, such as equipment, buildings, and land, that a company intends to use in the future to produce or sell its products. The amount paid for these assets, their cost, is reported on the balance sheet or in a note to the balance sheet. In addition, the amount of depreciation recorded on the assets since they were acquired is reported as accumulated depreciation, either on the balance sheet or in a note. The difference between the cost of these assets and accumulated depreciation is the amount actually used to compute total assets on the balance sheet. This amount generally is referred to as **net** property, plant, and equipment or net fixed assets. The cost of these assets sometimes is referred to as **gross** property, plant, and equipment.

The source of financing for plant assets does not affect the way the assets are reported on the balance sheet. Whether a company pays for the assets from cash it has accumulated, borrows money from creditors, or issues stock, the assets are still reported as plant assets. Plant assets acquired by capital leases also are included as part of property, plant, and equipment and are depreciated along with other assets.

Intangible assets are those that provide legal rights or benefits to a company. These assets include patents, copyrights, trademarks, and goodwill. A company benefits from these assets because it controls rights to certain property, processes, brands, or markets that give the company an advantage relative to its competitors.

Other assets include miscellaneous resources that are important to a particular company. These may include long-term receivables, long-term prepaid assets, buildings and equipment that a company is attempting to sell, and natural resources, such as timber, oil, or minerals.

The total amount reported by a company for its assets is the sum of current and long-term assets.

We will consider accounting for each of these types of assets in the sections that follow. We begin the discussion with plant assets, because these are the most common type of long-term assets and the most important for most companies.

PROPERTY, PLANT, AND EQUIPMENT

Objective 2

Apply appropriate measurement rules to the purchase, depreciation, and disposal of plant assets.

Plant assets include the land, buildings, and equipment a company uses in its operating activities. Favorite Cookie Company reported plant assets of $518,837 in 2008 (see Exhibit 1). That amount was net (after subtraction) of accumulated depreciation.

The transactions associated with plant assets include their purchase and disposal and their valuation on the balance sheet at the end of each fiscal period. The purchase and disposal of plant assets are recorded at cost, the amount paid for the assets or received when the assets are sold. The disposal of plant assets usually results in cash inflow and recognition of a gain or loss. Plant assets are reported on the balance sheet at cost less accumulated depreciation. Companies provide information about primary categories of plant assets in their balance sheets or in notes to their financial statements.

Land does not depreciate because it is not consumed. Companies generally buy land for office, manufacturing, and other facilities. Land used for these purposes is reported as part of property, plant, and equipment. The cost of consuming natural resources—oil or timber, for example—is described later in this chapter.

Plant Asset Cost

The cost of plant assets includes the amount paid for the assets plus the cost of transportation, site preparation, installation, and any construction necessary to make the assets usable for their intended purpose. The cost of land includes the cost of preparing the land for construction and use. Improvements to the land (such as paving and lighting) are treated as separate assets and are depreciated along with other plant assets.

CASE IN POINT

http://ingram.swlearning.com

Visit Procter & Gamble's home page to learn more about the company.

Reporting Long-Term Assets

Procter & Gamble provided the following information about its property and equipment in its 2004 annual report.

Consolidated Balance Sheets

Assets

	June 30	
Amounts in millions	**2004**	**2003**
Property, Plant and Equipment		
Buildings	**5,206**	4,729
Machinery and equipment	**19,456**	18,222
Land	**642**	591
	25,304	23,542
Accumulated depreciation	**(11,196)**	(10,438)
Net Property, Plant and Equipment	**14,108**	13,104

To illustrate, assume that on September 12, 2008, Favorite Cookie Company purchased a small parcel of property. The company paid $400,000 for the property, which included a building and office equipment. In addition, the company spent $10,000 in October to renovate the building.

Learning Note - If a capital lease is used to acquire plant assets, the present value of the future lease payments at the time the property is acquired is used as the cost of the assets.

To account for this acquisition, Favorite Cookie Company must separate the $400,000 cost of the property into its components: land, building, and equipment. This separation is necessary because the building and equipment will be depreciated, whereas the land will not be depreciated. The cost of the property is assigned to components on the basis of the relative fair market values of the various assets acquired. For example, assume that Favorite Cookie Company has the property appraised and determines that 70% should be allocated to the building, 20% to the land, and 10% to the equipment. It would record the $400,000 purchase as follows:

		Assets		=	Liabilities	+	Owners' Equity	
Date	**Accounts**	**Cash**	**Other Assets**				**Contributed Capital**	**Retained Earnings**
Sep. 12, 2008	Land		80,000					
	Buildings		280,000					
	Equipment		40,000					
	Cash	−400,000						

Assume that the $10,000 renovation cost included $7,500 for replacement of the building's roof and $2,500 for painting. Both of these costs relate to the building. However, the costs fall into two categories: those that extend the life or enhance the value of the property ($7,500 for roof replacement) and those that are ordinary repairs or maintenance ($2,500 for painting). **Expenditures made to acquire new plant assets or to extend the life or enhance the value of existing plant assets are known as *capital expenditures*.** Capital expenditures are recorded as assets because they create future benefits. **Expenditures to repair or maintain plant assets that do not extend the life or enhance the value of the assets are known as *operating expenditures*.** Operating expenditures are recorded as expenses because they are costs associated with the use or consumption of a resource.

Accordingly, the $10,000 renovation cost is recorded as follows:

		Assets		=	Liabilities	+	Owners' Equity	
Date	**Accounts**	**Cash**	**Other Assets**				**Contributed Capital**	**Retained Earnings**
Oct. 31, 2008	Buildings		7,500					
	Maintenance Expense							−2,500
	Cash	−10,000						

In addition to purchase and renovation costs, interest on debt used to finance the construction of assets is included as part of the cost of these assets. For example, if Favorite Cookie Company borrowed $100,000 at 8% for one year to finance construction of a building, the $8,000 interest paid on the loan would be assigned to the buildings account. This interest is capitalized (recorded as an asset) because it is part of the cost of constructing the asset. The total cost of the building, including interest, is depreciated over its useful life.

Depreciation

Buildings, equipment, and other plant assets that are consumed are depreciated over their estimated useful lives. **Depreciation** is the process of allocating the cost of plant assets to expense over the fiscal periods that benefit from their use. Because the actual consumption of a plant asset usually is impossible to determine, depreciation involves arbitrary allocations of costs. These allocations attempt to match the cost of consuming plant assets with the periods that benefit from using the assets. However, assumptions normally must be made about how much of the asset has been consumed. A variety of depreciation methods exist, but most fall into three general categories:

- ***Straight-line depreciation* allocates an equal amount of the cost of a plant asset to expense during each fiscal period of the asset's expected useful life.**
- ***Accelerated depreciation* allocates a larger portion of the cost of a plant asset to expense early in the asset's life.**
- ***Units-of-production depreciation* produces a level amount of depreciation expense per unit of output (rather than per fiscal period).**

Straight-Line Depreciation. Suppose that Favorite Cookie Company purchased equipment on January 1, 2007 at a cost of $50,000. Management expects the equipment to have a useful life of four years. At the end of four years, it expects to sell the equipment for $2,000 (called its residual value) and replace it with new equipment. The amount of depreciation the company should record over the life of the equipment is $48,000: cost minus residual value ($50,000 − $2,000). **Residual** or **salvage value** is the amount management expects to receive for an asset at the end of the asset's useful life. This amount may result from selling or trading in the asset. The residual value is zero for many assets.

Straight-line depreciation allocates $12,000 ($48,000 ÷ 4) of the cost to depreciation expense each year over the life of the asset:

Straight-line depreciation expense = (cost − residual value) ÷ expected life of asset

During 2007, Favorite Cookie Company would record depreciation expense on the equipment as follows:

		Assets		=	Liabilities	+	Owners' Equity	
Date	Accounts	Cash	Other Assets				Contributed Capital	Retained Earnings
Dec. 31, 2007	Depreciation Expense							−12,000
	Accumulated Depreciation		−12,000					

Accumulated Depreciation is a contra-asset account that offsets Equipment. The **net** or **book value** of a plant asset is the net cost of the asset after accumulated depreciation has been subtracted. A depreciation schedule describes the depreciation and book value of an asset over the asset's useful life. Exhibit 2 provides a depreciation schedule for the equipment purchased by Favorite Cookie Company in 2007.

An equal amount of depreciation is recorded each fiscal period. At the end of four years, the book value of the asset is $2,000, the amount that management expects to receive for the asset. The total amount of depreciation a company records each fiscal period is the sum of the amounts recorded for all of its individual plant assets. Therefore, a company prepares a depreciation schedule for each major type of plant asset.

Because depreciation is an estimation process, the amounts may change over time. For example, at the end of 2008, Favorite Cookie Company's managers may decide that they will be able to use the equipment for three more years (for a total life of five years), at which time the equipment will have a residual value of $2,000. As a result of this change in estimate, the equipment depreciation schedule would be revised as shown in Exhibit 3.

EXHIBIT 2
Straight-Line Depreciation Schedule

Year	Beginning Book Value	Depreciation Expense	Accumulated Depreciation	Ending Book Value
2007	$50,000	$12,000	$12,000	$38,000
2008	38,000	12,000	24,000	26,000
2009	26,000	12,000	36,000	14,000
2010	14,000	12,000	48,000	2,000

EXHIBIT 3
Revised Straight-Line Depreciation Schedule

Year	Beginning Book Value	Depreciation Expense	Accumulated Depreciation	Ending Book Value
2007	$50,000	$12,000	$12,000	$38,000
2008	38,000	12,000	24,000	26,000
*2009	26,000	8,000	32,000	18,000
*2010	18,000	8,000	40,000	10,000
*2011	10,000	8,000	48,000	2,000

***Changed from Exhibit 2.**

Depreciation expense for 2009 through 2011 is determined as follows:

Revised depreciation expense = (book value − residual value) ÷ estimated useful life
$8,000 = ($26,000 − $2,000) ÷ 3 years

A change in estimate affects depreciation in periods after the change is made. Amounts recorded in previous periods are not revised.

Straight-line depreciation is easy to compute and provides a reasonable estimate of the consumption of most plant assets. Consequently, it is the most commonly used method for determining depreciation in financial reports of major corporations.

Accelerated Depreciation. Accelerated depreciation allocates more depreciation expense to the earlier years of an asset's estimated life than to the later years. Several methods of computing accelerated depreciation are commonly used. One frequently used method is referred to as double-declining-balance. Double-declining-balance depreciation allocates to depreciation expense twice the straight-line rate times the book value of an asset. The straight-line rate is 1 divided by the estimated useful life of the asset. Thus, an asset with a life of four years has a straight-line rate of 1/4, or 25%. Double this rate would be 2/4, or 50%.

To illustrate, if Favorite Cookie Company used double-declining-balance depreciation for the equipment purchased at the beginning of 2007, it would compute depreciation for each year of the life of the asset as shown below.

Double-declining-balance depreciation expense = book value × (2 ÷ expected useful life)

The asset cannot be depreciated below its residual value, which is $2,000. Thus, the amount of depreciation expense recorded in 2010, the last year of the equipment's life, is $4,250 ($6,250 − $2,000), the amount needed to fully depreciate the asset, leaving a book value equal to the residual value.

Year	Depreciation Expense	=	Book Value	×	Depreciation Rate
2007	$25,000		$50,000		2/4
2008	12,500		25,000		2/4
2009	6,250		12,500		2/4
2010	4,250				

Note that book value, not cost, is used and the residual value is not subtracted in the calculation. For example, at the beginning of 2007, the original cost of $50,000 equals the book value. At the beginning of 2008, the book value is now $25,000 ($50,000 cost minus $25,000 accumulated depreciation).

Favorite Cookie Company should record $48,000 of depreciation over the life of the asset, just as when straight-line depreciation is used. The depreciation method does not change the total amount of depreciation recorded. It changes the amount allocated to each fiscal year.

Exhibit 4 provides a depreciation schedule for the equipment, assuming double-declining-balance depreciation.

EXHIBIT 4
Double-Declining-Balance Depreciation Schedule

Year	Beginning Book Value	Depreciation Expense	Accumulated Depreciation	Ending Book Value
2007	$50,000	$25,000	$25,000	$25,000
2008	25,000	12,500	37,500	12,500
2009	12,500	6,250	43,750	6,250
2010	6,250	4,250	48,000	2,000*

*The residual value

USING EXCEL

A spreadsheet contains functions for calculating depreciation. In Excel, the functions can be selected by clicking on the Function f_x button and selecting the Financial category. The SLN function calculates straight-line depreciation, and the DDB function calculates double-declining-balance depreciation. Double-clicking on the function name brings up a dialog box. Enter the cost, salvage value, and life of the asset. The life should be expressed in the appropriate time units (years or months for example), depending on the period for which depreciation expense is being calculated. For double-declining-balance depreciation, the period for which the depreciation is being calculated must also be entered. The period is a number relative to the beginning of the asset's life. For example, if depreciation is being calculated on an annual basis, the first year of an asset's life would be 1, the second year 2, and so forth. A dialog box appears below showing the data for an asset with a cost of $10,000, a salvage value of $1,000, and a life of five years. The calculation is for the first year of the asset's useful life (Period = 1). If the function were selected from cell A1, the cell would report the amount calculated by the function of $4,000.

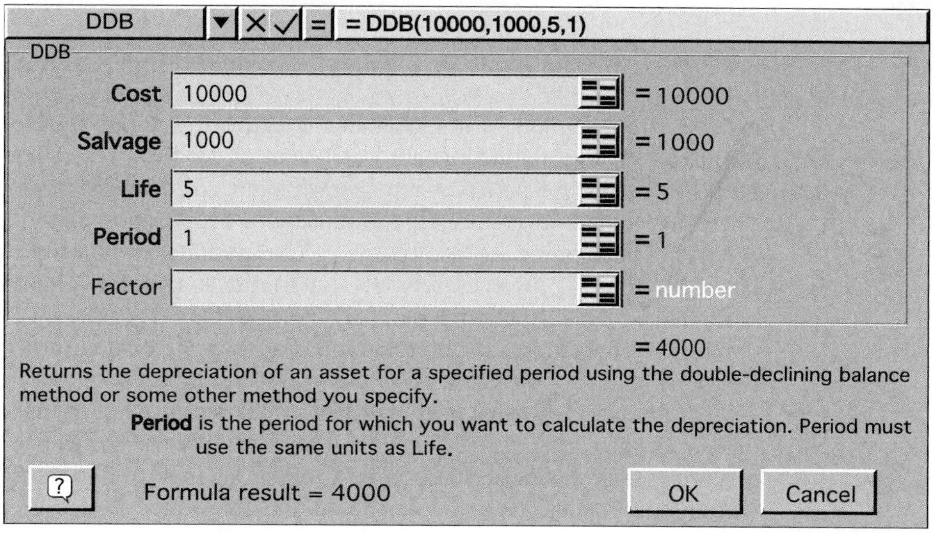

Reasons for Using Accelerated Depreciation. Accelerated depreciation methods are used for two primary reasons. In some cases, an asset is more useful earlier in its life than later, and the useful life may be difficult to estimate. For example, computer equipment becomes obsolete quickly. Accordingly, a company may accelerate the depreciation of computer equipment to ensure that most of the cost has been depreciated when the equipment is replaced.

A second, and more common, reason for using accelerated depreciation is for tax purposes. Depreciation expense is deductible in computing taxable income and income taxes. For example, assume that in 2007, Favorite Cookie Company reported $100,000 of income before depreciation and taxes. Exhibit 5 describes the effects on Favorite Cookie Company's income taxes of using straight-line and accelerated depreciation.

In 2007, straight-line depreciation expense (from Exhibit 2) results in higher pretax income, income taxes, and net income. Because double-declining-balance depreciation

EXHIBIT 5
Comparison of Straight-Line and Accelerated Depreciation Methods in 2007

	Straight-Line	Accelerated
Income before depreciation and taxes	$100,000	$100,000
Depreciation expense	12,000	25,000
Pretax income	$ 88,000	$ 75,000
Income taxes (35%)	30,800	26,250
Net income	$ 57,200	$ 48,750

CASE IN POINT

http://ingram.swlearning.com

Visit Procter & Gamble's home page to learn more about the company.

Disclosure of Depreciation Policy

In its 2004 annual report, Procter & Gamble provided the following description of its depreciation policy:

> *Property, plant and equipment are recorded at cost reduced by accumulated depreciation. Depreciation expense is recognized over the assets' estimated useful lives using the straight-line method. Machinery and equipment includes office furniture and equipment (15-year life), computer equipment and capitalized software (3- to 5-year lives) and manufacturing equipment (3- to 20-year lives). Buildings are depreciated over an estimated useful life of 40 years. Estimated useful lives are periodically reviewed and, where appropriate, changes are made prospectively. Where certain events or changes in operating conditions occur, asset lives may be adjusted and an impairment assessment may be performed on the recoverability of the carrying amounts.*

expense (from Exhibit 4) is higher in the earlier years, the taxable (pretax) income, income taxes, and net income are lower than under the straight-line method. For tax purposes, a company prefers to report lower pretax income and pay lower income taxes. Therefore, companies commonly use accelerated depreciation methods for tax purposes as a way of postponing the tax obligation. The specific method used depends on income tax regulations. Companies typically report the maximum amount of depreciation permitted by law for tax purposes. Larger amounts of depreciation expense reduce tax payments in the current fiscal period, thereby reducing cash outflows for tax purposes. By reducing its cash outflows, a company preserves more of its cash for other purposes.

For financial reporting purposes, companies prefer to report higher amounts of net income in the earlier years. Therefore, they generally use straight-line depreciation in preparing their financial statements. Companies may use straight-line depreciation when preparing their financial statements and accelerated depreciation when preparing their tax returns. Small companies often use accelerated depreciation methods for both purposes to avoid the need for two sets of accounting records. Note that *over the life of the asset*, the same total amount of depreciation expense is recognized under the straight-line method as under the accelerated methods. Thus, the same amount of total income tax is paid under those methods.

Companies disclose the accounting methods they use for recording and depreciating their plant assets in notes to their financial statements. These notes identify the depreciation method used and provide other relevant information.

The difference between straight-line and accelerated depreciation is a major source of deferred taxes. **Deferred taxes** are taxes that a company would owe if it used the same methods for preparing its tax return that it used for preparing its financial statements. For example, using the Exhibit 5 information, Favorite Cookie Company would record its taxes for 2007 as:

		Assets		=	Liabilities	+	Owners' Equity	
Date	**Accounts**	**Cash**	**Other Assets**				**Contributed Capital**	**Retained Earnings**
Dec. 31, 2007	Income Tax Expense							−30,800
	Income Tax Payable				26,250			
	Deferred Tax Liability				4,550			

Income tax payable is the amount Favorite Cookie Company owes based on its tax return. Income tax expense is the amount of tax it would owe if straight-line depreciation had been used for tax purposes. The difference between the payable and the expense is recorded as Deferred Taxes. Deferred taxes are the taxes Favorite Cookie Company has deferred (postponed) to some future period by using accelerated depreciation for tax purposes. Because the company expects to pay these taxes in the future, they are recorded as a long-term liability. Companies frequently report deferred taxes as long-term liabilities on their balance sheets.

Learning Note - Occasionally, a company will record a deferred tax charge. This charge appears on the balance sheet as a long-term asset. It represents a prepayment of taxes that the company will owe in the future.

Units-of-Production Depreciation. Some companies use the units-of-production method to depreciate production equipment and facilities across units of output. For example, suppose that at the beginning of 2008, Favorite Cookie Company purchased a truck to deliver goods to customers. The truck cost $30,000. Management expects the useful life of the truck to be 100,000 miles, at which time it will be sold for $10,000, and a new truck will be acquired. Rather than depreciating the truck over time, it will be depreciated based on mileage. A depreciation rate per mile for the truck can be computed as follows:

Units-of-production depreciation rate = (cost − residual value) ÷ estimated units
$0.20 per mile = ($30,000 − $10,000) ÷ 100,000 miles

If the truck were driven 12,000 miles in 2008, Favorite Cookie Company would record depreciation expense of $2,400 (12,000 miles × $0.20 per mile).

Companies often use the units-of-production method for production equipment. Also, it often is used by transportation and airline companies for depreciating trucks, automobiles, and airplanes.

Book and Market Value of Plant Assets. The book value of plant assets is the cost of the assets less accumulated depreciation. This amount is not an indication of the market value of the assets, which may be much higher than the book value in some cases. For example, land and buildings purchased by a company often increase in value over time because of inflation, increased demand for property, and increased construction costs. This difference between the market and book value of assets is an unrecorded asset. The market value of a company's stock is likely to include investors' estimates of the value of this unrecorded asset.

Disposing of Plant Assets

To dispose of plant assets—by retiring or selling them—a company must eliminate their cost and accumulated depreciation from its accounting records. For example, suppose that Favorite Cookie Company sells equipment on February 10, 2008. The equipment cost the company $20,000 when purchased. Accumulated depreciation on the equipment at the time it is sold is $14,000, and the company receives $8,000 for the equipment. It would record the sale as follows:

		Assets		=	Liabilities	+	Owners' Equity	
Date	Accounts	Cash	Other Assets				Contributed Capital	Retained Earnings
Feb. 10, 2008	Cash	8,000						
	Accumulated Depreciation		14,000					
	Equipment		−20,000					
	Gain on Asset Sale							2,000

This transaction eliminates the cost of the asset ($20,000) from Favorite Cookie Company's accounts. Also, it eliminates the accumulated depreciation taken on the asset ($14,000). The difference between the amount received ($8,000) and the book value of the asset at the time of the sale ($6,000 = $20,000 − $14,000) is recorded as a gain. This gain is reported as nonoperating income on the company's 2008 income statement. If the book value at the time of the sale had been greater than the amount received, Favorite Cookie Company would have recorded a Loss on Asset Sale.

Self-Study Problem #1

Banana Boat Company purchased equipment on January 1, 2007 at a cost of $400,000. The equipment had an expected life of three years and could be used to produce one million units of product. Its estimated residual value was $40,000. Income before depreciation and taxes in 2007 was $2 million. The company's tax rate was 35%.

Required

A. Prepare a depreciation schedule for the equipment for its three-year life, using straight-line and double-declining-balance depreciation methods.

B. Determine the amount of depreciation expense the company would record in 2007 if the units-of-production method were used and 300,000 units were produced.

C. Which of the three methods would result in the lowest tax liability for 2007?

The solution to Self-Study Problem 1 appears at the end of the chapter.

NATURAL RESOURCES

Objective 3

Apply appropriate measurement rules to the purchase and use of natural resources.

Paper, petroleum, and mining companies, among others, invest in natural resources. They purchase or lease land that contains timber, oil, or minerals. The cost of the land primarily reflects those natural resources.

The amount a company reports for natural resources on its balance sheet is the cost of the asset less depletion. ***Depletion*** **is the systematic allocation of the cost of natural resources to the periods that benefit from their use.** Assume that Silicon Company bought land containing minerals on April 1, 2007, for $8 million. The company would record the transaction as follows:

		Assets		=	Liabilities	+	Owners' Equity	
Date	Accounts	Cash	Other Assets				Contributed Capital	Retained Earnings
Apr. 1, 2007	Mineral Rights		8,000,000					
	Cash	−8,000,000						

Assume that the company estimated that the land contained 80,000 tons of minerals when it was purchased. The estimated cost per ton was $100 ($8,000,000 ÷ 80,000 tons). In 2007, Silicon mined the land and removed 16,000 tons of the minerals. These minerals then were sold to customers. The value of the asset consumed during 2007, \$1.6 million (\$100 × 16,000 tons), would be recorded in this way:

		Assets		=	Liabilities	+	Owners' Equity	
Date	**Accounts**	**Cash**	**Other Assets**				**Contributed Capital**	**Retained Earnings**
Dec. 31, 2007	Cost of Goods Sold							−1,600,000
	Mineral Rights		−1,600,000					

The amount reported by Silicon on its 2007 balance sheet for Mineral Rights would be \$6,400,000 (\$8,000,000 cost − \$1,600,000 accumulated depletion). The amount of the asset reported would decrease each year as additional minerals are mined and accumulated depletion increases.

This example assumes that the land has no real value apart from the value of the mineral deposits. If the land does have other value, that value would be recorded as a separate asset. Only the value of the minerals would be depleted.

GAAP require that companies report natural resources at their book value (cost − accumulated depletion). The market value of natural resources is not reported on the financial statements, although some companies disclose information about the current value of those assets in notes to their financial statements. Remember that market value can be much higher than book value. Companies that own oil and timber reserves, for example, have experienced dramatic increases in the market value of those resources in recent years because of rising demand. The market value of a company's stock reflects the unrecorded value of those assets.

LONG-TERM AND SHORT-TERM INVESTMENTS

Objective 4
Apply appropriate measurement rules to the purchase, valuation, and sale of long-term and short-term investments.

This section examines accounting for investments in debt and equity securities. It considers transactions and reporting issues for both short-term and long-term investments.

Types of Securities

Companies often invest in securities issued by other organizations. Securities include common and preferred stocks, bonds, certificates of deposit, and notes. Stocks are referred to as equity securities. Other securities are debt securities. If securities are readily exchangeable for cash (can be sold easily), they are **marketable securities.** A company never reports its own debt or equity securities as assets. Instead, those securities are reported as liabilities (debt) and stockholders' equity (equity securities).

Companies invest in marketable securities for many reasons. When there is a temporary surplus of cash, the cash is invested on a short-term basis to earn a return until cash is needed. Long-term investments meet different needs. Some are used to fund the future repurchase or repayment of a company's own debt or to provide for future retirement and other employee benefits. Often, investments in other companies are made to gain access to markets, resources, and technology controlled by these companies.

GAAP differentiate between two types of investments:

(1) investments that give the investor significant influence or control over the company issuing the securities, and

(2) investments that do not.

Investments That Yield Significant Influence or Control. These investments are always reported as a long-term asset. A company acquires significant influence over another company when it holds a large block of the second company's voting securities. Generally, this means 20% to 50% of the outstanding shares of common stock. When significant influence occurs, the equity method is used. A company acquires control over another firm by holding a very large block (usually a majority) of its voting securities. In this situation, the consolidation method is used. The equity and consolidation methods are discussed in the final section of this chapter.

Investments That Do Not Yield Significant Influence or Control. GAAP identify three categories of investments that do not yield significant influence or control. Each is treated differently in the financial statements. The three categories are as follows:

1. **Held-to-maturity securities** are investments in debt securities that the investor has the intent and ability to hold until the debt's maturity date. They are reported on the balance sheet as a long-term asset except during the year just prior to maturity when they should be reported as a current asset.
2. **Trading securities** are investments in either debt or equity securities that a company buys and sells on a regular basis. They are reported on the balance sheet under current assets.
3. **Available-for-sale securities** are investments in securities that a company could sell but that it does not trade regularly. These investments are reported as a current asset or noncurrent asset, depending on management's expectation regarding when the investments will be sold.

All investments in securities are recorded initially at cost. Cost includes brokerage commissions, fees, and taxes. (For illustrative purposes in this chapter, these additional costs are assumed to be zero.) Held-to-maturity securities (always debt securities) are reported on the balance sheet at **amortized cost**: original cost adjusted for amortization of premium or discount. **Trading securities and available-for-sale securities are reported on the balance sheet at current market value.** This is referred to as *mark-to-market accounting*.

Held-To-Maturity Securities

Only debt securities may fall into this category. To illustrate, assume that Big Foods Corporation bought Favorite Cookie Company bonds on January 1, 2008. Big Foods paid $208,201 for the bonds, which mature in 2012 at their face value of $200,000. The bonds pay annual interest of 8%. Interest payments are made on December 31. Big Foods intends to hold these bonds long-term and records the purchase of this investment as follows:

		Assets		=	Liabilities	+	Owners' Equity	
Date	**Accounts**	**Cash**	**Other Assets**				**Contributed Capital**	**Retained Earnings**
Jan. 1, 2008	Long-Term Investment		208,201					
	Cash	−208,201						

On December 31, 2008, Big Foods receives its first interest payment. The amount received is $16,000 (8% × $200,000 face value). Recall from our discussion in Chapter 9 that when bonds are issued at a price different from par, the premium or discount must be amortized. The interest earned each period is adjusted as the premium or discount is amortized over the life of the bonds. Because Big Foods paid $208,201 for Favorite

Cookie Company's bonds, it would amortize the $8,201 premium over the life of the bonds. Big Foods has determined that $1,426 of premium should be amortized upon receipt of the first interest payment. It would record the amortization along with the interest earned as follows:

		Assets		=	Liabilities	+	Owners' Equity	
Date	Accounts	Cash	Other Assets				Contributed Capital	Retained Earnings
Dec. 31, 2008	Cash	16,000						
	Long-Term Investment		−1,426					
	Interest Income							14,574

Cash received ($16,000) less the amortization ($1,426) during the period is reported as interest income for the period ($14,574). Assume Big Foods plans to hold the bonds until they mature in 2012. The bonds would be classified as held-to-maturity securities. At the end of its 2008 fiscal year, Big Foods must report its investment on the balance sheet at amortized cost of $206,775 ($208,201 cost − $1,426 amortization).

Trading Securities and Available-for-Sale Securities—Investments in Debt

If, instead, the bonds are held as trading securities or available-for-sale securities, they will be reported on the balance sheet at current market value. When the investment's amortized cost is different from its current market value, an unrealized holding gain or loss is recognized. The holding gain or holding loss is unrealized because actual sale of the investment has not yet occurred. Unrealized holding gains or losses are an indication of the gain or loss that would occur if the investment were sold at the balance sheet date.

To illustrate, assume the December 31, 2008 market price of Favorite Cookie Company bonds owned by Big Foods is $205,000. An adjusting entry is needed to update the balance in the long-term investment account from amortized cost of $206,775 ($208,201 − $1,426) to current market value of $205,000. That entry would appear as follows:

		Assets		=	Liabilities	+	Owners' Equity	
Date	Accounts	Cash	Other Assets				Contributed Capital	Retained Earnings
Dec. 31, 2008	Unrealized Holding Loss*						−1,775*	
	Long-Term Investment		−1,775					

***Amortized cost ($206,775) − current market value ($205,000) = $1,775 unrealized holding loss. This is included as part of Other Comprehensive Income in the stockholders' equity section of the balance sheet.**

The only difference in accounting for trading securities and available-for-sale securities is in how the Unrealized Holding Loss (or Gain) is reported in the financial statements. Trading securities are expected to be sold in the near future. Therefore, **for trading securities, the unrealized holding gain or loss is reported on the income statement as part of net income.** This gives an early signal to readers as to the likely outcome when the securities are sold. **Available-for-sale securities** are not expected to be sold in the near future. Therefore, **the unrealized holding gain or loss is reported as part of Other Comprehensive Income in the stockholders' equity section of the balance sheet.**

Trading Securities and Available-for-Sale Securities—Investments in Equity

The accounting for trading securities and available-for-sale securities is very similar. Both are recorded initially at cost and reported on the balance sheet at current market value. Assume that Big Foods Corporation purchased 10,000 shares of Favorite Cookie Company common stock for $12 per share on October 1, 2008. Assume these are available-for-sale securities that are not expected to be sold anytime soon. Big Foods would record the purchase as follows:

		Assets		=	Liabilities	+	Owners' Equity	
Date	**Accounts**	**Cash**	**Other Assets**				**Contributed Capital**	**Retained Earnings**
Oct. 1, 2008	Long-Term Investment		120,000					
	Cash	−120,000						

On December 31, 2008, the closing market price of Favorite Cookie Company stock was $14 per share. Thus, the value of Big Foods' investment has increased by $20,000 [($14 − $12) × 10,000 shares)]. Big Foods would record the increase in market value as follows:

		Assets		=	Liabilities	+	Owners' Equity	
Date	**Accounts**	**Cash**	**Other Assets**				**Contributed Capital**	**Retained Earnings**
Dec. 31, 2008	Long-Term Investment		20,000					
	Unrealized Holding Gain*						20,000*	

***This is included as part of Other Comprehensive Income in the stockholders' equity section of the balance sheet.**

Because these are available-for-sale securities, the Unrealized Holding Gain is reported on the balance sheet as a component of stockholders' equity. It is not part of net income. If the securities had been trading securities, the Unrealized Holding Gain would be reported on the income statement as part of net income. Either way, the Long-Term Investment will be reported on the balance sheet at current market value.

Big Foods' December 31, 2008 financial statements will combine the long-term investments and unrealized holding gain (or loss) accounts for both of its long-term investments. Big Foods owns bonds with a market value of $205,000 and stock with a market value of $140,000. Therefore, assuming both securities are available-for-sale, Big Foods will report its investments as shown in Exhibit 6.

If the investments were trading securities, the only difference would be that the $18,225 unrealized holding gain ($20,000 − $1,775) would be reported on the income statement rather than as part of other comprehensive income. In either case, Big Foods also would disclose the cost of its long-term investments ($328,201 = $208,201 for bonds + $120,000 for stock) on the balance sheet or in a note.

When Big Foods sells an investment, it records a realized gain or loss that is reported in computing net income on its income statement. For example, assume Big Foods' management changes its mind and sells Favorite Cookie Company stock on April 20, 2009, at

EXHIBIT 6
Balance Sheet Excerpts and Supporting Computations for Big Foods Corporation for Long-Term Investments

Balance Sheet December 31, 2008			
Assets		**Stockholders' equity**	
Long-term investments	$345,000	Other comprehensive income	$18,225
Computations			
Cost of bonds	$208,201	Unrealized holding loss on bonds	$ (1,775)
Amortization of premium	(1,426)		
Unrealized holding loss	(1,775)	Unrealized holding gain on stock	20,000
Cost of stock	120,000		
Unrealized holding gain	20,000	Net unrealized holding gain	$18,225
Long-term investments	$345,000		

a price of $17 per share. Big Foods has earned $50,000 on its investment [($17 − $12) × 10,000 shares]. It records the transaction as follows:

		Assets		=	Liabilities	+	Owners' Equity	
Date	**Accounts**	**Cash**	**Other Assets**				**Contributed Capital**	**Retained Earnings**
Apr. 20, 2009	Cash	170,000						
	Unrealized Holding Gain*						−20,000*	
	Long-Term Investment		−140,000					
	Investment Income							50,000

***This is included as part of Other Comprehensive Income in the stockholders' equity section of the balance sheet.**

This transaction records the realized gain ($50,000) and eliminates the long-term investment in stock and unrealized holding gain amounts that were recorded during 2008. The long-term investment amount of $140,000 is the cost ($120,000) plus the increase in market value that was added to the account on December 31, 2008 ($20,000). The realized gain ($50,000) would be reported by Big Foods as nonoperating income on its income statement for 2009. This is the amount Big Foods actually earned from its investment in Favorite Cookie Company stock.

As noted previously, the rules described above do not apply when a company owns a significant or controlling interest in another company. A company is considered by GAAP to have significant influence over another company when it owns 20% to 50% of the other company's common stock. This level of ownership suggests that the investor can influence management decisions of the issuing company. Therefore, special accounting rules, known as the **equity method**, are used to account for these investments. These rules are summarized in the appendix to this chapter.

Learning Note - Occasionally a firm will acquire nonmarketable securities. This means there is no active market for the security and it cannot readily be converted to cash. GAAP require the cost method be used to account for these investments. Under the cost method, the investment is recorded at cost and no further adjustments are made to the investment account. Dividends or interest received on such an investment are recorded as Investment Income.

If a company owns more than 50% of the common stock of another corporation, it controls the other corporation. In this situation, the investor is the parent corporation and the issuer of the stock is a subsidiary of the parent. The parent includes the subsidiary

EXHIBIT 7
Investments in Marketable Securities

Type of Investment	Recorded	Accounting Method	Treatment of Unrealized Holding Gain (Loss)
Acquires significant influence	At cost	Equity	none
Acquires control	At cost	Consolidation	none
Held-to-maturity	At cost	Amortized cost	none
Trading	At cost	Mark to market	Reported on income statement as Other Income
Available-for-sale	At cost	Mark to market	Report on balance sheet in Other Comprehensive Income

as part of its consolidated financial statements. That is, the financial statements of the parent treat the parent and subsidiary corporations as though they were one company. A summary of accounting for consolidations appears at the end of this chapter.

Short-Term Investments

Investments in short-term marketable securities are accounted for at market value. Investments are classified as short-term if management expects to sell the investments during the coming fiscal year. Short-term investments are reported as current assets. Therefore, they are separated from long-term investments on the balance sheet. The accounting procedures to record the purchase price and end-of-period adjustment for current market price are identical to those for long-term investments.

Exhibit 7 summarizes the appropriate treatment for investments in securities.

Self-Study Problem #2

Delta Can Company purchased 10,000 shares of Flatland Aluminum Company's common stock on June 1, 2007. Delta paid $230,000 for the stock. On December 1, 2007, Delta received a dividend check from Flatland for $25,000. The market value of Flatland's stock on December 31, 2007, the end of Delta's fiscal year, was $27 per share. On December 1, 2008, Delta received a dividend check from Flatland for $30,000. The market value of Flatland's stock on December 31, 2008, was $26 per share. Delta sold its investment in Flatland on March 5, 2009, for $245,000. Delta owned 5% of Flatland's common stock and had planned to keep its investment long term.

Required

A. Using the format presented in this chapter, record all transactions for Delta involving its investment in Flatland and explain the purpose of each transaction.

B. Calculate the amounts Delta would report on its 2007 and 2008 balance sheets for its investment in Flatland.

The solution to Self-Study Problem 2 appears at the end of the chapter.

INTANGIBLE ASSETS

Intangible assets include legal rights, such as copyrights, patents, brand names, and trademarks that a company owns. The purchase price and/or legal fees associated with acquiring those rights are recorded as assets and, with the exception of goodwill, are amortized over the life of the assets, usually on a straight-line basis.

Objective 5

Explain accounting issues associated with intangible and other long-term assets.

GAAP require that intangibles other than goodwill be amortized over a period of 40 years or less. (The longer the amortization period, the lower the expense recognized each year.) A company that purchases intangible assets for $1 million and amortizes those assets over 40 years would recognize $25,000 of amortization expense each year.

INTERNATIONAL

U.S. GAAP do not allow companies to report the estimated market value of their brand names, trademarks, and other intangibles as part of their assets. Only the costs associated with those items can be reported as assets on the balance sheet. Nevertheless, brand names and trademarks can be among a corporation's most valuable resources. For example, the **Coca-Cola** brand name has been estimated at a value of more than $25 billion. Many companies would report much higher asset and stockholders' equity amounts if they could include the market value of intangible assets. Great Britain and certain other countries allow corporations to report the estimated market value of intangible assets, which is why some British companies report higher asset and equity values than their U.S. counterparts.

An intangible asset reported by many companies is goodwill. *Goodwill* **is the excess of the purchase price of a company over the fair market value of its net assets** (assets − liabilities). To illustrate, assume that Big Foods Corporation purchased Value-Right Company on January 1, 2008, for $5 million. As part of the purchase negotiation, Value-Right Company's assets and liabilities were appraised and were determined to have current market values of $8 million and $3.5 million, respectively. Accordingly, the purchase resulted in Big Foods' recognizing $500,000 of goodwill:

Market value of Value-Right Company assets	$8,000,000
Market value of Value-Right Company liabilities	3,500,000
Market value of Value-Right Company net assets	$4,500,000
Amount paid by Big Foods Corporation	$5,000,000
Market value of Value-Right Company net assets	4,500,000
Goodwill (excess of amount paid over market value)	$ 500,000

Goodwill is common when one company purchases another company. Often the amount paid is greater than the value of identifiable assets. The purchaser is buying a company, not individual assets. The company as a whole may have more value than the sum of its assets because it is an established business. Its managers, employees, customers, suppliers, brand recognition, and other components add value that is not recognized on the balance sheet. Accordingly, goodwill is recorded as an indication of this value.

Goodwill remains on a company's balance sheet at cost unless the value of the goodwill is impaired. Goodwill is impaired when it becomes apparent the investment is less valuable than the purchaser originally expected. The balance of the goodwill account should be written down, and a loss should be recognized for the amount of the impairment.

OTHER LONG-TERM ASSETS

Long-term assets that are not included in one of the other primary categories (plant assets, long-term investments, or intangible assets) are considered other long-term assets.

An example of this type of asset is deferred charges. *Deferred charges* **are the assets that result when a company prepays expenses that produce long-term benefits.** Deferred charges typically are amortized over future periods. Start-up costs—the costs of the legal fees, support services, and advertising necessary to start a new business, division, or project—often are capitalized and reported as deferred charges. These costs are recorded as Organizational Costs or a similar asset account.

Certain other assets do not fit into standard asset categories. For example, plant assets that a company has removed from service and is trying to sell are listed as other assets, not as plant assets.

Some assets are specific to an industry or company—for example, software development costs in the computer industry. A description of those assets often is provided in the notes to the financial statements.

Most assets are recorded at cost when they are purchased. This cost is expensed over the life of the asset as the asset is consumed or as its value declines. When an asset is sold, a gain or loss equal to the difference between the book value of the asset and its selling price is recognized.

FINANCIAL REPORTING OF INVESTING ACTIVITIES

Objective 6

Summarize the effects of investing activities on a company's financial statements.

Investing activities affect the balance sheet, income statement, and statement of cash flows as described in Exhibit 8. Long-term assets (items a through d) appear on the balance sheet. The accumulated amount of holding gains and losses (item e) appears as an adjustment to stockholders' equity.

The income statement is affected by depreciation and amortization expense (item f), interest income (item g), and gains and losses from the sale of plant assets, long-term investments, and other long-term assets (item h).

Both the operating activities and the investing activities sections of the statement of cash flows are affected by investing activities. Depreciation and amortization expense (item i) is added to net income in computing operating cash flow using the indirect method. These are noncash expenses. Also, in computing operating cash flows, gains from the sale of long-term assets are subtracted and losses are added (item j). All cash

EXHIBIT 8 Financial Statement Presentation of Investing Activities

Balance Sheet

Assets

Current assets

(a) **Long-term investments**

(b) **Property, plant, and equipment**

(c) **Intangible assets**

(d) **Other assets**

Liabilities

Stockholders' Equity

Common stock

Retained earnings

(e) **Net holding gains (losses)**

Income Statement

Operating revenues

Operating expenses, except depreciation and amortization expense

(f) **Depreciation and amortization expense**

Operating income

Interest expense

(g) **Interest income**

(h) **Gains or (losses) from sale of long-term assets**

Pretax income

Income taxes

Net income

Statement of Cash Flows

Cash flow from operating activities:

Net income

(i) **Add depreciation and amortization expense**

(j) **(Subtract gains) add losses from sale of long-term assets**

Other adjustments

Net cash flow from operating activities

Cash flow from (for) investing activities:

(k) **Sale of property, plant, and equipment**

(l) **Sale of investments**

(m) **Other (purchases) or sales of long-term assets**

(n) **(Capital expenditures)**

(o) **(Purchase of investments)**

(p) **(Acquisitions)**

(q) **Net cash flow from (for) investing activities**

EXHIBIT 9
Investing Activities from Favorite Cookie Company's Statement of Cash Flows

Cash flow from (for) investing activities:	
Purchase of property and equipment	$(365,000)
Sale of property and equipment	8,000
Purchase of investments	(6,000)
Sale of investments	2,000
Net cash flow for investing activities	$(361,000)

flows associated with the sale of long-term assets are included in investing activities (items k, l, and m). Therefore, in terms of the operating activities section, the gain or loss is treated as a noncash item so that it is not included twice. Gains do not increase operating cash flows and losses do not reduce operating cash flows.

Cash received from the sale of long-term assets (items k, l, and m) and cash paid for long-term assets (items n, o, and p) are reported as investing activities. The total of these cash outflows and inflows is net cash from (for) investing activities (item q).

Exhibit 9 contains the investing activities section of Favorite Cookie Company's statement of cash flows for 2008. These amounts help explain changes in the company's long-term assets as presented on its balance sheet (Exhibit 1). Though the numbers on the cash flow statement do not always explain all changes in long-term assets, they should explain most of these changes. Some balance sheet changes are associated with noncash transactions. However, most changes in long-term assets involve the receipt or payment of cash and are reported in the investing activities section of the statement of cash flows.

Self-Study Problem #3

Silicon Company reported the following transactions for the year ended December 31, 2007:

- Sale of plant assets with a book value of $22,000 for $16,000, reporting a loss of $6,000
- Sale of securities with a book value of $10,000 for $14,000, reporting a gain of $4,000
- Depreciation and amortization expense of $8,000
- Interest and dividends from investments of $2,000
- Acquisitions of plant assets for $35,000
- Acquisitions of long-term investments for $10,000
- Net income of $50,000

Required Prepare the operating and investing sections of Silicon's cash flow statement, assuming that no other activities affected those sections. You can assume that Silicon received cash for the interest and dividend income in 2007.

The solution to Self-Study Problem 3 appears at the end of the chapter.

OTHER INVESTMENT ISSUES

Companies, especially large corporations, often own significant interests in other companies. As a general rule, if a company owns 20% to 50% of the common stock of another company, it is considered by GAAP to have *significant influence* over that company. If a company owns more than 50% of another company, it owns a *controlling interest* in the company. The following sections summarize accounting rules for these situations.

Equity Method

When one company owns 20% to 50% of the common stock of another company, it normally uses the equity method to account for its investment. The investment is recorded at cost. For example, assume that Big Foods Corporation purchased 30,000 shares of Little Market Corporation's 100,000 shares of common stock at a price of $20 per share on January 1, 2007. Big Foods Corporation would record the purchase as follows:

		Assets		=	Liabilities	+	Owners' Equity	
Date	**Accounts**	**Cash**	**Other Assets**				**Contributed Capital**	**Retained Earnings**
Jan. 1, 2007	Long-Term Investment		600,000					
	Cash	−600,000						

At the end of the 2007 fiscal year, Little Market reported a net income of $500,000 and paid dividends of $200,000. Under the equity method, Big Foods records 30% (the percentage of stock it owns) of Little Market's net income as investment income:

		Assets		=	Liabilities	+	Owners' Equity	
Date	**Accounts**	**Cash**	**Other Assets**				**Contributed Capital**	**Retained Earnings**
Dec. 31, 2007	Long-Term Investment		150,000					
	Investment Income							150,000

Little Market's net income increases its retained earnings. Therefore, the book value of Little Market increases by $500,000. Big Foods recognizes 30% of this increase as an increase in the value of its investment.

Dividends paid by Little Market reduce Little Market's retained earnings and book value. Therefore, Big Foods recognizes 30% of this decrease as a decrease in the value of its investment:

		Assets		=	Liabilities	+	Owners' Equity	
Date	**Accounts**	**Cash**	**Other Assets**				**Contributed Capital**	**Retained Earnings**
Dec. 31, 2007	Cash	60,000						
	Long-Term Investment		−60,000					

In this transaction, Big Foods receives cash from Little Market, but the value of Big Foods' investment decreases in proportion to the decrease in Little Market's retained earnings.

The equity method is appropriately named because it adjusts the investment account of the investor in proportion to changes in the book value of the investee's stockholders' equity. It ignores changes in market value. Investments that use the equity method often are listed separately from other investments on a company's balance sheet or are described in a note to the financial statements. Also, income from equity method investments often is separated from other income on a company's income statement. It is labeled *equity income* or a similar title. Investment income is a nonoperating-income item for most companies.

Consolidations

If a corporation owns more than 50% of the common stock of another company, it normally reports consolidated financial statements. These statements are issued by the parent corporation and include the financial activities of the parent and its subsidiaries. The process of consolidating a parent and its subsidiaries can be complex. Account balances for the parent and all of its subsidiaries are combined. Any intercompany transactions, such as sales by a subsidiary to the parent or a loan from the parent to the subsidiary, are eliminated. Only transactions of the parent and its subsidiaries with external parties are reported in the consolidated statements.

If the parent corporation does not own 100% of the common stock of a subsidiary, the portion that the parent does not own is known as **minority interest** or **noncontrolling interest**. The portion of a subsidiary's stockholders' equity that belongs to noncontrolling stockholders (owners other than the parent) is reported on the consolidated balance sheet as noncontrolling interest. This amount often appears after liabilities and before stockholders' equity. The portion of a subsidiary's net income that belongs to noncontrolling stockholders is reported on the consolidated income statement as noncontrolling interest in income. This amount is subtracted in determining the parent's consolidated net income because it is the portion of the subsidiary's net income not earned by the parent.

THINKING BEYOND THE QUESTION

HOW DO WE ACCOUNT FOR INVESTING ACTIVITIES?

This chapter described various types of long-term assets and how companies account for the acquisition, use, and disposal of these assets. Which assets a company invests in can be important decisions that affect the performance of the company. How do investing decisions affect a company's profitability and value?

Self-Study Problem Solutions

SSP11-1 A. Straight-line depreciation schedule ($400,000 − $40,000) ÷ 3 years = $120,000 per year

Year	Beginning Book Value	Depreciation Expense	Accumulated Depreciation	Ending Book Value
2007	$400,000	$120,000	$120,000	$280,000
2008	280,000	120,000	240,000	160,000
2009	160,000	120,000	360,000	40,000

Double-declining-balance depreciation schedule ($400,000 × 2/3 = $266,667)
($133,333 × 2/3 = $88,889)

Year	Beginning Book Value	Depreciation Expense	Accumulated Depreciation	Ending Book Value
2007	$400,000	$266,667	$266,667	$133,333
2008	133,333	88,889	355,556	44,444
2009	44,444	4,444	360,000	40,000

B. Units-of-production depreciation rate = ($400,000 − $40,000) ÷ 1,000,000 units = $0.36 per unit. Depreciation expense for 2007 = 300,000 units × $0.36 = $108,000.

C.

	Straight-Line	Double-Declining-Balance	Units-of-Production
Income before depreciation and taxes	$2,000,000	$2,000,000	$2,000,000
Depreciation expense	120,000	266,667	108,000
Income before taxes	1,880,000	1,733,333	1,892,000
Income taxes (35%)	658,000	606,667	662,200
Net income	$1,222,000	$1,126,666	$1,229,800

Double-declining-balance results in the lowest income tax liability for 2007.

SSP11-2 A.

		Assets		=	Liabilities	+	Owners' Equity	
Date	**Accounts**	**Cash**	**Other Assets**				**Contributed Capital**	**Retained Earnings**
June 1, 2007	Long-Term Investment		230,000					
	Cash	−230,000						
Dec. 1, 2007	Cash	25,000						
	Investment Income							25,000
Dec. 31, 2007	Long-Term Investment		40,000					
	Unrealized Holding Gain (Loss)*						40,000*	
Dec. 1, 2008	Cash	30,000						
	Investment Income							30,000
Dec. 31, 2008	Unrealized Holding Gain (Loss)*						−10,000*	
	Long-Term Investment		−10,000					
Mar. 5, 2009	Cash	245,000						
	Unrealized Holding Gain (Loss)*						−30,000*	
	Long-Term Investment		−260,000					
	Investment Income							15,000

***This is included as part of Other Comprehensive Income in the stockholders' equity section of the balance sheet.**

The transaction of 6/1/07 records the investment at cost. The transactions of 12/1/07 and 12/1/08 recognize dividends received as realized investment income. This income is reported on the income statement in computing net income for each fiscal year. The transaction of 12/31/07 records the increase in market value of the investment. This increase is an unrealized holding gain; it is not included as part of net income because an actual sale of the investment has not occurred. The transaction of 12/31/08 records a decrease in market value that is an unrealized holding loss. The loss is not included in computing net income because a sale has not occurred. The transaction of 3/5/09 recognizes a gain on the sale of the investment. This gain is reported as part of net income because the investment has been sold. Realized income and gains (or losses) are recorded when resources are received or investments are sold. Holding gains and losses are recorded when the market value of investments changes during a fiscal period, but the investments have not been sold.

B.

	2007	2008
Cost of investment	$230,000	$230,000
Holding gain	40,000	40,000
Holding loss		(10,000)
Market value of investment	$270,000	$260,000

SSP11-3

Silicon Company
Statement of Cash Flows
For the Year Ended December 31, 2007

Cash flow from operating activities	
Net income	$ 50,000
Adjustments for noncash items:	
Depreciation and amortization expense	8,000
Loss from sale of plant assets	6,000
Gain from sale of investments	(4,000)
Net cash flow from operating activities	$ 60,000
Cash flow for investing activities	
Capital expenditures	$(35,000)
Sale of plant assets	16,000
Purchase of investments	(10,000)
Sales of investments	14,000
Net cash flow for investing activities	$(15,000)

Interest and dividend income is part of net income. Assuming that cash was received for the interest and dividends, no adjustment would be made for this amount.

Define *Terms and Concepts Defined in This Chapter*

accelerated depreciation (404)
capital expenditures (404)
deferred charges (417)
depletion (410)
goodwill (417)
mark-to-market accounting (412)
operating expenditures (404)
straight-line depreciation (404)
units-of-production depreciation (404)

Review *Summary of Important Concepts*

1. Investing activities involve the acquisition, use, and disposal of long-term assets.
   a. Long-term investments are investments in stocks and bonds of other companies that managers expect to hold for longer than the coming fiscal year.
   b. Property, plant, and equipment are tangible assets used in a company's production and selling activities.

(Continued)

   c. Intangible assets are legal rights that a company has exclusive use of to create future profits.
   d. Other long-term assets are miscellaneous items that are not included in another category (e.g., property held for disposal).

2. Investments in plant assets are the most important long-term assets for most companies.
   a. Plant assets are recorded at cost when they are acquired.
   b. Plant assets are depreciated over their estimated useful lives.
      (1) Straight-line depreciation is used for financial reporting by most companies.
      (2) Accelerated depreciation methods often are used for computing taxable income.
      (3) Units-of-production depreciation may be used for machinery and equipment that has an estimated life in terms of units of activity rather than time.
   c. Plant assets are reported on the balance sheet at their book value (cost minus accumulated depreciation).
   d. When plant assets are sold, a gain or loss equal to the difference between the book value and the sale price of the assets is recognized.

3. Natural resources are recorded at cost, and depletion expense is recorded as the resources are consumed.

4. Long-term and short-term investments involve investments in debt or equity securities of other companies.
   a. Investments in securities are recorded at cost.
   b. Interest income is recorded in the period earned and usually is reported as non-operating income.
   c. Investments in debt securities are reported on the balance sheet at cost if the debt is to be held to maturity or at market value if it is not to be held to maturity.
   d. Investments in equity securities are reported at market value on the balance sheets of most companies.
   e. Holding gains or losses generally are reported as adjustments to stockholders' equity.
   f. Special accounting methods (the equity method and consolidation) are used when one company owns a significant interest (20% or more) in another company.

5. Intangible assets include legal rights, such as patents and copyrights, and goodwill.
   a. Intangible assets are recorded at cost and, except for goodwill, are amortized over their useful lives, not to exceed 40 years.
   b. Goodwill is the excess of the purchase price of a company over the market value of that company's net assets (assets minus liabilities).
   c. Goodwill is not amortized but is written down in value, and a loss is recognized, if its value is impaired.

6. Other long-term assets include deferred charges, plant assets held for sale, organization costs, and specialized assets that are not classified in one of the other asset categories.

7. Investing activities affect a company's balance sheet (particularly assets), income statement (depreciation and amortization expense, investment income, and gains and losses from sale of assets), and statement of cash flows (particularly the investing activities section).

8. As a general rule, special accounting methods are used when a company owns 20% or more of the common stock of another corporation.
   a. The equity method is used for investments of 20% to 50%.
   b. Consolidation is used when a company owns more than 50% of another company's common stock.

Questions

Q11-1 *Obj. 1* Archer Company produces sporting goods equipment. Identify and describe briefly the types of assets Archer is likely to own and report on its financial statements. (Hint: You may find it helpful to review Exhibit 1 in this chapter.)

Q11-2 *Obj. 1* The gross amount of property, plant, and equipment is usually different from the net amount of property, plant, and equipment. Explain the difference between the two terms and what they represent. In what way is one or the other of these terms related to book value?

Q11-3 *Obj. 2* Does it make sense to you that the cost of interest incurred to finance the construction of assets is included as part of the cost of the asset? Why or why not?

Q11-4 *Obj. 2* Do you agree that the units-of-production method always results in more rapid depreciation of an asset than does the straight-line method? Explain.

Q11-5 *Obj. 2* What is the difference between a capital expenditure and an operating expenditure? Explain how each is accounted for and why the treatment is different.

Q11-6 *Obj. 3* A friend says, "The accounting terms *depletion* and *depreciation* describe basically the same thing." Do you agree or disagree? Why?

Q11-7 *Obj. 3* The term *depletion expense* seldom appears on income statements, even if the company is a timber grower, mine owner, or owner of oil wells. If the cost of natural resources "harvested" never shows up on the income statement under depletion expense, how is this cost accounted for? Explain your answer.

Q11-8 *Obj. 4* Generally, under GAAP, market value is not used as the valuation basis for assets. Cost is used instead. For marketable securities, however, market value is frequently used. What's different about marketable securities that makes it reasonable for this class of asset to be reported at market value when most other assets are reported at cost?

Q11-9 *Obj. 4* Barbara is studying the annual reports of three different companies that her accounting group will use for its term project. She sees that two of the companies have made investments in the common stock of Microsoft, Inc. What bothers her is that one company has reported the investment as a current asset, while the other company has reported its investment as a long-term asset. Explain to Barbara why it is permissible, and preferable in certain circumstances, for the exact same type of asset to be reported differently.

Q11-10 *Obj. 4* Sometimes unrealized holding gains and losses are reported on the income statement. At other times they are reported on the balance sheet under stockholders' equity. What causes this difference in treatment? Does this different treatment make sense to you? Why or why not?

Q11-11 *Obj. 5* If market value is such a good basis for reporting certain marketable securities on the balance sheet, why not use market value as the basis for reporting intangible assets?

Q11-12 *Obj. 5* How does goodwill arise and come to be reported on a balance sheet? How is the amount calculated? What does goodwill represent?

Q11-13 *Obj. 6* Five years ago, Reeco Company paid $40,000 to acquire a building site. Since then the company has abandoned its expansion plans and yesterday sold the site for $65,800 in cash. How will this transaction be reported on the company's next cash flow statement? (Assume the indirect format is used.)

Q11-14 *Obj. 6* Explain how a manager can use accounting information as a means of controlling assets and ensuring their security.

Exercises

E11-1 Write a short definition for each of the terms listed in the *Terms and Concepts Defined in This Chapter* section.

E11-2
Obj. 1

Below is a list of accounts and year-end balances taken from the general ledger of Deep Drillers Inc.

Treasury stock	$ 3,000	Accumulated depreciation	$ 40,000
Building	160,000	Goodwill	10,000
Land	120,000	Storage tanks	90,000
Drilling equipment	230,000	Trademark	4,000
Accounts receivable	25,000	Oil wells	500,500
Dividend income	6,600	Investment in Susanna Co.*	195,600
Accounts payable	5,400	Construction in process	56,300
Common stock	250,000	Inventory of tools	36,000
Accumulated depletion	15,000		

***Deep Drillers owns 42% of Susanna's common stock.**

Prepare the long-term asset section of the balance sheet in good form. (Hint: Not all of the accounts need to be used.)

E11-3
Obj. 1

You are reviewing the balance sheet of Worldwide Technology, a manufacturer of assorted electronic components. You observe the following account classifications.

a. Intangible assets
b. Inventories
c. Investment in marketable securities
d. Property, plant, and equipment
e. Accounts receivable

For each of the classifications listed above, indicate whether it probably involves current assets or long-term assets. For each classification, give two examples of assets that might be reported there. Also indicate what attribute is being reported for each example you give (e.g., original cost, depreciated cost, market value, and so on).

E11-4
Obj. 1

The poorly trained bookkeeper at Flowing Water Company has shown you the long-term asset section of the company's balance sheet that he will soon distribute to stockholders. For your convenience, each item is identified with a letter. These letters will not appear in the finished document.

Long-term investments:	
(a) Machinery, net	$181,600
(b) Office supplies	8,710
(c) Land	78,000
Property, plant, and equipment:	
(d) Patents	27,000
(e) Processing plant, net	206,960
(f) Obsolete equipment awaiting sale, net	16,800
Intangible assets:	
(g) Prepaid insurance (for next three years)	21,000
(h) Common stock of Flower Corporation	83,000
Other long-term assets:	
(i) Cash	4,722
(j) Standby equipment, net (used only during peak production)	21,000
(k) Goodwill	14,000
(l) Investment in bonds of Beech Brothers, Inc.	46,000

Write down each of the four category headings above. After each heading, list the letters of the items you believe should be reported under that heading.

E11-5
Obj. 2

Camey Corporation purchased delivery equipment on January 1 at a cost of $300,000. The equipment is expected to have a useful life of seven years or 250,000 miles, and to have no salvage value. How much depreciation expense should be recorded during the first year using the straight-line, double-declining-balance, and units-of-production methods? During the year, the equipment was used for 80,000 miles. The company's fiscal year-end is December 31.

Assume that revenue for the year is $376,300 and that all expenses, other than for depreciation, total $225,492. Would the use of one depreciation method instead of another have a material effect on the income statement? Discuss. (Ignore taxes.)

E11-6 *Obj. 2* Cape Horn Company purchased a building on March 1, 1988, at a cost of $4,186,000. For financial reporting purposes, the building was being depreciated over 372 months at $10,500 per month. The remaining $280,000 of the cost was the estimated salvage value. The building was sold on October 31, 2007, for $7.2 million. An accelerated depreciation method allowed by the tax code was used to record depreciation for the tax return. As of October 31, 2007, the company had recorded $3.5 million of depreciation for tax purposes using an accelerated basis. Determine (a) the amount of gain or loss that should be reported on the income statement regarding the sale of the building, (b) the amount of gain or loss that should be reported on the tax return regarding the sale of the building, and (c) why a company would use straight-line depreciation for financial reporting purposes and accelerated depreciation for tax purposes.

E11-7 *Obj. 2* Jackson Hospital Inc. acquired new specialized diagnostic equipment at a cost of $480,000. The equipment had an estimated useful life of eight years and an estimated residual value of $30,000. Jackson uses the straight-line depreciation method. After five years, management determined that the equipment was in danger of becoming obsolete. During year 6, the estimated useful life of the equipment was revised to a total of seven years with a new estimated residual value of $20,000. Determine (a) the book value of the equipment that would be reported on the balance sheet at the end of year 5, and (b) the new amount of depreciation expense that would be reported on the year 6 and year 7 income statements. (c) Does the need for revision of the depreciation estimates indicate that a poor job of estimating was originally done? Discuss.

E11-8 *Obj. 2* Franchesca Company recorded the following transactions during its 2007 fiscal year:

a. Costs incurred for buildings under construction but not completed by year-end:

Labor	$350,000
Materials	675,000
Utilities	87,000
Special tools and equipment	22,000
Interest on construction loan	94,000

b. The cost of an addition to an existing building was $840,000.
c. The cost of repairs to equipment was $90,000. These repairs are required on a regular basis and do not affect the estimated useful life of the equipment.

How would each of these transactions affect Franchesca's financial statements for 2007? Assume cash had been paid for all costs by the end of the fiscal year.

E11-9 *Obj. 2* Leslie Company sells business stationery imprinted with a customer's business name and address. To do this, it purchased a printing machine costing $48,000 on January 1, 2004. The machine has an expected useful life of five years and an estimated salvage value of $3,000. Leslie Company uses straight-line depreciation for all of its depreciable assets.

On August 1, 2007, the manager of the print shop was persuaded to purchase a new machine that operated more efficiently. The old machine was sold at that time for $5,000.

a. Calculate the depreciation expense recorded on the old machine for each year of use.
b. Calculate any gain or loss on disposal of the old machine.
c. Show how information about the printing machine transactions would be reported on the statement of cash flows for years 2004 through 2007. Assume the indirect format is used.
d. How would the information about the printing machine affect the income statement for years 2004 through 2007?

E11-10 *Obj. 3* Modern Mining Company owns rights to coal reserves in several states. The rights cost the company $140 million. The reserves were expected to produce a total of 50 billion tons of coal. During the company's 2007 fiscal year, six billion tons of coal were mined from the reserves. Prior to 2007, 30 billion tons of coal had been mined. How much depletion expense should the

(Continued)

company record in 2007? At what amount should the company report the coal reserves on its balance sheet at the end of 2007? What effect would the depletion expense have on the company's cash flows in 2007?

E11-11 *Obj. 3* In 1975, the Big Tree Timber Company purchased 1,000 acres of recently cut forest land for $4,500,000. It planted new seedling trees at a cost of $1,200,000. Over the years, an additional $450,000 was spent thinning and monitoring the rapidly growing forest. Commercial harvest operations began on this property in 2007. During the year, 10% of the harvestable timber was cut and sold. Near year-end, a rival firm offered to purchase the remaining uncut timber (but not the land it is on) for a price of $30 million. Big Tree Timber turned down the offer and will harvest the remaining trees over the next four years. At that time, the acreage will be replanted with new seedlings. (a) What total amount of cost should be subject to depletion expense in this problem? Why? (b) What amount of depletion expense should be reported on the 2007 income statement? (c) What information discussed above should be reported on the year-end 2007 balance sheet? (d) What important information about Big Tree Timber Company will not be reported on the income statement or balance sheet? If it is not reported on the financial statements, how might this important information be communicated to interested parties?

E11-12 *Obj. 4* Long Shore Company purchased 1,000 shares of ABX Company's common stock for $30 each. It was a small investment, but Long Shore intended to hold the investment for the long term. At year-end, the total market value of the shares had increased to $33,500. Six months into the following year, Long Shore decided to sell the investment at its then-current market price of $35 per share. (a) Show how the initial purchase of the shares would be recorded in Long Shore's accounting system. (b) Show any entry to the accounting system that should be made at the end of the first year. (c) Show how the sale of the investment would be recorded in the accounting system.

E11-13 *Obj. 4* Julie McBeth Company made two short-term investments in marketable securities during the current fiscal year. At year-end, the following summary information was available.

a. Purchased 5% of the outstanding common shares of Duncan Company for $300,000 plus brokerage fees of $30,000.
b. Purchased 2% of the outstanding common shares of Macduff Company for $400,000 plus brokerage fees of $40,000.
c. At year-end, the Duncan shares had a market value of $350,000. The Macduff shares had a market value of $360,000. McBeth owned no other investments in common stock.

Show how the two purchases of stock and the year-end information would be entered into McBeth's accounting system. What information regarding these investments will you expect to see reported on the year-end balance sheet? Be specific as to account names, their location on the balance sheet, and dollar amounts.

E11-14 *Obj. 4* Isabella Company made small investments in the common stock of two companies during the current year. Isabella wishes to establish a long-term business relationship with each firm and purchased the shares as a good faith gesture. Each of the firms had millions of shares outstanding at the time.

a. Purchased 20,000 shares of Othello Company at $15 per share and paid a brokerage fee of $14,000.
b. Purchased 25,000 of the outstanding shares of Ferdinand Company for $16 per share and paid a brokerage fee of $18,000.
c. At year-end, the Othello shares had a market value of $350,000. The Ferdinand shares had a market value of $395,000.

At year-end, Isabella owned no other investments in common stock. Show how the two purchases of stock and the year-end information would be entered into Isabella's accounting system. What information regarding these investments will you expect to see reported on the year-end balance sheet? Be specific as to account names, their location on the balance sheet, and dollar amounts.

E11-15 *Obj. 4* Manatee Company purchased $800,000 of long-term bonds on January 1, 2007, at face value. The bonds pay interest at an 8% annual rate on each June 30 and December 31. Semiannual payments were received, as promised, on June 30, 2007, and December 31, 2007. Manatee's fiscal year ends December 31. At December 31, 2007, the market value of the bonds was $786,000. The bonds were sold on July 1, 2008 for $820,000. (a) Show how the purchase of the bonds and the receipt of the first interest payment would be entered into the accounting system. Indicate how information about this bond investment will be reported on Manatee's December 31, 2007, balance sheet if (b) management intends (and is able) to hold the bonds until maturity, or (c) management intends to hold the bonds for a few years and then sell them. Be sure to include the dollar amounts of any information that you suggest should be reported.

E11-16 *Obj. 4* Arkansas Company purchased 20,000 shares of Mena Company's common stock on May 15, 2005. Arkansas paid $380,000 for the stock. On September 12, 2005, Arkansas received a dividend check from Mena for $12,000. The market value of Mena's stock on December 31, 2005, was $24 per share. On September 12, 2006, Arkansas received a dividend check from Mena for $14,400. The market value of Mena's stock on December 31, 2006, was $22 per share. Arkansas sold its investment in Mena's stock on April 6, 2007, for $400,000. Throughout this period, Arkansas Company owned 8% of Mena's stock and intended for it to be a long-term investment.

1. Using the format presented in this chapter, record all transactions for Arkansas Company involving its investment in Mena and explain the purpose of each transaction.
2. Determine the amounts Arkansas Company would report on its 2005 and 2006 balance sheets (or notes) for its investment in Mena.

E11-17 *Obj. 5* Dundee Enterprises purchased 100% of Newberg Company's common stock for $200 million in cash. At the time of the purchase, the fair market value of Newberg's assets was $350 million. The fair market value of its liabilities was $180 million. (a) Explain the meaning of goodwill. (b) Why might a rational decision maker pay more than the fair market value of the assets acquired? (c) How does goodwill affect a company's financial reports? (d) What amount of goodwill should be recorded by Dundee? (e) What reason other than goodwill can you think of that might explain why a company would pay more than fair value when acquiring the assets of another firm?

E11-18 *Obj. 5* Joyful Sound Music Company purchased the net assets (i.e., assets minus liabilities) of Metrodome Company for $845,000. Metrodome is a retailer of music, instruments, and related items. Its net assets have been carried on its own books at a total of $530,000. An appraisal of all of Metrodome's assets and liabilities revealed a net fair market value of $783,000. Joyful is willing to pay extra because of Metrodome's very loyal retail customers, most of whom have dealt exclusively with the company for more than 30 years. (a) What is the amount of goodwill that Joyful should record at acquisition of Metrodome? (b) What might cause the purchased goodwill in this situation to become impaired?

E11-19 *Objs. 2, 5* Use the straight-line (SLN) and double-declining-balance (DDB) functions in Excel or another spreadsheet program to calculate the required amounts in the following situations.

a. Machinery was purchased at its invoice price of $296,016. This amount did not include sales tax of 6.15%. The estimated useful life was 13 years and residual value was estimated at $15,000. Use the straight-line depreciation method. (1) Determine the amount of depreciation for the first year of the machinery's use. (2) Determine the amount of depreciation for the eighth year of the machinery's use. (3) Determine the book value of the machinery at the end of the 12th year of use.
b. Computer equipment having an expected life of five years was purchased at a cost of $112,316. Because the new equipment differed from the old, minor remodeling of the office space was necessary at a cost of $6,152 before installation could occur. The computer equipment is expected to have a $5,000 residual value. Use the double-declining-balance method. (1) Determine the amount of depreciation for the first year of the equipment's life. (2) Determine the amount of depreciation for the fourth year of the equipment's life.
c. A patent was acquired at a cost of $1.3 million. The patent has a remaining legal life of 13 years, but technology is changing so rapidly in this industry that management believes the patent rights will be worthless at the end of six years. Straight-line amortization is used.

(Continued)

(1) Determine the amount of amortization for the fourth year of the patent's life. (2) Determine the book value of the patent at the end of six years.

E11-20 *Obj. 6* You are reviewing the balance sheet, income statement, and statement of cash flows of a large, well-known company. It has operations in several different lines of business and in several countries. As you inspect these financial statements, you are searching for information about the company's investing activities. First, define the term *investing activities*. Second, make a list, one for each of the three financial statements, of the information about investing activities that might be found on that statement. Carefully specify the information you might expect to see reported and indicate exactly where it would be found on the statement.

E11-21 *Obj. 6* Zirconium Graphics Company reported the following information for the year ended December 31:

a. Sale of plant assets having a book value of $30,000 for $22,000 cash
b. Sale of securities with a book value of $26,000 for $28,000 cash
c. Depreciation and amortization expense of $7,500
d. Interest and dividends received from investments totaling $4,000 in cash
e. Acquisitions of plant assets for $50,000 in cash
f. Acquisitions of long-term investments for $16,000 in cash
g. Net income of $60,000

Prepare the operating and investing sections of Zirconium's cash flow statement, assuming that no other activities affected those sections.

E11-22 *(Based on the Other Investment Issues section)* On January 1, Babcock Company acquired 4,800 shares of West Company's common stock at a price of $9 per share. Babcock did so to establish a long-term working relationship with West Company. At December 31, West reported net income of $30,000 and paid a $0.50 cash dividend on each of its 16,000 common shares. On that same date, the market value of West common stock was $11 per share. (a) Which accounting method should be used to account for this investment? Why? (b) Record all entries that should be made to the accounting system during the year as a result of this investment. (c) At what amount should the investment be reported on Babcock's end-of-year balance sheet? Show how you arrived at your solution.

Problems

P11-1 *Obj. 2* **COMPARING DEPRECIATION METHODS**

Clary Jensen Farms purchased power equipment with an expected useful life of four years or 1,000 hours of usage. The equipment was purchased on January 1, 2007, for $125,000. It is expected to have a salvage value of $5,000 at the end of four years. During 2007, the equipment was used for 260 hours. Assume that usage for the next three years will be 220 hours, 313 hours, and 207 hours, respectively.

Required

A. Prepare a depreciation schedule for the asset showing the book value and depreciation expense on the asset each year using the straight-line, double-declining-balance, and units-of-production methods.
B. Which method would you prefer to use for financial reporting purposes if you were general manager of the company? Which method would you prefer to use for tax purposes? Explain.
C. Which method has the greatest effect on cash flow each year? Why?

P11-2 *Obj. 2* **COMPARING DEPRECIATION METHODS AND CASH FLOW**

U.S. income tax law permits some assets to be depreciated using an accelerated method during the early years of an asset's life. In later years, a switch to the straight-line depreciation method is allowed if it produces more favorable tax results. (More favorable tax results occur when application of the straight-line method to the remaining book value of the asset produces a depreciation amount greater than that scheduled to be taken under the usual double-declining-balance method.) Pandora Company purchased equipment on March 1, 2007, at a cost of $2,100,000. The equipment was depreciated for a full year in 2007. It was expected to have a useful life of six years and no residual value.

Required

A. Prepare a schedule that shows the amount of depreciation that Pandora Company would take on the asset each year for tax purposes if it applied the usual double-declining-balance method over the asset's six-year life.
B. Prepare a similar schedule using the modified double-declining-balance method described above.
C. Show how the cash flow for taxes paid would differ under the straight-line method and the modified double-declining-balance method over the six-year period. The tax rate is 35%.
D. Summarize how the choice of a depreciation method affects cash flows for taxes.

P11-3 DETERMINING ACQUISITION COST AND FIRST-YEAR DEPRECIATION

Obj. 2

Matta Company has just acquired two assets:

1. New diagnostic equipment for the medical services division was acquired at an invoice price of $93,000. This did not include the 8.7% sales tax. Transportation cost of $2,650 was incurred to ship the equipment from the factory to Matta's medical center. During transit, the driver "forgot" to acquire a special required permit, and Matta was fined $425. When the equipment was unloaded at the medical center, eight feet of wall on the right side of the entry door had to be dismantled (and then rebuilt) to provide a larger opening to get the equipment into the building. The cost of labor and materials was $750. In addition, while the equipment was being moved through the opening, the left side of the doorway was inadvertently damaged. Fortunately, this cost only an additional $300 because workers were already on site. Setup and testing costs to calibrate the equipment properly before it could be used on patients cost another $2,700.
2. Manufacturing equipment was acquired by the semiconductor electronics division. The supplier of the equipment agreed to deliver the equipment, install it, and calibrate it to Matta's specifications, all as part of the negotiated selling price. Sales tax of 7.5% was not included in the selling price and was paid separately. Matta and the supplier agreed on the following terms: a $77,000 down payment, followed by three equal annual installment payments of $85,000 that include 8% interest on the unpaid balance. (Hint: Calculate the present value of the installment payments.)

Required

A. Matta's accounting staff has requested your advice and counsel as to the cost at which each of these assets should be entered into Matta's accounting records. Provide that advice, carefully specifying exactly how you came to each judgment you made.
B. Determine the amount by which net income would differ in the first year if Matta chose to use the straight-line depreciation method instead of double-declining-balance. Both assets have estimated useful lives of six years and zero estimated residual value.

P11-4 PURCHASE VERSUS SELF-CONSTRUCTION OF AN ASSET

Obj. 2

Arizona Company has outgrown its current office building and is considering a replacement. There are two options available.

1. An existing building and its land can be purchased for $5,500,000. The market value of the land alone is $100,000. The building can be renovated for $500,000. The estimated life of the building would be 20 years with no salvage value. Arizona can borrow the money needed for the purchase at an interest rate of 8%. The loan will be repaid in 14 equal annual payments made at the end of each year.

(Continued)

2. A new building can be constructed by the company for its own use. The following costs would be incurred:

Architect's plans	$ 120,000
Materials	1,700,000
Labor costs	3,500,000
Other fees and permits	150,000

The company already owns and has paid for the land, which cost $100,000. To help finance construction of the building, Arizona can obtain a one-year loan for $4,500,000 at an interest rate of 6%. The loan would be repaid in one year just as construction of the building was completed. The estimated life of the new building would be 25 years.

Required

A. Determine the equal annual payments to be made under the first option. What would be the interest expense incurred during the first year of the loan?
B. Calculate the projected yearly depreciation expense for the building under each option. Use the straight-line method.
C. What effects, arising from either of the two options, would appear on the statement of cash flows?
D. Mr. L. Horn, the controller, points out that the company can save money if it constructs its own building. He compared the cost of the existing building and land of $6,000,000 to the cost of the constructed building and land of $5,840,000. He wants to show the difference in the two amounts on the income statement as Gain on Construction. Do you support this idea? Why or why not?

P11-5 DEPRECIATION AND DISPOSAL OF ASSETS
Obj. 2

Diamondback Mfg. is buying a new grinding machine. The machine costs $124,000 and is assumed to have a salvage value of $4,000 in five years. The manufacturer's description of the machine indicates that it should operate for 30,000 hours. The company's accountant is trying to decide whether to depreciate the machine by the straight-line method, the double-declining-balance method, or the units-of-production method. The machine will be purchased on January 1 of the coming year.

Required

A. Set up depreciation schedules for the straight-line and double-declining-balance methods. (Hint: You may wish to use the SLN and DDB functions in an Excel spreadsheet.)
B. Using the units-of-production method, calculate the hourly rate and yearly depreciation, assuming the machine is used evenly throughout its life. Comment on the reasonableness of this assumption.
C. Assume that after using the machine for three-and-a-half years, a new and improved machine is purchased. The old machine is then sold for $25,000. Calculate any gain or loss on the sale of the machine under each of the three depreciation methods. (Note: When calculating the gain or loss for the units-of-production method, assume that the machine was not used equally each year. Instead, assume the actual hours used each year were 6,000, 7,000, 8,000, and 4,000. Discuss any differences found in the gain or loss.)
D. With regard to the year of disposal of the machine, indicate what would appear on the income statement and the statement of cash flows for each method. Assume the indirect method is used for the statement of cash flows.

P11-6 USING SPREADSHEET FUNCTIONS IN DEPRECIATION CALCULATIONS
Obj. 2

Rodriguez Company acquired sophisticated production equipment at a cost of $450,000. In addition, the firm paid $7,540 to have the equipment delivered and another $11,435 was spent on installation and testing. The annual cost paid to insure the equipment while used in production is $3,000. The expected life of the new equipment is six years, and the estimated salvage value is $40,000. Management, however, is concerned about changing technology in the industry. With each year that passes, it will become more and more likely that new production technology will render this equipment obsolete. Management needs to choose between use of straight-line depreciation and double-declining-balance. The company expects that income before depreciation expense and income taxes will be approximately $160,000 per year. The firm's corporate tax rate is 35%.

Required

A. Determine the cost of the equipment that should be recorded in the accounting system.
B. Use the straight-line (SLN) and double-declining-balance (DDB) functions from Excel or another spreadsheet program as an aid to constructing a schedule that shows (1) depreciation expense each year under each alternative and (2) ending book value each year under each alternative.
C. Prepare a projected income statement for the six years assuming straight-line depreciation is used. (You need to prepare only one projected income statement because all years yield exactly the same result.) Start with Income Before Depreciation and Taxes and conclude with Net Income.
D. Prepare projected income statements for all six years assuming double-declining-balance depreciation is used. Start with Income Before Depreciation and Taxes and conclude with Net Income.
E. Compare your results from parts C and D. Why is it important that a reader of financial statements consult the notes to the financial statements to determine the depreciation method in use?

P11-7 ETHICAL ISSUES AND DEPRECIATION POLICY

Obj. 2

Clemson Manufacturing Company produces specialty textiles. On January 1, it purchased a new weaving machine at a cost of $600,000. The machine has an expected life of five years and an estimated salvage value of $40,000. The company manager thinks the machine can be used to weave 4.0 million yards of fabric. The net income before depreciation and taxes in the first year was $3,600,000. The company's tax rate is 30%.

Required

A. Prepare a five-year depreciation schedule for the machinery under both straight-line and double-declining-balance methods. (Hint: You may wish to use the SLN and DDB functions in an Excel spreadsheet.)
B. Determine the amount of depreciation expense the company would incur during the first year if the units-of-production method were used and 1.2 million yards of fabric were produced.
C. Which of the three methods would result in the lowest income tax expense for the first year?
D. Which of the three methods would result in the highest net income for the first year?
E. Assume the income tax must be paid immediately at year-end. Assume also you are the chief executive officer (CEO) of the corporation and are paid a significant bonus based on reported profit for the year. Which accounting method would you recommend be used regarding this new equipment? Why?

P11-8 THE EFFECT OF DEPRECIATION ON NET INCOME AND TAXES

Obj. 2

McGuire Batt Company produces a wide line of insulation materials. On January 1, it acquired new production equipment at a cost of $1,200,000. The machine has an expected life of four years and an estimated salvage value of $80,000. The engineering specifications of this new equipment state that it will produce two million units of product over its useful life. For the first year, the company's net income before considering depreciation and taxes was $7.2 million. The company's tax rate was 35%.

Required

A. Prepare a four-year depreciation schedule for the machinery under both straight-line and double-declining-balance methods. (Hint: You may wish to use the SLN and DDB functions in an Excel spreadsheet.)
B. Determine the amount of depreciation expense the company would record on its income statement for the first year if the units-of-production method were used and 400,000 units were produced.

(Continued)

C. Which of the three methods would result in the lowest income tax expense for the first year?
D. Which of the three methods would result in the highest net income for the first year?

P11-9 **CHOICES IN DEPLETION AND DEPRECIATION METHODS**
Objs. 2, 3
Sioux City Minerals acquired a copper mine, paying $40,000,000. The mine is expected to be productive for 10 years and yield 500,000 tons of copper ore. At the end of that time, the property will be donated to the state. To produce the ore, the company purchased mining equipment at a cost of $4,800,000, which is expected to have a useful life of 12 years with no salvage.

Required

A. Assuming that 30,000 tons of ore were produced and sold in the first year of operations, calculate the depletion for the mine and the depreciation of the machinery.
B. Assume the same facts as in part A above, except that the machinery can be used only for this copper mine and will not be moved once the mine is abandoned. How do you believe the equipment should be depreciated in this case? Explain why. What would be the depletion and depreciation for the first year under your approach?
C. If the ore is sold for $120 per ton, calculate the profit under parts A and B above. If there is a difference in the two amounts, explain why.
D. Assume that after the first year, when 30,000 tons were produced, a mining engineer estimates that a total of 570,000 additional tons of ore can still be recovered from the mine. What would be the depletion of the mine and the depreciation of the machinery if 25,000 tons of copper were produced in the second year? (Assume straight-line depreciation.)
E. What would be the book values of the mine and the machinery at the end of the second year?

P11-10 **REPORTING INVESTMENTS**
Obj. 4
Keelson Enterprises manufactures automobiles and occasionally makes small investments in other corporations for long-term purposes. During its 2006 fiscal year, Keelson purchased 100,000 common shares (10%) of Milton Company for $3,500,000. Also, it purchased 5% of the common stock of Holmes Company for $2,690,000. During 2006, Keelson received $500,000 of dividends from Milton. At the end of the fiscal year, the investment in Milton had a market value of $3,100,000. The investment in Holmes had a market value of $2,800,000. Keelson owned no other stock investments during 2006. During its 2007 fiscal year, Keelson sold the Holmes investment for $2,900,000 and made a small investment in Balthasar Company for $1,930,000. During 2007, Keelson received $500,000 of dividends from Milton. At the end of 2007, the Milton investment had a market value of $3,350,000 and the Balthasar investment had a market value of $1,940,000. Keelson owned no other stock investments during 2007. All of Keelson's investments were properly accounted for as long-term investments.

Required

A. At year-end 2007, should these investments be classified as held-to-maturity, trading, or available-for-sale? Why?
B. Prepare a schedule calculating the amount Keelson would report for long-term investments on its balance sheet at the end of 2006 and 2007.
C. Prepare a schedule calculating the effect of Keelson's investment activities on its income for 2006 and 2007.

P11-11 **ACCOUNTING FOR INVESTMENTS IN SECURITIES**
Obj. 4
At December 31, 2007, Metro Medical Company owned small investments in the common stock of other firms as follows:

Company	Number of Shares Owned	Purchase Price per Share
1. Harbor Company	2,000	$18.75
2. Regency, Inc.	2,200	10.40
3. Hilton Products	1,400	26.00
4. Paxton Technology	750	45.00

Metro's management expects to sell its investments in Harbor and Paxton during the 2008 fiscal year. It does not, however, expect to sell its investments in Regency or Hilton at any time in the foreseeable future. The market value of each investment at the end of the 2007 fiscal year was as follows:

Harbor	$41,000
Regency	25,000
Hilton	34,200
Paxton	32,540

During 2007, Metro received $3,900 of dividends from Harbor and $1,700 of dividends from Hilton. Metro Company owned no other stock investments during 2007.

Required

A. Determine the amounts that should be reported on the December 31, 2007 balance sheet under the following classifications. Show how you determined each amount.
   1. Short-term investments
   2. Long-term investments
   3. Stockholders' equity

B. What information about these investments should appear on 2007's income statement? Be specific.

C. How is it helpful to readers of the financial statements to see information about the market value of common stock investments when Metro didn't pay those amounts to obtain the shares? Explain.

P11-12 ACCOUNTING FOR INVESTMENTS IN BONDS

Obj. 4

Nilani Company purchased 100 Arapaho Company bonds on April 1, 2007. The bonds pay interest semiannually on March 31 and September 30 at an annual coupon rate of 9%. The bonds sold at an effective yield of 8%. The effect of brokerage fees is included in computing the effective yield. The bonds mature on March 31, 2009, at their face value of $1,000 per bond. Nilani's fiscal year ends on September 30.

Required

A. Compute the price Nilani paid for Arapaho's bonds. (Hint: Determine the present value of the interest payments and principal repayment as demonstrated in Chapter 8.)

B. Prepare an amortization schedule for Nilani's investment.

C. Assume that the bonds are classified as held-to-maturity securities. Use the format presented in this chapter to show how the bond transactions would be entered into Nilani's accounting system in 2007, 2008, and 2009.

D. What is the total interest revenue from these bonds that Nilani will report on its 2007, 2008, and 2009 income statements? How does total interest revenue compare to Nilani's net cash flow from this bond investment during those same three years? Show your computations.

E. What does the result in part D suggest to you regarding the similarities and differences between accrual and cash-based measures?

P11-13 ACCOUNTING FOR INVESTMENTS IN BONDS

Obj. 4

On January 1, the Cheng Corporation purchased $10,000 of 5%, five-year bonds as a long-term investment. Interest is paid annually. The company is not involved in active trading of securities.

Required Using the format presented in the chapter, record each of the following transactions.

A. Record the purchase of the bonds for $10,000.

B. Record the receipt of the first interest payment on the bonds in part A.

C. Assuming the company intends to hold the bonds to maturity, what entry is necessary at the end of the first year if the market value of the bonds is $10,400 at that time?

D. Show how the answer to part C would differ if the company does not intend to hold the bonds to maturity.

E. Assume that the company purchased these bonds at a cost of $10,445. This price yields an effective rate of 4%.

F. Record the receipt of the first interest payment on the bonds purchased in part E.

G. Assuming the company intends to hold the bonds to maturity, prepare the necessary entry at the end of the first year to reflect the $10,400 market value of the bonds.

(Continued)

H. Show how the answer to part G would differ if the company does not intend to hold the bonds to maturity.
I. Report the carrying value (book value) of the bonds at the end of the first year in parts C, D, G, and H. Explain how the amounts have been calculated.
J. Prepare an amortization table for the bonds purchased in E, assuming the company holds the bonds to maturity. What is the total amount of cash received? What is the total amount of interest revenue? What is the difference between the two?

P11-14 INVESTMENTS IN DEBT SECURITIES

Obj. 4

On January 1, Gandini Company purchased $300,000 face value of Battaglia's 8.4% bonds at a price of $283,439. At this price, the bonds yielded 9% annually. At December 31, Gandini received an interest check on these bonds of $25,200. The market price of these bonds that day was $282,000.

Required

A. Using the format presented in this chapter, show the entries that would be made to the accounting system to record the purchase of this investment and receipt of the interest check. Assume this is a long-term investment.
B. Show how this investment should be reported in the year-end financial statements by completing the table of information that follows.

	If the bonds are . . .		
	Held-to-maturity securities	Trading securities	Available-for-sale securities
Accounting method to be used			
Amount of unrealized holding gain (loss) to be reported on income statement			
Amount of unrealized holding gain (loss) to be reported on balance sheet			
Amount of discount amortized during first year			
Balance of investment account on balance sheet at end of the first year			

P11-15 INVESTMENTS IN EQUITY SECURITIES

Obj. 4

On August 22, 2007, Burgess Company purchased 20,000 common shares of Radius Measurement Inc. at a price of $8 per share. Brokerage commissions, taxes, and transfer fees totaled an additional $800. At December 31, 2007, Burgess still owned the securities but the aggregate market value had declined to $148,000. This is a long-term investment.

Required

A. Using the format presented in this chapter, show the entries that would be made to the accounting system to record the purchase of these securities.
B. Show how this investment should be reported in the year-end 2007 financial statements by completing the table of information below.

	If the total number of Radius common shares outstanding totals		
	1 million	80,000	30,000
Accounting method to be used			
Amount of unrealized holding gain (loss) to be reported on income statement			
Amount of unrealized holding gain (loss) to be reported on balance sheet			
Balance of investment account on balance sheet			

C. Assume the investment in common stock was sold on January 23, 2008 at a price of $171,400. Use the format presented in this chapter to show the entry to record this event. Assume the investment has always been on the books as available-for-sale securities.

P11-16 DEPRECIATION, AMORTIZATION, AND DEPLETION

Objs. 2, 3, 5

The accounting staff at Golden Mining Company will soon prepare year-end entries to the accounting system to record the partial consumption of certain long-term assets. Your advice is sought regarding each of the following situations.

1. A mining site was acquired 10 years ago at a cost of $4,900,000. This included $700,000 to prepare an environmental impact statement, conduct a required survey, and build road access. The mine was expected to produce approximately 20 million tons of high-grade ore, after which the site could be sold for $500,000. This past year, 3.0 million tons were produced, processed, and sold.
2. Trucks and machinery having an estimated useful life of five years are being depreciated by the double-declining-balance method. These assets were purchased for $152,000 and have an estimated residual value of $22,000. This is the end of their third year in use.
3. A patent relating to the ore-refining process was purchased three years ago at a cost of $57,000. At the time of purchase, the patent had a remaining legal life of eight years. Management wants the required write-off of the patent's cost to have the minimum effect on net income that is allowed under the circumstances.

Required

A. Assist the accounting staff by suggesting the year-end entries that should be made to the accounting system for each of the situations above.
B. Assume the trucks and machinery have always been depreciated using the straight-line method. Assume further that it was determined during the current year that the estimated useful life would actually be a total of 10 years with a residual value of $2,000. What amount of depreciation expense would have been reported during each of the first two years under the straight-line method? What amount of depreciation expense will be reported for the current year and the years that follow under the straight-line method?

P11-17 ACCOUNTING FOR FIXED, NATURAL, AND INTANGIBLE ASSETS

Objs. 2, 3, 5

On the last day of the fiscal year, the chief financial officer of Fastrax Industries is reviewing several accounting matters. They are as follows:

1. Equipment purchased seven years ago at a cost of $475,000 was sold yesterday as scrap metal at a price of $3,000. It had originally been estimated to have a 10-year life with a $50,000 residual value. The straight-line method has been used.
2. Early in the current year, the mineral rights to a bauxite mine were acquired at a cost of $5.5 million. Mining consultants have estimated there are about 350,000 tons of recoverable ore that can be removed and processed.
3. Just yesterday, the company purchased a subsidiary company by paying the $3.0 million purchase price. Investigation prior to the acquisition reveals the market value of the subsidiary's identifiable assets totals $2.2 million.

Required Use the format presented in this chapter for parts A, B, C, and E.

A. Prepare the entry to record the current year's depreciation expense.
B. Prepare the entry to record yesterday's sale of old machinery. Also show how you arrived at the amounts you entered.
C. During the year just ended, 80,500 tons of bauxite ore were removed, processed, and sold from the mine. Prepare the appropriate entry to record the expense.
D. Explain what goodwill represents.
E. Prepare the entry to record the purchase of the subsidiary.

P11-18 ACCOUNTING FOR PLANT ASSETS

Objs. 2, 6

Garland Company purchased construction equipment on July 1, 2004, for $800,000. The equipment was expected to have a useful life of five years and a residual value of $50,000. On June 30, 2007, Garland no longer needed the equipment and sold it for $311,000. Garland's

(Continued)

accounting year ends on December 31. The company uses the straight-line depreciation method.

Required

A. Information about this equipment must be entered into the accounting system on July 1, 2004; December 31, 2004; December 31, 2005; December 31, 2006; and June 30, 2007. Show how that information should be entered, using the format shown in this chapter. (Hint: On June 30, 2007, be sure to record depreciation expense for the six months immediately preceding sale of the equipment.)

B. Why was a gain (or loss) recorded at the date of disposal? What caused this to occur? Does a loss mean that the company has been negligent in selling the asset? Does a gain on sale mean that the company has been skillful in selling the asset? Explain.

C. Calculate the cumulative net effect that all transactions involving the equipment had on Garland's pretax income from 2004 through 2007. Also, calculate the cumulative net effect that all transactions involving the equipment had on cash flows for this period. Explain the relationship between (1) the effect on pretax income and (2) the effect on cash flows.

P11-19 ETHICS IN FINANCIAL REPORTING

Obj. 6

Show-Me-the-Money Inc. is a medium-sized bank. The bank's stock is owned primarily by residents in the city where the bank operates. During the last decade, the bank lent money for numerous real estate developments. Most of the loans went to developers who constructed office space and expected to repay the loans from office rent. Aggressive lending and building practices resulted in overbuilding. A downturn in the local economy drastically reduced demand for office space. As a result, many of the buildings are now largely empty. Rent from the facilities is insufficient to pay interest on several of the bank's larger loans. The bank has permitted several borrowers to restructure their loans, providing a longer period of repayment and lower interest rates. The market value of the property backing these loans has decreased approximately 40% since its construction. The bank's proposed year-end balance sheet reports loans in the bank's long-term investment portfolio at $43 million. This amount is net of a loan loss reserve of $5 million. The balance sheet also includes $18 million of property among the bank's assets. This property was acquired through foreclosures on several loans. The property is valued at the present value of the original loan payments, including interest the bank expected from the original borrowers. The bank is collecting rent from tenants and expects to sell the property when real estate values return to higher levels. The bank's total assets are $80 million, and total stockholders' equity is $10 million. The bank's proposed income statement for the year reports profits of $6 million. The year-end audit is now underway, and the bank's auditors are reviewing the proposed financial statements. They have questioned management about its loans and property values. The auditors believe that the current market value of the loan portfolio is about $35 million. They are less sure about the value of the property. The bank's managers are arguing that the current market value of the loans is not relevant because they do not expect to sell the loans. Instead, they expect to hold the loans until they mature. Also, they do not plan to sell the property until they can recover the amount the bank invested.

Required Do you believe the investors and creditors of the bank will be well served by the financial statements that the bank's management proposes to report? Explain. Do you see any ethical problems with the way the bank's managers want to report its assets? Why? What problems may arise for the bank if it reports its loans at current market value?

P11-20 THE EQUITY METHOD

(Based on the Other Investment Issues section) On January 1, Schuster Company bought 2,400 of Helio Corporation's 10,000 outstanding shares of common stock as a long-term investment. The stock was acquired at a cost of $24,000. On December 31, Helio reported net income of $38,000 and paid dividends totaling $6,000. On the same date, the market value of Helio's common stock was $15 per share.

Required

A. Use the format presented in this chapter to show how the events described above would be entered into Schuster's accounting system.

B. Describe how this would be reported on Schuster's year-end financial statements by completing the table that follows.

Question	Solution
1. In which section of the balance sheet will this investment be reported? Be specific.	
2. What amount will be reported on the balance sheet for this investment? Show your work.	
3. What amount of income will be reported on the income statement related to this investment? Explain.	
4. What information will be reported about any unrealized holding gain or loss? Explain.	

P11-21 EXCEL IN ACTION

The Book Wermz expanded its operations in March 2008 by purchasing an existing chain of bookstores. The total cost of the purchase was $5 million. Of this amount, $2.2 million was allocated to the cost of buildings, $1.0 million to the cost of store equipment, and $275,000 to the cost of transportation equipment. The buildings have an estimated useful life of 30 years (360 months) and a salvage value of $100,000. The store equipment has an estimated useful life of five years (60 months) and a salvage value of $50,000. The transportation equipment has an estimated useful life of three years (36 months) or 90,000 miles and a salvage value of $75,000. The Book Wermz uses straight-line depreciation for financial reporting purposes. For income tax purposes, it uses double-declining-balance depreciation for buildings and store equipment and units-of-production depreciation for transportation equipment.

Required Use a spreadsheet to prepare a depreciation schedule for The Book Wermz for the assets described. The depreciation schedule will contain data for April through December 2008. Rows 1 through 3 should contain "The Book Wermz," "Depreciation Schedule," and "April-December 2008." Beginning in cell A5, list the following captions in column A: Asset, Cost, Salvage, Life (months), and Method. In column B, provide the data for Buildings that correspond to the captions in column A. Repeat the process for Store Equipment in column D and for Transportation Equipment in column F.

In cell A10 enter "Month," followed by the numbers 1 through 9 (corresponding to April through December) in cells A11 through A19. In cell B9, enter "Straight-Line." In cell C9, enter "Declining-Balance."

In cell B11, enter a function to calculate the straight-line depreciation for April for Buildings. Click on the Function button, select the Financial category, and select SLN from the Function name list. In the dialog box, enter the appropriate cell addresses for each of the values requested to complete the function. For example, enter $B$6 for cost. Make sure you include the $ sign in front of the cell references for cost, salvage, and life because the references are to fixed locations (cells B6 to B8). Once the calculation is completed for April, copy cell B11 to cells B12 to B19 to provide calculations for May through December. The amount of depreciation in each cell should be the same. In cell B20, calculate the total depreciation for 2008 using the Summation button.

In cell C11, enter a function to calculate the double-declining-balance depreciation for April for Buildings. Repeat the process used for straight-line depreciation, except use the DDB function in the Financial category. The references in the dialog box will be the same as those for straight-line depreciation. You will need to include a reference for Period. The reference is A11 for April. Do not enter $ signs for this reference because the reference will change for months May through December. You may leave the Factor reference blank. The factor is 2 for double-declining-balance, and 2 is the default for the DDB method. Once the calculation is made for April, copy cell C11 to cells C12 to C19. The amount of depreciation should be less

(Continued)

each month than the preceding month (declining balance). Total the column of depreciation amounts in cell C20.

In columns D and E, repeat the processes described above for Store Equipment.

In column F, enter data for Transportation Equipment and calculate straight-line depreciation. In column G enter data for the units-of-production method. In cell G10, enter the caption "Miles". In cells G11 through G19, enter the miles the equipment was used each month, as follows: 1500, 1800, 2000, 2800, 3000, 2500, 2700, 2600, and 2200. In cell H10, enter the caption "Expense." In cell H11, calculate the amount of depreciation for April using the equation =(($F6−$F7)/90000)*G13. Copy cell H11 to cells H12 through H19. Calculate totals for each column in row 20.

In columns I and J, calculate the total straight-line and accelerated depreciation amounts for each month. Total each column in row 20.

Calculate the tax savings to The Book Wermz of using accelerated depreciation for tax purposes. In column A, enter captions for "Total Accelerated," "Total Straight-line," "Difference," "Tax rate," and "Tax savings," beginning in cell A22. In column B, enter the amounts (cell references) that correspond with the total amounts. Use an equation to calculate the difference and assume a tax rate of 35%.

Format cells to provide a business appearance to the spreadsheet.

Suppose the life of the buildings was 380 months and the life of the store equipment was 72 months. How much depreciation would the company report and how much tax would it save?

P11-22 ETHICAL ISSUES AND INVESTING ACTIVITIES

Obj. 2

Since taking the company public with a recent stock issue, management at CMI ComWorld has been under pressure to meet earnings expectations from a variety of stakeholders. Provided below is a draft of the income statement prepared by the company's controller.

CMI ComWorld
Statement of Income
For the year ended 12/31/07

All numbers are in thousands	
Sales	$43,000
Cost of sales	28,000
Selling, general and administration	14,750
Net income	$ 250
Number of shares	1,000
Earnings per share	$0.25

During 2007 the company incurred repairs and maintenance expenditures of $1,000,000. The company's president reasoned that because routine maintenance reduces the likelihood of a mechanical breakdown, these expenditures benefit future years. Thus, the president instructed the controller to record the expenditures as an increase in fixed assets. When the controller questioned the president's instructions, the president responded as follows:

> "What's the problem? We'll put these expenditures on the balance sheet as fixed assets and depreciate them over a few years. It's just a matter of time until these expenditures show up on the income statement.
>
> Besides, if we fail to meet analysts' earnings expectations, or report a loss this year, our stock price will probably drop. Lots of innocent people will lose money. You don't want that on your conscience. Well, do you?"

Required

A. Do you agree with the president that repairs and maintenance expenditures should be recorded as a fixed asset? Why or why not?
B. Prepare the journal entry to undo the president's treatment of repairs and maintenance expenditures as a fixed asset.
C. Prepare an income statement that reflects your journal entry from part B.
D. Does the new income statement differ significantly from the draft prepared by the controller? Explain your results.

P11-23 MULTIPLE-CHOICE OVERVIEW OF THE CHAPTER

1. Which of the following is (are) used to determine how a given asset will be reported on the balance sheet?

	The Expected Period of Time Until the Asset Will Be Converted to Cash or Used Up	The Source of Financing that Was Used to Acquire the Asset
a.	Yes	Yes
b.	Yes	No
c.	No	Yes
d.	No	No

2. Belly-Acres Land Company made capital expenditures during the current year. At year-end, these expenditures should be reported on the
   a. income statement as expenses.
   b. balance sheet under current assets.
   c. balance sheet under long-term assets.
   d. statement of cash flows under operating activities.

3. The Song-in-My-Heart Record Store reported $20,000 of depreciation expense on assets acquired at the beginning of the current year. The assets' original cost was $50,000 with an estimated useful life of five years. The method used by Song-in-My-Heart for depreciating the assets was the
   a. straight-line method.
   b. cost recovery method.
   c. units-of-production method.
   d. double-declining-balance method.

4. The Shiny Metal Mining Company acquired mineral rights for $3,100,000. Geological studies indicate that two million tons of economically recoverable ore are likely to be present on the site. Subsequently, the rights to remaining minerals can be sold for approximately $300,000. The firm estimates that it will take about five years to mine the ore. In the first year, 600,000 tons of ore were recovered, processed, and sold. What is the amount of depletion for the first year?
   a. $930,000
   b. $840,000
   c. $620,000
   d. $560,000

5. Assuming an estimated useful life of three years and zero residual value, which of the following depreciation methods will always result in the least depreciation expense in the first year?
   a. Straight-line
   b. Double-declining-balance
   c. Units-of-production
   d. Cannot be determined from the information given

6. Boswell Company purchased its first investment in available-for-sale securities during the current year. At year-end, the current market value of the marketable securities is greater than the price paid to acquire them. As a result of this information, the company should report an unrealized holding
   a. loss on its income statement.
   b. gain on its income statement.
   c. loss on the balance sheet.
   d. gain on the balance sheet.

7. Hwan Manufacturing Company owns held-to-maturity bonds that were acquired at a premium. Each period that Hwan holds the investment, amortization of the premium will have which one of the following effects?
   a. The amount of interest revenue reported on the income statement will increase.
   b. The amount of cash received will decrease.
   c. The book value of the investment will decrease.
   d. The rate of return earned on the investment will decrease.

(Continued)

8. The excess of cost over the market value of identifiable net assets acquired in a purchase of another company should be reported in the financial statements as
   a. a current asset.
   b. an intangible asset.
   c. an expense of the period in which the acquisition occurs.
   d. a revenue of the period in which the acquisition occurs.

9. Which of the following is a *false* statement about intangible assets, other than goodwill?
   a. They have no physical substance.
   b. They have no real economic value.
   c. They can often be purchased or sold.
   d. They are amortized over their useful lives.

10. Khim Singer Company sold obsolete machinery that was no longer used in its factory. The transaction resulted in a loss being recorded in the company's accounting system. Information about this event will appear on which of the company's year-end financial statements?

	Income Statement	**Statement of Cash Flows (Indirect Format)**
a.	Yes	Yes
b.	Yes	No
c.	No	Yes
d.	No	No

11. *(Based on the Other Investment Issues section)* Farma Pharmaceutical Company has invested in the common stock of Bailey Biotech. The primary factor that will determine whether the equity method or the consolidation method is used to account for this is size of the
    a. investment.
    b. industry.
    c. parent company.
    d. total assets.

12. *(Based on the Other Investment Issues section)* On January 1 of the current year, Nancy Enterprises acquired 14,000 shares of the 40,000 outstanding shares of Tang Toys for $100,000. During the year, Tang Toys had net income of $50,000 and paid $10,000 in dividends. At December 31 of the current year, Nancy Enterprises should report what amount as its investment in Tang Toys?
    a. $96,500
    b. $103,500
    c. $114,000
    d. $117,500

Cases

C11-1 COMPARISON OF PURCHASE AND LEASING OF PLANT ASSETS

Objs. 2, 6

Swenson Company plans to acquire new chemical processing equipment on January 1, the beginning of the company's fiscal year. The equipment costs $2 million. Swenson can either borrow $2 million from a bank or lease the equipment. Both the bank and the leasing company believe that a 10% interest rate is appropriate, given Swenson's credit history. A lease would be accounted for as a capital lease (as discussed in Chapter 8). The equipment is expected to have a useful life of four years, which would be the same as the lease period. The equipment is expected to have zero residual value. Swenson normally uses the straight-line method to depreciate its equipment. The lease alternative would require year-end payments of $635,000 each year. If money is borrowed from a bank, four year-end payments would be required. Each payment would include one-fourth of the principal amount borrowed plus all of the interest expense that had been incurred on the unpaid balance during the year.

Required As the Chemical Division manager, you have been asked to evaluate the alternatives and to recommend the best choice for acquiring the equipment. Determine the comparative effects of purchasing versus leasing the equipment on Swenson's income statement, balance sheet, and statement of cash flows over the four-year period. Evaluate the alternatives and make a recommendation to top management.

C11-2 ANALYSIS OF INVESTMENT ACTIVITIES

Objs. 2, 4, 6

Selected information from **General Mills**' 2004 annual report and 10K is provided in Appendix A at the end of the text.

Required Review the annual report and write a short report in which you respond to each of the issues raised below.

A. Identify the accounting methods used by the company to account for plant assets, intangible assets, research and development costs, and advertising costs. (Hint: This information is disclosed in the notes to the financial statements.)
B. Identify the cost of each of the company's types of plant assets and the total amount of accumulated depreciation on these assets at the end of the most recent period reported.
C. Explain how the company reports its holdings of marketable securities in the financial statements. What percentage of the company's total assets is represented by marketable equity securities?
D. Explain the change in the company's plant asset accounts during the most recent year reported by an analysis of its investment activities and depreciation. (Hint: Because of certain accounting complexities, you won't be able to prove the change exactly. But see how much of the change you can explain.)

© PHOTODISC/GETTY IMAGES

Analysis of Investing Activities

12

HOW DO ASSETS CREATE VALUE FOR OUR BUSINESS?

Chapter 11 discussed investing activities, including accounting for the acquisition, use, and disposal of long-term assets. Decisions about long-term assets affect the profitability and value of a company. Property and equipment are necessary to support operating activities. Manufacturing companies require equipment and facilities to produce goods, and all companies require equipment and facilities to support administrative and sales functions. The amounts and types of assets a company acquires affect a company's expenses and cash flows. Good asset investments support additional sales and profits. Poor investments lead to higher expenses and reduced profits.

Maria and Stan have decided that, for Favorite Cookie Company to grow and become more valuable, it will need to produce its own goods. The company will need to invest in production equipment and facilities. They have to make decisions about the types and amounts of assets to acquire.

Food for Thought

If you are managing Favorite Cookie Company, what issues should you consider when deciding on the amounts and types of assets to use in the company? How should investors analyze the company's financial statements to assess management's investing decisions and the effects of these decisions on profits and company value?

Maria, president, Stan, vice president of operations, and Ellen, vice president of finance of Favorite Cookie Company, met to discuss investing plans for their company.

Maria: *We need to identify the equipment and facilities required for Favorite Cookie Company to become a manufacturing company. Is there anything special we need to consider?*

Ellen: *First, make sure the assets we acquire will permit us to produce the amount of goods we need and keep our production costs low enough so that we can make a profit.*

Stan: *Also, it's important for us to make sure the facilities and processes we use permit us to produce high-quality goods.*

Maria: *Do we have to trade off quality for cost? Are there other issues that affect our decision?*

Ellen: *We should consider how the assets we acquire will affect our cost structure. Some costs don't increase as sales increase, and other costs do. Cost structure can have an important effect on the profitability of Favorite Cookie Company.*

Objectives

Once you have completed this chapter, you should be able to:

1. Explain why investing decisions are important to a company and how they can affect its profits.
2. Explain how operating leverage affects a company's risk and profits.
3. Use financial statements to evaluate investing activities for various companies.
4. Explain how investing activities affect company value, and use accounting information to measure value-increasing activities.
5. Identify ways in which a company can use its assets to improve effectiveness and efficiency.
6. Explain why accounting information about long-term assets is useful for creditors.

INVESTING DECISIONS

Objective 1
Explain why investing decisions are important to a company and how they can affect its profits.

Maria, Stan, and Ellen continue to discuss investing activities for their new company. The three managers had decided earlier to finance their company primarily by issuing common stock. Their decisions now involve the types of long-term assets the company needs.

Maria observed: "We decided last week that we probably will need $5 million to fund production facilities and production and marketing costs. We assumed that we will require $4 million for plant assets. Now we should decide on the specific types of assets we'll need. We want to be sure that $5 million will be adequate."

"I have looked at various alternatives," Stan remarked, "and I have some estimates for us to consider. Our production process involves mixing ingredients to make cookie dough, shaping or forming the cookies, baking the cookies, examining the finished product for quality, and packaging the cookies for sale. Exhibit 1 illustrates the production process.

EXHIBIT 1 The Production Process for Favorite Cookie Company

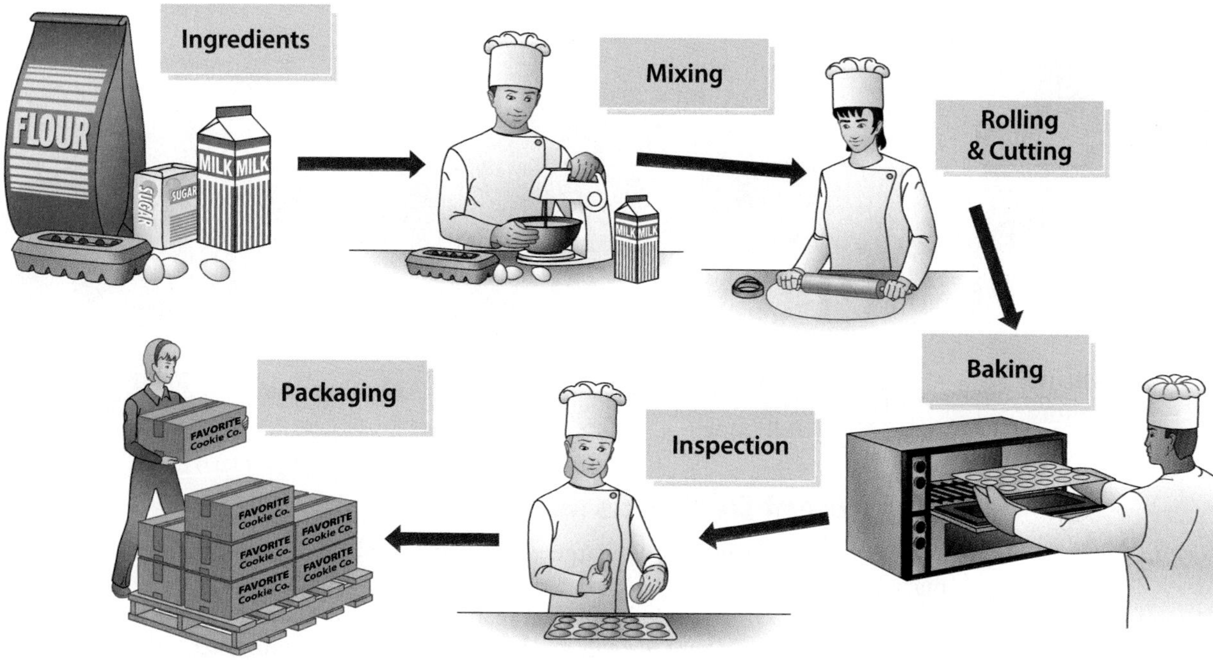

"Obviously," continued Stan, "we need equipment such as mixers and ovens. Also, we need equipment to move the materials between processes. We need enough building space to produce the product and provide storage for materials and finished goods."

"That seems fairly simple," Maria interrupted. "Can't we just buy what we need?"

"Well, it's not quite that simple," Stan responded. "We have to make some choices. For example, we have to decide how much of each type of equipment we need. We can start small and add more equipment as demand increases, but because the equipment has to be special-ordered, this will be a relatively expensive approach in the long run, assuming that our demand increases as we expect. If we start with smaller mixers and ovens, we will not be able to increase capacity very much once demand picks up.

"Perhaps the biggest decision we have to make," Stan continued, "is how much automation we want in the production process. We can use rather simple equipment that requires a lot of manual labor. For example, we can use pushcarts to move materials from one process to the next. Materials can be loaded into mixers and ovens by hand. And, we can use workers to inspect and package the finished products. These processes will require relatively large amounts of labor but will allow us to invest less in equipment.

"As an alternative, we can purchase more sophisticated equipment. Exhibit 2 shows this alternative. This equipment completes most of the processes with little human involvement. Conveyors can move materials to locations where ingredients are automatically loaded. The equipment prepares the dough, forms the cookies, and transfers them to ovens. Workers would have to make sure the equipment is functioning properly and make changes in settings for different types of cookies. This option calls for fewer employees. However, the employees would require more skills, so we would have to pay them more. Also, if we use automated equipment, we must acquire sufficient machinery to meet expected demand for the foreseeable future. It is expensive to increase the size of an automated production process, and therefore our initial investment will be larger than if we start with manual equipment.

"Thus, our basic choice is manual or automated equipment. If we select manual equipment, we can start with less investment and add equipment as demand increases. If we select automated equipment, we must invest more initially, but we will have the capacity we expect to need. Also, we will be able to produce a higher quality product. An automated production process is more reliable."

Maria observed, "This decision is more complicated than I had realized. What effect do the choices have on our expected profits?"

EXHIBIT 2 An Alternative Production Process for Favorite Cookie Company

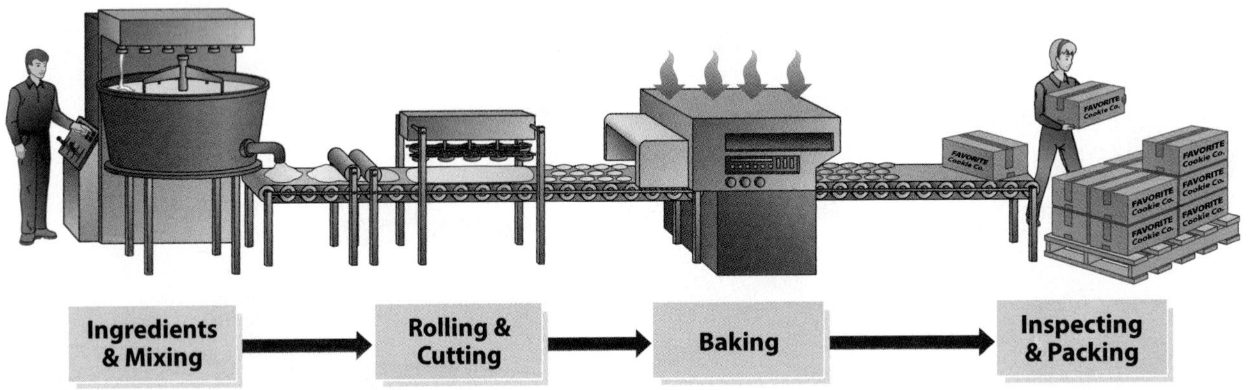

Investment Decisions and Profit

"The potential effects are quite large," Ellen responded. "Exhibit 3 provides some summary information.

"We expect sales of $3 million next year. That is the amount I assume in Exhibit 3," Ellen noted. "The amount we will need to invest initially in equipment differs between alternatives."

EXHIBIT 3
Expected Effects of Favorite Cookie Company's Investing Decisions with Sales of $3 Million

(In thousands)	Manual	Automated
Assets:		
Current assets	$ 1,000	$ 1,000
Plant assets	3,500	4,000
Total assets	$ 4,500	$ 5,000
Sales	$ 3,000	$ 3,000
Cost of ingredients	(800)	(800)
Depreciation	(250)	(300)
Wages and benefits	(780)	(700)
Other operating expenses	(1,000)	(1,000)
Operating income	170	200
Interest expense	(170)	(170)
Pretax income	—	30
Income taxes	—	(9)
Net income	$ —	$ 21

"If we use manual equipment, our initial equipment investment would be $3.5 million. The automated equipment alternative requires an initial investment of $4 million. Consequently, the amount of capital required to finance the company will be larger if we use automated equipment.

"The choice of equipment affects our projected income statement in two ways. The amount of depreciation differs because of the amounts invested in equipment. Annual depreciation expense will be lower for manual equipment. The choice also affects the amount of labor cost we can expect. The automated equipment alternative results in lower wages and benefits, saving us $80,000 next year. Other income statement amounts, except taxes, do not vary between the alternatives.

"The bottom line is, we should expect profit to be zero in the first year if we choose the manual equipment alternative. We earn a $21,000 profit if we choose automated equipment. Keep in mind, however, that we have to invest more money if we go with automated equipment."

"Okay," Stan remarked, "but what happens in the future? We expect sales to increase each year. Can we produce enough product to meet higher demand in the future?"

"The answer depends on which alternative we choose," Ellen answered. "Exhibit 4 provides similar information to Exhibit 3, assuming sales of $3.6 million, the amount we expect in the second year of operations.

"If we select the manual equipment, we will have to purchase an additional $250,000 of equipment to meet the higher demand. The advantage of using manual

EXHIBIT 4
Expected Effects of Favorite Cookie Company's Investing Decisions with Sales of $3.6 Million

(In thousands)	Manual	Automated
Assets:		
Current assets	$ 1,200	$ 1,440
Plant assets	3,750	4,000
Total assets	$ 4,950	$ 5,440
Sales	$ 3,600	$ 3,600
Cost of ingredients	(960)	(960)
Depreciation	(275)	(300)
Wages and benefits	(936)	(700)
Other operating expenses	(1,000)	(1,000)
Operating income	429	640
Interest expense	(170)	(170)
Pretax income	259	470
Income taxes	(78)	(141)
Net income	$ 181	$ 329

equipment is that we can start with less equipment and add more equipment as demand increases. For example, we can start with five mixers and add a sixth when we need it. If we use automated equipment, we must purchase large automated mixers and ovens to meet our expected sales of $3 million. However, we can increase production to $3.6 million without adding equipment. Another advantage of the automated equipment is that we can increase production without increasing labor costs. If we use manual machines, we will need additional employees to operate the new machinery.

"The result of these changes is that at $3.6 million of sales, depreciation and labor costs increase for the manual equipment alternative. Also, we will use more ingredients regardless of the type of equipment we use. Other costs do not increase, however. Therefore, our net income is positive for each alternative. The automated equipment alternative provides much higher income, however, as you can see in Exhibit 4."

"So it looks like the choice is clear," Maria concluded. "The automated equipment appears to be the best choice. It results in higher net income at the $3 and $3.6 million sales levels. Shouldn't we select that alternative?"

Investment Decisions and Risk

Objective 2
Explain how operating leverage affects a company's risk and profits.

"Probably," Ellen agreed. "But we need to consider the risk associated with each alternative. The automated equipment requires a larger investment. Also, we cannot reduce our costs very much if our sales don't meet expectations. Look at Exhibit 5, for example."

"In this exhibit, sales for next year are assumed to be $2.8 million, less than we expect but still a possibility. A real advantage of using manual equipment is apparent at this level. We can buy less equipment and still produce enough cookies to meet demand. Also, we can hire fewer employees and save some labor costs. Therefore, though we incur a loss, it is less than the loss incurred with the automated alternative. Also, the cash we save from buying less equipment will help us stay in business until demand increases.

"A disadvantage of the automated equipment is that we cannot reduce labor costs. We will need the same number of employees to operate and maintain the equipment whether we sell $2.8 million of product or $3.6 million. Once we have the automated equipment, our costs would remain fairly constant regardless of how much we produce. And, we can't downsize our operations and still stay in business. All of the equipment will be needed to manufacture any reasonable amount of product.

"Exhibit 6 illustrates the relation between sales and net income for each alternative. Manual equipment is the safer choice. If sales are lower than expected, we are more likely to survive if we invest in this equipment. On the other hand, we stand to make more money if we go with automated equipment."

EXHIBIT 5
Expected Effects of Favorite Cookie Company's Investing Decisions with Sales of $2.8 Million

(In thousands)	Manual	Automated
Assets:		
Current assets	$ 900	$ 900
Plant assets	3,400	4,000
Total assets	$ 4,300	$ 4,900
Sales	$ 2,800	$ 2,800
Cost of ingredients	(747)	(747)
Depreciation	(233)	(300)
Wages and benefits	(728)	(700)
Other operating expenses	(1,000)	(1,000)
Operating income	92	53
Interest expense	(170)	(170)
Pretax income	(78)	(117)
Income taxes	23	35
Net income	$ (55)	$ (82)

EXHIBIT 6 A Comparison of the Effects of Investment Decisions on Profits of Favorite Cookie Company

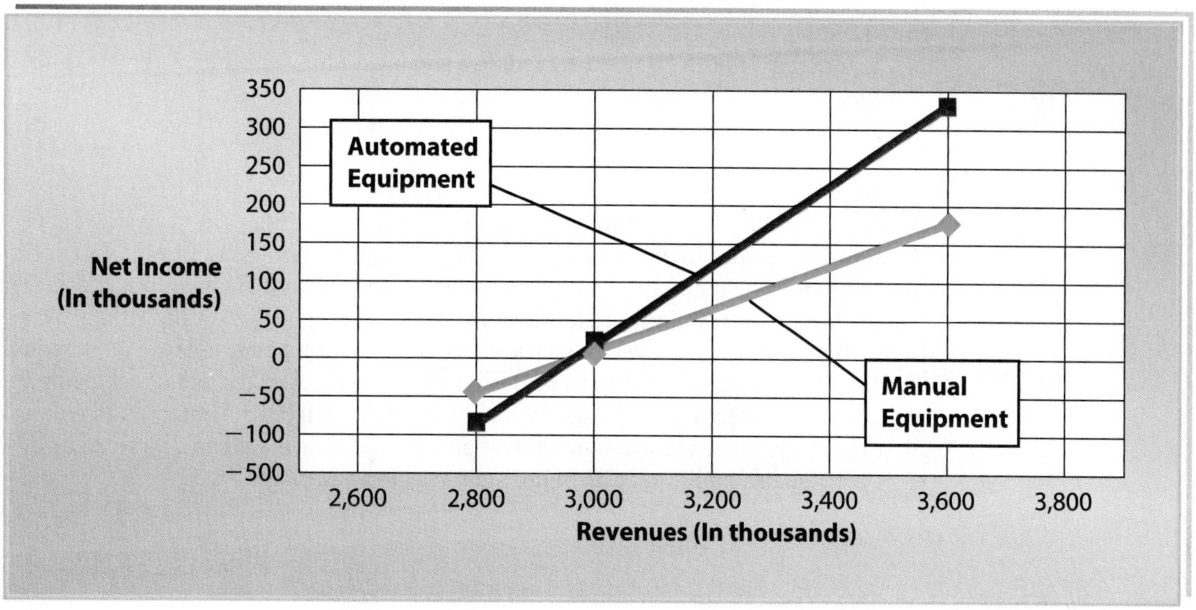

"The trade-off we are considering is typical of many companies," Ellen noted. "One alternative results in higher fixed costs than the other. **Fixed costs** are costs that do not increase in proportion to increases in sales. **Variable costs** are those that do increase in proportion to increases in sales. In our situation, if we go with automated equipment, most of our costs will be fixed. We can't cut costs much if sales are lower than expected, but we don't increase costs much if sales increase. Consequently, we lose more money if sales are low and make more money if sales are high than we would with an alternative that has fewer fixed costs. If we use manual equipment, our costs increase more rapidly as sales increase, but they also decrease more rapidly as sales decrease."

Ellen continued, "**The use of fixed costs to increase net income as sales increase is known as *operating leverage*.** Automation often results in higher operating leverage because a larger portion of total operating expenses is fixed. Other common causes of high operating leverage are large investments in plant assets and labor costs that don't change much in proportion to sales. High operating leverage increases risk, but it also increases the potential for high profits."

CASE IN POINT

The Effect of High Operating Leverage

Airlines are an example of companies with high operating leverage. It costs an airline about the same amount to fly an airplane whether it is full or empty. The cost of the airplane, the flight crew, maintenance, and fuel are largely fixed when a plane flies between two cities. The amount of revenue the airline earns depends on the number of tickets it sells. If the plane is full, the airline earns a good profit. If it is empty, the airline loses a lot of money. Other industries with high operating leverage are utilities, because they require a large investment in equipment regardless of how much they sell, and publishing companies. It costs almost as much to publish a book or magazine if one copy is sold as it does if a thousand copies are sold.

"We'll have to be sure our sales projections are accurate if we decide on automated equipment," Stan remarked. "But, I think it's the best choice for us."

"We know we have a good product," Maria added. "I think the advantages of automation are worth the risk. We'll have the production capacity we expect to need in the future."

"More importantly," Stan observed, "we will have a higher quality product. Once the equipment is working properly, it doesn't make many mistakes. We will save on waste from defective products, and we won't run as much risk of losing customers because of poor quality."

Ellen completed the conversation. "I agree. Also, we will be able to produce our product faster and deliver it to customers in a shorter period. I think the advantages of the automated equipment outweigh the risks of higher operating leverage. In addition, the company's financial leverage will be low because we are financing primarily with equity. Because our financial risk is low, we can afford higher operating risk. If sales are lower than expected, we won't run a major risk of not being able to pay creditors. Investors will expect high growth in profits. We have a better chance of achieving high growth with automated equipment because profits increase more rapidly as sales increase. If our revenues are much less than we expect or if we can't increase revenues each year, we probably won't be in business very long anyway."

Self-Study Problem #1

Financial statement information is presented below for Alchemy Corporation, a producer of pharmaceuticals. The company expects sales to increase by about 10% in 2007.

(In millions)	2006 Actual	2007 Expected
Sales	$988	$1,087
Cost of goods sold	(660)	(726)
Operating expenses	(294)	(300)
Operating income	34	61
Interest expense	(6)	(6)
Pretax income	28	55
Income taxes	(10)	(19)
Net income	$ 18	$ 36

Alchemy's management is considering automating much of the company's production process. The automation would result in about half of the company's cost of goods sold being fixed. Currently, most of these costs vary in proportion to sales, as shown in the financial numbers presented above.

Required

A. Assume that half ($330 million) of Alchemy's cost of goods sold in 2006 is fixed and that the other half increases in proportion to sales, an increase of 10%. Compute the company's expected cost of goods sold and net income in 2007. Assume that income taxes are 35% of pretax income. Round to the nearest million.

B. Compare your results with those presented above, which assume that cost of goods sold varies in proportion to sales. What effect would the automation have on Alchemy's profitability? What effect would it have on the company's risk? Explain your answer.

The solution to Self-Study Problem 1 appears at the end of the chapter.

INTERPRETATION OF INVESTING ACTIVITIES

Objective 3

Use financial statements to evaluate investing activities for various companies.

The first part of this chapter examined the investing decisions of managers and the effects of these decisions on a company's financial statements. This section examines financial statement information provided by actual corporations. We use this information to demonstrate how decision makers interpret the investing activities of companies and make decisions about companies' risk, return, and value attributes.

In the remaining sections of this chapter, we will consider the following issues as we look at the analysis of accounting information for the purpose of evaluating investing activities:

1. Identification of investing activities for one or more companies and fiscal periods
2. Consideration of asset growth for company profits and value
3. Measurement of the effects of asset growth
4. Examination of the effects of investing activities and growth on risk
5. Examination of creditors' use of accounting information about investing activities

Identifying Investing Activities

Exhibit 7 provides selected financial statement information for **Microsoft** and **Procter & Gamble.** As a first step in our analysis, we want to identify the companies' long-term assets and the changes in these assets resulting from investing activities.

It is apparent from Exhibit 7 that Microsoft is larger than Procter & Gamble in terms of total assets. However, most of Microsoft's assets are current assets. Procter & Gamble has more long-term assets than Microsoft. In addition to more property and equipment, Procter & Gamble has more intangible assets, particularly goodwill, than Microsoft. Intangible assets are part of the other long-term assets category in Exhibit 7. Goodwill results from acquisitions of companies, an activity in which Procter & Gamble has been

EXHIBIT 7 Selected Financial Statement Information for Microsoft and Procter & Gamble

	Microsoft		*Procter & Gamble*	
(In millions)	2004	2003	2004	2003
Balance Sheet				
Total current assets	$70,566	$58,973	$17,115	$15,220
Long-term assets:				
Property and equipment, at cost	6,489	6,078	25,304	23,542
Accumulated depreciation	(4,163)	(3,855)	(11,196)	(10,438)
Property and equipment, net	2,326	2,223	14,108	13,104
Long-term investments	12,210	13,692	—	—
Other long-term assets	7,287	6,844	25,825	15,382
Long-term assets	21,823	22,759	39,933	28,486
Total assets	$92,389	$81,732	$57,048	$43,706
Income Statement				
Total revenues	$36,835	$32,187	$51,407	$43,377
Depreciation and amortization expense	1,186	1,393	1,733	1,703
Net income	8,168	7,531	6,481	5,186
Statement of Cash Flows				
Cash flow from (for) investing activities:				
Purchase of property and equipment	$ (1,109)	$ (891)	$ (2,024)	$ (1,482)
Disposal of property and equipment	—	—	230	143
Purchase of investments, net	(1,632)	(5,259)	(121)	(107)
Other changes in long-term assets	(4)	(1,063)	(7,476)	(61)
Net investing cash flow	$ (2,745)	$ (7,213)	$(9,391)	$(1,507)

involved to a much larger extent than Microsoft. Long-term investments are a major component of Microsoft's long-term assets but are not a major item for Procter & Gamble.

Procter & Gamble grew faster from 2003 to 2004 than did Microsoft. Procter & Gamble's total assets increased by 30.5% [($57,048 − $43,706) ÷ $43,706] during this period while Microsoft's total assets increased by 13% [($92,389 − $81,732) ÷ $81,732]. Procter & Gamble's property and equipment grew by 7.7% [($14,108 − $13,104) ÷ $13,104] relative to Microsoft's growth of 4.6% [($2,326 − $2,223) ÷ $2,223]. The more rapid growth was associated with a larger increase in revenues for Procter & Gamble relative to Microsoft. Procter & Gamble's revenues grew 18.5% [($51,407 − $43,377) ÷ $43,377], and Microsoft's revenues grew 14.4% [($36,835 − $32,187) ÷ $32,187].

Other information about changes in long-term assets is provided by the investing activities section of the statement of cash flows. During the 2004 fiscal year, Procter & Gamble paid $2,024 million for additional property and equipment. It also paid $7,476 million to acquire other companies. These purchases and acquisitions were considerably larger than the $1,733 million of depreciation and amortization expense recorded by Procter & Gamble in 2004. For a company to grow, it must acquire assets in addition to those necessary to replace assets that are being consumed during a period. Microsoft's purchases of property and equipment in 2004 of $1,109 million was slightly less than the amount of depreciation and amortization expense of $1,186 million reported in 2004.

The Importance of Asset Growth

Objective 4

Explain how investing activities affect company value, and use accounting information to measure value-increasing activities.

Growth in assets is important to the value of a company and the wealth of its stockholders. For most companies, the ability to produce and sell products depends on having the necessary assets to support these activities. A manufacturing company must have equipment and facilities to produce goods. A merchandising company must have equipment and facilities to store, transport, display, and sell its goods. The amount a company can sell depends on how much it can produce or on how much it can make available to customers. Procter & Gamble's asset growth was associated with an increase in net income of 25.0% during the 2004 fiscal year [($6,481 − $5,186) ÷ $5,186] compared with an increase in net income of 8.5% for Microsoft [($8,168 − $7,531) ÷ $7,531].

Measuring the Effects of Growth

Additional investment and asset growth are valuable when a company uses these assets to generate higher profits. Additional investment is not valuable for its own sake. For example, if a company pays $1 million for an additional store, but it is not able to make a profit from the store, the investment is not a good decision.

A common measure of the outcome of a company's investment decisions is return on assets (ROA).

Return on Assets = Net Income ÷ Total Assets

Return on assets compares profits from producing and selling goods and services with the total amount invested in assets.

From Exhibit 7, we see that Microsoft's return on assets for 2004 was 8.8%.

0.088 = $8,168 ÷ $92,389

Procter & Gamble's return on assets for 2004 was 11.4%.

0.114 = $6,481 ÷ $57,048

Thus, compared with Microsoft, Procter & Gamble was creating a higher return on its investment in assets. For every dollar invested in assets by Microsoft, the company earned 8.8¢ of profit. For every dollar invested in assets by Procter & Gamble, it earned 11.4¢.

One way to examine events that affect a company's return on assets is to separate return on assets into components. Two primary components of return on assets are asset turnover and profit margin. *Asset turnover* **is the ratio of revenues to total assets:**

Asset Turnover = Revenues ÷ Total Assets

It is a measure of the ability of a company to use its assets to sell its products. Revenues include sales and service revenues that result from a business's primary operations. A company with a high asset turnover is more effective in using its assets than one with a low asset turnover.

Profit margin **(or** *return on sales***) is the ratio of net income to revenues:**

Profit Margin (or Return on Sales) = Net Income ÷ Revenues

It is a measure of the ability of a company to produce profits from its sales. A company with a high profit margin is more efficient in controlling costs than one with a low profit margin.

Return on assets is the product of asset turnover and profit margin.

Return on Assets = Asset Turnover × Profit Margin

We can determine Microsoft's and Procter & Gamble's asset turnover and profit margin from information in Exhibit 7. These amounts are provided in Exhibit 8.

A practical way to interpret asset turnover is to translate the ratio into dollars. Microsoft's asset turnover of 0.399 in 2004 means that the company was able to generate $0.40 of sales for every $1 it had invested in assets. In 2004, Procter & Gamble was able to generate $0.90 of sales for each dollar of investment. Therefore, Procter & Gamble was more effective than Microsoft in using its assets in 2004.

Similarly, we can translate profit margin into dollars. Microsoft's profit margin of 22.2% in 2004 means that the company was able to generate 22.2¢ of net income for every $1 of sales. Procter & Gamble's profit margin in 2004 was 12.6%.

Comparing asset turnover with profit margin provides information about why Procter & Gamble was earning a higher return on assets than Microsoft. Procter & Gamble earned a higher asset turnover, which more than offset the effect of its lower profit margin. Profitability depends on the ability of a company to use its assets to sell products and on the ability of a company to earn a profit from those sales. Procter & Gamble was doing a relatively good job of selling its products but was not earning as much profit on those sales as Microsoft.

As was discussed earlier for Favorite Cookie Company, operating leverage is a major factor in determining how much a company's net income is likely to increase as its revenues increase. Companies with high fixed costs, and therefore high operating leverage, experience larger increases in net income as revenues increase. The amount of operating leverage often is related to the proportion of a company's long-term assets to its total assets. This relationship is stronger when most of a company's long-term assets are property and equipment or goodwill (resulting from acquisitions). Depreciation and amortization expenses are fixed expenses. They do not change as a result of changes in

EXHIBIT 8

Asset Turnover and Profit Margin for Microsoft and Procter & Gamble

	Microsoft		Procter & Gamble	
	2004	2003	2004	2003
Asset Turnover	0.399	0.394	0.901	0.992
Profit Margin	0.222	0.234	0.126	0.120
Return on Assets	0.088	0.092	0.114	0.119

EXHIBIT 9
Operating Leverage Comparison

	Microsoft	Procter & Gamble
Revenue Growth	14.4%	18.5%
Net Income Growth	8.5%	25.0%
Operating Leverage Multiplier	0.59	1.35

sales volume. In contrast, if a company has a lot of inventory and other current assets or a lot of investments in securities, it is likely to exhibit higher proportions of variable expenses.

Microsoft is an example of a company with relatively low operating leverage in comparison to Procter & Gamble, which has high operating leverage. As Microsoft's revenues increase, many of its expenses also increase. In contrast, as Procter & Gamble's revenues increase, many of its expenses remain relatively fixed. Consequently, Procter & Gamble's net income increases more rapidly than Microsoft's as revenues increase. We can observe this difference by comparing the growth in net income for each company relative to the growth in revenues. Exhibit 9 reports this information for each company for 2004. Observe that Microsoft's revenue growth was higher than its net income growth. Procter & Gamble's revenue growth was lower than its net income growth.

The operating leverage multiplier in Exhibit 9 is the ratio of net income growth to revenue growth. Microsoft's net income grew at 59% of the rate of its revenue. Procter & Gamble's net income grew at 135% of the rate of its revenue. The difference is largely due to differences in operating leverage between the two companies, though it is not possible to rule out other factors from the available information.

In general, the more operating leverage a company has, the greater its net income will increase as its revenues increase. At the same time, if revenues decrease, a company with high operating leverage will exhibit a larger decrease in net income than a company with low operating leverage.

Self-Study Problem #2

Accounting information is provided below for two hardware companies that compete for customers.

	Moreco		DealRight	
(In millions)	2007	2006	2007	2006
Total assets	$48.3	$44.7	$120.6	$118.4
Revenues	67.9	61.0	159.1	143.2
Net income	5.3	4.2	9.5	10.0

Required

A. Compute asset turnover, profit margin, and return on assets for each year and company. Also, compute asset, revenue, and net income growth rates for each company from 2006 to 2007.

B. Evaluate the performance of each company with respect to the other and also in terms of changes from 2006 to 2007. Identify reasons for the differences in performance.

The solution to Self-Study Problem 2 appears at the end of the chapter.

THE EFFECT OF INVESTMENT ON EFFECTIVENESS AND EFFICIENCY

Objective 5

Identify ways in which a company can use its assets to improve effectiveness and efficiency.

Investment is important for a company. As a company acquires additional assets, it should be able to produce and sell more products and earn higher profits. Asset growth can increase a company's profits and return on assets if the additional assets improve the company's effectiveness and/or efficiency. Effectiveness increases when the dollar amount of sales increases more rapidly than the dollar amount of additional investment. As discussed in the previous section, we can observe this increase in effectiveness by examining the asset turnover ratio. Increases in asset turnover result when a company invests in new locations that produce large increases in sales. Asset turnover also increases when a company sells products in high demand. If a company has products in its stores that customers are not willing to buy, its sales will be low relative to the amount it has invested in assets. If it replaces these products with others that customers are interested in buying, its asset turnover will increase. Also, it can increase asset turnover by closing locations that do not create high sales and moving its assets to locations that produce higher sales.

Efficiency increases when a company is able to earn greater profit for each additional dollar of product it sells. Efficiency depends on reducing costs relative to the amount sold.

Effectiveness and efficiency often go together. For example, assume that Favorite Cookie Company invests $5 million in assets. It pays employees $700,000 in wages and benefits each year. Utilities and other costs amount to $300,000 per year. Average cost of goods sold for its products is 60% of sales revenues, and income taxes are 30% of pretax income. In 2008, the store sold $3.0 million of goods. Therefore, its net income would be as follows:

Sales	$ 3,000,000	
Cost of goods sold	(1,800,000)	60% of sales
Other operating expenses	(1,000,000)	
Pretax income	200,000	
Income taxes	(60,000)	
Net income	$ 140,000	

Suppose that by changing some of its product line, the company can increase sales to $3.3 million without any additional asset investment and without hiring additional employees or increasing utilities or other costs. Its net income would then be as follows:

Sales	$ 3,300,000	
Cost of goods sold	(1,980,000)	60% of sales
Other operating expenses	(1,000,000)	
Pretax income	320,000	
Income taxes	(96,000)	
Net income	$ 224,000	

Observe that an increase in sales of 10% (from $3 million to $3.3 million) results in an increase in net income of 60% (from $140,000 to $224,000). Exhibit 10 describes the effects of the increase in sales on the company's asset turnover, profit margin, and return on assets.

EXHIBIT 10

The Effect of a Sales Increase on Return on Assets

	Before	After
Sales Revenues (in millions)	$3	$3.3
Asset Turnover	0.600	0.660
Profit Margin	4.67%	6.79%
Return on Assets	2.80%	4.48%

The increase in sales improves the company's asset turnover. It is using its assets more effectively to generate more sales. No additional investment was made to create the additional sales. Company management found a better way to use the company's assets. Profit margin increased 45% (from 4.67% to 6.79%) as a result of the sales increase. This increase in profit margin resulted because many of the company's costs did not change in proportion to the increase in sales. Only cost of goods sold increased as sales increased. Therefore, the company's profits grew much more rapidly than its sales as a result of operating leverage. The more effective use of assets produced a dramatic increase in profits. Thus, a primary management decision involves finding the best locations and assets in which to invest and then using those assets effectively and efficiently to generate profits.

If a company's sales decrease, its profits often decrease more rapidly than its sales. Each dollar of lost sales is not matched by a dollar's decrease in expenses. For example, a company must employ sufficient workers to conduct its business, and so a decrease in sales often does not result in a proportional decrease in wages and benefits. Equipment and building costs often cannot be reduced in the short run. Therefore, profits decrease more rapidly than sales.

If sales decrease for any length of time, a company must find ways to reduce its investment so that it can eliminate unnecessary costs. Companies sell buildings, equipment, and other assets that are not being used effectively. Often these assets must be sold at less than their book values (cost minus accumulated depreciation), resulting in losses that reduce the company's already low net income. Also, a company may have to incur separation or relocation costs for employees who are terminated or moved to other locations. Thus, in the short run, downsizing a company usually results in extra costs and low net income or a net loss. If a company can close stores that are not profitable or get rid of assets it does not need, it may be able to become profitable and earn a return on assets that is competitive with those of other companies in its industry. If a company is not successful in these efforts, it is likely to be purchased by another company or to go out of business.

Thus, although asset growth is important to creating company value, growth must be accompanied by increases in sales and profits that compensate the company and its owners for the additional investment. If a company's growth is not effective, its additional investments reduce its return on assets. Eventually, the company is forced to sell assets that are not productive in an effort to return to a satisfactory level of profitability. This process often is costly and difficult. Investment in assets is essential. Effective asset growth increases company value. Growth also is risky. Investment in the wrong assets, investment in too many assets, or improper management of assets generally leads to poor profitability and can jeopardize a company's existence.

INVESTING ACTIVITIES AND CREDITOR DECISIONS

Objective 6

Explain why accounting information about long-term assets is useful for creditors.

A company's investing activities may be particularly important to its creditors. Companies often borrow money to acquire long-term assets. Accordingly, the ability of a company to repay creditors and pay interest usually is connected to its ability to use its long-term assets to generate profits and cash flows. If a company is unsuccessful in creating profits from its assets, it usually must sell a portion of its assets to create cash to repay its creditors. If the company is very unsuccessful and goes out of business, it sells its assets and uses the cash to pay off its debts. In some cases, specific debts are connected to particular assets that are used as security for the debts. If a company cannot repay these debts, the assets securing the debts must be transferred to creditors or sold to repay creditors.

Because of these relationships, the value of a company's long-term assets is particularly important to creditors. When a company's assets decrease in value, its debt becomes riskier. Consequently, accounting measurement rules traditionally are very conservative in the measurement of the value of assets, particularly tangible assets such as property, plant, and equipment. These rules attempt to ensure that a company does not overvalue assets on its balance sheet. Assets are recorded at cost and, except for certain financial assets that can be sold at market value, are not written up to a higher value, even if their market value increases. Thus, a building that is purchased for $1 million in 2007 is recorded at cost and is depreciated over its useful life. The amount reported on the balance sheet for the building will always be less than $1 million, regardless of how much the owner could receive if the building were sold.

Accounting standard setters in the United States have been reluctant to permit companies to write up their assets to market value for fear the amounts recorded would be highly subjective and might overstate asset value. In many cases, it is difficult to determine the market value of an asset. Further, the market value of an asset that is being used productively may be much higher than the market value of the same asset if it must be sold to repay debts.

Accounting measurement rules require companies to write down their assets, however, if the market values of the assets decrease below their book values. For example, assume that a company owns a building that it purchased for $1 million. Accumulated depreciation on the building at the end of 2007 was $600,000. Therefore, the book value at the end of 2007 was $400,000. At this time, the company determined that the market value of the building was $250,000. Accounting rules require the company to write down the asset by $150,000 ($400,000 − $250,000), recognizing a loss for this amount. This measurement rule, known as **lower of cost or market**, is intended to protect investors, particularly creditors, by ensuring that assets are not overstated.

Accounting rules in the United States differ from those of certain other countries with respect to the amount reported for long-term assets. Some countries—Great Britain, for example—permit companies to recognize increases in the market values of many assets. These increases in values also increase the stockholders' equities of these companies.

Self-Study Problem #3

Information is provided below for two paper products companies.

	Tenix Company		*Beson Company*	
(In millions)	2007	2006	2007	2006
Property and equipment	$471	$523	$214	$203
Total assets	654	708	323	308
Current liabilities	112	124	86	79
Long-term debt	435	440	125	130
Stockholders' equity	107	144	112	99
Asset impairment charge	(30)	—	—	—
Operating income	8	12	30	24
Interest expense	(38)	(39)	(10)	(9)

Required If you were a creditor of these companies, would you be concerned about the ability of either company to repay its debts? Explain your answer.

The solution to Self-Study Problem 3 appears at the end of the chapter.

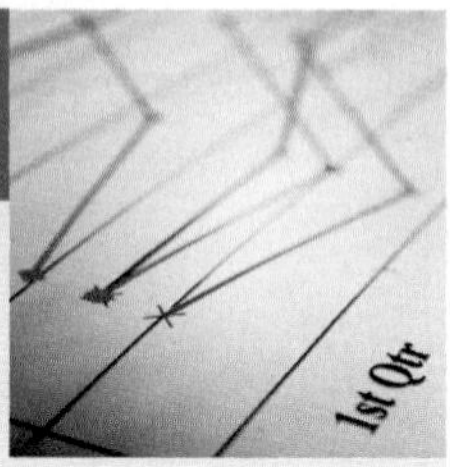

THINKING BEYOND THE QUESTION

HOW DO ASSETS CREATE VALUE FOR OUR BUSINESS?

Investing decisions affect a company's profits, risk, and value. Investment decisions that result in fixed costs increase risk and the ability of a company to create higher profits and sales. Managing risk involves selecting the amounts and types of long-term assets a company uses. Those decisions also affect performance measures such as return on assets. Asset costs affect net income as assets are consumed and total assets increase as more assets are acquired. A low return on assets is an indicator of poor investing decisions. If a company is not satisfied with its investing decisions and the performance of its assets, what can it do to improve that performance?

Self-Study Problem Solutions

SSP12-1 A. Expected cost of goods sold for 2007 = $693

$660 ÷ 2 =	$330	(half is fixed)
($660 ÷ 2) × 1.10 =	363	(half varies with sales, increasing by 10%)
Total cost of goods sold	$693	

(In millions)	**2006 Actual**	**2007 Expected**
Sales	$988	$1,087
Cost of goods sold	(660)	(693)
Operating expenses	(294)	(300)
Operating income	34	94
Interest expense	(6)	(6)
Pretax income	28	88
Income taxes (35%)	(10)	(31)
Net income	$ 18	$ 57

B. Because a portion of the cost of goods sold is fixed, these costs do not increase with sales. Therefore, the cost of goods sold is lower if the production process is automated and sales increase. Lower cost of goods sold results in higher net income.

Higher fixed costs increase operating leverage and increase the company's risk. Though profits are higher if sales increase, if sales decrease they will be lower than they would be with the nonautomated option. Fixed costs do not decrease in proportion to sales when sales decrease. Therefore, profits decrease more rapidly for companies with high operating leverage when sales decrease. Expenses that vary in proportion to sales decrease as sales decrease and, consequently, do not affect net income as much as fixed expenses do.

SSP12-2 A.

	Moreco		**DealRight**	
	2007	**2006**	**2007**	**2006**
Asset turnover	67.9 ÷ 48.3 = 1.406	61.0 ÷ 44.7 = 1.365	159.1 ÷ 120.6 = 1.319	143.2 ÷ 118.4 = 1.209
Profit margin	5.3 ÷ 67.9 = 0.078	4.2 ÷ 61.0 = 0.069	9.5 ÷ 159.1 = 0.060	10.0 ÷ 143.2 = 0.070
Return on assets	1.406 × 0.078 = 0.110	1.365 × 0.069 = 0.094	1.319 × 0.060 = 0.079	1.209 × 0.070 = 0.085
Asset growth	(48.3 − 44.7) ÷ 44.7 = 0.081		(120.6 − 118.4) ÷ 118.4 = 0.019	
Revenue growth	(67.9 − 61.0) ÷ 61.0 = 0.113		(159.1 − 143.2) ÷ 143.2 = 0.111	
Net income growth	(5.3 − 4.2) ÷ 4.2 = 0.262		(9.5 − 10.0) ÷ 10.0 = −0.05	

B. Moreco's return on assets increased from 2006 to 2007, while DealRight's return on assets decreased. Moreco's return on assets is higher in both years than DealRight's. Accordingly, Moreco is making better use of its assets to create profits.

Moreco's asset turnover increased from 2006 to 2007, as did DealRight's asset turnover. Therefore, both companies became more effective in using their assets to produce sales. Moreco's asset growth was higher than DealRight's, however. Therefore, Moreco was more successful in investing in productive assets, leading to higher sales and profits.

DealRight's major problem was a decrease in profit margin. DealRight became less efficient than Moreco. Moreco's profit margin increased. The greater increase in Moreco's profit margin could result from higher operating leverage. Moreco has more fixed costs that did not increase in proportion to sales. Another reason could be greater cost control. Some of DealRight's costs increased more rapidly than its sales, thus reducing profits.

SSP12-3 Creditors should be more concerned about Tenix Company than about Beson Company. Tenix reported a sizable decrease in plant assets. Much of this decrease was due to a writedown of assets because their market value was below their book value. Total plant assets are not much higher than long-term debt. Accordingly, the ability of Tenix to repay its debts in the event it went out of business is questionable. In addition, Tenix's profits are negative after deducting interest expense. The company is not earning sufficient profits to meet interest requirements. Tenix's performance is poor. Therefore, the likelihood that it could go out of business is relatively high, in which case it may have difficulty paying off all of its creditors.

Beson, in contrast, appears to be in relatively good shape. Its performance is strong, and its plant assets are large in proportion to long-term debt.

Define *Terms and Concepts Defined in This Chapter*

asset turnover (453)
operating leverage (449)
profit margin (453)
return on sales (453)

Review *Summary of Important Concepts*

1. The assets in which a company invests affect its profitability.
   a. Assets are necessary for a company to produce products and sell them to customers.
   b. Managers must determine the particular assets a company needs and how much of each type of asset it needs.
   c. Managers may have to choose among different assets that provide the same function.
   d. Choices concerning the amount and type of asset affect the capacity of a company to produce and sell products and the costs of those products.
2. Investing decisions often affect the proportion of a company's costs that are fixed or variable.
   a. High operating leverage results when a company has a lot of fixed costs.
   b. Costs that may be fixed are depreciation costs on assets and labor costs for workers who use those assets.
   c. A company with high fixed costs is riskier than one with low fixed costs because its profits change more rapidly as sales change.
   d. High operating leverage is an advantage when a company's sales are relatively high and when they increase. It is a disadvantage when sales are low or when they decrease.
3. A company's balance sheet and cash flow statement provide information about its investing activities.
   a. The balance sheet identifies the types and amounts of long-term assets that a company controls. Also, it provides a basis for determining increases and decreases in these amounts.

(Continued)

   b. The cash flow statement identifies amounts invested in long-term assets during a period and amounts received from the sale of these assets.
   c. Financial statement information is useful for measuring growth and change in a company's assets and, therefore, change in its ability to produce and sell products.

4. Asset growth increases a company's value by permitting it to increase sales and profits.
   a. Return on assets is a commonly used measure of a company's success in using its assets.
   b. Return on assets is affected by a company's effectiveness and efficiency.
   c. Asset turnover is a measure of effectiveness that considers the ability of a company to use its assets to create sales.
   d. Profit margin is a measure of efficiency that considers the ability of a company to create profits from its sales.
   e. Return on assets is the product of asset turnover times profit margin.

5. How a company uses its assets affects its effectiveness and efficiency.
   a. A company uses its assets effectively when it acquires the amounts of assets it needs to produce products it can sell and when it places these assets in locations that permit it to sell large quantities of products.
   b. If a company acquires too many assets, it can attempt to sell some assets to increase its profits and return on assets. In the short run, downsizing by selling unproductive assets usually is costly. In the long run, it may permit a company to survive and become competitive.
   c. A company uses its assets efficiently when it uses these assets to increase sales so that revenues increase faster than expenses.

6. Accounting information uses conservative values for most long-term assets.
   a. Conservatism results when increases in asset values above their cost or book value are not recorded but decreases in value are recorded.
   b. Conservatism protects the interests of creditors by ensuring that asset values are not overstated.
   c. If a company is unable to repay its debts, it may have to sell its assets to make these payments.

Questions

Q12-1 *Obj. 1* Why are investing activities critical to the success of a company?

Q12-2 *Obj. 1* How do investing activities affect a company's growth?

Q12-3 *Obj. 1* How do investing choices affect the choices available to a company in the future? Explain.

Q12-4 *Obj. 2* A friend who is approaching retirement is discussing her investment plan. She tells you that she wants to find a mutual fund that invests in stock of companies with high fixed costs, such as airlines, software developers, and publishers. "The higher fixed costs should make expenses more predictable, and earnings should be more reliable." What is your analysis of your friend's strategy?

Q12-5 *Obj. 3* The balance sheet and statement of cash flows provide information about a company's access to and use of cash. What differences would you expect to see in the information related to cash on these statements for a company reporting strong financial performance and a company reporting weak financial performance?

Q12-6 *Obj. 3* In reviewing a company's financial statements you observe that the company is consistently profitable and has consistent positive cash flows from operations and investing activities. Its cash flow from financing activities is consistently negative. What does this suggest to you about the company?

Q12-7 *Obj. 3* Why do some companies have a very large portion of total assets invested in property, plant, and equipment while other companies have just a small portion of assets invested in this manner?

Q12-8 *Obj. 3* What useful information can be obtained by comparing a firm's cost of plant, property, and equipment to the amount of its accumulated depreciation?

Q12-9 *Obj. 4* Why might a company wishing to increase its asset turnover acquire new assets? Wouldn't the greater amount of assets merely decrease asset turnover?

Q12-10 *Obj. 4* How do investing activities affect company value?

Q12-11 *Obj. 4* How is return on assets related to investing decisions?

Q12-12 *Obj. 5* Asset turnover is a measure of effectiveness. How can a firm increase its effectiveness?

Q12-13 *Obj. 5* How is it possible that profits can increase by 40% when sales increase by a much smaller amount?

Q12-14 *Obj. 6* Why is information about investing activities of interest to creditors?

Q12-15 *Obj. 6* Malcolm Greenlees is a friend who is planning to be a business manager. In a recent discussion about financial matters, Malcolm made the following statement. "A company's balance sheet measures the value of a company's resources. Investors can use this value for pricing the company's stock and for comparing the values of different companies. Creditors can use it for evaluating loan risk." How would you respond to Malcolm?

Exercises

Note: *Financial measurements have been presented in their simplest form in this chapter in order to place emphasis on thinking about the measurement and its connection with accounting, rather than on the complexities of calculation. Simplified calculations are also used in these end-of-chapter materials. In other texts, for example, return on assets may be calculated based on average total assets for the year, rather than on ending assets, and the income figure used may have the effects of interest and taxes removed.*

E12-1 Write a short definition for each of the terms listed in the *Terms and Concepts Defined in This Chapter* section.

E12-2 *Obj. 2* Sanders Company recorded sales revenues of $10 million for the year just ended. It recorded expenses totaling $9 million. Of these expenses, $4 million were expenses that would not have been different if sales revenue had been different. They were fixed expenses.

a. Prepare a table showing how much net income Sanders would have earned on sales of $8 million, $10 million, and $12 million.
b. Suppose the company's total expenses had been $9 million, and of that amount, the fixed expenses had been $6 million. The remaining expenses would have varied proportionately with sales revenue. Prepare a table showing how much net income Sanders would have earned on sales of $8 million, $10 million, and $12 million.
c. What conclusions about the effect of operating leverage on net income can you draw from this analysis?

E12-3 *Obj. 2* The Kolby and Kent companies both increased sales by 30% this year when compared with last year's results. Kolby's net income increased 40% as a result of the increased sales. Kent's net income increased 20%. Explain why differences in operating leverage may have resulted in a higher increase in net income for Kolby than for Kent. Provide a diagram to illustrate your explanation.

E12-4 *Obj. 2* Given below is selected information about two companies.

	Company A	Company B
Sales	$10,000	$10,000
Fixed costs	4,000	7,000
Variable costs	5,000	2,000

a. Calculate net income for each company.
b. What is operating leverage? Is it present in the operations of these two companies? If so, which company uses the greater amount of operating leverage?
c. If sales decrease by 10%, which company will report the higher net income?
d. If sales increase by 10%, which company will report the higher net income?

E12-5 *Obj. 3* Selected accounting information is provided below for two companies.

(In millions)	2004	2003	2002
Total assets:			
Sara Lee	$14,883	$15,450	$13,694
Merck & Co.	42,573	40,588	47,561
Depreciation and amortization:			
Sara Lee	734	674	582
Merck & Co.	1,451	1,314	1,231
Capital expenditures:			
Sara Lee	530	746	669
Merck & Co.	1,726	1,916	2,128

What trends in asset investments are apparent from the data presented? (Hint: Compare total assets, capital expenditures to total assets, and capital expenditures to depreciation and amortization for each year.)

E12-6 *Obj. 3* At the end of its most recent fiscal year, Shangri-La Company owned the following investments.

Investment	Historical Cost	Fair Market Value
A	$650,000	$765,000
B	840,000	730,000

Other assets had a book value of $2.4 million and liabilities had a book value of $2.8 million. Shangri-La's net income for 2007 was $280,000. If the company sold investment A at the end of the year for cash, what effect would the sale have on its financial statements and return on assets (ignoring the effect of income taxes)? Assume that assets are reported on the financial statements at historical cost. What effect would the sale of investment B have on the company's financial statements and return on assets? Compare these amounts to those that would be reported if no investments were sold. Does this example help explain why mark-to-market accounting is often required by GAAP? Discuss.

E12-7 *Objs. 3, 4* Following is selected information from **Dell Computer Corporation.**

Fiscal Year Ended (In millions)	January 30, 2004	January 31, 2003	February 1, 2002
Net revenue	$41,444	$35,404	$31,168
Net income	2,645	2,122	1,246
Cash from operations	3,670	3,538	3,797
Cash used in investing	(2,814)	(1,381)	(2,260)
Cash used in financing	(1,383)	(2,025)	(2,702)
Capital expenditures	(329)	(305)	(303)

With the information provided, calculate whatever ratios you believe are useful and describe the trends you observe.

E12-8 *Obj. 4* The following information is for **McDonald's Corporation** from its 2004 annual report.

(In millions)	2004	2003	2002
Revenues	$19,065	$17,140	$15,406
Net income	2,279	1,471	894
Total assets	27,838	25,838	23,971

Evaluate McDonald's Corporation's investing decisions by computing and analyzing its asset turnover, profit margin, and return on assets for 2002 through 2004.

E12-9 *Obj. 4* The following information was reported by **McDonald's Corporation** in its 2004 annual report.

(In millions)	2004	2003	2002
Cash flow from operating activities	$ 3,904	$ 3,269	$ 2,890
Total assets	27,838	25,838	23,971

Evaluate McDonald's Corporation's investing decisions by computing the ratio of cash flow from operating activities to total assets for 2002 through 2004. Compare the cash flow ratio with return on assets from E12-8. What do you conclude, given this information?

E12-10 *Obj. 4* Information is provided below for two companies that produce similar jewelry items for the same market.

	Lucy's Lockets		Desi's Delights	
(In thousands)	2008	2007	2008	2007
Sales	$630	$550	$650	$675
Net income	59	50	59	64
Total assets	500	450	875	880

Compute the asset turnover, profit margin, and return on assets for each company for each of the two years. Compare the performances of the two companies. Look at changes within each company and consider differences between the two companies.

E12-11 *Obj. 4* Given below is information about four companies.

	Able Co.	Baker Co.	Charlie Ltd.	Dilbert Inc.
Sales	$1,000	$2,000	$2,000	$600
Profit margin	0.18	0.06	0.11	0.24
Asset turnover	1.30	1.60	1.20	1.15

a. Which company generated the greatest profit?
b. Which company is the most efficient? Why?
c. Which company is the most effective? Why?
d. Which company has the greatest total assets?

E12-12 *Obj. 4* Following is information about current and projected sales and expenses for Squiggy Company. The company's total assets are also given.

	Current Sales	Decrease of 20%	Increase of 20%
Sales	$ 50,000	$ 40,000	$ 60,000
Less: Fixed costs	(10,000)	(10,000)	(10,000)
Variable costs	(10,000)	(8,000)	(12,000)
Net income	$ 30,000	$ 22,000	$ 38,000
Total assets	$ 25,000	$ 25,000	$ 25,000

a. Calculate the percentage changes in net income that would occur under each projection.
b. Calculate the percentage changes in return on assets, profit margin, and asset turnover that would occur under each projection.

E12-13 *Obj. 4* At a meeting of the top managers in your company, President Anne Thompson points out that stockholders have been pressuring the organization to increase return on assets. She asks for suggestions. Four of your colleagues respond in the following manner:

- "Sales, sales, sales. You've got to have more revenue to increase return."
- "Cut the expenses. How can you get a higher return if you don't keep more of your sales dollar?"
- "Expansion! More productive assets! Growth is the way to go."
- "No, no! Cut the assets! Sell those that will bring the best price!"

(Continued)

Evaluate your coworkers' comments. Will these strategies produce a definite increase in return on assets? What are the risks and rewards of each strategy?

E12-14 *Obj. 5* In a continuation of E12-13, another member of the group comments that to maximize return on assets, both efficiency and effectiveness are necessary. Explain what is meant by "efficiency" and "effectiveness," how they relate to return on assets, and whether you agree with your colleague's comment.

E12-15 *Obj. 5* Bumblebee Enterprises is considering adding another product line. Below are results from last year and pro forma (expected) results with the addition of the new line. Little change in sales from the current product lines is expected.

(In millions)	Last Year	Pro Forma
Sales	$260	$322
Net income	24	32
Total assets	300	372

Analyze the changes in effectiveness, efficiency, and return on assets that would be expected if the product line were added. Would you recommend addition of the product line?

E12-16 *Obj. 5* The following information is available for Cello Company:

	2008	2007	2006
Sales	$15,000	$ 8,000	$ 4,000
Net income	5,250	2,800	1,200
Average assets	30,000	20,000	10,000

Calculate the return on assets, profit margin, and asset turnover for each year and discuss the reasons for the change in return on assets over the three years.

E12-17 *Obj. 6* Winger Inc. is in the business of renting medical equipment for home health care. New government standards for lifts for disabled patients have rendered some equipment obsolete. Winger owns 10 four-year-old machines, each with a cost of $6,000. They have been depreciated using the straight-line method over an estimated life of 10 years. Since some parts can be used, they still have a resale value of approximately $1,000 each. Explain what accounting measure is required, what the effects on the financial statements will be (including amounts), and why this measure is important to creditors of Winger.

E12-18 *Obj. 6* Yarrow Company increased its investment in long-term assets by 20% in the past three years. This investment was financed by rapid increases in cash generated from operating activities. Cash from operating activities also was used to repay about 30% of Yarrow's long-term debt and to repurchase 10% of its common stock. What effect would you expect these events to have on the company's return on assets and return on equity? Does the company appear to be a good prospect for additional debt financing?

E12-19 *Objs. 3, 6* Abdullah Company reported the following information on its statement of cash flows.

(In millions)	2008	2007	2006
Net cash provided by operating activities	$ 3,195	$ 2,869	$ 2,688
Net cash from (used by) investing activities:			
Capital expenditures	(2,661)	(1,358)	(523)
Sales of equipment and property	293	305	257
Investments in other companies	(272)	0	0
Other	392	(627)	(924)
Total investing activities	$(2,248)	$(1,680)	$(1,190)
Net cash from (used by) financing activities:			
Payments on long-term debt	(547)	(648)	(2,130)
Repurchase of common stock	(994)	(740)	0
Other	627	200	614
Total financing activities	$ (914)	$(1,188)	$(1,516)

Interest expense for the past three years has been $372, $420, and $514. The company does not pay dividends. What information about the company's future prospects is communicated by its investing and financing activities during this period? Does the company appear to be a good prospect for new debt financing to be spent on additional capital assets?

Problems

P12-1 DETERMINING INVESTMENT STRATEGY FOR A NEW COMPANY

Objs. 1, 2

You have graduated with a business degree, and you have worked for three years for a small management consulting firm. Ivan Steeger (1352 Bull Run Road, Milltown, OR 97111) is a client who has been involved with several businesses in the past. He expects to be the major provider of equity capital for a new mail-order low-fat cookie business. His co-owners, who have baking expertise and a talent for developing recipes, will run the business.

The owners are about to meet to determine what equipment they will purchase for the business. Ivan gives you the following information about the business and their plans:

- Ivan will be providing about 25% of the financing; the remainder will be debt. Ivan will probably have to give his personal guarantee for much of the debt. The exact amount of debt will depend on the price of the equipment they decide to purchase.
- They expect business growth of about 20% for each of the first five years.
- All of the equipment has an expected life of at least five years. They will definitely purchase mixing and baking equipment. They must decide whether to add equipment that will shape cookies automatically, or hire employees to do the shaping.
- They also must decide what capacity they prefer in their initial equipment purchase. Smaller-capacity equipment would handle their expected demand for the first two years, operating eight hours a day. Equipment with twice the capacity would cost approximately 50% more.

Ivan asks for recommendations about discussion items for the meeting.

Required Write Ivan a letter in which you suggest major issues the owners should consider in making decisions about investments in equipment. You can assume that Ivan has some understanding of business terminology.

P12-2 THE EFFECT OF INVESTMENT STRATEGY AND OPERATING LEVERAGE ON RISK AND PROFITS

Objs. 1, 2

Following is a set of pro forma (or projected) income statements for a company. The columns labeled *A* are projected results for the company if it follows Strategy A. The columns labeled *B* are projected results for the company if it follows Strategy B.

	Low sales		Medium sales		High sales	
	A	B	A	B	A	B
Sales	$3,000	$3,000	$4,000	$4,000	$5,000	$5,000
Cost of sales	(180)	(180)	(240)	(240)	(300)	(300)
Depreciation	(315)	(450)	(355)	(450)	(395)	(450)
Wages expense	(1,300)	(1,500)	(1,600)	(1,500)	(1,800)	(1,500)
Other operating expenses	(1,000)	(1,000)	(1,000)	(1,000)	(1,000)	(1,000)
Operating income	205	(130)	805	810	1,505	1,750
Income tax (expense) or savings	(72)	46	(282)	(284)	(527)	(613)
Net income	$ 133	$ (84)	$ 523	$ 526	$ 978	$1,137

Required Study the information given and discuss each of the following.

A. The comparative risk of Strategy A versus Strategy B, as shown in the projected net income results
B. The company's operating leverage
C. The company's investment strategy

P12-3 EVALUATING THE EFFECTS OF OPERATING LEVERAGE ON PROFITS
Obj. 2

Yamhill County currently provides garbage removal services for two of the four small towns within its boundaries. In addition, it provides garbage removal services for residents who live in outlying rural areas. Each town has the option of contracting for garbage removal service from the county or providing service itself. Garbage volume and the resulting revenue from each town served is approximately the same; garbage volume for those who live in outlying rural areas is approximately that of two towns. Under the current situation, the following revenues and costs are incurred.

Revenue from garbage removal services	$2,000,000
Fixed expenses (don't change when revenues change)	600,000
Variable expenses (change proportionately when sales change):	
Wages	1,100,000
Truck maintenance	100,000

The Yamhill County commissioners are considering purchase of new garbage trucks that lift and crush the garbage more efficiently. This would double the fixed expenses and cut the existing variable expenses in half.

Required

A. Prepare a three-column pro forma income statement for the Yamhill County garbage service assuming the existing equipment continues in use. Show (1) the amount of projected net income if only outlying rural areas are served, (2) income if outlying rural areas plus those of two towns are served, and (3) income if outlying rural areas and four towns are served. Use the following format.

	Outlying rural areas only	Outlying rural areas plus two towns	Outlying rural areas plus four towns
Revenues			
Fixed expenses			
Variable expenses	______	______	______
Net income	======	======	======

B. Using the same format, prepare another three-column pro forma income statement showing garbage service with the new equipment under each of the three income situations listed in the first requirement.

C. Explain the effects that changing to new trucks could have on Yamhill County's profits and risks from the garbage service.

P12-4 COMPARING OPERATING LEVERAGE
Obj. 2

Information is provided below from the annual reports of two manufacturing companies operating in different industries.

	Solution Software, Inc.		Fashion Clothing Co.	
(In millions)	Sales	Earnings	Sales	Earnings
2004	$ 4,600	$1,150	$3,800	$300
2005	6,000	1,500	4,800	400
2006	8,700	2,200	6,500	550
2007	11,400	3,500	9,200	800
2008	14,500	4,500	9,500	850

Required Prepare a graph to illustrate the relationship between each company's earnings and its sales over the five years. Which company has the higher operating leverage? What effect does operating leverage have on the companies' operating income?

P12-5 COMPARING OPERATING LEVERAGE
Obj. 2

Information is provided on the following page from the 2004 annual reports of **Dell Computer Corporation** and **Tommy Hilfiger Corporation**.

(In millions)	Dell	Hilfiger
Net revenue	$ 41,444	$ 1,876
Cost of goods sold	(33,892)	(1,012)
Gross margin	7,552	864
Operating expenses	(4,008)	(666)
Operating income	$ 3,544	$ 198

Assume the cost of goods sold is variable and the operating expenses are half fixed and half variable.

Required

A. Compute Dell's projected operating income if sales decreased to 80% of current sales or increased to 120% of current sales.
B. Compute Hilfiger's projected operating income if sales decreased to 80% of current sales or increased to 120% of current sales.
C. Compare and discuss the results of your projections. Identify the company that has the higher operating leverage.

P12-6 OPERATING LEVERAGE AND RISK

Obj. 2

Financial statement information is presented below for Hillary Corporation, a producer of mountain climbing gear. The company expects sales to increase by about 20% in 2007.

(In millions)	2006 Actual	2007 Expected
Sales	$692	$830
Cost of goods sold	462	554
Operating expenses	206	247
Operating income	24	29
Interest expense	(5)	(5)
Pretax income	19	24
Income taxes	(7)	(8)
Net income	$ 12	$ 16

Hillary's management is considering automating much of the company's production process. The automation would result in about half of the company's cost of goods sold being fixed. Currently, most of these costs vary in proportion to sales, as shown in the financial numbers presented above.

Required

A. Assume that half ($231 million) of Hillary's cost of goods sold in 2006 is fixed and that the other half increases in proportion to sales, an increase of 20%. Compute the company's expected cost of goods sold.
B. Using the same assumptions as part A, compute expected net income for 2007. Assume that income taxes are 35% of pretax income. Round to the nearest million.
C. Compare your results with those presented above, which assume that cost of goods sold varies in proportion to sales. What effect would the automation have on Hillary's profitability? What effect would it have on the company's risk? Explain your answer.

P12-7 ASSESSING THE EFFECTS OF OPERATING LEVERAGE

Objs. 2, 3

Information is provided below from the financial statements of two companies for 2007.

2007	Jekyll	Hyde
Total assets	$30,000	$80,000
Total debt	10,000	50,000
Total equity	20,000	30,000
Sales	28,000	75,000
Operating expenses	20,000	60,000
Operating income	8,000	15,000
Interest expense	800	5,000
Pretax income	7,200	10,000
Income taxes (30%)	2,160	3,000
Net income	5,040	7,000

(Continued)

Jekyll's operating expenses include fixed costs of $5,000. Hyde's operating expenses include fixed costs of $50,000. All other operating expenses vary in proportion to sales for both companies. Assume that during 2008 sales for both companies increased by 20% from the amount reported, to $33,600 for Jekyll and to $90,000 for Hyde.

Required

A. Compute the net income Jekyll and Hyde would report for 2008 if sales increased by 20%.
B. Compute return on assets for Jekyll and Hyde in 2007 and 2008, assuming the increase in sales and no change in total assets.
C. Explain why the increase in sales would affect Jekyll and Hyde differently and explain which company is riskier.

P12-8 COMPARING CASH FLOWS

Obj. 3

Cash flow information is provided below for two companies in the health-care products industry. Cash outflows are shown in parentheses.

(In millions)	2004	2003	2002	Total
Johnson & Johnson				
Operating activities	$11,131	$10,595	$8,176	$29,902
Investing activities	(2,347)	(4,526)	(2,197)	(9,070)
Financing activities	(5,148)	(3,863)	(6,953)	(15,964)
Pfizer, Inc.				
Operating activities	$16,340	$11,713	$9,864	$37,917
Investing activities	(9,422)	4,850	(4,338)	(8,910)
Financing activities	(6,629)	(16,909)	(4,999)	(28,537)

Required Analyze the companies' cash flows for 2002 to 2004 and for the three years in total. Explain how the two companies compare in terms of their cash flow trends.

P12-9 ASSESSING ASSET AND INVESTMENT STRATEGY

Obj. 3

Widgets Inc. and Gizmos Inc. both manufacture accessories for computer users. The table below shows their investment policies and operating results for the past two years.

	Widgets Inc.		Gizmos Inc.	
(In thousands)	2007	2006	2007	2006
Plant and equipment	$2,400	$2,200	$4,300	$4,400
Accumulated depreciation	600	580	2,200	1,900
Total assets	5,000	4,300	8,000	8,100
Net income	432	320	(615)	(140)
Depreciation	320	290	520	541
Cash flow from operations	710	644	(105)	376
Cash flow from investing activities	(305)	(274)	205	56
New investment in plant and equipment	316	280	180	220

Required Explain what the preceding numbers tell you about the two companies' assets and investment policies. Include any information you find that would indicate financial problems within either company.

P12-10 COMPARING CASH FLOWS

Obj. 3

Cash flow information is provided below for two companies in the food products industry. Cash outflows are shown in parentheses.

(In millions)	2004	2003	2002	Total
Sara Lee				
Operating activities	$2,042	$1,824	$1,735	$5,601
Investing activities	(184)	(674)	(2,475)	(3,333)
Financing activities	(2,197)	(571)	470	(2,298)

(In millions)	2004	2003	2002	Total
Campbell Soup Co.				
Operating activities	$744	$873	$1,017	$2,634
Investing activities	(275)	(432)	(288)	(995)
Financing activities	(475)	(432)	(726)	(1,633)

Required Analyze the companies' cash flows for 2002 through 2004 and for the three years in total. Explain how the two companies compare in terms of their cash flow trends.

P12-11 COMPARING INVESTMENT ACTIVITIES

Objs. 3, 4

Selected information is provided below from the 2004 annual reports of **PepsiCo, Inc.** and **The Coca-Cola Company**.

(In millions except per share amounts)	PepsiCo	Coca-Cola
Current assets	$ 8,639	$ 12,094
Investments and other assets	5,759	9,306
Plant assets, net	8,149	6,091
Intangibles, net	5,440	3,836
Total assets	27,987	31,327
Current liabilities	6,752	10,971
Long-term debt	2,397	1,157
Shareholders' equity	13,572	15,935
Net income	4,212	4,847
Net sales	29,261	21,962
Interest expense	167	196
Depreciation and amortization	1,264	893
Net cash provided by operating activities	5,054	5,968
Net cash from (used) in investing activities	(2,330)	(503)
Net cash from (used) in financing activities	(2,315)	(2,261)
Earnings per share	2.47	2.00
Market value of equity	87,207	100,325

Required Use appropriate accounting ratios discussed in this chapter and any other ratios you think are helpful to compare the investing activities and performances of the two companies for 2004. What important differences exist in the investing and financing activities of the companies? How do these differences affect the risk and return of the companies? How would you expect these differences to affect the market-to-book value and book value-to-cash flow from operating activities ratios of the two companies?

P12-12 MEASURING THE RESULTS OF INVESTING ACTIVITIES

Obj. 4

Accounting information is provided below for two companies in the hair-care products industry.

	Faucett Company		Danson Industries	
(In millions)	2007	2006	2007	2006
Total assets	$33.8	$26.8	$84.4	$71.0
Sales	40.7	30.5	95.5	71.6
Net income	3.7	2.5	6.7	6.0

Required

A. Compute asset turnover, profit margin, and return on assets for each year and company. Also, compute asset growth for each company from 2006 to 2007.
B. Evaluate the performance of each company with respect to the other and also in terms of changes from 2006 to 2007. Identify reasons for the differences in performance.

P12-13 EVALUATING INVESTMENT DECISIONS

Objs. 4, 5

The information below was reported by PepsiCo, Inc. in its 2004 annual report.

(In millions)	2004	2003	2002
Net sales	$29,261	$26,971	$25,112
Net income	4,212	3,568	3,000
Cash flow from operating activities	5,054	4,328	4,627
Cash invested in other companies	(64)	(71)	(351)
Cash purchases of plant assets	(1,387)	(1,345)	(1,437)
Cash flow from investing activities	(2,330)	(2,271)	(527)
Cash dividends paid	(1,329)	(1,070)	(1,041)
Total assets	27,987	25,327	23,474

Required Identify and evaluate PepsiCo's investment decisions over the three years shown. Include in your analysis an examination of changes in efficiency and effectiveness.

P12-14 COMPARING INVESTMENT PERFORMANCE

Objs. 4, 5

The information below is for two companies in the same industry.

	Griffith Inc.		Johnson Inc.	
(In millions)	2008	2007	2008	2007
Sales	$8,223	$7,338	$9,430	$9,400
Net income	817	701	822	840
Total assets	7,250	6,490	8,347	8,350
Total liabilities	3,200	3,030	5,230	4,960
Market value	9,200	7,650	5,220	5,790

Required

A. Compute the asset turnover, profit margin, return on assets, and market to book value for each year and company. Also compute asset growth for each company from 2007 to 2008.

B. Compare the performances of the two companies over the two-year period with respect to effectiveness and efficiency.

C. Explain what reasons you find for the differences in the market value of the two companies. Could there be additional explanatory factors that do not appear in these numbers?

P12-15 INVESTING DECISIONS REGARDING PRODUCT LINES

Objs. 4, 5

The company for which you work has a significant investment in the stock of Star-Beasts Inc. (SBI), which currently manufactures one kind of toy, a large and lovable stuffed monster. SBI is considering expansion of its production facilities and would finance the expansion with long-term borrowing at an expected interest rate of 10%. The market would seem to support the manufacture and sale of 20% more monsters at the current profit margin. The added facilities would cost approximately $3.4 million. Alternatively, SBI could add one of two new lines: a mechanical dragon or a game called Starship Troopers.

The numbers below indicate current operating results and projections for the effects of added facilities for manufacturing the new lines. The numbers do not include interest on the new facilities or the company's 35% income tax rate.

(In thousands)	Current Operations	Addition of Dragons	Addition of Games
Sales	$9,860	$3,300	$2,900
Operating expenses	7,240	2,450	2,300
Interest expense	1,100	?	?
Total assets	8,422	?	?
Capital expenditures	?	3,450	1,800

Required

A. In addition to showing the current income statement, prepare pro forma income statements for SBI under each of the three strategies: expanding manufacturing of the current product and adding each of the new lines.

B. Determine the return on assets for the current situation and for each of the three strategies.

C. Indicate under which strategy you would feel most confident about the value of your company's investment, and explain why.

P12-16 EVALUATING INVESTMENT DECISIONS

Objs. 3, 4, 5

Creative Technology Inc. reported the following information in its 2007 annual report.

(In millions except EPS)	Total Assets	Long-Term Debt	Additions to Plant Assets	Net Income	Earnings per Share
2007	$31,471	$702	$4,032	$6,068	1.73
2006	28,880	448	4,501	6,945	1.93
2005	23,735	728	3,024	5,157	1.45
2004	17,504	400	3,550	3,566	1.01
2003	13,816	392	2,441	2,288	0.65

Required Using appropriate accounting ratios discussed in this chapter and any other ratios you think are helpful, evaluate the firm's investment decisions for the period from 2003 to 2007.

P12-17 COMPARING INVESTMENT PERFORMANCE

Objs. 4, 5

Information is provided below for **Tommy Hilfiger Corporation** and **Nike, Inc.**

	Hilfiger		Nike	
(In millions)	2004	2003	2004	2003
Total assets	$2,053	$2,028	$ 7,892	$ 6,821
Total liabilities	827	985	3,110	2,830
Revenues	1,876	1,888	12,253	10,697
Income (loss) from operations	198	(29)	1,550	1,229
Net income (loss)	132	(514)	946	474
Depreciation and amortization	77	88	299	252
Cash provided from operating activities	242	230	1,514	922
Cash used by investing activities	(84)	(72)	(947)	(216)
Cash used by financing activities	(164)	(125)	(399)	(607)
Cash used for additions to plant assets	(57)	(72)	(214)	(186)

Required

A. Compute the asset turnover, profit margin, and return on assets for each year and company.
B. Compare the effectiveness and efficiency of the two companies.
C. Compare the investing activities of the two companies over the two years and discuss your findings.

P12-18 ANALYZING ABILITY TO MEET DEBT PAYMENTS

Obj. 6

Sporting Life Inc. is a large retail chain of sporting goods stores. In a recent annual report, the following information was presented.

(In millions)	2007	2006	2005
Sales	$15,833	$15,668	$15,229
Operating income	1,455	1,341	893
Net income	662	536	266
Interest expense	304	418	499
Total assets	13,464	13,738	14,264
Long-term debt	3,057	3,919	4,606
Shareholders' equity	5,709	5,256	4,669
Cash provided by operating activities	1,690	1,573	1,220
Cash (used) by investing activities	(445)	(318)	(650)
Cash provided (used) by financing activities	(1,080)	(1,262)	(594)

Cash for investing activities was used primarily for property and equipment purchases. Cash used by financing activities was primarily to pay off long-term debt and acquire treasury stock.

Required

A. Assume that you work for an investment firm that has an opportunity to invest in notes that are part of Sporting Life's long-term debt. Write a short report in which you analyze the firm's ability to meet its debt payments, based on the information given.

(Continued)

B. Prepare a list of the most important additional pieces of information you would want before making a final decision about the investment. This list should include some accounting information; it might also include nonaccounting and nonquantitative items.

P12-19 ASSESSING CREDITWORTHINESS

Obj. 6 Year-end financial information is provided below for two companies that make baseball caps.

	Cobb Industries		Speaker Inc.	
(In millions)	**2007**	**2006**	**2007**	**2006**
Property, plant, and equipment	$283	$314	$171	$162
Total assets	392	424	259	246
Current liabilities	67	74	69	63
Long-term debt	261	264	100	104
Stockholders' equity	64	86	90	79
Asset impairment charge	(18)	—	—	—
Operating income	5	7	24	19
Interest expense	(23)	(24)	(8)	(7)

Required Study the information provided. If you were a creditor of these companies, would you be concerned about the ability of either company to repay its debts? Explain your answer.

P12-20 EXCEL IN ACTION

The Book Wermz reported sales for 2008 of $6,230,000. Cost of goods sold was 55% of sales, and operating expenses were $2,155,000. Interest expense was $190,000. Income taxes were 35% of pretax income. Total assets at the end of 2008 were $5,623,000.

Required Use the information provided to produce an income statement for The Book Wermz for the year ended December 31, 2008. Enter appropriate captions for the statement at the top of the spreadsheet and appropriate captions in column A. Enter amounts in column B. Use equations to calculate subtotals and totals. Calculate cost of goods sold as sales $\times$ 0.55 and income taxes as pretax income $\times$ 0.35.

Following the income statement, enter the total assets data and calculate asset turnover, profit margin, and return on assets. Enter captions in column A and calculations in column B. Use cell references to the income statement and total assets in these calculations.

Suppose that the company's management believes that it can increase sales by reducing product prices. Cutting the prices relative to the cost of goods sold would increase the ratio to 60%, but is expected to increase total sales to $7 million. Operating expenses and interest expense are relatively fixed and would not be affected by these changes. Total assets also would not be affected. In column C calculate the effects of the changes on the company's income statement and financial ratios. Copy the data from column B to column C and make changes as needed. Would the pricing change be advantageous to the company?

Another alternative for the company is to raise prices relative to cost of goods sold and significantly increase advertising. The increase in prices would reduce cost of goods sold to 50% of sales. The additional advertising expenses would increase operating expenses to $3 million. Total sales are expected to increase to $7.5 million. Interest expense and total assets would not be affected by these changes. In column D calculate the effects of the changes on income and the financial ratios. Would the company benefit from these changes?

P12-21 MULTIPLE-CHOICE OVERVIEW OF THE CHAPTER

1. As defined in this text, return on assets involves a comparison of total assets with
   a. net income.
   b. net income adjusted for dividends.
   c. net income adjusted for income taxes.
   d. net income adjusted for interest expense.

2. A high asset turnover indicates that a company
   a. buys and sells its long-term assets more frequently than most companies, so that it tends to operate with state-of-the-art equipment.
   b. generates a large amount of profit compared to its total assets.

c. generates a large amount of sales compared to its total assets.
d. uses fixed costs to increase net income as sales increase.

3. The substitution of fixed costs for variable costs affects which of the following most directly?
   a. Stockholders' equity
   b. Financial leverage
   c. Gross profit margin
   d. Operating leverage

4. A company with good investment opportunities normally can increase its stockholders' wealth by
   a. increasing the portion of net income paid out in dividends.
   b. investing in new assets.
   c. reducing the amount invested in new assets.
   d. reducing its rate of return on new assets.

5. Company A has a higher proportion of fixed to variable costs than Company B. Both have a positive net income. The sales revenues of both companies increased by 10%. You would expect
   a. Company A's expenses to increase more rapidly than Company B's.
   b. Company A's expenses to decrease while Company B's increase.
   c. Company A's net income to decrease while Company B's increases.
   d. Company A's net income to increase more rapidly than Company B's.

6. Company A and Company B are similar in size and in many other respects. The companies reported the following net cash flow from (used for) investing activities in their 2008 annual reports.

(In millions)	**2008**	**2007**	**2006**
Company A	$(460)	$(350)	$(265)
Company B	200	35	(80)

   From this information, you would expect
   a. Company A to be growing more rapidly than Company B.
   b. Company B to be growing more rapidly than Company A.
   c. Company B to have better investment alternatives than Company A.
   d. Company A to pay higher dividends than Company B.

7. Relative to Company A, Company B is more capital-intensive, has a higher debt to asset ratio, and pays out a smaller portion of its net income as dividends. Company A's asset growth rate has been larger than Company B's. From this information, it is likely that
   a. Company A is riskier than Company B.
   b. Company B is riskier than Company A.
   c. Company A has a higher market value than Company B.
   d. Company B has a higher market value than Company A.

8. Which of the following net cash flow patterns is typical of a company with high growth potential and strong financial performance?

	Cash Flow from Operating Activities	**Cash Flow from Investing Activities**
a.	Outflow	Outflow
b.	Outflow	Inflow
c.	Inflow	Inflow
d.	Inflow	Outflow

9. Which of the following is evidence of effective use of assets?
   a. Earning higher amounts of profit for each dollar of sales
   b. Selling long-term assets promptly when sales drop
   c. Increasing sales more rapidly than the dollar amount of additional investment
   d. Planning for assets that have high fixed cost and low variable cost, in order to make use of operating leverage

(Continued)

10. Under generally accepted accounting principles in the United States, most assets are valued on the balance sheet at
    a. cost.
    b. cost, or a lower value if they are impaired.
    c. cost, or a higher value if evidence of increase is verifiable.
    d. fair market value.

Cases

C12-1 EVALUATING INVESTMENT DECISIONS

Objs. 1, 3, 4

Selected information from **General Mills**' 2004 annual report and 10k is provided in Appendix A at the end of the text.

Required Review the annual report and write a short report in which you cover each of the following:

A. What major investing decisions did the company make from 2002 to 2004? Include decisions about disposing of as well as acquiring assets. (Hint: See note 2 to the financial statements, as well as the statement of cash flows.)
B. Evaluate the company's growth rate for total assets and net income from 2002 to 2004. (Hint: See the six-year financial summary.)
C. Compute return on assets, asset turnover, and profit margin for the company from 2002 to 2004. Does it appear that the company has made beneficial investing decisions?

C12-2 ANALYSIS OF AN ACQUISITION

Obj. 3

You are a financial analyst with a major corporation, High Hopes Company. You have been assigned the task of evaluating a potential acquisition candidate, Roll-the-Dice Inc. Selected accounting information for the two companies is presented below. Information for 2006 and 2007 reports actual company results. Results for 2008 are projected from information available at the beginning of the year.

(In millions)	2008	2007	2006
High Hopes Company			
Depreciation and amortization expense	$ 13.4	$ 13.1	$ 11.6
Operating income	46.3	42.7	37.5
Interest expense	4.9	5.1	5.5
Provision for income taxes	14.1	11.8	11.0
Net income	27.3	25.8	21.0
Total assets	305.7	292.1	274.8
Total liabilities	125.9	128.0	135.2
Total stockholders' equity	179.8	164.1	139.6
Net cash flow from operating activities	40.4	38.5	32.8
Net cash flow used for investing activities	(14.1)	(12.8)	(9.8)
Net cash flow used for financing activities	(25.3)	(25.7)	(23.0)
Roll-the-Dice Inc.			
Depreciation and amortization expense	$ 5.4	$ 5.2	$ 4.5
Operating income	22.8	19.3	12.9
Interest expense	3.7	3.5	3.0
Provision for income taxes	6.5	4.7	4.2
Net income	12.6	11.1	5.7
Total assets	114.3	111.0	93.4
Total liabilities	35.8	33.2	31.8
Total stockholders' equity	78.5	77.8	73.5
Net cash flow from operating activities	18.7	16.4	14.6
Net cash flow used for investing activities	(13.7)	(7.9)	(18.3)
Net cash flow from (used for) financing activities	(4.5)	(8.6)	3.8

The acquisition, if it were to occur, would result in High Hopes purchasing all of the common stock of Roll-the-Dice at a price of $130 million. To finance the acquisition, High Hopes plans to issue $130 million of long-term debt at 10.7% annual interest. The debt principal would be repaid in equal installments over 10 years. The interest would be paid annually on the unpaid principal. The fair market value of Roll-the-Dice's identifiable assets is $107 million. The fair market value of its liabilities is $35.8 million. Goodwill from the acquisition will not be amortized. There are no intercompany transactions between High Hopes and Roll-the-Dice. Assume that High Hopes' income tax rate is 34%.

Required Prepare a summary pro forma income statement and statement of cash flows for High Hopes for 2008, assuming it acquires Roll-the-Dice at the beginning of 2008. What recommendation would you make to High Hopes' management concerning the acquisition?

C12-3 RETURN-BASED BONUS, ETHICS, AND ACCOUNTING STANDARDS

Objs. 4, 6

Employees of the divisions of JX Controls Inc. receive a bonus of 4% of their salary in any year in which the divisional return on assets is above 10%. Toward the end of 2007, accountants for the fire alarm division projected the following year-end numbers:

Sales	$1,230,000
Cost of goods sold*	758,000
Other expenses†	322,000
Total divisional assets	1,590,000

**All products have the same gross margin.*
†All are fixed expenses.

At a meeting of divisional managers, Susan Torres, divisional vice president, told the group, "We've never received the bonus, although several other divisions have. Our employees work just as hard, and many of them really need the extra money for their families; I'd like us to get the bonus for them, as well as for ourselves. What ideas do you have for pulling it off?"

A variety of ideas were raised:

- "Let's do what we can about sales. We have an order for $40,000 in goods to be shipped in early January; could we get those out the door in December, and add that gross margin to this year's numbers?"
- "Sure—good idea. We might even accidentally overship by 20% and record the extra in this year's sales."
- "Could we slow down a bit on paying our bills? Wouldn't a few suppliers be willing to wait until January—maybe for about $50,000?"
- "We've got that old forming machine that hasn't been used for a year; it's really useless. It's on the books at $60,000 and is 70% depreciated, but it's worth only about $3,000 as scrap. Have we written it down?"
- "The projection includes that new $90,000 bending machine that just came in. We should have delayed ordering it—but we haven't booked it. Could we forget to record the machine and the payable until January?"

Required Write a short report reacting to the meeting. Determine which proposals would both be in accordance with accounting standards and actually raise return on assets. Calculate return on assets for the current projection and with the inclusion of those measures that meet these two tests. Also include your thoughts about the advantages and disadvantages of such a bonus system.

© PHOTODISC/GETTY IMAGES

Operating Activities

13

HOW DO WE ACCOUNT FOR OPERATING ACTIVITIES?

Operating activities involve selling goods and services, using assets, and using other resources, such as labor. Often these activities include transactions that occur in different fiscal periods. Accounting for these activities requires determining the appropriate period in which to recognize revenues and expenses and accounting for timing differences between when revenues and expenses are recognized and when related events occur. Determining revenues and expenses for a fiscal period sometimes requires estimates.

Food for Thought

Why is it necessary for a company to estimate revenues and expenses for a fiscal period? What factors should be considered when making the estimates? How do the estimates affect the reported financial information?

Maria, Stan, and Ellen discuss revenue and expense recognition for Favorite Cookie Company. Ellen, the vice president of finance, is aware that some of their activities will require estimates. She discusses these activities with Maria and Stan.

Ellen: *We have to make some decisions about how we will estimate some of our revenue and expense amounts.*

Stan: *Estimates? I thought accounting was all about identifying precise amounts.*

Ellen: *Actually, quite a few activities require estimation. For example, because we sell goods on credit, we will have to estimate the amount of doubtful accounts we expect each fiscal period.*

Maria: *Why can't we just write off accounts after we determine they cannot be collected?*

Ellen: *Accounting principles require that estimated amounts of doubtful accounts be recognized as expenses in the same fiscal period in which the goods were sold that created those accounts. Matching expenses with related revenues is important for proper measurement of operating results during a fiscal period.*

Stan: *Are there a lot of estimation issues we need to consider?*

Ellen: *There aren't too many for our company. A major consideration is the method we use for estimating inventory costs. Unit costs change over time, and we have to decide which costs to associate with goods sold during a period. It isn't reasonable for us to identify the exact cost of each unit we sell. Instead, we will need a systematic method of estimating that cost.*

Maria: *Does it really matter which method we use? Will it affect our income or cash flows?*

Ellen: *These decisions can affect our income statement and our cash flows, particularly as a result of their effect on tax payments. Let's examine some of these issues.*

Objectives

Once you have completed this chapter, you should be able to:

1. Identify the purpose and major components of an income statement.
2. Explain and apply rules for measuring revenues and receivables and reporting revenue transactions.
3. Describe reporting rules for inventories and cost of goods sold and compare reporting of inventories for merchandising and manufacturing companies.
4. Explain and apply rules for measuring cost of goods sold and inventories and describe the effects of income taxes on the choice of inventory estimation method.
5. Identify routine and nonroutine events that affect a company's income statement.

BASIC OPERATING ACTIVITIES

Objective 1
Identify the purpose and major components of an income statement.

The income statement reports the results of operating activities for a fiscal period on an accrual basis. Exhibit 1 provides the income statement for Favorite Cookie Company for 2007 and 2008. Early in 2008, the company expanded its operations by issuing common stock and some long-term debt. The financing was used to acquire property and plant to permit the company to produce its own cookies.

The first item on the income statement is net sales revenues. Companies with large amounts of service revenues report these in addition to sales revenues. Recall from Chapter 4, the term "operating revenues" is sometimes used to refer to sales and service revenues. Net revenues result from subtracting discounts and returns from gross revenues, as discussed in a later section. Cost of goods sold is subtracted from net sales revenue to compute gross profit. The expenses for marketing and distributing a company's products and managing its operations are subtracted from gross profit to calculate operating income. Nonoperating expenses or losses, such as interest expense, are subtracted and nonoperating income or gains are added to compute income before taxes. Income tax expense is subtracted from income before taxes to calculate net income. Finally, earnings per share is reported on a corporate income statement.

EXHIBIT 1
Income Statement for Favorite Cookie Company

For the Year Ended December 31,	2008	2007
Net sales revenue	$ 3,235,600	$ 686,400
Cost of goods sold	(1,954,300)	(457,600)
Gross profit	1,281,300	228,800
Selling, general and administrative expenses	(1,094,700)	(148,300)
Operating income	186,600	80,500
Interest expense	(20,400)	(4,800)
Pretax income	166,200	75,700
Income taxes	(49,860)	(22,710)
Net income	$ 116,340	$ 52,990
Earnings per share	$ 0.29	$ 0.13

REVENUES AND RECEIVABLES

Objective 2
Explain and apply rules for measuring revenues and receivables and reporting revenue transactions.

Operating revenues result from the sale of goods and services to customers. Operating revenues are the first items on the income statement and affect both cash and accounts receivable on the balance sheet, as illustrated in Exhibit 2. Cash received from customers is reported on the statement of cash flows, either directly, or indirectly as net income adjusted for the change in accounts receivable. Most companies recognize operating revenues at the time they transfer ownership of goods or services to customers. Ownership of most goods passes to the buyer at the time the goods are delivered or shipped to the buyer. Retail companies usually recognize revenues at the time a sale is made, when the customer takes possession of the goods. Most service companies recognize revenues at the time services are performed.

Manufacturing companies and some merchandising companies ship goods to customers. Ownership of these goods is transferred to the buyer at the location named in the sales terms. For example: When goods are shipped **FOB** (free on board) **destination**, ownership of goods is transferred to the customer when the goods are delivered (and the seller usually pays the shipping costs). When goods are shipped **FOB shipping point**, ownership passes to the customer when the goods are picked up by the shipper (and the buyer usually pays the shipping costs).

As a general rule, **revenue should be recognized when four criteria have been met:**

1. The selling company has completed most of the activities necessary to produce and sell the goods or services.
2. The selling company has incurred the costs associated with producing and selling the goods or services or can reasonably measure those costs.
3. The selling company can measure objectively the amount of revenue it has earned.
4. The selling company is reasonably sure that it is going to collect cash from the purchaser.

For most companies, these criteria have been met when goods are transferred or when services are provided to customers who pay for them or who are obligated to pay for them.

***Learning Note** - If the buyer pays for goods or services before the criteria for revenue recognition have been met, the seller recognizes **unearned revenue** (a liability). When the criteria are met, the seller recognizes the revenue and reduces the unearned revenue account.*

Special measurement and recognition issues arise when revenues are earned over an extended period, as from a long-term construction or service contract; when some customers can be expected to return a portion of goods purchased; when some customers are likely not to pay for their purchases; and when the seller provides a warranty for the goods or services sold.

Recognizing Revenue for Long-Term Contracts

Certain types of revenues create recognition problems because the activities that produce the revenues occur over more than one fiscal period. Revenues earned from long-term

EXHIBIT 2 The Effect of Sales and Services on the Financial Statements

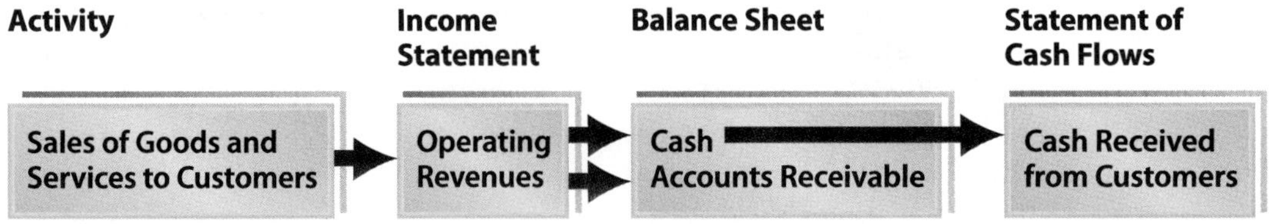

contracts often are recognized in proportion to the passage of time or in proportion to the amount of the contract that has been completed. For example, if a company contracts to provide maintenance services over a three-year period for $75,000, it might recognize $25,000 of revenue each year. In this case, the company assumes that it is going to provide approximately the same amount of service each year.

In the case of construction contracts—to construct an airplane or a building, for example—the seller usually estimates the portion of the contract that has been completed during a fiscal period. A corresponding portion of revenues then is recognized for that period. To illustrate, assume that Constructo Company contracts to construct a building for $20 million. The project will take three years to complete. At the end of 2007, the first year of the project, Constructo estimates that approximately 20% of the work has been completed. Therefore, it recognizes $4 million ($20 million × 20%) of revenue on the project for 2007. Also, it recognizes its costs associated with the project in computing net income for 2007.

CASE IN POINT

http://ingram.swlearning.com

Visit the Walt Disney Company's home page to learn more about the company.

Revenue Recognition Policies

Companies in the entertainment industry often earn revenues over an extended period as customers purchase tickets. **Walt Disney Company** is an example of this type of company. Disney's revenue recognition policy states:

> Revenue Recognition
>
> Broadcast advertising revenues are recognized when commercials are aired. Revenues from televison subscription services related to the Company's primary cable programming services are recognized as services are provided. Certain of the Company's contracts with cable service providers include annual programming commitments. In these cases, revenue subject to the commitment is deferred until the annual commitments are satisfied which generally results in revenue shifting from the first half of the year to the second.
>
> Revenues from advance theme park ticket sales are recognized when the tickets are used. Revenues from corporate sponsors at the theme parks are generally recognized over the period of the applicable agreements commencing with the opening of the related attraction.
>
> Revenues from the theatrical distribution of motion pictures are recognized when motion pictures are exhibited. Revenues from video sales are recognized on the date that video units are made widely available for sale by retailers. Revenues from the licensing of feature films and television programming are recorded when the material is available for telecasting by the licensee and when certain other conditions are met.
>
> Merchandise licensing advance and guarantee payments are recognized when the underlying royalties are earned.

(2004 Annual Report)

Sales Discounts and Returns

Revenues are reported on the income statement net of discounts and expected returns. A **discount** is a reduction in the normal sales price. Companies usually offer discounts from the normal price to encourage customers to buy large quantities of goods (a **quantity discount**) or to pay their accounts early (a **sales discount**). Discounts reduce revenues. Consequently, a company should record as revenue only the amount it actually expects to receive from a sale.

Suppose that Favorite Cookie Company sells goods priced at $5,000 to a customer on November 4, 2007, and offers a 2% discount if the customer pays in full within 10 days of the purchase. If the customer pays within the discount period (within the 10 days), Favorite Cookie Company earns revenue of $4,900 after subtracting the discount of $100 ($5,000 × 2%). If the customer does not pay within the discount period, Favorite Cookie Company earns $5,000.

Many companies record the sale at the full price ($5,000) and then deduct the discount if the customer pays within the discount period. For example, Favorite Cookie Company would record the sale as follows:

		Assets		=	Liabilities	+	Owners' Equity	
Date	Accounts	Cash	Other Assets				Contributed Capital	Retained Earnings
Nov. 4, 2007	Accounts Receivable		5,000					
	Sales Revenue							5,000

Then, if the customer pays within the discount period, the company would record this:

		Assets		=	Liabilities	+	Owners' Equity	
Date	Accounts	Cash	Other Assets				Contributed Capital	Retained Earnings
Nov. 10, 2007	Cash	4,900						
	Sales Discount							−100
	Accounts Receivable		−5,000					

The sales discount reduces the gross sales revenue of $5,000 to the net sales revenue of $4,900, the amount actually earned. The company reports net sales revenue on its income statement (see Exhibit 1).

Like sales discounts, **sales returns** are subtracted from sales revenues in reporting net operating revenues on the income statement. In certain industries, companies sell merchandise with the expectation that buyers will return some of that merchandise. Publishing companies, for example, often allow retailers to return unsold books and magazines for credit against the amount they owe.

Let's assume that Textbook Publishing Company sells $5 million of books during fiscal year 2007. It records sales revenues and accounts receivable in the amount of $5 million. From past experience, the company estimates that $500,000 of its 2007 sales will be returned in 2008. So Textbook Publishing should record an adjustment to its revenues and receivables at the end of 2007:

		Assets		=	Liabilities	+	Owners' Equity	
Date	Accounts	Cash	Other Assets				Contributed Capital	Retained Earnings
Dec. 31, 2007	Sales Returns							−500,000
	Allowance for Returns		−500,000					

Allowance for Returns reduces the amount of Accounts Receivable reported on the balance sheet, and Sales Returns reduces the amount of Sales Revenue on the income statement.

Future returns are estimated so that revenues for the fiscal period in which the sales were made can be measured more accurately. If Textbook Publishing waits until returns are received in 2008, its sales revenues for 2007 will be overstated on the 2007 income statement. A major principle of accounting is the **matching principle:** An effort is made to match revenues and expenses in the period in which they occur so that revenues, expenses, and net income are not misstated. Sales returns should be matched with the sales that result in the returns. The matching principle often requires that future events be estimated, such as the amount of future returns. These estimates are not completely accurate, but reported revenues and expenses usually are more correct when adjusted using these estimates than when no adjustment is made.

The amount of operating revenue a company reports on its income statement ($3,235,600 for Favorite Cookie Company in 2008 from Exhibit 1, for example) is the net amount of revenue earned after discounts and returns have been subtracted. Operating revenues usually are labeled "net operating revenues" or "net sales" as an indication that returns and discounts have been subtracted.

When actual goods are returned to a company, the amount of the return is written off against the allowance for returns account. Accounts Receivable is reduced by the amount of the return if the customer purchased on credit. Otherwise, a cash refund may be paid. In addition, Cost of Goods Sold and Merchandise are adjusted, assuming that the goods are put back into inventory to be resold. To illustrate, assume that Textbook Publishing received a return of $100,000 (sales price) on January 12, 2008, from a credit customer. The goods cost the company $75,000. Textbook Publishing would recognize the return in its accounts as follows:

		Assets		=	Liabilities	+	Owners' Equity	
Date	**Accounts**	**Cash**	**Other Assets**				**Contributed Capital**	**Retained Earnings**
Jan. 12, 2008	Allowance for Returns		100,000					
	Accounts Receivable		−100,000					
Jan. 12, 2008	Merchandise Inventory		75,000					
	Cost of Goods Sold							75,000

Observe that the balance of the cost of goods sold account is reduced by the cost of the goods returned.

CASE IN POINT

http://ingram.swlearning.com

Visit Time Warner Inc.'s home page to learn more about the company.

Merchandise Return Policy

Time Warner produces magazines, books, CDs, and other products. Its revenue recognition policy notes the following:

> Certain products, such as books and other merchandise, are sold to customers with the right to return unsold items. Revenues from such sales are recognized when the products are shipped, based on gross sales less a provision for future estimated returns based on historical experience.

(2004 Annual Report)

Uncollectible Accounts

Companies that sell goods and services on credit are likely to incur some bad debts. Some customers will be unable to pay for the goods and services they receive. Companies estimate the amount of receivables that are likely to be uncollectible and report this amount as a contra-asset such as **Allowance for Doubtful Accounts** or a similar title. This allowance is deducted from Accounts Receivable and the net amount of Accounts Receivable is reported on the balance sheet. The amount of the allowance is estimated at the end of fiscal periods, at least at the end of the fiscal year. For example, assume Favorite Cookie Company has a balance in Allowance for Doubtful Accounts of $1,000 at the end of its 2007 fiscal year before adjustments are made for the year. Management evaluates the company's credit sales and outstanding receivables and determines that the amount of the allowance account at the end of the year should be $5,000. Thus, the account would need to be increased by $4,000 ($5,000 balance needed − $1,000 current balance). As shown here, an expense of $4,000 would also be recognized.

		Assets		=	Liabilities	+	Owners' Equity	
Date	**Accounts**	**Cash**	**Other Assets**				**Contributed Capital**	**Retained Earnings**
Dec. 31, 2007	Doubtful Accounts Expense							−4,000
	Allowance for Doubtful Accounts		−4,000					

Companies base their estimates of the amount of doubtful accounts they expect on experience and on analysis of customer accounts. Some companies know from experience with their customers that a certain percentage of their credit sales is likely to become uncollectible. In other cases, the amount of uncollectible accounts changes in response to changes in general economic conditions. For example, during economic recessions, more people are out of work and many people earn less money than when the economy is strong. During these periods, the portion of uncollectible accounts associated with automobiles, houses, major appliances, and other goods purchased on long-term contracts increases, and sellers of these goods should increase their expected uncollectible accounts.

Many companies inspect their accounts receivable at year end to determine which accounts are at risk. Accounts that remain unpaid over a long period are more likely to be uncollectible. Consequently, companies often estimate that a higher percentage of older accounts will become uncollectible and use this information in estimating Doubtful Accounts Expense.

When a company identifies receivables as being uncollectible, those receivables are written off and the Allowance for Doubtful Accounts is adjusted. For example, assume that on February 12, 2008, Favorite Cookie Company determines that $800 owed by Home Goods Company cannot be collected because the company has gone out of business. Favorite Cookie Company would record the write off of the account as follows:

		Assets		=	Liabilities	+	Owners' Equity	
Date	**Accounts**	**Cash**	**Other Assets**				**Contributed Capital**	**Retained Earnings**
Feb. 12, 2008	Accounts Receivable		−800					
	Allowance for Doubtful Accounts		800					

The balance of the Allowance for Doubtful Accounts is reduced by the amount written off. Accounts Receivable are reduced. The specific account for Home Goods Company is written down to zero by this transaction. Note that an expense is not associated with this transaction. The expense was recorded at the end of 2007 when doubtful account expense was recorded based on estimates for the year. The sale to Home Goods Company occurred in 2007. Accordingly, the expense associated with not collecting the account was also recorded (as an estimate) in 2007.

Doubtful accounts expense is a selling expense. It results from a decision to sell goods to a customer on credit. The cost associated with this decision is the cost of a bad sales decision. Companies attempt to set credit policies so that they can avoid these costs. However, they must balance these costs with lost sales that would result if the company refused to sell goods on credit.

Warranty Costs

Companies, especially manufacturing companies, often offer warranties on goods they produce. A defective product can be returned to the seller for replacement or can be returned to the manufacturer for repair or replacement. The manufacturer incurs costs when goods are replaced or repaired, and these costs should be matched with the revenues resulting from the sale of the defective products. Therefore, companies estimate expected warranty costs each fiscal period and record these as expenses of the period in which goods were sold.

For example, when **Ford Motor Company** ships cars and trucks to dealers, it estimates the warranty costs it expects on these vehicles. These costs are recorded as expenses in the period in which revenues are recognized. Liabilities also are recognized for these expected obligations. Generally, warranty costs are combined with other financial statement items and are not reported separately in a company's financial statements. Most companies are not eager for customers or competitors to have information about their warranty costs.

As an illustration, assume Harris Company, a retailer, sells appliances with a 90-day warranty. From sales in March 2007, it estimates expected warranty costs of $12,000 will be incurred in April, May, and June to repair and replace defective parts. To match the expense with the sales, the expected costs are recorded at the end of March as follows:

		Assets		=	Liabilities	+	Owners' Equity	
Date	Accounts	Cash	Other Assets				Contributed Capital	Retained Earnings
Mar. 31, 2007	Warranty Expense							−12,000
	Warranty Obligations				12,000			

When actual warranty claims are received in April, May, and June, costs of these claims are written off through the liability account. No new expense is recognized. For example, assume that on May 15, Harris replaces a faulty motor on an appliance. The cost of the motor ($300) and labor to install the motor ($100) are recorded as follows:

		Assets		=	Liabilities	+	Owners' Equity	
Date	Accounts	Cash	Other Assets				Contributed Capital	Retained Earnings
May 15, 2007	Warranty Obligations				−400			
	Parts Inventory		−300					
	Wages Payable				100			

Revenues and expenses associated with selling goods and services should be recognized in the fiscal period in which the revenues are earned. Because the outcomes of some of the events associated with these revenues and expenses are not known until a later fiscal period, it is often necessary to estimate these effects. The estimates are recorded in the fiscal period in which the revenues are earned, and these amounts are adjusted in later periods when actual amounts are known. Doubtful accounts expense, sales returns, and warranty expense are all examples of these required estimates.

Self-Study Problem #1

Bonsai Company, a wholesaler of Asian foods, reported the following transactions for 2007:

1. Purchased $400,000 of merchandise inventory on credit.
2. Sold goods priced at $750,000 on credit.
3. The cost of merchandise sold to customers was $388,000.
4. Paid $384,000 to suppliers of merchandise.
5. Received $720,000 in cash from customers.
6. Granted $17,000 of sales discounts to customers for payment within the discount period.
7. Estimated that $10,000 of the year's credit sales would be uncollectible.
8. Wrote off $8,000 of accounts as uncollectible.

Required Using the format shown in this chapter, record each of the transactions and determine the amount of net income and net operating cash flow associated with these transactions.

The solution to Self-Study Problem 1 appears at the end of the chapter.

INVENTORIES AND COST OF GOODS SOLD

Objective 3
Describe reporting rules for inventories and cost of goods sold and compare reporting of inventories for merchandising and manufacturing companies.

To generate revenues, merchandising and manufacturing companies have to acquire or produce goods for sale. These activities increase Inventories on the balance sheet and reduce Cash and/or increase Accounts Payable, as illustrated in Exhibit 3. Once goods are sold, Inventories are reduced and Cost of Goods Sold is recognized. Therefore, the amount reported for inventories on the balance sheet is related to the amount reported for Cost of Goods Sold on the income statement and to Net Operating Cash Flow on the cash flow statement.

Accounting for Inventories and Cost of Goods Sold involves measurement and reporting rules. Measurement rules determine how costs are computed; reporting rules identify how these costs are reported on the income statement and the balance sheet.

Reporting Inventories and Cost of Goods Sold

Inventories and Cost of Goods Sold are reported by both merchandising and manufacturing companies. Inventory transactions of manufacturing companies are more complex than those of merchandising companies because manufacturing companies must account for the production of goods. We will begin with merchandising companies and then examine manufacturing companies.

EXHIBIT 3 The Effect of Inventory Transactions on the Financial Statements

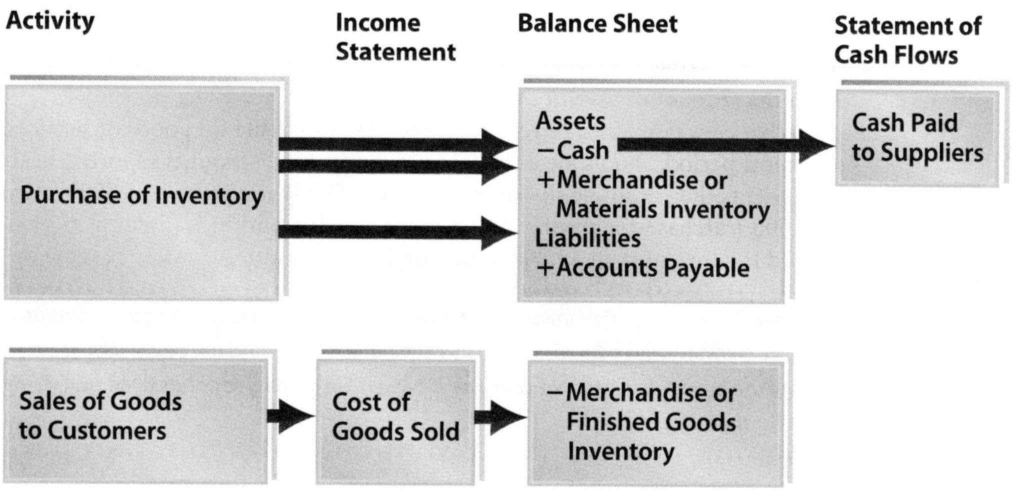

Merchandising Companies. Accounting for Merchandise Inventory is fairly simple. When it buys inventory, a company increases the balance of Merchandise Inventory. When it sells inventory, a company decreases the inventory account balance. Suppose that Favorite Cookie Company purchases $10,000 of inventory on May 4, 2007 on credit and sells $4,000 of that inventory on May 6. Favorite Cookie Company would record these transactions as follows:

		Assets		=	Liabilities	+	Owners' Equity	
Date	Accounts	Cash	Other Assets				Contributed Capital	Retained Earnings
May 4, 2007	Merchandise Inventory		10,000					
	Accounts Payable				10,000			
May 6, 2007	Cost of Goods Sold							−4,000
	Merchandise Inventory		−4,000					

The second transaction considers only the cost of the sale, not the amount of revenue earned.

A payment by Favorite Cookie Company on May 12 for half of the inventory purchased on May 4 would result in the following:

		Assets		=	Liabilities	+	Owners' Equity	
Date	Accounts	Cash	Other Assets				Contributed Capital	Retained Earnings
May 12, 2007	Accounts Payable				−5,000			
	Cash	−5,000						

This transaction reduces the payable and results in a cash payment to suppliers, which would be reported on the statement of cash flows.

In addition to recording the purchase and sales transactions that affect the financial statements, companies maintain detailed records that describe each item of inventory and the quantity purchased and sold. Those records help a company determine the number of units on hand, the demand for each item, and when to reorder. Also, these records are used for control purposes. Periodically, companies verify their inventory records by taking a physical count of inventory to make sure their records are consistent with the amount of inventory actually on hand.

Like sales discounts, **purchase discounts**, for paying for goods or services within the discount period, should be subtracted in computing amounts reported in the financial statements. For example, if Favorite Cookie Company receives a $200 discount on its $10,000 purchase for paying the account payable within a discount period, it should record the inventory at $9,800, reducing Inventory and Accounts Payable by $200.

Learning Note - The cost of inventory includes the amount paid for the goods plus any shipping costs paid by the buyer. Goods in transit between the seller and the buyer should be included as part of the buyer's inventory at year end if ownership of the goods has been transferred to the buyer at that time.

Manufacturing Companies. Accounting for the inventory transactions of a manufacturing company is more complex than that for a merchandising company because a manufacturing company produces inventory rather than purchasing it from a supplier. Most manufacturing companies separate their inventories into three categories: raw materials inventory, work-in-process inventory, and finished goods inventory. Exhibit 4 illustrates the relationships among these categories.

Raw materials inventory **includes the costs of component parts or ingredients that become part of the product being manufactured.** Raw materials are reported on the balance sheet as the cost of the components or ingredients a company has purchased that have not yet been placed into production. For example, the raw materials for Favorite Cookie Company would consist primarily of the flour, sugar, and other ingredients.

Work-in-process inventory **includes the costs of materials, labor, and overhead that have been applied to products that are in the process of being manufactured.** Materials costs are determined from the amounts paid for raw materials. As raw materials are used in the production process, the costs of these materials are transferred from Raw Materials Inventory to Work-in-Process Inventory. Labor costs, often referred to as direct labor, are added to Work-in-Process Inventory based on the amount earned by factory workers. Overhead costs include the costs of supplies, utilities, depreciation, maintenance, and similar items that are necessary for the manufacturing process.

Finished goods inventory **includes the costs of products that have been completed in the manufacturing process and are available for sale to customers.** These costs include the costs of the materials, labor, and overhead necessary to produce completed products.

EXHIBIT 4
Components of Manufacturing Inventory

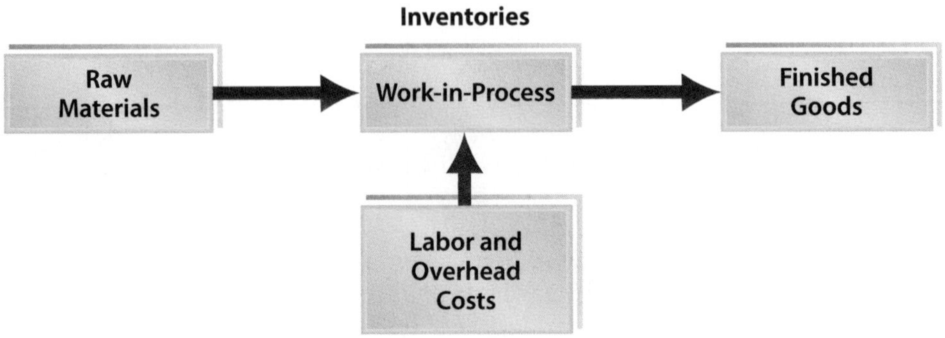

EXHIBIT 5
Computation of Manufacturing Inventory Costs

	January	February
Raw materials inventory		
Beginning balance	$ —	$ 3,000
Materials purchased during month	65,000	66,000
Material used in production	(62,000)	(67,000)
Ending balance	$ 3,000	$ 2,000
Work-in-process inventory		
Beginning balance	$ —	$ 4,000
Materials used in production	62,000	67,000
Labor costs	58,000	58,000
Overhead costs	42,000	42,000
Cost of goods completed	(158,000)	(161,000)
Ending balance	$ 4,000	$ 10,000
Finished goods inventory		
Beginning balance	$ —	$ 5,000
Cost of goods completed	158,000	161,000
Cost of goods sold	(153,000)	(163,000)
Ending balance	$ 5,000	$ 3,000

For example, assume that Favorite Cookie Company begins producing its own cookies early in January 2008. Exhibit 5 describes production activities for January and February.

At the beginning of January, Favorite Cookie Company has no manufacturing inventories. During January, the company purchases $65,000 of materials and uses $62,000 of materials. At the end of January, the company would report raw materials inventory of $3,000. That amount becomes the beginning materials inventory for February. If the company purchases $66,000 of materials in February and uses $67,000 of materials in production in February, it would report raw materials inventory of $2,000 at the end of February.

Work-in-process for January includes the costs of materials, labor, and overhead that went into production during January. The cost of goods that are completed during the month is transferred to finished goods inventory, leaving a balance of $4,000 for work-in-process inventory at the end of January. February's production begins with the $4,000 of inventory. Additional production costs of materials, labor, and overhead are added during February. The cost of completed goods is subtracted, leaving a balance of $10,000 at the end of February.

Finished goods inventory for January is the cost of goods completed during January less the cost of goods sold for the month. The ending balance of $5,000 is carried over as the beginning balance for February. The cost of goods completed during February is added and the cost of goods sold during February is subtracted, leaving a balance of $3,000 for finished goods inventory at the end of February.

Manufacturing companies do not recognize expenses for the materials, labor, and overhead used in the production process until goods are sold. Those expenses are part of the company's inventories until finished goods are sold. At that time, production costs are transferred to expense as Cost of Goods Sold. This accrual accounting procedure matches expenses with revenues in the period in which the revenues are recognized. The costs of goods that have not been sold at the end of the fiscal period are reported on the balance sheet as part of a company's inventories. Each inventory category (Raw Materials, Work-in-Process, and Finished Goods) may be reported on the balance sheet. In some cases, manufacturing companies report the amount of total inventories on the balance sheet and report the amounts of the various categories in a note.

CASE IN POINT

http://ingram.swlearning.com

Visit P&G's home page to learn more about the company.

Manufacturing Inventories

Procter & Gamble reported the following total manufacturing inventories in its 2004 annual report.

(In millions)	**2004**	**2003**
Inventories		
Raw materials	$1,191	$1,095
Work-in-process	340	291
Finished goods	2,869	2,254
Total manufacturing inventories	$4,400	$3,640

MEASURING INVENTORY

Objective 4
Explain and apply rules for measuring cost of goods sold and inventories and describe the effects of income taxes on the choice of inventory estimation method.

The examples presented in the previous sections are relatively straightforward because we assume that we know the cost of each inventory item. If a company sells 10 inventory items and each item costs $50, cost of goods sold is $500. A problem arises, however, when a company does not know the precise cost of an inventory item and the cost must be estimated. A major reason inventory costs are estimated is that the costs of merchandise, raw materials, labor, utilities, supplies, and other resources change over time.

Hydro Company sells and services agricultural irrigation equipment. On March 20, 2007, Hydro purchased 20 pump motors at $200 each. Hydro already had 8 identical motors on hand, for which it had paid $175 each. On March 22, 2007, a customer purchased one motor. Should the company record the cost of goods sold for the motor as $175 or as $200?

The decision about which cost to record ($175 or $200) affects both the income statement and the balance sheet. If $175 is used, this amount is subtracted from Merchandise Inventory and transferred to Cost of Goods Sold. All of the motors that cost $200 are left in Merchandise Inventory.

Most companies that sell products for which one unit of inventory is like other units of inventory estimate their cost of goods sold rather than trying to keep track of the cost of each individual unit. Exceptions to this practice are made when the cost of individual inventory items is large and one item is easily distinguished from another. For example, a car dealer keeps track of each car or truck in its inventory. For companies that estimate inventory costs, common methods are first-in, first-out (FIFO); last-in, first-out (LIFO); and weighted-average.

The *first-in, first-out method* assumes that the units of inventory acquired first are sold first. If Hydro used FIFO, it would record the cost of the motor sold on March 22 as $175 because this is the cost of the oldest items in Hydro's inventory.

The *last-in, first-out method* assumes that the last units of inventory acquired are the first sold. If Hydro used LIFO, it would record the cost of the motor sold on March 22 as $200 because this is the cost of the most recent items in Hydro's inventory.

The *weighted-average method* uses the average cost of units of inventory available during a period as the cost of units sold. Hydro's average inventory cost for pump motors on March 22 would be as follows:

	Units	**Cost per Unit**	**Total Cost**	
Beginning	8	$175	$1,400	
Purchased	20	200	4,000	
Total	28		$5,400	
Average cost per unit ($5,400 ÷ 28 units)				$192.86

Accordingly, Hydro would record cost of goods sold of $192.86 for the motor it sold on March 22.

Inventory estimation methods often are used even when a company knows which items of inventory are being sold. For example, Hydro could use LIFO for its motor sales even if the salesperson is sure that the motor delivered to the customer is one left over from last year. Most companies sell their oldest goods first, to avoid spoilage and obsolescence. But they may use LIFO to account for those goods anyway. LIFO often is used by companies because of its beneficial income tax effects.

Perpetual and Periodic Inventory Methods

The determination of inventory costs differs depending on whether a company uses perpetual or periodic inventory systems. *Perpetual inventory system* **refers to a system of recording cost of goods sold and updating inventory balances at the time goods are sold.** *Periodic inventory system* **refers to a system of recording cost of goods sold and updating inventory balances at the end of a fiscal period.** Because technology makes it feasible to identify costs at the time sales occur, the perpetual system is used by many companies.

Let's examine the effects of these inventory systems for Favorite Cookie Company. Suppose that the company has finished goods inventory of $3,000 at the end of February 2008. The inventory includes 150 cases of cookies at a cost of $20.00 per case. During March, the company completes a batch of 3,000 cases at a cost of $20.30 per case on March 8, a second batch of 3,000 cases at $20.60 on March 18, and a third batch of 3,000 cases at $20.90 on March 28. It shipped orders for 5,200 cases on March 20 and 3,600 cases on March 31. Exhibit 6 summarizes these events.

Perpetual System. To determine cost of goods sold using the perpetual system, calculate the cost at the time of each sale. On March 20, the company sold 5,200 cases. Using FIFO, the cost of these units would be $106,130, as shown in Exhibit 7. Using FIFO, the earliest inventory batches are sold first. Consequently, the March 1, March 8, and a portion of the March 18 batches are used in the calculation of Cost of Goods Sold.

The cost of goods sold using LIFO would be $106,460, as shown in Exhibit 7. Using LIFO, the most recent inventory layers are assumed to be sold first. Thus, for the March 20 sale, the cost of inventory from March 18 and a portion of cost of inventory from March 8 are included in cost of goods sold.

After the March 20 sale, Favorite Cookie Company would have 950 cases left in inventory. Using FIFO, the cost of these units is $20.60 per case, as shown in Exhibit 7. On March 20, a batch of 3,000 cases was produced. The company sold an additional 3,600 cases on March 31. The cost of these units using FIFO would be $74,955, as shown in Exhibit 8. The FIFO calculation assumes the units that cost $20.60 were sold along with a portion of the units from the March 28 batch.

Using LIFO, the inventory available on March 20, after the sales, included 150 cases that cost $20.00 per case and 800 cases that cost $20.30 per case. When goods are sold on March 31, the most recent goods available, those from March 28, are assumed to be sold first. Exhibit 8 shows the cost of goods sold for March 31 as $74,880, using LIFO.

EXHIBIT 6
Unit Costs and Sales for Favorite Cookie Company for March

	Units (Cases)	Unit Cost	Total Cost
March 1 Inventory	150	$20.00	$ 3,000
March 8 Batch	3,000	20.30	60,900
March 18 Batch	3,000	20.60	61,800
March 20 Sales	5,200		
March 28 Batch	3,000	20.90	62,700
March 31 Sales	3,600		
Total Cost of Goods Available for Sale			$188,400

EXHIBIT 7 Calculation of Perpetual Inventory Cost for March 20 Sales

	Units (Cases) Available	Units Sold March 20	Units Left	Unit Cost	Total Cost
FIFO Inventory Cost					
Beginning Inventory	150	150	0	$20.00	$ 3,000
March 8 Batch	3,000	3,000	0	20.30	60,900
March 18 Batch	3,000	2,050	950	20.60	42,230
Cost of Goods Sold		5,200			$106,130
Ending Inventory on March 20					
(cost from March 18)			950	20.60	$ 19,570
LIFO Inventory Cost					
Beginning Inventory	150	0	150	$20.00	$ 0
March 8 Batch	3,000	2,200	800	20.30	44,660
March 18 Batch	3,000	3,000	0	20.60	61,800
Cost of Goods Sold		5,200			$106,460
Ending Inventory on March 20					
(cost from March 1)			150	20.00	$ 3,000
(cost from March 8)			800	20.30	16,240
Total			950		$ 19,240

EXHIBIT 8 Calculation of Perpetual Inventory Cost for March 31 Sales

	Units (Cases) Available	Units Sold March 31	Units Left	Unit Cost	Total Cost
FIFO Inventory Cost					
Beginning Inventory	950	950	0	$20.60	$19,570
March 28 Batch	3,000	2,650	350	20.90	55,385
Cost of Goods Sold		3,600			$74,955
Ending Inventory on March 31					
(cost from March 28)			350	20.90	$ 7,315
LIFO Inventory Cost					
Beginning Inventory	150	0	150	$20.00	$ 0
March 8 Inventory	800	600	200	20.30	12,180
March 28 Batch	3,000	3,000	0	20.90	62,700
Cost of Goods Sold		3,600			$74,880
Ending Inventory on March 31					
(cost from March 1)			150	20.00	$ 3,000
(cost from March 8)			200	20.30	4,060
Total			350		$ 7,060

Thus, for the month of March:

	FIFO	LIFO
Total cost of goods sold	$181,085[1]	$181,340[2]
Ending inventory on March 31	7,315	7,060
Total goods available for sale during March	$188,400	$188,400

[1]($106,130 + $74,955)
[2]($106,460 + $74,880)

The weighted average method would calculate cost of goods sold based on the average cost of inventory available at the time of each sale. Exhibit 9 provides calculations for Favorite Cookie Company for March.

EXHIBIT 9
Calculation of Perpetual Average Inventory Cost for March Sales

	Units (Cases)	Unit Cost	Total Cost	Cost of Goods Sold
Beginning Inventory	150	$20.00	$ 3,000	
March 8 Batch	3,000	20.30	60,900	
March 18 Batch	3,000	20.60	61,800	
March 20 Average Cost	6,150	20.439	125,700	
March 20 Sales	5,200	20.439	106,283	$106,283
March 20 Inventory	950	20.439	19,417	
March 28 Batch	3,000	20.90	62,700	
March 31 Average Cost	3,950	20.789	82,117	
March 31 Sales	3,600	20.789	74,841	74,841
Ending Inventory	350	20.789	$ 7,276	$181,124

The company's inventory on March 20 includes 6,150 units at a combined cost of $125,700. Therefore, the average cost per unit is $20.439 ($125,700 ÷ 6,150 units). Cost of goods sold for the March 20 sale is $106,283 (5,200 units × $20.439), leaving an inventory of 950 units at a cost of $19,417 (950 units × $20.439).

When goods are sold on March 31, the average inventory cost is recalculated. March 31 inventory includes 3,950 units at a combined cost of $82,117. Therefore, the average cost per unit is $20.789 ($82,117 ÷ 3,950 units). Cost of goods sold for the March 31 sale is $74,841 (3,600 units × $20.789). Ending inventory for March is $7,276 (350 units × $20.789). Therefore, total cost of goods available for sale in March is $188,400 ($106,283 + $74,841 + $7,276), which agrees with the total under FIFO and under LIFO.

The average method is sometimes referred to as the **moving average method** when the perpetual system is used because the average unit cost is recalculated each time a sale is made based on units available at that date.

Periodic System. Using the periodic system, a company records inventory costs at the end of a fiscal period. Thus, Favorite Cookie Company would record the cost of all the goods it sold during March at the end of the month. The cost of goods sold for March would be $181,085 using FIFO and $181,340 using LIFO, as shown in Exhibit 10.

EXHIBIT 10 Calculation of Periodic Inventory Cost for March

Cost of Goods Sold for March	Units (Cases) Available	Units Sold	Units Left	Unit Cost	Total Cost
FIFO Inventory Cost					
Beginning Inventory	150	150	—	$20.00	$ 3,000
March 8 Batch	3,000	3,000	—	20.30	60,900
March 18 Batch	3,000	3,000	—	20.60	61,800
March 28 Batch	3,000	2,650	350	20.90	55,385
Cost of Goods Sold for March		8,800			$181,085[1]
Ending Inventory (from March 28)			350	20.90	$ 7,315[1]
LIFO Inventory Cost					
Beginning Inventory	150	—	150	$20.00	$ —
March 8 Batch	3,000	2,800	200	20.30	56,840
March 18 Batch	3,000	3,000	—	20.60	61,800
March 28 Batch	3,000	3,000	—	20.90	62,700
Cost of Goods Sold for March		8,800			$181,340[2]
Ending Inventory (from March 1)			150	20.00	$ 3,000
(from March 8)			200	20.30	4,060
Total			350		$ 7,060[2]

[1]**Total goods available for sale for March = $181,085 + $7,315 = $188,400.**
[2]**Total goods available for sale for March = $181,340 + $7,060 = $188,400.**

EXHIBIT 11
Calculation of Periodic Average Inventory Cost for March Sales

	Units (Cases)	Unit Cost	Total Cost
Beginning Inventory	150	$20.00	$ 3,000
March 8 Batch	3,000	20.30	60,900
March 18 Batch	3,000	20.60	61,800
March 28 Batch	3,000	20.90	62,700
Average Cost	9,150	20.59	188,400*
Cost of Goods Sold	8,800	20.59	181,193
Ending Inventory	350	20.59	$ 7,207

*Total goods available for sale in March

If the weighted average method is used, the cost of goods sold for a period is calculated from the total units available during the period and the combined cost of these units, as described in Exhibit 11. Favorite Cookie Company had 9,150 units available during March at a combined cost of $188,400. Therefore, the average cost per unit was $20.59 ($188,400 ÷ 9,150 units). Cost of goods sold for March is $181,193 (8,800 units × $20.59). Ending inventory for March is $7,207 (350 units × $20.59).

Under the periodic inventory system, as under the perpetual inventory system, all methods have the same total goods available for sale for March, $188,400.

Companies that use the periodic system may not keep track of units sold during each fiscal period. Instead, they may count the number of units available at the end of a period to determine how many units were sold. Generally, this approach is only used when it is not feasible or cost effective to keep track of units sold.

This method is frequently used for supplies or similar prepaid items for which it is not feasible to maintain detailed inventory records. For example, assume Favorite Cookie Company had 4 cases of copier paper at the beginning of March at a cost of $50 per case. During March, the company purchased 10 cases at a cost of $52 per case. A count at the end of March revealed that 2 cases remained on hand. Supplies expense and supplies on hand at the end of March could be calculated using FIFO as follows:

Beginning inventory	$ 200	4 cases × $50
Purchases	520	10 cases × $52
Supplies available	720	
Ending inventory	(104)	2 cases × $52
Supplies expense	$ 616	

Inventory Estimation and Income Taxes

The primary reason for the use of LIFO is the tax advantage LIFO provides to many companies. LIFO results in the most recent inventory costs being subtracted when computing net income. FIFO results in the oldest inventory costs being subtracted. In inflationary periods, the LIFO method usually produces a higher cost of goods sold and a lower pretax income than does the FIFO method. Accordingly, income taxes also are lower.

Exhibit 12 compares income statements for Favorite Cookie Company assuming the use of FIFO and LIFO. The LIFO column is identical to the income statement in Exhibit 1, which assumed the company used the LIFO method. If the company had used FIFO instead of LIFO, its cost of goods sold for 2008 would have been $1,946,800. The cost is lower because the company would have used the cost of its oldest inventory items when recording cost of goods sold, and the cost of most of the items it sells has increased during the year. The lower cost of goods sold results in higher gross profit, operating income, and pretax income. Selling, general, and administrative expenses and nonoperating items are not affected by the choice of inventory estimation method.

Income tax expense is higher if FIFO is used because the income tax rate Favorite Cookie Company pays on its pretax income is the same (about 30%) whether FIFO or

EXHIBIT 12
Income Statement for Favorite Cookie Company Using FIFO and LIFO Inventory Estimation

For the Year Ended December 31, 2008	FIFO	LIFO
Sales revenue	$ 3,235,600	$ 3,235,600
Cost of goods sold	(1,946,800)	(1,954,300)
Gross profit	1,288,800	1,281,300
Selling, general, and administrative expenses	(1,094,700)	(1,094,700)
Operating income	194,100	186,600
Interest expense	(20,400)	(20,400)
Pretax income	173,700	166,200
Income taxes	(52,110)	(49,860)
Net income	$ 121,590	$ 116,340

LIFO is used. Therefore, if FIFO is used, income tax expense is $52,110. If LIFO is used, income tax expense is $49,860. Consequently, if Favorite Cookie Company used FIFO, it would incur $2,250 in additional taxes compared with using LIFO. FIFO results in higher net income for Favorite Cookie Company, but it also results in higher income taxes.

INTERNATIONAL

Income tax regulations require that, in most cases, a company that uses LIFO to estimate cost of goods sold in computing its income taxes also must use LIFO to estimate cost of goods sold on its income statement. This rule, called a tax conformity rule, is unusual. Tax regulations normally permit companies to use different accounting measurement rules for estimating revenues and expenses for tax and income statement purposes. For example, a company can use accelerated depreciation for computing income taxes and straight-line depreciation for computing net income. As a result of this tax rule, a company often has to choose between reporting higher net income by using FIFO and paying lower taxes by using LIFO. Once a company chooses an inventory estimation method, it is required by GAAP to use the method consistently from year to year. A change from one method to another (from LIFO to FIFO, for example) is permitted only in infrequent circumstances when management can justify the change because of important changes in the company's business.

Learning Note - Most countries do not allow the use of LIFO. Therefore, multinational firms, including large U.S. corporations, normally use FIFO for inventories held in foreign countries even if they use LIFO for similar inventories held in the United States. Companies can use LIFO for some inventories and FIFO or the weighted-average method for others.

It is important to understand why many companies use LIFO even though it results in lower net income. To understand the reasoning, consider Favorite Cookie Company's operating cash flows. Although the choice of inventory method affects Cost of Goods Sold on the income statement, it has no effect on the amount of cash paid to suppliers. Assume the company paid $2 million for the inventory it purchased in 2008. Regardless of whether the company uses FIFO or LIFO, it still pays the same amount for this inventory. Also, the amounts of cash collected from customers and paid for other resources consumed in 2008 are the same, regardless of which inventory method the company uses. The only effect the company's inventory method has on its cash flows is the amount of income taxes it pays. Therefore, using LIFO reduces cash payments for taxes and leaves the company with more net cash flow from operating activities.

Remember that net income is an accrual-basis estimate of the net amount of cash a company will receive once it has collected cash from customers and paid for all resources consumed in operating activities. If Favorite Cookie Company uses FIFO, its net income is higher than if it uses LIFO, but its net operating cash flow is lower. Therefore, the higher income results from accounting estimation, not from real economic activity that creates additional resources for the company. Thus, if the company used FIFO, it might look as if it were performing better than if it used LIFO, but the appearance is deceiving. Actually, the company is performing better if it uses LIFO because of the lower tax payments. To understand and interpret net income, it is important to understand accounting measurement rules.

Companies that use FIFO normally do so for sound economic reasons. For example, if the cost of inventory decreases over time because of improvements in technology or increased competition, FIFO produces a tax advantage over LIFO. The oldest items in inventory cost more than the newest items. Including the cost of the oldest items in cost of goods sold reduces taxable income and income taxes. Accordingly, computer and other high-technology companies that experience decreases in inventory costs normally use FIFO.

Lower of Cost or Market Inventory Valuation. GAAP require companies to compare the costs determined through inventory estimation methods with the current market cost of the inventories on hand at the end of a fiscal year. **If current market costs are below the costs resulting from the use of an estimation method such as FIFO or LIFO, the inventories must be written down to the current market costs. This requirement is referred to as the *lower of cost or market inventory* rule.** Such writedowns are more common when FIFO is used because FIFO normally results in a higher estimated inventory value at year end. Therefore, FIFO inventory costs are more likely than LIFO costs to be higher than market.

A problem with reporting inventory at the lower of cost or market is that the market value of inventories is not always easy to determine. GAAP specify a procedure for computing market value that considers the current replacement cost and the amount a company expects to receive from selling the inventory less the profit it expects to earn from the inventory. Once a market value has been determined, it is compared with the cost of inventory. If the market value is less than cost, the inventory is written down to market.

Learning Note - An excess of market value over cost is not recognized through a valuation adjustment. This is another example of the conservatism of accounting measurement.

A writedown results in a loss that is recognized in the period in which the inventory decreases in value. To illustrate, assume that Tucker Company, which sells electronic equipment through its retail stores, acquired $500,000 of merchandise on August 18, 2007. By December 31, 2007, the end of the company's fiscal year, it had sold $300,000 of the merchandise. It was having difficulty selling the remaining $200,000 of merchandise because a competitor was marketing newer products at lower prices. Tucker estimated that the market value of its remaining inventory was $140,000 on December 31. Accordingly, it would recognize the decline in market value as follows:

		Assets		=	Liabilities	+	Owners' Equity	
Date	**Accounts**	**Cash**	**Other Assets**				**Contributed Capital**	**Retained Earnings**
Dec. 31, 2007	Loss on Inventory							−60,000
	Merchandise Inventory		−60,000					

Comparing Inventory Costs among Companies

GAAP require companies to disclose the methods they use to measure inventories and cost of goods sold. GAAP also require companies that use LIFO to disclose the effect of the method on the reported value of inventory. For example, **International Paper Co.** reported in its annual report for the fiscal year ended in 2004 that it used LIFO to determine most of its inventory costs. It also reported that these inventory costs were $170 million lower in 2004 than if FIFO had been used. International Paper's cost of goods sold was higher using LIFO. International Paper used LIFO because of its tax advantages. Furthermore, managers are aware that investors, creditors, and other users of accounting information who understand accounting methods recognize that higher net income is not beneficial unless it results from real economic improvement in a company's performance. Managers who use accounting methods to dress up their earnings to make them look better than they really are often lose the trust of investors and other users of financial statements when they learn of this type of behavior.

Case In Point

http://ingram.swlearning.com

Visit WorldCom's home page to learn more about the company.

The Importance of Reliable Accounting Information

WorldCom Inc. revealed in June 2002 that it had understated expenses by approximately $4 billion during 2001 and 2002 and that the company would have reported net losses during this period if the expenses had been stated correctly. The company's stock price dropped to around 9¢ per share after the information was released. At the beginning of 2002, the stock was trading at approximately $14 per share.

The FIFO, LIFO, and weighted-average methods are used by both merchandising and manufacturing companies. In recent years, however, many manufacturing companies have tried to reduce their inventories. Those companies buy materials as they are needed, "just in time" to be used in the manufacturing process. Materials are acquired at a rate sufficient to meet orders without accumulating large amounts of inventories. Companies that use just-in-time manufacturing procedures report relatively small amounts of inventory, and they expense almost all of their manufacturing costs each period as part of the cost of goods sold. For these companies, the method used to estimate inventory is less important than it is for companies with large inventories.

Self-Study Problem #2

Fashion Mart is a clothing retailer. During 2007, the company recorded $28 million of cost of goods sold. If it had used LIFO, it would have reported $30 million of cost of goods sold. The company's income tax rate was 35%. Sales revenue for the year was $45 million, and other expenses were $8 million.

Required

A. What would the difference in Fashion Mart's net income and cash flow from operating activities have been if it had used LIFO instead of FIFO in 2007?

B. What factors should the company consider in deciding which inventory estimation method to use?

The solution to Self-Study Problem 2 appears at the end of the chapter.

OTHER OPERATING ACTIVITIES AND INCOME STATEMENT ITEMS

In addition to operating revenues and cost of goods sold, operating expenses, other revenues and expenses, income taxes, and special items affect a company's income statement. The next two sections describe items that are reported in each of these categories.

Operating Expenses

Objective 5
Identify routine and nonroutine events that affect a company's income statement.

Most operating expenses other than cost of goods sold are period costs. Period costs are expensed in the fiscal period in which they occur. These costs usually reduce cash or other current assets or increase current liabilities on the balance sheet. The use of cash is a cash outflow on the statement of cash flows. Exhibit 13 illustrates these relationships.

EXHIBIT 13 The Effect of Period Costs on the Financial Statements

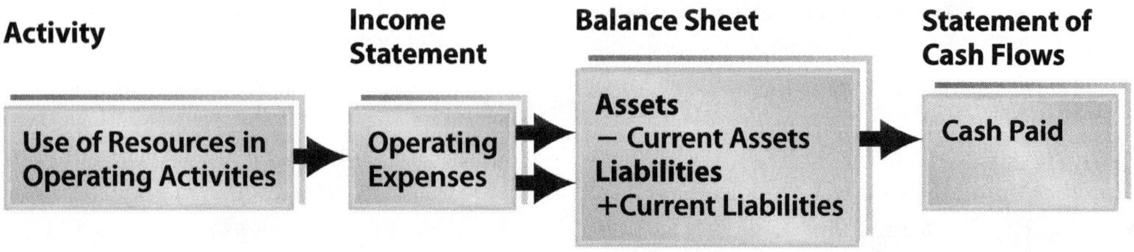

For most companies, period expenses result from marketing, research and development, and general administrative activities. Marketing costs include the costs of advertising, direct selling and distributing, depreciation of assets used primarily in selling activities, and the salaries and commissions of the sales force. Research and development costs are the costs of creating new products and production processes. Administrative costs include the depreciation of plant assets used in administrative activities (office buildings and equipment) and the salaries of managers and office workers.

The costs of certain operating activities are always expensed in the period in which the activities occur and resources are consumed. For example, GAAP require that research and development costs be expensed when they occur because of uncertainty about the future benefits to a company of these activities. In most cases, cash is paid for resources used in operating activities at about the time they are consumed. Accordingly, companies seldom use long-term debt (bonds or notes payable) to finance these activities.

The costs of other operating activities are expensed when certain events occur, which may be long before cash payments are made. As a result, long-term liabilities are associated with these items. A primary example is deferred compensation. Deferred compensation results when a company agrees to pay employee retirement benefits. These benefits are earned by employees as they work for the company. Therefore, the company recognizes expenses each period as the benefits are earned. Payments may be deferred for years, however, until benefits are paid to employees after they retire. Consequently, companies often record long-term liabilities associated with these future payments. The last section of this chapter describes deferred compensation expenses and liabilities in more detail.

Corporations often report operating expenses on one line on their income statements (see Exhibit 1 on page 477). Exceptions are made for some items, however. For example, GAAP require companies to report separately any unusual revenues or expenses that are material in amount. Separate reporting of these items calls attention to them. Among these types of items are expenses associated with restructuring a company's operations. Restructuring occurs when a company eliminates certain products, closes facilities, reduces its labor force, or sells off nonproductive assets. **International Paper**, for example, reported restructuring charges of $211 million for its fiscal year ended in 2004. These charges were associated with workforce reductions and facilities consolidations. These items are reported separately because they are not ordinary operating activities. Certain other expenses that are important to a company's operating activities—research and development expenses and depreciation expenses, for instance—also must be disclosed, either separately on the income statement or in notes to the financial statements. The last section of this chapter considers other income and expense items that often appear in corporate financial statements or notes to the statements.

Other Revenues and Expenses

Other revenues include interest and other investment income, such as dividends or gains from the sale of stocks and bonds. Other expenses include interest on short-term and long-term debt, including interest on capital lease obligations. These amounts are accrued. The amount of revenue reported is the amount earned, regardless of whether cash has been received. The amount of expense reported is the amount of obligation incurred during the current fiscal year, regardless of whether cash has been paid.

As shown in Exhibit 1, Favorite Cookie Company reported interest expense of $20,400. Items of this type are not part of the company's normal operating activities. Accordingly, they are reported after "operating income" to distinguish them from operating revenues and expenses. These activities are reported as part of the operating activities section of the statement of cash flows, however, because they are reported on the income statement.

Income Taxes

The income statement reports the amount of income taxes that a company would incur if its pretax income were all taxable in the current fiscal year. To determine the income tax expense reported on the income statement, most companies simply multiply their pretax income times the corporate tax rate. This rate includes federal and state income taxes and is adjusted for foreign taxes for multinational corporations. Consequently, the rate is not the same for all companies. The federal corporate tax rate in the United States was 35% on taxable income over $18.3 million in 2005. State and foreign tax rates vary.

For many companies, net income is the amount left after income taxes are deducted from pretax income. For other companies, special items (discussed in the next section) that affect net income are reported after income taxes.

Nonrecurring Gains and Losses

Certain gains and losses are reported separately on a company's income statement after the calculation of income associated with normal business activities. These items are reported separately because they are not expected to recur. The two types of nonrecurring items reported separately are discontinued operations and extraordinary items.

Discontinued operations **are product lines or major parts of a company from which the company will no longer derive income because it has sold or closed the facilities that produced the product line or that included that part of the company.** Two types of gains or losses associated with discontinued operations are reported. One is the gain or loss associated with operations that are being discontinued. Another is the gain or loss associated with the sale of the discontinued facilities.

For example, assume Beverly Company manufactures boats and sporting equipment. It decides to dispose of its boating division in 2007. On September 30, 2007, the company sells the division at a loss of $3 million, after taxes. From January 1 to September 30, 2007, the division earned a profit of $1.2 million, after taxes. The company would report these items separately on its income statement for the fiscal year ended December 31, 2007, as follows:

Income before taxes	$10,000,000
Provision for income taxes	(2,600,000)
Income before discontinued operations	7,400,000
Loss on sale of discontinued operations, net of tax effect of $850,000	(3,000,000)
Operating profit of discontinued operations, net of tax effect of $420,000	1,200,000
Net income	$ 5,600,000

Nonrecurring items are reported net of the tax effect associated with that item because if the nonrecurring item had not occurred, the associated tax effect would not have occurred either. Income taxes associated with normal business activities are reported separately as provision for income taxes or income tax expense. The tax effect usually offsets a reported gain or loss. A gain results in additional taxes. A loss results in tax savings because the loss can be deducted from other taxable income.

CASE IN POINT

http://ingram.swlearning.com

Visit General Motors' home page to learn more about the company.

Nonrecurring items are common in corporate income statements. As an example, **General Motors** reported the following information in its 2004 Income Statement (dollars in millions):

	2004	2003	2002
Income from continuing operations	2,805	2,862	1,975
(Loss) from discontinued operations	—	(219)	(239)
Gain on sale of discontinued operations	—	1,179	—
Net income	2,805	3,822	1,736

Extraordinary items **are gains or losses that are both unusual and infrequent for a particular company.** Losses associated with natural disasters often are reported as extraordinary items. The key to identifying those that are extraordinary is whether or not the event rarely occurs. For example, damage caused by an earthquake in California would not be considered an extraordinary loss since earthquakes are not rare in that area. However, damage caused by an earthquake in Nebraska might be considered extraordinary since that would be a rare event. Like discontinued operations, extraordinary items are reported net of taxes.

Net income is the amount earned by a company's stockholders (both preferred and common stockholders) during a fiscal period. **The amount earned by common stockholders is known as** *net income available for common stockholders* and is equal to net income minus any dividends paid to preferred stockholders. For example, if Harris Company reported net income of $156,000 and paid $13,000 in preferred dividends in 2007, its net income available for common stockholders would be $143,000 ($156,000 of net income − $13,000 of preferred dividends).

When a company reports nonrecurring items on its income statement, it also reports earnings per share separately for these items. In addition, earnings per share is based on income available for common stockholders. If Harris reported an extraordinary loss of $7,000 and had 20,000 shares of common stock outstanding throughout 2007, it would report earnings per share as follows:

Income before extraordinary items	$7.50 ($163,000 − $13,000) ÷ 20,000
Extraordinary loss (net of tax effect of $3,000)	(0.35) $7,000 ÷ 20,000
Net income	$7.15 ($156,000 − $13,000) ÷ 20,000

Self-Study Problem #3

King Company, a manufacturer of mattresses, reported the following items on its income statement for 2007.

A. Net operating revenues, $845,000
B. Cost of goods sold, $320,000
C. Selling and administrative expenses, $280,000
D. Research and development expenses, $78,000
E. Net interest expense, $4,000
F. Provision for income taxes, $50,000

G. Current year loss from discontinued operations of $30,000, net of tax benefit of $10,000
H. Loss from sale of discontinued operations of $100,000, net of tax benefit of $30,000
I. Cumulative effect (gain) of change in accounting principle of $120,000, net of tax of $40,000
J. Preferred stock dividends, $60,000

The company had 10,000 shares of common stock outstanding throughout the fiscal year.

Required Compute each of the following:

A. Operating income
B. Income (loss) from continuing operations, before taxes
C. Income (loss) before discontinued operations and the cumulative effect of the accounting change
D. Net income (loss)
E. Net income (loss) available for common shareholders
F. Earnings per share for continuing operations
G. Earnings per share for discontinued operations
H. Earnings per share for the cumulative effect of the accounting change
I. Earnings per share for net income (loss)

The solution to Self-Study Problem 3 appears at the end of the chapter.

OTHER TOPICS

This section describes three types of items that may appear on companies' income statements.

Equity Income

Equity income is income that a company earns using the equity method of accounting for investments in other companies (see Chapter 11). For example, assume that Alpha Company owns 40% of Beta Company's common stock and Beta reports net income of $10 million in 2007. Alpha would report $4 million ($10 million × 40%) of Beta's income as equity income on its 2007 income statement.

Noncontrolling Interest in Income

As discussed in Chapter 4, consolidated financial statements report the combined activities of a parent corporation and its subsidiaries as the operations of one company. When the parent owns less than 100% of a subsidiary's common stock, the portion it does not own is known as noncontrolling (or minority) interest. If Alpha Company owns 80% (the controlling interest) of Delta Company, the remaining 20% is noncontrolling interest. The portion of the subsidiary's net income attributable to noncontrolling interest is reported on the income statement as minority interest in income of consolidated subsidiaries. This amount is subtracted (assuming positive income) or added (assuming a loss) in computing net income because it is a portion of subsidiary income that has not been earned by the parent.

As an example, **International Paper** reported the following information on its 2004 income statement (in millions):

Earnings From Continuing Operations Before Income Taxes and Minority interest	$746
Income tax provision (benefit)	206
Minority interest expense, net of taxes	62
Earnings From Continuing Operations	478
Discontinued operations, net of taxes and minority interest	(513)
Net Earnings (Loss)	$ (35)

Deferred Compensation

Some operating expenses are not disclosed separately on the income statement but are described in detail in notes to the statement. For example, deferred employee compensation expenses are a subject of considerable disclosure by some companies. Deferred compensation involves retirement benefits, such as pensions and health-care benefits, provided to employees once they retire. If companies agree to provide these benefits, employees earn the benefits over the course of their working careers. The amount of benefits earned is determined by the wages employees earn and the length of time they work for a company. Consequently, companies incur expenses for these future benefits during the working careers of their employees.

To illustrate, assume that Alpha Company determines that the amount of benefits earned by employees at the end of 2007 is $60 million. This amount is referred to as the company's projected benefit obligation. If the fair market value of the assets Alpha has set aside to meet this obligation is $50 million, the company would report a pension liability of $10 million.

Projected benefit obligation	$60
Fair value of plan assets	50
Pension liability	$10

In addition to the liability, Alpha will report an expense associated with benefits earned by employees during 2007. Assume that benefits earned amounted to $8 million and earnings on pension plan assets amounted to $6 million. Alpha would report a net pension expense of $2 million.

Service cost (benefits earned)	$8
Return on plan assets	6
Net pension expense	$2

The calculation of deferred compensation costs is complex because it requires estimation of future benefits that will be earned by employees after they retire. Thus, a company must estimate how long employees will work, what amounts they will earn in the future, and how long they will receive benefits once they retire. The present values of these amounts then are estimated as a basis for determining the amount of funding currently required.

THINKING BEYOND THE QUESTION

HOW DO WE ACCOUNT FOR OPERATING ACTIVITIES?

This chapter considered the estimation and reporting of revenues and expenses. A company's income statement is affected by estimates of sales returns, doubtful accounts, warranty costs, inventory costs, and similar items. Also, it is affected by whether revenues and expenses require separate reporting and whether they are associated with recurring or nonrecurring activities. Why should stockholders and other decision makers care about estimation methods and in which part of the income statement a company reports its business activities?

Self-Study Problem Solutions

SSP13-1

		Assets		= Liabilities	+	Owners' Equity	
Item	**Accounts**	**Cash**	**Other Assets**			**Contributed Capital**	**Retained Earnings**
1.	Merchandise Inventory		400,000				
	Accounts Payable			400,000			
2.	Accounts Receivable		750,000				
	Sales Revenue						750,000
3.	Cost of Goods Sold						−388,000
	Merchandise Inventory		−388,000				
4.	Accounts Payable			−384,000			
	Cash	−384,000					
5.	Cash	720,000					
	Accounts Receivable		−720,000				
6.	Sales Discounts						−17,000
	Accounts Receivable		−17,000				
7.	Doubtful Accounts Expense						−10,000
	Allowance for Doubtful Accounts		−10,000				
8.	Allowance for Doubtful Accounts		8,000				
	Accounts Receivable		−8,000				

Income	
Gross sales revenue	$750,000
Sales discounts	−17,000
Net sales revenue	$733,000
Cost of goods sold	−388,000
Doubtful accounts expense	−10,000
Net income	$335,000

Cash Flow (Direct Method)	
Cash received from customers	$720,000
Cash paid to suppliers	384,000
Net operating cash flow	$336,000

Cash Flow (Indirect Method)	
Net income	$335,000
Increase in net receivables	−3,000
Increase in merchandise	−12,000
Increase in accounts payable	16,000
Net operating cash flow	$336,000

SSP13-2

A.

(In millions)	**FIFO**	**LIFO**
Sales revenue	$ 45.00	$ 45.00
Cost of goods sold	(28.00)	(30.00)
Other expenses	(8.00)	(8.00)
Pretax income	$ 9.00	$ 7.00
Income tax expense (35%)	(3.15)	(2.45)
Net income	$ 5.85	$ 4.55

Fashion Mart's cost of goods sold would have been $2 million larger using LIFO rather than FIFO. As a result, its net income would have been $1.3 million ($5.85 − $4.55) less if it had used LIFO. However, it would have incurred $0.7 million ($3.15 − $2.45) less in income taxes if it had used LIFO. Therefore, its net cash flow from operating activities would have been $0.7 million greater if it had used LIFO.

B. If Fashion Mart expects the costs of its inventory items to increase over time, LIFO will result in lower income taxes than FIFO. Therefore, the company will have higher net operating cash flow using LIFO. On the other hand, if the costs of inventory items are likely to decrease over time (perhaps because of improved production processes or greater competition among suppliers), FIFO will result in lower income taxes and higher net operating cash flow.

SSP13-3

	Net operating revenues	$845,000
	Cost of goods sold	(320,000)
	Selling and administrative expenses	(280,000)
	Research and development expenses	(78,000)
A.	Operating income	$167,000
	Net interest expense	(4,000)
B.	Income from continuing operations, before taxes	$163,000
	Provision for income taxes	(50,000)
C.	Income before discontinued operations and cumulative effect of accounting change	$113,000
	Discontinued operations:	
	Current period loss, net of tax of $10,000	(30,000)
	Loss from sale of discontinued operations, net of tax of $30,000	(100,000)
	Cumulative effect of change in accounting principle, net of tax of $40,000	120,000
D.	Net income	$103,000
	Preferred dividends	(60,000)
E.	Net income available for common shareholders	$ 43,000
	Earnings per share:	
F.	Continuing operations [($113,000 − 60,000) ÷ 10,000 shares]	$ 5.30
G.	Discontinued operations ($130,000 ÷ 10,000 shares)	(13.00)
H.	Cumulative effect of accounting change ($120,000 ÷ 10,000 shares)	12.00
I.	Net income available for common shareholders [($103,000 − $60,000) ÷ 10,000 shares]	$ 4.30

Define Terms and Concepts Defined in This Chapter

discontinued operations (497)
extraordinary items (498)
finished goods inventory (486)
first-in, first-out (FIFO) method (488)
last-in, first-out (LIFO) method (488)
lower of cost or market inventory (494)
net income available for common stockholders (498)
periodic inventory system (489)
perpetual inventory system (489)
raw materials inventory (486)
weighted-average method (488)
work-in-process inventory (486)

Review Summary of Important Concepts

1. The income statement reports the results of operating activities on an accrual basis.
2. Revenues result from the sale of goods and services to customers and increase cash and/or accounts receivable.
   a. Revenues should be recognized when all of the following events have occurred:
      (1) The seller has completed most activities necessary to produce and sell its products.
      (2) The seller has incurred the costs necessary to produce and sell its products or can reasonably estimate those costs.
      (3) The seller can measure objectively the amount of revenue it has earned.
      (4) The seller is reasonably sure of collecting cash from the buyer.

   b. Revenues from long-term contracts are recognized each fiscal period in proportion to the passage of time or the amount of work covered by the contract that has been completed.
   c. Sales discounts and returns are deducted from gross revenues in computing the amount of net revenue reported on the income statement.
   d. Uncollectible accounts expense is estimated each fiscal year to match the cost of expected doubtful accounts of customers with the revenues that resulted in the doubtful accounts.
   e. Warranty expenses are estimated each fiscal year to match these costs with revenues that resulted in the costs.

3. Companies purchase inventories, which are recorded as assets and are expensed as cost of goods sold when the inventory is sold to customers.
   a. Merchandise companies account for the purchase and sale of merchandise.
   b. Manufacturing companies account for raw materials inventories and for work-in-process and finished goods inventories, which include the costs of materials, direct labor, and manufacturing overhead.

4. Most companies estimate inventory and cost of goods sold amounts using one of three methods.
   a. First-in, first-out (FIFO) assumes that the units of inventory acquired first are sold first.
   b. Last-in, first-out (LIFO) assumes that the units of inventory acquired most recently are sold first.
   c. Weighted-average uses the average cost of inventory available to determine the cost of units sold.
   d. Perpetual inventory systems, which recognize cost of goods sold as inventory is sold, are used by most companies. Periodic inventory systems, which determine cost of goods sold from a count of inventory on hand at the end of a period, are used when the costs of perpetual systems exceed the benefits of timely inventory information.
   e. LIFO is used by many companies that experience increases in inventory costs over time because it results in lower income taxes and, therefore, higher net operating cash flow.
   f. Companies that use LIFO for determining their income taxes also must use LIFO in preparing their financial statements.
   g. If the market value of inventory at the end of a fiscal period is lower than the cost of the inventory, the inventory should be written down to market value, regardless of which inventory estimation method is used.

5. The income statement reports the effects of other operating activities.
   a. Operating expenses usually are period costs that reduce cash and/or increase liabilities.
   b. Some costs, such as research and development, are always expensed in the period in which they occur.
   c. Some activities, such as deferred compensation, are expensed as benefits are earned, though costs associated with providing the benefits are not incurred until years after the expenses are recognized.
   d. Income taxes are recorded by corporations based on federal, state, and foreign tax rates.

6. Nonrecurring items are reported after ordinary income and income taxes on the income statement and are reported net of tax effects.

7. Certain activities often are reported on the income statement or in notes to the financial statements.
   a. Equity income is income a company earns using the equity method of accounting for investments in other companies.
   b. Noncontrolling interest income is the portion of a subsidiary's net income that is allocated to noncontrolling interests (owners of the subsidiary other than the parent corporation).
   c. Deferred compensation arrangements often require a company to recognize a liability and expense for benefits earned by employees.

Questions

Q13-1 *Obj. 1* If the purpose of the income statement is to report the results of operating activities, why is there a section on the statement of cash flows that reports the results of operating activities?

Q13-2 *Obj. 1* Why is an income statement divided into so many different categories? Couldn't all the revenues and all the expenses each be totaled and then subtracted from each other to determine net income? Wouldn't this make accounting easier to learn?

Q13-3 *Obj. 1* A friend tells you, "I just ignore the income statement when I'm making an investment decision. All I care about is the cash, so that the company can pay me dividends. The balance sheet tells me about the cash the company's got; the cash flows statement tells me about its changes in cash. Who cares about the income statement? It's just a bunch of inaccurate stuff loaded with estimates." Do you agree with your friend's statements about the nature of the income statement and about its lack of importance? Explain why or why not.

Q13-4 *Obj. 2* When goods are sold FOB shipping point, the buyer usually pays the freight cost. Does this make sense? Why or why not?

Q13-5 *Obj. 2* Sales discounts and sales returns are accounted for as reductions of revenue. If they were accounted for as expenses, wouldn't the effect on net income be the same? Why not just treat sales discounts and sales returns as expenses?

Q13-6 *Obj. 3* Gross profit results from a company's transactions with its customers and suppliers. What types of transactions affect gross profit? How does the accounting for timing differences between cash flow and accrual measurements of these transactions affect financial statements?

Q13-7 *Obj. 3* At a meeting of your manufacturing team, a coworker groans: "We were working so hard to get the income for our bonus this year. Then they got all that raw material inventory in—and even paid for it. We don't need it yet. Why didn't they wait until January?" Will the raw materials inventory affect this year's income? Does it matter whether it was paid for this year or in January? Explain your answers.

Q13-8 *Obj. 3* On December 28, Hadley Company purchased goods FOB destination at a cost of $38,000. The goods arrived at Hadley's warehouse and were unloaded on January 5. Hadley's bookkeeper is unsure whether these goods should be included in merchandise inventory on the December 31 balance sheet. Should they? Why or why not?

Q13-9 *Obj. 4* A friend notes that when a company uses an accounting method such as LIFO, FIFO, or weighted-average, it is merely estimating (guessing) about the amount of inventory on hand. Is this true?

Q13-10 *Obj. 4* Some corporations use FIFO to estimate their inventory costs. Others use LIFO. What issues are important to this decision? What effect can the choice have on a company's net income and cash flow from operating activities?

Q13-11 *Obj. 4* When inventory prices are rising, the LIFO method yields lower net income and lower values for ending inventory than does FIFO. The opposite is true when prices are declining. Why is this the case?

Q13-12 *Obj. 4* GAAP require companies to report inventories on a lower of cost or market basis. What is the purpose of this measurement rule? What effect does it have on a company's financial statements?

Q13-13 *Obj. 5* You are aware that GAAP require expenditures for research and development to be charged to expense when incurred. This implies that such expenditures do not provide any benefit to future accounting periods. Do research and development expenditures have future economic benefit? If not, why not? If so, why might GAAP require companies to account for them as if they did not?

Q13-14 *Obj. 5* You are an investor in the common stock of Malapoosa Company. You notice in the firm's most recent annual report that net income was $3.75 million but that the net income available for common stockholders was only $3.0 million. Explain the difference between the two amounts.

Q13-15 *Obj. 5* An acquaintance with an interest in investing says, "Earnings per share is so complicated! I really only want one number—how much the company earned on my investment. But this company has earnings per share on income from continuing operations, on a discontinued segment, and on an extraordinary item, and then, finally, on net income. Which number is most important to me, as an investor?" Answer your acquaintance.

Exercises

E13-1 Write a short definition of each of the terms listed in the *Terms and Concepts Defined in This Chapter* section.

E13-2 *Obj. 1* At December 31, 2007, the general ledger of Hoffman Electric had the following account balances. All adjusting entries (except for income taxes at 35%) have been made. The company had 10,400 shares of common stock outstanding during the year.

Accounts payable	$ 8,950	Equipment	$ 80,300
Accounts receivable	14,970	Gain on sale of land	4,800
Accrued liabilities	21,000	Interest expense	1,420
Accumulated depreciation	15,300	Merchandise	18,465
Advertising expense	9,968	Land	30,000
Cash	9,530	Retained earnings*	57,984
Common stock	36,000	Sales revenue	260,772
Cost of goods sold	102,690	Utilities expense	9,002
Depreciation expense	13,510	Wages expense	59,780

***Balance at January 1, 2007**

Prepare an income statement in good form. (Hint: See Exhibit 1.)

E13-3 *Obj. 1* An excerpt from **Alcoa**'s 2004 Statement of Consolidated Income is provided below.*

Statement of Consolidated Income
(In millions, except per-share amounts)

For the year ended December 31	**2004**
Sales	$23,478
Other income, net	289
	23,767
Cost of goods sold	18,623
Selling, general, administrative, and other expenses	1,284
Research and development expenses	182
Provision for depreciation, depletion and amortization	1,204
Interest expense	270
	21,563
Income from continuing operations before taxes on income	2,204
Provision for taxes on income	557
Income from continuing operations before minority interests' share	1,647
Less: Minority interests' share	245
Income from continuing operations	1,402
Loss from discontinued operations	(92)
Net Income	$ 1,310

(Continued)

Earnings (loss) per Share	
Basic:	
Income from continuing operations	$1.61
Loss from discontinued operations	(0.11)
Net income	$1.50
Diluted:	
Income from continuing operations	$1.60
Loss from discontinued operations	(0.11)
Net income	$1.49

***Minor changes have been made to simplify the presentation.**

Briefly explain each item presented on the income statement. (Minority interest may be ignored if you are not studying the Other Topics section at the end of the chapter.) How much gross profit did Alcoa report for 2004?

E13-4 *Obj. 2* San Miguel Company manufactures specialized industrial equipment. The equipment often is sold under credit terms that provide for payment over a two- or three-year period. A substantial prepayment is required before equipment is manufactured. The purchaser accepts title to the equipment at the time it is received. San Miguel also sells service contracts on the equipment it sells. These multiyear contracts stipulate that San Miguel will provide periodic maintenance on the equipment and will repair the equipment if it breaks down. Explain (a) when San Miguel should recognize revenue from its equipment sales and (b) when it should recognize service contract revenue. In each case, explain why this revenue timing is proper.

E13-5 *Obj. 2* Goodman Company sold merchandise during its 2007 fiscal year. The total sales price of the merchandise was $30 million. Because of quantity sales discounts, the company billed its customers $29.1 million for the merchandise. Goodman sells goods to retailers who have a right to return the merchandise within 90 days if it does not sell. Goodman expects a return rate of 6% of the amount sold. How much revenue should Goodman recognize for 2007? Justify your answer.

E13-6 *Obj. 2* At year-end 2007, Fenton Company reported gross accounts receivable of $3,650,000 and an allowance for doubtful accounts of $450,000. During its fiscal 2008 year, it recorded sales of $18,600,000 on credit and collected $18,750,000 from customers. It wrote off $165,000 of bad debts and estimated that it required an allowance for doubtful accounts at the end of 2008 equal to 3% of its 2008 sales. (a) Use the format presented in this chapter to identify how each of the year 2008 events would be entered into the accounting system. (b) What was the net amount of accounts receivable reported by Fenton on its 2008 balance sheet?

E13-7 *Obj. 2* For each of the following transactions of Yeats Machinery, indicate in which month or months the related revenue or expense should appear in the monthly income statement, and why.

a. In January, the firm receives an order for a $200,000 machine, along with a 30% cash deposit. The machine is manufactured in March and April, and is delivered to the customer on April 16. The remainder of the price is collected in May.
b. Components to be used in manufacturing the above machine are received in February and paid for in March.
c. Workers are paid for the work on the machine in April and May. Quarterly payments for their health insurance are made in June. Workers also will receive pension benefits at some point because of the work they did during this period. (Hint: Health insurance and pension benefits are part of the cost of labor.)
d. The company estimates there is a 5% chance that it will have to replace parts of the machine during the two-year warranty period.

E13-8 *Obj. 2* Geyser Company began operations in 2007. It had credit sales of $4 million and cash sales of $1 million. The chief accountant decided to estimate doubtful accounts expense at 5% of total credit sales. During the year, $3.5 million of the credit sales were collected from customers and by the end of the year, $150,000 had been written off as uncollectible.

At the end of the second year of operations, credit sales were $6 million and cash sales were $1.5 million. The accountant decided that it would be more accurate to base doubtful accounts expense on ending Accounts Receivable. Accordingly, it was estimated that the ending balance of Allowance for Doubtful Accounts should have a balance equal to 8% of Accounts Receivable. During the year, $5.4 million was collected from customers and $180,000 was written off as uncollectible.

For each of the two years, determine the following amounts:

a. The ending balance of Accounts Receivable
b. The estimated Doubtful Accounts Expense
c. The ending balance in the Allowance for Doubtful Accounts

E13-9 *Obj. 2* During 2007, Vitro Construction Company started a two-year construction project having a total contract price of $2,000,000. At December 31, 2007, the firm's construction engineers estimated that the project was 35% completed. To date, 35% of the budgeted $1,300,000 in costs had been incurred.

What amounts of (a) revenue, (b) expense, and (c) gross profit should be reported by this company at the end of 2007?

E13-10 *Obj. 2* Sandoval Inc. signed a $40 million contract to build a new office building. The company expected that the project would take about two and one-half years. During the first year, the company incurred the following costs:

Raw materials	$4 million
Direct labor	6 million
Overhead (insurance, equipment rental, etc.)	2 million

At the end of the first year, management is very pleased with its construction to date. The costs incurred are consistent with the estimate that the project is 40% completed.

Determine the amount of (a) revenue and (b) expense that the builder should report on its income statement at the end of the first year.

E13-11 *Objs. 2, 3* Boris Inc. purchased an inventory item for $400 on February 27, 2007, and paid the bill on March 12. On April 4, Boris sold the item for $625; the customer paid in full on May 15. Use the format presented in the chapter to identify how each of these events would affect Boris's account balances. What is the net effect of these transactions on Boris's 2007 income statement? What is the net effect on total assets?

E13-12 *Objs. 2, 3* During the year, Nifty Threads Company, a popular clothing store, had the following transactions:

1. Nifty Threads purchased $600,000 of clothing from several manufacturers, on credit.
2. The company sold clothing on credit at prices totaling $855,000.
3. The cost of clothing sold to customers was $491,000.
4. The company received a discount of $35,000 on its purchases.
5. The company received $788,000 in cash from customers.
6. The company paid $565,000 to the clothing manufacturers.
7. The company granted $22,000 of sales discounts to customers for payment within the discount period.
8. The company estimated that $16,000 of the year's credit sales would be uncollectible.
9. The company wrote off $12,000 as uncollectible.

a. Using the format shown in this chapter, record each of the transactions.
b. Determine the amount of net income and net operating cash flow associated with these transactions.

E13-13 *Objs. 2, 3* Dockery Company purchased a truckload of 1,000 small motors for an invoice price of $60 each on January 28. Since the company paid the bill within 10 days, on February 6, it received a 2% discount. It then sold the parts to Green Manufacturing for $75 each on March 27; since Green paid within 10 days, on April 5, it was granted a 1% discount. Calculate the full effect of these transactions on Dockery's monthly income statements for January, February, March, and April.

E13-14 *Objs. 1, 2, 3* Think carefully about each of the following statements. For each one, indicate whether you believe it to be always true, generally true, generally false, or always false. For any item you judge to fall into the last three categories, describe your reasoning.

(Continued)

a. Sales discounts are reported on the income statement as an operating expense.
b. When a company writes off an uncollectible account against Allowance for Doubtful Accounts, the net amount of Accounts Receivables reported on the balance sheet does not change.
c. Jabba Company purchased inventory for its retail store. Jabba should include in the cost of this inventory the amount charged by the freight company to deliver the goods to Jabba's store.
d. Most retail stores will report three categories of inventory: raw materials, work-in-process, and finished goods.
e. When merchandise is sold to customers, the entries to Sales Revenue and Accounts Receivable will be for different amounts than the entries to Merchandise and Cost of Goods Sold.
f. A purchase of merchandise for later resale to customers has no effect on the income statement.
g. Purchase discounts received from vendors should be deducted when determining and reporting the cost of merchandise.
h. **Ford Motor Company** just received 1,000 steering wheels for a particular line of cars it manufactures. The cost of these items should be recorded initially in Work-in-Process Inventory.
i. The cost of wages earned by factory employees should be reported on the income statement as Wages Expense during the accounting period in which employees earned them.
j. Diggin' Deep Company, a gold mining firm, sold gold bars to Lookin' Good, Inc. The second firm is a manufacturer of jewelry. Diggin' Deep sold finished goods but Lookin' Good bought raw materials.

E13-15 *Obj. 4*

Dickinson Company is a wholesaler of garden supplies. At the beginning of the year, the company owned 100 bags of Power-Gro lawn fertilizer at a cost of $8 per bag. Before the spring gardening season, it purchased its entire supply of Power-Gro for the year, 500 bags at $8.30 each and 400 bags at $8.50 each. During the year, it sold 880 bags for $12 each. (a) Calculate ending inventory, cost of goods sold, and gross profit under three cost estimating procedures: periodic FIFO, periodic LIFO, and weighted-average. (b) Which results in the highest gross profit? The lowest? Why?

E13-16 *Obj. 4*

BirminghaMetals Inc. reported ending inventories of $1,721 million at year-end 2007 and $2,013 million at year-end 2008. It used periodic LIFO for most of its inventories. If it had used periodic FIFO, it would have reported inventories of $2,015 for 2007 and $2,575 for 2008. Assuming an income tax rate of 35%, what effect did the use of periodic LIFO instead of periodic FIFO have on the company's reported net income and income taxes?

E13-17 *Obj. 4*

Domestic Company sells kitchen appliances. During the year just ended, the company sold 210,000 units and recorded cost of goods sold totaling $42 million. If periodic LIFO had been used, the company would have reported $44 million of cost of goods sold. Inventory to replace the units sold was purchased during the year for $45 million. The year-end Accounts Receivable balance did not differ from the prior year-end. The company's income tax rate was 30%. Sales revenue for the year was $60 million and other expenses (all paid in cash) were $12 million.

a. What would net income have been if Domestic had used periodic LIFO instead of periodic FIFO?
b. What would the company's cash flow from operating activities have been if it had used periodic LIFO instead of periodic FIFO?
c. Does the inventory method that results in increased net income also produce increased operating cash flow? Explain why or why not.

E13-18 *Objs. 2, 3*

Ten transactions are shown on the next page as they were entered into the accounting system. For each, explain the event that caused the entry to be made.

		Assets		= Liabilities	+	Owners' Equity
Event	**Accounts**	**Cash**	**Other Assets**		**Contributed Capital**	**Retained Earnings**
a.	Accounts Receivable		50,000			
	Sales Revenue					50,000
b.	Inventory		−8,000			
	Cost of Goods Sold					−8,000
c.	Cash	2,000				
	Accounts Receivable		−2,000			
d.	Inventory		35,000			
	Accounts Payable			35,000		
e.	Inventory		−5,000			
	Accounts Payable			−5,000		
f.	Doubtful Accounts Expense					−800
	Allowance for Doubtful Accounts		−800			
g.	Accounts Receivable		−400			
	Allowance for Doubtful Accounts		400			
h.	Cash	980				
	Accounts Receivable		−1,000			
	Sales Discounts					−20
i.	Allowance for Returns		−300			
	Sales Returns					−300
j.	Warranty Expense					−250
	Warranty Obligations			250		
Totals		2,980	67,900	30,250		40,630

E13-19 *Obj. 4* The following information regarding inventory transactions is available for the month of May.

Date	Type of Event	Number of Units	Unit Cost	Total Cost
May 1	Beginning inventory	100	$12	$1,200
3	Purchase	50	14	700
12	Sale	70		
15	Sale	60		
20	Purchase	100	15	1,500
28	Sale	60		

Determine the correct balances at May 31 for Merchandise Inventory and Cost of Goods Sold under each of the following inventory methods: (a) periodic FIFO, (b) periodic LIFO, and (c) weighted-average.

E13-20 *Obj. 4* Small Part Company had the following information regarding inventory transactions available at the end of October. Year-to-date Cost of Goods Sold at October 1 was $236,700.

Date	Type of Event	Number of Units	Unit Cost	Total Cost
October 1	Beginning inventory	9,000	$10	$ 90,000
4	Purchase	3,000	12	36,000
11	Sale	8,000		
15	Sale	2,000		
22	Purchase	10,000	14	140,000
29	Sale	5,000		

(Continued)

Determine the correct year-to-date balances at October 31 for Merchandise Inventory and Cost of Goods Sold under each of the following inventory methods: (a) periodic FIFO, (b) periodic LIFO, and (c) weighted-average.

E13-21 *Obj. 4* Randolph Company is a retailer that sells appliances to institutions such as schools, universities, and state governments. During the month of January, Randolph Company recorded the following information:

	Units	Unit Cost	Total Cost
January 1 inventory	550	$300	$165,000
Purchases January 5	100	305	30,500
Sales January 7	300		
Purchases January 10	600	310	186,000
Sales January 31	500		

Assuming Randolph Company uses a perpetual FIFO inventory system, determine the cost of goods sold and value of the ending inventory.

E13-22 *Obj. 4* Using the data provided in E13-21, calculate the cost of goods sold and value of the ending inventory if Randolph Company uses a perpetual LIFO inventory system.

E13-23 *Obj. 5* A partial income statement is shown below for Mavis Company.

(In thousands)	**2007**
Income before extraordinary items and taxes	$4,523
Provision for income taxes	1,036
Income before extraordinary items	$3,487
Extraordinary loss from condemnation of land for a freeway (net of tax benefits of $322)	644
Net income	$2,843

Earnings per share	**Basic**	**Diluted**
Income before extraordinary items	$1.16	$1.00
Extraordinary items	0.21	0.19
Net income	$0.95	$0.81

(a) Why are earnings per share presented for both before and after the extraordinary items? (b) On how many shares was Mavis computing basic earnings per share? Diluted earnings per share? (c) What kinds of items might account for the additional shares used for the calculation of diluted earnings per share?

E13-24 *Obj. 5* The Hot Aire Company reported the following items on its income statement for 2007.

a. Net operating revenues, $956,000
b. Cost of goods sold, $312,000
c. Selling and administrative expenses, $245,000
d. Research and development expenses, $122,000
e. Net interest expense, $8,500
f. Provision for income taxes, $85,920
g. Current year loss from discontinued operations of $24,000, net of tax benefit of $7,680
h. Loss from sale of discontinued operations of $89,000, net of tax benefit of $24,480
i. Preferred stock dividends, $48,000

The company had 25,000 shares of common stock outstanding throughout the fiscal year.

Compute each of the following:

A. Operating income
B. Income (loss) from continuing operations, before taxes
C. Income (loss) before discontinued operations
D. Net income (loss)
E. Net income (loss) available for common shareholders
F. Earnings per share from continuing operations

G. Earnings per share from discontinued operations
H. Earnings per share from net income (loss)

E13-25 *Obj. 5* The Florida Boatworks Company had the following income statement items for the year 2007.

Income from continuing operations, before taxes	$250,000
Current year loss from discontinued operations	(10,500)
Gain from sale of discontinued operations	3,250
Extraordinary loss from hurricane	(21,000)
Tax rate, applicable to all income statement items	30%
Number of shares of common stock outstanding during 2007	80,000

a. Beginning with "Income from continuing operations, before taxes," prepare the remaining sections of the income statement.
b. Calculate earnings per common share for all sections of the income statement. The company has no preferred stock outstanding.

E13-26 *Objs. 2, 3, 5* Explain whether each of the following would be expensed on the income statement in 2007 or in some later year, and why.

a. Inventory purchased in 2007 but sold in 2008.
b. Estimated warranty costs for goods sold in 2007; the warranty servicing will take place in 2008 and 2009.
c. Bad debts caused by 2007 sales; the actual bad receivables will not be identified until a later year.
d. Research and development costs incurred in 2007 but aimed at producing a better product in later years.

Problems

P13-1 INCOME STATEMENT PREPARATION
Obj. 1

On January 1, 2007, Pete Everett began Leafy Green Corporation, a salad bar supply business, by investing $5,000 cash and a delivery van worth $7,200 in exchange for 1,000 shares of $2 par common stock. Pete expects the van to have a remaining life of three years with no salvage value; he plans to use straight-line depreciation. Two friends invested $2,000 each, receiving 150 shares of stock each.

The next day, Leafy Green borrowed $8,400 at 8% annual interest for operating funds. The loan is to be repaid or refinanced in three months.

Salad ingredients for the month of January cost $8,500; Leafy Green has paid for 75% of this. The company has delivered prepared salad bar materials to three customers, each of whom has been billed $5,500; two of the three have paid. No ingredients were on hand at the end of the month.

Other operating expenses, paid in cash, were $6,000.

Required Prepare an income statement for Leafy Green Corporation for the month of January 2007. Include earnings per share.

P13-2 REVENUE RECOGNITION
Obj. 2

Several situations in which the timing of revenue is in doubt are listed below.

a. An appliance manufacturer sent out a truckload of dishwashers FOB destination in late January; they arrived February 2 and were paid for in March. Monthly income statements are prepared.
b. A magazine publisher sold two-year subscriptions for a monthly publication.
c. An auto dealer sold five-year service contracts for cash at the time of the auto sale.
d. A home decorating center sold wallpaper with a 60-day right to return of up to 25% of an order. For the past several years, returns have been fairly consistent, with one in 10 customers returning some paper; the average return is 1.2 rolls.

(Continued)

e. A bridge construction firm is involved in only one project at a time; the average project takes three years. The contract price is firm and definitely collectible; total costs of the project can be estimated.

Required First, explain what events generally must occur before any revenue is recognized. Then discuss when each of the above situations should result in revenue recognition, and why.

P13-3 REVENUE RECOGNITION

Obj. 2

The following excerpt is from **Unisys Corporation**'s 2004 Form 10k.

> **Revenue Recognition.** Revenue from hardware sales is recognized upon shipment and the passage of title. . . . Revenue from software licenses is recognized at the inception of the initial license term and upon execution of an extension to the license term. . . . Revenue from equipment and software maintenance is recognized on a straight-line basis as earned over the lives of the respective contracts. . . . Revenue from operating leases is recognized on a monthly basis over the term of the lease and for sales-type leases at the inception of the lease term . . . For contracts accounted for on the percentage-of-completion basis, revenue and profit recognized in any given accounting period is based on estimates of total projected contract costs, the estimates are continually reevaluated and revised, when necessary, throughout the life of a contract.

Required What is meant by revenue recognition? Why does Unisys use different revenue recognition principles for different types of revenue? What are the critical events for each of these types of revenue? Why is estimation involved in revenue recognition for the multiyear, fixed-price contracts?

P13-4 COMPUTING ACCOUNTS RECEIVABLE

Obj. 2

Georgia Company reported accounts receivable of $16.5 million at the end of its 2007 fiscal year. This amount was net of an allowance for doubtful accounts of $1,800,000. During 2008, Georgia sold $56.5 million of merchandise on credit. It collected $57.9 million from customers. Accounts valued at $1,980,000 were written off as uncollectible during 2008. Georgia's management estimates that 10% of the year-end Accounts Receivable balance will be uncollectible.

Required Answer each of the following questions:

A. What amount will Georgia report for accounts receivable and the allowance for doubtful accounts at the end of 2008?
B. What is the Doubtful Accounts Expense for 2008?
C. How will the accounts receivable and allowance accounts be presented on the balance sheet? Show the balance sheet.
D. Why do companies record expenses for doubtful accounts based on estimates from receivables or sales during the prior year rather than recording the expenses when accounts are written off in a future period?
E. If estimated uncollectibles as a percentage of sales or receivables were to increase over several years, what information might this provide to decision makers?

P13-5 INVENTORY TRANSACTIONS OF MANUFACTURING COMPANIES

Obj. 3

Evans Company began the year with $850,000 of raw materials inventory, $1,400,000 of work-in-process inventory, and $620,000 of finished goods inventory. During the year, the company purchased $3,550,000 of raw material and used $3,720,000 of raw materials in production. Labor used in production for the year was $2,490,000. Overhead was $1,380,000. Cost of goods sold for the year was $7,200,000. The ending balance of Finished Goods Inventory was $530,000.

Required Use Exhibit 5 in the chapter as a format for developing a schedule to show the effect of these events on Evans' inventory accounts for the year.

P13-6 CLASSIFICATION OF MANUFACTURING COSTS

Obj. 3

The following information is taken from the records of the Carolby Company, a manufacturer of lawn furniture. Indicate whether the cost of each item should be included as part of the finished goods cost or should be treated as an expense. For the items that become part of the cost of finished goods, indicate whether each should be designated as materials, labor, or factory overhead.

a. Salaries of sales office staff
b. Electric utilities for the factory area
c. Office supplies
d. Paint and miscellaneous plastic parts
e. Depreciation on factory equipment
f. Depreciation on delivery vans
g. Salaries of factory foremen
h. Miscellaneous factory supplies
i. Steel rods used for chair frames
j. Plastic sheets used for table tops
k. Salaries of furniture assemblers
l. Insurance on the factory
m. Insurance on the administrative offices
n. Advertising in trade magazines
o. Lawn furniture sold to retailers
p. Rental of storage facilities for materials
q. Rental of storage facilities for finished goods

Required Briefly explain your reasoning for classifying the various items as part of the cost of goods manufactured or as an expense.

P13-7 INVENTORIES

Objs. 3, 4

Modern Industries manufactures a variety of computer parts and accessories in a rapidly changing technological environment. At year-end 2007, it reported the following comparative information regarding inventories.

(In millions)	**2007**	**2006**
Raw materials and parts	$14	$16
Work in process	28	31
Finished goods	25	28
Total inventories	$67	$75

The 2007 income statement reflected cost of sales of $3,165 million. In the operating activities section of the statement of cash flows, the $8 million decrease in inventories was added to net income. Notes to the financial statements included the following:

- Inventories are reported at the lower of cost (first-in, first-out) or market. If the cost of the inventories exceeds their market (replacement) value, a writedown to market value is taken currently.
- The company participates in a highly competitive industry that is characterized by rapid changes in technology, frequent introductions of new products, short product life cycles, and downward pressures on prices and margins.

Required Answer the following questions related to Modern Industries' inventories.

A. Describe the nature of each of the three inventories listed on the balance sheet. When does each become an expense?
B. Why is the inventory decrease added to net income on the statement of cash flows?
C. Many U.S. corporations use the LIFO inventory method to save income taxes. Why might a computer industry manufacturer like this firm decide to use FIFO instead? Explain.

P13-8 INVENTORY TRANSACTIONS AND PERIODIC INVENTORY COSTING METHODS

Objs. 3, 4

Culture Music Store had the following selected account balances on October 1.

Merchandise inventory (1,000 units)	$ 7,000
Accounts receivable	15,000
Allowance for doubtful accounts	(1,200)
Warranty obligations	500

(Continued)

Goods are sold with a 60-day money-back guarantee against defects. During October, the following transactions occurred.

1. The store purchased 4,000 units of inventory on credit at a total invoice cost of $32,000. The goods, which were received in October, were purchased FOB destination and the seller paid freight costs of $250.
2. During the first week of the month, 700 units were sold on credit at prices averaging $12 each.
3. A clerk noticed that 50 recordings purchased in part 1 were mislabeled. These units were returned to the vendor for full credit.
4. During the second week, a cash-only sale was held and 1,200 units sold at an average price of $10 each.
5. Customers returned a total of 53 units that had been sold in part 2. The goods were in salable condition and returned to the shelf.
6. The vendor was paid in full for the goods purchased in part 1.
7. Checks were received from customers who purchased goods in part 2. All took the 2% discount that was offered for paying within 10 days.
8. A total of 1,600 units were sold during the rest of the month at prices averaging $13. Three-quarters of the sales were on credit.
9. At month-end, management estimated that 10% of the goods sold in parts 4 and 8 would be returned as defective.
10. Also at month-end, management estimated that $344 of this period's credit sales would be uncollectible.

Required

A. Show how each of the transactions would be entered into the accounting system assuming the firm uses the perpetual FIFO inventory method.

B. Prepare an income statement for the month of October assuming that operating expenses (other than warranty expense and doubtful accounts expense) totaled $2,500 and the company's tax rate is 35%.

C. By what amount would net income have been different if the perpetual LIFO method had been used? Prepare a schedule that proves your solution.

D. By what amount would net cash flow from operating activities have been different if the perpetual LIFO method has been used? Explain your solution.

P13-9 ACCOUNTING ERRORS REGARDING OPERATING ACTIVITIES

Obj. 3

At year-end, the accounting department at Bell-Jones Industries had prepared the following balance sheet and income statement.

Balance sheet

Cash	$ 58,000
Accounts receivable	215,000
Less: Allowance for returns	9,000
Allowance for doubtful accounts	(3,000)
Merchandise	136,000
Buildings and equipment	413,000
Less: Accumulated depreciation	(107,800)
Land	79,000
Total assets	$ 799,200
Accounts payable	$ 108,200
Wages payable	25,000
Warranty obligations	61,000
Common stock	300,000
Retained earnings	305,000
Total liabilities and stockholders' equity	$ 799,200

Income statement

Net sales	$ 1,855,000
Service contracts	792,000
Cost of goods sold	(1,298,500)
Operating expenses:	
Wages	(537,300)
Rent	(60,000)
Advertising	(282,000)
Doubtful accounts	0
Depreciation	(26,800)
Warranties	(55,000)
Operating income	$ 387,400
Interest revenue	1,350
Income before taxes	388,750
Provision for taxes	136,063
Net income	$ 252,687

Just prior to the arrival of the outside auditors, one of the accounting staff brought a list of items to the chief financial officer. The staff member was concerned that these items had not been properly accounted for in the financial statements.

1. A source document showing a customer's return of goods had been missing until just now and had not been processed through the accounting system. The goods had been sold on account to the customer for $9,000 during the current year and were returned to the warehouse for sale to others. The company's normal gross profit on sales is 30%.
2. Just before year-end, inventory had been purchased on credit at a cost of $60,000, FOB destination. By year-end, it had not yet arrived but it had been included in the ending inventory anyway.
3. At the end of the prior year, there was $80,000 of inventory in transit from a supplier. The goods had been purchased FOB shipping point but had not yet arrived. The goods had been included in last year's ending inventory anyway.
4. An error had been made in computing the warranty costs for goods sold during the current year. A total of $55,000 had been charged to Warranty Expense, but the correct amount was $75,000.
5. Near year-end, a $100,000 service contract was obtained from a major customer. It was a renewal of an existing contract that would otherwise have expired during the coming year. Because this type of work had been performed many times before for this customer, the contract was entered into the accounting system as a credit sale during the year just ended. Collection of the cash will occur as the services are performed.
6. The adjusting entry to allowance for returns had not yet been recorded at year-end. Using the firm's usual approach, an additional $10,300 should be recorded.
7. No adjusting entry had been made at year-end to account for doubtful accounts. Using the firm's usual approach, $5,960 should be charged to expense.

Required

A. Show any entries to the accounting system that you believe should be made as a result of this information. If an item does not require an entry, explain why.

B. What is the proper amount of operating income that should be reported for the period? Prepare a schedule to show how you determined this amount.

P13-10 IDENTIFYING PERPETUAL INVENTORY COSTING METHODS

Obj. 3

At the end of the first quarter, yesterday, a staff accountant prepared the information below. It is a schedule of merchandise inventory and cost of goods sold under each of the three most common costing methods: perpetual LIFO, perpetual FIFO, and perpetual weighted-average. Unfortunately, she forgot to label which one was which and today is her day off.

Schedule of merchandise inventory and cost of goods sold

Summary of inventory transactions:

Beginning inventory: March 1 = 9,000 units at $10 each
Purchases: March 3 = 3,000 units at $12 each
March 24 = 10,000 units at $14 each
Sales: March 11 = 7,000 units at $15
March 15 = 2,000 units at $15
March 30 = 4,000 units at $17

Costing results using method A:	Merchandise Inventory	Cost of Goods Sold
March 1 beginning balances	$ 90,000	$236,700
March 3 purchase	36,000	—
March 11 sale	−73,500	73,500
March 15 sale	−21,000	21,000
March 24 purchase	140,000	—
March 30 sale	−52,760	52,760
March 31 ending balances	$118,740	$383,960

(continued)

Costing results using method B:	Merchandise Inventory	Cost of Goods Sold
March 1 beginning balances	$ 90,000	$236,700
March 3 purchase	36,000	—
March 11 sale	−70,000	70,000
March 15 sale	−20,000	20,000
March 24 purchase	140,000	—
March 30 sale	−50,000	50,000
March 31 ending balances	$126,000	$376,700

Costing results using method C:	Merchandise Inventory	Cost of Goods Sold
March 1 beginning balances	$ 90,000	$236,700
March 3 purchase	36,000	—
March 11 sale	−76,000	76,000
March 15 sale	−20,000	20,000
March 24 purchase	140,000	—
March 30 sale	−56,000	56,000
March 31 ending balances	$114,000	$388,700

Required

A. Match each set of cost results above with the inventory costing method used to generate it. (Hint: In which direction are prices moving?)

B. Prove your results by showing how the amount for the first sale was computed under each method.

P13-11 PERIODIC INVENTORY ESTIMATION AND INCOME CONTROL

Obj. 4

Rousseau Company uses the periodic LIFO inventory estimation method. At the beginning of the current fiscal year, the company's inventory consisted of the following:

Units	Unit Cost	Total Cost
8,000	$22	$176,000
4,000	23	92,000
2,000	32	64,000
2,000	34	68,000
16,000		$400,000

These units were produced over several years, during which inventory costs had increased rapidly. During the current year, Rousseau produced 20,000 additional units of inventory at an average cost of $36 per unit. The average sales price of units sold during the year was $55.

Required Answer the following questions.

A. What would be Rousseau's gross profit and average gross profit per unit if it sold 20,000, 24,000, 28,000, or 36,000 units during the year?

B. Assume that Rousseau sold 36,000 units during the year. How many units would it need to produce to minimize the tax effect of its gross profit? How many units would it need to produce to maximize its gross profit?

C. If you were a manager of Rousseau and you wanted to control the amount of gross profit reported by the company, what could you do? If you wanted to develop an accounting standard that could prevent this type of management manipulation of income, what kind of standard might you propose?

P13-12 ACCOUNTING CHOICE DECISIONS

Obj. 4

Harris Company reported sales revenue of $12 million for the year. The company uses FIFO for inventory estimation purposes. Cost of goods sold was $3.5 million. If the company had used

LIFO, its cost of goods sold would have been $4.3 million. The company reported depreciation expense of $1.2 million on a straight-line basis. If the company had used accelerated depreciation, it would have reported depreciation expense of $1.7 million. Other expenses, excluding income tax, were $3 million. The company's income tax rate was 30%.

Required

A. Compute Harris's net income as reported and as it would have been reported if LIFO and accelerated depreciation had been used.
B. What effect would the choice of accounting methods have on the company's cash flows from operating activities during the year if the same methods were used for both financial reporting and tax purposes?

P13-13 PERPETUAL AND PERIODIC INVENTORY SYSTEMS

Obj. 4

Records of the Genesis Corporation reveal the following information about inventory during the year.

January 1	Beginning inventory	1,000 units	@ $10
March 15	Purchase of inventory	3,500 units	@ $12
July 21	Sale of inventory	4,000 units	
September 12	Purchase of inventory	1,600 units	@ $14
October 31	Sale of inventory	1,200 units	

The company's accountant is trying to decide whether to determine Cost of Goods Sold using the perpetual inventory system (calculating Cost of Goods Sold after every sale) or the periodic inventory system (calculating Cost of Goods Sold at the end of the year only). Assume the company uses the LIFO method for inventory costing.

Required Using the information given above, answer each of the following questions.

A. How many units have been sold? How many units remain in ending inventory?
B. What is Cost of Goods Sold using the perpetual method? The periodic method? What is the cost of ending inventory for each method?
C. Is there a difference in net income for each method? Why? (Assume for purposes of this question that Sales Revenue is $85,000 and all other expenses are $5,600.)
D. What are the advantages of using perpetual? Using periodic?

P13-14 PREPARING AN INCOME STATEMENT

Objs. 1, 5

Lawson Company's accounting system listed the following information for the company's 2007 fiscal year (in millions):

Average common shares outstanding	2.5
Cost of goods sold	$173.2
Extraordinary gain	19.4
Gain on sale of securities	7.4
General and administrative expenses	73.3
Income taxes (35% of pretax income)	
Interest expense	10.0
Interest income	5.7
Loss associated with cumulative effect of accounting change	4.0
Loss from discontinued operations	12.3
Sales of merchandise	318.6
Selling expenses	28.5

Required Prepare an income statement for Lawson Company for the year ended December 31, 2007. Assume that the tax rate of 35% applies to special items as well as ordinary income. (Hint: Discontinued operations are listed before extraordinary items, which are listed before accounting changes.)

P13-15 INTERPRETING AN INCOME STATEMENT

Objs. 1, 5 Worldwide Corporation reported the following income statement for 2008.

(In millions)	2008	2007	2006
Product sales	$ 3,355	$ 3,298	$ 3,236
Service sales	2,941	2,591	2,543
Sales of products and services	6,296	5,889	5,779
Cost of products sold	(2,549)	(2,523)	(2,508)
Cost of services sold	(1,931)	(1,754)	(1,743)
Costs of products and services sold	(4,480)	(4,277)	(4,251)
Provision for restructuring	(86)	(23)	(249)
Marketing, administration, and general expenses	(1,686)	(1,184)	(1,313)
Other income and expenses, net	149	(288)	(154)
Interest expense	(233)	(134)	(165)
Loss from continuing operations before income taxes and minority interest in income of consolidated subsidiaries	(40)	(17)	(353)
Income taxes	7	13	116
Minority interest in income of consolidated subsidiaries	(11)	(9)	(9)
Loss from continuing operations	(44)	(13)	(246)
Discontinued operations, net of income taxes:			
Income from operations	135	90	71
Estimated loss on disposal of discontinued operations	(76)		(95)
Income (loss) from discontinued operations	59	90	(24)
Income (loss) before cumulative effect of change in accounting principle	15	77	(270)
Cumulative effect of change in accounting principle			
Postemployment benefits			(56)
Net income (loss)	$ 15	$ 77	$ (326)

Required Answer each of the following questions.

A. For 2008, calculate the gross profit on product sales and on service sales. Why are these shown separately?
B. What is a "provision for restructuring"? What is a "discontinued segment"? Why is it that the restructuring provision is part of operating income, but the discontinued segment is not?
C. Some businesses show interest expense in a separate section with a title like "Other Revenues and Expenses," below Income from Operations. Would Worldwide's operating income have been positive in the years presented if it did not include interest expense?
D. Why is "income taxes" a positive number, not an expense?
E. What is a "cumulative effect of change in accounting principle"?
F. Which would be of more use in attempting to predict the financial future of the company: income from continuing operations or the final net income numbers, including the discontinued operations and the effect of the change in accounting principle?
G. Why are the effects of the discontinued segment and the change in accounting principle presented net of any tax effect?

P13-16 PRESENTATION OF THE INCOME STATEMENT

Objs. 1, 5 Pelican Enterprises had the following account balances in its general ledger at June 30, 2007, the end of the company's fiscal year. All adjusting entries (except for the accrual of income taxes at 30%) had been entered. The company had an average of 900,000 shares of common stock outstanding during the year.

General ledger account balances (in thousands)

Accounts receivable	$ 349	Land	$1,980
Accumulated depreciation	922	Loss on sale of old machinery	255
Advertising expense	1,224	Merchandise inventory	471
Buildings and equipment	4,811	Notes payable, long-term	150
Cash	482	Preferred stock, 7%	300
Common stock	2,400	Prepaid advertising	54
Cost of goods sold	3,660	Rent expense	546
Depreciation expense	102	Rent payable	450
Extraordinary gain on extinguishment of debt	40	Retained earnings	513
		Sales revenue	6,930
Investments, long-term	250	Service revenue	3,382
Interest revenue	44	Wages expense	855
Interest expense	124	Wages payable	32

Required

A. Prepare an income statement in good form, including earnings per share information.

B. Have the closing entries been made to the accounting system? How can you tell? (Hint: You might want to review the accounting cycle in Chapter 3.)

C. What is the amount of net income available to common stockholders? Why is this important information?

D. Why do you think that GAAP require that gross profit, operating income, pretax income, and net income be separately disclosed?

P13-17 THE EFFECT OF ACCOUNTING CHOICES

Objs. 2, 4, 5

Ginsberg Company is a recently formed, publicly traded company. At the end of its most recent fiscal year, the company reported the following information.

a. Sales revenues were $13,680,000, and 360,000 units were sold. Credit sales were $10,000,000. Uncollectible accounts associated with credit sales are estimated to be between 3% and 4%.

b. At the beginning of the year, 140,000 units of inventory were on hand at a unit cost of $10 per unit; during the year, 250,000 units were purchased at $10.50, and, later, 150,000 units were purchased at $11.50 per unit.

c. Plant assets included equipment with a book value of $3,375,000 and buildings with a book value of $8,260,000. The equipment has an estimated remaining useful life of between four and seven years. The buildings have an estimated remaining useful life of between 25 and 35 years.

d. Intangible assets (excluding goodwill) cost $1,200,000 and have a remaining useful life of no less than 10 years.

e. The company has the option of adopting a new accounting standard for the fiscal year. If the standard is adopted, the cumulative effect of the accounting change, before the tax effect, will be a loss of $1,100,000.

f. The company's tax rate is 34%. Other operating expenses were $6,245,000. Interest expense was $460,000. There were 500,000 shares of common stock outstanding throughout the year.

Management has not yet made decisions about how to treat items a through e. A choice is necessary in each instance. The chief financial officer has asked you to determine the range of net income that might be reported depending on the choices that are made.

Required Prepare two different pro forma (projected) income statements for the year.

A. With the first income statement, show the minimum net income the company could report under GAAP.

B. With the second income statement, show the maximum net income that could be reported under GAAP.

C. What does this suggest to you about comparing the reported net income of one firm versus the others?

P13-18 IDENTIFYING OPERATING ACTIVITIES FROM ENTRIES TO THE ACCOUNTING SYSTEM

Objs. 2, 3, 4, 5

Goose Hollow Company had the following entries to its accounting system during a recent week.

		Assets		=	Liabilities	+	Owners' Equity	
Event	**Accounts**	**Cash**	**Other Assets**				**Contributed Capital**	**Retained Earnings**
a.	Accounts Receivable		18,000					
	Sales Revenue							18,000
	Merchandise Inventory		−14,600					
	Cost of Goods Sold							−14,600
b.	Merchandise Inventory		−33,000					
	Accounts Payable				−33,000			
c.	Cash	4,365						
	Accounts Receivable		−4,500					
	Sales Discount							−135
d.	Allowance for Doubtful Accounts		1,100					
	Accounts Receivable		−1,100					
e.	Cash	−2,500						
	Accounts Payable				−2,500			
f.	Accounts Receivable		−6,000					
	Allowance for Returns		6,000					
	Merchandise Inventory		4,200					
	Cost of Goods Sold							4,200
g.	Finished Goods Inventory		13,000					
	Work-in-Process Inventory		−13,000					
h.	Warranty Expense							−15,750
	Warranty Obligations				15,750			
i.	Allowance for Returns		−8,300					
	Sales Returns							−8,300
j.	Doubtful Accounts Expense							−3,740
	Allowance for Doubtful Accounts		−3,740					
k.	Merchandise Inventory		−800					
	Loss on Inventory							−800

Required Study each entry and write a short description of the event that occurred to cause the entry.

P13-19 REPORTING EQUITY INCOME, NONCONTROLLING INTEREST, AND PENSION INFORMATION

(Based on the Other Topics section.) A partial income statement for Half Moon Inc. is reported below.

Half Moon Inc. Partial Income Statement For Year Ending December 31, 2007	
Sales revenue	$3,504,600
•	
•	
•	
Operating income	$ 587,300
Equity income in related company (Able Co.)	40,000
Income before income taxes	$ 627,300
Provision for income taxes	219,500
Income before noncontrolling interests	$ 407,800
Noncontrolling interest in net income of subsidiary (Baker Co.)	(2,466)
Net income	$ 405,334

In addition, the following disclosure was found in the notes to the financial statements.

Note 7:	Projected benefit obligation	$1,500,000
	Fair value of plan assets	1,300,000
	Pension liability	$ 200,000
	Service cost	$ 103,400
	Return on plan assets	100,100
	Net pension expense	$ 3,300

Required Explain each of the following.

A. What information is conveyed by the line labeled "Equity income in related company"? Describe the situation that must prevail for this line to appear on an income statement.
B. What information is conveyed by the line labeled "Noncontrolling interest in net income of subsidiary"? Describe the situation that must prevail for this line to appear on an income statement. Why is this amount subtracted in this case?
C. What information is conveyed by each of the first three lines of Note 7?
D. What information is conveyed by each of the second set of three lines of Note 7?

P13-20 EXCEL IN ACTION

The Book Wermz purchases books for all of its stores through a central purchasing department. Books are then shipped to different stores for sale. One of the company's largest selling items is an edition of Webster's dictionary. A large volume of sales occurs in August and September each year to students returning to school. At the beginning of August 2007, the company's inventory of dictionaries included 245 units purchased on April 12, 2007 at $27.00 per unit, 360 units purchased on May 3, 2007 at $29.00 per unit, and 1,000 units purchased on July 24, 2007 at $32.00 per unit. No purchases were made in August. The Book Wermz sold 1,447 units of the dictionary during August.

Required Use a spreadsheet to prepare a schedule of Cost of Goods Sold and Ending Inventory for the dictionary for August. Show both FIFO and LIFO inventory numbers.

Enter the captions illustrated on the next page at the top of the spreadsheet.

	A	B	C	D	E	F	G
1	The Book Wermz						
2	Inventory of Webster's Dictionary						
3	August 31, 2007						
4							
5	FIFO Basis						
6				Cost of Goods Sold		Ending Inventory	
7	Date Purchased	Units Available	Cost per Unit	Units	Cost	Units	Cost

Beginning in row 8, enter data in each column for each of the purchase dates. In the Cost of Goods Sold columns, enter the number of units sold and the cost of these units (units sold × cost per unit) from each inventory layer[1] using the FIFO method. In the Ending Inventory columns, provide the same data for units remaining in inventory at the end of August. Use formulas for all calculations so that if the units available or cost per unit numbers changed, these changes would automatically be updated in columns D–G.

In row 11, sum columns B and D–G, using the Summation button.

Beginning in row 13, repeat the captions, data, and calculations using the LIFO method. You can copy the data from the FIFO section, select cell A13, and paste the data. Then make any needed changes for the LIFO calculations.

Beginning in row 21, provide a calculation of the amount of income taxes the company would save if it used the LIFO method in August. The company's income tax rate was 35%. Place captions in column A and calculations in column B. The calculations should report the amount of LIFO cost, FIFO cost, the excess of LIFO over FIFO costs, the company's income tax rate, and the tax savings.

Format the schedule using underlines, commas, and appropriate alignment so that it is easy to read and has a formal appearance.

Suppose the number of units available from the April purchase was 545 and the cost of the May purchase was $31.00 per unit. What would cost of goods sold be for August for the dictionaries? What would the ending inventory be at the end of August?

[1]Each purchase represents an inventory layer. For example, Book Wermz has a beginning inventory layer of 245 units at $27.00 per unit. The company acquired additional inventory layers at $29.00 and $32.00 per unit.

P13-21 MULTIPLE-CHOICE OVERVIEW OF THE CHAPTER

1. The excess of sales revenues over cost of goods sold for a fiscal period is
   a. net income.
   b. income before taxes.
   c. operating income.
   d. gross profit.

2. Timing differences between sales revenues recognized during a fiscal period and cash collected from customers during the period affects the change in the balance of
   a. accounts receivable.
   b. unearned revenue.
   c. gross profit.
   d. allowance for doubtful accounts.

3. A transaction to estimate the amount of doubtful accounts expense for a fiscal period would affect the
   a. accounts receivable and doubtful accounts expense accounts.
   b. allowance for doubtful accounts and doubtful accounts expense accounts.
   c. allowance for doubtful accounts and accounts receivable accounts.
   d. allowance for doubtful accounts and sales revenue accounts.

4. Universal Joint Company publishes a monthly periodical, *Grease Today*. At the beginning of March, the company's unearned revenues included 1,200 one-year subscriptions at $36 each. During March, the company received 200 new subscriptions. The March issue

was shipped to all subscribers on March 25. The amount of subscription revenue the company should recognize in March is

a. $7,200.
b. $4,200.
c. $3,600.
d. $600.

5. Inventory prices on the balance sheet are closest to current costs for a company that estimates its inventories using
   a. FIFO.
   b. LIFO.
   c. weighted-average.
   d. a method that cannot be determined from the information given.

6. A company will report the highest net income if
   a. it uses LIFO inventory, with rising prices and increasing inventory levels.
   b. it uses LIFO inventory estimating, under all conditions.
   c. it uses FIFO inventory, with rising prices and increasing inventory levels.
   d. it uses FIFO inventory estimating, under all conditions.

7. Warranty expense should appear in the income statement in the period when
   a. the product is manufactured.
   b. the product is sold.
   c. a defective item is repaired or replaced.
   d. the warranty period ends and all expense is known.

8. Merchandise in transit at the end of the accounting period that has been shipped FOB shipping point should be included in the ending inventory of
   a. the buyer.
   b. the seller.
   c. both the buyer and the seller.
   d. the freight company.

9. Redford Company reported net income of $40 million for its most recent fiscal year. The company recorded interest expense of $10 million for the year. Also, it paid preferred dividends of $2 million and common dividends of $5 million. The average number of common shares outstanding for the year was 10 million. The company would report earnings per share of common stock for the year of
   a. $4.00.
   b. $3.80.
   c. $3.30.
   d. $2.30.

10. Given the following information, determine Cost of Goods Sold for the month using the perpetual LIFO method.

Date	Event	Units	Unit Cost
May 1	Beginning inventory	100	$5
5	Purchase of inventory	10	6
12	Sale of inventory	20	
18	Purchase of inventory	10	7
23	Purchase of inventory	10	8
28	Sale of inventory	25	

    a. $225
    b. $285
    c. $325
    d. $425

11. When a periodic inventory system is used, cost of goods sold is calculated as
    a. beginning inventory + purchases − ending inventory.
    b. beginning inventory + purchases + ending inventory.

(Continued)

c. ending inventory + purchases − beginning inventory.
d. beginning inventory + ending inventory − purchases.

12. A major disadvantage of a periodic inventory system is
    a. the added expense of applying it.
    b. the required technology for applying it.
    c. the lesser degree of control and information it provides.
    d. the requirement for an inventory count, which is never necessary with a perpetual system.

13. *(Based on the Other Topics section.)* Deferred compensation, such as pension benefits and health care for retirees, should be expensed
    a. when a plan is adopted.
    b. while employees are working.
    c. when employees retire.
    d. when paid to retirees.

Cases

C13-1 EXAMINING OPERATING ACTIVITIES

Objs. 2, 4, 5

Selected information from **General Mills**' 2004 annual report and 10K is provided in Appendix A at the end of the text.

Required Review the annual report and answer each of the following questions.

A. What was the primary inventory estimation method used by General Mills? What is the effect on the company's cost of goods sold and operating income of using this primary method as compared to other methods? (Hint: Look at Notes 1c and 6. The "Reserve for LIFO" is an estimate of the difference between FIFO and LIFO values.)
B. What was the amount of General Mills' allowance for doubtful accounts for 2004? Did the relationship between estimated doubtful accounts and net sales change from 2002 to 2004?
C. How much did General Mills report for depreciation and amortization and for interest expense in 2004? How much cash did General Mills pay for depreciation, amortization, and interest in 2004? (Hint: See the income statement, cash flow statement, and Note 13.)

C13-2 THE EFFECT OF ACCOUNTING CHOICES ON REPORTED RESULTS

Objs. 2, 3, 4

Sunlight Incorporated and Moonbeam Enterprises both began operations on the first day of 2007. Both operate in the same industry, sell the same products, and have many of the same customers. Both companies have just reported financial results at the end of 2007. By a remarkable coincidence, the sales revenue reported by both companies was exactly the same. Overall, however, Moonbeam's net income was approximately 75% greater than Sunlight's. You are a little surprised by this because it was generally thought by those in the industry that Sunlight had been the better managed and more successful firm.

Income Statements for Year 2007	Sunlight Incorporated	Moonbeam Enterprises
Sales revenue	$31,000	$31,000
Cost of goods sold	20,000	18,600
Gross profit	$11,000	$12,400
Operating expenses:		
Depreciation	1,100	1,100
Insurance	550	610
Supplies	1,300	1,300
Uncollectible accounts	1,240	310
Warranties	620	0
Wages	1,500	1,570
Total operating expenses	6,310	4,890
Operating income	4,690	7,510
Interest expense	900	900
Pretax income	3,790	6,610
Income tax expense	1,298	2,314
Net income	$ 2,492	$ 4,296
Earnings per share	$ 1.25	$ 2.15

Upon reviewing the notes that accompany the financial statements, however, you observe the following.

1. At year-end, Sunlight recorded allowances in its accounting system for expected sales discounts (of $113) and expected sales returns ($1,345). Moonbeam, while having the same types of products and customers, did not believe it had enough information to record estimates after only one year in business.
2. Both companies reported sales totaling 1,200 units. Sunlight recognizes revenue when goods are shipped to customers. Moonbeam recognizes revenue when the order is received. As of year-end, the last 100 units that Moonbeam has reported as sales have not yet been shipped to customers because Moonbeam is temporarily out of stock. An employee forgot to re-order the item on time and now the manufacturer's plant is down for annual maintenance at year-end. Production is scheduled to resume on January 15. As soon as these units are received at Moonbeam's warehouse, they will be shipped to the customers who ordered them.
3. Moonbeam used the perpetual FIFO method of inventory estimation, but Sunlight used perpetual LIFO. Both companies had the same inventory costs and reported inventory transactions as follows.

Event	Units	Cost per Unit	Total Cost
Beginning inventory	0	$ 0	$ 0
Purchase	200	12	2,400
Purchase	500	15	7,500
Sales	300		
Purchase	400	17	6,800
Sales	500		
Purchase	300	19	5,700
Sales	300		
Sales*	100		

As the wholesale cost of goods increased during the year, both firms increased selling prices, too. This last batch of sales (as reported by each firm) was sold at $30 per unit. Unlike other sales, this batch of goods was sold for cash and no returns were allowed.

4. At year-end, both companies were concerned about uncollectible accounts. Being new in the business, neither firm had much history upon which to base an estimate. Nevertheless, Sunlight estimated that approximately 4% of sales would be uncollectible. Moonbeam was more optimistic and estimated the rate at only 1%.
5. The companies differ in how they account for warranty expenses. Sunlight's management estimated the cost of future warranty claims (for goods sold during the year just

ended) and recorded an expense for that amount. Moonbeam decided that the amount would be immaterial and it would just charge these claims to expense in the later years when they were paid.

Required Which firm had the better financial results for its first year of operation? Why? Prepare any tables or schedules that you think would support your conclusion or be helpful to illustrate the basis for your conclusion.

© PHOTODISC/GETTY IMAGES

14 Analysis of Operating Activities

HOW DO OPERATIONS CREATE VALUE FOR OUR BUSINESS?

A goal of operating activities is to create value for customers who purchase a company's products. By creating value for customers, a company also can create value for its owners. To do this, a company must produce and sell its products efficiently and effectively. The opportunities, challenges, and uncertainties that arise from operating activities require managers to make operating decisions. Accounting information describes the results of operating activities. It can be used to identify and evaluate management decisions. Also, it can help decision makers form expectations about a company's economic future and make decisions that will affect that future.

Company managers like Stan, Maria, and Ellen make strategic decisions that determine how a company will compete in its product markets. The managers, investors, creditors, and other stakeholders must then evaluate how successful the strategy has been.

Food for Thought

As an advisor to the managers of Favorite Cookie Company, what issues do you think they should consider when deciding on the strategy the company will use to compete? How can managers and other decision makers evaluate how well the strategy is working?

Maria, Stan, and Ellen are meeting to decide on an operating strategy for Favorite Cookie Company.

Maria: *Our company operates in a very competitive industry. We need to determine how we are going to price our products and what competitive strategy we will use to create sales and profits.*

Stan: *We have to sell our products at a relatively high price to make a profit. I realize that our sales volume will decrease if our prices are too high, but I was hoping we could depend on the high quality of our products to create sales.*

Ellen: *I think we should focus on the quality of our products. Our cookies appeal to customers who are willing to pay for the added flavor and consistent quality. Our operating strategy should focus on what makes our products special.*

Maria: *Okay, let's figure out how we can make that strategy work and the effect the strategy should have on the performance of the company.*

Objectives

Once you have completed this chapter, you should be able to:

1. Explain the relationship between product pricing and sales volume in creating revenues and profits.
2. Explain how operating strategy affects a company's return on assets.
3. Define cost leadership and product differentiation, and explain how companies use these strategies to create profits.
4. Evaluate operating performance by using accrual and cash flow measures.
5. Examine return on equity and explain how operating, investing, and financing activities are interconnected.
6. Describe the primary components of an accounting system and how they are useful for understanding business activities.

OPERATING DECISIONS

Objective 1

Explain the relationship between product pricing and sales volume in creating revenues and profits.

After their discussions of financing and investing activities described in previous chapters, Maria, president, Stan, vice president of operations, and Ellen, chief financial officer of Favorite Cookie Company, met to discuss operating activities of their company. "In our previous discussions, we decided to finance our company primarily with common stock and to invest in automated equipment for our production process," Maria began. "Now, we need to make some operating decisions. In particular, we need to determine how to price our products so that they continue to be competitive and profitable. First, let's think about the basic factors that affect profitability. Net income is revenues minus expenses. Return on assets is net income divided by total assets.

Net income = revenues − expenses
Return on assets = net income ÷ total assets

"Return on assets provides a simple measure for evaluating how well we use our assets to create profits. We need to determine how to create a return on assets that will satisfy our stockholders. We have already decided on an automated production process that will require an initial investment in assets of $5 million. Also, expenses created by this process are mostly fixed. Exhibit 1 summarizes, from our prior discussions, our expected initial investment and expected operating results for the next two years.

EXHIBIT 1

Summary of Expected Assets and Expected Operating Results for Favorite Cookie Company

(In thousands) Assets	Initial Investment	Operating Results	Year 1	Year 2
Current assets	$1,000	Sales revenues	$ 3,000	$ 3,600
Plant assets	4,000	Cost of ingredients	(800)	(960)
Total assets	$5,000	Depreciation	(300)	(300)
		Wages and benefits	(700)	(700)
		Other operating expenses	(1,000)	(1,000)
		Operating income	200	640
		Interest expense	(20)	(20)
		Pretax income	180	620
		Income taxes	(54)	(186)
		Net income	$ 126	$ 434

Maria continued: "We expect our return on assets to be only 2.5% ($126 ÷ $5,000) in the first year. By the second year, we expect to be earning a higher profit, and we believe our future profitability will be much higher. If our investment in assets remains at approximately $5 million, our return on assets should increase to 8.7% in year two. What we can see from Exhibit 1 is that assets and expenses are pretty well determined by our production process and will not increase much until we can sell more of our product than we can produce. The real issue, then, is how to generate as much revenue as possible from our product."

Stan observed, "What I hear you saying is this: The major purpose of our company is to earn a satisfactory return for our stockholders by creating value for our customers. We have a valuable product, and we can produce it efficiently. Though these are necessary attributes of a successful business, they do not guarantee our success. We have to develop a strategy for creating profits by competing with other producers."

"Right," Maria said. "And, again, the basics are pretty straightforward. Revenue depends on two factors, number of units sold (generally referred to as sales volume) and price per unit.

Sales revenues = sales volume × price per unit

The more units we sell at a given price, the more revenue we earn. More revenue means higher net income and higher return on assets."

"Also, we know that sales volume and price are indirectly related," Ellen noted. "As price goes up, sales volume goes down. Therefore, we need to determine a price that will allow us to maximize our revenues. What we can charge is affected by the prices charged by our competitors and what our customers are willing to pay. You've looked at the competition, Stan. What are your thoughts on this matter?"

"The industry is dominated by a few major producers," Stan replied. "All of these companies produce very similar products. Consequently, competition is based largely on price. Each company attempts to sell its products at as low a price as possible. All of the companies charge about the same amount. One company cannot raise its prices without losing customers. If a company's prices get much higher than those of other companies, customers simply will buy from a competitor who sells at a lower price. Producers, then, must set prices that are close to their competitors' and that allow them to earn a reasonable profit. The most efficient producers earn the most money because they keep their production and marketing costs low. To keep these costs low, it is usually necessary to produce in high volume because so many of the costs are fixed, as we have seen for our company. Companies have to invest a lot in plant assets to get into this business. Therefore, they have to sell a lot of product to cover the costs of their investment and earn a reasonable return on assets."

DEVELOPING AN OPERATING STRATEGY

Objective 2
Explain how operating strategy affects a company's return on assets.

"Companies in our industry don't earn a huge profit on each item sold," Ellen continued. "A commonly used measure of profitability relative to amount of sales is profit margin, or return on sales. **Profit margin** is the ratio of net income to sales, or operating revenues, and is a measure of a company's ability to create profit from its sales.

Profit margin = net income ÷ sales revenues

Average profit margin in our industry is about 7%. A practical way of thinking about this measure is that companies earn 7¢ for each $1 of revenue they earn.

"Because profit margin is fairly low," Ellen went on, "companies must sell a lot of product to earn a reasonable profit. A commonly used measure of sales volume relative to total investment is asset turnover. **Asset turnover** is the ratio of sales, or operating revenues, to total assets and is a measure of a company's ability to generate sales from its investment in assets.

Asset turnover = sales revenues ÷ total assets

"Average asset turnover in our industry is 1.2. A practical way of thinking about this measure is that companies generate $1.20 of sales revenue for each $1 invested in assets.

"You can see that **return on assets** is a combination of profit margin and asset turnover.

Return on assets = profit margin × asset turnover

$$\frac{\text{Net income}}{\text{Total assets}} = \frac{\text{net income}}{\text{sales revenues}} \times \frac{\text{sales revenues}}{\text{total assets}}$$

Therefore, average return on assets in our industry is 8.4% = 7% profit margin × 1.2 asset turnover. This should be our target for the second year of operations."

"Our products are different from most competing products, however," Maria interjected. "We can compete by offering quality and taste that are not available from our competitors. Our marketing research has demonstrated that our customers are willing to pay more for our products than for those of our competitors."

"That's what we're counting on," Stan replied. "We can't price our products too much above those of our competitors, but we can command a premium because of the distinct quality and taste we offer. Thus, we can expect customers to pay a bit more for our products than for those of our competitors.

"Exhibit 2 contains some estimated sales figures for years 1 and 2. Scenario 1 estimates revenues using average industry prices and expected unit sales for Favorite Cookie Company. Scenario 2 estimates revenues using a 10% premium over the average industry price. Expected unit sales will be lower in scenario 2 than in scenario 1 because of the higher price. I don't expect the decrease in sales volume to be very large, however, because of the added value of our products. I think most customers will pay a higher price if we can make them aware of the higher quality.

"As you can see from the first scenario, if we charge average industry prices, we will fall below our expected total sales revenues of $3 million in year 1 and $3.6 million in year 2. The 10% premium gets us to our target sales revenue levels each year."

Maria asked, "If the higher price produces more revenue, why not use a higher premium, say 20%? Why should we be content with a 10% premium? Surely our quality justifies the higher price."

"We have to be careful," Stan answered. "We are marketing a new product, and customers will have to determine for themselves that it is a better product than they can get from our competitors. We expect sales to increase each year as more customers discover our product. If we start out with too high a price, however, customers will be discouraged from trying our product. Our marketing people have done some market tests, and they believe a premium of much above 10% will slow sales considerably over the first few years. Our primary challenge in the first couple of years is to get the product into the hands of customers. Once they are sold on its value, we can consider higher prices.

EXHIBIT 2
Estimated Sales Volume at Different Price Levels for Favorite Cookie Company

	Units		Revenues	
Unit Price	Year 1	Year 2	Year 1	Year 2
Scenario 1: Sell at average industry price				
$27	108,000	130,000	$2,916,000	$3,510,000
Scenario 2: Sell at premium price (10% above industry average)				
$30	100,000	120,000	$3,000,000	$3,600,000

EXHIBIT 3
Expected Return on Assets for Favorite Cookie Company in Year 2

Estimated sales revenues	$3,600,000	
Estimated net income	434,000	
Estimated assets	5,000,000	
Profit margin	12.06%	$434,000 ÷ $3,600,000
Asset turnover	0.720	$3,600,000 ÷ $5,000,000
Return on assets	8.68%	12.06% × 0.720

"Also, a 10% premium earns us a competitive return in the second year. Exhibit 3 computes our expected profit margin, asset turnover, and return on assets in year 2. At estimated sales of $3.6 million, we expect to earn a profit of $434,000 (from Exhibit 1). Assuming that we maintain a total investment in assets of $5 million, we will earn a return on assets of 8.68% in year 2, which is slightly above the industry average of 8.4%."

"Is it reasonable to expect our total assets to stay at $5 million, Ellen?" Maria asked.

"I think so," Ellen responded. "We won't need much additional plant investment, and I think we can keep current assets fairly constant. I don't see anything wrong with Stan's estimates."

Stan continued, "You can see that our asset turnover is lower than average—0.72 (Exhibit 3), compared with 1.2 for the industry. We are not going to sell enough product, even if we sell at the industry average price, to generate a high asset turnover. Our product is too new. It will take several years for us to build sales volume. Our asset turnover should increase over time.

"We make up for the low asset turnover with a high profit margin, however. Our expected profit margin is a little over 12% (Exhibit 3), compared with 7% for the industry. As asset turnover increases, a high profit margin will earn us a much higher return than the industry average. A key to our success is sales volume. If we can increase sales each year without incurring a lot of additional expenses, we should make a lot of money."

Maria and Ellen nodded in agreement. "Now let's see if we can make our plans work," Maria said, closing the meeting.

Self-Study Problem #1

Information is presented below for two appliance companies.

(In thousands)	Ardmore	Bellwood
Sales revenues	$ 800	$800
Net income	100	80
Total assets	1,000	800

Required

A. Compute profit margin, asset turnover, and return on assets for each company.

B. Compare the operating strategies of the two companies and explain which company is doing the better job with its strategy.

C. Using the information presented, discuss how each company could improve its profits and return on assets.

The solution to Self-Study Problem 1 appears at the end of the chapter.

INTERPRETATION OF OPERATING ACTIVITIES

Objective 3

Define cost leadership and product differentiation, and explain how companies use these strategies to create profits.

To create profits and value for stockholders, a company must use its assets effectively to create and sell products demanded by customers. Also, it must operate efficiently so that revenues exceed expenses. Companies that are more effective and efficient earn higher profits and are more valuable than less effective and less efficient companies. Asset turnover is a measure of effectiveness. A company that sells more of its products will have a higher asset turnover than a company with the same amount of assets that sells less of its product. Profit margin is a measure of efficiency. A company that is efficient in controlling costs and converting resources into products will have a higher profit margin than a company with the same amount of sales that is less efficient.

Asset turnover and profit margin are not the same for all companies, even those that are highly profitable and create high value. Among highly profitable companies, asset turnover is higher for some and profit margin is higher for others. These components of return on assets provide useful information about companies' operating activities. To illustrate, consider the information in Exhibit 4.

This exhibit provides information for **Microsoft** and **Procter & Gamble**. It compares profit margin, asset turnover, and return on assets for the companies. Microsoft is a larger company than Procter & Gamble. Procter & Gamble has a smaller profit margin but a higher asset turnover than Microsoft in both years.

Cost Leadership and Product Differentiation Strategies

Differences in profit margin and asset turnover among companies are not accidents. The strategies companies use to create profits differ. To generate high returns, companies with lower asset turnovers, like Microsoft, must generate high profit margins. Thus, they must carefully control production and selling costs to make sure they earn a reasonable profit on each dollar of product sold. Observe from Exhibit 4 that Microsoft earned 22.2¢ on each dollar of sales in 2004, compared with 12.6¢ for Procter & Gamble.

Companies like Microsoft can earn higher profit margins because they sell products that are differentiated from their competitors' products. These products offer certain qualities or features that build a customer following. Microsoft is known worldwide for its software products. Customers are willing to pay more for Microsoft's products than for competitor products offered by other companies, some of which are sold at a much lower cost or are provided without cost.

Procter & Gamble also sells some specialized products, but its products are less distinct from competitors than Microsoft's products. Its products command less of a premium. Consequently, Procter & Gamble depends more on asset turnover to generate a return than does Microsoft. Low profit margin companies must sell in high volumes to make a profit. Therefore, high asset turnover is essential to their success.

Because they must keep their prices low to generate high sales volume, low profit margin companies must keep their operating expenses low so they can earn a profit. These companies use a **cost leadership strategy** to generate profits. They lead their competitors in selling high quantities of products by keeping the prices of these products

EXHIBIT 4

Profit Margin, Asset Turnover, and Return on Assets for Microsoft and Procter & Gamble

	Microsoft		*Procter & Gamble*	
(In millions)	2004	2003	2004	2003
Net income	$ 8,168	$ 7,531	$ 6,481	$ 5,186
Total revenues	36,835	32,187	51,407	43,377
Total assets	92,389	81,732	57,048	43,706
Asset turnover	0.399	0.394	0.901	0.992
Profit margin	22.2%	23.4%	12.6%	12.0%
Return on assets	8.8%	9.2%	11.4%	11.9%

EXHIBIT 5
Cost Leadership and Product Differentiation as Alternative Operating Strategies

Operating Strategy	Profit Margin	Asset Turnover
Cost Leadership	Low	High
Product Differentiation	High	Low

competitive. High profit margin companies use a **product differentiation strategy**. They compete by offering products with special features or qualities that customers are willing to buy at a premium.

Exhibit 5 illustrates these operating strategies. **Cost leadership and product differentiation are two ends of a competitive spectrum.** Microsoft and Procter & Gamble are not at either end of the spectrum. However, Microsoft falls closer toward the product differentiation end than Procter & Gamble does. Most companies fall somewhere between the two ends of the spectrum. In fact, many companies offer several products or product lines of the same type to compete across the spectrum. For example, manufacturers of TVs and other electronic equipment offer products in various sizes and with various features to appeal to customers who want a low-cost product and to those who want special features. Most automobile companies offer brands and models of various sizes and with various features. Some of these brands or models are targeted toward customers who are looking primarily for economical transportation. Others are targeted toward customers who are looking primarily for style or comfort.

Both asset turnover and profit margin are important for all companies. A company using a cost leadership strategy relies on high sales volume. It cannot ignore profit margin, however. Because this type of company earns a relatively low profit margin, a small drop in this margin can make a big difference in the company's profitability. Cost leadership and product differentiation describe different ways in which companies compete to earn a profit. Both Microsoft and Procter & Gamble have gained success by effectively selling products and efficiently controlling costs.

A company's operating strategy determines the types of decisions that are important for the company's success. Cost leadership companies typically buy and sell in high volume. They keep their operations streamlined to keep costs low. Usually, few specialized customer services are offered. Sales facilities typically are not elaborate. Advertising often emphasizes low prices and convenient "one-stop" shopping. Little research and development activity takes place.

Product differentiation companies produce and sell specialized products. They emphasize service quality and often use elaborate selling facilities—compare the facilities of brand-name stores in a typical mall with those of discount stores like **Wal-Mart**, for example. Advertising emphasizes the high quality or special features of their products and how these products are better than products offered by competitors. An attempt is made to build brand loyalty. Research and development activities often are critical for these companies. For example, **Microsoft** has become one of the most profitable software companies by continuing to develop products that are not available from other producers.

Comparing Accrual and Cash Flow Measures of Operating Performance

Objective 4
Evaluate operating performance by using accrual and cash flow measures.

Return on assets measures performance using accrual-based net income. Operating cash flow is also an important measure of operating activities. If a company does not convert its profits into cash, the profits are a misleading performance indicator. The ratio of **operating cash flow to total assets** is useful for comparing the operating cash flows of different companies. It is a measure of cash flow generated during a period through the use of assets to produce and sell goods and services.

Exhibit 6 provides operating cash flow to total assets information for Microsoft and Procter & Gamble. Consistent with its return on assets, Microsoft's operating cash flows were lower than those of Procter & Gamble in both years. Procter & Gamble was converting a larger portion of its earnings into cash than was Microsoft in these years.

EXHIBIT 6
A Comparison of Operating Cash Flows for Microsoft and Procter & Gamble

	Microsoft		Procter & Gamble	
(In millions)	2004	2003	2004	2003
Net income	$ 8,168	$ 7,531	$6,481	$5,186
Depreciation and amortization	1,186	1,393	1,733	1,703
Other adjustments	5,272	6,873	1,148	1,811
Net cash from operations	14,626	15,797	9,362	8,700
Operating cash flows to total assets	15.8%	19.3%	16.4%	19.9%

The operating activities sections of the statements of cash flows shown in Exhibit 6 provides information about the changes in cash flows from 2003 to 2004. Net cash flow was substantially higher than net income because of depreciation and amortization expenses that did not require cash payments and changes in current asset and liability accounts.

The statement of cash flows is useful for identifying the amount of cash a company is generating from its operating activities. Both Microsoft and Procter & Gamble were creating large amounts of cash from operations, though Microsoft's operating cash flow decreased from 2003 to 2004.

Further Evaluation of Operating Strategy

As we have discussed, profit margin and asset turnover are useful measures for understanding and evaluating a company's operating strategy. Each of these ratios can be separated into other ratios for more detailed analysis of a company's operating activities. For example, assets can be divided into individual asset categories for a more detailed examination of turnover. The categories that are most often examined are inventory and receivables. Inventory turnover and receivables turnover compare income statement numbers with balance sheet numbers.

Inventory turnover **is the ratio of cost of goods sold (from the income statement) to inventory (from the balance sheet); it measures the success of a company in converting its investment in inventory into sales.** Though inventory is necessary for many companies, it is expensive for a company to maintain large amounts of inventory. If the amount of inventory increases relative to selling activities, as measured by cost of goods sold, a company is less effective in using its resources. A major decrease in inventory turnover or a ratio that is lower than that of similar companies indicates that a company is investing too heavily in inventory for the amount of product it is selling.

Exhibit 7 provides selected financial statement information for Microsoft and Procter & Gamble. The exhibit provides several financial ratios for the two companies. Inventory turnover was higher for Microsoft than for Procter & Gamble in both years. The higher ratio indicates that Microsoft was selling its inventory faster than Procter & Gamble.

A ratio related to inventory turnover is *day's sales in inventories,* **the ratio of inventory to average daily cost of goods sold.** Average daily cost of goods sold is computed by dividing cost of goods sold by 365. This ratio measures the average number of days for a company to sell its total inventory, or how many days' supply of inventory it keeps on hand. Procter & Gamble maintains higher inventory levels than Microsoft. These ratios increased for both companies from 2003 to 2004. An increase in day's sales in inventories signals that a company is not selling its products as quickly and often is a sign that the company is likely to become less profitable. Sales for both Microsoft and Procter & Gamble are strong and inventory levels are low, however.

Accounts receivable turnover **is the ratio of sales revenues (from the income statement) to accounts receivable (from the balance sheet); it measures a company's ability to convert revenues into cash.** A higher ratio indicates that a greater portion of sales is being collected in cash during a period. Microsoft had higher amounts of receivables relative to sales in both years. Therefore, its accounts receivable turnover was lower in both years.

EXHIBIT 7 Selected Financial Statement Information and Ratios for Microsoft and Procter & Gamble

	Microsoft		Procter & Gamble	
(In millions)	2004	2003	2004	2003
Sales revenues	$ 36,835	$ 32,187	$ 51,407	$ 43,377
Cost of goods sold	6,716	6,059	25,076	22,141
Gross profit	30,119	26,128	26,331	21,236
Income from operations	27,801	22,642	9,827	7,853
Interest expense	—	—	629	561
Net income	8,168	7,531	6,481	5,186
Accounts receivable	5,890	5,196	4,062	3,038
Inventories	640	421	4,400	3,640
Property and equipment	2,326	2,223	14,108	13,104
Total assets	92,389	81,732	57,048	43,706
Total liabilities	17,564	16,820	39,770	27,520
Total shareholders' equity	74,825	64,912	17,278	16,186
Market value	293,000	269,000	122,000	112,000
Inventory turnover (cost of sales ÷ inventory)	10.5	14.4	5.7	6.1
Days' sales in inventories (inventory ÷ (cost of sales ÷ 365))	34.8	25.4	64.0	60.0
Accounts receivable turnover (sales ÷ receivables)	6.3	6.2	12.7	14.3
Average collection period (receivables ÷ (sales ÷ 365))	58.4	58.9	28.8	25.6
Fixed asset turnover (sales ÷ plant assets)	15.8	14.5	3.6	3.3
Gross profit margin (gross profit ÷ sales)	81.8%	81.2%	51.2%	49.0%
Operating profit margin (operating income ÷ sales)	75.5%	70.3%	19.1%	18.1%
Financial leverage (assets ÷ equity)	1.2	1.3	3.3	2.7
Times interest earned (operating income ÷ interest expense)			15.6	14.0
Return on assets (net income ÷ assets)	8.8%	9.2%	11.4%	11.9%
Return on equity (ROA × financial leverage)	10.6%	12.0%	37.6%	32.1%
Market to book value (market value ÷ equity)	3.9	4.1	7.1	6.9

A ratio related to accounts receivable turnover is *average collection period*, **the ratio of accounts receivable to average daily sales.** Average daily sales are computed by dividing sales revenue by 365. This ratio measures how long it takes a company, on average, to collect its receivables. The ratio was higher in both years for Microsoft. An increase in the ratio may signal that a company is having difficulty collecting cash from its customers. There is no indication that this is a problem for either Microsoft or Procter & Gamble.

Another turnover ratio is *fixed asset turnover*, **the ratio of sales revenues to fixed assets (property and equipment).** The ratio measures the effectiveness of a company in using its investment in fixed assets to create sales. The ratio was higher for Microsoft than Procter & Gamble in both years. Microsoft generates higher sales relative to its investment in fixed assets than Procter & Gamble.

Asset turnover, inventory turnover, day's sales in inventories, accounts receivable turnover, average collection period, and fixed asset turnover are primarily effectiveness measures. They indicate how well a company is using its assets to sell its products and collect cash from its customers.

In addition to examining turnover ratios to evaluate effectiveness, we can examine changes in the components of profit margin to provide additional information about a company's efficiency. Two commonly used components are gross profit margin and operating profit margin. Both ratios compare income statement numbers with other income statement numbers.

Gross profit margin **is the ratio of gross profit (sales revenues minus cost of goods sold) to sales revenues; it measures efficiency in the production or purchase of goods for sale.** A high gross profit margin indicates that a company is controlling its product costs. Product costs are the costs of merchandise for merchandising companies and production costs for manufacturing companies. A decrease in gross profit margin or a margin lower than that of similar companies indicates that a company is not efficient in producing or purchasing goods for sale. Exhibit 7 indicates that Procter & Gamble's gross profit margins were lower than those of Microsoft.

Operating profit margin **is the ratio of operating income (sales revenues minus operating expenses) to sales revenues.** When compared with gross profit margin, operating profit margin is an indicator of a company's efficiency in controlling operating costs other than product costs. These costs are primarily period expenses associated with selling and administrative activities. Consequently, operating profit margin can be used to evaluate a company's efficiency in controlling its selling and administrative costs.

Microsoft's operating profit margin increased from 70.3% in 2003 to 75.5% in 2004 (Exhibit 7). Microsoft's operating profit margin was much higher in both years than was Procter & Gamble's. The differences reflect Microsoft's low cost of goods sold numbers. Most of Microsoft's costs are not product related costs.

Linking Operating and Investing Activities with Financing Activities

Objective 5

Examine return on equity and explain how operating, investing, and financing activities are interconnected.

Return on assets (and operating cash flow to assets) links a company's operating activities (profits or operating cash flows) with its investing activities (total assets). Thus, return on assets measures the ability of a company to use its investments to generate operating results. Completing the link among operating, investing, and financing activities requires that we examine financial leverage and return on equity.

Recall from Chapter 10 that return on equity is return on assets times financial leverage as measured by the assets to equity ratio. Thus, return on equity is a summary measure of the success of a company's financing, investing, and operating activities. We can separate return on equity into three components.

Return on Equity = Profit Margin × Asset Turnover × Financial Leverage

$$\frac{\text{Net Income}}{\text{Equity}} = \frac{\text{Net Income}}{\text{Sales Revenues}} \times \frac{\text{Sales Revenues}}{\text{Total Assets}} \times \frac{\text{Total Assets}}{\text{Equity}}$$

Profit margin measures the ability of a company to operate efficiently to produce profits (operating activities). Asset turnover measures the ability of a company to create sales (operating activities) from investments in assets (investing activities). Assets to equity measures the capital structure (financing activities) used by a company to pay for its assets (investing activities). Companies can use each of these components to improve their returns to stockholders and their company value.

Exhibit 7 includes return on equity and market to book value ratios for Microsoft and Procter & Gamble. Procter & Gamble has higher financial leverage than Microsoft. This leverage worked in favor of Procter & Gamble. Financial leverage resulted in higher return on equity than in return on assets.

Financial leverage can result in higher return for a company's stockholders. However, the higher return is associated with greater financial risk because debt and interest must be paid. Another ratio that is used to measure financial risk is *times interest earned,* **the ratio of operating income (income before interest and taxes) to interest expense.** The ratio is larger when a company incurs relatively small amounts of interest. From Exhibit 7, we can see that Procter & Gamble was incurring much higher interest expense and a lower times interest earned than Microsoft, which has no interest-paying debt. Procter & Gamble's market to book value was higher in both years.

A company's value depends on its operating activities in relation to its investing and financing activities. All of these activities are interrelated and must be considered together to understand a company's performance. Financial statements are a major source of information for measuring and evaluating these activities. They provide information about both the results of activities for a period and changes in results from one period to the next. Thus, both return on assets and equity and the amount of change in return on assets and equity from one period to the next are important for evaluating performance. Companies with high and increasing returns usually are more valuable than companies with low and decreasing returns.

Learning Note - In this book, we have discussed some major issues that are important for understanding financial accounting information and using this information to evaluate performance. We have focused on those issues that we believe are most important. Our discussion has not included many other issues that are relevant for understanding and using accounting information because space prohibits coverage of all relevant topics. Other topics are covered in more advanced accounting and business courses.

Self-Study Problem #2

Information is provided below for two companies that produce and sell plastic containers.

	Caseopia		**Dragoon**	
(In thousands)	**2008**	**2007**	**2008**	**2007**
Sales revenues	$750	$700	$320	$300
Cost of goods sold	450	420	208	180
Gross profit	300	280	112	120
Operating expenses	120	135	50	43
Operating income	180	145	62	77
Net income	100	87	37	46
Accounts receivable	46	43	23	20
Inventories	82	80	50	42
Total assets	960	900	500	450

Required

A. Compute profit margin, gross profit margin, operating profit margin, asset turnover, accounts receivable turnover, inventory turnover, and return on assets for each company.

B. Use these ratios to evaluate the operating activities of each company and to compare the companies' performance.

The solution to Self-Study Problem 2 appears at the end of the chapter.

THE BIG PICTURE

In this final section, we summarize the primary topics covered in this book. It is important to see how each topic fits into the overall story in order to understand the importance of accounting as a business tool.

Exhibit 8 illustrates the role of accounting in the business decision process. A business is a transformation process in which (1) financial resources are obtained through

EXHIBIT 8
Accounting and Business Decisions

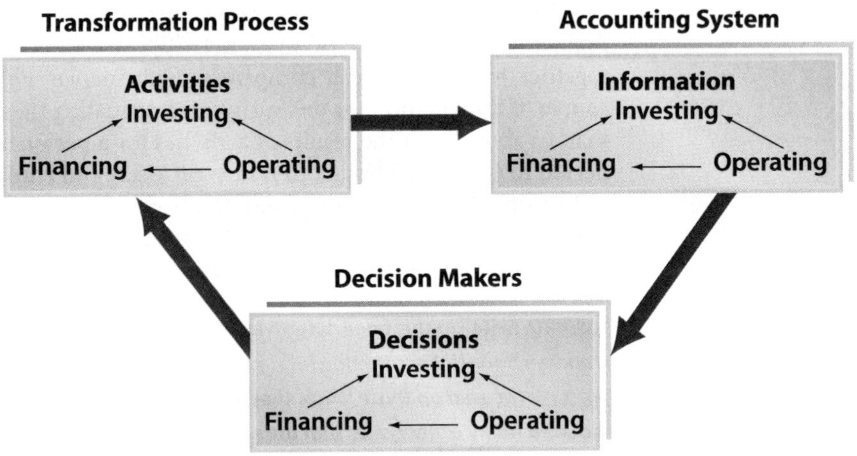

financing activities, (2) financial resources are used to acquire other resources through investing activities, and (3) resources are used to produce and sell goods and services through operating activities. Accounting is an information system for measuring and reporting the transformation of resources into goods and services and the sale or transfer of these goods and services to customers. Thus, the accounting system provides information about activities that have occurred in the transformation process. This information is used by decision makers both to evaluate past activities and to plan for future activities that are part of the transformation process. Accordingly, the accounting system links past events to future events.

Objective 6
Describe the primary components of an accounting system and how they are useful for understanding business activities.

Accounting information plays a crucial role in business decisions. Accounting information, like any other information, tells only a partial story. Certain aspects of a company's activities are measured, summarized, and reported. Other aspects are ignored. Assumptions and estimations are necessary to measure certain activities for which more specific, timely information is not available. Thus, the picture of a company provided by accounting information is incomplete and does not fully represent the actual company. The picture that is presented depends on the particular set of rules used to measure and report the company's activities. Organizations that set accounting standards, like the FASB, influence the type of picture that is presented.

Accounting information provides a representation of a company. The company is too complex to be represented completely. An information system identifies certain attributes of the company and summarizes a large amount of complex data to make them useful to decision makers. As a result, the representation of the company is only an approximation of the company. Rules used by the system affect how the company is represented. A different set of rules would result in a different representation. Accordingly, if decision makers are to use the representation provided by the system, they need to understand the system so that they are not misled by differences between the representation and the actual company. Consequently, it is essential for those who use accounting information to make business decisions to understand major components of the accounting system.

Exhibit 9 provides a more detailed description of the accounting system. The primary components of the system include measurement rules, processing and storage procedures, reporting rules, and reports.

Measurement rules determine which attributes of the transformation process enter the accounting system. Measurement units used to measure activities in the transformation process are primarily dollar values, based on the historical costs of resources acquired or used in the transformation process. Transactions (primarily exchanges of resources) are measured on an accrual basis. This basis recognizes events in the transformation process when they cause resources to increase or decrease, rather than when cash is received or paid. These events are recognized in specific fiscal periods so that activities in the transformation process can be determined and evaluated on a timely

EXHIBIT 9
The Accounting Information System

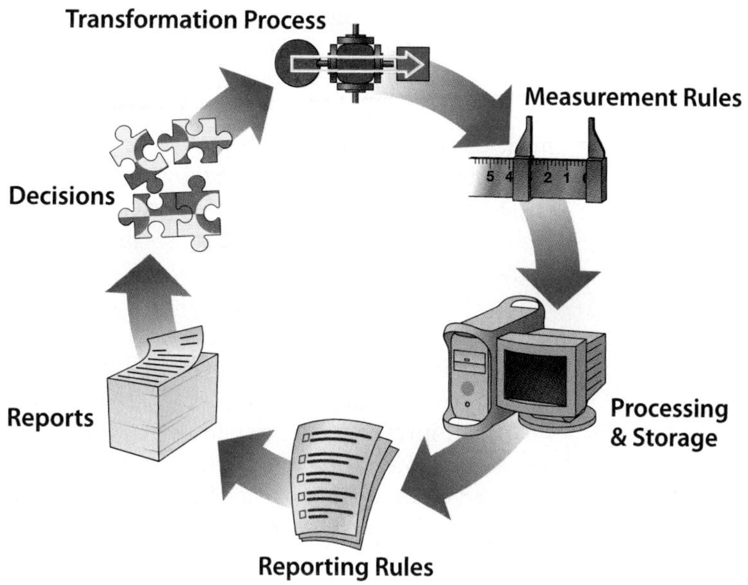

basis. Expenses are matched with revenues in the period in which resources are consumed. The matching of expenses with revenues in particular fiscal periods requires estimation of the financial effects of some events. For example, depreciation and inventory estimation are used to allocate asset costs to specific periods. Accounting measurement rules often are conservative. These rules recognize expenses or losses in the period in which an asset is likely to have been consumed or impaired or in which a liability is likely to have been incurred. Revenues or gains often are deferred, however, until all events that created the revenue or gain have been completed. Conservatism recognizes that the financial effects of events often are estimates and attempts to ensure that revenues and profits are not overstated by optimistic managers. The values of certain resources that are difficult to measure objectively, such as management or employee skills and brand names, are excluded from accounting measurement.

Processing and storage procedures determine how information from the transformation process enters the accounting system and how this information is summarized and stored so that it can be provided to decision makers. Double-entry bookkeeping has been the traditional method of recording transactions in an accounting system. Each transaction is recorded in two or more accounts, which are information categories that can be classified into five types: assets, liabilities, owners' equity, revenues, and expenses. The accounting cycle is a process for entering, processing, and summarizing accounting information. The process involves (1) examining business activities, (2) recording transactions, (3) updating account balances, (4) making end-of-period adjustments, (5) preparing financial statements, and (6) closing revenue and expense accounts. In most businesses, many of these steps are performed by computer programs. Internal control procedures ensure the accuracy of information in the accounting system.

Reporting rules determine the type and format of information reported by an accounting system. Reporting rules govern the separation of accounting information into individual financial statements. The rules specify the order of accounts or activities and the amount of detail reported in financial statements and accompanying notes. Direct and indirect formats for reporting the statement of cash flows are examples of reporting rules. Other examples include requirements that companies report their accounting policies and certain measurement rules in notes to financial statements. In general, reporting rules require companies to provide sufficient information in their financial statements or accompanying notes so that users are fully informed about the companies' financial activities. Reporting rules also specify the timing of reports. For example, most corporations are required to provide annual reports and quarterly updates to their stockholders. In addition to general reports such as financial statements, specific reporting rules may be used to design reports for special uses, such as those for managers and taxing authorities.

Accounting reports are the summary documents provided to decision makers. Financial statements (income statement, balance sheet, statement of cash flows, and statement of stockholders' equity) are the primary financial accounting reports. These statements usually are accompanied by notes that explain numbers or activities in the statements. Financial statements reported to external decision makers usually are accompanied by an audit report that expresses the auditor's opinion about whether the statements fairly present the company's financial position and results of operations. Accounting reports also may contain explanations by company management about events reported in the financial statements.

Decisions of managers, owners, creditors, and others depend, in part, on their understanding of the information reported by a company's accounting system. Managers make financing, investing, and operating decisions that determine the future of a company. These decisions rely on information about past financing, investing, and operating activities, and on estimation of the effects of decisions on future activities. Owners, creditors, and other users evaluate managers' financing, investing, and operating activities. They use accounting information to assess how well a company has performed and how well it is likely to perform in the future.

Information about financing activities identifies a company's capital structure and the particular types of debt and equity a company uses to finance its assets. Financial statements help users determine the effects of financial leverage on profitability and the ability of a company to meet its debt obligations. They provide information about when obligations will become due and about changes in financing, such as new borrowing, repaying debt, and selling and repurchasing stock.

Information about investing activities identifies both the types of assets a company has acquired and the changes in these assets over time. Financial statement users can assess whether a company is growing (by acquiring additional assets) and whether those assets are being used productively to generate additional sales and profits. Information about assets also is useful for evaluating uncertainty about future profits if a company's sales are lower than expected. Companies with high operating leverage (high fixed to total costs) are sensitive to sales volatility because they cannot reduce many of their costs—for example, those associated with production facilities—in the short run.

Information about operating activities identifies how well a company is able to use its assets to create sales and to control production and selling costs so that it earns a profit. This information also is useful for assessing a company's ability to convert profits to cash and its ability to pay dividends or invest in growth opportunities. Separate reporting of unusual or nonrecurring events helps users distinguish ordinary events from those requiring special analysis.

Exhibit 10 summarizes information derived from financial statements for evaluating a company's performance and assessing its value. Company value is depicted on the top line of the illustration as being derived primarily from a company's ability to earn profits. Profits, in turn, depend on a company's ability to sell goods and services (revenues) and its ability to use resources efficiently in producing and selling those products (expenses). Revenues and expenses depend on a company's investment in assets that can be used to produce and sell its products. A larger investment in assets should permit a company to generate higher revenues, but it also results in higher expenses. The ability of a company to invest in assets depends on financing available from debt and equity. The amounts of debt and equity and the mix of debt relative to equity affect investment decisions and operating results. Profits from operating results also are a source of equity through retained earnings.

Accounting measures such as profit margin and asset turnover summarize relationships among the various activities that create company value. Profit margin links profits to revenues. Asset turnover links revenues to assets. Return on assets links profits to assets. Return on equity links revenues to equity and encompasses all of the

EXHIBIT 10 Using Accounting Information to Make Decisions About Company Value

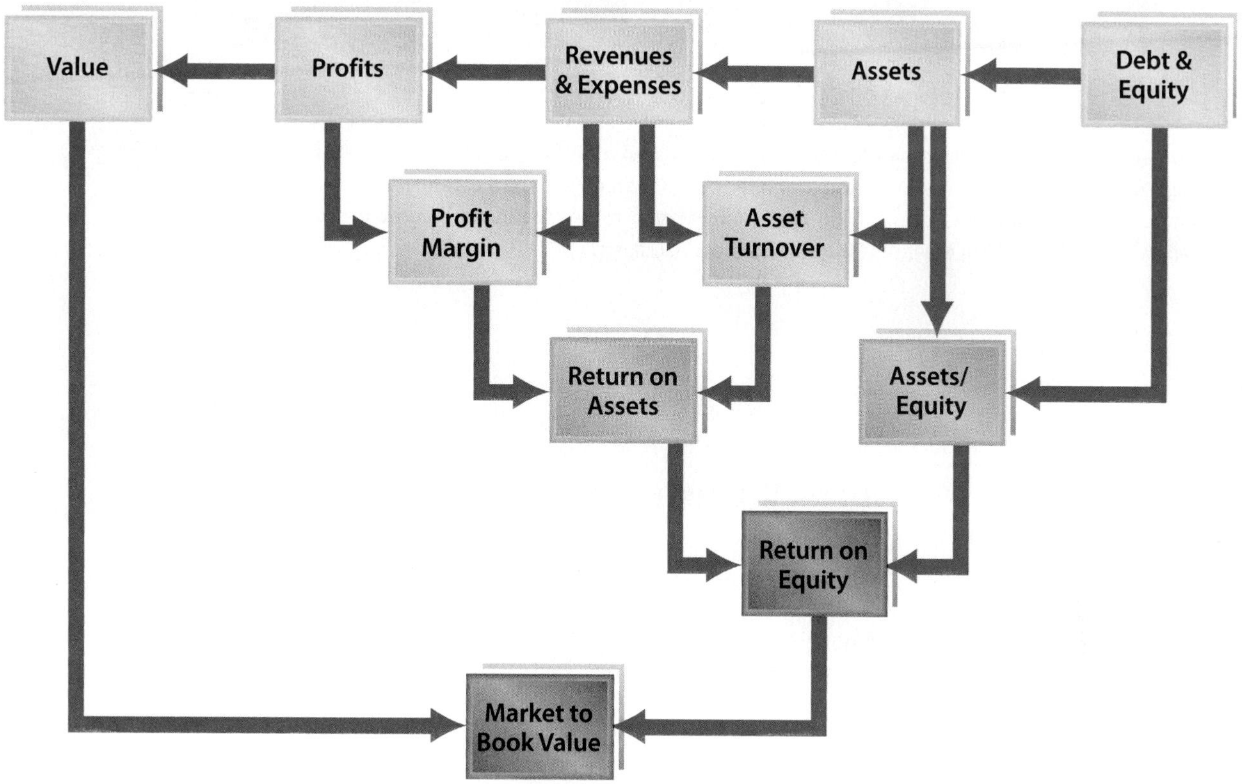

accounting relationships from profits through revenues and expenses, assets, debt, and equity. Therefore, it incorporates all of the activities in a company's transformation process: financing, investing, and operating. Finally, market to book value links company value (market value of stockholders' equity) to accounting numbers. When the accounting performance measures depicted in the exhibit are high, company value typically is high.

Consequently, understanding accounting information is important for understanding company value. Understanding the accounting system, including the rules used to measure and report information and the procedures used to capture and summarize this information, is critical to understanding accounting information. The primary goal of this book has been to help you understand the components of the accounting system, how they work, and how they can be used to understand business activities.

Self-Study Problem #3

To understand a company's operating activities, it is important to understand the relationships among operating, investing, and financing activities and to understand the accounting system that provides information about these activities.

Required Explain why.

The solution to Self-Study Problem 3 appears at the end of the chapter.

THINKING BEYOND THE QUESTION

HOW DO OPERATIONS CREATE VALUE FOR OUR BUSINESS?

Companies use different strategies to earn profits. Successful use of these strategies results in high return on the company's investment and a high return for its stockholders. A careful review of a company's financial statements can provide useful information for evaluating the company's performance. Why is accounting essential for good business decisions?

Self-Study Problem Solutions

SSP14-1 A. Profit margin = net income ÷ sales revenues

Ardmore: 12.5% = \$100 ÷ \$800
Bellwood: 10% = \$80 ÷ \$800

Asset turnover = sales revenues ÷ total assets

Ardmore: 0.8 = \$800 ÷ \$1,000
Bellwood: 1.0 = \$800 ÷ \$800

Return on assets = profit margin × asset turnover

Ardmore: 10.0% = 12.5% × 0.8
Bellwood: 10.0% = 10% × 1.0

B. Ardmore appears to charge higher prices for its products than Bellwood. It earns more for each dollar of sales (12.5¢ for Ardmore versus 10¢ for Bellwood). Bellwood sells more of its product than Ardmore, however. It sells \$1 of product for each \$1 invested in assets, whereas Ardmore sells 80¢ for each \$1 invested. By charging lower prices, Bellwood is able to sell more product.

Ardmore earns a higher net income than Bellwood, but each company earns the same return on assets. Therefore, neither company is more profitable than the other relative to their investments in assets. We can conclude that each company is profitable, but the companies use different strategies to create their profits. Ardmore apparently sells products with features or quality that are more desirable than those of Bellwood. Customers are willing to pay more for these products, though they purchase fewer of them. Bellwood competes by selling lower-price products and by selling a higher volume than Ardmore.

C. The primary factors involved in creating a high return on assets are revenues, expenses, and assets. Revenues depend on sales price and volume. Companies are more effective if they can sell more of their products to earn higher revenues without increasing expenses. Companies increase revenues by increasing sales prices if they sell the same number of units. Also, they increase revenues by increasing sales volume if they sell at the same price. They earn higher net income if they reduce expenses without decreasing sales revenues. Finally, companies increase return on assets by reducing the amount of assets they need to earn a given amount of net income. Companies are more efficient if they reduce assets or expenses without reducing revenues. Thus, companies become more profitable by becoming more effective or efficient.

SSP14-2 A.

	Caseopia		Dragoon	
	2008	2007	2008	2007
Profit margin	$100 ÷ $750 = 13.3%	$87 ÷ $700 = 12.4%	$37 ÷ $320 = 11.6%	$46 ÷ $300 = 15.3%
Gross profit margin	$300 ÷ $750 = 40.0%	$280 ÷ $700 = 40.0%	$112 ÷ $320 = 35.0%	$120 ÷ $300 = 40.0%
Operating profit margin	$180 ÷ $750 = 24.0%	$145 ÷ $700 = 20.7%	$62 ÷ $320 = 19.4%	$77 ÷ $300 = 25.7%
Asset turnover	$750 ÷ $960 = 0.781	$700 ÷ $900 = 0.778	$320 ÷ $500 = 0.640	$300 ÷ $450 = 0.667
Accounts receivable turnover	$750 ÷ $46 = 16.304	$700 ÷ $43 = 16.279	$320 ÷ $23 = 13.913	$300 ÷ $20 = 15.000
Inventory turnover	$450 ÷ $82 = 5.488	$420 ÷ $80 = 5.250	$208 ÷ $50 = 4.160	$180 ÷ $42 = 4.286
Return on assets	$100 ÷ $960 = 10.4%	$87 ÷ $900 = 9.7%	$37 ÷ $500 = 7.4%	$46 ÷ $450 = 10.2%

B. Dragoon's return on assets was higher than Caseopia's in 2007. During 2008, Caseopia's return on assets increased while Dragoon's decreased, so that Caseopia's return was higher in 2008. Several factors account for these changes. Dragoon's profit margin decreased while Caseopia's increased. This change was due to a decrease in Dragoon's gross profit margin and an increase in Caseopia's operating profit margin. Dragoon was less efficient in 2008 than in 2007 in controlling production costs, and Caseopia was more efficient in controlling selling and administrative costs. Asset turnover increased slightly for Caseopia and decreased slightly for Dragoon. Accounts receivable turnover was lower in 2008 than in 2007 for Dragoon. Dragoon's performance was worse in 2008 than in 2007, primarily due to its lower profit margin. Caseopia's performance was better in 2008, primarily due to its higher profit margin. Caseopia's profit margin and asset turnover ratios were higher in 2008 than Dragoon's, indicating that it was the better-performing company.

SSP14-3 Operating activities involve the production and sale of goods and services. Producing and selling products requires investment in assets that are used in the production and selling processes. As a company increases in size by investing in additional assets, it should be able to produce and sell more products. Thus, revenues, expenses, and operating cash flows are affected by a company's assets. Assets are financed by debt and equity, including retained earnings. Consequently, the more assets a company has, the more debt and equity it requires. The types of financing a company uses affect its financial leverage. The types of assets it uses affect its operating leverage. Increases in financial and operating leverage increase uncertainty about a company's future profitability. Therefore, operating, investing, and financing activities are linked; one type of activity has a major effect on the other types of activities. Operating activities cannot be evaluated separately from investing and financing activities. Relationships among these activities are important for understanding a company's past performance and potential future performance.

A company's accounting system provides information for understanding the company's financing, investing, and operating activities. This information has to be interpreted by decision makers. Interpretation depends on understanding how the information was created. For example, accounting systems use measurement and reporting rules to determine what information will be reported to decision makers and how activities will be measured. These rules result in a particular presentation of a company's activities; the presentation would be different if other rules were used. Users should understand that accounting information, like any information, provides only an approximation of the underlying company. Not all aspects of a company are reported. Those that are reported are determined by the system. Therefore, understanding the information and being able to use it effectively to make decisions requires the decision maker to understand the biases and limitations of the information system.

Define Terms and Concepts Defined in This Chapter

accounts receivable turnover (534)
average collection period (535)
day's sales in inventories (534)
fixed asset turnover (535)
gross profit margin (535)
inventory turnover (534)
operating profit margin (536)
times interest earned (536)

Review Summary of Important Concepts

1. Operating decisions involve choices about how a company will produce and sell products to earn revenues and make a profit.
   a. Sales revenue depends on sales volume and price per unit, which are indirectly related. An increase in price usually results in a decrease in volume.
   b. The prices a company can charge for its products depend on what customers are willing to pay based on the value of the products to them and the prices charged by competitors.
   c. If a market is highly competitive and companies in the market produce very similar products, the companies usually will compete on the basis of price. They will keep their prices low to attract customers and will depend on high sales volume to earn a profit.
   d. If a company can distinguish its products from competitors' products by special features or qualities, it can charge a higher price and earn more per unit from customers who are willing to pay for these features or qualities.
   e. Asset turnover measures the volume of sales (in dollars) relative to a company's investment in assets. Companies that compete using low prices require high asset turnover to earn a high profit and return on assets.
   f. Profit margin measures the amount of income a company can earn on its sales. Companies that compete using special product features use high profit margin to earn a high profit and return on assets.

2. The operating strategies that companies select depend on the types of products they produce and sell.
   a. Companies that rely on low costs use a cost leadership strategy and require high asset turnover.
   b. Companies that rely on product features use a product differentiation strategy and require high profit margin.
   c. Product differentiation companies normally rely on brand-name identification, advertising of product features, and research and development activities to a greater extent than cost leadership companies.
   d. Many companies provide different products and product lines to compete in both cost leadership and product differentiation markets.

3. Various measures can be used to evaluate the success of a company's operating strategy.
   a. Profit margin, asset turnover, and return on assets are commonly used measures.
   b. The ratio of operating cash flow to assets measures a company's ability to convert its profits into cash.
   c. Inventory turnover measures a company's ability to convert its investment in inventory into sales.
   d. Day's sales in inventories measures the average number of days for a company to sell its total inventory, or how many days' supply of inventory it keeps on hand.
   e. Accounts receivable turnover measures a company's ability to convert its credit sales into cash.
   f. Average collection period measures how long it takes a company to collect its receivables.
   g. Fixed asset turnover measures the effectiveness of a company in using its investment in fixed assets to create sales.

h. Gross profit margin measures a company's efficiency in the production or purchase of goods for sale.
i. Operating profit margin measures a company's efficiency in controlling selling and administrative expenses in addition to its efficiency in controlling product costs.
j. Return on equity includes the effect of financing in evaluating overall company performance and links operating, investing, and financing activities.
k. Times interest earned measures the ability of a company to meet its interest requirements.

4. Accounting provides information about a company's transformation process to help decision makers identify and evaluate past activities and plan for and form expectations about future activities.
   a. To use accounting information effectively, decision makers must understand the accounting system that provides the information.
   b. The system consists of measurement rules, processing and storage procedures, reporting rules, and reports that provide particular types of information about a company's activities.
   c. Decision makers who understand how information is produced by the accounting system can use this information to assess performance and company value.

Questions

Q14-1 *Obj. 1* Sales at Tulip Manufacturing Company are expected to double during the coming year. The company has unused capacity available and should be able to handle the new business. If a large portion of the company's costs are fixed, what would you expect to happen to profits during the coming year?

Q14-2 *Obj. 1* Sales at Borderline Insurance Agency are expected to double during the coming year. The company has been growing in recent years but generally has no trouble hiring more agents or leasing additional equipment when needed. If a large portion of the company's costs are variable, what would you expect to happen to profits during the coming year?

Q14-3 *Obj. 2* The sales manager at Buff & Tuff Health Machines has just completed a sales presentation to staff indicating that the firm will, from now on, pursue a product differentiation strategy. He notes that this should have the effect of increasing the company's asset turnover ratio with only a minor decrease in its profit margin. Does the sales manager's presentation make sense? Why or why not?

Q14-4 *Obj. 2* Generic Chemical Inc. produces standardized products that become raw materials for other companies. Each company's goods are chemically identical to those of any other company. In general, would you expect this firm to have a high profit margin, high asset turnover, both, or neither? Why?

Q14-5 *Obj. 2* Mystic Communications leads its industry in product innovation. Its financial success has been the result of creating innovative products, getting them to market quickly, and building consumer acceptance. By the time competitors develop effective alternative products, Mystic has moved on to other new products and markets. The cost of maintaining facilities to invent and produce these products is high. Would you expect this company to have a high profit margin, high asset turnover, both, or neither? Why?

Q14-6 *Obj. 3* What are the primary differences between cost leadership and product differentiation?

Q14-7 *Obj. 3* How are the cost leadership and product differentiation strategies used to improve return on assets and profitability? In particular, how would you expect the choice of strategy to affect the components of return on assets reported by companies using these strategies?

Q14-8 *Obj. 3* A marketing manager in your company tells you, "We've got this great product—it's really special, much better than the competition's. But we just can't sell very much because our prices are

(Continued)

so high. We'd make much more money if we lowered the prices." Do you agree? Why or why not? What other information would you want to have before making a final pricing decision?

Q14-9 *Obj. 4* Under normal operating conditions, what relationship do you expect to find between net income and net cash flow from operations? Which will be higher? Why? What will the major reconciling items be between the two?

Q14-10 *Obj. 4* Concerning net income and net cash flow from operations, will trends in one tend to be followed by changes in the other? Explain. What trends might appear in a company with financial problems?

Q14-11 *Obj. 4* The company you work for has a good return on assets, but inventory turnover and receivables turnover are low for your industry. You also have ongoing cash flow problems. Is there a connection? Explain the connection between inventory turnover, receivables turnover, and the generation of cash flow from operations.

Q14-12 *Obj. 5* Why should the growth and variability of earnings affect the value of a company's common stock? Explain.

Q14-13 *Obj. 5* Return on assets and return on equity are measures of performance. What is the difference between the two measures? Be specific.

Q14-14 *Obj. 5* Think about how the nature of financing, investing, and operating activities differ. What is meant by "operating strategy"? How might one decide what strategy is most appropriate for a particular company?

Exercises

E14-1 Write a short definition of each of the terms listed in the *Terms and Concepts Defined in This Chapter* section.

E14-2 *Obj. 1* You are preparing for a meeting at which your company will discuss its selling price for a new product. You have already made the decision to invest $2.3 million in production facilities with a capacity to produce 350,000 units per year. Fixed expenses, including depreciation and minimal advertising, will be $300,000 per year. Variable expenses will be $4 per unit. Your marketing people have developed three sales scenarios:

a. At a price of $7 per unit, below much of the competition, you sell 200,000 units per year.
b. At a price of $9 per unit, the average among the competition, you sell 135,000 units per year.
c. At a price of $7 per unit, with an additional $400,000 per year spent to advertise your low price, you sell 300,000 units per year.

Prepare a schedule (according to the following format) that shows the pro forma (or expected) profit from each scenario.

	Strategy A	Strategy B	Strategy C
Unit price			
Estimated sales in units			
Sales revenue			
Variable expenses			
Fixed expenses			
Additional advertising			
Total expenses			
Pro forma operating profit			

Which scenario would you recommend? Why?

E14-3 *Obj. 1* The Lakeside Symphony Association is a not-for-profit organization. The primary function of the association is to operate the Lakeside Symphony Orchestra for the benefit of local citizens.

The board of directors of the organization is discussing ticket prices for the upcoming season. Ticket receipts do not cover all costs of a concert; donations must be solicited for the remainder, but finding enough donors is difficult, and funds are always scarce.

Each concert has fixed orchestra costs of approximately $28,000, primarily for paying the musicians. The only variable costs are programs, tickets, and refreshments served at a reception following the concert; these total about $2 per attendee. Orchestra managers estimate that they can sell 1,300 tickets for the average concert at $12, 1,100 tickets at $15, or 800 tickets at $20.

Which option do you recommend? Why? Are the financial measurements used in this chapter appropriate for a not-for-profit situation like this? Why or why not? What nonfinancial considerations should enter into the decision?

E14-4
Obj. 1
Garden Company has the capacity to produce 200,000 tillers. Variable costs are $30 per tiller. Fixed costs are $1,500,000. Should the company aim to sell 200,000 at $100 each, 160,000 at $125 each, or 125,000 at $160 each? Explain your recommendation. What will the company have to do to carry out the strategy you recommend?

E14-5
Obj. 2
Three companies have the following financial results:

	Company A	Company B	Company C
Profit margin	0.05	0.40	0.25
Asset turnover	6.00	0.75	1.20
Return on assets	30%	30%	30%

What can you conclude about the financial results and the operating strategy of each company?

E14-6
Objs. 2, 3
Selected information from the annual report of **Home Depot Inc.** is provided below. The report is for the fiscal year ended January 30, 2005.

(In millions)	
Net sales	$73,094
Net income	5,001
Total assets	38,907

Calculate Home Depot's profit margin, asset turnover, and return on assets. In comparison with the companies shown in Exhibit 4 in this chapter, what strategy does Home Depot appear to be using to generate profits?

E14-7
Objs. 2, 3
Selected information from the 2004 annual reports of **Hershey Foods Corp.** and **Wm. Wrigley Jr. Co.** is provided below. Both companies are prominent in the sugar and confectionary products industry.

(In millions)	Hershey Foods	Wrigley
Net sales	$4,429	$3,649
Net income	591	493
Total assets	3,798	3,167

Compare the operating strategies of the two companies by calculating profit margin, asset turnover, and return on assets. Which company appears to be doing the better job with its strategy?

E14-8
Objs. 2, 3
The numbers below are from the records of two small local restaurants.

	Pat's Place	Henry's Hangout
Sales	$220,000	$190,000
Net income	80,000	30,000
Total assets	530,000	210,000

What do these numbers tell you about the operating strategy for each restaurant? What could each do to improve its return on assets?

E14-9 *Objs. 2, 3* The numbers below are from the 2004 annual reports of two major airlines.

	Southwest Airlines		Delta Air Lines	
(In millions)	**2004**	**2003**	**2004**	**2003**
Sales	$ 6,530	$5,937	$15,002	$14,087
Net income (loss)	313	442	(5,198)	(773)
Total assets	11,337	9,878	21,801	25,939

Calculate return on assets, asset turnover, and profit margin. Which airline appears to be more successful? Do you find evidence of differences in operating strategies, or do both appear to compete on the same basis? What could the less successful line do to improve profits?

E14-10 *Obj. 3* Styles, Inc., a clothing manufacturer, reported the information given below over a three-year period.

	2008	2007	2006
Sales	$ 9,000	$ 6,000	$3,000
Net income	1,683	852	288
Total assets	20,036	10,650	3,692
Inventory	1,500	960	500
Cost of goods sold	5,500	3,500	1,800
Fixed assets	4,000	2,500	1,500

(a) Compute the firm's profit margin, asset turnover, day's sales in inventory, fixed asset turnover, and return on assets for each year shown. (b) Discuss the company's operating strategy over this time period.

E14-11 *Obj. 4* Selected summary information is presented below for two companies.

	Fasani Enterprises		Thunderbird Corporation	
(In millions)	**2008**	**2007**	**2008**	**2007**
Total assets	$7,446	$6,512	$8,452	$7,786
Net sales	6,812	5,746	8,910	7,388
From the statement of cash flows:				
Net income	$ 414	$ 366	$ 312	$ 816
Depreciation and amortization	366	314	268	244
Decrease (increase) in receivables	12	(8)	(326)	(262)
Decrease (increase) in inventories	174	116	84	(32)
Increases (decrease) in payables	264	124	(114)	(62)
Cash flow from operations	$1,230	$ 912	$ 224	$ 704

a. Calculate the ratios of cash flow from operations to net income and to total assets.
b. Evaluate the success of each company at using assets to generate cash flow from operations.
c. What are the major causes of the difference between net income and cash flow for the two companies?

E14-12 *Obj. 4* Information is provided below from the 2004 annual report of the **Walt Disney Company**.

(In millions)	**2004**	**2003**	**2002**
Net earnings (loss)	$ 2,345	$1,267	$1,236
Net cash from operating activities	4,370	2,901	2,286
Net cash from (for) investing activities	(1,484)	(1,034)	(3,176)
Net cash from (for) financing activities	(2,701)	(1,523)	1,511

(a) Evaluate Disney's performance over the three years presented. Would you characterize the company as growing, stable, or declining? (b) Is it surprising that the change in net earnings differs from the change in net cash from operating activities over the period? Which measure of operating activities is more stable? Why?

E14-13 *Obj. 4* Information is provided on the following page for **Federated Department Stores**, owner of the department store chains Bloomingdale's and Macy's. The amounts given are from Federated's unaudited fourth quarter report for the year ended January 29, 2005.

(In millions)	Fiscal 2004	Fiscal 2003
Sales	$15,630	$15,264
Cost of goods sold	9,297	9,099
Operating income	1,400	1,341
Net income (loss)	689	693
Accounts receivable	3,418	3,213
Merchandise inventories	3,120	3,215
Total assets	14,885	14,550
Cash provided by operating activities	1,507	1,776

Calculate inventory turnover, accounts receivable turnover, gross profit margin, and operating profit margin. Compare your results with those for Wal-Mart shown below. To what extent are the differences explained by the differing operating strategies of the two retailers?

	Wal-Mart	
	2004	2003
Inventory turnover	7.5	7.3
Accounts receivable turnover	204	146
Gross profit margin	22%	22%
Operating profit margin	6%	6%

E14-14 *Obj. 4* Following is an income statement for Crystal Corporation. Calculate three ratios that indicate efficiency and interpret the results.

Crystal Corporation
Income Statement
For the Year Ending December 31, 2007

Sales revenue		$50,000
Less: Cost of goods sold		25,000
Gross profit		$25,000
Other operating expenses:		
Advertising	$3,000	
Utilities	3,500	
Wages	2,500	9,000
Operating income		$16,000
Less: Income taxes		5,600
Net income		$10,400

E14-15 *Obj. 4* Footpedal Enterprises has been in business for five years. This past year was the best year yet, as demonstrated by several indicators shown below.

	2008	2007	2006	2005	2004
Inventory turnover	5.2	4.7	4.3	4.5	4.1
Accounts receivable turnover	6.0	5.7	5.4	5.4	5.3
Gross profit margin	23.2	22.8	22.9	22.6	21.8
Operating profit margin	12.1	12.0	11.9	11.8	11.9

Your new assistant wonders why upper management is so happy that the inventory turnover, the accounts receivable turnover, the gross profit margin, and the operating profit margin all increased this year. Explain why an increase in each of these items is a positive indicator.

E14-16 *Obj. 4* The selected information on the following page has been taken from the last two annual reports of Rasheed Company.

(Continued)

	2008	2007
Accounts receivable	$ 1,466	$ 1,330
Merchandise inventory	2,093	1,947
Total assets	13,707	12,829
Total stockholders' equity	4,386	4,180
Sales revenue	14,472	13,971
Cost of goods sold	11,481	11,606
Operating income	1,636	1,509
Net income	1,170	1,020
Interest expense	1,000	900
Fixed assets	8,000	7,500

a. Compute each of the following ratios for both years.
   1. Inventory turnover
   2. Accounts receivable turnover
   3. Gross profit margin
   4. Operating profit margin
   5. Profit margin
   6. Asset turnover
   7. Return on assets
   8. Return on equity
   9. Times interest earned
   10. Day's sales in inventory
   11. Average accounts receivable collection period
   12. Fixed asset turnover

b. Has the company's financial performance improved or deteriorated during the most recent year? Was the firm more effective, more efficient, both, or neither? Which factors contributed to the improvement? Did any factors hurt overall performance? Explain.

E14-17 *Obj. 4* Your assistant has just provided you with your company's latest financial results. Unfortunately, several of the numbers are smudged and unreadable. They are each represented below by a letter.

Balance sheet (as of month-end)	
Cash	$ 482
Accounts receivable	(a)
Merchandise inventory	(b)
Buildings and equipment	3,411
Accumulated depreciation	(922)
Investments, long-term	250
Land	980
Total assets	$ (c)
Accounts payable	$ 977
Notes payable, long-term	(d)
Common stock	3,400
Retained earnings	1,491
Total liabilities and equity	$ (e)

Income statement (as of month-end)		
Sales revenue		$10,377
Cost of goods sold		6,226
Gross profit		(f)
Operating expenses:		
Advertising	$350	
Depreciation	500	
Rent	(g)	
Wages	376	(h)
Income before taxes		$ 1,945
Income taxes (35%)		(i)
Net income		$ (j)

Summary ratio values

1. Accounts receivable turnover	5.62
2. Inventory turnover	7.15
3. Return on assets	18.27
4. Return on equity	(k)

Determine the missing amounts above. (Round amounts to the nearest dollar.)

E14-18 *Obj. 5* The following information was taken from the 2004 annual report of **General Electric Company** (in millions).

Net income	$ 16,593
Interest expense	11,907
Total assets	750,330
Total stockholders' equity	110,284

Calculate return on assets and return on equity. What conclusions can you draw about the effect of financial leverage on return to stockholders? Will financial leverage benefit stockholders under all conditions?

E14-19 *Obj. 5* Bootstrap Computer Company reported the following summary information in its annual report.

	2007
Sales	$27,000
Net income	5,049
Total assets	60,108
Stockholders' equity	40,070
Fixed assets	25,000
Income before interest & taxes	10,278
Interest expense	2,500

a. Compute each of the following ratios:
   i. Profit margin
   ii. Asset turnover
   iii. Return on assets
   iv. Return on equity
   v. Fixed asset turnover
   vi. Times interest earned
b. Explain how the return on equity measure includes information about all three activities in the transformation process.

E14-20 *Obj. 5* The following summary information is taken from the annual reports of **McDonald's Corporation** and **Wendy's International.** All amounts are in millions.

	McDonald's		Wendy's	
	2004	2003	2004	2003
Sales revenue	$19,065	$17,141	$3,635	$3,149
Operating income	3,541	2,832	227	418
Net income	2,279	1,471	52	236
Total assets	27,838	25,838	3,198	3,133
Stockholders' equity	14,202	11,982	1,716	1,759

a. Compute profit margin, asset turnover, return on assets, financial leverage, and return on equity for both firms for both years.
b. Which company is more profitable? What similarities or differences do you observe in how these two companies earned their profits during the periods shown?

E14-21 *Objs. 5, 6* Market to book value links company value to accounting numbers. It is related to a variety of attributes. Complete the table below by indicating whether the value of each attribute indicates a high market to book value company or a low one. The first item is completed as an example.

Attribute	Magnitude of Attribute	Expected Company Value
Asset growth	High	High
Debt to assets	Low	
Dividend payout	Low	
Equity growth	Low	
Investing cash outflow	High	
Operating cash inflow	Low	
Research and development expenditure	High	
Return on assets	Low	
Return on equity	High	
Sales growth	High	

E14-22 *Obj. 6* Accounting reports provide a variety of information for evaluating a company. For each accounting number in the following list, write the letter from the description in the right-hand column that indicates the type of information provided by the number.

Accounting Information	Description
______ Asset turnover	a. Ability to create value for stockholders from operating activities
______ Financial leverage	b. Measures the effectiveness of a company in using its investment in fixed assets to create sales
______ Growth in assets	c. Ability to generate sales from total investment
______ Growth in equity	d. Ability to generate profit from sales
______ Growth in sales	e. Use of debt to increase return to stockholders
______ Growth in return on equity	f. The ratio of operating income to interest expense
______ Investing cash flow	g. Direction and amount of change in future return on equity
______ Operating cash flow	h. Potential for higher return
______ Profit margin	i. The ratio of accounts receivable to average daily sales
______ Research and development	j. Reinvestment of earnings to increase value of company for stockholders
______ Return on assets	k. Reinvestment of operating cash to increase value of company for stockholders
______ Return on equity	l. Growth potential through innovation
______ Fixed asset turnover	m. Ability to create value from total investment
______ Times interest earned	n. Source of cash for new investment and payments to stockholders
______ Day's sales in inventory	o. Ratio of inventory to average daily cost of goods sold
______ Average accounts receivable collection period	p. Potential for additional sales from increased investment

E14-23 *Obj. 6* Following is the income statement and balance sheet of a company that just sold stock to the public for the first time.

Balance sheet at July 31, 2007	
Cash	$ 3,500
Accounts receivable	2,000
Inventory	1,700
Buildings, net	18,000
Total assets	$25,200
Accounts payable	$ 1,500
Wages payable	500
Common stock	10,000
Retained earnings	13,200
Total liabilities and equity	$25,200

Income statement for July 2007	
Sales revenue	$5,000
Cost of sales	1,000
Gross profit	$4,000
Operating expenses:	
Wages	500
Depreciation	400
Interest	200
Operating income	$2,900
Income taxes	1,015
Net income	$1,885

The following terms are described under Objective 6 in this chapter. Find and list examples of each of these concepts in the financial statements above.

a. Measurement units
b. Historical costs
c. Accrual basis
d. Fiscal periods
e. Matched
f. Estimation

Problems

P14-1 RETURN ANALYSIS

Obj. 2

Information is provided below for three manufacturers from their 2004 annual reports.

(In millions)	Caterpillar, Inc. (agricultural machinery)	Kellogg Co. (foods)	Eli Lilly & Co. (pharmaceuticals)
Net sales	$30,251	$ 9,614	$13,858
Net income (loss)	2,035	891	1,810
Total assets	43,091	10,790	24,867
Total stockholders' equity	7,467	2,257	10,920

Required

A. Calculate asset turnover, profit margin, return on assets, and return on equity for each company.

B. Evaluate the relationship between asset turnover and profit margin and between return on assets and return on equity for the companies.

P14-2 EVALUATING OPERATING STRATEGIES

Obj. 2

Information is presented below for two furniture companies.

(In thousands)	Colony	Vernon
Operating revenues	$1,360	$1,440
Net income	180	130
Total assets	1,900	1,370
Fixed assets	1,400	1,000

Required

A. Compute profit margin, asset turnover, fixed asset turnover, and return on assets for each company.

B. Compare the operating strategies of the two companies and explain which company is doing the better job with its strategy.

C. Using the information presented, discuss how each company could improve its profits and return on assets.

P14-3 OPERATING STRATEGY DECISIONS AND PRODUCT PRICING

Objs. 1, 2, 3

You are working as an assistant to the vice president for marketing at Long Life Incorporated, a startup manufacturer of a healthy, minimally refined breakfast cereal. Since little processing will be done, much of the cost of the product will be in the premium ingredients. The company will be investing $3 million in processing and packaging facilities to produce a maximum of 15,000 cases of cereal per month. It will advertise and market only in a restricted regional area in the foreseeable future, although expansion is possible in the long run. Fixed costs for operating the facility will be approximately $85,000 per month. Variable costs, primarily for ingredients and labor, are expected to be approximately $17 per case.

In the past, most cereals of this sort have been sold at specialty stores for high prices. However, in recent years, some have moved into supermarkets at prices that are competitive with those of traditional cereals. A marketing research study has given you estimated results after the first year for three possible scenarios:

1. Sell to supermarkets for $29 per case, spend $25,000 per month on advertising, and sell approximately 11,000 cases per month. The average price grocery stores pay competitors

(Continued)

for a case of this size is $30, and $25,000 is a minimal monthly budget for advertising in the local area.

2. Sell to supermarkets for $31 per case, spend $40,000 per month on advertising, and sell approximately 12,000 cases per month.
3. Sell to specialty stores for $34 per case, spend only $7,000 per month advertising in health food periodicals, and sell approximately 7,500 cases per month.

Required

A. Prepare a schedule (using the format below) that shows the pro forma (or expected) profit from each scenario.

B. Write a report for your company president and vice presidents in which you analyze each of the above strategies and make a recommendation concerning which one to choose.

C. Also include discussion of any long-term trends and other outside factors that you feel should be considered in making this strategic decision.

	Strategy 1	Strategy 2	Strategy 3
Selling price per case			
Estimated monthly sales (cases)			
Sales revenue			
Expenses:			
Fixed, per month			
Advertising, per month			
Variable per case			
Total monthly expenses			
Pro forma monthly profit			
Pro forma annual profit			
% return on $3 million investment			

P14-4 PRODUCT PRICING DECISIONS

Objs. 1, 3

You have been hired as a marketing manager for NuTech Appliance Company. The company manufactures major home appliances, such as refrigerators, stoves, and dishwashers. NuTech is about to add a new dishwasher to its lineup. The new appliance will have standard features, appearance, and quality, except that it will be considerably quieter than similar models from the competition.

The president of the company, Marta Feliz, has asked you to prepare a memo describing the factors you believe the company should consider in pricing the new product.

Required Write a memo to Feliz. Describe the measurement or measurements you would hope to maximize through a pricing decision. Then explain what factors should be considered, including information from within and outside of the company. Describe estimates that you would want to develop before making a final pricing decision.

P14-5 ASSESSING OPERATING STRATEGIES

Objs. 2, 3

Discount Shoes and Elegant Footwear are both retail shoe companies. Both have outlets in major cities throughout the United States. Discount Shoes uses a cost leadership strategy, and Elegant Footwear uses a product differentiation strategy.

Required Answer each of the following questions.

A. What differences would you expect to observe between the two companies with respect to the location and design of their stores, the types of products they sell, and the types of service they provide?

B. Compare the companies' expected sales revenues, cost of goods sold, operating expenses, merchandise inventory, and plant assets based on the strategies they use to generate profits.

P14-6 COMPARING OPERATING STRATEGIES

Objs. 2, 3

Companies' operating strategies often result in differences in the following attributes: (a) types of products, (b) sales price per unit, (c) profit margin, (d) asset turnover, and (e) amount invested in assets.

Required Discuss the types of competitive strategies a company might use and how each strategy would affect each of the attributes listed on the previous page. What factors are likely to affect the strategy selected by a company?

P14-7 ACCRUAL- AND CASH-BASED MEASUREMENT OF SUCCESS

Objs. 2, 3, 4

The information below is extracted from the 2004 annual reports of two personal computer companies.

	Dell		Apple	
(In millions)	**2004**	**2003**	**2004**	**2003**
Sales	$41,444	$35,404	$8,279	$6,207
Net income	2,645	2,122	276	69
Total assets	19,311	15,470	8,050	6,815
Operating cash flow	3,670	3,538	934	289

Required Use appropriate analytical tools, including ratios, to answer the following questions.

A. Which company is more successful at generating net income from its assets?
B. Does this greater success result from the company using its assets more effectively to generate sales or from its generating greater profit from its sales? How do the profit margins compare?
C. Which company is more successful at generating cash flow from its assets?

P14-8 ANALYZING CASH FLOW FROM OPERATIONS

Obj. 4

Selected information is presented below for two companies that compete in the same industry.

	Park Enterprises		Schleifer, Inc.	
	2008	2007	2008	2007
Sales revenue	$1,811	$1,476	$1,967	$2,212
Cost of goods sold	1,391	1,137	1,773	1,641
Ending accounts receivable	317	314	299	386
Ending inventory	115	216	132	355
From the statement of cash flows:				
Net income	$ 131	$ 79	$ (163)	$ 85
Depreciation and amortization	29	21	31	25
(Increase) decrease in accounts receivable	(21)	(86)	87	(70)
(Increase) decease in inventory	100	(14)	223	(137)
Increase (decrease) in accounts payable and other current liabilities	121	62	(32)	55
Other items	(19)	26	(41)	(5)
Cash flow from operations	$ 341	$ 88	$ 105	$ (47)

Required Using this information, examine the details of how each company generates cash from operations.

A. Determine which company requires less time to convert inventory to sales. Consider this in relation to gross profit margins.
B. Determine which company requires less time to collect its receivables from its customers.
C. For each company and each year, examine and comment on the differences between net income and cash flow from operations. What does this show you about the operating strengths or weaknesses of the companies?

P14-9 EVALUATING OPERATING PERFORMANCE

Obj. 4

The following information was taken from the 2008 annual report of Hogar Products, Inc. The company manufactures a wide variety of household products.

Year ended December 31	**2008**	**2007**	**2006**
(In millions, except per share data)			
Net sales	$3,720	$3,336	$2,973
Cost of products sold	2,548	2,260	2,020
Gross income	$1,172	$1,076	$ 953
Selling, general, and administrative expenses	583	498	462
Trade names and goodwill amortization	55	32	24
Operating income	$ 534	$ 546	$ 467
Nonoperating (income) expenses:			
Interest expense	(60)	(76)	(59)
Other, net	211	15	18
Income before taxes	$ 685	$ 485	$ 426
Income taxes	289	192	169
Net income	$ 396	$ 293	$ 257
Earnings per share:			
Basic	$ 2.44	$ 1.81	$ 1.60
Diluted	$ 2.38	$ 1.80	$ 1.60

Required

A. How much did sales grow from 2006 to 2007 and from 2007 to 2008?
B. Restate each item on the income statement (except earnings per share) as a percent of net sales. [Hint: Sales always = 100%; 2008 cost of product sold = 68.5% ($2,548 ÷ $3,720).]
C. What have the changes in relative revenues and expenses had on operating income and net income over the three-year period?
D. What conclusions can you draw about the company's operating leverage? Are most of its costs fixed or variable?

P14-10 EVALUATING OPERATING PERFORMANCE AND EFFICIENCY

Obj. 4

Information is provided below for **Coca-Cola Company** and **PepsiCo Inc.** for the years 2002–2004.

	Coca-Cola			**PepsiCo**		
(In millions)	**2004**	**2003**	**2002**	**2004**	**2003**	**2002**
Sales	$21,962	$21,044	$19,564	$29,261	$26,971	$25,112
Gross profit	14,324	13,282	12,459	15,855	14,592	13,615
Operating profit	5,698	5,221	5,458	5,259	4,781	4,295
Net income	4,847	4,347	3,050	4,212	3,568	3,000

Required

A. Compute the three ratios that reflect operating efficiency.
B. Discuss the operating performance of Coca-Cola and PepsiCo using the information you obtained in part A.

P14-11 EVALUATING OPERATING PERFORMANCE AND EFFECTIVENESS

Obj. 4

Information is provided below for Coca-Cola Company and PepsiCo Inc. for 2004 and 2003.

	Coca-Cola		**PepsiCo**	
(In millions)	**2004**	**2003**	**2004**	**2003**
Sales	$21,962	$21,044	$29,261	$26,971
Cost of goods sold	7,638	7,762	13,406	12,379
Net income	4,847	4,347	4,212	3,568
Total assets	31,327	27,342	27,987	25,327
Accounts receivable, net	2,171	2,091	2,999	2,830
Inventories	1,420	1,252	1,541	1,412
Cash from operations	5,968	5,456	5,054	4,328

Required

A. Prepare a schedule showing the values of three turnover ratios for each company for the two years shown.
B. Discuss the effectiveness of Coca-Cola and PepsiCo using the results of these turnover ratios.
C. Using this information, discuss the cash operating performance of Coca-Cola and PepsiCo.

P14-12 ANALYZING CASH FLOW FROM OPERATIONS

Obj. 4

Information is provided below for **Hasbro Inc.** and **PepsiCo Inc.**

	Hasbro		PepsiCo	
(In millions)	**2004**	**2003**	**2004**	**2003**
Net income	$ 196	$ 158	$ 4,212	$ 3,568
Depreciation and amortization	146	164	1,264	1,221
Increase (decrease) from changes in current assets and liabilities:				
Accounts and notes receivable	76	(13)	(130)	(220)
Inventories	(16)	35	(100)	(49)
Prepaid expenses and other current assets	29	8		
Accounts payable, accrued liabilities, and income taxes payable	(90)	17	(52)	171
Other adjustments	18	85	(140)	(363)
Cash flows from operations	$ 359	$ 454	$ 5,054	$ 4,328
Sales	$2,998	$3,139	$29,261	$26,971
Cost of sales	1,252	1,288	13,406	12,379
Accounts receivable, net	579	608	2,999	2,830
Inventories	195	169	1,541	1,412
Total assets	3,241	3,163	27,987	25,327

Required

A. Compare the two companies as to their ratios of operating cash flow to total assets and their ratios of operating cash flow to net income.
B. Compare the two companies as to their ability to convert revenues to cash.

P14-13 LINKING OPERATING, INVESTING, AND FINANCING ACTIVITIES

Objs. 3, 4, 5

Information is provided below for **Minnesota Mining and Manufacturing Corporation** (known as 3M) and **Eastman Chemical Co.** for 2004 and 2003.

	3M Corp.		Eastman Chemical	
(In millions)	**2004**	**2003**	**2004**	**2003**
Net sales	$20,011	$18,232	$6,580	$5,800
Net income (loss)	2,990	2,403	170	(270)
Total assets	20,708	17,600	5,872	6,244
Total stockholders' equity	10,378	7,885	1,184	1,043

Required

A. Calculate profit margin, asset turnover, return on assets, financial leverage, and return on equity.
B. Discuss the results and compare the companies' effectiveness, efficiency, operating strategy, use of investments in assets, and financing activity.

P14-14 COMPARING RESULTS FROM DIFFERENT OPERATING STRATEGIES

Objs. 3, 5

Big Bend Inc. and Longbow Ltd. have both been in the chemical business for several decades. Each has developed a strong reputation in the industry and both are known for strong management. Big Bend tends to sell specialty products in small batches that are custom made. Longbow operates more in large-scale sales of commodity-type products that become raw material for a wide variety of plastics and polymers. Selected information is presented below for two recent fiscal periods.

	Big Bend		Longbow	
(In millions)	2008	2007	2008	2007
Total assets	$34.2	$30.2	$ 38.2	$ 36.1
Total stockholders' equity	9.96	8.82	17.3	16.3
Sales revenue	40.3	35.9	206.5	193.3
Net income	3.68	3.13	6.4	5.8

Required

A. Considering only the brief written descriptions of the two firms, would you expect one or the other to use a product differentiation strategy? Or cost leadership strategy? Explain.
B. Compute the profit margin, asset turnover, and return on assets for 2008 for both firms. Are your expectations from part A borne out by the data for 2008?
C. What changes in profit margin, asset turnover, and return on assets have occurred between 2007 and 2008?
D. Compute the return on equity for both firms for both years.
E. Which is a more successful strategy, product differentiation or cost leadership? Explain.

P14-15 EVALUATING GROWTH AND VALUE

Obj. 5

Information is provided below from the 2004 annual reports of **Sara Lee Corporation** and **Dell Computer.**

(In millions)	2004	2003	2002	2001	2000
Sara Lee					
Total assets	$14,883	$15,450	$13,694	$10,167	$11,611
Common stockholders' equity	2,948	2,052	1,742	1,122	1,234
Sales	19,566	18,291	17,628	16,632	16,454
Dell					
Total assets	$19,311	$15,470	$13,535	$13,670	$11,471
Common stockholders' equity	6,280	4,873	4,694	5,622	5,308
Sales	41,444	35,404	31,168	31,888	25,265

Required

A. Calculate the annual growth in assets, common equity, and sales for each company from 2000 through 2004. (Hint: To compute the growth rate from year to year, use the following formula—[(later year amount − earlier year amount) ÷ earlier year amount].)
B. Evaluate and compare the two companies' growth rates. As an investor, would the difference in growth rates make one firm more attractive as an investment than the other? Explain.

P14-16 CONNECTING OPERATING ACTIVITIES, FINANCING ACTIVITIES, AND VALUE
Obj. 5

Billboards–R–Us and Outdoor SignCorp have the following selected information available.

	2008	2007	2006	2005
Billboards–R–Us:				
Total assets	$12,431	$11,665	$10,862	$ 9,989
Stockholders' equity	3,939	3,326	3,551	3,382
Net income (millions)	804	199	704	761
Diluted earnings per share	1.62	0.37	1.40	1.54
Market value per share	28.50	20.63	24.25	24.81
Total market value	13,680	9,902	11,761	11,810
Outdoor SignCorp:				
Total assets	$ 6,101	$ 5,533	$ 4,828	$ 4,077
Stockholders' equity	2,246	1,816	1,390	1,528
Net income (millions)	740	694	331	644
Diluted earnings per share	5.48	5.17	2.45	4.78
Market value per share	97.13	77.00	67.50	69.13
Total market value	13,112	10,326	9,113	9,311

Required

A. Calculate the return on assets, return on equity, and market to book value for each year.
B. Evaluate the effects that operating activities and financing activities appear to have had on the value of each company to its stockholders.
C. Has the stock price responded as you would expect? Explain.

P14-17 EVALUATING OPERATING PERFORMANCE
Obj. 5

Information is provided below for two companies that produce and sell audio-magnification devices for the hearing impaired.

	John, Inc.		Roberta Company	
	2008	2007	2008	2007
Sales revenue	$ 825	$ 770	$ 352	$ 330
Cost of goods sold	540	504	250	216
Gross profit	285	266	102	114
Operating expenses	168	189	70	60
Operating income	117	77	32	54
Interest expense	30	20	10	8
Income before tax	87	57	22	46
Tax	30	20	8	16
Net income	57	37	14	30
Accounts receivable	78	73	39	34
Inventories	139	136	85	71
Fixed assets	900	850	600	550
Total assets	1,630	1,530	850	765

Required

A. For each company and each year, compute the following measures:
   1. Profit margin
   2. Gross profit margin
   3. Operating profit margin
   4. Asset turnover
   5. Accounts receivable turnover
   6. Inventory turnover
   7. Return on assets
   8. Fixed asset turnover
   9. Times interest earned
   10. Day's sales in inventory
   11. Average collection period for accounts receivable

(Continued)

B. For each year, prepare a schedule summarizing which company had the better value of each ratio.
C. Prepare a schedule that shows, for each company, whether the value of each ratio improved or declined.
D. Which firm had the stronger operating performance during the periods studied? Briefly summarize why.

P14-18 USEFULNESS AND LIMITATIONS OF FINANCIAL STATEMENT INFORMATION
Obj. 6

You work as part of a team that selects parts suppliers for a large manufacturer. Your company is highly dependent on your suppliers, and you want long-term relationships. You want suppliers who are financially stable, without cash flow problems. If they need more capacity in order to grow with you, you want them to be able to attract additional investors.

One of your team members claims that financial statements tell you everything you need to know to determine the future stability and growth potential of a supplier. Another claims that financial statements are useless in the process, and that talking with the people in the company is the only route to judging its future.

Required Discuss the strengths and weaknesses of financial statements in assisting you as you try to determine the stability and growth potential of possible suppliers. What can you learn about a company from a standard set of financial statements? What are the limitations of financial statements? What would you look at in the statements to judge a supplier's ability to remain in business and avoid cash flow problems? What relationships in the statements would help you judge whether the company could attract additional capital for growth?

P14-19 VALUE OF ACCOUNTING AND AUDITING STANDARDS
Obj. 6

In the United States, the Financial Accounting Standards Board sets measurement and reporting standards for financial statements. For large companies, the Securities and Exchange Commission imposes some additional standards. The Public Company Accounting Oversight Board (PCAOB) is a nonprofit corporation created by the Sarbanes-Oxley Act of 2002 (SOX) to develop auditing standards and to oversee the audits of public companies. Similar bodies perform these functions in other countries. A major effort is being made to set worldwide standards.

Required Describe and evaluate these standards, answering the following questions.

A. What are measurement and reporting standards?
B. Why are measurement and reporting standards important to users of financial statements?
C. What is an audit?
D. Why are auditing standards important to financial statement users?
E. What advantages and disadvantages do you see to having separate accounting and auditing standards for each country?

P14-20 EXCEL IN ACTION

Accounting information is provided below for The Book Wermz and two of its competitors for the fiscal year ending December 31, 2008.

	The Book Wermz	Book Farm	Special Editions
Sales	$6,230,000	$20,584,000	$4,896,200
Cost of goods sold	3,426,500	13,390,200	2,153,100
Operating expense	2,155,000	5,212,600	1,852,000
Interest expense	190,000	670,500	106,000
Inventory	1,987,600	5,845,000	2,246,000
Total assets	5,623,000	13,254,000	6,895,000
Stockholders' equity	3,370,000	6,687,000	4,826,000

Required Enter the data in a spreadsheet. Use the data to prepare an income statement for each company to include gross profit, operating income, pretax income, and net income. The income tax rate for each company is 35% of pretax income. Use formulas for computed values so that changes in any of the numbers shown above will be recomputed automatically in the spreadsheet. Format the income statement appropriately.

Following the income statement, enter the balance sheet data for each company.

Use the income statement and balance sheet data to calculate the following ratios, which should follow the balance sheet data: gross profit margin, operating profit margin, profit margin, inventory turnover, asset turnover, return on assets, financial leverage (assets/equity), and return on equity. The calculations should use cell references to the income statement and balance sheet data. Each ratio should include four digits to the right of the decimal.

Following the ratios, provide a brief response to the following questions.

1. Which company appears to be using a cost leadership strategy most effectively?
2. Which company appears to be using a product differentiation strategy most effectively?
3. What strategy does The Book Wermz appear to be following and how effective has this strategy been?
4. What effect has financial leverage had on the companies' ratios?

Format each response so that it appears as wrapped text in a cell that is the width of the columns used to enter data in the spreadsheet.

Include the following captions at the top of the spreadsheet: "Financial Analysis Comparison", followed by "December 31, 2008". Captions should be centered over the spreadsheet columns in which accounting information appears.

P14-21 MULTIPLE-CHOICE OVERVIEW OF THE CHAPTER

1. If a company sets its product price too high, the primary danger is that
   a. asset turnover will be too low.
   b. gross profit margin will be too low.
   c. inventory turnover will be too high.
   d. accounts receivable turnover will be reduced.

2. A company's profit margin is the ratio of its earnings to its
   a. total assets.
   b. total liabilities.
   c. operating income.
   d. operating revenues.

3. A company that follows a product differentiation strategy tends to have
   a. high profit margin and asset turnover.
   b. low profit margin and asset turnover.
   c. high profit margin and low asset turnover.
   d. low profit margin and high asset turnover.

4. Chrysanthemum Company reported a profit margin of 5% and an asset turnover of 2.0 for the fiscal year. The company's return on assets for the year was
   a. 10%.
   b. 3%.
   c. 2.5%.
   d. 2%.

5. Which company is likely to have the lowest ratio of cash flow from operations to net income?
   a. A shrinking company that is reducing inventory and receivables
   b. A growing company with increasing inventory and receivables
   c. A company with new, expensive assets and high depreciation charges
   d. A company with a growing deferred tax liability

6. High receivables turnover is evidence of
   a. extension of credit to customers who are poor credit risks.
   b. high sales volume.
   c. low efficiency.
   d. rapid collection of cash from customers.

7. A tendency to sell products rapidly is evidenced by
   a. low asset turnover.
   b. high inventory turnover.

(Continued)

c. high operating leverage.
d. a cost leadership operating strategy.

8. Which of the following is the strongest indicator of a high-value company?
   a. High market to book value
   b. High gross profit margin
   c. High financial leverage
   d. High ratio of operating cash flow to net income

9. The difference between a company's return on assets and its return on equity can be explained by the company's
   a. operating leverage.
   b. asset turnover.
   c. financial leverage.
   d. profit margin.

10. Accounting can best be defined as
   a. a precise reporting system for giving decision makers a total picture of all events occurring in a business entity.
   b. an information system for measuring the transformation process in a business entity and reporting results to decision makers.
   c. a procedure for recording the transactions of a business entity, usually using a system of debits and credits.
   d. a set of rules, developed by standard-setting bodies, for measuring and reporting.

Cases

C14-1 ANALYSIS OF OPERATING ACTIVITIES

Objs. 3, 4, 5

Selected information from **General Mills**' 2004 annual report and 10K is provided in Appendix A at the end of the text.

Required Review the annual report and answer each question or follow the directions given.

A. Compute profit margin, asset turnover, and return on assets for the company for 2003 to 2004. Evaluate the changes you see in these measures over the three years.
B. Compare your ratio calculations with those in Exhibit 4. Based on this and any other evidence contained in the annual report, does it appear that General Mills is using a cost leadership strategy or a product differentiation strategy?
C. Compute receivables turnover, inventory turnover, and gross profit margin for 2004 and 2003. Evaluate any changes you find.
D. Compute the return on equity for 2004 and 2003 and compare it with the return on assets. Do the changes in return on equity result more from changes in net income or from changes in the amount of stockholders' equity?
E. Financial statements present only a partial, highly summarized view of a company. Assume that you are considering investing in General Mills' common stock. List several items that are contained in the statements but are based on estimates.

C14-2 ANALYSIS OF AN INVESTMENT

Objs. 4, 5

You are an investment analyst. Some of your clients have talked with you about an investment they are considering in a new company, Beach Front Resorts. This company will construct condominiums and rent them to tourists. The total investment required for the project is \$5.5 million. Individual investors are expected to invest not less than \$100,000 each. They could borrow up to this amount at 10% annual interest. The development will contain 50 units that will cost \$80,000 per unit to construct. Land for the development will cost \$250,000, and \$300,000 will be held in reserve for first-year operating costs for the year beginning January 1, 2007. The remaining investment capital will be used for furnishings, streets, parking lots, sidewalks, and landscaping. Buildings will be depreciated over a 20-year period. Other depreciable assets will be depreciated over five years. Straight-line depreciation will be used.

Based on an analysis of similar developments in the area, units should rent for an average of $1,300 per week. Each unit should rent for at least 25 weeks per year. On the average, each unit is expected to rent for 30 weeks per year. Maintenance and operating costs are expected to average $200 per unit-week for 52 weeks. Management costs will be $250,000 per year. A reserve fund will be established with annual reinvestments of profits of $200,000 for future repair and replacement of property. The remaining profits will be distributed to investors in proportion to their investments. The company is not subject to income tax.

Required

A. Calculate the net income and cash flow to investors from operating activities expected from the project in 2007, assuming average rentals of 25 and 30 weeks. Assume that cash flows are equivalent to revenues and expenses except for depreciation. Which is more relevant to the investment decision, net income or cash flow? Why?
B. Assume that investors could expect to receive net cash flows from their investments for 10 years at the amounts expected for 2007. At the end of 10 years, they expect to be able to sell their investments for $1.2 million. What is the present value of the cash flows, assuming 25-week and 30-week average rentals each year? The expected rate of return is 10%.
C. What effect does the company's operating leverage have on its expected operating results?
D. Would you recommend that your clients invest in Beach Front Resorts? What factors are important to this decision other than those considered above?

C14-3 MAKING AN INVESTMENT DECISION

Objs. 4, 5

A friend has given you a hot tip on an investment opportunity in a business venture. You would have to invest $20,000 in the business for a 10% ownership share. The business would import goods from South America and sell them in several large cities in the United States.

The total investment in the company will be $500,000, including debt of $300,000 at 12% interest. The investment will be used to acquire merchandise, equipment, and facilities, and to cover initial operating costs. Expected sales each year will be $1,000,000, though sales could be as low as $700,000. Annual expenses include wages of $100,000 plus sales commissions of 15% of sales, transportation costs of 8% of sales, cost of goods sold of 30% of sales, depreciation of $80,000, insurance and miscellaneous costs of $30,000, and interest. The debt will be repaid along with interest in equal annual installments over a five-year period. The business will operate for five years and then be liquidated. The expected liquidation value is $200,000, after repayment of debt. Each year $100,000 will be reinvested for asset replacement and upkeep. The remaining cash flows will be distributed to the owners.

Required

A. Prepare an income statement for the company for the first year assuming (1) expected sales and (2) minimum sales.
B. Calculate return on assets, return on equity, profit margin, and asset turnover for results based on (1) and (2) above.
C. Determine the annual debt payment and prepare an amortization schedule for the first two years.
D. Prepare a cash flow statement for the company for year 1 based on (1) and (2) in part A above, assuming that all cash flows are approximately equal to revenues and expenses except depreciation. Also, calculate the cash distribution to owners.
E. Assuming that you require a 12% return on your investment, would you invest in this business if annual sales are $1,000,000? If annual sales are $700,000? (Hint: Compare the present value of expected cash distributions to the cost of the investment.)
F. Should you invest in this company? Support your opinion with material from parts A through E and any other factors that you feel are relevant. Evaluate any risks involved, including those related to high financial or operating leverage.

Appendix A

GENERAL MILLS, INC.
EXCERPTS FROM 2004 ANNUAL REPORT

2004 ANNUAL REPORT

GENERAL MILLS

GENERAL MILLS AT A GLANCE

U.S. RETAIL

In the United States, we market our products through a variety of outlets including grocery store chains, cooperatives, mass merchandisers, membership stores and wholesalers. Our U.S. Retail business is divided into six major marketing divisions: Big G Cereals, Meals, Pillsbury USA, Baking Products, Snacks and Yoplait-Colombo yogurt.

SELECTED BRANDS

Cheerios
Betty Crocker
Wheaties
Gold Medal
Pillsbury
Hamburger Helper
Old El Paso
Totino's
Yoplait
Green Giant
Progresso
Bisquick
Nature Valley
Cascadian Farm
Grands!
Chex Mix
Pop•Secret
Bugles

NET SALES BY DIVISION

$7.76 Billion in total

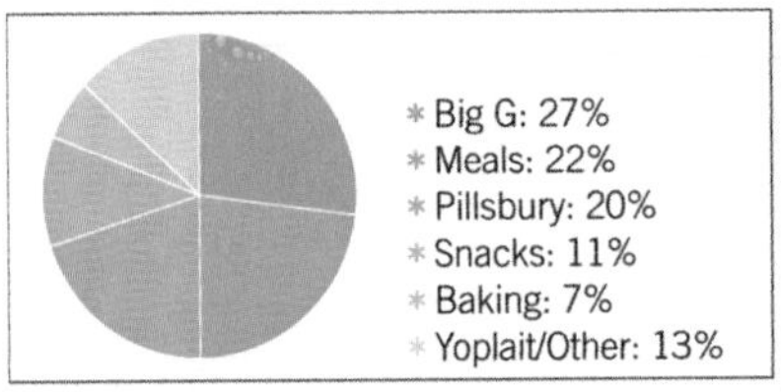

NET SALES GROWTH BY DIVISION

(in millions)

	2004	2003	Growth
Big G Cereals	$2,071	$1,998	4%
Meals	1,749	1,702	3
Pillsbury USA	1,518	1,438	6
Yoplait/Other	1,011	932	8
Snacks	828	788	5
Baking Products	586	549	7

BAKERIES & FOODSERVICE

General Mills markets mixes and unbaked, partially baked and fully baked dough products to retail, supermarket and wholesale bakeries under the *Pillsbury* and *Gold Medal* trademarks. We also market a variety of branded and specialty products, such as cereals, baking mixes, dinner products and yogurt, to restaurants, cafeterias, convenience stores and foodservice distributors.

BAKERIES & FOODSERVICE CUSTOMERS

Distributors/Restaurants
Foodservice Distributors
Quick Service Restaurants
Casual Dining Restaurants

Bakery Channels
Traditional Bakeries
Supermarket Bakeries
Supercenter Bakeries
Wholesale Bakeries

Convenience Stores/Vending

NET SALES BY CUSTOMER SEGMENT

$1.76 Billion in total

INTERNATIONAL

Our international businesses consist of operations and sales in Canada, Europe, Latin America and the Asia/Pacific region. In these regions, we sell numerous local brands, in addition to internationally recognized brands such as *Häagen-Dazs* ice cream, *Old El Paso* Mexican foods and *Green Giant* vegetables. These international businesses have sales and marketing organizations in 33 countries.

NET SALES BY REGION

$1.55 Billion in total

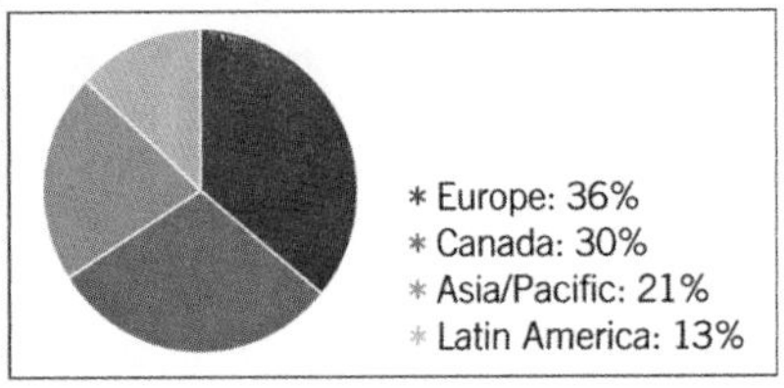

JOINT VENTURES

General Mills is a partner in several joint ventures. Cereal Partners Worldwide is our joint venture with Nestlé. Snack Ventures Europe is a partnership with PepsiCo. We have four Asian joint ventures that sell *Häagen-Dazs* ice cream, and 8th Continent is our U.S. soy products joint venture with DuPont.

NET SALES BY JOINT VENTURE

$1.21 Billion proportionate share

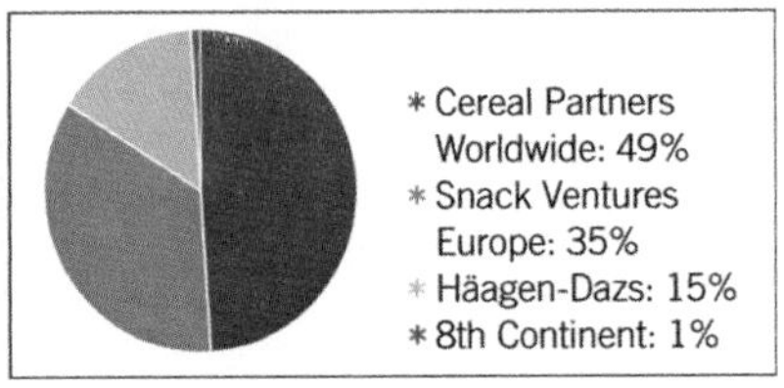

TABLE OF CONTENTS

2004 financial highlights

In Millions, Except Per Share Data

Fiscal Year Ended	May 30, 2004	May 25, 2003	Change
Net Sales	$11,070	$10,506	5%
Net Earnings	1,055	917	15
Earnings Per Share:			
Basic	2.82	2.49	13
Diluted	2.75	2.43	13
Diluted, Before Identified Items*	2.85	2.65	8
Average Common Shares Outstanding:			
Basic	375	369	2
Diluted	384	378	2
Dividends Per Share	$ 1.10	$ 1.10	–

**See page 16 for a summary of Identified Items.*

NET SALES
(dollars in millions)

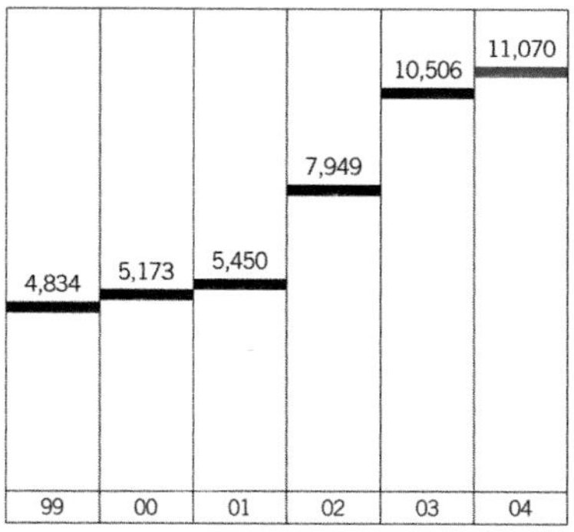

NET EARNINGS
(dollars in millions, comparable for goodwill)

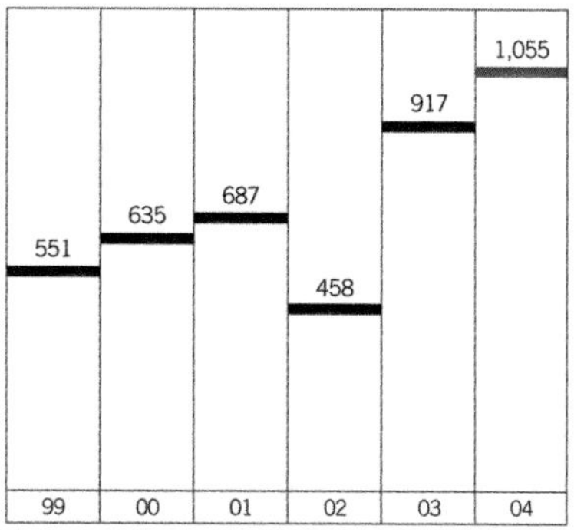

DILUTED EARNINGS PER SHARE
(dollars, comparable for goodwill)

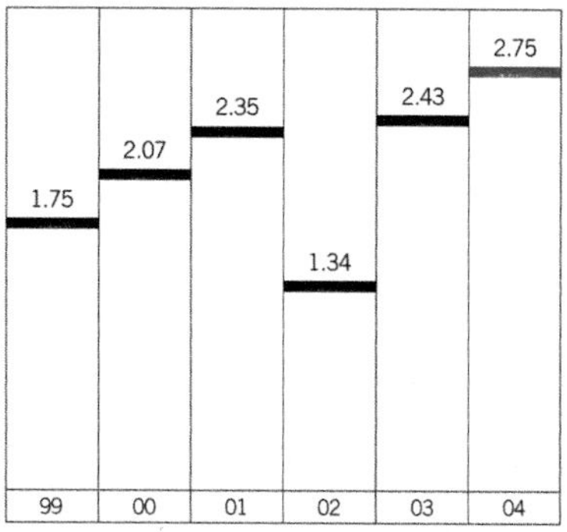

2 *

to our shareholders

General Mills achieved good sales and earnings gains in 2004, which included the benefit of an extra week in the fiscal period. For the 53-week year ended May 30, 2004:

* Net sales increased 5 percent to $11.07 billion.
* Net earnings exceeded $1 billion for the first time, growing 15 percent to $1.06 billion.
* And diluted earnings per share grew 13 percent to $2.75, up from $2.43 last year.

The extra week contributed approximately 8 cents to our earnings per share, so on a 52-week comparable basis, our net earnings would have grown 12 percent and our diluted earnings per share would have increased 10 percent, to $2.67.

Strong cash flow enabled us to exceed our debt-reduction goal for 2004, pay out nearly 40 percent of earnings as dividends and make all of our planned capital investments to support future growth. General Mills' debt levels increased significantly in conjunction with our October 2001 acquisition of Pillsbury. We are committed to paying down $2 billion in net debt by the end of fiscal 2006 and targeted $450 million of that total in 2004. In fact, we reduced our debt balance by $572 million. This has improved our financial condition and puts us in good shape relative to our three-year debt-reduction goal.

During 2004, we also invested more than $650 million in capital projects that will support future business growth and productivity savings. And we returned approximately $410 million in cash to shareholders as dividends.

While our earnings results were good overall, they fell short of our initial expectations for the year due to three principal factors. First, prices for a number of key ingredients increased sharply, and our 2004 commodity costs were much higher than we planned – over $100 million above our 2003 expense. Second, the recent popularity of low-carbohydrate diets slowed sales in several of our major product categories. And third, our Bakeries and Foodservice business fell well short of targeted results in 2004. Net sales for this business segment declined 2 percent to $1.76 billion and operating profits of $132 million were down 15 percent. These results were due in part to the low-carbohydrate trend and higher supply chain costs. But the earnings decline in this segment also reflects disruption caused by our own manufacturing realignment actions and by decisions to eliminate low-margin product lines in a number of categories.

Net sales for our largest business segment, U.S. Retail, grew 5 percent in 2004 to $7.76 billion. Unit volume increased 4 percent, or 2 percent on a 52-week comparable basis. This was in line with consumer purchase trends, as composite

U.S. RETAIL LEADING MARKET POSITIONS

Dollars in Millions, Fiscal 2004	Category Sales	Category Sales Growth	Our Retail Sales Growth	Our Dollar Share	Rank
Ready-to-eat Cereals	$7,600	–1%	–2%	31%	2
Refrigerated Yogurt	3,160	7	6	37	1
Frozen Vegetables	2,200	1	–1	21	1
Mexican Products	2,130	2	–	15	2
Ready-to-serve Soup	1,760	7	12	26	2
Refrigerated Dough	1,580	–1	–3	69	1
Dessert Mixes	1,470	3	4	38	1
Frozen Baked Goods	900	3	6	21	1
Microwave Popcorn	890	2	6	20	2
Frozen Hot Snacks	850	4	11	26	2
Dry Dinners	660	–7	3	65	1
Fruit Snacks	620	4	2	60	1

Source: ACNielsen plus Wal-Mart projections, 52 versus 52-week basis

3

retail sales for the company's major product lines also grew 2 percent over the same period. Operating profit for this business segment grew 3 percent, slower than sales growth primarily due to increased commodity costs.

Our consolidated international businesses had a strong year. Net sales increased 19 percent to $1.55 billion, with favorable currency translation contributing 11 points of that growth. Unit volume rose 5 percent overall, including a 6 percent volume increase for our Canadian business, and 12 percent growth for our operations in the Asia/Pacific region. International operating profits grew faster than sales, rising 31 percent to reach $119 million.

After-tax profits from joint venture operations grew 21 percent to reach $74 million. Cereal Partners Worldwide (CPW), our joint venture with Nestlé, posted a 9 percent unit volume increase. Volume for Snack Ventures Europe (SVE), our venture with PepsiCo, grew 4 percent. Our share of after-tax profits from these two ventures combined was $58 million, up 29 percent for the year. Our Häagen-Dazs joint ventures in Asia recorded another year of growth. And in the United States, our 8th Continent soy products venture with DuPont made excellent progress building distribution and market share for our *8th Continent* refrigerated soymilk varieties.

Our financial results for both 2004 and 2003 included certain costs primarily related to our acquisition of Pillsbury. These costs are the restructuring and other exit costs identified on our consolidated statements of earnings, and merger-related costs that are included in selling, general and administrative expenses. We separately identify these costs (which are discussed in detail in the Form 10-K that appears beginning on page 19 of this report) because they represent expenses associated with an infrequently occurring event, and we believe identifying them improves the comparability of year-to-year results from operations. Excluding these identified costs, General Mills' earnings per share would have totaled $2.85 in 2004 and $2.65 in 2003. A table on page 16 of this report provides a reconciliation of our earnings per share with and without these identified items.

General Mills' earnings growth in 2004 was not reflected in market price appreciation for our stock and, as a result, total return to shareholders for the year fell short of our longer-term performance. The market price of General Mills' common stock declined slightly in fiscal 2004 and total return to shareholders, including dividends, was just 1 percent. This was below the overall market's performance, as the S&P 500 Index generated a 22 percent return over the same one-year period. In contrast, General Mills has outperformed the market over the longer

DILUTED EPS EXCLUDING IDENTIFIED ITEMS
(dollars)

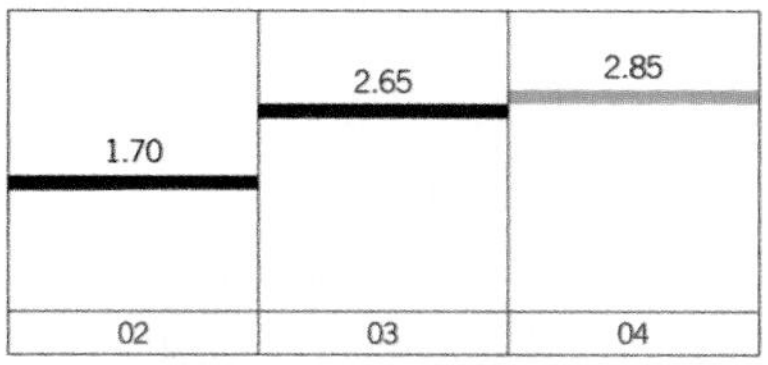

See page 16 for a reconciliation of this non-GAAP measure.

DEBT BALANCE
(dollars in millions)

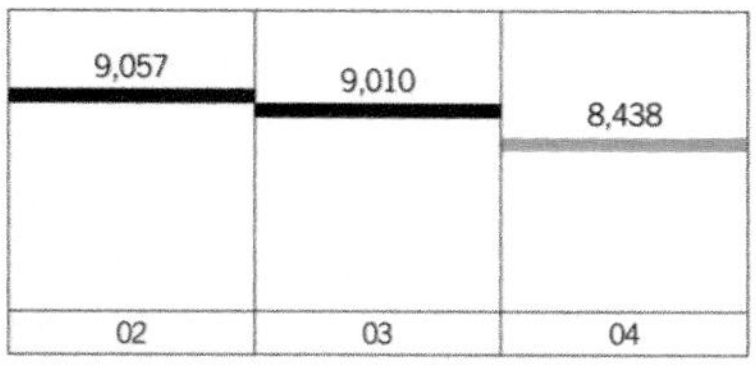

Total adjusted debt plus minority interests; see page 16 for a reconciliation of this non-GAAP measure.

4 *

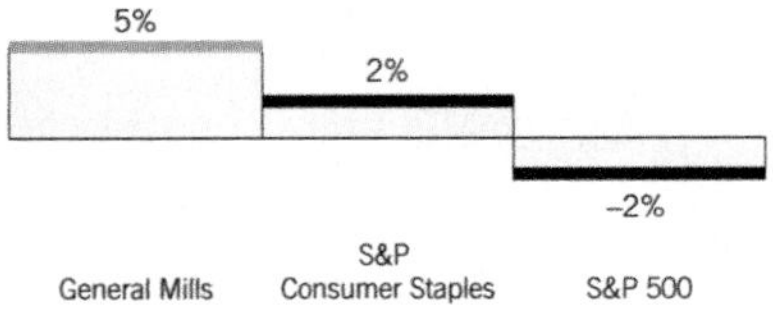

term. For the most recent five-year period, total return to General Mills shareholders has averaged more than 5 percent annually, while the S&P 500 Index has delivered a negative 2 percent average annual return.

We are committed to sustaining our long-term record of superior shareholder returns in the years ahead. Our plans continue to focus on four central growth strategies:

* Product innovation, which drives unit volume and market share gains.
* Channel expansion, to ensure our products are available everywhere people buy food.
* International expansion, to build our brands in fast-growing markets around the world.
* Margin expansion, to grow our earnings faster than sales.

We think our business portfolio offers excellent prospects for future growth. Our U.S. Retail brands hold leading market positions in a number of attractive food categories, as shown in the table on page 2, and we see plenty of opportunities to build these brands with innovation focused on health news, variety and convenience. Our Bakeries and Foodservice business is well-positioned to compete for a growing share of away-from-home food sales. And our International businesses have established solid niche positions in key markets throughout Europe, Asia and Latin America that will provide excellent growth opportunities for years to come.

In fiscal 2005, we face several challenges that will hinder earnings growth. Our business plan includes actions designed to offset those challenges. The first obvious hurdle is the fact that we'll have one less week of business in 2005 going up against 53-week results in 2004. But beyond that, commodity prices have continued to move up – our 2005 business plan assumes a $165 million increase in commodity costs compared to our 2004 expense. Energy costs will be higher, as will our salary and benefits expense. And from an operations perspective, we need to stabilize trends in our Bakeries and Foodservice segment.

To partially offset the higher input costs we're experiencing, we've increased list prices on certain product lines. We also plan to increase merchandised price points for certain products. These actions won't entirely cover our higher costs, however. We'll need productivity to help cover some of our input cost inflation. We have a target to capture at least $150 million in supply chain productivity during 2005, and we'll continue to control administrative costs companywide. We've also identified opportunities

* I to r: Steve Sanger, Steve Demeritt, Ray Viault

to reconfigure certain manufacturing activities to improve our cost structure.

The key driver of our results in 2005 will be the level of product innovation we bring to our brands and business categories. The number of new products will outpace the record level of 2004. And more importantly, our product innovation will bring meaningful, new health and convenience benefits to consumers. You'll see some of these ideas described on the following pages of this report.

We expect our product innovation, productivity initiatives and pricing actions to offset the hurdles we see in 2005 and enable us to meet or exceed our 2004 level of earnings per share. And we expect another year of strong cash flows. We will be returning increased cash to shareholders with a 13 percent increase in our dividend. The new quarterly rate of 31 cents per share is effective with the dividend payable Aug. 2, 2004. The annual dividend of $1.24 represents a payout of approximately 45 percent of our 2004 reported earnings per share. General Mills has now paid shareholder dividends without interruption or reduction for 106 years.

We'll have some changes in leadership responsibilities as a result of Vice Chairman Ray Viault's planned retirement in October following eight years with General Mills and a distinguished 30-year career in the food industry. The operating divisions that currently report to Ray will be reporting to Ken Powell, who has been named an executive vice president for General Mills. Ken is returning to Minneapolis after serving for the past five years as chief executive officer for Cereal Partners Worldwide, our joint venture with Nestlé. Several additional senior executives also have assumed new responsibilities. Information on our senior management team appears on page 15 of this report.

In closing this letter, we would like to acknowledge the talent and hard work of our more than 27,000 General Mills colleagues worldwide. The caliber of General Mills' people and the strength of our unique culture give us great confidence in the future prospects for your company.

Sincerely,

STEPHEN W. SANGER
Chairman of the Board
and Chief Executive Officer

STEPHEN R. DEMERITT
Vice Chairman

RAYMOND G. VIAULT
Vice Chairman

July 29, 2004

ITEM 7 — *Management's Discussion and Analysis of Financial Condition and Results of Operation.*

EXECUTIVE OVERVIEW

General Mills is a global consumer foods company. We develop differentiated food products and market these value-added products under unique brand names. We work continuously on product innovation to improve our established brands and to create new products that meet consumers' evolving needs and preferences. In addition, we build the equity of our brands over time with strong consumer-directed marketing and innovative merchandising. We believe our brand-building strategy is the key to winning and sustaining leading share positions in markets around the globe.

Our businesses are organized into three segments. Our U.S. Retail segment accounted for approximately 70 percent of our fiscal 2004 net sales, and reflects business with a wide variety of grocery stores, specialty stores, drug and discount chains, and mass merchandisers operating throughout the United States. Our major product categories in this business segment are ready-to-eat cereals, meals, refrigerated and frozen dough products, baking products, snacks, yogurt and organic foods. Our Bakeries and Foodservice segment generated approximately 16 percent of fiscal 2004 net sales. This business segment consists of products marketed to retail and wholesale bakeries, and to commercial and noncommercial foodservice distributors and operators throughout the United States and Canada. The remaining 14 percent of our fiscal 2004 net sales was generated by our consolidated International businesses. These include a retail business in Canada that largely mirrors our U.S. retail product mix, along with retail and foodservice businesses competing in key markets in Europe, Latin America and the Asia/Pacific region.

In addition to these consolidated operations, we participate in several joint ventures. We record our proportionate share of after-tax earnings or losses from these ventures. In fiscal 2004, joint ventures accounted for $74 million of our after-tax earnings.

Our fundamental business goal is to generate superior returns for our shareholders over the long term by delivering consistent growth in sales and earnings, coupled with an attractive dividend yield. We have met this objective over the most recent five-year period (fiscal 1999 to 2004), as General Mills' total return to shareholders has averaged 5 percent while the S&P 500 Index has posted a negative 2 percent average annual return over this period. However, in the most recent fiscal year the 22 percent return of the S&P 500 Index outperformed our 1 percent return.

We achieved good sales and earnings gains in fiscal 2004, which included the benefit of an extra week. For the 53-week period ended May 30, 2004, our net sales grew 5 percent and diluted earnings per share grew 13 percent. Details of our financial results are provided in the Results of Operations section below. Our cash flow in 2004 was strong, enabling us to pay out almost 40 percent of earnings as dividends, make significant fixed asset investments to support future growth and productivity, and reduce the balance of our adjusted debt plus minority interests by $572 million (see definition of adjusted debt on page 14 of this report). We have prioritized debt repayment as a use of cash for the three-year period through fiscal 2006. Our goal is to reduce the balance of our adjusted debt plus minority interests by a cumulative $2 billion by the end of 2006, and thereby improve our fixed charge coverage to the levels we demonstrated prior to our acquisition of Pillsbury in October 2001.

While our earnings results in 2004 were good overall, they fell short of our initial expectations for the year due to three principal factors. First, higher commodity costs reduced our gross margin. Second, the recent popularity of low-carbohydrate diets slowed sales in several of our major product categories. And finally, our Bakeries and Foodservice business fell well short of targeted results, due in part to the low-carbohydrate trend and higher supply chain costs. These results also reflect disruption caused by our own manufacturing realignment actions and decisions to eliminate low-margin product lines in a number of customer categories.

In fiscal 2005, we face several challenges that will hinder earnings growth. The first obvious hurdle is the fact that we will have one less week of business in 2005 going up against 53-week results in 2004. But beyond that, commodity prices continue to rise — our 2005 business plan assumes a significant increase in commodity costs compared to our 2004 expense. Energy costs and our salary and benefit expense are expected to be higher. And from an operations perspective, we need to stabilize trends in our Bakeries and Foodservice segment.

To partially offset the higher input costs we are experiencing, we have increased list prices on certain product lines. We also plan to increase merchandised price points for certain products. However, these actions won't entirely cover our increased costs. We plan to capture additional supply chain productivity during 2005, and we will continue to control administrative costs companywide. We also have identified opportunities to reconfigure certain manufacturing activities to improve our cost structure.

We believe the key driver of our results in 2005 will be the success of our product innovation, which is critical to achieving unit volume growth. Our business plans include new product activity and innovations that respond to consumers' interest in health and nutrition, convenience and new flavor varieties.

RESULTS OF OPERATIONS — 2004 vs. 2003

Net sales for the company increased 5 percent for the year compared to sales in fiscal 2003. Excluding the effect of the 53rd week, net sales increased 4 percent. The components of net sales growth are shown in the following table:

Components of Net Sales Growth
Fiscal 2004 vs. Fiscal 2003

Unit Volume Growth:	
52 vs. 52-week Basis (as if fiscal 2004 contained 52 weeks)	+2 pts
53rd week	+1 pt
Price/Product Mix/Foreign Currency Exchange	+3 pts
Trade and Coupon Promotion Expense	−1 pt
Net Sales Growth	+5%

The unit volume growth in fiscal 2004 contributed approximately $130 million in gross margin improvement (net sales less cost of sales) over fiscal 2003. However, gross margin increased by only $89 million. Increased cost of sales, driven primarily by more than $100 million in commodity cost increases, could not be fully covered by net pricing realization. As a result, gross margin as a percent of net sales decreased from 42 percent in fiscal 2003 to 41 percent in fiscal 2004.

Selling, general and administrative costs decreased by $29 million from fiscal 2003 to fiscal 2004, driven by a $36 million decrease in merger-related costs. These merger-related costs are infrequently occurring items related to the planning and execution of the integration of Pillsbury, including consulting, system conversions, relocation, training and communications.

Net interest expense decreased 7 percent from $547 million in fiscal 2003 to $508 million in fiscal 2004, primarily due to favorable interest rates. We have in place a net amount of interest rate swaps that convert $79 million of floating rate debt to fixed rates. Our portfolio of interest rate swaps has an average life of 4.0 years and has an average fixed rate of 5.3 percent. Taking into account the effect of all of our interest rate swaps, the average interest rate on our total outstanding debt as of May 30, 2004 was approximately 5.8 percent.

Restructuring and other exit costs were $26 million in fiscal 2004, as described in more detail in Note Three to the consolidated financial statements. Approximately $11 million was related to plant closures in the Netherlands, Brazil and California. We recorded an additional $7 million primarily related to adjustments of costs associated with previously announced closures of manufacturing facilities. In addition, we recorded $8 million for severance, primarily related to realignment actions in our Bakeries and Foodservice organization. Our fiscal 2003 results included restructuring and other exit costs of $62 million. These costs also are discussed in Note Three.

Our effective income tax rate was 35 percent in fiscal 2004 and 2003.

After-tax earnings from joint venture operations grew 21 percent to reach $74 million in fiscal 2004, compared with $61 million reported a year earlier. Profits for Cereal Partners Worldwide (CPW), our joint venture with Nestlé, and Snack Ventures Europe (SVE), our joint venture with PepsiCo, together grew to $58 million, 29 percent higher than last year's profits. Häagen-Dazs joint ventures profits were partially offset by continued marketing investment for 8th Continent, the Company's soy products joint venture with DuPont. These two ventures combined for $16 million of profit. General Mills' proportionate share of joint venture net sales grew to $1.2 billion, compared to $1.0 billion in fiscal 2003.

Average diluted shares outstanding were 384 million in fiscal 2004, up 2 percent from 378 million in fiscal 2003 primarily due to stock option exercises.

Net income increased to $1,055 million in fiscal 2004, from $917 million in 2003. Net income per diluted share of $2.75 in 2004 was up 13 percent from $2.43 in 2003 as a result of the increased income from operations. We exceeded our debt reduction goal for the year, retiring $572 million of adjusted debt plus minority interests, a key internal measure that we define in our Capital Structure table on page 14.

Operating Segment Results

U.S. Retail Segment

Net sales for our U.S. Retail operations totaled $7.76 billion in fiscal 2004, compared to $7.41 billion in fiscal 2003. The components of net sales growth are shown in the following table:

Components of U.S. Retail Net Sales Growth
Fiscal 2004 vs. Fiscal 2003

Unit Volume Growth:	
52 vs. 52-week Basis (as if fiscal 2004 contained 52 weeks)	+2 pts
53rd week	+2 pts
Price/Product Mix	+2 pts
Trade and Coupon Promotion Expense	−1 pt
Net Sales Growth	+5%

Unit volume grew 4 percent versus fiscal 2003 fueled by an increase in product and marketing innovation. Without the 53rd week, unit volume grew 2 percent. All of our U.S. Retail divisions experienced volume growth for the year:

U.S. Retail Unit Volume Growth
Fiscal 2004 vs. Fiscal 2003

Yoplait	+10%
Snacks	+5
Baking Products	+4
Meals	+3
Pillsbury USA	+2
Big G Cereals	+2
Total U.S. Retail	+4%
52 vs. 52-week Basis (as if fiscal 2004 contained 52 weeks)	+2%

Big G cereal volume grew 2 percent in 2004, with contributions from new products including *Berry Burst Cheerios*, and gains by several key established brands such as *Honey Nut Cheerios* and *Reese's Puffs*. Yoplait yogurt volume increased 10 percent with continued growth from established lines plus contributions from *Yoplait Nouriche* yogurt beverages. Snacks division volume was up 5 percent, led by growth in fruit snacks and granola bars. Meals division unit volume rose 3 percent with contributions from the line of *Progresso* Rich & Hearty soups introduced during the year, and from *Betty Crocker* dinner mixes. Unit volume growth of 2 percent for Pillsbury USA reflected gains for *Totino's* pizza and hot snacks, frozen breakfast items (toaster strudel, waffles) and frozen baked goods. Baking Products division unit volume was up 4 percent.

Retail dollar sales for the Company's major brands also grew 2 percent overall on a 52 vs. 52-week basis as measured by ACNielsen plus projections for Wal-Mart:

Retail Dollar Sales Growth (52 vs. 52-week Basis)
Fiscal 2004 vs. Fiscal 2003

	General Mills Retail Sales Growth
Composite Retail Sales	+2%
Major Product Lines:	
Grain Snacks	+12%
Ready-to-serve Soup	+12
Refrigerated Yogurt	+6
Dessert Mixes	+4
Dry Dinners	+3
Fruit Snacks	+2
Ready-to-eat Cereals	−2
Refrigerated Dough	−3

Source: ACNielsen plus Wal-Mart Projections

The unit volume growth in fiscal 2004 contributed approximately $125 million in gross margin improvement over fiscal 2003, but gross margin increased by only $54 million. Increased cost of sales, driven primarily by more than $90 million in commodity cost increases, could not be fully covered by net pricing realization. As a result, gross margin as a percent of net sales decreased from 48 percent in fiscal 2003 to 46 percent in fiscal 2004.

Selling, general and administrative costs decreased by $1 million from fiscal 2003 to fiscal 2004.

Operating profits grew to $1.81 billion, up from $1.75 billion in fiscal 2003.

ITEM 8 — *Financial Statements and Supplementary Data.*

REPORT OF MANAGEMENT RESPONSIBILITIES

The management of General Mills, Inc. is responsible for the fairness and accuracy of the consolidated financial statements. The statements have been prepared in accordance with accounting principles that are generally accepted in the United States, using management's best estimates and judgments where appropriate. The financial information throughout this Annual Report on Form 10-K is consistent with our consolidated financial statements.

Management has established a system of internal controls that provides reasonable assurance that assets are adequately safeguarded and transactions are recorded accurately in all material respects, in accordance with management's authorization. We maintain a strong audit program that independently evaluates the adequacy and effectiveness of internal controls. Our internal controls provide for appropriate separation of duties and responsibilities, and there are documented policies regarding use of Company assets and proper financial reporting. These formally stated and regularly communicated policies demand highly ethical conduct from all employees.

The Audit Committee of the Board of Directors meets regularly with management, internal auditors and independent auditors to review internal control, auditing and financial reporting matters. The independent auditors, internal auditors and employees have full and free access to the Audit Committee at any time.

The independent auditors, KPMG LLP, were retained to audit our consolidated financial statements. Their report follows.

S. W. Sanger
Chairman of the Board and
Chief Executive Officer

J. A. Lawrence
Executive Vice President and
Chief Financial Officer

July 29, 2004

REPORT OF INDEPENDENT REGISTERED PUBLIC ACCOUNTING FIRM

The Stockholders and the Board of Directors
General Mills, Inc.:

We have audited the accompanying consolidated balance sheets of General Mills, Inc. and subsidiaries as of May 30, 2004 and May 25, 2003, and the related consolidated statements of earnings, stockholders' equity and cash flows for each of the fiscal years in the three-year period ended May 30, 2004. Our audits also included the financial statement schedule listed in Item 15(a)2. These consolidated financial statements are the responsibility of the Company's management. Our responsibility is to express an opinion on these consolidated financial statements based on our audits.

We conducted our audits in accordance with the standards of the Public Company Accounting Oversight Board (United States). Those standards require that we plan and perform the audit to obtain reasonable assurance about whether the financial statements are free of material misstatement. An audit includes examining, on a test basis, evidence supporting the amounts and disclosures in the financial statements. An audit also includes assessing the accounting principles used and significant estimates made by management, as well as evaluating the overall financial statement presentation. We believe that our audits provide a reasonable basis for our opinion.

In our opinion, the consolidated financial statements referred to above present fairly, in all material respects, the financial position of General Mills, Inc. and subsidiaries as of May 30, 2004 and May 25, 2003, and the results of their operations and their cash flows for each of the fiscal years in the three-year period ended May 30, 2004 in conformity with accounting principles generally accepted in the United States of America. Also, in our opinion, the related financial statement schedule, when considered in relation to the basic consolidated financial statements taken as a whole, presents fairly, in all material respects, the information set forth therein.

KPMG LLP

Minneapolis, Minnesota
June 29, 2004

GENERAL MILLS, INC.
CONSOLIDATED STATEMENTS OF EARNINGS
In Millions, Except Per Share Data

Fiscal Year Ended	May 30, 2004	May 25, 2003	May 26, 2002
Net Sales	$11,070	$10,506	$7,949
Costs and Expenses:			
Cost of sales	6,584	6,109	4,662
Selling, general and administrative	2,443	2,472	2,070
Interest, net	508	547	416
Restructuring and other exit costs	26	62	134
Total Costs and Expenses	9,561	9,190	7,282
Earnings before Taxes and Earnings from Joint Ventures	1,509	1,316	667
Income Taxes	528	460	239
Earnings from Joint Ventures and Other Adjustments	74	61	30
Net Earnings	$ 1,055	$ 917	$ 458
Earnings per Share			
Earnings per Share – Basic	$ 2.82	$ 2.49	$ 1.38
Average Number of Common Shares	375	369	331
Earnings per Share – Diluted	$ 2.75	$ 2.43	$ 1.34
Average Number of Common Shares – Assuming Dilution	384	378	342

See accompanying notes to consolidated financial statements. Adjustments have been made to the original to simplify the presentation.

GENERAL MILLS, INC.
CONSOLIDATED BALANCE SHEETS
In Millions

	May 30, 2004	May 25, 2003
ASSETS		
Current Assets:		
Cash and cash equivalents	$ 751	$ 703
Receivables, less allowance for doubtful accounts of $19 in 2004 and $28 in 2003	1,010	980
Inventories	1,063	1,082
Prepaid expenses and other current assets	222	184
Deferred income taxes	169	230
Total Current Assets	3,215	3,179
Land, Buildings and Equipment at cost, net	3,111	2,980
Goodwill	6,684	6,650
Other Intangible Assets	3,641	3,622
Other Assets	1,797	1,796
Total Assets	$18,448	$18,227
LIABILITIES AND EQUITY		
Current Liabilities:		
Accounts payable	$ 1,145	$ 1,303
Current portion of long-term debt	233	105
Notes payable	583	1,236
Other current liabilities	796	800
Total Current Liabilities	2,757	3,444
Long-term Debt	7,410	7,516
Deferred Income Taxes	1,773	1,661
Other Liabilities	961	1,131
Total Liabilities	12,901	13,752
Minority Interests	299	300
Stockholders' Equity:		
Cumulative preference stock, none issued	–	–
Common stock, 502 shares issued	5,680	5,684
Retained earnings	3,722	3,079
Less common stock in treasury, at cost, shares of 123 in 2004 and 132 in 2003	(3,921)	(4,203)
Unearned compensation	(89)	(43)
Accumulated other comprehensive income	(144)	(342)
Total Stockholders' Equity	5,248	4,175
Total Liabilities and Equity	$18,448	$18,227

See accompanying notes to consolidated financial statements.

GENERAL MILLS, INC.
CONSOLIDATED STATEMENTS OF CASH FLOWS
In Millions

Fiscal Year Ended	May 30, 2004	May 25, 2003	May 26, 2002
Cash Flows – Operating Activities:			
Net earnings	$ 1,055	$ 917	$ 458
Adjustments to reconcile net earnings to cash flow:			
Depreciation and amortization	399	365	296
Deferred income taxes	109	27	93
Changes in current assets and liabilities, excluding effects from businesses acquired	(186)	246	37
Tax benefit on exercised options	63	21	46
Cumulative effect of change in accounting principle	–	–	3
Pension and other postretirement activity	(21)	(56)	(105)
Restructuring and other exit costs	26	62	134
Other, net	16	49	(46)
Cash provided by continuing operations	1,461	1,631	916
Cash used by discontinued operations	–	–	(3)
Net Cash Provided by Operating Activities	1,461	1,631	913
Cash Flows – Investment Activities:			
Purchases of land, buildings and equipment	(628)	(711)	(506)
Investments in businesses, intangibles and affiliates, net of investment returns and dividends	(2)	(261)	(3,688)
Purchases of marketable securities	(7)	(63)	(46)
Proceeds from sale of marketable securities	129	57	70
Proceeds from disposal of land, buildings and equipment	36	14	21
Proceeds from disposition of businesses	–	–	939
Other, net	2	(54)	(61)
Net Cash Used by Investment Activities	(470)	(1,018)	(3,271)
Cash Flows – Financing Activities:			
Change in notes payable	(1,023)	(2,330)	2,688
Issuance of long-term debt	576	2,048	3,485
Payment of long-term debt	(248)	(334)	(427)
Proceeds from minority interest investors	–	148	150
Common stock issued	192	96	139
Purchases of common stock for treasury	(24)	(29)	(2,436)
Dividends paid	(413)	(406)	(358)
Other, net	(3)	(78)	28
Net Cash (Used) Provided by Financing Activities	(943)	(885)	3,269
Increase (Decrease) in Cash and Cash Equivalents	48	(272)	911
Cash and Cash Equivalents – Beginning of Year	703	975	64
Cash and Cash Equivalents – End of Year	$ 751	$ 703	$ 975
Cash Flow from Changes in Current Assets and Liabilities, Excluding Effects from Businesses Acquired:			
Receivables	$ (22)	$ 31	$ 265
Inventories	24	(20)	(12)
Prepaid expenses and other current assets	(15)	(28)	12
Accounts payable	(167)	67	(90)
Other current liabilities	(6)	196	(138)
Changes in Current Assets and Liabilities	$ (186)	$ 246	$ 37

See accompanying notes to consolidated financial statements.

GENERAL MILLS, INC.
CONSOLIDATED STATEMENTS OF STOCKHOLDERS' EQUITY
In Millions, Except Per Share Data

	$.10 Par Value Common Stock (One Billion Shares Authorized)							
	Issued		Treasury					
	Shares	Amount	Shares	Amount	Retained Earnings	Unearned Compen-sation	Accumulated Other Compre-hensive Income	Total
Balance at May 27, 2001	408	$ 745	(123)	$ (3,014)	$ 2,468	$ (54)	$ (93)	$ 52
Comprehensive Income:								
Net earnings					458			458
Other comprehensive income, net of tax:								
Cumulative effect of adopting SFAS No. 133							(158)	(158)
Net change on hedge derivatives							(114)	(114)
Net change on securities							(11)	(11)
Foreign currency translation							(4)	(4)
Minimum pension liability adjustment							4	4
Other comprehensive income							(283)	(283)
Total comprehensive income								175
Cash dividends declared ($1.10 per share), net of income taxes of $1					(358)			(358)
Shares issued for acquisition	94	4,902	40	992				5,894
Shares repurchased from Diageo			(55)	(2,318)				(2,318)
Stock compensation plans (includes income tax benefits of $53)	–	46	6	176				222
Shares purchased			(3)	(119)				(119)
Put and call option premiums/settlements, net	–	40	–	(9)				31
Unearned compensation related to restricted stock awards						(29)		(29)
Earned compensation and other						26		26
Balance at May 26, 2002	**502**	**$5,733**	**(135)**	**$(4,292)**	**$2,568**	**$(57)**	**$(376)**	**$ 3,576**
Comprehensive Income:								
Net earnings					917			917
Other comprehensive income, net of tax:								
Net change on hedge derivatives							(4)	(4)
Net change on securities							(5)	(5)
Foreign currency translation							98	98
Minimum pension liability adjustment							(55)	(55)
Other comprehensive income							34	34
Total comprehensive income								951
Cash dividends declared ($1.10 per share), net of income taxes of less than $1					(406)			(406)
Stock compensation plans (includes income tax benefits of $21)	–	25	4	118				143
Shares purchased			(1)	(29)				(29)
Put and call option premiums/settlements, net	–	(74)	–	–				(74)
Unearned compensation related to restricted stock awards						(11)		(11)
Earned compensation and other						25		25
Balance at May 25, 2003	**502**	**$5,684**	**(132)**	**$(4,203)**	**$3,079**	**$(43)**	**$(342)**	**$ 4,175**
Comprehensive Income:								
Net earnings					1,055			1,055
Other comprehensive income, net of tax:								
Net change on hedge derivatives							101	101
Net change on securities							(10)	(10)
Foreign currency translation							75	75
Minimum pension liability adjustment							32	32
Other comprehensive income							198	198
Total comprehensive income								1,253
Cash dividends declared ($1.10 per share), net of income taxes of less than $1					(412)			(412)
Stock compensation plans (includes income tax benefits of $5)	–	(4)	10	306				302
Shares purchased			(1)	(24)				(24)
Unearned compensation related to restricted stock awards						(77)		(77)
Earned compensation and other						31		31
Balance at May 30, 2004	**502**	**$5,680**	**(123)**	**$(3,921)**	**$3,722**	**$(89)**	**$(144)**	**$ 5,248**

See accompanying notes to consolidated financial statements.

GENERAL MILLS, INC.
NOTES TO CONSOLIDATED FINANCIAL STATEMENTS

1. SUMMARY OF SIGNIFICANT ACCOUNTING POLICIES

Preparing our consolidated financial statements in conformity with accounting principles generally accepted in the United States requires us to make estimates and assumptions that affect reported amounts of assets, liabilities, disclosures of contingent assets and liabilities at the date of the financial statements, and the reported amounts of revenues and expenses during the reporting period. Actual results could differ from our estimates.

(A) PRINCIPLES OF CONSOLIDATION – Our consolidated financial statements include parent company operations and majority-owned subsidiaries as well as General Mills' investment in and share of net earnings or losses of 20- to 50-percent-owned companies, which are recorded on an equity basis.

Our fiscal year ends on the last Sunday in May. Fiscal year 2004 consisted of 53 weeks, and fiscal 2003 and 2002 each consisted of 52 weeks. Our wholly owned international operations, with the exception of Canada and our export operations, are reported for the 12 calendar months ended April 30. The results of the acquired Pillsbury operations are reflected from November 1, 2001.

(B) LAND, BUILDINGS, EQUIPMENT AND DEPRECIATION – Buildings and equipment are depreciated over estimated useful lives, primarily using the straight-line method. Buildings are usually depreciated over 40 to 50 years, and equipment is depreciated over three to 15 years. Depreciation charges for fiscal 2004, 2003 and 2002 were $376 million, $347 million and $283 million, respectively. Accelerated depreciation methods generally are used for income tax purposes. When an item is sold or retired, the accounts are relieved of its cost and related accumulated depreciation; the resulting gains and losses, if any, are recognized.

(C) INVENTORIES – Inventories are valued at the lower of cost or market. We generally use the LIFO method of valuing inventory because we believe that it is a better match with current revenues. However, FIFO is used for most foreign operations, where LIFO is not recognized for statutory purposes.

(D) INTANGIBLE ASSETS – Goodwill represents the difference between the purchase prices of acquired companies and the related fair values of net assets acquired and accounted for by the purchase method of accounting. On May 28, 2001, we adopted Statement of Financial Accounting Standards (SFAS) No. 142, "Goodwill and Intangible Assets." This Statement eliminated the amortization of goodwill and intangibles with indefinite lives, primarily acquired brand intangibles, and instead requires that they be tested annually for impairment. See Note One (O) for the effects of this adoption. We capitalize the costs of software internally developed or externally purchased for internal use. The costs of patents, copyrights and other amortizable intangible assets are amortized evenly over their estimated useful lives.

(E) RECOVERABILITY OF LONG-LIVED ASSETS – We review long-lived assets, including identifiable intangibles and goodwill, for impairment when events or changes in circumstances indicate that the carrying amount of an asset may not be recoverable. An asset is deemed impaired and written down to its fair value if estimated related future cash flows are less than its carrying amount.

(F) FOREIGN CURRENCY TRANSLATION – For most of our foreign operations, local currencies are considered the functional currency. Assets and liabilities are translated using exchange rates in effect at the balance sheet date. Results of operations are translated using the average exchange rates during the period. Translation effects are classified within Accumulated Other Comprehensive Income in Stockholders' Equity.

(G) FINANCIAL INSTRUMENTS – See Note One (O) for a description of our adoption of SFAS No. 133, "Accounting for Derivative Instruments and Hedging Activities." We use interest rate swaps, currency swaps, and forward and option contracts to manage risks generally associated with foreign exchange rate, interest rate and commodity market volatility. All hedging instruments are designated and effective as hedges. If the underlying hedged transaction ceases to exist or if the hedge becomes ineffective, all changes in fair value of the related derivatives that have not been settled are recognized in current earnings. Instruments that do not qualify for hedge accounting are marked to market with changes recognized in current earnings. We do not hold or issue derivative financial instruments for trading purposes and we are not a party to leveraged derivatives. See Note Seven for additional information related to our financial instruments.

(H) REVENUE RECOGNITION – We recognize sales upon shipment to our customers. Reported sales are net of certain coupon and trade promotion costs. Coupons are expensed when distributed based on estimated redemptions. Trade promotions are expensed based on estimated participation and performance levels for offered programs. We generally do not allow a right of return. However, on a limited case-by-case basis with prior approval, we may allow customers to return product in saleable condition for redistribution to other customers or outlets. These returns are recorded as reductions of net sales in the period of the return.

(I) SHIPPING AND HANDLING – Shipping and handling costs associated with internal movements of inventories are recorded as cost of sales and recognized when the related finished product is shipped to the customer. Shipping costs associated with the distribution of finished product to our customers are recorded as selling, general and administrative expense and are recognized when the related finished product is shipped to the customer. The amount recorded in selling, general and administrative expense was $352 million, $345 million and $243 million in fiscal 2004, 2003 and 2002, respectively.

(J) RESEARCH AND DEVELOPMENT – All expenditures for research and development are charged against earnings in the year incurred. The charges for fiscal 2004, 2003 and 2002 were $158 million, $149 million and $131 million, respectively.

(K) ADVERTISING COSTS – Advertising expenses (including production and communication costs) for fiscal 2004, 2003 and 2002 were $512 million, $519 million and $489 million, respectively. Prepaid advertising costs (including syndication properties) of $25 million and $31 million were reported as assets at May 30, 2004, and May 25, 2003, respectively. We expense the production costs of advertising the first time that the advertising takes place.

(L) STOCK-BASED COMPENSATION – We use the intrinsic value method for measuring the cost of compensation paid in Company common stock. This method defines our cost as the excess of the stock's market value at the time of the grant over the amount that the employee is required to pay. Our stock option plans require that the employee's payment (i.e., exercise price) be the market value as of the grant date. The following table illustrates the pro forma effect on net earnings and earnings per share if the company had applied the fair value recognition provisions of SFAS No. 123, "Accounting for Stock-Based Compensation," to stock-based employee compensation.

In Millions, Except Per Share Data, Fiscal Year	2004	2003	2002
Net earnings, as reported	$1,055	$ 917	$ 458
Add: Stock-based employee compensation expense included in reported net earnings, net of related tax effects	17	13	10
Deduct: Total stock-based employee compensation expense determined under fair value based method for all awards, net of related tax effects	(67)	(68)	(84)
Pro forma net earnings	$1,005	$ 862	$ 384
Earnings per share:			
Basic – as reported	$ 2.82	$2.49	$1.38
Basic – pro forma	$ 2.68	$2.34	$1.16
Diluted – as reported	$ 2.75	$2.43	$1.34
Diluted – pro forma	$ 2.62	$2.29	$1.13

The weighted average fair values at grant date of the options granted in fiscal 2004, 2003 and 2002 were estimated as $8.54, $8.24 and $11.77, respectively, using the Black-Scholes option-pricing model with the following weighted average assumptions:

Fiscal Year	2004	2003	2002
Risk-free interest rate	3.9%	3.8%	5.1%
Expected life	7 years	7 years	7 years
Expected volatility	21%	21%	20%
Expected dividend growth rate	10%	9%	8%

The Black-Scholes model requires the input of certain key assumptions, does not give effect to restrictions that are placed on employee stock options, and therefore may not provide a reliable measure of fair value.

(M) EARNINGS PER SHARE – Basic Earnings per Share (EPS) is computed by dividing net earnings by the weighted average number of common shares outstanding. Diluted EPS includes the effect of all dilutive potential common shares (primarily related to outstanding in-the-money stock options).

(N) CASH AND CASH EQUIVALENTS – We consider all investments purchased with an original maturity of three months or less to be cash equivalents. Cash and cash equivalents totaling $117 million and $211 million at May 30, 2004 and May 25, 2003, respectively, are designated as collateral for certain derivative liabilities.

2. ACQUISITIONS

On October 31, 2001, we acquired the worldwide Pillsbury operations from Diageo plc (Diageo). Pillsbury, based in Minneapolis, Minnesota, built a portfolio of leading food brands, such as *Pillsbury* refrigerated dough, *Green Giant, Old El Paso, Progresso* and *Totino's*. Pillsbury had sales of $6.1 billion (before EITF Issue 01-09 reclassification) in its fiscal year ended June 30, 2001, including businesses subsequently divested.

The transaction was accounted for as a purchase. Under terms of the agreement between General Mills and Diageo, we acquired Pillsbury in a stock and cash transaction. Consideration to Diageo included 134 million General Mills common shares. Under a stockholders' agreement, Diageo had a put option to sell directly to us 55 million shares of General Mills common stock at a price of $42.14 per share, which Diageo exercised on November 1, 2001. Therefore, those 55 million shares were valued at a total of $2,318 million. The 79 million shares of General Mills common stock retained by Diageo were valued at $3,576 million based on the three-day average trading price prior to the closing of $45.27 per share. Therefore, the total stock consideration was $5,894 million. The cash paid to Diageo and assumed debt of Pillsbury on October 31, 2001 totaled $3,830 million. Under terms of the agreement, Diageo held contingent value rights that required payment to Diageo on April 30, 2003, of $273 million based on the average price of General Mills stock of $45.55 per share for the 20 trading days prior to that date and the 79 million shares Diageo held. As a result, the total acquisition consideration (exclusive of direct acquisition costs) was $9,997 million.

In order to obtain regulatory clearance for the acquisition of Pillsbury, we arranged to divest certain dessert and specialty products businesses on November 13, 2001, for $316 million. On December 26, 2001, Nestlé USA exercised its right to buy the 50 percent stake that it did not already own in Ice Cream Partners USA LLC, a joint venture, for $641 million. Net proceeds from these transactions were used to reduce our debt level.

The stockholders' agreement between General Mills and Diageo, as amended, includes a standstill provision, under which Diageo is precluded from buying additional shares in General Mills for a 20-year period following the close of the transaction, or for three years following the date on which Diageo owns less than 5 percent of General Mills' outstanding shares, whichever is earlier. The agreement also generally requires pass-through voting by Diageo, so its shares will be voted in the same proportion as the other General Mills shares are voted.

The allocation of the purchase price was completed in fiscal 2003. Intangible assets included in the final allocation of the purchase price were acquired brands totaling $3.5 billion and goodwill of $5.8 billion. Deferred income taxes of $1.3 billion, associated with the brand intangibles, were also recorded.

Presented below is a condensed balance sheet disclosing the final purchase price allocation with the amounts assigned to major asset and liability captions of the acquired Pillsbury business at the date of acquisition (in millions):

Current Assets	$ 1,245
Land, Buildings and Equipment	1,002
Investments and Assets to be Sold	1,006
Other Noncurrent Assets	263
Brand Intangibles	3,516
Goodwill	5,836
Total Assets	12,868
Current Liabilities	(1,328)
Deferred Income Taxes	(1,087)
Other Noncurrent Liabilities	(456)
Total Liabilities	(2,871)
Purchase Consideration	$ 9,997

5. BALANCE SHEET INFORMATION

The components of certain balance sheet accounts are as follows:

In Millions	May 30, 2004	May 25, 2003
Land, Buildings and Equipment:		
Land	$ 53	$ 55
Buildings	1,290	1,180
Equipment	3,419	3,005
Construction in progress	557	689
Total land, buildings and equipment	5,319	4,929
Less accumulated depreciation	(2,208)	(1,949)
Net land, buildings and equipment	$ 3,111	$ 2,980
Goodwill:		
Total goodwill	$ 6,770	$ 6,736
Less accumulated amortization	(86)	(86)
Goodwill	$ 6,684	$ 6,650
Other Intangible Assets:		
Intangible assets not subject to amortization		
Brands	$ 3,516	$ 3,516
Pension intangible	6	7
Intangible assets not subject to amortization	3,522	3,523
Intangible assets subject to amortization, primarily capitalized software	$ 197	$ 154
Less accumulated amortization	(78)	(55)
Intangible assets subject to amortization	119	99
Total other intangible assets	$ 3,641	$ 3,622
Other Assets:		
Prepaid pension	$ 1,148	$ 1,084
Marketable securities, at market	30	160
Investments in and advances to affiliates	422	362
Miscellaneous	197	190
Total other assets	$ 1,797	$ 1,796
Other Current Liabilities:		
Accrued payroll	$ 230	$ 243
Accrued interest	186	178
Accrued taxes	249	129
Miscellaneous	131	250
Total other current liabilities	$ 796	$ 800

The changes in the carrying amount of goodwill for fiscal 2002, 2003 and 2004 are as follows:

In Millions	U.S. Retail	Bakeries and Foodservice	International	Pillsbury Unallocated Excess Purchase Price	Total
Balance at May 27, 2001	$ 745	$ 59	$ –	$ –	$ 804
Pillsbury transaction	–	–	–	7,669	7,669
Balance at May 26, 2002	$ 745	$ 59	$ –	$ 7,669	$ 8,473
Activity including translation	–	–	10	(1,833)	(1,823)
Allocation to segments	4,279	1,146	411	(5,836)	–
Balance at May 25, 2003	$5,024	$1,205	$421	$ –	$ 6,650
Activity including translation	–	–	34	–	34
Balance at May 30, 2004	$5,024	$1,205	$455	$ –	$ 6,684

The Pillsbury acquisition valuation and purchase price allocation was completed in fiscal 2003. The activity during fiscal 2003 primarily reflects the allocation of the purchase price to brand intangibles, net of tax, and the contingent value rights payment to Diageo (see Note Two, "Acquisitions").

Intangible asset amortization expense was $23 million, $18 million and $13 million for fiscal 2004, 2003 and 2002, respectively. Estimated amortization expense for the next five fiscal years (in millions) is as follows: $23 in 2005, $21 in 2006, $16 in 2007, $12 in 2008 and $12 in 2009.

As of May 30, 2004, a comparison of cost and market values of our marketable securities (which are debt and equity securities) was as follows:

In Millions	Cost	Market Value	Gross Gain	Gross Loss
Held to maturity:				
Debt securities	$ –	$ –	$–	$ –
Equity securities	2	2	–	–
Total	$ 2	$ 2	$–	$ –
Available for sale:				
Debt securities	$48	$48	$–	$ –
Equity securities	4	6	2	–
Total	$52	$54	$2	$ –

As of May 30, 2004 and May 25, 2003, respectively, $25 million and $53 million was designated as collateral for certain derivative liabilities.

Realized gains from sales of marketable securities were $20 million, $14 million and $15 million in fiscal 2004, 2003 and 2002, respectively. The aggregate unrealized gains and losses on available-for-sale securities, net of tax effects, are classified in Accumulated Other Comprehensive Income within Stockholders' Equity.

Scheduled maturities of our marketable securities are as follows:

In Millions	Held to Maturity Cost	Held to Maturity Market Value	Available for Sale Cost	Available for Sale Market Value
Under one year (current)	$–	$–	$26	$26
From 1 to 3 years	–	–	3	3
From 4 to 7 years	–	–	5	5
Over 7 years	–	–	14	14
Equity securities	2	2	4	6
Totals	$2	$2	$52	$54

6. INVENTORIES

The components of inventories are as follows:

In Millions	May 30, 2004	May 25, 2003
Raw materials, work in process and supplies	$ 234	$ 221
Finished goods	793	818
Grain	77	70
Reserve for LIFO valuation method	(41)	(27)
Total Inventories	$1,063	$1,082

At May 30, 2004, and May 25, 2003, respectively, inventories of $765 million and $767 million were valued at LIFO. LIFO accounting decreased fiscal 2004 earnings by $.02 per share and had a negligible impact on fiscal 2003 and 2002 earnings. Results of operations were not materially affected by a liquidation of LIFO inventory. The difference between replacement cost and the stated LIFO inventory value is not materially different from the reserve for LIFO valuation method.

13. INTEREST EXPENSE

The components of net interest expense are as follows:

In Millions, Fiscal Year	2004	2003	2002
Interest expense	$537	$589	$445
Capitalized interest	(8)	(8)	(3)
Interest income	(21)	(34)	(26)
Interest, net	$508	$547	$416

During fiscal 2004, 2003 and 2002, we paid interest (net of amount capitalized) of $490 million, $502 million and $346 million, respectively.

Appendix B

SOURCES OF INFORMATION ABOUT COMPANIES AND INDUSTRIES

Many college and public libraries offer print and electronic resources that provide information about companies and industries. The following listing describes some of the resources you may find useful. The listing is not comprehensive. Check with your librarian for other resources that may be available in your library.

Industry Classification

http://ingram.swlearning.com
Visit the NAICS home page to access the NAICS codes.

http://ingram.swlearning.com
Visit the OSHA home page to find these SIC codes.

- The *North American Industry Classification System* (NAICS) categorizes companies using an industry classification code. Companies with the same classification code produce similar products. Other reference materials often use NAICS codes to identify companies and industries.
- The *Standard Industrial Classification Manual* provides an earlier system for classifying companies and industries. Some reference materials still use Standard Industrial Classification (SIC) codes to organize information.

Business Periodicals

http://ingram.swlearning.com
You can access articles from these periodicals via their home pages.

- *Business Week* provides general coverage of a wide variety of business issues, including individual companies and industries.
- *Fortune* provides descriptive articles on many companies and industries. Special issues provide rankings of companies by sales, both overall and within industries.
- *Forbes* provides descriptive articles on many companies and industries. Special issues provide summary information for large companies.
- *The Wall Street Journal* provides daily coverage of major events related to specific companies and industries as well as the overall economy.

Company Profiles

http://ingram.swlearning.com
Access more complete company profiles by visiting the applicable company home pages.

- *Hoover's Handbook of American Business* gives profiles of companies, including overview, history, financial data, products and brands, and major competitors.
- *Standard & Poor's Corporation Records* provides a brief profile and financial information on public companies. *Standard & Poor's Stock Reports* also provides a brief profile but includes more information about the company's stock. Information from both sources is also included in the electronic database from Standard & Poor's called *NetAdvantage.*
- *Mergent* (formerly *Moody's*) *Industrial Manual* provides profiles of companies, including history, subsidiaries, financial information, and a description of the company's long-term debt and equity offerings. Other manuals cover other industries, such as transportation and public utilities. This information is also available in Mergent's electronic database called *FIS Online.*

- *Thomson Research* (formerly *Global Access*) is an electronic database that contains extensive information on companies such as financial information, stock data, and so on.
- *Factiva.com* (formerly *Dow Jones Interactive*) provides several ways to research a company. Look at company filings, review stock price history, or search for articles about the company in the Publications Library.
- *Value Line Investment Survey* provides analysis and commentary on major industries and companies.
- *EDGAR* offers free access to public company filings with the Securities and Exchange Commission.
- A company's annual report to the shareholders often contains useful information about its products and markets in addition to their financial statements. Many companies now post their annual report on their Web site. Use your favorite search engine (e.g., Google at http://www.google.com/) to search for the company's home page. Look for an "Information for Investors" or "Investor Relations" section to find the company's annual report.
- *International Directory of Company Histories* is a large multi-volume set that gives extensive background information on the history of individual companies.

Industry Profiles

- *Standard & Poor's Industry Surveys* provides detailed analysis of over 50 major industries. This information is also contained in the electronic database from Standard & Poor's called *NetAdvantage*.
- *Encyclopedia of American Industries* gives profiles of industries arranged by SIC code. Almost every code has a profile, so information can be quite specific.
- *U.S. Industry & Trade Outlook* (formerly *U.S. Industrial Outlook*) contains information on major industries in the United States, along with forecasts of future prospects.
- *Manufacturing & Distribution USA* gathers industry statistics from the U.S. Census Bureau and other sources and organizes them by SIC code.
- *Marketresearch.com* contains market research reports on individual industries and types of products.

Articles in Magazines and Newspapers

There are numerous databases that allow the user to search for articles on a given topic, company, or industry. Even general-subject databases usually contain a large number of articles on business topics. Here are a few examples of databases that are particularly useful for the business researcher:

- *ABI/INFORM* is a database covering over a thousand business-related magazines and journals. Search for articles about a topic, a company, or an industry. Many articles are available full-text.
- *Business Source Elite* is another database that covers a huge number of business magazines and journals, with many offered full-text.
- *Lexis-Nexis Academic Universe* provides access to articles in thousands of magazines, journals, and newspapers. It also contains information from other types of sources such as radio and television programs.
- The Publications Library in *Factiva.com* contains thc full-text of thousands of business magazines, trade journals, and news releases.

Government Information

The federal government gathers huge amounts of data about the economy, trade, and industry. Much of this information is now distributed freely on the Web. Here are a few examples:

http://ingram.swlearning.com

Visit applicable government sites to access these data.

- *Economic Indicators* includes the gross national product, consumer price indexes, unemployment rates, interest rates, and many more commonly used economic statistics.

- The Federal Reserve Banks gather economic data about their various regions and share the data through publications on their Web sites.
- *Survey of Current Business* provides more detailed economic data, as well as articles about foreign investment, personal income, and other economic topics.
- *The U.S. Census Bureau* gathers huge amounts of data and offers it to the public. Note particularly the Economic Census, where you can find data on individual industries at the national, state, or local level.
- *Statistical Abstract of the United States* gathers into one place the most frequently requested statistics gathered by all the various departments and agencies of the federal government.

Industry Ratios

Industry averages for a variety of ratios and other accounting measures are available in *RMA* (formerly Robert Morris Associates) *Annual Statement Studies*, Dun & Bradstreet's *Industry Norms & Key Business Ratios*, and Leo Troy's *Almanac of Business and Industrial Financial Ratios*.

Glossary

A

accelerated depreciation
A depreciation method that allocates a larger portion of the cost of a plant asset to expense early in the asset's life. (11)

account
A record of increases and decreases in the dollar amount associated with a specific resource or activity. (2)

accounting
An information system for the measurement and reporting of the transformation of resources into goods and services and the sale or transfer of these goods and services to customers. (1)

accounting cycle
The process of recording, summarizing, and reporting accounting information. (3)

accounts payable
A liability account that identifies an obligation to pay suppliers in the near future. (3)

accounts receivable
An asset account that increases when goods are sold on credit. (3)

accounts receivable turnover
The ratio of sales revenues (from the income statement) to accounts receivable (from the balance sheet); it measures a company's ability to convert revenues into cash. (14)

accrual accounting
A form of accounting in which revenues are recognized when they are earned and expenses are recognized when they are incurred. (3)

accrued expenses
Expenses recognized prior to the payment of cash. (3)

accrued liabilities
Liabilities that record the obligation to make payments for expenses that have been incurred or for assets that have been acquired but for which payment has not been made. (3)

accrued revenue
Revenue recognized prior to the receipt of cash. (3)

accumulated depreciation
A contra-asset account used to identify the total amount of depreciation recorded for a company's assets. (3)

adjusting entry
A transaction recorded in the accounting system to ensure the correct account balances are reported for a particular fiscal period. (3)

application software
The computer programs that permit data to be recorded and processed. (7)

articulation
The relationship among financial statements in which the numbers on one statement explain numbers on other statements. (4)

asset turnover
The ratio of revenues to total assets. (12)

assets
Resources controlled by a business. (2)

attestation
an auditor's affirmation of the fairness of financial statements and other information. (6)

audit
A detailed, systematic investigation of a company's accounting records and procedures for the purpose of determining the reliability of financial reports. (1, 6)

auditing standards
Procedures used in conducting an audit to help auditors form an opinion about the fairness of the audited statements. (6)

average collection period
The ratio of accounts receivable to average daily sales. (14)

B

balance sheet
A financial statement that identifies a company's assets and claims to those assets by creditors and owners at a specific date. (2)

business activities
Events that occur when a business acquires, uses, or sells resources or claims to those resources. (2)

business organization
Organizations that sell their goods and services to make a profit. (1)

C

capital expenditures
Expenditures made to acquire new plant assets or to extend the life or enhance the value of existing plant assets. (11)

capital stock
See *common stock*. (9)

capital structure
The relative amounts of debt and equity used by a company to finance its assets. (10)

cash
The financial resources in the form of coins and currency, bank deposits, and short-term investments that can be converted easily into currency and that can be used to pay for resources and obligations of a company. (2)

charter
The legal right granted by a state that permits a corporation to exist. (9)

closing entries
Transactions that reset the balances of each revenue and expense account to zero and transfer these balances to Retained Earnings. (3)

commitment
A promise to engage in some future activity that will have an economic effect. (9)

common stock
The stock that conveys primary ownership rights in a corporation (also called capital stock). (4, 9)

comprehensive income
The change in a company's owners' equity during a period that is the result of all non-owner transactions and activities. (4)

computer network
A set of hardware devices that are linked so they can exchange data among themselves using software. (7)

consolidated financial statements
A report that includes the activities of the parent and its subsidiaries as though they were one company. (4)

contingency
An existing condition that may result in an economic effect if a future event occurs. (9)

contra account
An account that offsets another account. (3)

contracts
Legal agreements for the exchange of resources and services. (1)

contributed capital
An owners' equity account that identifies amounts contributed to a company by its owners; the direct investment made by stockholders in a corporation. (2, 9)

control accounts
Summary accounts that maintain totals for all subsidiary accounts of a particular type. (7)

corporation
A legal entity with the right to enter into contracts; the right to own, buy, and sell property; and the right to sell stock. (1)

cost of goods sold
An expense that identifies the cost to the company of the goods transferred to customers. (2)

cost of services sold
The cost of material, labor, and other resources consumed directly in producing services sold during a period. (4)

creditor
A person or organization who loans financial resources to an organization. (1)

credits
Decreases in elements on the left (assets) side of the accounting equation and increases in elements on the right (liabilities and owners' equity) side. (2)

current assets
Cash or other resources that management expects to convert to cash or consume during the next fiscal year. (4)

current liabilities
Those obligations that management expects to fulfill during the next fiscal year. (4)

current ratio
Current assets divided by current liabilities. (4, 10)

D

database
A set of computerized files in which company data are stored in a form that facilitates retrieval and updating of the data. (7)

database management system
Controls database functions to ensure data are recorded properly and are accessed only by authorized users. (7)

date of declaration
Date on which a corporation's board of directors announces that a dividend will be paid. (9)

date of payment
Date on which the dividends are mailed to those receiving dividends. (9)

date of record
Date used to determine those owners who will receive the dividend. (9)

day's sales in inventories
The ratio of inventory to average daily cost of goods sold. (14)

debits
Increases in elements on the left (assets) side of the accounting equation and decreases in elements on the right (liabilities and owners' equity) side. (2)

deferred charges
The assets that result when a company prepays expenses that produce long-term benefits. (11)

deferred expenses
Expenses recognized after the payment of cash. (3)

deferred revenue
Revenue recognized after cash has been received. (3)

depletion
The process of allocating the cost of natural resources to expenses in the periods that benefit from their use. (4, 11)

depreciation
The allocation of the cost of assets to the fiscal periods that benefit from the assets' use. (3)

discontinued operations
Product lines or major parts of a company from which the company will no longer derive income because it has sold or closed the facilities that produced the product line or that included that part of the company. (13)

discussion memorandum
A document that identifies accounting issues and alternative approaches to resolving the issues. (6)

dividends
Distributions of cash or stock by a corporation to its stockholders. (4)

E

earnings per share
A measure of the earnings performance of each share of common stock during a fiscal period. (4)

e-business
Using computer networks, such as the Internet, to make customer sales. (7)

effective business
An organization that is successful in providing goods and services demanded by customers. (1)

efficient business
An organization that keeps the costs of resources consumed in providing goods and services low relative to the selling prices of these goods and services. (1)

enterprise resource planning (ERP) systems
Systems that integrate most of the business information functions as a basis for management decisions. (7)

expense
The amount of resources consumed in the process of acquiring and selling goods and services. (2)

exposure draft
A document that describes a proposed accounting standard. (6)

extraordinary items
Gains or losses that are both unusual and infrequent for a particular company. (13)

F

FASB conceptual framework
A set of objectives, principles, and definitions to guide the development of new accounting standards. (6)

financial accounting
The process of preparing, reporting, and interpreting accounting information that is provided to external decision makers. (1)

Financial Accounting Standards Board (FASB)
The primary organization for setting accounting standards for businesses in the United States since 1973. (6)

financial leverage (FL)
The use of debt to increase a company's return on equity; total assets divided by total stockholders' equity. (10)

financial statements
Reports that summarize the results of a company's accounting transactions for a fiscal period. (2)

financing activities
Events that occur when owners or creditors provide resources to a company or when a company transfers resources to owners or creditors. (2)

finished goods inventory
The costs of products that have been completed in the manufacturing process and are available for sale to customers. (13)

first-in, first-out (FIFO) method
Inventory method that assumes that the units of inventory acquired first are sold first. (13)

fiscal period
Any time period for which a company wants to report its financial activities. (2)

fixed asset turnover
The ratio of sales revenues to fixed assets (property and equipment). (14)

fixed assets
Long-term, tangible resources (also called plant assets). (4)

G

General Accounting Office (GAO)
The primary federal government agency that oversees accounting in the federal government. (6)

general ledger
The primary ledger a company uses to record its account balances; contains records for each control account. (3, 7)

generally accepted accounting principles (GAAP)
Standards developed by professional accounting organizations to identify appropriate accounting and reporting procedures. (1)

going concern
An organization with an indefinite life that is sufficiently long that, over time, all currently incomplete transactions will be completed. (6)

goodwill
The excess of the price paid for a company over the fair market value of the net assets (assets less liabilities) of the acquired company. (11)

Governmental Accounting Standards Board (GASB)
The organization that sets accounting standards for state and local governmental units. (6)

governmental and nonprofit organizations
Organizations that provide goods or, more typically, services without the intent of making a profit. (1)

gross profit
The difference between the selling price of goods or services sold to customers during a period and the cost of the goods or services sold. (4)

gross profit margin
The ratio of gross profit (sales revenues minus cost of goods sold) to sales revenues; it measures efficiency in the production or purchase of goods for sale. (14)

H

historical cost
The purchase or exchange price of an asset or liability at the time it is acquired or incurred. (4)

I

income statement
A financial statement that reports revenues and expenses for a fiscal period as a means of determining how well a company has performed in creating profit for its owners. (2)

information
Facts, ideas, and concepts that help us understand the world. (1)

intangible assets
Long-term legal rights resulting from the ownership of patents, copyrights, trademarks, and similar items. (4)

interest
The cost of borrowing that is paid to creditors in addition to the repayment of principal. (2)

internal controls
Procedures a company uses to protect its assets and ensure the accuracy of its accounting information. (6)

International Accounting Standards Board (IASB)
The organization that recommends accounting standards that it believes are appropriate for a broad range of global activities involving companies in many nations. (6)

inventory turnover
The ratio of cost of goods sold (from the income statement) to inventory (from the balance sheet); it measures the success of a company in converting its investment in inventory into sales. (14)

investing activities
Activities involving the acquisition or disposal of long-term resources used by a business. (2)

J

journal
A chronological record of a company's transactions. (3)

L

last-in, first-out (LIFO) method
Inventory method that assumes that the last units of inventory acquired are the first sold. (13)

ledger
A file in which each of a company's accounts and the balances of those accounts are maintained. (3)

liability
The claim of a creditor to a company's resources. (2)

liquid assets
Resources that can be converted to cash in a relatively short period. (4)

long-term investments
Occur when a company lends money to or purchases stock issued by other organizations and does not intend to sell those investments in the coming fiscal year. (4)

long-term liabilities
Obligations not classified as current liabilities. (4)

lower of cost or market inventory
Situation where the inventories must be written down to the current market costs if current market costs are below the costs resulting from the use of an estimation method such as FIFO or LIFO. (13)

M

management's discussion and analysis (MD&A)
A section on a corporate annual report that explains important events and changes in performance during the years presented in the financial statements. (6)

managerial accounting (management accounting)
The process of preparing, reporting, and interpreting accounting information for use by an organization's internal decision makers. (1)

manufacturing companies
Organizations that produce goods that they sell to consumers, to merchandising companies, or to other manufacturing companies. (1)

mark-to-market accounting
Process of trading securities and available-for-sale securities being reported on the balance sheet at current market value. (11)

market
Any location or process that permits resources to be bought and sold. (1)

matching principle
An accounting concept which requires companies to recognize the expenses used to generate revenue in the same accounting period in which the revenues are recognized. (3)

merchandise inventory
An asset account that identifies the cost of goods a company has purchased that are available for sale to customers. (2)

merchandising companies
Organizations that sell to consumers goods that are produced by other companies. (1)

moral hazard
The condition that exists when agents have superior information to principals and are able to make decisions that favor their own interests over those of the principals. (1)

mutual agency
A legal right that permits a partner to enter into contracts and agreements that are binding on all members of a partnership. (1)

N

net income
The amount of profit earned by a business during a fiscal period. (2)

net income available for common stockholders
The amount earned by common stockholders. (13)

notes payable
A liability account used to identify amounts a company owes to creditors with whom a formal agreement, or note, has been signed. (2)

O

operating activities
Activities necessary to acquire and sell goods and services. (2)

operating expenditures
Expenditures to repair or maintain plant assets that do not extend the life or enhance the value of the assets. (11)

operating expenses
Costs of resources consumed as part of operating activities during a fiscal period and that are not directly associated with specific goods or services. (4)

operating income
The excess of gross profit over operating expenses. (4)

operating leverage
The use of fixed costs to increase net income as sales increase. (12)

operating profit margin
The ratio of operating income (sales revenues minus operating expenses) to sales revenue. (14)

organization
A group of people who work together to develop, produce, and/or distribute goods or services. (1)

owners' equity
A contribution by owners to a business, along with any profits that are kept in the business. (2)

P

paid-in capital in excess of par value
The amount in excess of the stock's par value received by a corporation from the sale of its stock. (9)

par value
The value assigned to each share of stock by a corporation in its corporate charter. (9)

parent
The controlling corporation. (4)

partnership
A business owned by two or more persons, with no legal identity distinct from that of the owners. (1)

periodic inventory system
Inventory system of recording cost of goods sold and updating inventory balances at the end of a fiscal period. (13)

perpetual inventory system
Inventory system of recording cost of goods sold and updating inventory balances at the time goods are sold. (13)

plant assets
Long-term, tangible resources (also called fixed assets). (4)

posting
The process of transferring transactions to specific accounts in a company's ledger. (3)

preemptive right
The right of stockholders to maintain the same percentage of ownership when new shares are issued. (9)

preferred stock
Stock with a higher claim on dividends and assets than common stock. (9)

prepaid expense
An asset account that identifies a resource that has been paid for but not used. (3)

principal
The amount a company borrows. (2)

profit
The difference between the price a seller receives for goods or services and the total cost to the seller of all resources consumed in developing, producing, and selling those goods or services during a particular period. (1)

profit margin
The ratio of net income to sales (also called return on sales). (12)

property and equipment
Long-term, tangible assets that are used in a company's operations. (4)

proprietorship
A business owned by one person, with no legal identity distinct from that of the owner. (1)

R

raw materials inventory
the costs of component parts or ingredients that become part of the product being manufactured. (13)

relational database
A set of related files that are linked so that files can be updated and information can be retrieved from the files efficiently. (7)

retail companies
See *merchandising companies.* (1)

retained earnings
A subcategory of owners' equity that are the accumulated profits of a business that have been reinvested in the business. (2)

return on assets (ROA)
The ratio of net income to total assets; net income divided by total assets (2, 10)

return on equity (ROE)
Net income divided by stockholders' equity. (10)

return on investment (ROI)
The amount of profits earned by a business that could be paid to owners. (1)

return on sales
See *profit margin.* (12)

revenue
The amount a company expects to receive when it sells goods or services. (2)

risk
Uncertainty about an outcome. (1)

S

sales revenue
Revenue that identifies the amount a company earns from selling its products. (2)

Securities Act of 1933
Legislation that required most corporations to file registration statements before selling stock to investors. (6)

Securities and Exchange Commission (SEC)
A federal agency that was given responsibility for overseeing external financial reporting by publicly traded corporations. (6)

Securities Exchange Act of 1934
Legislation that required corporations to provide annual financial reports to stockholders. (6)

service companies
Organizations that sell services rather than goods. (1)

shareholders
See *stockholders.* (1)

stakeholders
Those who have an economic interest in an organization and those who are affected by its activities. (1)

statement of cash flows
A financial statement that reports events that affected a company's cash account during a fiscal period. (2)

statement of stockholders' equity
A financial statement that reports changes in a corporation's owners' equity for a fiscal period. (4)

Statements of Financial Accounting Standards
FASB standards that establish acceptable accounting procedures or financial report content. (6)

stock
A certificate of ownership that represents an equal share in the ownership of a corporation. (1)

stock dividends
Shares of stock distributed by a company to its current stockholders without charge to the stockholders. (9)

stock rights
Authorization for existing stockholders to purchase new shares. (9)

stock split
The issuance by a corporation of a multiple of the number of shares of stock outstanding before the split. (9)

stockholders
Owners of a corporation. (1)

straight-line depreciation
A depreciation method that allocates an equal amount of the cost of a plant asset to expense during each fiscal period of the asset's expected useful life. (11)

subsidiaries
The companies owned or controlled by the parent corporation. (4)

subsidiary accounts
Accounts that record financial data about individual items of importance to a company, such as transactions for individual customers, suppliers, or products. (7)

supply-chain management
The interaction of a company and its suppliers. (7)

T

table
A file that contains data represented as rows and columns. (7)

times interest earned
The ratio of operating income (income before interest and taxes) to interest expense. (14)

total revenue
The amount earned from selling goods and services. (4)

transactions
Descriptions of business activities (or events) that are measured in dollar values and recorded in accounts. (2)

treasury stock
Stock repurchased by a company from its stockholders. (9)

U

unearned revenue
A liability account that results when a company receives cash from a customer for goods or services to be provided in the future. (3)

units-of-production depreciation
A depreciation method that produces a level amount of depreciation expense per unit of output (rather than per fiscal period). (11)

W

weighted-average method
Inventory method that uses the average cost of units of inventory available during a period as the cost of units sold. (13)

work-in-process inventory
The costs of materials, labor, and overhead that have been applied to products that are in the process of being manufactured. (13)

working capital
The difference between current assets and current liabilities. (4)

working capital ratio
The ratio of current assets to current liabilities. (4)

Index

D

E

F

M

N

O

P

Q

R